VW Polo
Owners Workshop Manual
Peter T Gill

Models covered

(5638 - 384 - 6BA4)

Polo Hatchback 'Mk V'
Petrol: 1.2 litre (1198cc) 3-cyl & 1.4 litre (1390cc) non-turbo
Turbo-diesel: 1.2 litre (1199cc) & 1.6 litre (1598cc)

Does NOT cover 1.2 litre 4-cyl TSI, 1.4 litre 'Twincharger' or 1.4 litre 'ACT' (turbo) petrol models, nor bi-fuel models
Does NOT cover revised Polo range introduced July 2014

© Haynes Group Limited 2014

ABCDE
FGHIJ
K

A book in the **Haynes Owners Workshop Manual Series**

ISBN 978 0 85733 638 5

British Library Cataloguing in Publication Data
A catalogue record for this book is available from the British Library.

Printed in India

Haynes Group Limited
Sparkford, Yeovil, Somerset BA22 7JJ, England

Haynes North America, Inc
2801 Townsgate Road, Suite 340, Thousand Oaks, CA 91361

The manufacturer's authorised representative in the EU for product safety is:

HaynesPro BV
Stationsstraat 79 F, 3811MH Amersfoort, The Netherlands
gpsr@haynes.co.uk

Disclaimer

There are risks associated with automotive repairs. The ability to make repairs depends on the individual's skill, experience and proper tools. Individuals should act with due care and acknowledge and assume the risk of performing automotive repairs.

The purpose of this manual is to provide comprehensive, useful and accessible automotive repair information, to help you get the best value from your vehicle. However, this manual is not a substitute for a professional certified technician or mechanic.

This repair manual is produced by a third party and is not associated with an individual vehicle manufacturer. If there is any doubt or discrepancy between this manual and the owner's manual or the factory service manual, please refer to the factory service manual or seek assistance from a professional certified technician or mechanic.

Even though we have prepared this manual with extreme care and every attempt is made to ensure that the information in this manual is correct, neither the publisher nor the author can accept responsibility for loss, damage or injury caused by any errors in, or omissions from, the information given.

Contents

Contents

REPAIRS & OVERHAUL

Engine and associated systems

Transmission

Brakes and suspension

Body equipment

Wiring diagrams

REFERENCE

Index

The VW Polo range covered by this manual was introduced to the UK market in October 2009. Using the same new platform as its VW Group sister cars, the Seat Ibiza Mk IV and Audi A1, the car represents a substantial update on the preceding Polo range. The new Mk 5 Polo, follows the styling from the Mk 6 Golf, and is 44mm longer, 32mm wider and 13mm lower than the previous Polo.

The 1.2 litre (3-cylinder) and 1.4 litre (4-cylinder) petrol engines are derived from well-proven units, which have appeared in the previous VW Polo.

The 1.2 litre diesel engine was added to the range in February 2010, and is new for the VW Polo. The 1.6 litre diesel engine has been seen in the VW Golf before, but is new to the Polo.

All the engines are of overhead camshaft design, mounted transversely, with the transmission mounted on the left-hand side. A five-speed manual transmission is available with a seven speed DSG transmission optional, on some models.

All models have fully independent front suspension. The rear suspension is semi-independent, with suspension struts, trailing arms and a 'self-steering' torsion beam axle. The compact rear springs are mounted separately from the shock absorbers, to minimise intrusion into the rear load space. The speed-sensitive power steering system fitted to all models has an electric hydraulic pump, rather than an engine-driven one.

A wide range of standard and optional equipment is available within the Polo range to suit most tastes. All models have electric mirrors, tinted glass, four airbags, power steering and ABS as standard, with central locking, electric windows, and air conditioning available further up the range.

Provided that regular servicing is carried out in accordance with the manufacturer's recommendations, the VW Polo should prove a reliable and economical small car. The engine compartment is well designed, and most of the items needing frequent attention are easily accessible.

Your VW Polo manual

The aim of this manual is to help you get the best value from your car. It can do so in several ways. It can help you decide what work must be done (even should you choose to get it done by a garage). It will also provide information on routine maintenance and servicing, and give a logical course of action and diagnosis when random faults occur. However, it is hoped that you will use the manual by tackling the work yourself. On simpler jobs it may even be quicker than booking the car into a garage and going there twice, to leave and collect it. Perhaps most important, a lot of money can be saved by avoiding the costs a garage must charge to cover its labour and overheads.

The manual has drawings and descriptions to show the function of the various components so that their layout can be understood. Tasks are described and photographed in a clear step-by-step sequence. The illustrations are numbered by the Section number and paragraph number to which they relate – if there is more than one illustration per paragraph, the sequence is denoted alphabetically.

References to the 'left' or 'right' of the car are in the sense of a person in the driver's seat, facing forwards.

Acknowledgements

Thanks are due to Draper tools Limited, who provided some of the workshop tools, and to all those people at Sparkford who helped in the production of this manual.

This manual is not a direct reproduction of the vehicle manufacturers' data, and its publication should not be taken as implying any technical approval by the vehicle manufacturers or importers.

We take great pride in the accuracy of information given in this manual, but car manufacturers make alterations and design changes during the production run of a particular car of which they do not inform us. No liability can be accepted by the authors or publishers for loss, damage or injury caused by any errors in, or omissions from, the information given.

Working on your car can be dangerous. This page shows just some of the potential risks and hazards, with the aim of creating a safety-conscious attitude.

General hazards

Scalding

• Don't remove the radiator or expansion tank cap while the engine is hot.
• Engine oil, transmission fluid or power steering fluid may also be dangerously hot if the engine has recently been running.

Burning

• Beware of burns from the exhaust system and from any part of the engine. Brake discs and drums can also be extremely hot immediately after use.

Crushing

• When working under or near a raised vehicle, always supplement the jack with axle stands, or use drive-on ramps.
Never venture under a car which is only supported by a jack.
• Take care if loosening or tightening high-torque nuts when the vehicle is on stands. Initial loosening and final tightening should be done with the wheels on the ground.

Fire

• Fuel is highly flammable; fuel vapour is explosive.
• Don't let fuel spill onto a hot engine.
• Do not smoke or allow naked lights (including pilot lights) anywhere near a vehicle being worked on. Also beware of creating sparks (electrically or by use of tools).
• Fuel vapour is heavier than air, so don't work on the fuel system with the vehicle over an inspection pit.
• Another cause of fire is an electrical overload or short-circuit. Take care when repairing or modifying the vehicle wiring.
• Keep a fire extinguisher handy, of a type suitable for use on fuel and electrical fires.

Electric shock

• Ignition HT and Xenon headlight voltages can be dangerous, especially to people with heart problems or a pacemaker. Don't work on or near these systems with the engine running or the ignition switched on.

• Mains voltage is also dangerous. Make sure that any mains-operated equipment is correctly earthed. Mains power points should be protected by a residual current device (RCD) circuit breaker.

Fume or gas intoxication

• Exhaust fumes are poisonous; they can contain carbon monoxide, which is rapidly fatal if inhaled. Never run the engine in a confined space such as a garage with the doors shut.
• Fuel vapour is also poisonous, as are the vapours from some cleaning solvents and paint thinners.

Poisonous or irritant substances

• Avoid skin contact with battery acid and with any fuel, fluid or lubricant, especially antifreeze, brake hydraulic fluid and Diesel fuel. Don't syphon them by mouth. If such a substance is swallowed or gets into the eyes, seek medical advice.
• Prolonged contact with used engine oil can cause skin cancer. Wear gloves or use a barrier cream if necessary. Change out of oil-soaked clothes and do not keep oily rags in your pocket.
• Air conditioning refrigerant forms a poisonous gas if exposed to a naked flame (including a cigarette). It can also cause skin burns on contact.

Asbestos

• Asbestos dust can cause cancer if inhaled or swallowed. Asbestos may be found in gaskets and in brake and clutch linings. When dealing with such components it is safest to assume that they contain asbestos.

Special hazards

Hydrofluoric acid

• This extremely corrosive acid is formed when certain types of synthetic rubber, found in some O-rings, oil seals, fuel hoses etc, are exposed to temperatures above 4000C. The rubber changes into a charred or sticky substance containing the acid. *Once formed, the acid remains dangerous for years. If it gets onto the skin, it may be necessary to amputate the limb concerned.*
• When dealing with a vehicle which has suffered a fire, or with components salvaged from such a vehicle, wear protective gloves and discard them after use.

The battery

• Batteries contain sulphuric acid, which attacks clothing, eyes and skin. Take care when topping-up or carrying the battery.
• The hydrogen gas given off by the battery is highly explosive. Never cause a spark or allow a naked light nearby. Be careful when connecting and disconnecting battery chargers or jump leads.

Air bags

• Air bags can cause injury if they go off accidentally. Take care when removing the steering wheel and trim panels. Special storage instructions may apply.

Diesel injection equipment

• Diesel injection pumps supply fuel at very high pressure. Take care when working on the fuel injectors and fuel pipes.

⚠️ *Warning: Never expose the hands, face or any other part of the body to injector spray; the fuel can penetrate the skin with potentially fatal results.*

Remember...

DO

• Do use eye protection when using power tools, and when working under the vehicle.

• Do wear gloves or use barrier cream to protect your hands when necessary.

• Do get someone to check periodically that all is well when working alone on the vehicle.

• Do keep loose clothing and long hair well out of the way of moving mechanical parts.

• Do remove rings, wristwatch etc, before working on the vehicle – especially the electrical system.

• Do ensure that any lifting or jacking equipment has a safe working load rating adequate for the job.

DON'T

• Don't attempt to lift a heavy component which may be beyond your capability – get assistance.

• Don't rush to finish a job, or take unverified short cuts.

• Don't use ill-fitting tools which may slip and cause injury.

• Don't leave tools or parts lying around where someone can trip over them. Mop up oil and fuel spills at once.

• Don't allow children or pets to play in or near a vehicle being worked on.

The following pages are intended to help in dealing with common roadside emergencies and breakdowns. You will find more detailed fault finding information at the back of the manual, and repair information in the main chapters.

If your car won't start and the starter motor doesn't turn

- ☐ If it's a model with automatic transmission, make sure the selector is in P or N.
- ☐ Open the bonnet and make sure that the battery terminals are clean and tight.
- ☐ Switch on the headlights and try to start the engine. If the headlights go very dim when you're trying to start, the battery is probably flat. Get out of trouble by jump starting (see next page) using a friend's car.

If your car won't start even though the starter motor turns as normal

- ☐ Is there fuel in the tank?
- ☐ Has the engine immobiliser been deactivated? This should happen automatically, on inserting the ignition key. However, if a replacement key has been obtained (other than from a VW dealer); it may not contain the transponder chip necessary to deactivate the system.
- ☐ Is there moisture on electrical components under the bonnet? Switch off the ignition, and then wipe off any obvious dampness with a dry cloth. Spray a water-repellent aerosol product (WD-40 or equivalent) on electrical connectors like those shown in the photos. Pay special attention to the DIS ignition module's wiring connector. (Note that diesel engines don't usually suffer from damp).

A Check the condition and security of the battery connections (remove the cover first).

B Check the fuses and fusible links in the fusebox located on top of the battery.

C Check the wiring to the ignition coils beneath the engine top cover (petrol models only).

Check that electrical connections are secure (with the ignition switched off) and spray them with a water-dispersant spray like WD-40 if you suspect a problem due to damp.

D Check that the starter motor wiring is secure.

Jump starting

Jump starting will get you out of trouble, but you must correct whatever made the battery go flat in the first place. There are three possibilities:

1 *The battery has been drained by repeated attempts to start, or by leaving the lights on.*

2 *The charging system is not working properly (alternator drivebelt slack or broken, alternator wiring fault or alternator itself faulty).*

3 *The battery itself is at fault (electrolyte low, or battery worn out).*

When jump-starting a car, observe the following precautions:

✓ Before connecting the booster battery, make sure that the ignition is switched off.

Caution: Remove the key in case the central locking engages when the jump leads are connected

✓ Ensure that all electrical equipment (lights, heater, wipers, etc) is switched off.

✓ Take note of any special precautions printed on the battery case.

✓ Make sure that the booster battery is the same voltage as the discharged one in the vehicle.

✓ If the battery is being jump-started from the battery in another vehicle, the two vehicles MUST NOT TOUCH each other.

✓ Make sure that the transmission is in neutral (or PARK, in the case of automatic transmission).

Budget jump leads can be a false economy, as they often do not pass enough current to start large capacity or diesel engines. They can also get hot.

1 Connect one end of the red jump lead to the positive (+) terminal of the flat battery

2 Connect the other end of the red lead to the positive (+) terminal of the booster battery.

3 Connect one end of the black jump lead to the negative (-) terminal of the booster battery

4 Connect the other end of the black jump lead to a bolt or bracket on the engine block, well away from the battery, on the vehicle to be started.

5 Make sure that the jump leads will not come into contact with the fan, drive-belts or other moving parts of the engine.

6 Start the engine using the booster battery and run it at idle speed. Switch on the lights, rear window demister and heater blower motor, then disconnect the jump leads in the reverse order of connection. Turn off the lights etc.

Wheel changing

⚠️ *Warning: Do not change a wheel in a situation where you risk being hit by other traffic. On busy roads, try to stop in a lay-by or a gateway. Be wary of passing traffic while changing the wheel – it is easy to become distracted by the job in hand.*

Preparation

☐ When a puncture occurs, stop as soon as it is safe to do so.

☐ Park on firm level ground, if possible, and well out of the way of other traffic.

☐ Use hazard warning lights if necessary.

☐ If you have one, use a warning triangle to alert other drivers of your presence.

☐ Apply the handbrake and engage first or reverse gear (or Park on models with automatic transmission).

☐ Chock the wheel diagonally opposite the one being removed – a couple of large stones will do for this.

☐ If the ground is soft, use a flat piece of wood to spread the load under the jack.

Changing the wheel

1 The spare wheel and tools are stored in the luggage compartment. Lift out the jack and wheel changing tools from the centre of the spare wheel.

2 Unscrew the retainer and lift out the wheel.

3 On steel wheels, use the wire hook and wheel brace to remove the wheel trim from the wheel.

4 On alloy wheels, use the plastic puller from the tool kit to remove the cover from each wheel bolt, including the anti-theft bolt.

5 Slacken each wheel bolt by half a turn (using the special splined adapter for the anti-theft bolt).

6 Locate the jack below the reinforced point on the sill (don't jack the vehicle at any other point of the sill) and on firm ground, then turn the jack handle clockwise until the wheel is raised clear of the ground.

7 Unscrew the wheel bolts (using the special splined adapter for the anti-theft bolt) and remove the wheel. Fit the spare wheel, and screw in the bolts. Lightly tighten the bolts with the wheelbrace then lower the vehicle to the ground.

8 Securely tighten the wheel bolts in the sequence shown then refit the wheel trim/ hub cap. Stow the punctured wheel back in the spare wheel well. Note that the wheel bolts should be tightened to the specified torque at the earliest possible opportunity.

Finally . . .

☐ Stow the jack and tools in the spare wheel.

☐ Check the tyre pressure on the wheel just fitted. If it is low, or if you don't have a pressure gauge with you, drive slowly to the nearest garage and inflate the tyre to the correct pressure.

Note: *If a temporary 'space-saver' spare wheel has been fitted, special conditions apply to its use. This type of spare wheel is only intended for use in an emergency, and should not remain fitted any longer than it takes to get the punctured wheel repaired. While the temporary wheel is in use, ensure it is inflated to the correct pressure, do not exceed 50 mph (80 kph), and avoid harsh acceleration, braking or cornering.*

Identifying leaks

Puddles on the garage floor or drive, or obvious wetness under the bonnet or underneath the car, suggest a leak that needs investigating. It can sometimes be difficult to decide where the leak is coming from, especially if an engine undershield is fitted. Leaking oil or fluid can also be blown rearwards by the passage of air under the car, giving a false impression of where the problem lies.

⚠ *Warning: Most automotive oils and fluids are poisonous. Wash them off skin, and change out of contaminated clothing, without delay.*

HAYNES HiNT *The smell of a fluid leaking from the car may provide a clue to what's leaking. Some fluids are distinctively coloured. It may help to remove the engine undershield, clean the car carefully and to park it over some clean paper overnight as an aid to locating the source of the leak.*
Remember that some leaks may only occur while the engine is running.

Sump oil

Engine oil may leak from the drain plug...

Oil from filter

...or from the base of the oil filter.

Gearbox oil

Gearbox oil can leak from the seals at the inboard ends of the driveshafts.

Antifreeze

Leaking antifreeze often leaves a crystalline deposit like this.

Brake fluid

A leak occurring at a wheel is almost certainly brake fluid.

Power steering fluid

Power steering fluid may leak from the pipe connectors on the steering rack.

Towing

When all else fails, you may find yourself having to get a tow home – or of course you may be helping somebody else. Long-distance recovery should only be done by a garage or breakdown service. For shorter distances, DIY towing using another car is easy enough, but observe the following points:

☐ Use a proper tow-rope – they are not expensive. The vehicle being towed must display an ON TOW sign in its rear window.

☐ Always turn the ignition key to the 'On' position when the vehicle is being towed, so that the steering lock is released, and the direction indicator and brake lights work.

☐ A rear towing eye is provided below the right-hand side of the rear bumper. Remove the plastic cover.

☐ The front towing eye is located in the tool kit, and is screwed into position behind the cover on the right-hand side of the front bumper (**see illustration**). The eye has a **left-hand thread**, which means it screws in **anti-clockwise**.

☐ Before being towed, release the handbrake and select neutral on the transmission.

☐ On models with automatic transmission, special precautions apply. If in doubt, do not tow, or transmission damage may result.

☐ Note that greater-than-usual pedal pressure will be required to operate the brakes, since the vacuum servo unit is only operational with the engine running.

☐ On models with power steering, greater-than-usual steering effort will also be required.

☐ The driver of the car being towed must keep the tow-rope taut at all times to avoid snatching.

☐ Make sure that both drivers know the route before setting off.

☐ Only drive at moderate speeds and keep the distance towed to a minimum. Drive smoothly and allow plenty of time for slowing down at junctions.

Introduction

There are some very simple checks which need only take a few minutes to carry out, but which could save you a lot of inconvenience and expense.

These checks require no great skill or special tools, and the small amount of time they take to perform could prove to be very well spent, for example:

☐ Keeping an eye on tyre condition and pressures, will not only help to stop them wearing out prematurely, but could also save your life.

☐ Many breakdowns are caused by electrical problems. Battery-related faults are particularly common, and a quick check on a regular basis will often prevent the majority of these.

☐ If your car develops a brake fluid leak, the first time you might know about it is when your brakes don't work properly. Checking the level regularly will give advance warning of this kind of problem.

☐ If the oil or coolant levels run low, the cost of repairing any engine damage will be far greater than fixing the leak, for example.

Underbonnet check points

◄ **1.4 litre petrol**

A Engine oil level dipstick
B Engine oil filler cap
C Coolant expansion tank
D Brake fluid reservoir
E Power steering fluid reservoir
F Screen washer fluid reservoir
G Battery

◄ **1.2 litre diesel**

A Engine oil level dipstick
B Engine oil filler cap
C Coolant expansion tank
D Brake fluid reservoir
E Power steering fluid reservoir
F Screen washer fluid reservoir
G Battery

Engine oil level

Before you start

✔ Make sure that the car is on level ground.
✔ Check the oil level before the car is driven, or at least 10 minutes after the engine has been switched off.

HAYNES HiNT *If the oil is checked immediately after driving the vehicle, some of the oil will remain in the upper engine components, resulting in an inaccurate reading on the dipstick.*

The correct oil

Modern engines place great demands on their oil. It is very important that the correct oil for your car is used (see *Lubricants and fluids*).

Car care

● If you have to add oil frequently, you should check whether you have any oil leaks. Place some clean paper under the car overnight, and check for stains in the morning. If there are no leaks, then the engine may be burning oil.

● Always maintain the level between the upper and lower dipstick marks. If the level is too low, severe engine damage may occur. Oil seal failure may result if the engine is overfilled by adding too much oil.

1 The dipstick is often brightly coloured for easy identification (see *Underbonnet check points* for exact location). Withdraw the dipstick, and then use a clean rag or paper towel to wipe the oil from it. Insert the clean dipstick into the tube as far as it will go, then withdraw it again.

3 Oil is added through the filler cap aperture. Unscrew the cap.

2 Note the level on the end of the dipstick. It is satisfactory for the level to be anywhere in the dotted area. The notches on the dipstick represent the absolute MAX and MIN marks. There are different dipsticks used, depending on engine.

4 Top-up the oil level, using a funnel may help to reduce spillages. Place some cloth rags around the filler cap aperture if required. Add the oil slowly, checking the level on the dipstick frequently. Avoid overfilling (see *Car care*).

Coolant level

Warning: Do not attempt to remove the expansion tank pressure cap when the engine is hot, as there is a very great risk of scalding. Do not leave open containers of coolant about, as it is poisonous.

Car care

● With a sealed-type cooling system, adding coolant should not be necessary on a regular basis. If frequent topping-up is required, it is likely there is a leak. Check the radiator, all hoses and joint faces for signs of staining or wetness, and rectify as necessary.

● It is important that antifreeze is used in the cooling system all year round, not just during the winter months. Don't top up with water alone, as the antifreeze will become diluted.

1 The coolant level varies with the temperature of the engine. When the engine is cold, the coolant level should be between the MIN and MAX marks.

2 If topping-up is necessary, wait until the engine is cold. Slowly unscrew the cap to release any pressure present in the cooling system, and remove the cap.

3 Add a mixture of water and the specified antifreeze (see *Lubricants and fluids*) to the expansion tank until the coolant level is halfway between the level marks. Refit the cap and tighten it securely. **Note:** *Some antifreeze is supplied pre-mixed ('ready to use'), and that no more water should be added to it.*

Brake (and clutch) fluid level

Note: *On manual transmission models, the fluid reservoir also supplies the clutch master cylinder with fluid*

Before you start

✔ Make sure that the car is on level ground.
✔ Cleanliness is of great importance when dealing with the braking system, so take care to clean around the reservoir cap before topping-up. Use only clean brake fluid.

Safety first!

● If the reservoir requires repeated topping-up this is an indication of a fluid leak somewhere in the system, which should be investigated immediately.

● If a leak is suspected, the car should not be driven until the braking system has been checked. Never take any risks where brakes are concerned.

⚠ *Warning: Brake fluid can harm your eyes and damage painted surfaces, so use extreme caution when handling and pouring it. Do not use fluid that has been standing open for some time, as it absorbs moisture from the air, which can cause a dangerous loss of braking effectiveness.*

1 The MIN and MAX marks are indicated on the reservoir. The fluid level must be kept between the marks at all times. Note that the level will drop naturally as the brake pad linings wear, but must never be allowed to fall below the MIN mark.

2 If topping-up is necessary, first wipe clean the area around the filler cap to prevent dirt entering the hydraulic system. Unscrew and remove the reservoir cap.

3 Carefully add fluid, taking care not to spill it onto the surrounding components. Use only the specified fluid (see *Lubricants and fluids*); mixing different types can cause damage to the system. On completion, securely refit the cap and wipe away any spilt fluid.

Washer fluid level

● Screenwash additives not only keep the windscreen clean during bad weather, they also prevent the washer system freezing in cold weather – which is when you are likely to need it most. Don't top-up using plain water, as the screenwash will become diluted, and will freeze in cold weather.

 Warning: On no account use engine coolant antifreeze in the screen washer system – this may damage the paintwork.

1 The screen wash fluid reservoir is located on the right-hand side of the engine compartment, behind the headlight. Pull up the filler cap to release it from the reservoir.

2 When topping-up the reservoir, a screen wash additive should be added in the quantities recommended on the bottle.

Battery

Caution: Before carrying out any work on the vehicle battery, read the precautions given in 'Safety first!' at the start of this manual.

✔ Make sure that the battery tray is in good condition, and that the clamp is tight. Corrosion on the tray, retaining clamp and the battery itself can be removed with a solution of water and baking soda. Thoroughly rinse all cleaned areas with water. Any metal parts damaged by corrosion should be covered with a zinc-based primer, and then painted.

✔ Periodically (approximately every three months), check the charge condition of the battery as described in Chapter 5A. A 'magic eye' charge indicator is fitted to the standard battery – if the indicator shows green, then the battery is in good condition and charged up. If the indicator turns darker, eventually to black, then the battery requires charging. If the indicator shows clear/yellow, then the electrolyte is low and in a critical condition, and should be topped-up with distilled water. If charging the battery does not return the eye to green, the battery should be scrapped

✔ If the battery is flat, and you need to jump start your vehicle, see *Roadside Repairs*.

1 The battery is located in the front left-hand corner of the engine compartment.

2 Check the security and condition of all the battery and fuse connections. The exterior of the battery should be inspected periodically for damage such as a cracked case or cover.

3 If corrosion (white, fluffy deposits) is evident, remove the cables from the battery terminals (refer to *Disconnecting the battery* in the Reference chapter at the end of this manual), clean them with a small wire brush, then refit them. Automotive stores sell a tool for cleaning the battery post . . .

4 . . . as well as the battery cable clamps. **Note:** *VW specifically prohibit the use of grease on the battery terminals.*

Tyre condition and pressure

It is very important that tyres are in good condition, and at the correct pressure - having a tyre failure at any speed is highly dangerous. Tyre wear is influenced by driving style - harsh braking and acceleration, or fast cornering, will all produce more rapid tyre wear. As a general rule, the front tyres wear out faster than the rears. Interchanging the tyres from front to rear ("rotating" the tyres) may result in more even wear. However, if this is completely effective, you may have the expense of replacing all four tyres at once!

Remove any nails or stones embedded in the tread before they penetrate the tyre to cause deflation. If removal of a nail does reveal that the tyre has been punctured, refit the nail so that its point of penetration is marked. Then immediately change the wheel, and have the tyre repaired by a tyre dealer.

Regularly check the tyres for damage in the form of cuts or bulges, especially in the sidewalls. Periodically remove the wheels, and clean any dirt or mud from the inside and outside surfaces. Examine the wheel rims for signs of rusting, corrosion or other damage. Light alloy wheels are easily damaged by "kerbing" whilst parking; steel wheels may also become dented or buckled. A new wheel is very often the only way to overcome severe damage.

New tyres should be balanced when they are fitted, but it may become necessary to re-balance them as they wear, or if the balance weights fitted to the wheel rim should fall off. Unbalanced tyres will wear more quickly, as will the steering and suspension components. Wheel imbalance is normally signified by vibration, particularly at a certain speed (typically around 50 mph). If this vibration is felt only through the steering, then it is likely that just the front wheels need balancing. If, however, the vibration is felt through the whole car, the rear wheels could be out of balance. Wheel balancing should be carried out by a tyre dealer or garage.

1 Tread Depth - visual check
The original tyres have tread wear safety bands (B), which will appear when the tread depth reaches approximately 1.6 mm. The band positions are indicated by a triangular mark on the tyre sidewall (A).

2 Tread Depth - manual check
Alternatively, tread wear can be monitored with a simple, inexpensive device known as a tread depth indicator gauge.

3 Tyre Pressure Check
Check the tyre pressures regularly with the tyres cold. Do not adjust the tyre pressures immediately after the vehicle has been used, or an inaccurate setting will result.

Tyre tread wear patterns

Shoulder Wear

Underinflation (wear on both sides)
Under-inflation will cause overheating of the tyre, because the tyre will flex too much, and the tread will not sit correctly on the road surface. This will cause a loss of grip and excessive wear, not to mention the danger of sudden tyre failure due to heat build-up.
Check and adjust pressures
Incorrect wheel camber (wear on one side)
Repair or renew suspension parts
Hard cornering
Reduce speed!

Centre Wear

Overinflation
Over-inflation will cause rapid wear of the centre part of the tyre tread, coupled with reduced grip, harsher ride, and the danger of shock damage occurring in the tyre casing.
Check and adjust pressures

If you sometimes have to inflate your car's tyres to the higher pressures specified for maximum load or sustained high speed, don't forget to reduce the pressures to normal afterwards.

Uneven Wear

Front tyres may wear unevenly as a result of wheel misalignment. Most tyre dealers and garages can check and adjust the wheel alignment (or "tracking") for a modest charge.
Incorrect camber or castor
Repair or renew suspension parts
Malfunctioning suspension
Repair or renew suspension parts
Unbalanced wheel
Balance tyres
Incorrect toe setting
Adjust front wheel alignment
Note: *The feathered edge of the tread which typifies toe wear is best checked by feel.*

Wiper blades

1 Check the condition of the wiper blades: if they are cracked or show signs of deterioration, or if the glass swept area is smeared, renew them. For maximum clarity of vision, wiper blades should be renewed annually.

2 To remove a windscreen wiper blade, turn the ignition on, then turn the ignition off, and press the wiper switch stalk down once. This places the arms in the 'service' position. Lift the wiper from the screen and press the securing clip ...

3 ... slide the blade upwards from the end of the wiper arm, taking care not to allow the wiper arm to spring back and damage the windscreen. When completed, return the blades to the park position by pressing the wiper switch stalk again.

4 To remove the rear wiper blade, press the securing clip (arrowed), and remove as described for the front wiper blades.

Electrical systems

✔ Check all external lights and the horn. Refer to the appropriate Sections of Chapter 12 for details if any of the circuits are found to be inoperative.

✔ Visually check all accessible wiring connectors, harnesses and retaining clips for security, and for signs of chafing or damage.

HAYNES HiNT *If you need to check your brake lights and indicators unaided, back up to a wall or garage door and operate the lights. The reflected light should show if they are working properly.*

1 If a single indicator light, brake light or headlight has failed, it is likely that a bulb has blown and will need to be renewed. Refer to Chapter 12 for details. If both brake lights have failed, it is possible that the brake light switch operated by the brake pedal has failed. Refer to Chapter 9 for details.

2 If more than one indicator light or headlight has failed, it is likely that either a fuse has blown or that there is a fault in the circuit (see *Electrical fault finding* in Chapter 12). The main fuses are in the fusebox beneath a cover on the right-hand end of the facia panel.

3 Additional heavy duty fuses and fusible links are in the fusebox located on top of the battery. To renew a blown fuse, pull it from its location in the fusebox, using the plastic pliers provided. Fit a new fuse of the same rating, available from car accessory shops. It is important that you find the reason that the fuse blew (see *Electrical fault finding* in Chapter 12).

Lubricants and fluids

Note: *Using lubricants and fluids that do not meet the VW standard may invalidate the warranty*

Engine (petrol):

Standard (distance/time) service interval	Multigrade engine oil, viscosity SAE 5W/40 to 20W/50 - VW 502 00
LongLife (variable) service interval	VW LongLife engine oil VW 503 00 or VW 504 00

Engine (diesel):

Standard (distance/time) service interval	Multigrade engine oil, viscosity SAE 5W/40 to 20W/50
Engines without particulate filter	VW 505 01
Engines with particulate filter	VW 507 00
LongLife (variable) service interval	VW LongLife engine oil
Engines without particulate filter	VW 507 00
Engines with particulate filter	VW 507 00
Cooling system	VW additive G12 plus-plus (TL-VW 774 G) or G12 plus (TL-VW 774 F) - antifreeze and corrosion protection
Manual transmission	VW G50 synthetic gear oil, viscosity SAE 75W/90 - G 052 512 A2
DSG semi-automatic transmission	G 052 145
Braking system	Hydraulic fluid to DOT 4 VW 501 14 (part no. B 000 750)
Power steering fluid	VW hydraulic oil G 004 000 M2

Tyre pressures

Note: *The recommended tyre pressures for Polo models are given on a sticker attached to the inside of the fuel filler flap. The pressures given are for the original-equipment tyres – the recommended pressures may vary if any other make or type of tyre is fitted; check with the tyre manufacturer or supplier for latest recommendations. The following pressures are typical.*

	Front	Rear
Petrol models:		
Normal load	2.2 bar (32 psi)	2.0 bar (29 psi)
Full load	2.4 bar (35 psi)	2.6 bar (38 psi)
Diesel models:		
Normal load	2.3 bar (33 psi)	2.1 bar (30 psi)
Full load	2.5 bar (36 psi)	2.7 bar (39 psi)

Note: *Where a space-saver spare tyre is fitted, its pressure must be 4.2 bar (61 psi).*

Chapter 1 Part A:
Routine maintenance and servicing – petrol models

Contents

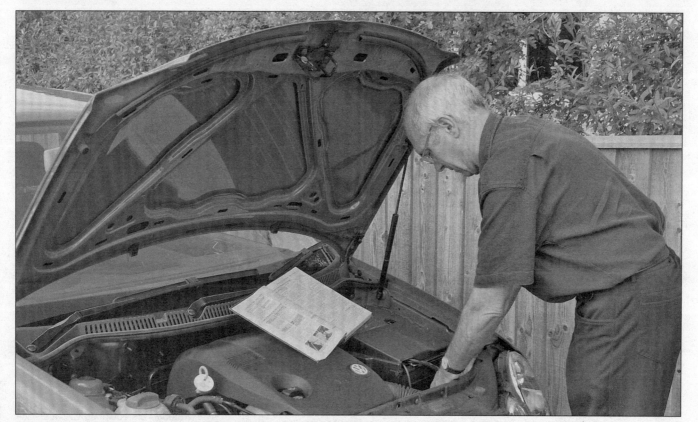

Degrees of difficulty

| Easy, suitable for novice with little experience | Fairly easy, suitable for beginner with some experience | Fairly difficult, suitable for competent DIY mechanic | Difficult, suitable for experienced DIY mechanic | Very difficult, suitable for expert DIY or professional |

Lubricants and fluids . . . . Refer to end of *Weekly checks* on page 0•16

Engine codes

1.2 litre:
SOHC . . . . CHFA
DOHC . . . . CGPA and CGPB
1.4 litre . . . . CGGB

Capacities

Engine oil – including filter (approximate)

1.2 litre . . . . 2.8 litres
1.4 litre . . . . 3.2 litres

Cooling system

1.2 litre . . . . 5.1 litres
1.4 litre . . . . 5.5 litres

Transmission

Manual transmission - Type 02T . . . . 2.0 litres
DSG transmission (optional for 1.4 litre engine). . . . . 1.7 litres

Fuel tank (approximate) . . . . 45 litres

Cooling system

Antifreeze mixture:
40% antifreeze . . . . Protection down to -25°C
50% antifreeze . . . . Protection down to -35°C
Note: *Refer to antifreeze manufacturer for latest recommendations.*

Ignition system

	Type	Electrode gap
Spark plugs:		
1.2 litre:		
Engine codes CHFA, CGPA & CGPB	VW 101 905 618 A	1.0 – 1.1 mm
	VW 101 905 601 F	1.0 – 1.1 mm
1.4 litre:		
Engine codes CGGB	VW 101 905 601 F	1.0 – 1.1 mm

Brakes

Brake pad minimum thickness:
Including backing plate:
Front . . . . 7.0 mm
Rear . . . . 7.6 mm
Friction lining only:
Front and rear . . . . 2.0 mm
Rear brake shoe friction material minimum thickness . . . . 1.5 mm

Torque wrench settings

	Nm	lbf ft
Manual transmission 02T:		
Filler/level and drain plug:		
Multi-splined (12-point) plug	25	18
Hexagon (Allen key) plug	30	22
Oil filter housing cap (1.2 litre engines)	25	18
Roadwheel bolts	120	89
Spark plugs (1.2 litre engines)	30	22
Spark plugs (1.4 litre engines)	25	18
Sump drain plug	30	22

Maintenance schedule

The maintenance intervals in this manual are provided with the assumption that you, not the dealer, will be carrying out the work. These are the minimum intervals recommended by us for cars driven daily. If you wish to keep your car in peak condition at all times, you may wish to perform some of these procedures more often. We encourage frequent maintenance, since it enhances the efficiency, performance and resale value of your car.

When the vehicle is new, it should be serviced by a dealer service department (or other workshop recognised by the vehicle manufacturer as providing the same standard of service) in order to preserve the warranty. The vehicle manufacturer may reject warranty claims if you are unable to prove that servicing has been carried out as and when specified, using only original equipment parts or parts certified to be of equivalent quality.

Longlife service schedule

All VW models are equipped with a service interval display indicator in the instrument panel. Every time the engine is started the panel will illuminate for approximately 20 seconds with service information. With the standard fixed interval display, the service intervals are in accordance with specific distances and time periods. With the LongLife display, the service interval is variable. Once the service interval has been reached, the display will flash 'OIL service' for an oil change service or 'INSP service' for an inspection service.

For models using the LongLife schedule, the occurrence of either service reminder on the display unit will depend on how the car is being used (number of starts, length of journeys, vehicle speeds, brake pad wear, bonnet opening frequency, fuel consumption, oil level and oil temperature). For example, if a vehicle is being used under extreme driving conditions, the service may occur at 10 000 miles, whereas, if the vehicle is being used under moderate driving conditions, it may occur at 20 000 miles, although the maximum length of time between INSP services is 2 years. It is important to realise that this system is completely variable according to how the vehicle is being used, and therefore the service should be carried out when indicated on the display. **Note:** *Models with the variable service*

interval system are equipped with an engine oil level sensor, brake pad wear indicator, and a variable service indicator.

The LongLife variable service intervals are only applicable to models with a PR number of QG1 (>2012) or QI6 (2013>). This number is shown in the vehicle Service Schedule booklet, on a service interval plate inside the luggage compartment **(see illustration)** or on the Next Service sticker located on the driver's door pillar). With the variable (LongLife) service interval on models with these PR numbers, the engine must **only** be filled with the recommended **LongLife** engine oil (see *Lubricants and fluids*).

After completing a service, VW technicians use a special instrument to reset the service display to the next service interval, and a print-out is put in the vehicle service record. The display can be reset by the owner as described in Section 5, but note that for models using the LongLife interval, the procedure will automatically reset the schedule to an amended

0.5 Vehicle Data Sticker location

LongLife interval, in which oil renewal and brake pad checks are based on distance/time while every other system remains LongLife. To have the display reset to the full LongLife schedule, it is necessary to take the car to a VW dealer who will use a special instrument to encode the on-board computer.

Every 250 miles or weekly
- [ ] Refer to *Weekly checks*

'OIL service' on display
- [ ] Renew the engine oil and filter (Section 3)

Note: *Frequent oil and filter changes are good for the engine. We recommend changing the oil at least once a year.*
- [ ] Check the front and rear brake pad thickness (Section 4)
- [ ] Reset the service interval display (Section 5)

'INSP service' on display
Note: *In addition to the items given above.*
- [ ] Check the condition of the exhaust system and its mountings (Section 6)
- [ ] Check all underbonnet components and hoses for fluid and oil leaks (Section 7)
- [ ] Check the condition of the auxiliary drivebelt (Section 8 and Section 25)
- [ ] Check the coolant antifreeze concentration (Section 9)
- [ ] Check the brake hydraulic circuit for leaks and damage (Section 10)
- [ ] Check the headlight beam adjustment (Section 11)
- [ ] Renew the pollen filter element (Section 12)
- [ ] Check the manual transmission oil level (Section 13)
- [ ] Check the underbody protection for damage (Section 14)
- [ ] Check the condition of the driveshafts (Section 15)
- [ ] Check the steering and suspension components for condition and security (Section 16)
- [ ] Check the battery condition, security and electrolyte level (Section 17)
- [ ] Lubricate all hinges and locks (Section 18)
- [ ] Check the condition of the airbag unit(s) (Section 19)

'INSP service' on display (continued)
- [ ] Check the operation of the windscreen/tailgate/headlight washer system(s) (as applicable) (Section 20)
- [ ] Check the engine management self-diagnosis memory for faults (Section 21)
- [ ] Carry out a road test and check exhaust emissions (Section 22)

Every 40 000 miles or 4 years, whichever comes first
Note: *Many dealers perform these tasks at every second INSP service.*
- [ ] Renew the air filter element (Section 23)
- [ ] Renew the spark plugs (Section 24)
- [ ] Check the condition of the auxiliary drivebelt (Section 8 and Section 25)
- [ ] Check the power steering hydraulic fluid level (Section 26)
- [ ] Check the DSG transmission fluid level (Section 27)
- [ ] Renew the timing belt and tensioner – 1.4 litre engines only* (Section 28)

* VW specify timing belt inspection after the first 55 000 miles and then every 20 000 miles, but does not have a renewal interval time. However, if the car is used mainly for short journeys, we recommend that the timing belt be renewed at 55 000 miles when the first Inspection takes place. The belt renewal interval is very much up to the individual owner, bearing in mind that severe engine damage will result if the belt breaks in use.
* 1.2 litre petrol engines have a maintenance-free timing chain fitted.

Every 2 years
- [ ] Renew the brake (and clutch) fluid (Section 29)
- [ ] Renew the coolant** (Section 30)

** This work is not included in the VW schedule, and should not be required if the recommended VW G12 LongLife coolant antifreeze/inhibitor is used.

Underbonnet view – 1.4 litre model

1 Engine oil filler cap
2 Engine oil dipstick
3 Coolant expansion tank
4 Windscreen/headlight washer fluid reservoir
5 Power steering fluid reservoir
6 Ignition coils and spark plugs (under cover)
7 Fuel injectors
8 Brake master cylinder fluid reservoir
9 Brake ABS unit
10 Engine management ECU
11 Battery
12 Alternator
13 Air filter housing
14 Suspension upper mounting

Front underbody view – 1.4 litre model

1 Sump drain plug
2 Manual transmission oil filler/level plug
3 Rear engine mounting/link
4 Driveshaft
5 Front suspension subframe
6 Front suspension lower arm
7 Steering track rod
8 Front brake caliper
9 Exhaust flexible front pipe
10 Radiator bottom coolant hose
11 Air conditioning compressor
12 Radiator electric cooling fan
13 Auxiliary drivebelt

Rear underbody view – 1.2 litre model

1 Fuel tank
2 Rear axle assembly
3 Rear suspension coil
    spring
4 Rear shock absorber
5 Exhaust rear silencer
6 Rear axle assembly front
    mountings
7 Handbrake cables
8 Fuel tank filler neck
9 Spare wheel well

Maintenance procedures

1 Introduction

This Chapter is designed to help the home mechanic maintain his/her car for safety, economy, long life and peak performance.

The Chapter contains a master maintenance schedule, followed by Sections dealing specifically with each task in the schedule. Visual checks, adjustments, component renewal and other helpful items are included. Refer to the accompanying illustrations of the engine compartment and the underside of the car for the locations of the various components.

Servicing your car will provide a planned maintenance programme, which should result in a long and reliable service life. This is a comprehensive plan, so maintaining some items, but not others, will not produce the same results.

As you service your car, you will discover that many of the procedures can – and should – be grouped together, because of the particular procedure being performed, or because of the proximity of two otherwise unrelated components to one another. For example, if the car is raised for any reason, the exhaust can be inspected at the same time as the suspension and steering components.

The first step in this maintenance programme is to prepare yourself before the actual work begins. Read through all the Sections relevant to the work to be carried out, then make a list and gather all the parts and tools required. If a problem is encountered, seek advice from a parts specialist, or a dealer service department.

2 Regular maintenance

1 If, from the time the car is new, the routine maintenance schedule is followed closely, and frequent checks are made of fluid levels and high-wear items, as suggested throughout this manual, the engine will be kept in relatively good running condition, and the need for additional work will be minimised.

2 It is possible that there will be times when the engine is running poorly due to the lack of regular maintenance. This is even more likely if a used car, which has not received regular and frequent maintenance checks, is purchased. In such cases, additional work may need to be carried out, outside of the regular maintenance intervals.

3 If engine wear is suspected, a compression test (refer to Chapter 2A or Chapter 2B) will provide valuable information regarding the overall performance of the main internal components. Such a test can be used as a basis to decide on the extent of the work to be carried out. If, for example, a compression test indicates serious internal engine wear, conventional maintenance as described in this Chapter will not greatly improve the performance of the engine, and may prove a waste of time and money, unless extensive overhaul work is carried out first.

4 The following series of operations are those most often required to improve the performance of a generally poor-running engine:

Primary operations

a) Clean, inspect and test the battery (See 'Weekly checks').

b) Check all the engine-related fluids (See 'Weekly checks').

c) Check the condition and tension of the auxiliary drivebelt (Section 8).

d) Renew the spark plugs (Section 24).

e) Check the condition of the air filter, and renew if necessary (Section 23).

f) Check the condition of all hoses, and check for fluid leaks (Section 7).

5 If the above operations do not prove fully effective, carry out the following secondary operations:

Secondary operations

All items listed under *Primary operations*, plus the following:

a) Check the charging system (see Chapter 5A).

b) Check the ignition system (see Chapter 5B).

c) Check the fuel system (see Chapter 4A).

'OIL service' on display

3 Engine oil and filter renewal

1 Frequent oil and filter changes are the most important maintenance procedures, which can be undertaken by the DIY owner. As engine oil ages, it becomes diluted and contaminated, which leads to premature engine wear.

2 Before starting this procedure, gather all the necessary tools and materials. Also make sure that you have plenty of clean rags and newspapers handy, to mop-up any spills. Ideally, the engine oil should be warm, as it will drain better, and more built-up sludge will be removed with it. Take care, however, not to touch the exhaust or any other hot parts of the engine when working under the car. To avoid any possibility of scalding, and to protect yourself from possible skin irritants and other harmful contaminants in used engine oils, it is advisable to wear gloves when carrying out this work. Access to the underside of the car will be greatly improved if it can be raised on a lift, driven onto ramps, or jacked up and supported

on axle stands (see *Jacking and vehicle support*). Whichever method is chosen, make sure that the car remains level, or if it is at an angle, that the drain plug is at the lowest point. Where necessary, undo the retaining screws and remove the engine undershield(s), then also remove the engine top cover where applicable.

3 Using a socket and wrench or a ring spanner, slacken the drain plug about half a turn **(see illustrations)**. Position the draining container under the drain plug, and then remove the plug completely **(see Haynes Hint)**. Recover the sealing washer from the drain plug (the sealing ring may be part of the drain plug, and cannot be renewed separately).

4 Allow some time for the old oil to drain, noting that it may be necessary to reposition the container as the oil flow slows to a trickle.

5 After all the oil has drained, wipe off the drain plug with a clean rag, and fit a new sealing washer (or fit a complete new drain plug with sealing washer). Clean the area around the drain plug opening, and refit the plug. Tighten the plug to the specified torque.

6 If the filter is also to be renewed, move the container into position under the oil filter. On 1.2

litre engines, the filter is located beneath a cap on the front right-hand end of the engine. On 1.4 litre engines, the filter is a canister-type, which is located on the front of the cylinder block.

7 On 1.2 litre engines, unscrew the cap several turns from the oil filter housing until its sealing face is level with the side peg. Leave the cap in this position for at least one minute, to allow the oil to drain from the filter and housing. Cover the alternator with cloth rags, to prevent entry of oil. Completely unscrew the cap and withdraw it together with the filter. If the filter is stuck to the cap, tap the cap bottom extension lightly on a wooden base to release the filter. Using a screwdriver, remove the O-ring seal from the cap and discard it – a new one must be used when refitting **(see illustrations)**.

8 On 1.4 litre engines, using an oil filter removal tool if necessary, slacken the filter initially, then unscrew it by hand the rest of the way **(see illustration)**. Hold the oil filter in an upright position as it is being removed, then empty the remaining oil from inside the filter into the container. Check the old filter to make sure that its rubber sealing ring has not stuck to the engine. If it has, carefully remove it.

3.3a The engine oil drain plug location on the sump

3.3b The seal is integral with the plug

HAYNES HiNT

Keep the drain plug pressed into the sump while unscrewing it by hand the last couple of turns. As the plug releases, move it away sharply so the stream of oil issuing from the sump runs into the container, not up your sleeve.

3.7a Unscrew the cap and remove the oil filter

3.7b Tap the bottom extension of the cap to release the filter

3.8 Oil filter location – 1.4 litre engines

9 Use a clean rag to remove all oil, dirt and sludge from the filter housing and cap, or filter sealing area on the cylinder block (as applicable).

10 On 1.2 litre engines, fit a new O-ring seal to the cap, and then insert the new filter in the housing and screw on the cap. Tighten the cap to the specified torque. Wipe away any excess oil.

11 On 1.4 litre engines, apply a light coating of clean engine oil to the sealing ring on the new filter, and then screw it into position on the engine. Tighten the filter firmly by hand only – **do not** use any tools. Wipe away any excess oil.

12 Remove the old oil and all tools from under the car. Refit the engine undershield(s), tighten the retaining screws securely, and then lower the car to the ground. Also refit the engine top cover where applicable.

13 Remove the dipstick, and then unscrew the oil filler cap from the cylinder head cover. Fill the engine, using the correct grade and type of oil (see *Lubricants and fluids*). An oil can spout or funnel may help to reduce spillage **(see illustration)**. Pour in half the specified quantity of oil first, and then wait a few minutes for the oil to run to the sump. Continue adding oil a small quantity at a time until the level is up to the maximum mark on the dipstick. Refit the filler cap.

14 Start the engine and run it for a few minutes; check for leaks around the oil filter seal and the sump drain plug. Note that there may be a few seconds delay before the oil pressure warning light goes out when the engine is started, as the oil circulates through the engine oil galleries and the new oil filter (where fitted) before the pressure builds up.

15 Switch off the engine, and wait a few minutes for the oil to settle in the sump once more. With the new oil circulated and the filter completely full, recheck the level on the dipstick, and add more oil as necessary.

16 Dispose of the used engine oil safely, with reference to *General repair procedures* in the *Reference* section of this manual.

4 Brake pad/lining check

Front and rear disc brakes

1 The outer brake pads can be checked without removing the wheels; by observing the brake pads through the holes in the wheels **(see illustration)**. If necessary, remove the wheel trim. The thickness of the pad lining must not be less than the dimension given in the Specifications.

2 If the outer pads are worn near their limits, it is worthwhile checking the inner pads as well. Jack up car and support it on axle stands (see *Jacking and vehicle support*). Remove the roadwheels.

3 Use a steel rule to check the thickness of the brake pads, and compare with the

3.13 Use a funnel to reduce spillage when adding engine oil

minimum thickness given in the Specifications **(see illustration)**.

4 For a comprehensive check, the brake pads should be removed and cleaned. The operation of the caliper can then also be checked, and the condition of the brake disc itself can be fully examined on both sides. Refer to Chapter 9, Section 4.

5 If any pad's friction material is worn to the specified minimum thickness or less, all four pads at the front or rear, as applicable, must be renewed as a set. Never renew the pads on just one wheel, as uneven braking will result.

6 On completion of the check, refit the roadwheels and lower the car to the ground.

Rear drum brakes

7 Chock the front wheels, then jack up the rear of the car and support it on axle stands (see *Jacking and vehicle support*).

8 For a quick check, the thickness of friction material remaining on one of the brake shoes can be observed through a hole in the brake backplate, which is exposed by prising out the rubber sealing grommet. If a rod of the same diameter as the specified minimum friction material thickness is placed against the shoe friction material, the amount of wear can be assessed. A torch or inspection light will probably be required. If the friction material on any shoe is worn down to the specified minimum thickness or less, all four shoes must be renewed as a set.

4.3 The thickness (a) of the brake pads must not be less than the specified amount

4.1 The outer brake pads can be observed through the holes in the wheels

9 For a comprehensive check, the brake drum should be removed and cleaned. This will allow the wheel cylinders to be checked, and the condition of the brake drum itself to be fully examined (see Chapter 9, Section 10).

10 On completion of the check, refit the roadwheels where removed, and lower the car to the ground.

5 Resetting the service interval display

1 After all necessary maintenance work has been completed; the service interval display must be reset. VW technicians use a special dedicated instrument to do this, and a printout is then put in the vehicle service record. It is possible for the owner to reset the display as described in the following paragraphs, but note that the procedure will automatically reset the display to a 10 000 mile interval. To continue with the 'variable' intervals which take into consideration the number of starts, length of journeys, vehicle speeds, brake pad wear, bonnet opening frequency, fuel consumption, oil level and oil temperature, the display must be reset by a VW dealership using the special dedicated instrument.

Models up to 2013

2 To reset the display, follow the procedures below **(see illustration)**:
   a) Switch off the ignition.
   b) Press and hold down the trip reset

5.2 Press reset button (A) and then clock setting button (B)

button '0.0/SET' beneath the speedometer.
c) Switch the ignition on.
d) Release the reset button '0.0/SET'.
e) Then briefly press the clock setting button beneath the rev counter (within 20 seconds).
f) The display will then switch back to its original display.

Models from 2014

3 To reset the oil change display, follow the procedures as described above, for models up to 2013.
4 To reset the inspection service display, follow the procedures below:

a) Switch the hazard warning lights on.

b) With ignition switched off, press the trip reset button '0.0/SET' and hold down.
c) Switch the ignition on.
d) Release the reset button '0.0/SET'.
e) Then briefly press the clock setting button beneath the rev counter (within 20 seconds).
f) The display will then switch back to its original display.

'INSP service' on display

6 Exhaust system check

1 With the engine cold (at least an hour after the car has been driven), check the complete exhaust system from the engine to the end of the tailpipe. The exhaust system is most easily checked with the car raised on a hoist, or supported on axle stands, so that the exhaust components are readily visible and accessible (see *Jacking and vehicle support*).
2 Check the exhaust pipes and connections for evidence of leaks, severe corrosion and damage. Make sure that all brackets and mountings are in good condition, and that all relevant nuts and bolts are tight. Leakage at any of the joints or in other parts of the system will usually show up as a black sooty stain in the vicinity of the leak.
3 Rattles and other noises can often be traced to the exhaust system, especially the brackets and mountings. Try to move the pipes and silencers. If the components are able to come into contact with the body or suspension parts, secure the system with new mountings. Otherwise separate the joints (if possible) and twist the pipes as necessary to provide additional clearance.

7 Hose and fluid leak check

1 Visually inspect the engine joint faces, gaskets and seals for any signs of water or

oil leaks. Pay particular attention to the areas around the camshaft cover, cylinder head, oil filter and sump joint faces. Bear in mind that, over a period of time, some very slight seepage from these areas is to be expected – what you are really looking for is any indication of a serious leak. Should a leak be found, renew the offending gasket or oil seal by referring to the appropriate Chapters in this manual.
2 Also check the security and condition of all the engine-related pipes and hoses. Ensure that all cable-ties or securing clips are in place and in good condition. Clips that are broken or missing can lead to chafing of the hoses, pipes or wiring, which could cause more serious problems in the future.
3 Carefully check the radiator hoses and heater hoses along their entire length. Renew any hose that is cracked, swollen or deteriorated. Cracks will show up better if the hose is squeezed. Pay close attention to the hose clips that secure the hoses to the cooling system components. Hose clips can pinch and puncture hoses, resulting in cooling system leaks.
4 Inspect all the cooling system components (hoses, joint faces, etc) for leaks **(see Haynes Hint)**. Where any problems of this nature are found on system components, renew the component or gasket with reference to Chapter 3.
5 Where applicable, inspect the automatic transmission fluid cooler hoses for leaks or deterioration.
6 With the car raised, inspect the petrol tank and filler neck for punctures, cracks and other damage. The connection between the filler neck and tank is especially critical. Sometimes a rubber filler neck or connecting hose will leak due to loose retaining clamps or deteriorated rubber.
7 Carefully check all rubber hoses and metal fuel lines leading away from the petrol tank. Check for loose connections, deteriorated hoses, crimped lines, and other damage. Pay particular attention to the vent pipes and hoses, which often loop up around the filler neck and can become blocked or crimped. Follow the lines to the front of the car, carefully inspecting them all the way. Renew damaged sections as necessary.
8 From within the engine compartment, check the security of all fuel hose attachments and pipe unions, and inspect the fuel hoses and vacuum hoses for kinks, chafing and deterioration.

9 Where applicable, check the condition of the power steering fluid hoses and pipes.

8 Auxiliary drivebelt check

1 Apply the handbrake, and then jack up the front of the car and support it on axle stands (see *Jacking and vehicle support*).
2 Using a socket on the crankshaft pulley bolt, turn the engine slowly clockwise so that the full length of the auxiliary drivebelt can be examined. Look for cracks, splitting and fraying on the surface of the belt; check also for signs of glazing (shiny patches) and separation of the belt plies. Use a mirror to check the underside of the drivebelt **(see illustration)**. If damage or wear is visible, or if there are traces of oil or grease on it, the belt should be renewed (see Section 25).

9 Antifreeze check

1 The cooling system should be filled with the recommended G12 antifreeze and corrosion protection fluid – **do not** mix this antifreeze with any other type. Over a period of time, the concentration of fluid may be reduced due to topping-up (this can be avoided by topping-up with the correct antifreeze mixture – see Specifications) or fluid loss. If loss of coolant has been evident, it is important to make the necessary repair before adding fresh fluid.
2 With the engine **cold**, carefully remove the cap from the expansion tank. If the engine is not completely cold, place a cloth rag over the

8.2 Checking the underside of the auxiliary drivebelt with a mirror

A leak in the cooling system will usually show up as white – or rust-coloured deposits on the area adjoining the leak.

cap before removing it, and remove it slowly to allow any pressure to escape.

3 Antifreeze checkers (hydrometers) are available from car accessory shops. Draw some coolant from the expansion tank and observe how many plastic balls are floating in the checker. Usually, 2 or 3 balls must be floating for the correct concentration of antifreeze, but follow the tool manufacturer's instructions.

4 If the concentration is incorrect, it will be necessary to either withdraw some coolant and add antifreeze, or alternatively drain the old coolant and add fresh coolant of the correct concentration (see Section 30).

10 Brake hydraulic circuit check

1 Check the entire brake hydraulic circuit for leaks and damage. Start by checking the master cylinder in the engine compartment. At the same time, check the vacuum servo unit and ABS units for signs of fluid leakage.

2 Raise the front and rear of the car and support it on axle stands (see *Jacking and vehicle support*). Check the rigid hydraulic brake lines for corrosion and damage.

3 Check that the flexible hydraulic hoses to the front brake calipers are not twisted or chafing on any of the surrounding suspension components. To carry out this check, turn the steering fully to both sides to make this check. Also check that the hoses are not brittle or cracked.

4 Lower the car to the ground after making the checks.

11 Headlight beam adjustment

1 Accurate adjustment of the headlight beam is only possible using optical beam-setting equipment, and this work should therefore be carried out by a VW dealer or service station with the necessary facilities.

2 Basic adjustments can be carried out in an emergency, and further details are given in Chapter 12, Section 8 and Chapter 12, Section 9.

12 Pollen filter element renewal

1 The pollen filter is located on the heater assembly, and is removed into the passenger footwell.

2 Reach under the glovebox, and slide the two retaining catches on the pollen filter lower cover towards each other, to release and remove the cover **(see illustrations)**.

3 Withdraw the filter downwards from the heater assembly, and remove from inside the car **(see illustration)**.

12.2a Slide the catches (arrowed) towards each other...   **12.2b ...and remove the pollen filter lower cover**

12.3 Withdraw the pollen filter into the passenger footwell   **12.4 Separate the filter from the frame (where fitted), noting the airflow arrows**

4 Where fitted, separate the filter from the frame, noting the fitted direction of the airflow arrows, which should be towards the driver's side **(see illustration)**.

5 Fit the new filter to the frame (where applicable), with the airflow arrows pointing in the direction noted on removal. Insert the pollen into the heater assembly, and then refit the lower cover. Slide the two catches apart, to secure the cover to the housing.

13 Manual transmission oil level check

1 Park the car on a level surface. For improved access to the filler/level plug, apply the handbrake, and then jack up the front of the car and support it on axle stands (see *Jacking and vehicle support*), but note that the rear of the car should also be raised to ensure an accurate level check. The oil level must be checked before the car is driven, or at least 5 minutes after the engine has been switched off. If the oil is checked immediately after driving the car, some of the oil will remain distributed around the transmission components, resulting in an inaccurate level reading.

2 As applicable, undo the retaining screws and remove the engine undershield. Wipe clean the area around the transmission filler/level plug, which is situated on the rear, inner face of the transmission, above the engine rear mounting/torque link **(see illustration)**.

3 There are two types of filler/drain plugs fitted to this transmission; if the multi-splined plug is fitted a special tool will be required (VW tool number 3257, though alternatives may be available). Since the plug will almost certainly be very tight, badly fitting substitute tools are unlikely to work, and damage may be caused to the plug's splines.

4 The oil level should reach the lower edge of the filler/level hole. A certain amount of oil will have gathered behind the filler/level plug, and will trickle out when it is removed; this does **not** necessarily indicate that the level is correct. To ensure that a true level is established, wait until the initial trickle has stopped, and then add oil as necessary until a trickle of new oil can be seen emerging. The level will be correct when the flow ceases; use only good-quality oil of the specified type.

13.2 Manual transmission oil filler/level plug location

15.1 Check the condition of the driveshaft gaiter (arrowed)

5 If the transmission has been overfilled so that oil flows out when the filler/level plug is removed, check that the car is completely level (front-to-rear and side-to-side), and allow the surplus to drain off into a suitable container.

6 When the oil level is correct, refit the filler/level plug and tighten it to the specified torque. Wipe off any spilt oil then refit the engine undershield(s), tighten the retaining screws securely, and lower the car to the ground.

14 Underbody protection check

Raise and support the car on axle stands (see *Jacking and vehicle support*). Using a torch or lead light, inspect the entire underside of the car, paying particular attention to the wheel arches. Look for any damage to the flexible underbody coating, which may crack or flake off with age, leading to corrosion (note, however, that there are plastic underbody panels to protect the underside of the vehicle). Also check that the wheel arch liners are securely attached with any clips provided – if they come loose, dirt may get in behind the liners and defeat their purpose. If there is any damage to the underseal, or any corrosion, it should be repaired before the damage gets too serious.

15 Driveshaft check

1 With the car raised and securely supported on stands, slowly rotate the roadwheel. Inspect the condition of the outer constant velocity (CV) joint rubber gaiters, squeezing the gaiters to open out the folds. Check for signs of cracking, splits or deterioration of the rubber, which may allow the grease to escape, and lead to water and grit entry into the joint. Also check the security and condition of the retaining clips. Repeat these checks on the inner joints **(see illustration)**. If any damage or deterioration is found, the gaiters should be renewed (see Chapter 8, Section 3).

16.4 Check for wear in the hub bearings by grasping the wheel and trying to rock it

2 At the same time, check the general condition of the CV joints themselves by first holding the driveshaft and attempting to rotate the wheel. Repeat this check by holding the inner joint and attempting to rotate the driveshaft. Any appreciable movement indicates wear in the joints, wear in the driveshaft splines, or a loose driveshaft retaining bolt.

16 Steering and suspension check

1 Raise the front and rear of the car, and securely support it on axle stands (see *Jacking and vehicle support*).
2 Visually inspect the track rod end balljoint dust cover, the lower front suspension balljoint dust cover, and the steering rack-and-pinion gaiters for splits, chafing or deterioration. Any wear of these components will cause loss of lubricant, together with dirt and water entry, resulting in rapid deterioration of the balljoints or steering gear.
3 Check the power steering fluid hoses for chafing or deterioration, and the pipe and hose unions for fluid leaks. Also check for signs of fluid leakage under pressure from the steering gear rubber gaiters, which would indicate failed fluid seals within the steering gear.
4 Grasp the roadwheel at the 12 o'clock and 6 o'clock positions, and try to rock it **(see illustration)**. Very slight free play may be felt, but if the movement is appreciable, further

17.1 Unclip the plastic cover

investigation is necessary to determine the source. Continue rocking the wheel while an assistant depresses the footbrake. If the movement is now eliminated or significantly reduced, it is likely that the hub bearings are at fault. If the free play is still evident with the footbrake depressed, then there is wear in the suspension joints or mountings.
5 Now grasp the wheel at the 9 o'clock and 3 o'clock positions, and try to rock it as before. Any movement felt now may again be caused by wear in the hub bearings or the steering track rod balljoints. If the inner or outer balljoint is worn, the visual movement will be obvious.
6 Using a large screwdriver or flat bar, check for wear in the suspension mounting bushes by levering between the relevant suspension component and its attachment point. Some movement is to be expected as the mountings are made of rubber, but excessive wear should be obvious. Also check the condition of any visible rubber bushes, looking for splits, cracks or contamination of the rubber.
7 With the car standing on its wheels, have an assistant turn the steering wheel back-and-forth about an eighth of a turn each way. There should be very little, if any, lost movement between the steering wheel and roadwheels. If this is not the case, closely observe the joints and mountings previously described, but in addition check the steering column universal joints for wear, and the rack-and-pinion steering gear itself.
8 Check for any signs of fluid leakage around the front suspension struts and rear shock absorber. Should any fluid be noticed, the suspension strut or shock absorber is defective internally, and should be renewed. **Note:** *Suspension struts/shock absorbers should always be renewed in pairs on the same axle to ensure correct handling.*
9 The efficiency of the suspension strut/shock absorber may be checked by bouncing the car at each corner. Generally speaking, the body will return to its normal position and stop after being depressed. If it rises and returns on a rebound, the suspension strut/shock absorber is probably suspect. Examine also the suspension strut/shock absorber upper and lower mountings for any signs of wear.

17 Battery check

1 The battery is located in the front, left-hand corner of the engine compartment. Release the clip at the back, and then hinge the plastic cover forwards to gain access to the battery positive (+) terminal **(see illustration)**.
2 Where necessary, open the plastic cover (on the right-hand side of the battery) to gain access to the fuses.
3 Release the retaining clips at the front of the

plastic cover to access the wiring terminals on the top of the battery **(see illustration)**.

4 Check that both battery terminals and all connections are securely attached and are free from corrosion. **Note:** *Before disconnecting the terminals from the battery, refer to 'Disconnecting the battery' in the Reference Chapter at the end of this manual.*

5 Check the battery casing for signs of damage or cracking and check the battery retaining clamp bolt is securely tightened. If the battery casing is damaged in any way the battery must be renewed (see Chapter 5A, Section 3).

6 Some models are fitted with a battery with a small window that shows the state of the battery electrolyte. The window is located on the top of the battery **(see illustration)**, near the negative terminal. If the window is green, the battery is in good condition and charged up. If the window is black, the battery is flat and should be charged. If the window is colourless or yellow, the electrolyte is in a critical condition. If charging the battery does not return the window to green, the battery should be scrapped.

7 On completion of the check, make sure the covers are securely back in position.

18 Hinge and lock lubrication

1 Lubricate the hinges of the bonnet, doors and tailgate with a light general-purpose oil. Similarly, lubricate all latches, locks and lock strikers. At the same time, check the security and operation of all the locks, adjusting them if necessary (see Chapter 11, Section 11).

2 Lightly lubricate the bonnet release mechanism and cable with suitable grease.

19 Airbag unit check

Inspect the exterior condition of the airbag(s) for signs of damage or deterioration. If an airbag shows signs of damage, it must be renewed (see Chapter 12, Section 25 and Chapter 12, Section 26). Note that it is not permissible to attach any stickers to the surface of the airbag, as this may affect the deployment of the unit.

20 Windscreen/tailgate/ headlight washer system check

1 Check that each of the washer jet nozzles are clear and that each nozzle provides a strong jet of washer fluid.

2 The tailgate jet should be aimed to spray at the centre of the screen, using a pin.

3 The windscreen washer nozzles can be adjusted up and down as required.

17.3 Fused links on top of the battery

4 Especially during the winter months, make sure that the washer fluid concentration is sufficient to avoid freezing.

21 Engine management self-diagnosis memory fault check

A VW dealer or a specialist using diagnostic equipment should carry out this work. The diagnostic socket is located beneath the driver's side of the facia, above the accelerator pedal **(see illustration)**.

22 Road test and exhaust emissions check

Instruments and electrical equipment

1 Check the operation of all instruments and electrical equipment, including the air conditioning system, where applicable.

2 Make sure that all instruments read correctly, and switch on all electrical equipment in turn, to check that it functions properly.

Steering and suspension

3 Check for any abnormalities in the steering, suspension, handling or road 'feel'.

4 Drive the car, and check that there are no unusual vibrations or noises that may indicate wear in the driveshafts, wheel bearings, etc.

5 Check that the steering feels positive, with no excessive 'sloppiness', or roughness, and check for any suspension noises when cornering and driving over bumps.

Drivetrain

6 Check the performance of the engine, clutch (where applicable), gearbox/transmission and driveshafts.

7 Listen for any unusual noises from the engine, clutch and gearbox/transmission.

8 Make sure the engine runs smoothly at idle, and there is no hesitation on accelerating.

9 Check that, where applicable, the clutch action is smooth and progressive, that the drive is taken up smoothly, and that the pedal

17.6 Window to check battery condition (arrowed)

travel is not excessive. Also listen for any noises when the clutch pedal is depressed.

10 Check that all gears can be engaged smoothly without noise, and that the gear lever action is smooth and not abnormally vague or 'notchy'.

11 Listen for a metallic clicking sound from the front of the car, as the car is driven slowly in a circle with the steering on full-lock. Carry out this check in both directions. If a clicking noise is heard, this indicates wear in a driveshaft joint, in which case renew the joint if necessary.

Braking system

12 Make sure that the car does not pull to one side when braking, and that the wheels do not lock when braking hard.

13 Check that there is no vibration through the steering when braking.

14 Check that the handbrake operates correctly without excessive movement of the lever, and that it holds the car stationary on a slope.

15 Test the operation of the brake servo unit as follows. With the engine off, depress the footbrake four or five times to exhaust the vacuum. Hold the brake pedal depressed, and then start the engine. As the engine starts, there should be a noticeable 'give' in the brake pedal as vacuum builds up. Allow the engine to run for at least two minutes, and then switch it off. If the brake pedal is depressed now, it should be possible to detect a hiss from the servo as the pedal is depressed. After about four or five applications, no further hissing

21.1 Diagnostic socket location

should be heard, and the pedal should feel considerably harder.

16 Under controlled emergency braking, the pulsing of the ABS unit must be felt at the footbrake pedal.

Exhaust emissions check

17 Although not part of the manufacturer's maintenance schedule, this check will normally be carried out on a regular basis according to the country the car is operated in. Currently in the UK, exhaust emissions testing is included as part of the annual MOT test after the car is 3 years old.

Every 40 000 miles or 4 years

23 Air filter element renewal

1.2 litre engines

1 Undo the screws and lift the cover from the air filter housing located on the left-hand rear corner of the engine compartment (see illustrations). If required, release the retaining clip and disconnect the air intake hose from the upper cover.

2 Note how the element is fitted, then remove it (see illustration).

3 Remove any debris and wipe clean the interior of the housing.

4 Fit the new air filter element in position, ensuring that the edges are securely seated.

5 Refit the cover and secure with the screws. If removed, secure the air intake hose to the upper cover with the retaining clip.

1.4 litre engines

6 Undo the screws and lift the front edge of the air filter cover, and then disengage it from the rear edge (see illustrations). If required, release the retaining clip and disconnect the breather pipe from the left-hand side of the upper cover.

7 Note its fitted position, then lift the element from the housing (see illustration).

8 Remove any debris and wipe clean the interior of the housing.

9 Fit the new filter element in position.

10 Refit the cover and tighten the screws securely. If removed, fit the breather pipe to the upper cover making sure it is clipped back in position.

24 Spark plug renewal

1 The correct functioning of the spark plugs is vital for the correct running and efficiency of the engine. It is essential that the plugs fitted are appropriate for the engine (a suitable type is specified at the beginning of this Chapter). If this type is used and the engine is in good condition, the spark plugs should not need attention between scheduled renewal intervals. Spark plug cleaning is rarely necessary, and should not be attempted unless specialised equipment is available, as damage can easily be caused to the firing ends.

2 Remove the engine top cover.

3 The HT coils must now be pulled from the tops of the spark plugs. VW technicians use a special tool to do this as the coils are very tight in their holders, however, a length of strong welding rod or similar, bent at right-angles at one end, will do the task. Hook the rod under the wiring connector/HT coil then pull directly upwards (see illustrations).

23.1a Undo the retaining screws...

23.1b ...remove the upper cover...

23.2 ...and remove the air filter element

23.6a Undo the air filter cover screws (arrowed)...

23.6b ...and lift the cover from place

23.7 ...Remove the air filter element

24.3a Use a bent metal rod to release the HT coils...

24.3b ...then remove them from the cylinder head

24.5 Using a deep socket to remove the spark plugs

24.10a If single-electrode plugs are being fitted, check the electrode gap using a feeler gauge...

24.10b ...or a wire gauge...

24.11 ...and if necessary adjust the gap by bending the electrode

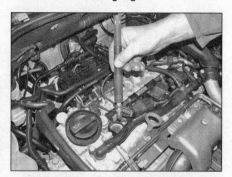

24.12 Using a piece of rubber hose to avoid cross threading the spark plugs

4 It is advisable to remove the dirt from the spark plug recesses using a clean brush, vacuum cleaner or compressed air before removing the plugs, to prevent dirt dropping into the cylinders.

5 Unscrew the plugs using a spark plug spanner, suitable box spanner or a deep socket and extension bar **(see illustration)**. Keep the socket aligned with the spark plug – if it is forcibly moved to one side, the ceramic insulator may be broken off. The use of a universal joint socket will be helpful. As each plug is removed, examine it as follows.

6 Examination of the spark plugs will give a good indication of the condition of the engine. If the insulator nose of the spark plug is clean and white, with no deposits, this is indicative of a weak mixture or too hot a plug (a hot plug transfers heat away from the electrode slowly, a cold plug transfers heat away quickly).

7 If the tip and insulator nose are covered with hard black-looking deposits, then this is indicative that the mixture is too rich. Should the plug be black and oily, and then it is likely that the engine is fairly worn, as well as the mixture being too rich.

8 If the insulator nose is covered with light tan to greyish-brown deposits, then the mixture is correct and it is likely that the engine is in good condition.

9 The spark plug electrode gap is of considerable importance as, if it is too large or too small, the size of the spark and its efficiency will be seriously impaired. On engines fitted with multi-electrode spark plugs, it is recommended that the plugs are

renewed rather than attempting to adjust the gaps. On other spark plugs, the gap should be set to the value given by the manufacturer.

10 To set the gap on single electrode plugs, measure it with a feeler blade and then bend open, or closed, the outer plug electrode until the correct gap is achieved. The centre electrode should never be bent, as this may crack the insulator and cause plug failure, if nothing worse. If using feeler blades, the gap is correct when the appropriate-size blade is a firm sliding fit **(see illustrations)**.

11 Special spark plug electrode gap adjusting tools are available from most motor accessory shops, or from some spark plug manufacturers **(see illustration)**.

12 Before fitting the spark plugs, check that the threaded connector sleeves are tight, and that the plug exterior surfaces and threads are clean. It's often difficult to screw in new spark plugs without cross-threading them – this can be avoided using a piece of rubber hose **(see illustration)**.

 HAYNES HiNT *It is very often difficult to insert spark plugs into their holes without cross-threading them. To avoid this possibility, fit a short length of rubber hose over the end of the spark plug. The flexible hose acts as a universal joint to help align the plug with the plug thread, the hose will slip on the spark plug, preventing thread damage to the aluminium cylinder head.*

13 Remove the rubber hose (if used), and tighten the plug to the specified torque using the spark plug socket and a torque wrench. Refit the remaining spark plugs in the same manner.

14 Reconnect the ignition coils using a reversal of the removal procedure, then refit the engine top cover.

25 Auxiliary drivebelt check and renewal

1 The poly-vee drivebelt drives the alternator and where fitted, the air conditioning compressor.

2 On all engines, the drivebelt tension is adjusted automatically by a spring-tensioned idler.

Checking

3 See Section 8 for information on checking the condition of the drivebelt. When the belt is removed, check all pulleys are free from any damage and are secure. Also check that the alternator and air-conditioning compressor are mounted securely.

Renewal

4 For improved access, apply the handbrake, and then jack up the front of the vehicle and support it on axle stands (see *Jacking and vehicle support*). Remove the right-hand front roadwheel, and then remove the inner wheel arch liner **(see illustration)**.

25.4 Remove inner wheel arch liner

25.6 Use a spanner to turn the tensioner and release the auxiliary drivebelt – 1.2 litre engines

25.7a Turn the tensioner with a spanner – 1.4 litre engine with air conditioning…

25.7b …and lock it in position with a metal rod/drill bit (arrowed)

5 If the drivebelt is to be re-used, mark it for clockwise direction to ensure it is refitted the same way round.

6 On 1.2 litre engines, lever off the cover (where fitted) from the tensioner pulley, then use a Torx key or spanner (as applicable) to turn the pulley anti-clockwise against the tension spring **(see illustration)**. If necessary, the tensioner may be retained with a metal rod (drill bit) inserted through the hole in the pulley arm and body, to lock it in position.

7 On 1.4 litre engines, use a spanner to turn the tensioner central bolt clockwise to release the tension on the drivebelt **(see illustrations)**. If necessary, the tensioner may be retained with a metal rod (drill bit) inserted through the hole in the pulley and body, to lock it in position.

8 Note how the drivebelt is routed, then remove it from the crankshaft pulley, alternator pulley and air conditioning compressor pulley (where fitted).

9 Locate the new drivebelt around the pulleys, then by holding the pressure of the tensioner with a spanner, remove the locking pin. Slowly release the pressure on the spanner, so that the tensioner takes up the slack in the belt. Check that the belt is located correctly in the multi-grooves in the pulleys.

10 Start the engine and check that the drivebelt runs, as it should over the pulleys. Make sure that all tools and hands are kept clear of the drivebelt with the engine running.

11 With the engine stopped, refit the inner wheel arch liner and roadwheel, and then lower the vehicle to the ground.

26 Power steering hydraulic fluid level check

1 Turn the front roadwheels to the straight-ahead position without starting the engine. If the car has been left standing for an hour or more, the power steering fluid will be cold (below 50ºC), and the 'cold' level markings must be used. If, however, the engine is at normal temperature (above 50ºC), the fluid will be hot, and the 'hot' level markings must be used.

2 The reservoir for the Electrically Powered Hydraulic Steering (EPHS) is located on the front left-hand corner of the engine compartment. **Note:** *On some models with a high-capacity battery, the battery and tray must be removed in order to access the reservoir filler cap.* The fluid level is checked with the dipstick attached to the reservoir filler cap. Unscrew the cap from the hydraulic fluid reservoir, and wipe clean the integral dipstick with a clean cloth **(see illustration)**.

3 Screw on the cap hand-tight then unscrew it again and check the fluid level on the dipstick. The fluid level must be between the MIN (or lower) and MAX (or upper) marks **(see illustrations)**. If the fluid is cold (below 50ºC), it must be at least above the lower level mark or MIN. If the fluid is hot (above 50ºC), it must not be above the upper level mark or MAX.

4 If the level is above the maximum level mark, syphon off the excess amount. If it is below the minimum level mark, add the specified fluid as necessary *(see Lubricants and fluids)*, but in this case also check the system for leaks **(see illustration)**. On completion, screw on the cap and tighten. Refit the battery and tray where removed.

26.2 Unscrew the cap from the hydraulic fluid reservoir (arrowed)

26.3a The power steering fluid level must be between the upper and lower marks

26.3b Alternative power steering cap markings

26.4 Topping-up the fluid level

27 DSG transmission fluid level check

The DSG semi-automatic transmission fitted to 1.4 litre petrol engines is the 7-speed dual clutch (0AM) transmission. The transmission is filled for life, and does not have an oil level checking procedure. If there has been an oil leak from the transmission, after the leak has been rectified, renew the transmission oil as described in Chapter 7B, Section 6.

28 Timing belt and tensioner renewal (1.4 litre engines)

Refer to Chapter 2B, Sections 6 and 7, for renewal on 1.4 litre engines.

Every 2 years

29 Brake (and clutch) fluid renewal

⚠️ *Warning: Brake hydraulic fluid can harm your eyes and damage painted surfaces, so use extreme caution when handling and pouring it. Do not use fluid that has been standing open for some time, as it absorbs moisture from the air. Excess moisture can cause a dangerous loss of braking effectiveness.*

1 The procedure is similar to that for the bleeding of the hydraulic system as described in Chapter 9, Section 2, except that the brake fluid reservoir should be emptied by syphoning, using a clean poultry baster or similar before starting, and allowance should be made for the old fluid to be expelled when bleeding a section of the circuit. Since the clutch hydraulic system also uses fluid from the brake system reservoir, it should also be bled at the same time by referring to Chapter 6, Section 2.

2 Working as described in Chapter 9, Section 2, open the first bleed screw in the sequence, and pump the brake pedal gently until nearly all the old fluid has been emptied from the master cylinder reservoir.

3 Top-up to the MAX level with new fluid, and continue pumping until only the new fluid remains in the reservoir, and new fluid can be seen emerging from the bleed screw. Tighten the screw, and top the reservoir level up to the MAX level line.

4 Work through all the remaining bleed screws in the sequence until new fluid can be seen at all of them. Be careful to keep the master cylinder reservoir topped-up to above the MIN level at all times, or air may enter the system and greatly increase the length of the task.

5 When the operation is complete, check that all bleed screws are securely tightened, and that their dust caps are refitted. Wash off all traces of spilt fluid, and recheck the master cylinder reservoir fluid level.

6 On models with a manual transmission unit, once the brake fluid has been changed the clutch fluid should also be renewed. Referring to Chapter 6, Section 2, bleed the clutch until new fluid is seen to be emerging from the slave cylinder bleed screw, keeping the master cylinder fluid level above the MIN level line at all times to prevent air entering the system. Once the new fluid emerges, securely tighten the bleed screw then disconnect and remove the bleeding equipment. Securely refit the dust cap then wash off all traces of spilt fluid.

7 Ensure the master cylinder fluid level is correct (see *Weekly checks*) and thoroughly check the operation of the brakes and (where necessary) clutch before taking the car on the road.

30 Coolant renewal

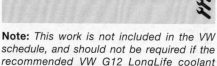

Note: *This work is not included in the VW schedule, and should not be required if the recommended VW G12 LongLife coolant anti-freeze/inhibitor is used. However, if standard antifreeze/inhibitor is used, the work should be carried out at the recommended interval.*

⚠️ *Warning: Wait until the engine is cold before starting this procedure. Do not allow antifreeze to come in contact with your skin, or with the car's painted surfaces. Rinse off spills immediately with plenty of water. Never leave antifreeze lying around in an open container, or in a puddle in the driveway or on the garage floor. Children and pets are attracted by its sweet smell, but antifreeze can be fatal if ingested.*

Cooling system draining

1 With the engine completely cold, unscrew the expansion tank cap.

2 Firmly apply the handbrake then jack up the front of the car and support it on axle stands (see *Jacking and vehicle support*). Undo the retaining screws and remove the engine under shield to gain access to the base of the radiator.

3 Position a suitable container beneath the bottom hose fitting to the left-hand end of the radiator. **Note:** *On some models there is a coolant drain plug, which is fitted to a plastic elbow between the bottom hose and the radiator.* Unscrew the drain plug and pull it out slightly (there is no need to remove it completely) and allow the coolant to drain into the container **(see illustration)**. If desired, a length of tubing can be fitted to the drain outlet to direct the flow of coolant during draining. Where no drain outlet is fitted to the hose end fitting, remove the retaining clip and disconnect the bottom hose from the radiator to drain the coolant.

4 On engines with an oil cooler, to fully drain the system, also disconnect one of the coolant hoses from the oil cooler which is located at the front of the cylinder block.

5 If the coolant has been drained for a reason other than renewal then, provided it is clean, it can be re-used.

6 Once all the coolant has drained, securely tighten the radiator drain plug or reconnect the bottom hose to the radiator (as applicable). Where necessary, also reconnect the coolant hose to the oil cooler and secure it in position with the retaining clip. Refit the undershield(s), tighten the retaining screws securely.

Cooling system flushing

7 If the recommended VW coolant has not been used and coolant renewal has been neglected, or if the antifreeze mixture has become diluted, the cooling system may gradually lose efficiency, as the coolant passages become restricted due to rust, scale deposits, and other sediment. The cooling system efficiency can be restored by flushing the system clean.

8 The radiator should be flushed separately from the engine, to avoid excess contamination.

30.3 Unscrew the drain plug and allow the coolant to drain into the container

30.18 Filling the cooling system

Radiator flushing

9 To flush the radiator first tighten the radiator drain plug (where applicable).

10 Disconnect the top and bottom hoses and any other relevant hoses from the radiator.

11 Insert a garden hose into the radiator top inlet. Direct a flow of clean water through the radiator, and continue flushing until clean water emerges from the radiator bottom outlet.

12 If after a reasonable period the water still does not run clear, the radiator can be flushed with a good proprietary cleaning agent. It is important that the manufacturer's instructions are followed carefully. If the contamination is particularly bad, insert the hose in the radiator bottom outlet, and reverse-flush the radiator.

Engine flushing

13 To flush the engine, remove the thermostat (see Chapter 3, Section 4).

14 With the bottom hose disconnected from the radiator, insert a garden hose into the thermostat housing. Direct a clean flow of water through the engine, and continue flushing until clean water emerges from the radiator bottom hose.

15 When flushing is complete, refit the thermostat and reconnect the hoses.

Cooling system filling

16 Before attempting to fill the cooling system, ensure the drain plug (where applicable) is securely closed and make sure that all hoses are securely connected and their retaining clips are in good condition. If the recommended VW coolant is not being used, ensure that a suitable antifreeze mixture is used all year round, to prevent corrosion of the engine components (see following sub-Section).

17 Remove the coolant temperature sensor from the coolant distribution housing on the left-hand end of the cylinder head with reference to Chapter 3, Section 6.

18 Remove the expansion tank filler cap and slowly fill the system with coolant **(see illustration)**, until bubble-free coolant runs from the temperature sensor hole, then refit the sensor immediately. Continue to fill the system until the level is up to the MAX level mark on the expansion tank. Help to bleed the air from the system by repeatedly squeezing the radiator bottom hose.

19 Refit the cap to the expansion tank, then run the engine at a fast idle speed until the cooling fan cuts in. Wait for the fan to stop then switch the engine off and allow the engine to cool.

20 When the engine has cooled, check the coolant level with reference to *Weekly checks*. Top-up the level if necessary, and refit the expansion tank cap.

Antifreeze mixture

21 If the recommended VW coolant is not being used, the antifreeze should always be renewed at the specified intervals. This is necessary not only to maintain the antifreeze properties, but also to prevent corrosion, which would otherwise occur as the corrosion inhibitors become progressively less effective.

22 Always use an ethylene glycol based antifreeze that is suitable for use in mixed-metal cooling systems. The quantity of antifreeze and levels of protection are indicated in the Specifications.

23 Before adding antifreeze, the cooling system should be completely drained, preferably flushed, and all hoses checked for condition and security.

24 After filling with antifreeze, a label should be attached to the expansion tank, stating the type and concentration of antifreeze used, and the date installed. Any subsequent topping-up should be made with the same type and concentration of antifreeze.

25 Do not use engine antifreeze in the windscreen/tailgate washer system, as it will damage the paintwork. A screen wash additive should be added to the washer system in the quantities stated on the bottle.

Airlocks

26 If, after draining and refilling the system, symptoms of overheating are found which did not occur previously, then the fault is almost certainly due to trapped air at some point in the system, causing an airlock and restricting the flow of coolant; usually, the air is trapped because the system was refilled too quickly.

27 If an airlock is suspected, first try gently squeezing all visible coolant hoses. A coolant hose, which is full of air, feels quite different to one full of coolant, when squeezed. After refilling the system, most airlocks will clear once the system has cooled, and been topped up.

28 While the engine is running at operating temperature, switch on the heater and heater fan, and check for heat output. Provided there is sufficient coolant in the system, any lack of heat output could be due to an airlock in the system.

29 Airlocks can have more serious effects than simply reducing heater output - a severe airlock could reduce coolant flow around the engine. Check that the radiator top hose is hot when the engine is at operating temperature - a top hose that stays cold could be the result of an airlock (or a non-opening thermostat).

30 If the problem persists, stop the engine and allow it to cool down **completely**, before unscrewing the expansion tank filler cap or loosening the hose clips and squeezing the hoses to bleed out the trapped air. In the worst case, the system will have to be at least partially drained (this time, the coolant can be saved for re-use) and flushed to clear the problem.

Chapter 1 Part B:
Routine maintenance and servicing – diesel models

Contents

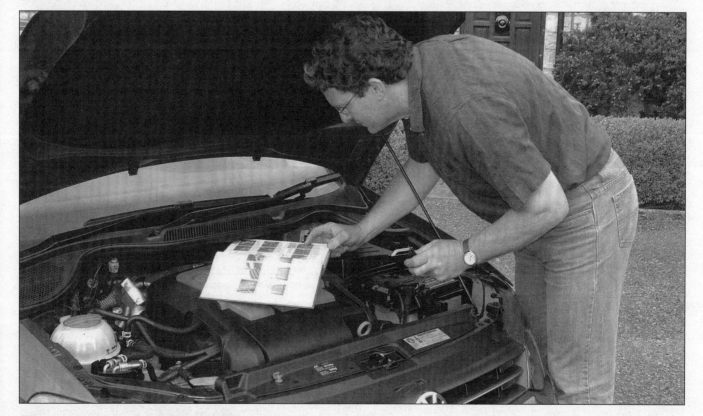

Degrees of difficulty

Easy, suitable for novice with little experience	**Fairly easy,** suitable for beginner with some experience	**Fairly difficult,** suitable for competent DIY mechanic	**Difficult,** suitable for experienced DIY mechanic	**Very difficult,** suitable for expert DIY or professional

Lubricants and fluids . . . . Refer to the end of *Weekly checks* on page 0•16

Engine codes
1.2 litre . . . . CFWA
1.6 litre . . . . CAYB, CAYC and CLNA

Capacities

Engine oil (including filter)
1.2 litre engines . . . . 4.3 litres
1.6 litre engines . . . . 4.3 litres

Cooling system
1.2 litre engines . . . . 6.2 litres
1.6 litre engines . . . . 6.6 litres

Transmission
Manual transmission - Type 02R . . . . 2.0 litres
DSG transmission (optional for 1.6 litre engines) . . . . 1.7 litres

Fuel tank (approximate) . . . . 45 litres

Cooling system
Antifreeze mixture:
  40% antifreeze . . . . Protection down to -25°C
  50% antifreeze . . . . Protection down to -35°C
Note: *Refer to antifreeze manufacturer for latest recommendations.*

Brakes
Brake pad minimum thickness:
  Front and rear (friction lining only) . . . . 2.0 mm
Rear brake shoe friction material minimum thickness . . . . 1.5 mm

Torque wrench settings

	Nm	lbf ft
Alternator mounting bolt	20	15
Manual transmission 02R:		
Filler/level and drain plug	35	26
Roadwheel bolts	120	89
Sump drain plug	30	22

Maintenance schedule

The maintenance intervals in this manual are provided with the assumption that you, not the dealer, will be carrying out the work. These are the minimum intervals recommended by us for cars driven daily. If you wish to keep your car in peak condition at all times, you may wish to perform some of these procedures more often. We encourage frequent maintenance, since it enhances the efficiency, performance and resale value of your car.

When the vehicle is new, it should be serviced by a dealer service department (or other workshop recognised by the vehicle manufacturer as providing the same standard of service) in order to preserve the warranty. The vehicle manufacturer may reject warranty claims if you are unable to prove that servicing has been carried out as and when specified, using only original equipment parts or parts certified to be of equivalent quality.

Longlife service schedule

All VW models are equipped with a service interval display indicator in the instrument panel. Every time the engine is started the panel will illuminate for approximately 20 seconds with service information. With the standard fixed interval display, the service intervals are in accordance with specific distances and time periods. With the LongLife display, the service interval is variable. Once the service interval has been reached, the display will flash 'OIL service' for an oil change service or 'INSP service' for an inspection service.

For models using the LongLife schedule, the occurrence of either service reminder on the display unit will depend on how the car is being used (number of starts, length of journeys, vehicle speeds, brake pad wear, bonnet opening frequency, fuel consumption, oil level and oil temperature). For example, if the car is being used under extreme driving conditions, the service may occur at 10 000 miles, whereas, if the car is being used under moderate driving conditions, it may occur at 20 000 miles, although the maximum length of time between INSP services is 2 years. It is important to realise that this system is completely variable according to how the car is being used, and therefore the service should be carried out when indicated on the display.

Note: *Models with the variable service interval system are equipped with an engine oil level*

sensor, brake pad wear indicator, and a variable service indicator.

The LongLife variable service intervals are only applicable to models with a PR number of QG1 (>2012) or QI6 (2013>). This number is shown in the vehicle Service Schedule booklet, on a service interval plate inside the luggage compartment **(see illustration)** or on the Next Service sticker located on the driver's door pillar). With the variable (LongLife) service interval on models with these PR numbers, the engine must **only** be filled with the recommended **LongLife** engine oil (see *Lubricants and fluids*).

After completing a service, VW technicians use a special instrument to reset the service display to the next service interval, and a print-out is put in the vehicle service record. The display can be reset by the owner as described in Section 5, but note that for models using the LongLife interval, the procedure will automatically reset the schedule to an amended LongLife interval, in which oil renewal and brake pad checks are based on distance/time while every other system remains LongLife. To have the display reset to the full LongLife schedule, it is necessary to take the car to a VW dealer who will use a special instrument to encode the on-board computer.

0.5 Vehicle Data Sticker location

Every 250 miles or weekly
- [ ] Refer to *Weekly checks*

'OIL service' on display
- [ ] Renew the engine oil and filter (Section 3)

Note: *Frequent oil and filter changes are good for the engine. We recommend changing the oil at least once a year.*
- [ ] Check the front and rear brake pad thickness (Section 4)
- [ ] Reset the service interval display (Section 5)

'INSP service' on display
In addition to the items listed above, carry out the following:
- [ ] Check the condition of the exhaust system and its mountings (Section 6)
- [ ] Check all underbonnet components and hoses for fluid and oil leaks (Section 7)
- [ ] Check the condition of the auxiliary drivebelt (Section 8 and Section 25)
- [ ] Check the coolant antifreeze concentration (Section 9)
- [ ] Check the brake hydraulic circuit for leaks and damage (Section 10)
- [ ] Check the headlight beam adjustment (Section 11)
- [ ] Renew the pollen filter element (Section 12)
- [ ] Check the manual transmission oil level (Section 13)
- [ ] Check the underbody protection for damage (Section 14)
- [ ] Check the condition of the driveshafts (Section 15)
- [ ] Check the steering and suspension components for condition and security (Section 16)
- [ ] Check the battery condition, security and electrolyte level (Section 17)
- [ ] Lubricate all hinges and locks (Section 18)
- [ ] Check the condition of the airbag unit(s) (Section 19)
- [ ] Check the operation of the windscreen/tailgate/head-light washer system(s) (as applicable) (Section 20)

'INSP service' on display (continued)
- [ ] Check the engine management self-diagnosis memory for faults (Section 21)
- [ ] Carry out a road test and check exhaust emissions (Section 22)

Every 40 000 miles or 4 years, whichever comes first
Note: *Many dealers perform these tasks with every second INSP service.*
- [ ] Renew the air filter element (Section 23)
- [ ] Renew the fuel filter (Section 24)
- [ ] Check the condition of the auxiliary drivebelt (Section 8 and Section 25)
- [ ] Check the power steering hydraulic fluid level (Section 26)
- [ ] Check the DSG transmission fluid level (Section 27)
- [ ] Renew the timing belt and tensioner* (Section 28)

* *VW specify timing belt renewal after 130,000 miles. However, if the car is used mainly for short journeys, or in a high dust area, we recommend that the timing belt be renewed earlier at 75,000 miles. The belt renewal interval is very much up to the individual owner, bearing in mind that severe engine damage will result if the belt breaks in use.*

Every 2 years
- [ ] Renew the brake (and clutch) fluid (Section 29)
- [ ] Renew the coolant* (Section 30)

* *This work is not included in the VW schedule, and should not be required if the recommended VW G12 LongLife coolant antifreeze/inhibitor is used.*

Every 75 000 miles then every 20 000 miles thereafter
- [ ] Check the particulate filter* (Section 31)

Underbonnet view - 1.2 litre diesel model

1   Engine oil filler cap
2   Engine oil dipstick
3   Oil filter
4   Coolant expansion tank
5   Fuel filter
6   Windscreen/headlight washer fluid reservoir
7   Master cylinder brake fluid reservoir
8   Front suspension strut upper mounting
9   Air cleaner housing
10 Engine management ECU
11 Battery
12 Alternator
13 High-pressure fuel pump
14 Power steering fluid reservoir

Front underbody view - 1.2 litre diesel model

1   Sump drain plug
2   Manual transmission drain plug
3   Engine rear mounting/link
4   Driveshaft
5   Front suspension subframe
6   Front suspension lower arm
7   Steering track rod
8   Front brake caliper
9   Front flexible exhaust pipe
10 Intercooler hose for turbocharger
11 Air conditioning compressor
12 Radiator electric cooling fan

Rear underbody view - 1.2 litre diesel model

1 Fuel tank
2 Rear axle assembly
3 Rear suspension coil spring
4 Rear shock absorber
5 Exhaust rear silencer
6 Rear axle assembly front mountings
7 Handbrake cables
8 Fuel tank filler neck
9 Spare wheel well

Maintenance procedures

1 Introduction

This Chapter is designed to help the home mechanic maintain his/her car for safety, economy, long life and peak performance.

The Chapter contains a master maintenance schedule, followed by Sections dealing specifically with each task in the schedule. Visual checks, adjustments, component renewal and other helpful items are included. Refer to the accompanying illustrations of the engine compartment and the underside of the car for the locations of the various components.

Servicing your car will provide a planned maintenance programme, which should result in a long and reliable service life. This is a comprehensive plan, so maintaining some items but not others will not produce the same results.

As you service your car, you will discover that many of the procedures can – and should – be grouped together, because of the particular procedure being performed, or because of the proximity of two otherwise unrelated components to one another. For example, if the car is raised for any reason, the exhaust can be inspected at the same time as the suspension and steering components.

The first step in this maintenance programme is to prepare yourself before the actual work begins. Read through all the Sections relevant to the work to be carried out, then make a list and gather all the parts and tools required. If a problem is encountered, seek advice from a parts specialist, or a dealer service department.

2 Regular maintenance

1 If, from the time the car is new, the routine maintenance schedule is followed closely, and frequent checks are made of fluid levels and high-wear items, as suggested throughout this manual, the engine will be kept in relatively good running condition, and the need for additional work will be minimised.

2 It is possible that there will be times when the engine is running poorly due to the lack of regular maintenance. This is even more likely if a used car, which has not received regular and frequent maintenance checks, is purchased. In such cases, additional work may need to be carried out, outside of the regular maintenance intervals.

3 If engine wear is suspected, a compression test (refer to Chapter 2C or Chapter 2D) will provide valuable information regarding the overall performance of the main internal components. Such a test can be used as a basis to decide on the extent of the work to be carried out. If, for example, a compression test indicates serious internal engine wear, conventional maintenance as described in this Chapter will not greatly improve the performance of the engine, and may prove a waste of time and money, unless extensive overhaul work is carried out first.

4 The following series of operations are those most often required to improve the performance of a generally poor-running engine:

Primary operations

a) Clean, inspect and test the battery (See 'Weekly checks').
b) Check all the engine-related fluids (See 'Weekly checks').

c) *Check the condition and tension of the auxiliary drivebelt (Section 8).*

d) *Check the condition of the air filter, and renew if necessary (Section 23).*

e) *Check the condition of all hoses, and check for fluid leaks (Section 7).*

5 If the above operations do not prove fully effective, carry out the following secondary operations:

Secondary operations

All items listed under *Primary operations*, plus the following:

a) *Check the charging system (see Chapter 5A).*

b) *Check the preheating system (see Chapter 5C).*

c) *Renew the fuel filter (Section 24) and check the fuel system (see Chapter 4B).*

'OIL service' on display

3 Engine oil and filter renewal

1 Frequent oil and filter changes are the most important preventative maintenance procedures, which can be undertaken by the DIY owner. As engine oil ages, it becomes diluted and contaminated, which leads to premature engine wear.

2 Before starting this procedure, gather all the necessary tools and materials. Also make sure that you have plenty of clean rags and newspapers handy, to mop-up any spills. Ideally, the engine oil should be warm, as it will drain better, and more built-up sludge will be removed with it. Take care, however, not to touch the exhaust or any other hot parts of the engine when working under the vehicle. To avoid any possibility of scalding, and to protect yourself from possible skin irritants and other harmful contaminants in used engine oils, it is advisable to wear gloves when carrying out this work. Access to the underside of the vehicle will be greatly improved if it can be raised on a lift, driven onto ramps, or jacked up and supported on axle stands (see *Jacking and vehicle support*). Whichever method is chosen, make sure that the vehicle remains level, or if it is at an angle, that the drain plug is at the lowest point. Undo the retaining screws and remove the engine undertray, then also remove the engine top cover **(see illustrations)**.

3 Slacken the sump drain plug about half a turn. Position the draining container under the drain plug, and then remove the plug completely **(see illustrations and Haynes Hint)**. To drain all oil from the engine, loosen the cap from the top of the oil filter housing using a socket or spanner - this will allow the oil to drain from the filter housing into the sump.

4 Allow some time for the old oil to drain, noting that it may be necessary to reposition the container as the oil flow slows to a trickle.

5 After all the oil has drained, wipe off the drain plug with a clean rag, and fit a new sealing washer. Clean the area around the drain plug opening, and refit the plug. Tighten the plug securely. **Note:** *On some engines, the sealing washer is integral with the drain plug. On these engines, the drain plug must be renewed.*

6 Place absorbent cloths around the oil filter housing to catch any spilt oil. On 1.6 litre

3.2a **Undo the undertray screws (arrowed)...**

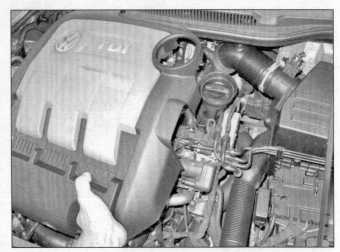

3.2b **...and remove the engine cover**

3.3a **Undo the sump drain plug**

3.3b **The seal is integral with the plug**

HAYNES HiNT

Keep the drain plug pressed into the sump while unscrewing it by hand the last couple of turns. As the plug releases, move it away sharply so the stream of oil issuing from the sump runs into the container, not up your sleeve.

3.6 Remove the solenoid - arrowed

3.7a Use a 32mm socket to unscrew the filter cap…

3.7b …and withdraw the filter and cap…

engines, unbolt the bracket and unclip the solenoid valve from above the oil filter **(see illustration)**.

7 Fully unscrew the cap from the top of the oil filter and remove it together with the filter element. Recover the large sealing ring from the cap, and the small sealing ring from the centre rod. Unclip the filter element from the cap and dispose of it **(see illustrations)**.

8 Using a clean rag, wipe all oil and sludge from the inside of the filter housing and cap.

9 Fit new sealing rings, then refit the assembly and tighten to the specified torque. Make sure the filter element is engaged with the cap and the correct way up **(see illustrations)**. Wipe up any spilt oil before refitting the engine top cover.

10 Remove the old oil and all tools from under the car then refit the undertray and lower the car to the ground. Also refit the engine top cover.

3.7c …then slide the old filter from the cap

11 Remove the dipstick, and then unscrew the oil filler cap from the cylinder head cover. Fill the engine, using the correct grade and type of oil (see *Lubricants and fluids*). An

3.9a The new filter comes with three O-ring seals

oil can spout or funnel may help to reduce spillage. Pour in half the specified quantity of oil first **(see illustration)**, then wait a few minutes for the oil to run to the sump (see

3.9b Fit the three seals to the oil filter cap in the positions shown…

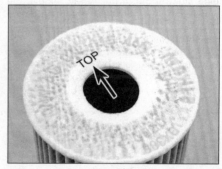

3.9c …then slide the new filter to the cap…

3.9d …noting 'TOP' on the filter for correct fitting

3.9e Lubricate the O-ring seals with clean engine oil…

3.9f …then refit to the oil filter housing

3.11 Pour in half the specified quantity of oil first, wait, then add the rest

Weekly checks). Continue adding oil a small quantity at a time until the level is up to the maximum mark on the dipstick. Refit the filler cap.

12 Start the engine and run it for a few minutes; check for leaks around the oil filter cap and the sump drain plug. Note that there may be a few seconds delay before the oil pressure warning light goes out when the engine is started, as the oil circulates through the engine oil galleries and the new oil filter before the pressure builds-up.

⚠ *Warning: Do not increase the engine speed above idling while the oil pressure light is illuminated, as considerable damage can be caused to the turbocharger.*

13 Switch off the engine, and wait a few minutes for the oil to settle in the sump once more. With the new oil circulated and the filter completely full, recheck the level on the dipstick, and add more oil as necessary.

14 Dispose of the used engine oil safely, with reference to *General repair procedures* in the *Reference* section of this manual.

4 Brake pad/lining check

Front and rear disc brakes

1 The outer brake pads can be checked without removing the wheels, by observing the brake pads through the holes in the wheels **(see illustration)**. If necessary, remove the wheel trim. The thickness of the pad lining must not be less than the dimension given in the Specifications.

2 If the outer pads are worn near their limits, it is worthwhile checking the inner pads as well. Jack up car and support it on axle stands (see *Jacking and vehicle support*). Remove the roadwheels.

H31925

4.3 The thickness (a) of the brake pads must not be less than the specified amount

4.1 The outer brake pads can be observed through the holes in the wheels

3 Use a steel rule to check the thickness of the brake pads, and compare with the minimum thickness given in the Specifications **(see illustration)**.

4 For a comprehensive check, the brake pads should be removed and cleaned. The operation of the caliper can then also be checked, and the condition of the brake disc itself can be fully examined on both sides. Refer to Chapter 9, Section 4.

5 If any pad's friction material is worn to the specified minimum thickness or less, all four pads at the front or rear, as applicable, must be renewed as a set.

6 On completion of the check, refit the roadwheels and lower the car to the ground.

Rear drum brakes

7 Chock the front wheels, then jack up the rear of the car and support it on axle stands (see *Jacking and vehicle support*).

8 For a quick check, the thickness of friction material remaining on one of the brake shoes can be observed through a hole in the brake backplate, which is exposed by prising out the rubber sealing grommet. If a rod of the same diameter as the specified minimum friction material thickness is placed against the shoe friction material, the amount of wear can be assessed. A torch or inspection light will probably be required. If the friction material on any shoe is worn down to the specified minimum thickness or less, all four shoes must be renewed as a set.

5.2 Press reset button (A) and then clock setting button (B)

9 For a comprehensive check, the brake drum should be removed and cleaned. This will allow the wheel cylinders to be checked, and the condition of the brake drum itself to be fully examined (see Chapter 9, Section 10).

10 On completion of the check, refit the roadwheels where removed, and lower the car to the ground.

5 Resetting the service interval display

1 After all necessary maintenance work has been completed; the service interval display must be reset. VW technicians use a special dedicated instrument to do this, and a printout is then put in the vehicle service record. It is possible for the owner to reset the display as described in the following paragraphs, but note that the procedure will automatically reset the display to a 10 000 mile interval. To continue with the 'variable' intervals which take into consideration the number of starts, length of journeys, vehicle speeds, brake pad wear, bonnet opening frequency, fuel consumption, oil level and oil temperature, the display must be reset by a VW dealership using the special dedicated instrument.

Models up to 2013

2 To reset the display, follow the procedures below **(see illustration)**:

a) *Switch off the ignition.*

b) *Press and hold down the trip reset button '0.0/SET' beneath the speedometer.*

c) *Switch the ignition on.*

d) *Release the reset button '0.0/SET'.*

e) *Then briefly press the clock setting button beneath the rev counter (within 20 seconds).*

f) *The display will then switch back to its original display.*

Models from 2014

3 To reset the oil change display, follow the procedures as described above, for models up to 2013.

4 To reset the inspection service display, follow the procedures below:

a) *Switch the hazard warning lights on.*

b) *With ignition switched off, press the trip reset button '0.0/SET' and hold down.*

c) *Switch the ignition on.*

d) *Release the reset button '0.0/SET'.*

e) *Then briefly press the clock setting button beneath the rev counter (within 20 seconds).*

f) *The display will then switch back to its original display.*

'INSP service' on display

6 Exhaust system check

1 With the engine cold (at least an hour after the car has been driven), check the complete exhaust system from the engine to the end of the tailpipe. The exhaust system is most easily checked with the car raised on a hoist, or supported on axle stands, so that the exhaust components are readily visible and accessible (see *Jacking and vehicle support*).
2 Check the exhaust pipes and connections for evidence of leaks, severe corrosion and damage. Make sure that all brackets and mountings are in good condition, and that all relevant nuts and bolts are tight. Leakage at any of the joints or in other parts of the system will usually show up as a black sooty stain in the vicinity of the leak.
3 Rattles and other noises can often be traced to the exhaust system, especially the brackets and mountings. Try to move the pipes and silencers. If the components are able to come into contact with the body or suspension parts, secure the system with new mountings. Otherwise separate the joints (if possible) and twist the pipes as necessary to provide additional clearance.

7 Hose and fluid leak check

1 Visually inspect the engine joint faces, gaskets and seals for any signs of water or oil leaks. Pay particular attention to the areas around the camshaft cover, cylinder head, oil filter and sump joint faces. Bear in mind that, over a period of time, some very slight seepage from these areas is to be expected – what you are really looking for is any indication of a serious leak. Should a leak be found, renew the offending gasket or oil seal by referring to the appropriate Chapters in this manual.
2 Also check the security and condition of all the engine-related pipes and hoses. Ensure that all cable-ties or securing clips are in place and in good condition. Clips that are broken or missing can lead to chafing of the hoses, pipes or wiring, which could cause more serious problems in the future.
3 Carefully check the radiator hoses and heater hoses along their entire length. Renew any hose, which is cracked, swollen or deteriorated. Cracks will show up better if the hose is squeezed. Pay close attention to the hose clips that secure the hoses to the cooling system components. Hose clips can pinch and puncture hoses, resulting in cooling system leaks.
4 Inspect all the cooling system components

(hoses, joint faces, etc.) for leaks (see Haynes Hint). Where any problems of this nature are found on system components, renew the component or gasket with reference to Chapter 3.
5 Where applicable, inspect the automatic transmission fluid cooler hoses for leaks or deterioration.
6 With the car raised, inspect the petrol tank and filler neck for punctures, cracks and other damage. The connection between the filler neck and tank is especially critical. Sometimes a rubber filler neck or connecting hose will leak due to loose retaining clamps or deteriorated rubber.
7 Carefully check all rubber hoses and metal fuel lines leading away from the petrol tank. Check for loose connections, deteriorated hoses, crimped lines, and other damage. Pay particular attention to the vent pipes and hoses, which often loop up around the filler neck and can become blocked or crimped. Follow the lines to the front of the car, carefully inspecting them all the way. Renew damaged sections as necessary.
8 From within the engine compartment, check the security of all fuel hose attachments and pipe unions, and inspect the fuel hoses and vacuum hoses for kinks, chafing and deterioration.
9 Check the condition of the power steering fluid hoses and pipes.

8 Auxiliary drivebelt check

1 Apply the handbrake, and then jack up the front of the car and support it on axle stands (see *Jacking and vehicle support*).
2 Using a socket on the crankshaft pulley bolt, turn the engine slowly clockwise so that the full length of the auxiliary drivebelt can be examined. Look for cracks, splitting and fraying on the surface of the belt; check also for signs of glazing (shiny patches) and separation of the belt plies. Use a mirror to

HAYNES HiNT

A leak in the cooling system will usually show up as white – or rust-coloured deposits on the area adjoining the leak.

check the underside of the drivebelt (see illustration). If damage or wear is visible, or if there are traces of oil or grease on it, the belt should be renewed (see Section 25).

9 Antifreeze check

1 The cooling system should be filled with the recommended G12 antifreeze and corrosion protection fluid – do not mix this antifreeze with any other type. Over a period of time, the concentration of fluid may be reduced due to topping-up (this can be avoided by topping-up with the correct antifreeze mixture – see Specifications) or fluid loss. If loss of coolant has been evident, it is important to make the necessary repair before adding fresh fluid.
2 With the engine cold, carefully remove the cap from the expansion tank. If the engine is not completely cold, place a cloth rag over the cap before removing it, and remove it slowly to allow any pressure to escape.
3 Antifreeze checkers are available from car accessory shops. Draw some coolant from the expansion tank and observe how many plastic balls are floating in the checker. Usually, 2 or 3 balls must be floating for the correct concentration of antifreeze, but follow the manufacturer's instructions.
4 If the concentration is incorrect, it will be necessary to either withdraw some coolant and add antifreeze, or alternatively drain the old coolant and add fresh coolant of the correct concentration (see Section 30).

10 Brake hydraulic circuit check

1 Check the entire brake hydraulic circuit for leaks and damage. Start by checking the master cylinder in the engine compartment. At the same time, check the vacuum servo unit and ABS units for signs of fluid leakage.
2 Raise the front and rear of the car and support it on axle stands (see *Jacking and*

8.2 Checking the underside of the auxiliary drivebelt with a mirror

12.2a Slide the catches towards each other...

12.2b ...and remove the pollen filter lower cover

12.3 Withdraw the pollen filter into the passenger footwell

12.4 Separate the filter from the frame (where fitted), noting the airflow arrows

vehicle support). Check the rigid hydraulic brake lines for corrosion and damage.

3 Check that the flexible hydraulic hoses to the front brake calipers are not twisted or chafing on any of the surrounding suspension components. To carry out this check, turn the steering fully to both sides to make this check. Also check that the hoses are not brittle or cracked.

4 Lower the car to the ground after making the checks.

11 Headlight beam adjustment

1 Accurate adjustment of the headlight beam is only possible using optical beam-setting equipment, and this work should therefore be carried out by a VW dealer or service station with the necessary facilities.

13.2 Oil drain plug (A) oil filler/level plug (B)

2 Basic adjustments can be carried out in an emergency, and further details are given in Chapter 12, Section 8 and Chapter 12, Section 9.

12 Pollen filter element renewal

1 The pollen filter is located on the heater assembly, and is removed into the passenger footwell.

2 Reach under the glovebox, and slide the two retaining catches on the pollen filter lower cover towards each other, to release and remove the cover (see illustrations).

3 Withdraw the filter downwards from the heater assembly, and remove from inside the car (see illustration).

4 Where fitted, separate the filter from the

13.3 Removing the oil filler/level plug

frame, noting the fitted direction of the airflow arrows, which should be towards the driver's side (see illustration).

5 Fit the new filter to the frame (where applicable), with the airflow arrows pointing in the direction noted on removal. Insert the pollen into the heater assembly, and then refit the lower cover. Slide the two catches apart, to secure the cover to the housing.

13 Manual transmission oil level check

1 Park the car on a level surface. For improved access to the filler/level plug, apply the handbrake, then jack up the front of the car and support it on axle stands (see *Jacking and vehicle support*), but note that the rear of the car should also be raised to ensure an accurate level check. The oil level must be checked before the car is driven, or at least 5 minutes after the engine has been switched off. If the oil is checked immediately after driving the car, some of the oil will remain distributed around the transmission components, resulting in an inaccurate level reading.

2 As applicable, undo the retaining screws and remove the engine undershield. Wipe clean the area around the transmission filler/level plug which is situated on the front, left-hand end of the transmission (see illustration).

3 The transmission has a hex fitting on its filler/level plug, which means it can be unscrewed with a large Allen key or bit (see illustration). Ensure that the tool used is a good fit in the plug, and take care when loosening to avoid personal injury from surrounding components, as the plug will be tight.

4 The oil level should reach the lower edge of the filler/level hole. A certain amount of oil will have gathered behind the filler/level plug, and will trickle out when it is removed; this does **not** necessarily indicate that the level is correct. To ensure that a true level is established, wait until the initial trickle has stopped, then add oil as necessary until a trickle of new oil can be seen emerging. The level will be correct when the flow ceases; use only good-quality oil of the specified type.

5 If the transmission has been overfilled so that oil flows out when the filler/level plug is removed, check that the car is completely level (front-to-rear and side-to-side), and allow the surplus to drain off into a suitable container.

6 When the oil level is correct, refit the filler/level plug and tighten it to the specified torque. Wipe off any spilt oil then refit the engine undershield(s), tighten the retaining screws securely, and lower the car to the ground.

14 Underbody protection check

Raise and support the car on axle stands

(see *Jacking and vehicle support*). Using a torch or lead light, inspect the entire underside of the car, paying particular attention to the wheel arches. Look for any damage to the flexible underbody coating, which may crack or flake off with age, leading to corrosion (note, however, that there are plastic underbody panels to protect the underside of the vehicle). Also check that the wheel arch liners are securely attached with any clips provided – if they come loose, dirt may get in behind the liners and defeat their purpose. If there is any damage to the underseal, or any corrosion, it should be repaired before the damage gets too serious.

15 Driveshaft check

1 With the car raised and securely supported on stands, slowly rotate the roadwheel. Inspect the condition of the outer constant velocity (CV) joint rubber gaiters, squeezing the gaiters to open out the folds. Check for signs of cracking, splits or deterioration of the rubber, which may allow the grease to escape, and lead to water and grit entry into the joint. Also check the security and condition of the retaining clips. Repeat these checks on the inner joints **(see illustration)**. If any damage or deterioration is found, the gaiters should be renewed (see Chapter 8, Section 3).
2 At the same time, check the general condition of the CV joints themselves by first holding the driveshaft and attempting to rotate the wheel. Repeat this check by holding the inner joint and attempting to rotate the driveshaft. Any appreciable movement indicates wear in the joints, wear in the driveshaft splines, or a loose driveshaft retaining bolt.

16 Steering and suspension check

1 Raise the front and rear of the car, and securely support it on axle stands (see *Jacking and vehicle support*).
2 Visually inspect the track rod end balljoint dust cover, the lower front suspension balljoint dust cover, and the steering rack-and-pinion gaiters for splits, chafing or deterioration. Any wear of these components will cause loss of lubricant, together with dirt and water entry, resulting in rapid deterioration of the balljoints or steering gear.
3 Check the power steering fluid hoses for chafing or deterioration, and the pipe and hose unions for fluid leaks. Also check for signs of fluid leakage under pressure from the steering gear rubber gaiters, which would indicate failed fluid seals within the steering gear.
4 Grasp the roadwheel at the 12 o'clock and

15.1 Check the condition of the driveshaft gaiter (arrowed)

6 o'clock positions, and try to rock it **(see illustration)**. Very slight free play may be felt, but if the movement is appreciable, further investigation is necessary to determine the source. Continue rocking the wheel while an assistant depresses the footbrake. If the movement is now eliminated or significantly reduced, it is likely that the hub bearings are at fault. If the free play is still evident with the footbrake depressed, then there is wear in the suspension joints or mountings.
5 Now grasp the wheel at the 9 o'clock and 3 o'clock positions, and try to rock it as before. Any movement felt now may again be caused by wear in the hub bearings or the steering track rod balljoints. If the inner or outer balljoint is worn, the visual movement will be obvious.
6 Using a large screwdriver or flat bar, check for wear in the suspension mounting bushes by levering between the relevant suspension component and its attachment point. Some movement is to be expected as the mountings are made of rubber, but excessive wear should be obvious. Also check the condition of any visible rubber bushes, looking for splits, cracks or contamination of the rubber.
7 With the car standing on its wheels, have an assistant turn the steering wheel back-and-forth about an eighth of a turn each way. There should be very little, if any, lost movement between the steering wheel and roadwheels. If this is not the case, closely observe the joints and mountings previously described, but in addition check the steering column universal joints for wear, and the rack-and-pinion steering gear itself.

17.1 Unclip the plastic cover

16.4 Check for wear in the hub bearings by grasping the wheel and trying to rock it

8 Check for any signs of fluid leakage around the front suspension struts and rear shock absorber. Should any fluid be noticed, the suspension strut or shock absorber is defective internally, and should be renewed. **Note:** *Suspension struts/shock absorbers should always be renewed in pairs on the same axle to ensure correct handling.*
9 The efficiency of the suspension strut/shock absorber may be checked by bouncing the car at each corner. Generally speaking, the body will return to its normal position and stop after being depressed. If it rises and returns on a rebound, the suspension strut/shock absorber is probably suspect. Examine also the suspension strut/shock absorber upper and lower mountings for any signs of wear.

17 Battery check

1 The battery is located in the front, left-hand corner of the engine compartment. Release the clip at the back, and then hinge the plastic cover forwards to gain access to the battery positive (+) terminal **(see illustration)**.
2 Where necessary, open the plastic cover (on the right-hand side of the battery) to gain access to the fuses.
3 Release the retaining clips at the front of the plastic cover to access the wiring terminals on the top of the battery **(see illustration)**.
4 Check that both battery terminals and all connections are securely attached and are free from corrosion. **Note:** *Before disconnecting*

17.3 Fused links on top of the battery

17.6 Window to check battery condition (arrowed)

the terminals from the battery, refer to 'Disconnecting the battery' in the Reference Chapter at the end of this manual.

5 Check the battery casing for signs of damage or cracking and check the battery retaining clamp bolt is securely tightened. If the battery casing is damaged in any way the battery must be renewed (see Chapter 5A, Section 3).

6 Some models are fitted with a battery with a small window that shows the state of the battery electrolyte. The window is located on the top of the battery (see illustration), near the negative terminal. If the window is green, the battery is in good condition and charged up. If the window is black, the battery is flat and should be charged. If the window is colourless or yellow, the electrolyte is in a critical condition. If charging the battery does not return the window to green, the battery should be scrapped.

7 On completion of the check, make sure the covers are securely back in position.

18 Hinge and lock lubrication

1 Lubricate the hinges of the bonnet, doors and tailgate with a light general-purpose oil. Similarly, lubricate all latches, locks and lock strikers. At the same time, check the security and operation of all the locks, adjusting them if necessary (see Chapter 11, Section 11).

2 Lightly lubricate the bonnet release mechanism and cable with suitable grease.

21.1 Diagnostic socket location

19 Airbag unit check

Inspect the exterior condition of the airbag(s) for signs of damage or deterioration. If an airbag shows signs of damage, it must be renewed (see Chapter 12, Section 25 and Chapter 12, Section 26). Note that it is not permissible to attach any stickers to the surface of the airbag, as this may affect the deployment of the unit.

20 Windscreen/tailgate/ headlight washer system check

1 Check that each of the washer jet nozzles is clear and that each nozzle provides a strong jet of washer fluid.

2 The tailgate jet should be aimed to spray at the centre of the screen, using a pin.

3 The windscreen washer nozzles can be adjusted up and down as required.

4 Especially during the winter months, make sure that the washer fluid concentration is sufficient to avoid freezing.

21 Engine management self-diagnosis memory fault check

A VW dealer or a specialist using diagnostic equipment should carry out this work. The diagnostic socket is located beneath the driver's side of the facia, above the accelerator pedal (see illustration).

22 Road test and exhaust emissions check

Instruments and electrical equipment

1 Check the operation of all instruments and electrical equipment including the air conditioning system.

2 Make sure that all instruments read correctly, and switch on all electrical equipment in turn, to check that it functions properly.

Steering and suspension

3 Check for any abnormalities in the steering, suspension, handling or road 'feel'.

4 Drive the car, and check that there are no unusual vibrations or noises that may indicate wear in the driveshafts, wheel bearings, etc.

5 Check that the steering feels positive, with no excessive 'sloppiness', or roughness,

and check for any suspension noises when cornering and driving over bumps.

Drivetrain

6 Check the performance of the engine, clutch, gearbox and driveshafts.

7 Listen for any unusual noises from the engine, clutch and gearbox.

8 Make sure the engine runs smoothly at idle, and there is no hesitation on accelerating.

9 Check that the clutch action is smooth and progressive, that the drive is taken up smoothly, and that the pedal travel is not excessive. Also listen for any noises when the clutch pedal is depressed.

10 Check that all gears can be engaged smoothly without noise, and that the gear lever action is smooth and not abnormally vague or 'notchy'.

11 Listen for a metallic clicking sound from the front of the car, as the car is driven slowly in a circle with the steering on full-lock. Carry out this check in both directions. If a clicking noise is heard, this indicates wear in a driveshaft joint, in which case renew the joint if necessary.

Braking system

12 Make sure that the car does not pull to one side when braking, and that the wheels do not lock when braking hard.

13 Check that there is no vibration through the steering when braking.

14 Check that the handbrake operates correctly without excessive movement of the lever, and that it holds the car stationary on a slope.

15 Test the operation of the brake servo unit as follows. With the engine off, depress the footbrake four or five times to exhaust the vacuum. Hold the brake pedal depressed, and then start the engine. As the engine starts, there should be a noticeable 'give' in the brake pedal as vacuum builds-up. Allow the engine to run for at least two minutes, and then switch it off. If the brake pedal is depressed now, it should be possible to detect a hiss from the servo as the pedal is depressed. After about four or five applications, no further hissing should be heard, and the pedal should feel considerably harder.

16 Under controlled emergency braking, the pulsing of the ABS unit must be felt at the footbrake pedal.

Exhaust emissions check

17 Although not part of the manufacturer's maintenance schedule, this check will normally be carried out on a regular basis according to the country the car is operated in. Currently in the UK, exhaust emissions testing is included as part of the annual MOT test after the car is 3 years old.

Every 40 000 miles or 4 years

23 Air filter element renewal

1 The air filter is housed in the air cleaner, which is situated on the left-hand side of the inner wing, behind the battery.
2 Undo the six retaining screws and lift the cover from the top of the air cleaner body **(see illustration)**.
3 If required, disconnect the wiring connector from the air mass meter, then release the retaining clip and disconnect the air intake hose from the upper cover **(see illustration)**.
4 Release the air filter element from the upper cover.
5 Remove any debris that may have collected inside the air cleaner housing. Make sure the O-ring is in position in the lower part of the housing **(see illustration)**, before refitting the new filter element.
6 Fit a new air filter element in position, ensuring that it is located correctly.
7 Refit the air cleaner upper cover and secure in position with the six retaining screws.

24 Fuel filter renewal

1 The fuel filter is mounted on the right-hand inner wing (right as seen from the driver's seat) **(see illustration)**. Position a container underneath the filter unit and pad the surrounding area with rags to absorb any fuel that may be spilt.
Caution: Be prepared for an amount of fuel loss.
2 Disconnect the quick-release couplings from the top of the fuel filter and move the two fuel hoses to one side, noting their fitted position for refitting.
3 Release the securing clips from around the upper edge of the fuel filter, and then withdraw it upwards from the filter mounting bracket.
4 Fit the new fuel filter into the mounting bracket, making sure the filter is fitted in the position noted on removal and the clips are secure around the upper edge of the filter.
5 Reconnect the fuel supply hose (from the fuel tank) to the inlet side of the filter, then fit a vacuum pump to the other side of the fuel filter and draw the fuel up into the filter. When the filter has been filled with fuel, refit the outlet fuel hose (to the fuel rail) back to the filter **(see illustrations)**. Remove the collecting container and rags from around the filter.
6 Start and run the engine at idle, and then check around the fuel filter for fuel leaks.
Note: *It may take a few seconds of cranking before the engine starts.*
7 Raise the engine speed to about 2000 rpm several times, and then allow the engine to idle again. Observe the fuel flow through the transparent hose leading to the fuel injection pump and check that it is free of air bubbles.

25 Auxiliary drivebelt check and renewal

Check

1 See Section 8, for information on checking the condition of the drivebelt.
2 There are two different types of tensioner fitted to diesel engines; the routing of the belt is the same, although the procedure for belt renewal is different.
3 When the belt is removed, check all pulleys are free from any damage and are secure. Also check that the alternator and air-conditioning compressor are mounted securely.

Renewal

4 For improved access, apply the handbrake, and then jack up the front of the vehicle and support it on axle stands (see *Jacking and vehicle support*).
5 Remove the right-hand front roadwheel, then remove the access panel from the inner wheel arch.

With tensioner spring element

6 Use a spanner on the centre bolt and turn the tensioner clockwise. Lock the tensioner in its released position by inserting a locking pin (Allen key or similar) through the lug into the tensioner body **(see illustrations)**.

23.2 Remove the cover...

23.3 ...disconnect wiring connector, if required

23.5 Make sure the O-ring seal is fitted correctly

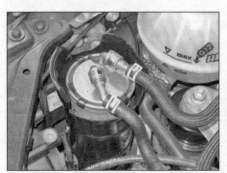
24.1 Location of fuel filter

24.5a Using a rubber bulb with one way valve to draw fuel...

24.5b ...or using a vacuum pump

25.6a Turn the tensioner clockwise...

25.6b ...and lock the tensioner in position

25.7 Note the fitted position of the belt before removal

25.8 With the locking pin removed, slowly take up the slack in the belt

7 Note how the drivebelt is routed, then remove it from the crankshaft pulley (**see illustration**), alternator pulley, and air conditioning compressor pulley (as applicable).

8 Locate the new drivebelt on the pulleys, then by holding the pressure of the tensioner with a spanner, remove the locking pin. Slowly release the pressure on the spanner (**see illustration**), so that the tensioner takes up the slack in the belt. Check that the belt is located correctly in the multi-grooves in the pulleys.

9 Start the engine and check that the drivebelt runs, as it should over the pulleys. Make sure that all tools and hands are kept clear of the drivebelt with the engine running.

10 With the engine stopped, refit the access panel and roadwheel, and then lower the vehicle to the ground. Refit the engine top cover if removed.

With tensioner roller

11 Undo the tensioner roller retaining bolt, and remove the tensioner roller from the engine. Note the retaining bolt is below the tensioner roller, and goes up through the mounting bracket in a vertical direction (**see illustration**). Discard the retaining bolt, as a new one will be required for refitting.

12 Note how the drivebelt is routed, then remove it from the crankshaft pulley, alternator pulley, and air-conditioning compressor pulley (as applicable).

13 Locate the new drivebelt on the pulleys, then fit the tensioner roller, making sure its guide pin is located correctly in the mounting bracket.

14 Fit the new retaining bolt, and then tighten to the following five stages:
  a) Tighten bolt by hand at this point.
  b) Tighten bolt until it reaches stop.
  c) Turn the bolt back through 90°
  b) Tighten bolt to 30Nm.
  c) Tighten a further 90°

15 When tensioner roller is fitted and the belt is tensioned, check the tensioner retaining bolt. The part of the bolt that has protruded out through the upper end of the mounting bracket (behind the tensioner roller) must not protrude more than 2.5mm higher than the outer surface of the tensioner roller. This ensures that the bolt has been tightened to its end stop.

16 Start the engine and check that the drivebelt runs, as it should over the pulleys. Make sure that all tools and hands are kept clear of the drivebelt with the engine running.

17 With the engine stopped, refit the access panel and roadwheel, and then lower the vehicle to the ground. Refit the engine top cover if removed.

25.11 Auxiliary drivebelt with tensioner roller

H48704

1) Auxiliary belt
2) Tensioner roller
3) Crank pulley/vibration damper
4) Securing bolt
5) Dowel
6) Mounting brackt
7) Tensioning roller securing bolt

26 Power steering hydraulic fluid level check

1 Turn the front roadwheels to the straight-ahead position without starting the engine. If the car has been left standing for an hour or more, the power steering fluid will be cold (below 50ºC), and the 'cold' level markings must be used. If, however, the engine is at normal temperature (above 50ºC), the fluid will be hot, and the 'hot' level markings must be used.

2 The reservoir for the Electrically Powered Hydraulic Steering (EPHS) is located on the front left-hand corner of the engine compartment. **Note:** *On some models with a high capacity battery, the battery and tray must be removed in order to access the reservoir filler cap.* The fluid level is checked with the dipstick attached to the reservoir filler cap. Unscrew the cap from the hydraulic fluid reservoir, and wipe clean the integral dipstick with a clean cloth **(see illustration)**.

3 Screw on the cap hand-tight, then unscrew it again and check the fluid level on the dipstick. The fluid level must be between the MIN (or lower) and MAX (or upper) marks **(see illustrations)**. If the fluid is cold (below 50ºC), it must be at least above the lower level mark or MIN. If the fluid is hot (above 50ºC), it must not be above the upper level mark or MAX.

4 If the level is above the maximum level mark, syphon off the excess amount. If it is below the minimum level mark, add the specified fluid as necessary (see *Lubricants and fluids*), but in this case also check the system for leaks **(see illustration)**. On completion, screw on the cap and tighten. Refit the battery and tray where removed.

27 DSG transmission fluid level check

The DSG semi-automatic transmission fitted

26.2 Unscrew the cap from the hydraulic fluid reservoir - arrowed

26.3b Alternative power steering cap markings

to 1.6 litre diesel engines is the 7-speed dual clutch (0AM) transmission. The transmission is filled for life, and does not have an oil level checking procedure. If there has been an oil leak from the transmission, after the leak has been rectified, renew the transmission oil as described in Chapter 7B, Section 6.

26.3a The power steering fluid level must be between the upper and lower marks

26.4 Topping-up the fluid level

28 Timing belt and tensioner renewal

Refer to Chapter 2C for 1.2 litre engines or Chapter 2D for 1.6 litre engines.

Every 2 years

29 Brake (and clutch) fluid renewal

⚠ Warning: Brake hydraulic fluid can harm your eyes and damage painted surfaces, so use extreme caution when handling and pouring it. Do not use fluid that has been standing open for some time, as it absorbs moisture from the air. Excess moisture can cause a dangerous loss of braking effectiveness.

1 The procedure is similar to that for the bleeding of the hydraulic system as described in Chapter 9, Section 2, except that the brake fluid reservoir should be emptied by syphoning, using a clean poultry baster or similar before starting, and allowance should be made for the old fluid to be expelled when bleeding a section of the circuit. Since the

clutch hydraulic system also uses fluid from the brake system reservoir, it should also be bled at the same time by referring to Chapter 6, Section 2.

2 Working as described in Chapter 9, open the first bleed screw in the sequence, and pump the brake pedal gently until nearly all the old fluid has been emptied from the master cylinder reservoir.

3 Top-up to the MAX level with new fluid, and continue pumping until only the new fluid remains in the reservoir, and new fluid can be seen emerging from the bleed screw. Tighten the screw, and top the reservoir level up to the MAX level line.

4 Work through all the remaining bleed screws in the sequence until new fluid can be seen at all of them. Be careful to keep the master cylinder reservoir topped-up to above the MIN level at all times, or air may enter the system and greatly increase the length of the task.

5 When the operation is complete, check that all bleed screws are securely tightened, and that their dust caps are refitted. Wash off all traces of spilt fluid, and recheck the master cylinder reservoir fluid level.

6 On models with a manual transmission unit, once the brake fluid has been changed the clutch fluid should also be renewed. Referring to Chapter 6, Section 2, bleed the clutch until new fluid is seen to be emerging from the slave cylinder bleed screw, keeping the master cylinder fluid level above the MIN level line at all times to prevent air entering the system. Once the new fluid emerges, securely tighten the bleed screw then disconnect and remove the bleeding equipment. Securely refit the dust cap then wash off all traces of spilt fluid.

7 Ensure the master cylinder fluid level is correct (see *Weekly checks*) and thoroughly check the operation of the brakes and clutch before taking the car on the road.

30.3a Disconnect hose from the circulation pump – 1.6 litre engine

30.3b Disconnect hose from the circulation pump – 1.2 litre engine

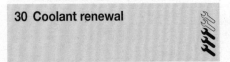

30 Coolant renewal

Note: *This work is not included in the VW schedule, and should not be required if the recommended VW G12 LongLife coolant antifreeze/inhibitor is used. However, if standard antifreeze/inhibitor is used, the work should be carried out at the recommended interval.*

⚠ *Warning: Wait until the engine is cold before starting this procedure. Do not allow antifreeze to come in contact with your skin, or with the car's painted surfaces. Rinse off spills immediately with plenty of water. Never leave antifreeze lying around in an open container, or in a puddle in the driveway or on the garage floor. Children and pets are attracted by its sweet smell, but antifreeze can be fatal if ingested.*

Cooling system draining

1 With the engine completely cold, unscrew the expansion tank cap.
2 Firmly apply the handbrake then jack up the front of the car and support it on axle stands (see *Jacking and vehicle support*). Undo the retaining screws and remove the engine under shield to gain access to the base of the radiator.
3 Position a suitable container beneath the bottom hose fitting to the left-hand end of the radiator. **Note:** *On some models there*

30.18 Filling the cooling system

is a coolant drain plug, which is fitted to a plastic elbow between the bottom hose and the radiator. Unscrew the drain plug and pull it out slightly (there is no need to remove it completely) and allow the coolant to drain into the container. If desired, a length of tubing can be fitted to the drain outlet to direct the flow of coolant during draining. Where no drain outlet is fitted to the hose end fitting, remove the retaining clip and disconnect the bottom hose from the radiator or the coolant hose to the auxiliary electric pump, to drain the coolant **(see illustrations)**.
4 On engines with an oil cooler, to fully drain the system, also disconnect one of the coolant hoses from the oil cooler which is located at the front of the cylinder block.
5 If the coolant has been drained for a reason other than renewal then, provided it is clean, it can be re-used.
6 Once all the coolant has drained, securely tighten the radiator drain plug or reconnect the bottom hose to the radiator (as applicable). Where necessary, also reconnect the coolant hose to the oil cooler and secure it in position with the retaining clip. Refit the undershield(s), tighten the retaining screws securely.

Cooling system flushing

7 If the recommended VW coolant has not been used and coolant renewal has been neglected, or if the antifreeze mixture has become diluted, the cooling system may gradually lose efficiency, as the coolant passages become restricted due to rust, scale deposits, and other sediment. The cooling system efficiency can be restored by flushing the system clean.
8 The radiator should be flushed separately from the engine, to avoid excess contamination.

Radiator flushing

9 To flush the radiator first tighten the radiator drain plug (where applicable).
10 Disconnect the top and bottom hoses and any other relevant hoses from the radiator.
11 Insert a garden hose into the radiator top inlet. Direct a flow of clean water through the radiator, and continue flushing until clean water emerges from the radiator bottom outlet.

12 If after a reasonable period, the water still does not run clear, the radiator can be flushed with a good proprietary cleaning agent. It is important that the manufacturer's instructions are followed carefully. If the contamination is particularly bad, insert the hose in the radiator bottom outlet, and reverse-flush the radiator.

Engine flushing

13 To flush the engine, remove the thermostat (see Chapter 3, Section 4).
14 With the bottom hose disconnected from the radiator, insert a garden hose into the thermostat housing. Direct a clean flow of water through the engine, and continue flushing until clean water emerges from the radiator bottom hose.
15 When flushing is complete, refit the thermostat and reconnect the hoses.

Cooling system filling

16 Before attempting to fill the cooling system, ensure the drain plug (where applicable) is securely closed and make sure that all hoses are securely connected and their retaining clips are in good condition. If the recommended VW coolant is not being used, ensure that a suitable antifreeze mixture is used all year round, to prevent corrosion of the engine components (see following sub-Section).
17 Remove the coolant temperature sensor from the coolant distribution housing on the left-hand end of the cylinder head with reference to Chapter 3, Section 6.
18 Remove the expansion tank filler cap and slowly fill the system with coolant **(see illustration)**, until bubble-free coolant runs from the temperature sensor hole, then refit the sensor immediately. Continue to fill the system until the level is up to the MAX level mark on the expansion tank. Help to bleed the air from the system by repeatedly squeezing the radiator bottom hose.
19 Refit the cap to the expansion tank, then run the engine at a fast idle speed until the cooling fan cuts in. Wait for the fan to stop then switch the engine off and allow the engine to cool.
20 When the engine has cooled, check the coolant level with reference to *Weekly checks*. Top-up the level if necessary, and refit the expansion tank cap.

Antifreeze mixture

21 If the recommended VW coolant is not being used, the antifreeze should always be renewed at the specified intervals. This is necessary not only to maintain the antifreeze properties, but also to prevent corrosion that would otherwise occur as the corrosion inhibitors become progressively less effective.
22 Always use an ethylene glycol based antifreeze, which is suitable for use in mixed-metal cooling systems. The quantity of antifreeze and levels of protection are indicated in the Specifications.
23 Before adding antifreeze, the cooling

system should be completely drained, preferably flushed, and all hoses checked for condition and security.

24 After filling with antifreeze, a label should be attached to the expansion tank, stating the type and concentration of antifreeze used, and the date installed. Any subsequent topping-up should be made with the same type and concentration of antifreeze.

25 Do not use engine antifreeze in the windscreen/tailgate washer system, as it will damage the paintwork. A screen wash additive should be added to the washer system in the quantities stated on the bottle.

Airlocks

26 If, after draining and refilling the system, symptoms of overheating are found which did not occur previously, then the fault is almost certainly due to trapped air at some point in the system, causing an airlock and restricting the flow of coolant; usually, the air is trapped because the system was refilled too quickly.

27 If an airlock is suspected, first try gently squeezing all visible coolant hoses. A coolant hose, which is full of air, feels quite different to one full of coolant, when squeezed. After refilling the system, most airlocks will clear once the system has cooled, and been topped up.

28 While the engine is running at operating temperature, switch on the heater and heater fan, and check for heat output. Provided there is sufficient coolant in the system, any lack of heat output could be due to an airlock in the system.

29 Airlocks can have more serious effects than simply reducing heater output - a severe airlock could reduce coolant flow around the engine. Check that the radiator top hose is hot when the engine is at operating temperature - a top hose that stays cold could be the result of an airlock (or a non-opening thermostat).

30 If the problem persists, stop the engine and allow it to cool down **completely**, before unscrewing the expansion tank filler cap or loosening the hose clips and squeezing the hoses to bleed out the trapped air. In the worst case, the system will have to be at least partially drained (this time, the coolant can be saved for re-use) and flushed to clear the problem.

31 Particulate filter check

Eventually, the amount of ash deposited in the particle filter by the filtration process will cause a blockage, and engine running problems. VW state that the maximum amount of ash is 60g. At this point, the particle filter must be renewed. Unfortunately, the mass of the ash can only be established using dedicated VW diagnostic equipment, connected to the vehicle through the diagnostic plug under the drivers side of the facia. Consequently, we recommend this task is entrusted to a VW dealer or suitably equipped specialist.

Chapter 2 Part A:
1.2 litre petrol engine in-car repair procedures

Contents

Degrees of difficulty

Easy, suitable for novice with little experience	**Fairly easy,** suitable for beginner with some experience	**Fairly difficult,** suitable for competent DIY mechanic	**Difficult,** suitable for experienced DIY mechanic	**Very difficult,** suitable for expert DIY or professional

Specifications

General

Type	Three-cylinder in-line, chain-driven single (SOHC) or double (DOHC) overhead camshaft, four-stroke, liquid-cooled
Cubic capacity	1198 cc
Manufacturer's engine codes*:	
1.2 litre SOHC (6V)	CHFA
1.2 litre DOHC (12V)	CGPA and CGPB
Maximum power output:	
CHFA and CGPB	44 kW at 5200 rpm
CGPA	51 kW at 5400 rpm
Maximum torque output:	
CHFA and CGPB	108 Nm at 3000 rpm
CGPA	112 Nm at 3000 rpm
Bore	76.5 mm
Stroke	86.9 mm
Compression ratio:	
CHFA	10.8 : 1
CGPA and CGPB	10.4 : 1
Compression pressures (oil temperature 30°C minimum):	
New	10.0 to 15.0 bars
Minimum	7.0 bars
Maximum difference between cylinders	3.0 bars
Firing order	1 – 3 – 2
No 1 cylinder location	Crankshaft pulley end
Direction of crankshaft rotation	Clockwise (when viewed from right-hand side of car)

* Note: *See 'Vehicle identification' at the end of this manual for the location of engine code markings.*

Lubrication system

Oil pump type	Chain-driven from crankshaft
Oil pressure (oil temperature 80°C):	
Minimum @ idling	0.3 to 0.7 bar
Minimum @ 2000 rpm	2.0 bar
Maximum @ high rpm	7.0 bar

Camshaft

Camshaft endfloat (maximum)	0.20 mm

Torque wrench settings

	Nm	lbf ft
Air conditioning compressor	23	17
Auxiliary drivebelt tensioner and guide pulley	40	30
Camshaft bearing caps (DOHC engines):		
Stage 1	10	7
Stage 2	Angle-tighten a further 90°	
Camshaft cover (SOHC engines):		
Stage 1	6	4
Stage 2	Angle-tighten a further 90°	
Camshaft position sensor	8	6
Camshaft sprocket:		
DOHC:		
Stage 1	50	37
Stage 2	Angle-tighten a further 90°	
SOHC:		
Stage 1	20	15
Stage 2	Angle-tighten a further 90°	
Coolant pump pulley	22	16
Crankshaft pulley*:		
SOHC engines:		
Stage 1	90	66
Stage 2	Angle-tighten a further 90°	
DOHC engines:		
Stage 1	150	110
Stage 2	Angle-tighten a further 180°	
Cylinder head bolts:		
Stage 1	30	22
Stage 2	Angle-tighten a further 90°	
Stage 3	Angle-tighten a further 90°	
Cylinder head cover/housing:		
SOHC engines:		
Stage 1	6	4
Stage 2	Angle-tighten a further 90°	
DOHC engines:		
Stage 1	10	7
Stage 2	Angle-tighten a further 90°	
Engine lifting eye	20	15
Flywheel bolts (new)*:		
Stage 1	60	44
Stage 2	Angle-tighten a further 90°	
Left-hand engine mounting:		
Mounting to body:		
Stage 1	50	37
Stage 2	Angle-tighten a further 90°	
Mounting to transmission:		
Stage 1	40	30
Stage 2	Angle-tighten a further 90°	
Oil filter cap	25	18
Oil filter housing	24	18
Oil level and temperature sender	8	6
Oil pressure switch	25	18
Oil pump	24	18
Oil pump chain tensioner	15	11
Oil pump sprocket:		
Stage 1	20	15
Stage 2	Angle-tighten a further 90°	
Rear mounting link:		
To transmission:		
Stage 1	30	22
Stage 2	Angle-tighten a further 90°	
To subframe:		
Stage 1	40	30
Stage 2	Angle-tighten a further 90°	
Right-hand engine mounting:		
Pedestal to engine	45	33
Mounting to body:		
Stage 1	20	15
Stage 2	Angle-tighten a further 90°	
Intermediate bracket to pedestal:		
Stage 1	30	22
Stage 2	Angle-tighten a further 90°	
Sump bolts	9	7

Torque wrench settings (continued)

	Nm	lbf ft
Sump oil drain plug	30	22
Timing chain guide (DOHC engines)	15	11
Timing chain hydraulic tensioner	15	11
Timing cover:		
SOHC engines (see illustration 5.19a):		
Bolt 3	45	33
Bolts 1 and 2	45	33
Bolts 22 and 23	25	18
All other bolts	10	7
SOHC engines (see illustration 5.19b):		
Bolts 1, 2 and 3	50	37
Bolts 4 and 5	25	18
Bolts 6, 7, 8, 11 and 14, and all other bolts:		
Stage 1	8	6
Stage 2	Angle-tighten a further 90°	
Timing chain tensioner guide pivot	18	13

*Use thread-locking compound.

1 General information

How to use this Chapter

This Part of Chapter 2 describes those repair procedures that can reasonably be carried out on the engine while it remains in the car. If the engine has been removed from the car and is being dismantled, as described in Part E, any preliminary dismantling procedures can be ignored.

Note that while it may be possible physically to overhaul certain items while the engine is in the car, such tasks are not usually carried out as separate operations, and usually require the execution of several additional procedures (not to mention the cleaning of components and of oilways); for this reason, all such tasks are classed as major overhaul procedures, and are described in Part E of this Chapter.

Caution: The pistons, connecting rods and crankshaft must not be removed on these engines. If these components are excessively worn or damaged, the complete cylinder block and pistons must be renewed as an assembly.

Part E describes the removal of the engine/transmission from the car and the full overhaul procedures that can then be carried out.

Engine description

The engine is an overhead camshaft (OHC), in-line three-cylinder unit, which is mounted transversely at the front of the car, with the manual transmission bolted to the left-hand end of the engine. **Note:** *This engine is not available with automatic or DSG transmissions.*

The engine is available with a single overhead camshaft (SOHC) as engine code CHFA, or with double overhead camshafts (DOHC, 12-valve) as engine codes CGPA and CGPB. The cylinder block is identical on both engines, and incorporates a gear-driven

balance shaft. **Note:** *The engine code may be found on the vehicle data sticker, by the spare wheel.*

Caution: It is not permitted to dismantle the balance shaft and gears.

The cylinder block, cylinder head and valve cover are all cast in aluminium alloy. The cylinder bores are machined in the cylinder block. The crankshaft has four main bearings, and thrustwashers are fitted to number 3 main bearing to control crankshaft endfloat. A balance shaft is located in a housing beneath the cylinder block, and is driven by a gear located on the end of the crankshaft.

Camshaft drive is by chain from the crankshaft, and the chain is tensioned by a hydraulic tensioner. The valves are closed by coil springs and the camshafts actuate the valves by roller rockers and hydraulic tappets. On the SOHC engine there are 2 valves per cylinder, and on the DOHC engine there are 4 valves per cylinder. The flywheel is located on a flange at the left-hand end of the crankshaft. The main bearings and the big-end bearings are of shell type, whilst the connecting rod small-end bearings are of the bronze bush type, being pressed into the connecting rod and reamed to suit.

The oil pump is chain-driven from the end of the crankshaft. Oil is drawn from the sump through a strainer and circulated through an externally mounted filter to the various engine components.

Operations with engine in car

The following work can be carried out with the engine in the car:

a) *Compression pressure – testing.*
b) *Crankshaft pulley – removal and refitting.*
c) *Timing cover – removal and refitting.*
d) *Timing chain – renewal.*
e) *Timing chain tensioner and sprockets – removal and refitting.*
f) *Camshaft(s) and hydraulic tappets – removal and refitting.*
g) *Cylinder head – removal and refitting*.*
h) *Cylinder head – decarbonising.*

i) *Sump – removal and refitting.*
j) *Oil pump – removal, overhaul and refitting.*
k) *Crankshaft oil seals – renewal.*
l) *Engine/transmission mountings – inspection and renewal.*
m) *Flywheel – removal, inspection and refitting.*

* *Cylinder head dismantling procedures are detailed in Chapter 2E.*

2 Compression test – description and interpretation

1 When engine performance is down, or if misfiring occurs which cannot be attributed to the ignition or fuel systems, a compression test can provide diagnostic clues as to the engine's condition. If the test is performed regularly, it can give warning of trouble before any other symptoms become apparent.

2 The engine must be fully warmed-up to normal operating temperature, the battery must be fully charged, and the spark plugs must be removed (Chapter 1A, Section 24). The aid of an assistant will also be required.

3 Disable the ignition system by unplugging the wiring plug from the ignition coil module or HT coils. Also, disconnect the wiring from the fuel injectors. Note: This may generate a fault code in the engine management memory, and it will be necessary to have this code erased by a VW dealer on completion of the test.

4 Fit a compression tester to the No 1 cylinder spark plug hole – the type of tester which screws into the plug thread is to be preferred.

5 Have the assistant hold the throttle wide open and crank the engine on the starter motor; after one or two revolutions, the compression pressure should build-up to a maximum figure and then stabilise. Record the highest reading obtained.

6 Repeat the test on the remaining cylinders, recording the pressure in each.

7 All cylinders should produce very similar pressures, of the order of 10 to 15 bars.

3.7 Fit new O-rings before refitting the camshaft end caps

Any one cylinder reading below 10 bars, or a difference of more than 3 bars between cylinders, suggests a fault.

8 Note that the compression should build-up quickly in a healthy engine; low compression on the first stroke, followed by gradually increasing pressure on successive strokes, indicates worn piston rings.

9 A low compression reading on the first stroke, which does not build-up during successive strokes, indicates leaking valves or a blown head gasket (a cracked head could also be the cause).

10 If the pressure in any cylinder is reduced to 10 bars or less, carry out the following test to isolate the cause. Introduce a teaspoonful of clean oil into that cylinder through its spark plug hole and repeat the test.

11 If the addition of oil temporarily improves the compression pressure, this indicates that bore or piston wear is responsible for the

pressure loss. No improvement suggests that leaking or burnt valves, or a blown head gasket, may be to blame.

12 A low reading from two adjacent cylinders is almost certainly due to the head gasket having blown between them; the presence of coolant in the engine oil will confirm this.

13 If one cylinder is about 20 percent lower than the others and the engine has a slightly rough idle; a worn camshaft lobe could be the cause.

14 On completion of the test, refit the spark plugs and reconnect the ignition system. Refit the fuel injector wiring. Have any fault code (see paragraph 3) erased by a VW dealer.

3 Engine assembly and valve timing marks – general information and usage

1 Top dead centre (TDC) is the highest point in its travel up-and-down its cylinder bore that each piston reaches as the crankshaft rotates. While each piston reaches TDC both at the top of the compression stroke and again at the top of the exhaust stroke, for the purpose of timing the engine, TDC refers to the No 1 piston position at the top of its compression stroke.

2 No 1 piston and cylinder are at the right-hand end of the engine. Note that the crankshaft rotates clockwise when viewed from the right-hand side of the car.

3 Disconnect the battery negative lead (refer to *Disconnecting the battery* in the *Reference* Chapter). Remove all the spark plugs as described in Chapter 1A, Section 24.

3.9a Fit the camshaft TDC tools...

3.9b ...and tighten the bolts

3.9c Crankshaft TDC tool

3.9d Crankshaft TDC tool fitted through the cylinder block rear flange

Engine code CHFA

Note: *VW TDC setting tools T10120 and T10121 will be required for this procedure. Alternatively, pattern setting tools may be obtained from a car accessory shop.*

4 Unbolt the camshaft position sensor from the cylinder head cover.

5 Unbolt the crankshaft position/speed sender from the cylinder block rear flange.

6 Insert the camshaft TDC tool in the cylinder head cover hole, then turn the engine with a socket on the crankshaft pulley bolt until the TDC tool fully enters the hole in the camshaft. The engine is now at TDC compression for No 1 cylinder and the remaining TDC tool can be inserted through the cylinder block rear flange into the hole in the flywheel.

Engine codes CGPA and CGPB

Note: *VW TDC setting tools T10123 and T10121 will be required for this procedure. Alternatively, pattern setting tools may be obtained from a car accessory shop.*

7 At the left-hand end of the cylinder head, unbolt the caps from the ends of the inlet and exhaust camshafts. **Note:** *New O-rings must be fitted before refitting the caps* **(see illustration).**

8 Unbolt the crankshaft position/speed sender from the cylinder block rear flange.

9 Turn the engine with a socket on the crankshaft pulley bolt until the grooves at the left-hand ends of the camshafts are both horizontal. Now insert the tools T10123 into the camshafts and secure with the bolts. The engine is now at TDC compression for No 1 cylinder and the remaining TDC tool can be inserted through the cylinder block rear flange into the hole in the flywheel **(see illustrations).**

All engines

10 If necessary, as a further check that No 1 cylinder is on its compression stroke, remove the TDC tools and turn the engine back a little from the position described in paragraph 6 or 9. Now turn the engine forwards again to TDC with a finger placed over No 1 spark plug hole. If No 1 piston is rising on a compression stroke, pressure will be felt building-up as the engine is turned forwards to TDC.

11 Once No 1 cylinder has been positioned at TDC on the compression stroke, TDC for any of the other cylinders can then be located by rotating the crankshaft clockwise 240° at a time and following the firing order (see Specifications).

4 Crankshaft pulley – removal and refitting

Removal

1 Remove the engine top cover and air filter as applicable.

2 Mark the auxiliary drivebelt for normal rotation to ensure correct refitting. Note the routing of the drivebelt for ease of refitting.

3 Where fitted, lever off the cover from the

centre of the drivebelt tensioner roller, then use a 50 mm Torx key to turn the tensioner anti-clockwise to the stop. Hold the tensioner in this position and remove the drivebelt from the pulleys. Release the tensioner or, if preferred, retain the tensioner in this position by inserting a suitable pin/drill bit through the hole provided.

4 Have an assistant engage 4th gear and apply firm pressure to the footbrake pedal, then loosen the crankshaft pulley bolt and remove it together with the pulley **(see illustrations)**. VW state that the bolt must be renewed whenever removed.

Refitting

5 Locate the pulley and new bolt on the end of the crankshaft, then tighten it to the specified torque and angle while holding it stationary using the method for removal **(see illustration)**.

6 Locate the auxiliary drivebelt on the pulleys while holding the tensioner against the spring pressure, then release the tensioner making sure that the ribs of the drivebelt locate correctly in the pulley grooves. Refit the cover to the centre of the tensioner roller.

7 Refit the engine top cover and air filter as applicable.

---

5 Timing cover –
removal and refitting

Removal

1 Remove the engine top cover and air filter as applicable.

2 Apply the handbrake, then jack up the front of the car and support it on axle stands (see *Jacking and vehicle support*). Remove the right-hand front roadwheel. For improved access, also remove the right-hand front wheel arch liner.

3 Mark the auxiliary drivebelt for direction of rotation to ensure correct refitting. Lever off the cover from the centre of the drivebelt tensioner roller, then use a 50 mm Torx key to turn the tensioner anti-clockwise to the stop. Hold the tensioner in this position and remove the drivebelt from the pulleys. Release the tensioner or, if preferred, retain the tensioner in this position by inserting a suitable pin/drill bit through the hole provided **(see illustration)**.

5.11 Removing the oil level dipstick tube mounting bolt

4.4a Unscrew the crankshaft pulley bolt...

4.5 Angle-tightening the crankshaft pulley bolt

4 Hold the coolant pump pulley stationary using an oil filter strap or similar tool, then unscrew the retaining bolts and remove the pulley from the drive flange.

5 On models with air conditioning, unbolt the auxiliary drivebelt guide pulley from the cylinder block.

6 Unbolt the auxiliary drivebelt tensioner and pulley from the cylinder block.

7 Remove the alternator as described in Chapter 5A, Section 5.

8 Unclip the coolant expansion tank purge hose, and place it to one side.

9 Have an assistant engage 4th gear and apply firm pressure to the footbrake pedal, then use a multi-splined key to loosen the crankshaft pulley bolt and remove it together with the pulley. Alternatively, use a homemade tool to retain the pulley **(see illustrations 4.4a & 4.4b)**. VW state that the bolt must be renewed whenever removed.

5.12 Engine support bar attached to the right-hand end of the engine

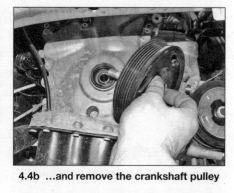

4.4b ...and remove the crankshaft pulley

5.3 Insert a suitable pin/drill bit to retain the auxiliary drivebelt tensioner

10 Remove the sump as described in Section 9. If necessary, remove the exhaust front pipe as described in Chapter 4C, Section 4, to provide additional working room.

11 Unbolt and remove the oil level dipstick tube **(see illustration)** and, where applicable, remove the oil level/temperature sender from the cylinder block.

12 The right-hand end of the engine must now be supported while the engine mounting is removed, and the engine then held in a safe position in order to carry out the remaining work. To do this, use a hoist or support bar attached to the engine lifting eyes – this is preferable to using a trolley jack beneath the engine **(see illustration)**. With the engine supported, remove the right-hand engine mounting with reference to Section 14.

13 Unbolt the PCV valve (crankcase ventilation) from the timing cover and recover the O-ring **(see illustration)**.

5.13 Removing the PCV valve (crankcase ventilation) from the timing cover

5.14a Removing the timing cover

5.14b If necessary, unscrew the bolts...

5.14c ...and remove the oil separator from the timing cover

14 Progressively unscrew and remove all of the retaining bolts, then remove the timing cover from the engine. If necessary, tap the cover lightly to release the sealant, and then withdraw the cover from the location dowels **(see illustrations)**.

15 With the cover removed, slide the sleeve and O-ring from the end of the crankshaft. **Note:** *This is necessary, as the sleeve must be assembled onto the crankshaft **after** refitting the timing cover.*

16 If the timing cover has been removed in order to carry out other work (i.e. timing chain or cylinder head removal), the pistons must be positioned away from their TDC positions as a precaution against them touching the valves. To do this, temporarily refit the crankshaft pulley, then insert and tighten the crankshaft pulley bolt, using the TDC locking tool to hold the crankshaft stationary. Now, remove the locking tool and turn the crankshaft 45° anti-clockwise.

Refitting

17 Before refitting, carefully clean away all residues of sealant from the cover and engine. Also, check that the cover M6 retaining bolts still have thread sealant on their threads, and if not, renew them.

18 Apply a 3.0 mm diameter bead of sealant to the inside of the cover, making sure that the bead is on the inside of the bolt holes **(see illustrations)**. Do not forget the upper and lower centre holes. **Note:** *The timing cover*

5.18a Apply a bead of sealant as shown – SOHC engine

5.18b Apply a bead of sealant as shown – DOHC engine

A	3.0 mm bead	C	Joint between cylinder
B	Location dowels		block and head

A	3.0 mm bead	C	Joint between cylinder
B	Location dowels		block and head

5.18c Applying the sealant to the timing cover

must be refitted within 15 minutes of applying the sealant to the cylinder head. Apply a little sealant to the joint between the cylinder head and block on the engine, at the front and rear points where the cover makes contact.

19 Carefully locate the timing cover on the engine, insert the bolts, and progressively tighten them to the specified torque in sequence **(see illustrations)**. Note that there are different torques according to the position of the bolts, and on engine codes CGPA and CGPB, some bolts require a torque plus angle-tightening.

20 Refit the sleeve to the end of the crankshaft together with a new O-ring. VW state that the cover oil seal must not be lubricated with either oil or grease.

21 The remainder of refitting is a reversal of removal.

6 Timing chain, tensioner and sprockets – removal, inspection and refitting

Engine code CHFA

Removal

1 Set the engine to TDC as described in Section 3 and insert the locking tools.

2 Remove the timing cover as described in Section 5 and position No 1 piston/crankshaft 45° anti-clockwise from its TDC position.

3 The timing chain tensioner rail must now be released from the chain and the hydraulic tensioner locked. To do this, press the lower end of the rail rearwards so that it forces the piston into the hydraulic tensioner, then insert a suitable 3.0 mm diameter tool through the holes provided to retain the piston.

4 Unscrew and remove the retaining bolt and withdraw the sprocket from the end of the camshaft, at the same time disengaging it from the timing chain. VW state that it is in order to use their TDC tool to hold the camshaft stationary, however, if a pattern tool is used, we recommend that a sprocket retaining tool be made out of a length of metal bar, with two long bolts positioned to engage the holes in the sprocket.

5 Remove the sump as described in Section 9.

6 Unbolt the plastic cover from the oil pump, then hold the sprocket stationary and unscrew the retaining bolt – discard the bolt as a new one must be used on refitting. Slide the small sprocket from the end of the crankshaft and place the chain and sprockets to one side. **Note:** *The sprocket is not keyed to the crankshaft.*

7 Slide the crankshaft sprocket together with the timing chain from the crankshaft. **Note:** *The sprocket is keyed to the crankshaft.*

8 Slide the tensioner rail from its upper pivot.

5.19a Timing chain cover bolt tightening sequence – SOHC engine

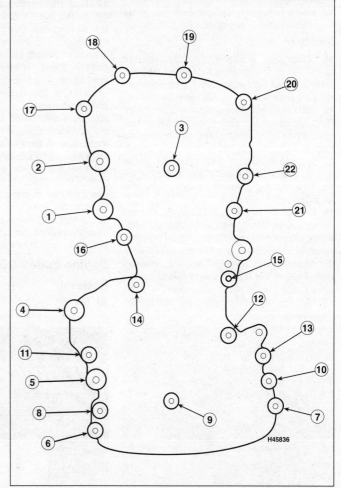

5.19b Timing chain cover bolt tightening sequence – DOHC engine

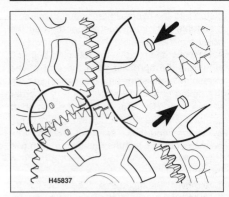

6.19 Balance shaft gear alignment indents

If necessary, unbolt the remaining guide rail and hydraulic tensioner from the cylinder block.

Inspection

9 Thoroughly clean all components, and then examine the timing chain and oil pump drive chain for excessive wear. Also check the sprocket teeth for wear. If the engine has covered a high mileage, the chain and sprockets should be renewed as a matter of course.

10 The crankshaft pulley bolt must be renewed whenever removed.

Refitting

11 Check that the camshaft is still positioned at TDC with the locking tool fitted and the retaining bolt tightened. No 1 piston should still be positioned before TDC (see Section 3).

12 Slide the tensioner rail onto its upper pivot. Refit the guide rail and hydraulic tensioner, and tighten the mounting bolts to the specified torque.

13 Engage the crankshaft sprocket in the timing chain and locate the sprocket on the end of the crankshaft, making sure it is engaged with the groove.

14 Engage the oil pump drive sprocket (small) with the drive chain, then locate the sprocket on the end of the crankshaft. Engage the large sprocket in the chain; position the sprocket on the oil pump and screw on the new retaining bolt. Tighten the bolt to the specified torque while holding the sprocket stationary.

15 Refit the oil pump plastic cover and tighten the screws.

6.25 Insert a 3.0 mm diameter drill bit in the hole to retain the timing chain tensioner piston

16 Refit the sump with reference to Section 9.

17 Clean the contact surfaces of the camshaft and sprocket and engage the sprocket with the timing chain. Locate the sprocket on the end of the camshaft and insert the retaining bolt, loosely at this stage so that the sprocket can move freely on the locked camshaft.

18 Press the lower end of the timing chain tensioner rail rearwards, remove the locking tool, and release the rail to tension the timing chain.

19 Turn the crankshaft slowly clockwise 45° so that No 1 piston is at TDC, and insert the locking tool through the cylinder block rear flange into the flywheel – note that the crankshaft should be turned *slowly* to the TDC position; if it is turned too far, turn it back and start again. The indents on the balance shaft gears must also be aligned with each other **(see illustration)**.

20 Apply slight anti-clockwise pressure to the camshaft sprocket with the holding tool (paragraph 4), then tighten the retaining bolt to the torque and angle given in the Specifications.

21 Turn the engine through two complete revolutions, then check that the TDC tools can be fitted to the camshaft and flywheel. Remove the tools.

22 Unbolt and remove the crankshaft pulley from the end of the crankshaft, then refit the timing cover with reference to Section 5.

Engine codes CGPA and CGPB

Removal

23 Set the engine to TDC as described in Section 3 and insert the locking tools.

24 Remove the timing cover as described in Section 5 and position No 1 piston/crankshaft 45° anti-clockwise from its TDC position.

25 The timing chain tensioner rail must now be released from the chain and the hydraulic tensioner locked. To do this, press the lower end of the rail rearwards so that it forces the piston into the hydraulic tensioner, then insert a suitable 3.0 mm diameter tool through the holes provided to retain the piston **(see illustration)**.

26 Identify the inlet and exhaust camshaft sprockets for position, then unscrew and remove their retaining bolts and withdraw the sprockets, at the same time disengaging them from the timing chain. VW state that it is in order to use their TDC tool to hold the camshafts stationary while loosening the sprocket retaining bolt, however, if pattern tools are used, we recommend that a sprocket retaining tool be made out of a length of metal bar, with two long bolts positioned to engage the holes in the sprocket **(see illustrations)**.

27 Remove the sump as described in Section 9.

28 Unbolt the plastic cover from the oil pump, then hold the sprocket stationary and unscrew the retaining bolt – discard the bolt as a new one must be used on refitting. Slide the small sprocket from the end of the crankshaft and place the chain and sprockets to one side. **Note:** *The sprocket is not keyed to the crankshaft.*

29 Slide the crankshaft sprocket together with the timing chain from the crankshaft **(see illustration)**. **Note:** *The sprocket is keyed to the crankshaft.*

30 Slide the tensioner rail from its upper pivot. If necessary, unbolt the remaining guide rail and hydraulic tensioner from the cylinder block **(see illustrations)**.

Inspection

31 Thoroughly clean all components, and then examine the timing chain and oil pump drive chain for excessive wear. Also check the sprocket teeth for wear. If the engine has covered a high mileage, the chain and sprockets should be renewed as a matter of course.

32 The crankshaft pulley bolt must be renewed whenever removed.

6.26a Hold the sprocket while loosening the bolt...

6.26b ...then remove the bolt and sprocket

6.29 Removing the timing chain sprocket from the crankshaft

6.30a Slide the tensioner rail from its upper pivot...

6.30b ...then unbolt the remaining guide rail

6.30c Removing the timing chain tensioner

Refitting

33 Check that the camshafts are still positioned at TDC with the locking tools fitted and the retaining bolts tightened. No 1 piston should still be positioned before TDC (see Section 3).

34 Slide the tensioner rail onto its upper pivot. Refit the guide rail and hydraulic tensioner, and tighten the mounting bolts to the specified torque.

35 Engage the crankshaft sprocket in the timing chain and locate the sprocket on the end of the crankshaft, making sure it is engaged with the groove.

36 Engage the oil pump drive sprocket (small) with the drive chain, then locate the sprocket on the end of the crankshaft. Engage the large sprocket in the chain; position the sprocket on the oil pump and screw on the new retaining bolt. Tighten the bolt to the specified torque while holding the sprocket stationary.

37 Refit the oil pump plastic cover and tighten the screws.

38 Refit the sump with reference to Section 9.

39 Clean the contact surfaces of the camshafts and sprockets and engage the sprockets with the timing chain. Locate the sprockets on the end of the camshafts and insert the retaining bolts, loosely at this stage so that the sprockets can move freely on the locked camshafts.

40 Press the lower end of the timing chain tensioner rail rearwards, remove the locking tool, and release the rail to tension the timing chain.

41 Turn the crankshaft slowly clockwise 45° so that No 1 piston is at TDC, and insert the locking tool through the cylinder block rear flange into the flywheel – note that the crankshaft should be turned *slowly* to the TDC position; if it is turned too far, turn it back and start again. The indents on the balance shaft gears must also be aligned with each other **(see illustration 6.19)**.

42 Apply slight anti-clockwise pressure to the camshaft sprocket with the holding tool (paragraph 4), then tighten the retaining bolt to the torque and angle given in the Specifications. The angle-tightening can be made by marking the bolt and sprocket with dabs of paint **(see illustration)**.

43 Turn the engine through two complete revolutions, then check that the TDC tools

can be fitted to the camshaft and flywheel. Remove the tools.

44 Unbolt and remove the crankshaft pulley from the end of the crankshaft, then refit the timing cover with reference to Section 5.

---

7 Camshaft(s) and hydraulic tappets – removal, inspection and refitting

Engine code CHFA

Removal

1 Remove the timing cover as described in Section 5.

2 Remove the camshaft sprocket as described in Section 6.

3 Progressively unscrew the retaining bolts from the cylinder head cover/housing. Lift the cover/housing from the cylinder head. If it is tight, tap it with a wooden or hide mallet. Discard the bolts, as new ones must be used during refitting.

4 Lift the camshaft from the cylinder head.

5 Obtain a suitable box with compartments for each of the roller/rocker arms and hydraulic tappets, so that they can be identified for their correct position to ensure correct refitting. Remove the rocker arms and hydraulic tappets and place them in the box.

6 Clean away the sealant from the cylinder head and cover, and also clean the camshaft bearings.

Inspection

7 Visually inspect the camshaft for evidence of

6.42 Mark the bolt and sprocket to apply the tightening angle

wear on the surfaces of the lobes and journals. Normally their surfaces should be smooth and have a dull shine; look for scoring, erosion or pitting, and areas that appear highly polished, indicating excessive wear. Accelerated wear will occur once the hardened exterior of the camshaft has been damaged, so always renew worn items.

8 If the machined surfaces of the camshaft appear discoloured or blue, it is likely that it has been overheated at some point, probably due to inadequate lubrication.

9 To measure the camshaft endfloat, temporarily locate it on the cylinder head without the rockers and hydraulic tappets. Anchor a DTI gauge to the end of the cylinder head and align the gauge probe with the camshaft axis. Push the camshaft to one end of the cylinder head as far as it will travel, then rest the DTI gauge probe on the end of the camshaft, and zero the gauge display. Push the camshaft as far as it will go to the other end of the cylinder head, and record the gauge reading. Verify the reading by pushing the camshaft back to its original position and checking that the gauge indicates zero again. Repeat the checking procedure for the remaining camshaft.

10 Check that the camshaft endfloat measurement is within the limit given in the Specifications. Wear outside of this limit is unlikely to be confined to any one component, so renewal of the camshaft and cover must be considered.

11 Inspect the hydraulic tappets for obvious signs of wear or damage, and renew if necessary. Check that the oil holes in the tappets are free from obstructions.

Refitting

12 Remove the crankshaft TDC locking tool, then turn the engine anti-clockwise by 45° so that none of the pistons are at their TDC position.

13 Lubricate the roller/rocker arms and hydraulic tappets with engine oil and refit them to their correct positions on the cylinder head. Check that the arms are located correctly on the valve stems and hydraulic tappets.

14 Apply a film of grease to the camshaft bearing surfaces in the cylinder head and cover/housing.

7.15 Grease the shaded areas (A) and apply a 2.0 to 3.0 mm wide bead (B) of sealant as shown

Arrows indicate areas to keep clear

7.16 Position the camshaft TDC cut-out as shown

A Location dowels

15 Apply a 2.0 to 3.0 mm wide bead of sealant as shown **(see illustration)** to the cylinder head. Make sure that the sealant is not allowed onto the camshaft bearing surfaces, and make sure that the bead runs around the inside of the bolt holes. **Note:** *The cylinder head cover must be refitted within 15 minutes of applying the sealant to the cylinder head.*

16 Carefully lay the camshaft on the cylinder head with the TDC cut-out just above the upper face of the head, and pointing forwards towards the exhaust manifold position. Refit the cylinder head cover/housing, making sure that the location dowels enter the holes in the head **(see illustration)**.

17 Insert *new* retaining bolts and initially hand-tighten all of them.

18 Tighten the retaining bolts to the specified torque and angle given in the Specifications, and in sequence **(see illustration)**.

19 Refit the camshaft sprocket with reference to Section 6.

20 Refit the timing cover as described in Section 5.

Engine codes CGPA and CGPB

Removal

21 Remove the timing cover as described in Section 5.

22 Remove the camshaft sprockets as described in Section 6.

23 Remove the ignition coils with the power output stage. Note that VW technicians use a special tool (T10094) to remove the coils, however, a length of bent welding rod or similar hooked under the wiring plugs, may be used to extract the coils.

24 Unscrew the cylinder head cover bolts in the **reverse** order to that shown for tightening in paragraph 41, and remove them.

25 Remove the cylinder head cover complete with camshafts from the cylinder head **(see illustration)**. If it is tight, use a mallet or rubber hammer to tap the top of the cover in several places in order to release it from the locating dowels.

26 Clean away the sealant from the cylinder head and cover.

27 With the cylinder head cover on the bench, loosen the camshaft bearing cap/housing bolts in the **reverse** order to that shown for tightening in paragraph 36. Lift the caps/housings from the cover **(see illustration)**. Identify the caps/housings for location to ensure correct refitting.

28 Identify each camshaft for location and position, then lift them out from the cylinder head cover **(see illustration)**. **Note:** *The inlet camshaft has a lug that is positioned over the hole for the Hall sender.*

29 Obtain a suitable box with compartments for each of the roller/rocker arms and hydraulic

7.18 Cylinder head cover/housing bolt tightening sequence

7.25 Remove the cylinder head cover complete with camshafts

7.27 Removing camshaft bearing caps

7.28 Removing the camshafts from the cylinder head cover

7.29a Remove the roller/rocker arms and hydraulic tappets from the cylinder head...

tappets, so that they can be identified for their correct position. Remove the rocker arms and hydraulic tappets from the cylinder head and place them in the box **(see illustrations)**.

30 Clean the camshaft bearing surfaces in the cover and caps/housings.

Inspection

31 Refer to paragraphs 7 to 11, but note that the camshafts and caps/housings will have to be temporarily refitted to the cover to measure the endfloat.

Refitting

32 Remove the crankshaft TDC locking tool, then turn the engine anti-clockwise by 45º so that none of the pistons are at their TDC position.

33 Lubricate the roller/rocker arms and hydraulic tappets with engine oil and refit them to their correct positions on the cylinder head **(see illustration)**.

34 Apply a film of grease to the camshaft bearing surfaces in the caps/housings and cover.

35 Carefully locate the camshafts in their

7.29b ...and place them in the box

correct positions in the cover, noting that the lug on the inlet camshaft must be positioned over the hole for the Hall sender.

36 Refit the bearing caps/housings and initially hand-tighten the retaining bolts. It is important that the caps are not tilted as the bolts are tightened. Tighten the bolts in sequence **(see illustration)** to the torque and angle given in the specifications.

7.33 Fitting the roller/rocker arms to the hydraulic tappets

37 Apply a 2.0 to 3.0 mm wide bead of sealant as shown **(see illustrations)** to the cylinder head cover. Make sure that the sealant is not allowed onto the camshaft bearing surfaces, and make sure that the bead runs around the inside of the bolt holes. **Note:** *The cylinder head cover must be refitted within 15 minutes of applying the sealant to the cylinder head.*

38 Check that the roller/rocker arms are

7.36 Camshaft bearing cap/housing bolt tightening sequence

7.37a Apply a bead of sealant as shown – DOHC engine

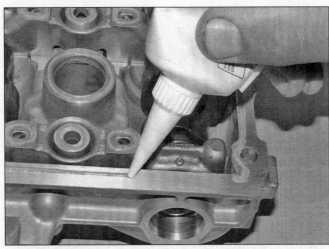

7.37b Apply the sealant carefully to the cylinder head cover

7.41 Cylinder head cover bolt tightening sequence

correctly located on the valve stems and hydraulic tappets.

39 Lower the cover onto the cylinder head making sure that the location dowels enter their holes correctly.

40 Insert *new* retaining bolts and initially hand-tighten all of them.

41 Tighten the retaining bolts to the specified torque and angle given in the Specifications, and in sequence **(see illustration)**.

42 Refit the ignition coils and power output stage, followed by the pipe sections.

43 Refit the camshaft sprockets (Section 6) and timing cover (Section 5).

8 Cylinder head –
removal, inspection and refitting

Removal

1 Remove the timing cover as described in Section 5. Also, if required, remove the inlet and exhaust manifolds.

2 Remove the camshaft sprocket(s) as described in Section 6.

3 On engine code CHFA (SOHC) remove the camshaft and hydraulic tappets as described in Section 7.

4 On engine codes CGPA and CGPB (DOHC)

8.7 Cylinder block with head removed

remove the cylinder head cover complete with camshafts, and then remove the hydraulic tappets as described in Section 7. It is not necessary to remove the camshafts from the cover unless it is specifically required to work on them.

5 Progressively slacken the cylinder head bolts in the **reverse** order to that given for tightening in paragraph 20. Remove the cylinder head bolts. **Note:** *The bolts must not be re-used – obtain new ones.*

6 With all the bolts removed, lift the cylinder head from the block (together with the inlet and exhaust manifolds, if not removed). If the cylinder head is stuck, tap it with a soft-faced mallet to break the joint. **Do not** insert a lever into the gasket joint.

7 Lift the cylinder head gasket from the block **(see illustration)**.

8 If desired, the inlet and exhaust manifolds can be removed from the cylinder head with reference to the relevant part of Chapter 4.

Inspection

9 Dismantling and inspection of the cylinder head is covered in Part E of this Chapter.

10 The mating faces of the cylinder head and block must be perfectly clean before refitting the head.

11 Use a scraper to remove all traces of gasket and carbon, also clean the tops of

8.17a Cylinder head locating dowel on the block

the pistons. Take particular care with the aluminium surfaces, as the soft metal is easily damaged.

12 Make sure that debris is not allowed to enter the oil and water passages – this is particularly important for the oil circuit, as carbon could block the oil supply to the camshaft and crankshaft bearings. Using adhesive tape and paper, seal the water, oil and bolt holes in the cylinder block. To prevent carbon entering the gap between the pistons and bores, smear a little grease in the gap. After cleaning a piston, rotate the crankshaft to that the piston moves down the bore, and then wipe out the grease and carbon with a cloth rag. Clean the other piston crowns in the same way.

13 Check the head and block for nicks, deep scratches and other damage. If slight, they may be removed carefully with a file. More serious damage may be repaired by machining, but this is a specialist job. If warpage of the cylinder head is suspected, use a straight-edge to check it for distortion, as described in Part E of this Chapter.

Refitting

14 Ensure that the cylinder head bolt holes in the cylinder block are clean and free of oil. Syringe or soak up any oil left in the bolt holes. This is most important in order that the correct bolt tightening torque can be applied, and to prevent the possibility of the block being cracked by hydraulic pressure when the bolts are tightened.

15 Ensure that the crankshaft has been turned to position No 1 piston slightly down its bore from the TDC position (refer to timing chain refitting in Section 6). This will eliminate any risk of piston-to-valve contact as the cylinder head is refitted.

16 Where applicable, refit the inlet and exhaust manifolds to the cylinder head.

17 Ensure that the cylinder head locating dowels are in place in the cylinder block, and then fit a new cylinder head gasket

8.17b Typical cylinder head gasket markings

8.19 Lightly oil the threads and heads of the bolts

over the dowels, ensuring that the part number is uppermost **(see illustrations)**. Where applicable, the OBEN/TOP marking should also be uppermost. Note that VW recommend that the gasket is only removed from its packaging immediately prior to fitting.

18 Lower the cylinder head into position on the gasket, ensuring that it engages correctly over the dowels.

19 Lightly oil the threads and heads of the new cylinder head bolts, then insert them and screw in as far as possible by hand **(see illustration)**.

20 Working in sequence, tighten all the

cylinder head bolts to the specified Stage 1 torque **(see illustrations)**.

21 Again working in sequence, tighten all the cylinder head bolts through the specified Stage 2 angle **(see illustration)**.

22 Finally, tighten all the cylinder head bolts, in sequence, through the specified Stage 3 angle.

23 Refit the hydraulic tappets, camshaft(s) and cylinder head cover with reference to Section 7.

24 Refit the camshaft sprocket(s) as described in Section 6.

25 Refit the timing cover as described in Section 5.

9 Sump – removal and refitting

Removal

1 Apply the handbrake, then jack up the front of the car and support securely on axle stands (see *Jacking and vehicle support*).

2 Remove the securing screws and withdraw the engine undershield.

3 Drain the engine oil as described in Chapter 1A, Section 3.

4 Where fitted, disconnect the wiring connector from the oil level/temperature sender on the sump.

5 Unscrew and remove the bolts securing the sump to the cylinder block, and then withdraw the sump **(see illustration)**. If necessary, release the sump by tapping with a soft-faced mallet.

Refitting

6 Commence refitting by thoroughly cleaning the mating faces of the sump and cylinder block. Ensure that all traces of old sealant are removed.

7 Ensure that the cylinder block mating face of the sump is free from all traces of old sealant, oil and grease, and then apply a 2.0 to 4.0 mm

8.20a Cylinder head bolt tightening sequence – SOHC engine

8.20b Cylinder head bolt tightening sequence – DOHC engine

8.20c Tightening the bolts to the torque setting

8.21 Tightening the bolts through the specified angle

9.5 Unscrew the bolts around the edge of the sump

9.7 Applying a bead of sealant to the sump

10.2a Unbolt the plastic cover from the oil pump...

10.2b ...and use a tool to hold the sprocket while the retaining bolt is loosened...

10.2c ...then remove the bolt and sprocket

thick bead of silicone sealant (D 176404 A2 or equivalent) to the sump. Note that the sealant should be run around the inside of the bolt holes in the sump (see illustration). The sump must be fitted within 5 minutes of applying the sealant.

8 Offer the sump up to the cylinder block, then refit the retaining bolts, and progressively tighten them in diagonal sequence to the specified torque.

9 Reconnect the wiring to the oil level/temperature sender on the sump.

10.4a Unscrew the mounting bolts...

10.4b ...and remove the oil pump

10.5a Removing the oil pump chain and sprocket...

10.5b ...then unbolt and remove the tensioner

10 Refit the engine undershield and lower the car to the ground.

11 Allow at least 30 minutes from the time of refitting the sump for the sealant to dry, then refill the engine with oil, with reference to Chapter 1A, Section 3.

10 Oil pump, drive chain and sprockets – removal, inspection and refitting

Removal

1 Remove the sump as described in Section 9. It is not necessary to remove the timing cover unless renewing the timing chain.

2 Unbolt the plastic cover from the oil pump, then hold the sprocket stationary and unscrew the retaining bolt (see illustrations). Discard the bolt as a new one must be used on refitting.

3 Swivel the chain tensioner outwards and release the sprocket from the oil pump. Leave the sprocket hanging in the chain.

4 Unscrew the mounting bolts and withdraw the oil pump from the dowels in the cylinder block (see illustrations).

5 If it is required to remove the oil pump chain and tensioner, first remove the timing cover as described in Section 5. Mark the chain and sprockets to ensure they are refitted the original way around. Slide the small sprocket from the end of the crankshaft, and then remove both sprockets from the chain. Note: *The sprocket is not keyed to the crankshaft.* Unbolt and remove the tensioner (see illustrations).

Inspection

6 Thoroughly clean all components, then examine the oil pump drive chain for excessive wear. Also check the sprocket teeth for wear. If the engine has covered a high mileage, the chain and sprockets should be renewed as a matter of course.

7 The crankshaft pulley bolt must be renewed whenever removed.

Refitting

8 If removed, refit the oil pump drive chain as follows. Refit the tensioner, then engage the small sprocket with the drive chain, then locate the sprocket on the end of the crankshaft making sure that it is the correct way around.

9 Locate the oil pump on the cylinder block dowels, insert the mounting bolts and tighten them to the specified torque.

10 Where removed, engage the oil pump sprocket in the chain. Swivel the chain tensioner outwards, then position the sprocket on the oil pump and screw on the new retaining bolt. Tighten the bolt to the specified torque and angle while holding the sprocket stationary.

11 Refit the oil pump plastic cover and tighten the screws.

12 Refit the sump with reference to Section 9.

12.3 Removing the old oil seal

12.5a Locate the new oil seal in the timing cover...

12.5b ...and use a suitable socket to tap it into position

11 Oil pressure warning light switch – removal and refitting

Removal

1 The oil pressure warning light switch is located on the left-hand end of the cylinder head.

2 Disconnect the wiring connector and wipe clean the area around the switch.

3 Unscrew the switch from the cylinder head and remove it, along with its sealing washer. If the switch is to be left removed from the engine for any length of time, plug the cylinder head aperture.

Refitting

4 Examine the sealing washer for signs of damage or deterioration and if necessary renew.

5 Refit the switch, complete with washer, and tighten it to the specified torque.

6 Securely reconnect the wiring connector then check and, if necessary, top-up the engine oil as described in *Weekly checks*.

12 Crankshaft oil seals – renewal

Right-hand oil seal

1 Remove the crankshaft pulley as described in Section 4, then note the fitted depth of the oil seal in the timing cover.

2 Slide the sleeve from the end of the crankshaft. **Note:** *This is necessary, as the sleeve must be assembled onto the crankshaft through the oil seal.* If necessary, remove the sleeve-sealing O-ring from the crankshaft. If the sleeve is reluctant to move, the timing cover must be removed as described in Section 5.

3 Carefully lever the old seal out of the timing cover using a suitable flat-bladed screwdriver **(see illustration)**, taking great care not to damage the cover or crankshaft. Alternatively, punch or drill two small holes opposite each other in the seal, then screw a self-tapping

12.6a Refit the O-ring seal...

12.8 Note the fitted depth of the oil seal before removing it

screw into each and pull on the screws with pliers to extract the seal.

4 Clean the seal housing.

5 Note that the new oil seal **must not** be oiled or greased, and the contact surfaces of the timing cover must be completely dry. New oil seals are provided with a fitting adapter. Locate the adapter and new seal over the crankshaft and onto the timing cover, and press it into position until it is at the fitted depth previously noted. If necessary, the seal can be tapped into position using a suitable tubular drift, such as a socket, which bears only on the hard outer edge of the seal **(see illustrations)**. Note that the sealing lips must face inwards.

6 If necessary, locate a new O-ring seal on the crankshaft, and then carefully insert the sleeve through the new oil seal onto the crankshaft **(see illustrations)**.

7 Refit the crankshaft pulley as described in Section 4.

12.6b ...and insert the sleeve

Left-hand oil seal

8 Remove the flywheel as described in Section 13, then note the fitted depth of the oil seal in the timing cover **(see illustration)**.

9 Carefully punch or drill two small holes opposite each other in the seal. Screw a self-tapping screw into each hole, and pull on the screws with pliers to extract the seal **(see illustration)**.

10 Clean the cylinder block/crankcase, and polish off any burrs or raised edges on the crankshaft, which may have caused the seal to fail in the first place.

11 Note that the new oil seal **must not** be oiled or greased, and the contact surfaces of the housing and crankshaft must be completely dry. New oil seals are provided with a fitting adapter. Locate the adapter and new seal over the crankshaft and into the housing, and press it into position until it is at the fitted depth previously noted **(see**

12.9 Removing the crankshaft left-hand (flywheel end) oil seal

12.11a Locate the adapter and new oil seal over the crankshaft...

12.11b ...and tap it into position

is critical and, if not done accurately, the hardness of the teeth will be destroyed.

7 If it is felt necessary, use the correct-size tap to clean the threads in the crankshaft of any old thread-locking fluid.

Refitting

8 Clean the mating surfaces of the flywheel and crankshaft, and then refit the rear plate and locate the flywheel on the crankshaft.

9 If the new flywheel retaining bolts are not supplied with their threads already pre-coated **(see illustration)**, apply a suitable thread-locking compound to the threads of each bolt. Fit the bolts, tightening them by hand only at this stage.

10 Lock the flywheel using the method employed on dismantling, and tighten the retaining bolts to the specified torque wrench and angle settings **(see illustration)**.

11 Refit the clutch as described in Chapter 6, Section 6, and then remove the locking tool and refit the transmission as described in Chapter 7A, Section 3.

illustrations). If necessary, the seal can be tapped into position using a suitable tubular drift, such as a socket, which bears only on the hard outer edge of the seal. Note that the sealing lips must face inwards.

12 Refit the flywheel as described in Section 13.

13 Flywheel –
removal, inspection and refitting

Removal

1 Remove the transmission as described in Chapter 7A, Section 3, and then remove the clutch assembly as described in Chapter 6, Section 6.

2 Prevent the flywheel from turning by locking the ring gear teeth **(see illustration)**, or by bolting a strap between the flywheel and the cylinder block/crankcase.

3 Unscrew and remove the flywheel retaining bolts; discard the bolts, as they must be renewed whenever they are disturbed.

4 Remove the flywheel, and if necessary remove the engine rear plate **(see illustration)**. Do not drop the flywheel, as it is very heavy. **Note:** *The bolt holes are offset, so it is only possible to fit the flywheel in one position.*

Inspection

5 If the clutch mating surface of the flywheel is deeply scored, cracked or otherwise damaged, the flywheel must be renewed, unless it is possible to have it surface-ground. Seek the advice of a VW dealer or engine reconditioning specialist.

6 If the ring gear teeth are badly worn, it must be renewed, but this job is best left to a VW dealer or engine reconditioning specialist. The temperature to which the new ring gear must be heated for installation (150°C minimum)

14 Engine/transmission
mountings –
inspection and renewal

Inspection

1 If improved access is required, jack up the front of the car, and support it securely on axle stands (see *Jacking and vehicle support*). Remove the securing screws and remove the engine under shield.

2 Check the mounting rubbers to see if they are cracked, hardened or separated from the metal at any point; renew the mounting if any such damage or deterioration is evident.

3 Check that all the mountings are securely tightened; use a torque wrench to check if possible.

4 Using a large screwdriver or a crowbar, check for wear in the mounting by carefully levering against it to check for free play. Where this is not possible, enlist the aid of an assistant to move the engine/transmission back-and-forth, or from side-to-side, whilst you observe the mounting. While some free play is to be expected, even from new components, excessive wear should be obvious. If excessive free play is found, check first that the fasteners are correctly secured, and then renew any worn components as described in the following paragraphs.

5 When working on the right-hand mounting and rear lower mounting (torque arm), remove the mounting as a complete unit. VW state that the mounting bracket-to-flexible mounting nut/bolt should not be slackened, see following procedures for each individual mounting.

Renewal

Right-hand mounting

Note: *New mounting securing bolts will be required on refitting.*

13.2 Home-made tool used to hold the flywheel/driveplate stationary

13.4 Removing the engine rear plate

13.9 Fitting the new flywheel retaining bolts

13.10 Tighten the bolts to the specified torque angle

14.9 Undo the earth cable securing nut – arrowed

14.10a Undo the mounting bracket to engine bolts - arrowed

14.10b Undo the mounting bracket-to-body bolts - arrowed

14.16 Transmission mounting bolts – arrowed

14.17 Mounting bracket to transmission mounting bolts - arrowed

14.21 Rear lower torque arm mounting bolts – arrowed

6 Attach a hoist and lifting tackle to the engine lifting brackets on the cylinder head, and raise the hoist to just take the weight of the engine. Alternatively the engine can be supported on a trolley jack under the engine. Use a block of wood between the sump and the head of the jack, to prevent any damage to the sump.

7 To gain access to the engine mounting-to-body bolts, undo the two screws and move the coolant reservoir to one side, leaving the coolant hoses connected.

8 Unclip any wiring harness, pipes or hoses from over the upper mounting bracket and move them to one side.

9 Undo the securing nut and disconnect the earth wiring connector (where fitted), from the top of the engine mounting bracket **(see illustration)**.

10 Unscrew the three bolts securing the mounting bracket-to-engine, and the four bolts securing the engine mounting-to-body, then remove the complete right-hand mounting from the engine compartment **(see illustrations)**.

Caution: Do NOT undo the engine mounting centre nut, securing the bracket to the flexible mounting.

11 Refitting is a reversal of removal, but use new mounting securing bolts, and tighten all fixings to the specified torque.

Left-hand mounting

Note: *New mounting bolts will be required on refitting.*

12 Remove the air filter housing as described in Chapter 4A, Section 2.

13 Remove the battery, as described in Chapter 5A, Section 3.

14 Attach a hoist and lifting tackle to the engine lifting brackets on the engine/transmission, and raise the hoist to just take the weight. Alternatively the engine/transmission can be supported on a trolley jack under the transmission. Use a block of wood between the transmission and the head of the jack, to prevent any damage to the transmission.

15 Release any relevant wiring or hoses from the clips on the battery tray, then unscrew the three securing bolts and remove the battery tray. Disconnect the drain hose from the front of the tray as it is being removed.

16 Unscrew the two bolts securing the mounting to the transmission bracket, and the three remaining bolts securing the mounting to the body **(see illustration)**, then lift the mounting from the engine compartment.

17 To remove the mounting bracket from the transmission, remove the left-hand front wheel and wheel arch liner, then lower the transmission slightly and undo the three retaining bolts **(see illustration)**.

18 Refitting is a reversal of removal, but use new mounting securing bolts, and tighten all fixings to the specified torque.

Rear lower mounting (torque arm)

Note: *New mounting bolts will be required on refitting.*

19 Apply the handbrake, then jack up the front of the car and support securely on axle stands (see *Jacking and vehicle support*). Remove the engine undershield for access to the rear mounting (torque arm).

20 Support the rear of the transmission beneath the final drive housing. To do this, use a trolley jack and block of wood, or alternatively wedge a block of wood between the transmission and the subframe.

21 Working under the car, unscrew and remove the bolt securing the mounting to the subframe and the two bolts securing the mounting to the transmission **(see illustration)**, then withdraw the complete mounting from under the car.

Caution: Do NOT undo the lower mounting centre bolt, securing the bracket to the flexible mounting.

22 Refitting is a reversal of removal, but use new mounting securing bolts, and tighten all fixings to the specified torque.

Notes

Chapter 2 Part B:
1.4 litre petrol engine in-car repair procedures

Contents

Degrees of difficulty

Easy, suitable for novice with little experience	**Fairly easy,** suitable for beginner with some experience	**Fairly difficult,** suitable for competent DIY mechanic	**Difficult,** suitable for experienced DIY mechanic	**Very difficult,** suitable for expert DIY or professional

Specifications

General

Type	Four-cylinder in-line, belt-driven double overhead camshaft (DOHC), four stroke, 16-valve, liquid-cooled
Cubic capacity	1390 cc
Manufacturer's engine code*	CGGB
Maximum power output	63 kW @ 5000 rpm
Maximum torque output	132 Nm @ 3800 rpm
Bore	76.5 mm
Stroke	75.6 mm
Compression ratio	10.5 : 1
Compression pressures (oil temperature 30°C minimum):	
New	10.0 to 15.0 bars
Minimum	7.0 bars
Maximum difference between cylinders	3.0 bars
Firing order	1 – 3 – 4 – 2
No 1 cylinder location	Crankshaft pulley end
Direction of crankshaft rotation	Clockwise (when viewed from right-hand side of car)

* Note: *See 'Vehicle identification' at the end of this manual for the location of engine code markings.*

Camshafts

Camshaft endfloat (maximum)	0.15 mm
Camshaft bearing running clearance	No figure specified
Camshaft run-out	No figure specified

Lubrication system

Oil pump type	Gear type, driven directly from front of crankshaft
Oil pressure (oil temperature 80°C):	
Minimum @ idling	0.3 to 0.7 bar
Minimum @ 2000 rpm	2.0 bar
Maximum @ high rpm	7.0 bar

Torque wrench settings

	Nm	lbf ft
Alternator	20	15
Ancillary (alternator, etc) bracket mounting bolts	50	37
Auxiliary drivebelt tensioner securing bolt:		
M8 bolt:		
Stage 1	20	15
Stage 2	Angle-tighten a further 90°	
M10 bolt	45	33
Big-end bearing caps bolts*:		
Stage 1	30	22
Stage 2	Angle-tighten a further 90°	
Camshaft carrier bolts*:		
Stage 1	10	7
Stage 2	Angle-tighten a further 90°	
Camshaft left-hand endplate bolts	10	7
Camshaft sprocket bolts*:		
Stage 1	20	15
Stage 2	Angle-tighten a further 90°	
Clutch pressure plate mounting bolts*:		
Stage 1	60	44
Stage 2	Angle-tighten a further 90°	
Coolant pump bolts	20	15
Crankcase breather (oil separator) bolts	10	7
Crankshaft oil seal housing bolts	12	9
Crankshaft pulley/sprocket bolt*:		
Stage 1	150	110
Stage 2	Angle-tighten a further 180°	
Cylinder head bolts*:		
Stage 1	30	22
Stage 2	Angle-tighten a further 90°	
Stage 3	Angle-tighten a further 90°	
Engine/transmission left-hand mounting to transmission*:		
Stage 1	40	30
Stage 2	Angle-tighten a further 90°	
Engine/transmission left-hand mounting to body*:		
Stage 1	50	37
Stage 2	Angle-tighten a further 90°	
Engine/transmission rear mounting bracket to transmission*:		
Stage 1	30	22
Stage 2	Angle-tighten a further 90°	
Engine/transmission rear mounting link to subframe*:		
Stage 1	40	30
Stage 2	Angle-tighten a further 90°	
Engine/transmission right-hand mounting to engine*:		
Stage 1	20	15
Stage 2	Angle-tighten a further 90°	
Engine/transmission right-hand mounting to body*:		
Stage 1	30	22
Stage 2	Angle-tighten a further 90°	
Engine-to-automatic transmission bolts:		
M12 bolts	80	59
M10 cylinder block-to-transmission bolts	60	44
M10 sump-to-transmission bolts	25	18
Engine-to-manual transmission bolts	80	59
Engine-to-manual transmission cover plate bolts	10	7
Exhaust manifold nuts	25	18
Exhaust pipe-to-manifold nuts	40	30
Flywheel/driveplate bolts*:		
Stage 1	60	44
Stage 2	Angle-tighten a further 90°	
Knock sensor	20	15
Oil cooler securing nut	25	18
Oil drain plug	30	22
Oil level/temperature sensor-to-sump bolts	10	7
Oil pick-up pipe securing bolts	10	7
Oil pressure warning light switch	25	18
Oil pump securing bolts*	12	9

Torque wrench settings (continued)

	Nm	lbf ft
Sump:		
Sump-to-cylinder block bolts:		
Metal sump	15	11
Aluminium sump	13	10
Sump-to-transmission bolts	45	33
Timing belt idler pulley bolt	50	37
Timing belt outer cover bolts:		
Small bolts	10	7
Large bolts	20	15
Timing belt rear cover bolts:		
Small bolts	10	7
Large bolt (coolant pump bolts)	20	15
Timing belt tensioner:		
Main timing bolt tensioner bolt	20	15
Secondary timing belt tensioner bolt	20	15

* Note: *Use new fasteners*

1 General information

Using this Chapter

This Part of Chapter 2 describes those repair procedures that can reasonably be carried out on the engine while it remains in the car. If the engine has been removed from the car and is being dismantled as described in Part E, any preliminary dismantling procedures can be ignored.

Note that while it may be possible physically to overhaul items such as the piston/connecting rod assemblies while the engine is in the car, such tasks are not usually carried out as separate operations, and usually require the execution of several additional procedures (not to mention the cleaning of components and of oil ways); for this reason, all such tasks are classed as major overhaul procedures, and are described in Part E of this Chapter. *Caution: The crankshaft must not be removed on these engines. If the crankshaft or main bearing surfaces are worn or damaged, the complete crankshaft/cylinder block assembly must be renewed.*

Part E describes the removal of the engine/transmission from the car and the full overhaul procedures that can then be carried out.

Engine description

The engine is a water-cooled, double overhead camshaft, in-line four-cylinder unit, with an aluminium-alloy cylinder block and cylinder head. It is mounted transversely at the front of the car, with the transmission bolted to the left-hand side of the engine.

The crankshaft is of five-bearing type, and thrustwashers are fitted to the centre main bearing to control crankshaft endfloat. The crankshaft and main bearings are matched to the alloy cylinder block, and it is not possible to reassemble the crankshaft and cylinder block once the components have been separated. If the crankshaft or bearings are worn, the complete cylinder block/crankshaft assembly must be renewed.

The inlet camshaft is driven by a toothed belt from the crankshaft sprocket, and the exhaust camshaft is driven from the inlet camshaft by a second toothed belt. The camshafts are located in a camshaft carrier, which is bolted to the top of the cylinder head.

The valves are closed by coil springs, and run in guides pressed into the cylinder head; the camshafts actuate the valves by roller rockers and hydraulic tappets. There are four valves per cylinder, two inlet valves and two exhaust valves.

The oil pump is driven directly from the end of the crankshaft. Oil is drawn from the sump through a strainer, and then forced through an externally mounted, renewable filter. From there, it is distributed to the cylinder head, where it lubricates the camshaft journals and hydraulic tappets, and also to the crankcase, where it lubricates the main bearings, connecting rod big-ends, gudgeon pins and cylinder bores.

Engine coolant is circulated by a pump, driven by the main timing belt. For details of the cooling system, refer to Chapter 3.

Repairs with engine in car

The following operations can be performed without removing the engine:
a) *Compression pressure – testing.*
b) *Camshaft carrier – removal and refitting.*
c) *Crankshaft pulley – removal and refitting.*
d) *Timing belt covers – removal and refitting.*
e) *Timing belt(s) – removal, refitting and adjustment.*
f) *Timing belt tensioner and sprockets – removal and refitting.*
g) *Camshaft oil seal(s) – renewal.*
h) *Camshafts and hydraulic tappets – removal, inspection and refitting.*
i) *Cylinder head – removal and refitting*.*
j) *Sump – removal and refitting.*
k) *Oil pump – removal, overhaul and refitting.*
l) *Crankshaft oil seals – renewal.*
m) *Engine/transmission mountings – inspection and renewal.*
n) *Flywheel – removal, inspection and refitting.*
* *Cylinder head dismantling procedures are detailed in Chapter 2E, with details of camshaft and hydraulic tappet removal.*

Note: *It is possible to remove the pistons and connecting rods (after removing the cylinder head and sump) without removing the engine. However, this is not recommended. Work of this nature is more easily and thoroughly completed with the engine on the bench, as described in Chapter 2E.*

2 Compression test – description and interpretation

1 When engine performance is down, or if misfiring occurs which cannot be attributed to the ignition or fuel systems, a compression test can provide diagnostic clues as to the engine's condition. If the test is performed regularly, it can give warning of trouble before any other symptoms become apparent.

2 The engine must be fully warmed-up to normal operating temperature, the battery must be fully charged and the spark plugs must be removed. The aid of an assistant will be required.

3 Disable the ignition system by disconnecting the wiring plug from the ignition coils.

4 Fit a compression tester to the No 1 cylinder spark plug hole. The type of tester that screws into the plug thread is preferred.

5 Have the assistant hold the throttle wide open and crank the engine for several seconds on the starter motor. Note: The throttle will not operate until the ignition is switched on. After one or two revolutions, the compression pressure should build up to a maximum figure and then stabilise. Record the highest reading obtained.

6 Repeat the test on the remaining cylinders, recording the pressure in each.

7 All cylinders should produce very similar pressures. Any difference greater than that specified indicates the existence of a fault. Note that the compression should build-up quickly in a healthy engine. Low compression on the first stroke, followed by gradually increasing pressure on successive strokes, indicates worn piston rings. A low

3.4a Crankshaft pulley timing mark aligned with TDC mark on timing belt cover

3.4b Timing mark scribed on inner flange of pulley aligned with TDC mark on timing belt cover

3.5 Crankshaft sprocket tooth with chamfered edge aligns with cast arrow on oil pump

compression reading on the first stroke, which does not build-up during successive strokes, indicates leaking valves or a blown head gasket (a cracked head could also be the cause). Deposits on the undersides of the valve heads can also cause low compression.

8 If the pressure in any cylinder is reduced to the specified minimum or less, carry out the following test to isolate the cause. Introduce a teaspoonful of clean oil into that cylinder through its spark plug hole and repeat the test.

9 If the addition of oil temporarily improves the compression pressure, this indicates that bore or piston wear is responsible for the pressure loss. No improvement suggests that leaking or burnt valves, or a blown head gasket, may be to blame.

10 A low reading from two adjacent cylinders is almost certainly due to the head gasket having blown between them and the presence of coolant in the engine oil will confirm this.

11 If one cylinder is about 20 percent lower than the others and the engine has a slightly rough idle; a worn camshaft lobe could be the cause.

12 On completion of the test, refit the spark plugs and reconnect the ignition wiring.

3 Engine assembly and valve timing marks – general information and usage

General information

1 TDC is the highest point in the cylinder that each piston reaches as it travels up and down when the crankshaft turns. Each piston reaches TDC at the end of the compression stroke and again at the end of the exhaust stroke, but TDC generally refers to piston position on the compression stroke. No 1 piston is at the timing belt end of the engine.

2 Positioning No 1 piston at TDC is an essential part of many procedures, such as timing belt removal and camshaft removal.

3 The design of the engines covered in this Chapter is such that piston-to-valve contact may occur if the camshaft or crankshaft is turned with the timing belt removed. For this reason, it is important to ensure that the camshaft and crankshaft do not move in relation to each other once the timing belt has been removed from the engine.

4 The crankshaft pulley has a marking which, when aligned with a corresponding reference marking on the timing belt cover, indicates that No 1 piston (and hence also No 4 piston) is at TDC. Note that on some models, the crankshaft pulley timing mark is located on the outer flange of the pulley. In order to make alignment of the timing marks easier, it is advisable to remove the pulley (see Section 4) and, using a set-square, scribe a corresponding mark on the inner flange of the pulley (see illustrations).

5 Note that there is also a timing mark that can be used with the crankshaft sprocket – this is useful if the crankshaft pulley and timing belt have been removed. When No 1 piston is at TDC, the crankshaft sprocket tooth with the chamfered inner edge aligns with a cast arrow on the oil pump (see illustration).

6 The camshaft sprockets are equipped with TDC positioning holes. When the positioning holes are aligned with the corresponding holes in the camshaft carrier, No 1 piston is at TDC on the compression stroke (see illustration).

7 Additionally, on some models, the flywheel/driveplate has a TDC marking, which can be observed by unscrewing a protective plastic cover from the transmission bellhousing. The mark takes the form of a notch in the edge of the flywheel on manual transmission models, or an O marking on automatic transmission models. Note that it is not possible to use these marks on all models due to the limited access available to view the marks.

Setting No 1 cylinder to TDC

Note: *Suitable locking pins will be required to lock the camshaft sprockets in position during this procedure. On some engines, it may be necessary to use a small engineer's mirror to view the timing marks from under the wheel arch.*

3.6 Camshaft sprocket positioning holes (arrowed) aligned

8 Before starting work, make sure that the ignition is switched off (ideally, the battery negative lead should be disconnected).

9 Remove the air cleaner assembly as described in Chapter 4A, Section 2.

10 If desired, to make the engine easier to turn, remove all of the spark plugs as described in Chapter 1A, Section 24.

11 Apply the handbrake, then jack up the front of the car and support on axle stands (see *Jacking and vehicle support*).

12 Remove the right-hand front roadwheel, then remove the securing screws and/or clips, and remove the appropriate engine undershields to enable access to the crankshaft pulley.

13 Remove the upper timing belt cover as described in Section 5.

14 Turn the engine clockwise, using a spanner on the crankshaft pulley bolt, until the TDC mark on the crankshaft pulley or flywheel/driveplate is aligned with the corresponding mark on the timing belt cover or transmission casing, and the locking pin holes in the camshaft sprockets are aligned with the corresponding holes in the camshaft carrier.

15 If necessary, to give sufficient clearance for the camshaft locking tool to be engaged with the camshaft sprockets, unbolt the air cleaner support bracket from the engine mounting. Similarly, if necessary, unbolt the power steering fluid reservoir and move it to one side, leaving the fluid hoses connected.

16 A suitable tool will now be required to lock the camshaft sprockets in the TDC position. A special VW tool is available for this purpose, but a suitable tool can be improvised using two M8 bolts and nuts, and a short length of steel bar. With the camshaft sprocket positioned as described in paragraph 14, measure the distance between the locking pin hole centres, and drill two corresponding 8 mm holes in the length of steel bar. Slide the M8 bolts through the holes in the bar, and secure them using the nuts.

17 Slide the tool into position in the holes in the camshaft sprockets, ensuring that the pins (or bolts) engage with the holes in camshaft carrier **(see illustration)**. The engine is now locked in position, with No 1 piston at TDC on the compression stroke.

4 Crankshaft pulley – removal and refitting

Removal

1 Disconnect the battery negative lead (refer to *Disconnecting the battery* in the *Reference* Chapter at the end of this manual).

2 For improved access, jack up the front of the car, and support securely on axle stands (see *Jacking and vehicle support*). Remove the right-hand front roadwheel. Also remove

3.17 Tool used to lock camshaft sprockets at TDC (engine and timing belt removed)

the engine top cover and where necessary disconnect the ventilation hose.

3 Remove the securing screws and/or release the clips, and withdraw the relevant engine undershield(s) to enable access to the crankshaft pulley.

4 If necessary (for any later work to be carried out), turn the crankshaft using a socket or spanner on the crankshaft pulley bolt, until the relevant timing marks align (see Section 3).

5 Remove the auxiliary drivebelt, as described in Chapter 1A, Section 25.

6 To prevent the crankshaft from turning as the pulley bolt is slackened, a tool similar to that shown can be used. Engage the tool with two of the slots in the pulley **(see illustration)**.

7 Counterhold the pulley, and slacken the pulley bolt (take care – the bolt is very tight) using a socket and a suitable extension.

8 Unscrew the bolt, and remove the pulley **(see illustration)**.

9 Refit the crankshaft pulley securing bolt, with a spacer washer positioned under its head, to retain the crankshaft sprocket.

Refitting

10 Unscrew the crankshaft pulley/sprocket bolt used to retain the sprocket, and remove the spacer washer, then refit the pulley to the sprocket. Ensure that the locating pin on the sprocket engages with the corresponding hole in the pulley.

11 Oil the threads of the new crankshaft pulley bolt. Prevent the crankshaft from turning as during removal, then fit the new pulley securing bolt, and tighten it to the

4.8 Removing the crankshaft pulley

4.6 Counterhold the crankshaft pulley using a tool similar to that shown

specified torque, in the two stages given in the Specifications.

12 Refit the auxiliary drivebelt as described in Chapter 1A, Section 25.

13 Refit the engine undershield(s) and top cover.

14 Refit the roadwheel, lower the car to the ground, and reconnect the battery negative lead.

5 Timing belt covers – removal and refitting

Upper outer cover

1 Remove the air cleaner assembly as described in Chapter 4A, Section 2. Also remove the engine top cover and, where necessary, disconnect the ventilation hose.

2 Release the two securing clips, and lift the cover from the engine **(see illustration)**.

3 Refitting is a reversal of removal.

Lower outer cover

4 Remove the crankshaft pulley, as described in Section 4.

5 Release the two cover securing clips, located at the rear of the engine, and unscrew the two lower securing bolts, and the single bolt securing the cover to the engine mounting bracket. Withdraw the cover downwards from the engine **(see illustrations)**.

6 Refitting is a reversal of removal, but refit the crankshaft pulley with reference to Section 4.

5.2 Removing the upper outer timing belt cover

5.5a Release the two securing clips (arrowed)...

5.5b ...then unscrew the two lower securing bolts (arrowed)...

5.5c ...and the single bolt securing the cover to the engine mounting bracket...

5.5d ...and withdraw the lower timing belt cover

5.8 Removing the idler pulley/bracket assembly (viewed with engine removed)

5.9 Unscrew rear timing belt cover bolt next to engine right-hand lifting eye

Rear timing belt cover

Note: *As the rear timing belt cover securing bolts also secure the coolant pump, it is advisable to drain the cooling system (see Chapter 1A, Section 30) before starting this procedure, and to renew the coolant pump seal/gasket (see Chapter 3, Section 7) before refitting the cover. Refill the cooling system with reference to Chapter 1A, Section 30.*

7 Remove the timing belt as described in Section 6.

8 Unbolt the timing belt idler pulley/bracket assembly **(see illustration)**.

9 Unscrew the rear timing belt cover securing bolt located next to the engine right-hand lifting eye **(see illustration)**.

10 Unscrew the two securing bolts, and remove the rear timing belt cover. Note that the bolts also secure the coolant pump **(see illustration)**.

5.10 Removing the rear timing belt cover (viewed with engine removed)

11 Refitting is a reversal of removal, but tighten the timing belt idler pulley/bracket bolt to the specified torque, and refit the timing belt as described in Section 6.

6 Timing belt(s) – removal and refitting

Removal

1 These engines have two timing belts; the main timing belt drives the inlet camshaft from the crankshaft, and the secondary timing belt drives the exhaust camshaft from the inlet camshaft.

Main timing belt

2 Disconnect the battery negative lead (refer to *Disconnecting the battery* in the *Reference* Chapter at the end of this manual).

6.13 Slacken the tensioner bolt, lever the tensioner anti-clockwise, then retighten

3 Remove the air cleaner assembly as described in Chapter 4A, Section 2. Also remove the engine top cover and, where necessary, disconnect the ventilation hose.

4 Remove the upper and lower timing belt covers as described in Section 5.

5 Refit the crankshaft pulley securing bolt, with a spacer washer positioned under its head, to retain the crankshaft sprocket.

6 Turn the crankshaft to position No 1 piston at TDC on the compression stroke, and lock the camshaft sprockets in position, as described in Section 3.

7 Unscrew the securing screw, and move the power steering fluid reservoir clear of the working area, leaving the fluid hoses connected. Where necessary, unclip the charcoal canister hose from the reservoir.

8 Where applicable, on models with air conditioning, unscrew the securing bolt, and remove the auxiliary drivebelt idler pulley.

9 Attach a hoist and lifting tackle to the right-hand (timing belt end) engine lifting bracket, and raise the hoist to just take the weight of the engine.

10 Remove the complete engine right-hand mounting assembly, as described in Section 19. Also, unbolt the mounting bracket from the cylinder block.

11 Unscrew the four securing bolts, and remove the engine right-hand mounting bracket from the engine.

12 If either of the timing belts are to be refitted, mark their running directions to ensure correct refitting.

13 Engage a suitable Allen key with the hole in the main timing belt tensioner plate, then

6.14 Removing the main timing belt

6.17a Slacken the tensioner bolt, and lever the tensioner clockwise...

6.17b ...then unscrew the bolt and remove the tensioner

slacken the tensioner bolt, lever the tensioner anti-clockwise using the Allen key (to release the tension on the belt), and retighten the tensioner bolt **(see illustration)**.

14 Temporarily remove the camshaft sprocket locking tool, then slide the main timing belt from the sprockets, noting it's routing **(see illustration)**. Refit the camshaft sprocket locking tool once the timing belt has been removed.

15 Turn the crankshaft a quarter-turn (90°) anti-clockwise to position No's 1 and 4 pistons slightly down their bores from the TDC position. This will eliminate any risk of piston-to-valve contact if the crankshaft or camshaft is turned whilst the timing belt is removed.

Secondary timing belt

16 Once the main timing belt has been removed, to remove the secondary timing belt, proceed as follows.

17 Engage a suitable Allen key with the hole in the secondary timing belt tensioner plate, then slacken the tensioner bolt, and lever the tensioner clockwise using the Allen key (to release the tension on the belt). Unscrew the securing bolt, and remove the secondary timing belt tensioner **(see illustrations)**.

18 Temporarily remove the camshaft sprocket locking tool, and slide the secondary timing belt from the sprockets **(see illustration)**. Refit the sprocket locking tool once the belt has been removed.

Refitting

Secondary timing belt

19 Check that the camshaft sprockets are still locked in position by the locking pins.

20 Temporarily remove the camshaft sprocket locking tool, and fit the secondary timing belt around the camshaft sprockets. Make sure that the belt is as tight as possible on its top run between the sprockets (but note that there will be some slack in the belt). If the original belt is being refitted, observe the running direction markings. Refit the camshaft sprocket locking tool once the belt has been fitted to the sprockets.

21 Check that the secondary timing belt tensioner pointer is positioned on the far right of the tensioner backplate.

22 Lift the lower run of the secondary

timing belt using the tensioner, and fit the tensioner securing bolt (if necessary turn the tensioner with an Allen key until the bolt hole in the tensioner aligns with the bolt hole in the cylinder head). Make sure that the lug on the tensioner backplate engages with the core plug hole in the cylinder head **(see illustration)**.

23 Use the Allen key to turn the tensioner anti-clockwise until the tensioner pointer aligns with the lug on the tensioner backplate, with the lug positioned against the left-hand stop in the core plug hole **(see illustration)**. Tighten the tensioner bolt to the specified torque.

24 Turn the crankshaft a quarter-turn (90°) clockwise to reposition No's 1 and 4 pistons at TDC. Ensure that the crankshaft sprocket tooth with the chamfered inner edge is aligned with the corresponding mark on the oil pump housing **(see illustration)**.

6.18 Removing the secondary timing belt

6.23 Turn the tensioner anti-clockwise to align the tensioner pointer and the lug

Main timing belt

25 Where applicable, ensure that the secondary drivebelt has been refitted and tensioned, then again temporarily remove the camshaft sprocket locking tool, and fit the main timing belt around the sprockets. If the original belt is being refitted, observe the running direction markings. Work in an anti-clockwise direction, starting at the coolant pump sprocket, followed by the tensioner roller, crankshaft sprocket, idler pulley, inlet camshaft sprocket and the second idler pulley. Once the belt has been refitted, refit the camshaft sprocket locking tool.

26 Ensure that the tensioner bolt is slack, then engage an Allen key with the hole in the tensioner plate, and turn the plate clockwise until the tension indicator pointer is aligned with the centre of the cut-out in the backplate. Tighten the tensioner securing bolt to the specified torque.

6.22 Ensure the backplate lug engages correctly with the core plug hole

6.19 Crankshaft sprocket tooth with chamfered edge aligned with cast arrow on oil pump

7.3 Turn tensioner anti-clockwise to position shown before fitting. Cut-out engages with bolt (A)

27 Remove the camshaft sprocket locking tool.

28 Using a spanner or socket on the crankshaft pulley bolt, turn the engine through two complete turns in the normal direction of rotation, until the crankshaft sprocket tooth with the chamfered inner edge is aligned with the corresponding mark on the oil pump housing **(see illustration 6.19)**. Check that the locking tool can again be fitted to lock the camshaft sprockets in position – if not, one or both of the timing belts may have been incorrectly fitted.

29 With the crankshaft timing marks aligned, and the camshaft sprockets locked in position, check the tension of the timing belts. The secondary and main belt tension indicators should be positioned as described in paragraphs 23 and 25 respectively – if not, repeat the appropriate tensioning procedure, then recheck the tension.

7.8a Removing the smaller...

7.13 Refitting the crankshaft sprocket. Pulley locating pin (arrowed) must be outermost

30 When the belt tension is correct, refit the engine right-hand mounting bracket, and tighten the securing bolts to the specified torque.

31 Disconnect the hoist and lifting tackle from the engine lifting bracket.

32 Where applicable, refit the auxiliary drivebelt idler pulley.

33 Refit the lower outer timing belt cover, with reference to Section 5 if necessary.

34 Refit the crankshaft pulley as described in Section 4.

35 Refit the upper outer timing belt cover.

36 Refit the air cleaner assembly, and reconnect the battery negative lead.

7 Timing belt tensioner and sprockets – removal, inspection and refitting

Tensioner

Main timing belt

1 Remove the main timing belt as described in Section 6.

2 Unscrew the main timing belt tensioner bolt, and remove the tensioner from the engine.

3 Engage an Allen key with the hole in the tensioner plate, and turn the tensioner anti-clockwise to the position shown **(see illustration)**.

4 Refit the tensioner to the engine, ensuring that the cut-out in the tensioner backplate engages with the bolt on the cylinder block **(refer to illustration 7.3)**. Refit the tensioner securing bolt, and tighten by hand.

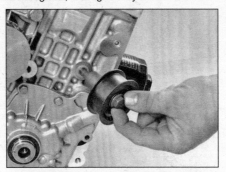

7.8b ...and larger timing belt idler pulleys

7.18 Ensure sprocket lug (1) engages with camshaft notch (2)

5 Refit and tension the main timing belt as described in Section 6.

Secondary timing belt

6 Removal and refitting of the tensioner is described as part of the timing belt removal procedure in Section 6.

Main timing belt idler pulleys

7 Remove the timing belt as described in Section 6.

8 Unscrew the securing bolt and remove the relevant idler pulley. Note that the smaller pulley (the idler pulley nearest the inlet manifold side of the engine) can be removed complete with its mounting bracket (unbolt the mounting bracket bolt, leaving the pulley attached to the bracket) **(see illustrations)**.

9 Refit the relevant idler pulley and tighten the securing bolt to the specified torque. Note that if the smaller idler pulley has been removed complete with its bracket; ensure that the bracket locates over the rear timing belt cover bolt on refitting.

10 Refit and tension the main timing belt as described in Section 6.

Crankshaft sprocket

11 Remove the main timing belt as described in Section 6.

12 Unscrew the crankshaft pulley, and the washer used to retain the sprocket, and withdraw the sprocket from the crankshaft.

13 Commence refitting by positioning the sprocket on the end of the crankshaft, noting that the pulley locating pin must be outermost **(see illustration)**. Temporarily refit the pulley securing bolt and washer to retain the sprocket.

14 Refit the main timing belt as described in Section 6.

Camshaft sprockets

15 Remove the main and secondary timing belts as described in Section 6. Ensure that the crankshaft has been turned a quarter-turn (90°) anti-clockwise to position No's 1 and 4 pistons slightly down their bores from the TDC position. This will eliminate any risk of piston-to-valve contact if the crankshaft or camshaft is turned whilst the timing belt is removed.

16 The relevant camshaft sprocket bolt must now be slackened. The camshaft must be prevented from turning as the sprocket bolt is unscrewed – **do not** rely solely on the sprocket locking tool for this. To hold the sprocket, make up a tool, and use it to hold the sprocket stationary by means of the holes in the sprocket **(refer to illustration 7.19)**.

17 Unscrew the camshaft sprocket bolt, and withdraw the sprocket from the end of the camshaft, noting which way round it is fitted.

18 Commence refitting by offering the sprocket up to the camshaft, ensuring that lug on the sprocket engages with the notch in the end of the camshaft. If both camshaft sprockets have been removed, note that the double sprocket (for the main and secondary timing belts) should be fitted to the inlet camshaft, and note that the exhaust camshaft sprocket must be fitted first **(see illustration)**.

19 Fit a new sprocket securing bolt, then use the tool to hold the sprocket stationary, as during removal, and tighten the bolt to the specified torque, in the two stages given in the Specifications **(see illustration)**.

20 Refit the secondary and main timing belts as described in Section 6.

Coolant pump sprocket

21 The coolant pump sprocket is integral with the coolant pump. Refer to Chapter 3, Section 7, for details of coolant pump removal.

8 Camshaft carrier – removal and refitting

Removal

1 Disconnect the battery negative lead (refer to *Disconnecting the battery* in the *Reference* Chapter at the end of this manual).

2 Remove the main and secondary timing belts, as described in Section 6.

3 Disconnect the wiring and remove the ignition coils from the spark plugs (see Chapter 1A, Section 24), then remove the cable guide.

4 Disconnect the inlet camshaft position sensor wiring connector **(see illustration)**.

5 Where fitted, unscrew the bolt securing the exhaust gas recirculation solenoid valve to the end of the camshaft carrier **(see illustration)**. Move the valve to one side.

7.19 Tighten the sprocket securing bolt using a suitable tool to hold the sprocket stationary

6 Disconnect the wiring plug from the oil pressure warning light switch, located at the front left-hand corner of the camshaft carrier. Release the wiring harness from the clip on the end of the camshaft carrier, and move the wiring to one side **(see illustrations)**.

7 Remove the rear timing belt cover securing bolt, located next to the engine right-hand lifting eye **(see illustration)**.

8 Working progressively from the centre out, in a diagonal sequence, slacken and remove the camshaft carrier securing bolts **(see illustration)**.

9 Carefully lift the camshaft carrier from the cylinder head. The camshafts can be removed from the carrier, as described in Section 9.

Refitting

10 Commence refitting by thoroughly cleaning all traces of old sealant, and all traces of oil and grease, from the mating faces

8.4 Disconnect the wiring connector from the inlet camshaft position sensor

of the cylinder head and camshaft carrier. Ensure that no debris enters the cylinder head or camshaft carrier.

11 Ensure that the crankshaft is still positioned a quarter-turn (90°) anti-clockwise from the TDC position, and that the camshafts are locked in position with the locking tool, as described in Section 3.

12 Check that the valve rockers are correctly located on the valves, and securely clipped into position on the hydraulic tappets.

13 Apply a thin, even coat of sealant (VW AMV 188 003, or equivalent) to the cylinder head mating face of the camshaft carrier **(see illustration)**. Do not apply the sealant too thickly, as excess sealant may enter and block the oilways, causing engine damage.

14 Carefully lower the camshaft carrier onto the cylinder head, until the camshafts rest on the rockers. Note that the camshaft carrier locates on dowels in the cylinder head; if

8.5 Unbolt the exhaust gas recirculation solenoid valve from the camshaft carrier

8.6a Disconnect the oil pressure warning light switch wiring plug...

8.6b ...then release the wiring from the clip on the end of the camshaft carrier

8.7 Remove the timing belt rear cover bolt next to the engine right-hand lifting eye

8.8 Removing the camshaft carrier securing bolts

8.13 Spread sealant on the camshaft carrier's cylinder head mating face

8.16 Tightening a camshaft carrier bolt through the specified Stage 2 angle

desired, to make fitting easier, two guide studs can be made up as follows:

a) Cut the heads off two M6 bolts, then cut slots in the top of each bolt to enable the bolt to be unscrewed using a flat-bladed screwdriver.

b) Screw one bolt into each of the camshaft carrier bolt locations at opposite corners of the cylinder head.

c) Lower the camshaft carrier over the bolts to guide it into position on the cylinder head.

15 Fit new camshaft carrier securing bolts, and tighten them progressively, working from the centre out, in a diagonal sequence (i.e. tighten all bolts through one turn, then tighten all bolts through a further turn, and so on). Ensure that the camshaft carrier sits squarely on the cylinder head as the bolts are tightened, and make sure that the carrier engages with the cylinder head dowels. Where applicable, once the camshaft carrier contacts the surface of the cylinder head, unscrew the two guide studs, and fit the two remaining new camshaft carrier securing bolts in their place.

16 Tighten the camshaft carrier securing bolts to the specified torque, in the two stages given in the Specifications **(see illustration)**.

17 Leave the camshaft carrier sealant to dry for approximately 30 minutes before carrying out any further work on the cylinder head or camshaft carrier.

18 Once the sealant has been allowed to dry, refit the rear timing belt cover bolt.

19 Reconnect the oil pressure warning light switch wiring plug, and clip the wiring into position on the end of the camshaft carrier.

20 Refit the exhaust gas recirculation solenoid valve bracket to the camshaft carrier, and tighten the securing bolt. Make sure that the lug on the camshaft carrier endplate engages with the corresponding hole in the solenoid valve bracket.

21 Reconnect the camshaft position sensor wiring connector.

22 Refit the cable guide and reconnect the ignition coils to the spark plugs.

23 Refit the secondary and main timing belts, as described in Section 6.

24 Reconnect the battery negative lead.

---

9 Camshafts – removal, inspection and refitting

Removal

1 Remove the camshaft carrier as described in Section 8.

2 Remove the camshaft sprockets, with reference to Section 7 if necessary.

3 If the inlet camshaft is to be removed, unscrew the securing bolt, and remove the inlet camshaft position sensor **(see illustration)**.

4 Remove the relevant camshaft carrier endplate **(see illustration)**.

5 Carefully withdraw the relevant camshaft from the endplate end of the camshaft carrier, taking care not to damage the bearing surfaces of the camshaft and housing as the camshaft is withdrawn **(see illustration)**.

Inspection

6 Visually inspect the camshafts for evidence of wear on the surfaces of the lobes and journals. Normally their surfaces should be smooth and have a dull shine; look for scoring, erosion or pitting and areas that appear highly polished, indicating excessive wear. Accelerated wear will occur once the hardened exterior of the camshaft has been damaged, so always renew worn items. **Note:** If these symptoms are visible on the tips of the camshaft lobes, check the corresponding rocker, as it will probably be worn as well.

7 If the machined surfaces of the camshaft appear discoloured or blue, it is likely that it has been overheated at some point, probably due to inadequate lubrication. This may have distorted the shaft, so check the run-out as follows: place the camshaft between two V-blocks and using a DTI gauge, measure the run-out at the centre journal. No maximum run-out figure is quoted by the manufacturers, but it should be obvious if the camshaft is excessively distorted.

8 To measure camshaft endfloat, temporarily refit the relevant camshaft to the camshaft carrier, and refit the camshaft sealing plate to the rear of the camshaft carrier. Anchor a DTI gauge to the timing belt end of the camshaft carrier and align the gauge probe with the camshaft axis. Push the camshaft to one end of the camshaft carrier as far as it will travel, then rest the DTI gauge probe on the end of the camshaft, and zero the gauge display. Push the camshaft as far as it will go to the other end of the camshaft carrier, and record the gauge reading. Verify the reading by pushing the camshaft back to its original position and checking that the gauge indicates zero again.

9 Check that the camshaft endfloat measurement is within the limit listed in the Specifications. Wear outside of this limit may be cured by renewing the relevant camshaft carrier endplate, although wear is unlikely to be confined to any one component, so renewal of the camshafts and camshaft carrier must be considered.

Refitting

10 Refitting is a reversal of removal, bearing in mind the following points:

a) Before refitting the camshaft, renew the camshaft oil seals, with reference to Section 11.

b) Lubricate the bearing surfaces in the camshaft carrier, and the camshaft lobes before refitting the camshaft(s).

c) Refit the camshaft sprocket(s) with reference to Section 7, noting that if both sprockets have been removed, the exhaust camshaft sprocket must be fitted first.

d) Refit the camshaft carrier as described in Section 8.

9.3 Remove the inlet camshaft position sensor

9.4 Remove the camshaft carrier endplate

9.5 Withdraw the camshaft from the camshaft carrier

10 Rockers and hydraulic tappets – removal, inspection and refitting

Removal

1 Remove the camshaft carrier, as described in Section 8.
2 As the components are removed, keep them in strict order, so that they can be refitted in their original locations.
3 Unclip the rockers from the hydraulic tappets, and lift them from the cylinder head **(see illustration)**.
4 Carefully lift the hydraulic tappets from their bores in the cylinder head. It is advisable to store the tappets (in order) upright in an oil bath whilst they are removed from the engine.

Inspection

5 Check the tappet bores in the cylinder head for signs of scoring or damage. If significant scoring or damage is found, it may be necessary to renew the cylinder head and the complete set of tappets.
6 Inspect the hydraulic tappets for obvious signs of wear or damage, and renew if necessary. Check that the oil holes in the tappets are free from obstructions.
7 Check the valve, tappet, and camshaft contact faces of the rockers for wear or damage, and also check the rockers for any signs of cracking. Renew any worn or damaged rockers.
8 Inspect the camshaft lobes, as described in Section 9.

Refitting

9 Oil the tappet bores in the cylinder head, and the hydraulic tappets themselves, then carefully slide the tappets into their original bores **(see illustration)**.
10 Oil the rocker contact faces of the tappets, and the tops of the valve stems, then refit the rockers to their original locations, ensuring that the rockers are securely clipped onto the tappets.
11 Check the endfloat of each camshaft, as described in Section 9, then refit the camshaft carrier as described in Section 8.

11 Camshaft oil seals – renewal

Right-hand oil seals

1 Remove the main and secondary timing belts as described in Section 6.
2 Remove the relevant camshaft sprocket as described in Section 7.
3 Drill two small holes into the existing oil seal, diagonally opposite each other. Take great care to avoid drilling through into the seal housing or camshaft sealing surface. Thread two self-tapping screws into the holes,

10.3 Removing a rocker (hydraulic tappets arrowed)

and using a pair of pliers, pull on the heads of the screws to extract the oil seal.
4 Clean out the seal housing and the sealing surface of the camshaft by wiping it with a lint-free cloth. Remove any swarf or burrs that may cause the seal to leak.
5 Lubricate the lip and outer edge of the new oil seal with clean engine oil, and push it over the camshaft until it is positioned above its housing. To prevent damage to the sealing lips, wrap some adhesive tape around the end of the camshaft.
6 Using a hammer and a socket of suitable diameter, drive the seal squarely into its housing. **Note:** *Select a socket that bears only on the hard outer surface of the seal, not the inner lip that can easily be damaged.*
7 Refit the relevant camshaft sprocket with reference to Section 7.
8 Refit and tension the secondary and main timing belts as described in Section 6.

Left-hand oil seals

9 The camshaft left-hand oil seals take the form of O-rings located in the grooves in the camshaft carrier endplates.
10 Unscrew the securing bolts, and remove the relevant camshaft endplate.
11 Prise the old O-ring from the groove in the endplate.
12 Lightly oil the new O-ring, and carefully locate it in the groove in the endplate **(see illustration)**.
13 Refit the endplate, and tighten the securing bolts to the specified torque.

11.12 Renew the camshaft carrier endplate O-ring

10.9 Oil the tappets before fitting

12 Cylinder head – removal, inspection and refitting

Note: *The cylinder head must be removed with the engine cold.*

Removal

1 Disconnect the battery negative lead (refer to *Disconnecting the battery* in the *Reference* Chapter at the end of this manual).
2 Drain the cooling system as described in Chapter 1A, Section 30.
3 Remove the main and secondary timing belts as described in Section 6.
4 As the engine is currently supported using a hoist attached to the engine lifting brackets bolted to the cylinder head, it is now necessary to attach a suitable bracket to the cylinder block, so that the engine can still be supported as the cylinder head is removed.
5 A suitable bracket can be bolted to the cylinder block using spacers, and a long bolt screwed into the hole located next to the coolant pump **(see illustration)**. Ideally, attach a second set of lifting tackle to the hoist, adjust the lifting tackle to support the engine using the bracket attached to the cylinder block, and then disconnect the lifting tackle attached to the bracket on the cylinder head. Alternatively, temporarily support the engine under the sump using a jack and a block of wood, and then transfer the lifting tackle from the bracket on the cylinder head to the bracket bolted to the cylinder block.

12.5 Home-made engine lifting bracket fitted next to the coolant pump

12.6 Disconnect the radiator hoses from the cylinder head coolant housing

12.8 Unscrew the dipstick tube bracket bolt from the cylinder head

12.9 Disconnect the EGR pipe from the throttle body and recover the gasket

12.10 Lift the inlet manifold back from the engine

6 Release the hose clips, and disconnect the two radiator hoses from the coolant housing at the transmission end of the cylinder head **(see illustration)**. Similarly, release the hose clips and disconnect the remaining three small

12.11 Unbolt the wiring bracket from the cylinder head right rear corner

coolant hoses from the rear of the coolant housing.
7 Remove the air cleaner assembly, complete with the air trunking, as described in Chapter 4A, Section 2.

8 Unscrew the bolt securing the oil level dipstick tube bracket to the cylinder head, then lift the dipstick tube, and turn it to one side, to clear the working area **(see illustration)**. Release the wiring harnesses from the clip on the dipstick tube bracket. Note that the dipstick tube bracket bolt also secures the inlet manifold.
9 Where fitted, unscrew the two securing bolts and disconnect the exhaust gas recirculation (EGR) pipe from the throttle body and recover the gasket **(see illustration)**. Also unscrew the bolt securing the EGR pipe bracket to the coolant housing.
10 Unscrew the six securing bolts (three upper and three lower) and lift the inlet manifold back from the engine **(see illustration)**. Ensure that the inlet manifold is adequately supported in the engine compartment, and take care not to strain any wires, cables or hoses. Recover the O-rings if they are loose.
11 Unbolt the wiring connector bracket from the right-hand rear corner of the cylinder head **(see illustration)**.
12 Disconnect the wiring plug from the coolant temperature sensor, located in the coolant housing at the transmission end of the cylinder head, then unclip the wiring harnesses from the coolant housing, and move them to one side **(see illustrations)**.
13 Disconnect the vacuum hose from the exhaust gas recirculation (EGR) valve (where applicable).
14 Unclip the wiring from the bracket attached to the exhaust heat shield, then unscrew the securing bolts (two upper bolts and one lower bolt), and remove the heat shield **(see illustrations)**.
15 Disconnect the exhaust front section from the manifold with reference to Chapter 4C, Section 5. If desired, the exhaust manifold can be removed as follows:
  a) *Unscrew the union nut securing the EGR pipe to the exhaust manifold, and remove the EGR pipe (where applicable).*
  b) *Unscrew the exhaust manifold securing nuts, then lift off the manifold and recover the gasket.*
16 Remove the camshaft carrier, with reference to Section 8.
17 Pull out the metal clip securing the plastic coolant pipe to the coolant housing at the

12.12a Disconnect the coolant temperature sensor wiring plug...

12.12b ...then unclip the wiring harnesses and move them to one side

12.14a Unclip the wiring from the bracket on the exhaust heat shield...

12.14b ...then remove the heat shield

left-hand rear corner of the cylinder head **(see illustration)**.
18 Progressively slacken the cylinder head bolts in order, then unscrew and remove the bolts **(see illustration)**.
19 With all the bolts removed, lift the cylinder head from the block. If the cylinder head is stuck, tap it with a soft-faced mallet to break the joint. **Do not** insert a lever into the gasket joint. As the cylinder head is lifted off, release the coolant pump pipe from the thermostat housing on the cylinder head.
20 Lift the cylinder head gasket from the block.

Inspection

21 Dismantling and inspection of the cylinder head is covered in Part E of this Chapter. Additionally, check the condition of the coolant pump pipe-to-thermostat housing O-ring, and renew if necessary.

Refitting

22 The mating faces of the cylinder head and block must be perfectly clean before refitting the head. Use a scraper to remove all traces of gasket and carbon, also clean the tops of the pistons. Take particular care with the aluminium surfaces, as the soft metal is easily damaged. Make sure that debris is not allowed to enter the oil and water passages – this is particularly important for the oil circuit, as carbon could block the oil supply to the camshaft and crankshaft bearings. Using adhesive tape and paper, seal the water, oil and bolt holes in the cylinder block. To prevent carbon entering the gap between the pistons and bores, smear a little grease in the gap. After cleaning a piston, rotate the crankshaft to that the piston moves down the bore, and then wipe out the grease and carbon with a cloth rag. Clean the other piston crowns in the same way.
23 Check the head and block for nicks, deep scratches and other damage. If slight, they may be removed carefully with a file. More serious damage may be repaired by machining, but this is a specialist job.
24 If warpage of the cylinder head is suspected, use a straight-edge to check it for distortion, as described in Part E of this Chapter.
25 Ensure that the cylinder head bolt holes in the crankcase are clean and free of oil.

12.17 Pull out the coolant pipe-to-housing metal clip (engine removed for clarity)

Syringe or soak up any oil left in the bolt holes. This is most important in order that the correct bolt tightening torque can be applied, and to prevent the possibility of the block being cracked by hydraulic pressure when the bolts are tightened.
26 Ensure that the crankshaft has been turned to position No's 1 and 4 pistons slightly down their bores from the TDC position (see Section 6). This will eliminate any risk of piston-to-valve contact as the cylinder head is refitted. Also ensure that the camshaft sprockets are locked in the TDC position using the locking tool, as described in Section 3.
27 Ensure that the cylinder head locating dowels are in place in the cylinder block, and then fit a new cylinder head gasket over the dowels, ensuring that the part number is uppermost. Where applicable, the OBEN/TOP marking should also be uppermost **(see illustrations)**. Note that VW recommend that the gasket is only removed from its packaging immediately prior to fitting.
28 Lower the cylinder head into position on the gasket, ensuring that it engages correctly over the dowels. As the cylinder head is lowered into position, ensure that the coolant pump pipe engages with the thermostat housing (use a new O-ring if necessary).
29 Fit the new cylinder head bolts, and screw them in as far as possible by hand.
30 Working progressively, in sequence, tighten all the cylinder head bolts to the specified Stage 1 torque **(see illustration)**.
31 Again working progressively, in sequence, tighten all the cylinder head bolts through the specified Stage 2 angle.

12.18 Cylinder head bolt slackening sequence

32 Finally, tighten all the cylinder head bolts, in sequence, to the specified Stage 3 torque.
33 Reconnect the lifting tackle to the engine right-hand lifting bracket on the cylinder head, then adjust the lifting tackle to support the engine. Once the engine is adequately supported using the cylinder head bracket, disconnect the lifting tackle from the bracket bolted to the cylinder block, and unbolt the improvised engine lifting bracket from the cylinder block. Alternatively, remove the trolley jack and block of wood from under the sump.
34 Refit the clip securing the plastic coolant pipe to the coolant housing.
35 Refit the camshaft carrier as described in Section 8.
36 Further refitting is a reversal of removal, bearing in mind the following points:
a) Refit the exhaust manifold and reconnect the EGR pipe, and/or reconnect the exhaust front section to the manifold, as described in Section 4C, Section 5.
b) Refit the inlet manifold using new O-rings.
c) Reconnect the EGR pipe (where applicable) to the throttle body using a new gasket.
d) Refit the secondary and main timing belts as described in Section 6.
e) Ensure that all wires, pipes and hoses are correctly reconnected and routed, as noted before removal.
f) Tighten all fixings to the specified torque, where applicable.
g) On completion, refill the cooling system as described in Chapter 1A, Section 30.

12.27a Ensure that the dowels (arrowed) are in place in the cylinder block...

12.27b ...and the gasket part number and OBEN/TOP markings are uppermost

12.30 Cylinder head bolt tightening sequence

14.3 Position chamfered tooth (A) as shown

13 Sump –
removal and refitting

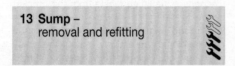

Removal

1 Disconnect the battery negative lead (refer to *Disconnecting the battery* in the *Reference* Chapter at the end of this manual).
2 Chock the rear wheels and apply the handbrake, then jack up the front of the car and support it on axle stands (see *Jacking and vehicle support*). Remove the engine undertray.
3 Drain the engine oil, then clean and refit the engine oil drain plug, tightening it to the specified torque wrench setting. If the engine is nearing the service interval when the oil and filter are due for renewal, it is recommended that the filter is also removed and a new one fitted. After reassembly, the engine can then be replenished with fresh engine oil. Refer to Chapter 1A, Section 3, for further information.
4 Remove the exhaust front pipe with reference to Chapter 4C, Section 5.
5 Disconnect the wiring from the oil level/ temperature sender.

6 Unscrew the two bolts securing the sump rear flange to the transmission.
7 Progressively unscrew and remove the sump retaining bolts.
8 Break the joint by striking the sump with the palm of the hand, then lower the sump away from the engine and withdraw it.
9 While the sump is removed, take the opportunity to clean the oil pump pick-up/ strainer pipe mesh using a suitable solvent. Inspect the strainer mesh for signs of clogging or splitting and renew if necessary, referring to Section 14, for further information.

Refitting

10 Thoroughly clean all traces of sealant and oil from the mating surfaces of the cylinder block/crankcase and sump, and then use a clean rag to wipe out the sump and the engine's interior.
11 Apply a 2.0 to 3.0 mm diameter bead of sealant to the sump mating flange, making sure that the bead is around the inner edges of the bolt holes. The bead must not exceed 3.0 mm diameter. **Note:** *The sump must be refitted within 5 minutes of applying the sealant.*
12 When refitting the sump, to guide the sump into position on the cylinder block mating face, two guide studs can be improvised by cutting the heads off two M6 bolts, and cutting slots in the ends of the bolts so that they can later be unscrewed using a flat-bladed screwdriver. Screw the guide studs into two diagonally opposite sump securing bolt holes.
13 Offer the sump into position, then refit the sump bolts and tighten them to the specified torque. Once the sump is held securely in position, unscrew the guide studs, and refit the remaining two sump securing bolts.
14 Insert the two rear flange bolts and tighten them to the specified torque.
15 Reconnect the wiring to the oil level/ temperature sender.
16 Refit the exhaust front pipe with reference to Chapter 4C, Section 5.
17 Refit the engine undertray and lower the car to the ground.
18 Reconnect the battery negative lead.
19 Refill the engine with oil as described in Chapter 1A, Section 3.

14 Oil pump –
removal, inspection and refitting

Removal

1 Remove the main timing belt as described in Section 6.
2 Turn the crankshaft a quarter-turn (90°) clockwise to reposition No's 1 and 4 pistons at TDC. Ensure that the crankshaft sprocket tooth with the chamfered inner edge is aligned with the corresponding mark on the oil pump housing.
3 Turn the crankshaft to move the crankshaft sprocket three teeth anti-clockwise away from the TDC position. The third tooth to the right of the tooth with the ground-down outer edge must align with the corresponding mark on the oil pump housing (**see illustration**). This procedure positions the crankshaft correctly to enable oil pump refitting.
4 Remove the timing belt tensioner as described in Section 7.
5 Remove the sump as described in Section 13.
6 Unscrew the securing bolts and remove the oil pick-up pipe from the oil pump. Recover the gasket.
7 Remove the crankshaft sprocket; noting which way round it is fitted.
8 Unscrew the securing bolts, noting their locations to ensure correct refitting, and remove the oil pump (**see illustration**). Recover the gasket.

Inspection

9 No spare parts are available for the oil pump, and if worn or faulty the complete pump must be renewed.
10 To inspect the oil pump rotors, remove the securing screws, and lift off the oil pump rear cover (**see illustration**).
11 Note that the rotors fit with the punched dots on the edges of the rotors facing the oil pump cover (**see illustration**).
12 Lift out the rotors, and inspect them for wear and damage. If there are any signs of wear or damage, the complete oil pump assembly must be renewed.
13 Lubricate the contact faces of the rotors

14.8 Removing the oil pump

14.10 Lifting off the oil pump rear cover

14.11 Note that the rotors fit with the punched dots (arrowed) facing the oil pump cover

14.15 Prise the crankshaft oil seal from the oil pump

with clean engine oil, then refit the rotors to the pump, ensuring that the punched dots on the edges of the rotors face the pump cover.

14 Refit the pump cover, and tighten the screws securely.

15 Using a flat-bladed screwdriver, prise the crankshaft oil seal from the oil pump, and discard it **(see illustration)**.

16 Thoroughly clean the oil seal seat in the oil pump.

17 Press or drive a new oil seal into position in the oil pump, using a socket or tube of suitable diameter **(see illustration)**. Ensure that the seal seats squarely in the oil pump. Ensure that the socket or tube bears only on the hard outer ring of the seal, and take care not to damage the seal lips. Press or drive the seal into position until it is seated on the shoulder in the housing. Make sure that the closed end of the seal is facing outwards.

Refitting

18 Commence refitting by cleaning all traces of old gasket and sealant from the mating faces of the cylinder block and oil pump.

19 Wind a length of tape around the end of the crankshaft to protect the oil seal lips as the oil pump is slid into position.

20 Fit a new oil pump gasket over the dowels in the cylinder block **(see illustration)**.

21 Turn the inner oil pump rotor to align one of the drive cut-outs in the edge of the inner rotor with the line mark on the oil pump rear cover **(see illustration)**.

22 Lightly oil the four tips of the oil pump drive cam on the end of the crankshaft.

23 Coat the lips of the crankshaft oil seal with a thin film of clean engine oil.

24 Slide the oil pump into position over the end of the crankshaft until it engages with the dowels, taking care not to damage the oil seal, and ensuring that the inner rotor engages with the drive cam on the crankshaft **(see illustration)**.

25 Fit new oil pump securing bolts to the locations noted before removal, and tighten them to the specified torque **(see illustration)**.

26 Remove the tape from the end of the crankshaft, then refit the crankshaft sprocket, noting that the pulley locating pin must be outermost. Temporarily refit the securing bolt and washer to retain the sprocket.

27 Refit the oil pick-up pipe, using a new gasket, and tighten the securing bolts to the specified torque **(see illustration)**.

28 Refit the sump as described in Section 13.

29 Refit the timing belt tensioner as described in Section 7.

30 Refit the main timing belt as described in Section 6.

15 Oil pressure relief valve – removal, inspection and refitting

The oil pressure relief valve is an integral part of the oil pump. The valve piston and spring are located to the side of the oil pump rotors and can be inspected once the oil pump has been removed from the engine and the rear cover has been removed (see Section 14). If any sign of wear or damage is found the oil pump assembly will have to be renewed; the relief valve piston and spring are not available separately.

16 Oil pressure warning light switch – removal and refitting

Removal

1 The oil pressure warning light switch is fitted to the left-hand end of the cylinder head. To gain access to the switch, remove the air cleaner as described in Chapter 4A, Section 2.

2 Disconnect the wiring connector and wipe clean the area around the switch **(see illustration)**.

14.17 Driving a new oil seal into the oil pump using a socket

14.20 Fit a new gasket over the dowels in the cylinder block

14.21 Align one of the rotor drive cut-outs (1) with the oil pump rear cover mark (2)

14.24 Slide the oil pump over the crankshaft. Note the tape used to protect the oil seal

14.25 Fit the new oil pump securing bolts to the locations (arrowed) noted before removal

14.27 Fit a new oil pick-up pipe gasket

16.2 Disconnecting the oil pressure switch wiring connector

3 Unscrew the switch from the cylinder head and remove it along with its sealing washer. If the switch is to be left removed from the engine for any length of time, plug the hole in the cylinder head.

Refitting

4 Examine the sealing washer for signs of damage or deterioration and if necessary renew.
5 Refit the switch, complete with washer, and tighten it to the specified torque.
6 Securely reconnect the wiring connector then refit the air cleaner. Check and, if necessary, top-up the engine oil as described in *Weekly checks*.

17 Crankshaft oil seals – renewal

Right-hand oil seal

1 Remove the main timing belt as described in Section 6, and the crankshaft sprocket with reference to Section 7.
2 To remove the seal without removing the oil pump, drill two small holes diagonally opposite each other, insert self-tapping screws, and pull on the heads of the screws with pliers.
3 Alternatively, the oil seal can be removed with the oil pump (see Section 14).
4 Thoroughly clean the oil seal seating in the oil pump.
5 Wind a length of tape around the end of the crankshaft to protect the oil seal lips as the seal is fitted.

18.3 Flywheel locked in position with a home-made tool

6 Fit a new oil seal to the oil pump, pressing or driving it into position using a socket or tube of suitable diameter. Ensure that the socket or tube bears only on the hard outer ring of the seal, and take care not to damage the seal lips. Press or drive the seal into position until it is seated on the shoulder in the oil pump. Make sure that the closed end of the seal is facing outwards.
7 Refit the crankshaft sprocket with reference to Section 7, and the main timing belt as described in Section 6.

Left-hand oil seal

8 The crankshaft left-hand oil seal is integral with the housing, and must be renewed as an assembly, complete with the crankshaft speed/position sensor wheel. The sensor wheel is attached to the oil seal/housing assembly, and is a press-fit on the crankshaft flange. VW special tool T10017 is required to fit this assembly and, in the workshop, we found that there is no means of accurately aligning the sensor wheel on the crankshaft without the tool (there is no locating key, and there are no alignment marks). If the sensor wheel is not precisely aligned on the crankshaft, the crankshaft speed/position sensor will send incorrect TDC signals to the engine management ECU, and the engine will not run correctly (the engine may not run at all). As the appropriate special tool is only available to VW dealers, there is no alternative but to have the new assembly fitted by a VW dealer.

18 Flywheel/driveplate – removal, inspection and refitting

Removal

1 Remove the manual transmission as described in Chapter 7A, Section 3, and remove the automatic transmission as described in Chapter 7B, Section 2.
2 On manual transmissions, remove the clutch assembly as described in Chapter 6, Section 6.
3 Lock the flywheel/driveplate in position using a homemade locking tool, fabricated from a piece of scrap metal **(see illustration)**.

18.9 Apply locking fluid to the new flywheel bolts, if necessary

Bolt it to one of the transmission bellhousing mounting holes. Mark the position of the flywheel/driveplate with respect to the crankshaft using a dab of paint.
4 Slacken and withdraw the mounting bolts, then lift off the flywheel/driveplate.
Caution: Get an assistant to help, as the flywheel is extremely heavy.

Inspection

5 If the flywheel's clutch mating surface is deeply scored, cracked or otherwise damaged, the flywheel must be renewed. However, it may be possible to have it surface-ground; seek the advice of a VW dealer or engine reconditioning specialist.
6 On automatic transmissions, if the driveplate is cracked or otherwise damaged, the driveplate must be renewed.
7 If the ring gear is badly worn or has missing teeth, the flywheel/driveplate must be renewed.

Refitting

8 Clean the mating surfaces of the flywheel/driveplate and crankshaft. Remove any remaining locking compound from the threads of the crankshaft holes, using the correct-size tap, if available.

> **HAYNES HiNT** If a suitable tap is not available, cut two slots down the threads of one of the old flywheel bolts with a hacksaw, and use the bolt to remove the locking compound from the threads.

9 If the new flywheel/driveplate retaining bolts are not supplied with their threads pre-coated, apply a suitable thread-locking compound to the threads of each bolt **(see illustration)**.
10 Offer up the flywheel/driveplate to the crankshaft, using the alignment marks made during removal, and fit the new retaining bolts.
11 Lock the flywheel/driveplate using the method employed on dismantling, and tighten the retaining bolts to the specified torque and angle.
12 Refit the clutch as described in Chapter 6, Section 6 and then remove the locking tool
13 Refit the manual transmission as described in Chapter 7A, Section 3 and the automatic transmission as described in Chapter 7B, Section 2.

19 Engine/transmission mountings – inspection and renewal

Inspection

1 If improved access is required, jack up the front of the car, and support it securely on axle stands (see *Jacking and vehicle support*). Remove the securing screws and remove the engine under shield.

2 Check the mounting rubbers to see if they are cracked, hardened or separated from the metal at any point; renew the mounting if any such damage or deterioration is evident.

3 Check that all the mountings are securely tightened; use a torque wrench to check if possible.

4 Using a large screwdriver or a crowbar, check for wear in the mounting by carefully levering against it to check for free play. Where this is not possible, enlist the aid of an assistant to move the engine/transmission back-and-forth, or from side-to-side, whilst you observe the mounting. While some free play is to be expected, even from new components, excessive wear should be obvious. If excessive free play is found, check first that the fasteners are correctly secured, and then renew any worn components as described in the following paragraphs.

Caution: Do NOT undo the centre bolt, securing the bracket to the flexible mounting.

5 When working on the right-hand mounting and rear lower mounting (torque arm), remove the mounting as a complete unit. VW state that the mounting bracket-to-flexible mounting nut/bolt should not be slackened, see following procedures for each individual mounting.

Renewal

6 The engine mountings on the 1.4 litre engine are similar to those fitted on the 1.2 litre petrol models, see Chapter 2A, Section 14, for the removal and refitting procedures of the engine mountings.

Chapter 2 Part C:
1.2 litre diesel engine in-car repair procedures

Contents

Degrees of difficulty

Easy, suitable for novice with little experience	Fairly easy, suitable for beginner with some experience	Fairly difficult, suitable for competent DIY mechanic	Difficult, suitable for experienced DIY mechanic	Very difficult, suitable for expert DIY or professional

Specifications

General

Type	Three-cylinder in-line, belt-driven double overhead camshaft (DOHC), four-stroke, liquid-cooled
Cubic capacity	1199 cc
Manufacturer's engine code*	CFWA
Maximum power output	55 kW @ 4200 rpm
Maximum torque output	180 Nm @ 2000 rpm
Bore	79.5 mm
Stroke	80.5 mm
Compression ratio	16.5 :1

Compression pressures (oil temperature 80°C minimum):

New	25.0 to 31.0 bars
Minimum	19.0 bars
Maximum difference between cylinders	5.0 bars
Firing order	1 – 2 – 3
No.1 cylinder location	Timing belt end

* Note: See 'Vehicle identification' at the end of this manual for the location of engine code markings.

Lubrication system

Oil pump type	Gear type, chain-driven from crankshaft
Oil pressure switch (green)	0.5 bar

Oil pressure (oil temperature 80°C):

Minimum @ idling	0.8 bar
Minimum @ 2000 rpm	1.5 bar
Maximum @ high rpm	5.0 bar

Torque wrench settings

	Nm	lbf ft
Ancillary (alternator, etc) bracket mounting bolts*:		
Stage 1 (all six bolts)..	40	30
Stage 2 (for two lower bolts).................................	Angle-tighten a further 45°	
Stage 2 (for four upper bolts)	Angle-tighten a further 90°	
Auxiliary drivebelt tensioner securing bolt:		
Stage 1...	20	15
Stage 2...	Angle-tighten a further 180°	
Big-end bearing caps bolts*:		
Stage 1...	30	22
Stage 2...	Angle-tighten a further 90°	
Camshaft retaining frame bolts	10	7
Camshaft cover bolts...	10	7
Camshaft sprocket hub centre bolt	100	74
Camshaft sprocket-to-hub bolts*:		
Stage 1...	20	15
Stage 2...	Angle-tighten a further 45°	
Common rail bolts	22	16
Coolant pump bolts..	15	11
Crankshaft oil seal housing bolts..............................	15	11
Crankshaft pulley-to-sprocket bolts*:		
Stage 1...	10	7
Stage 2...	Angle-tighten a further 90°	
Crankshaft sprocket bolt*:		
Stage 1...	120	89
Stage 2...	Angle-tighten a further 90°	
Cylinder head bolts*:		
Stage 1...	30	22
Stage 2...	60	44
Stage 3...	Angle-tighten a further 90°	
Stage 4...	Angle-tighten a further 90°	
Engine mountings:		
RH engine mounting*:		
Mounting bracket to engine:		
Stage 1...	40	30
Stage 2...	Angle-tighten a further 180°	
Mounting to body:		
Stage 1...	40	30
Stage 2...	Angle-tighten a further 90°	
Mounting to bracket:		
Stage 1...	60	44
Stage 2...	Angle-tighten a further 90°	
LH engine/transmission mounting*:		
Mounting to body:		
Stage 1...	40	30
Stage 2...	Angle-tighten a further 90°	
Mounting to bracket on transmission:		
Stage 1...	60	44
Stage 2...	Angle-tighten a further 90°	
Rear mounting link*:		
Link-to-transmission:		
Short (front) bolt:		
Stage 1...	40	30
Stage 2...	Angle-tighten a further 90°	
Long (rear) bolt:		
Stage 1...	60	44
Stage 2...	Angle-tighten a further 90°	
Link-to-subframe:		
Stage 1...	100	74
Stage 2...	Angle-tighten a further 90°	
Flywheel*:		
Stage 1...	60	44
Stage 2...	Angle-tighten a further 90°	
Fuel pump hub nut..	95	70
Fuel pump sprocket bolts*		
Stage 1...	20	15
Stage 2...	Angle-tighten a further 90°	

Torque wrench settings (continued)

	Nm	lbf ft
Main bearing cap bolts*:		
Stage 1	65	48
Stage 2	Angle-tighten a further 90°	
Oil cooler screws	11	7
Oil drain plug*	30	22
Oil filter housing-to-cylinder block bolts*:		
Stage 1	14	10
Stage 2	Angle-tighten a further 180°	
Oil filter cover	25	18
Oil level/temperature sensor-to-sump bolts	9	7
Oil pressure warning light switch	22	16
Oil pump/balancer shaft chain tensioner securing bolts*:		
Stage 1 (centre bolt)	8	6
Stage 2 (bolt to front of engine)	8	6
Stage 3 (bolt to rear of engine)	8	6
Stage 4 (centre bolt)	Angle-tighten a further 90°	
Stage 5 (bolt to front of engine)	Angle-tighten a further 90°	
Stage 6 (bolt to rear of engine)	Angle-tighten a further 90°	
Oil pump/balancer shaft securing bolts:		
Stage 1	14	10
Stage 2	Angle-tighten a further 180°	
Oil pump/balancer shaft cover securing bolts	8	6
Oil pump/balancer shaft idler sprocket securing bolt	23	16
Piston oil spray jet bolt	27	19
Sump:		
Sump-to-cylinder block bolts	13	9
Sump-to-transmission bolts	40	30
Thermostat housing	15	11
Timing belt outer cover bolts	10	7
Timing belt tensioner roller securing nut:		
Stage 1	20	15
Stage 2	Angle-tighten a further 45°	
Timing belt idler pulleys:		
Lower idler roller nut	20	15
Upper idler roller (small) bolt	15	11
Upper idler roller (large) bolt*:		
Stage 1	50	37
Stage 2	Angle-tighten a further 90°	

*Do not re-use fasteners

1 General information

How to use this Chapter

This Part of Chapter 2 describes those repair procedures that can reasonably be carried out on the engine while it remains in the vehicle. If the engine has been removed from the vehicle and is being dismantled as described in Part E, any preliminary dismantling procedures can be ignored.

Note that while it may be possible physically to overhaul certain items while the engine is in the vehicle, such tasks are not usually carried out as separate operations, and usually require the execution of several additional procedures (not to mention the cleaning of components and of oilways); for this reason, all such tasks are classed as major overhaul procedures, and are described in Part E of this Chapter.

Engine description

Throughout this Chapter, engines are referred to by type, and are identified and referred to by the manufacturer's code letters. A listing of all engines covered, together with their code letters, is given in the Specifications at the start of this Chapter.

The engine is a water-cooled, double overhead camshafts (DOHC), in-line three-cylinder unit, with cast-iron cylinder blocks and aluminium-silicone alloy cylinder heads. All are mounted transversely at the front of the vehicle, with the transmission bolted to the left-hand end of the engine.

The crankshaft is of four-bearing type, and thrustwashers are fitted to No.3 main bearing to control crankshaft endfloat.

Drive for the exhaust camshaft is by a toothed timing belt from the crankshaft, with the intake camshaft driven by interlocking gears at the left-hand end of both camshafts. The gears incorporate a toothed backlash

compensator element. Each camshaft is mounted at the top of the cylinder head, and is secured by a bearing frame/ladder.

The valves are closed by coil springs, and run in guides pressed into the cylinder head. The valves are operated by roller rocker arms incorporating hydraulic tappets.

The gear-type oil pump is driven by a chain from the right-hand (timing belt) end of the crankshaft. Oil is drawn from the sump through a strainer, and then forced through an externally mounted, renewable filter. From there, it is distributed to the cylinder head, where it lubricates the camshaft journals and hydraulic tappets, and also to the crankcase, where it lubricates the main bearings, connecting rod big-ends, gudgeon pins and cylinder bores. A coolant-fed oil cooler is fitted to the oil filter housing on all engines. Oil jets are fitted to the base of each cylinder – these spray oil onto the underside of the pistons, to improve cooling.

A balancer shaft unit is fitted to the

underside of the cylinder block, and this incorporates the oil pump. A chain then drives both the balance shaft and oil pump from the crankshaft sprocket.

All engines are fitted with a combined brake servo vacuum pump, driven by the camshaft on the transmission end of the cylinder head.

On all engines, engine coolant is circulated by a pump, driven by the timing belt. For details of the cooling system, refer to Chapter 3.

Operations with engine in car

The following operations can be performed without removing the engine:

a) Compression pressure – testing.
b) Camshaft cover – removal and refitting.
c) Crankshaft pulley – removal and refitting.
d) Timing belt covers – removal and refitting.
e) Timing belt – removal, refitting and adjustment.
f) Timing belt tensioner and sprockets – removal and refitting.
g) Camshaft oil seals – renewal.
h) Camshafts and hydraulic tappets – removal, inspection and refitting.
i) Cylinder head – removal and refitting.
j) Cylinder head and pistons – decarbonising.
k) Sump – removal and refitting.
l) Oil pump/balance shaft unit – removal, overhaul and refitting.
m) Crankshaft oil seals – renewal.
n) Engine/transmission mountings – inspection and renewal.
o) Flywheel/driveplate – removal, inspection and refitting.

Note: It is possible to remove the pistons and connecting rods (after removing the cylinder head and sump) without removing the engine. However, this is not recommended. Work of this nature is more easily and thoroughly completed with the engine on the bench, as described in Chapter 2E.

2 Compression and leakdown tests – description and interpretation

Compression test

Note: A compression tester suitable for use with diesel engines will be required for this test.

1 When engine performance is down, or if misfiring occurs which cannot be attributed to the ignition or fuel systems, a compression test can provide diagnostic clues as to the engine's condition. If the test is performed regularly, it can give warning of trouble before any other symptoms become apparent.

2 The engine must be fully warmed-up to normal operating temperature, the battery must be fully charged, and you will require the aid of an assistant.

3 Remove the glow plugs as described in Chapter 5C, Section 2, and then fit a compression tester to the No.1 cylinder glow plug hole. The type of tester that screws into the plug thread is preferred. **Note:** Part of the glow plug removal procedure is to disconnect the fuel injector wiring plugs. As a result of the plugs being disconnected and the engine cranked, faults may be stored in the ECU memory. These must be erased after the compression test.

4 Have your assistant crank the engine for several seconds on the starter motor. After one or two revolutions, the compression pressure should build-up to a maximum figure and then stabilise. Record the highest reading obtained.

5 Repeat the test on the remaining cylinders, recording the pressure in each.

6 The cause of poor compression is less easy to establish on a diesel engine than on a petrol engine. The effect of introducing oil into the cylinders (wet testing) is not conclusive, because there is a risk that the oil will sit in the recess on the piston crown, instead of passing to the rings. However, the following can be used as a rough guide to diagnosis.

7 All cylinders should produce very similar pressures. Any difference greater than that specified indicates the existence of a fault. Note that the compression should build-up quickly in a healthy engine. Low compression on the first stroke, followed by gradually increasing pressure on successive strokes, indicates worn piston rings. A low compression reading on the first stroke, which does not build-up during successive strokes, indicates leaking valves or a blown head gasket (a cracked head could also be the cause).

8 A low reading from two adjacent cylinders is almost certainly due to the head gasket having blown between them and the presence of coolant in the engine oil will confirm this.

9 On completion, remove the compression tester, and refit the glow plugs, with reference to Chapter 5C, Section 2.

10 Reconnect the wiring to the injector solenoids. Finally, have a VW dealer or suitably equipped specialist erase any fault codes from the ECU memory.

3.8 The alignment mark (arrowed) on the crankshaft sprocket should be almost vertical

Leakdown test

11 A leakdown test measures the rate at which compressed air fed into the cylinder is lost. It is an alternative to a compression test, and in many ways it is better, since the escaping air provides easy identification of where pressure loss is occurring (piston rings, valves or head gasket).

12 The equipment required for leakdown testing is unlikely to be available to the home mechanic. If poor compression is suspected, have the test performed by a suitably equipped garage.

3 Engine assembly and valve timing marks – general information and usage

General information

1 TDC is the highest point in the cylinder that each piston reaches as it travels up-and-down when the crankshaft turns. Each piston reaches TDC at the end of the compression stroke and again at the end of the exhaust stroke, but TDC generally refers to piston position on the compression stroke. No 1 piston is at the timing belt end of the engine.

2 Positioning No 1 piston at TDC is an essential part of many procedures, such as timing belt removal and camshaft removal.

3 The design of the engines covered in this Chapter is such that piston-to-valve contact may occur if the camshaft or crankshaft is turned with the timing belt removed. For this reason, it is important to ensure that the camshaft and crankshaft do not move in relation to each other once the timing belt has been removed from the engine.

Setting TDC on No 1 cylinder

Note: VAG special tool T10050 is required to lock the crankshaft sprocket in the TDC position. Alternatively obtain a tool from automotive tool specialists. Try asttools.co.uk.

4 Raise the front of the vehicle and support it securely on axle stands (see Jacking and vehicle support). Remove the front right-hand road wheel, then release the fasteners and remove the lower section of the wheelarch liner.

5 Remove the auxiliary drivebelt as described in Chapter 1B, Section 25.

6 Remove the crankshaft pulley/vibration damper as described in Section 5.

7 Remove the timing belt outer covers as described in Section 6.

8 Using a spanner or socket on the crankshaft sprocket bolt, turn the crankshaft in the normal direction of rotation (clockwise) until the alignment mark on the face of the sprocket is almost vertical **(see illustration)**, and the hole in the camshaft sprocket hub aligns with the hole in the cylinder head.

9 While in this position it should be possible to insert the VAG tool T10050 to lock the

crankshaft, and a 6 mm diameter rod/drill bit to lock the camshafts **(see illustrations)**. **Note:** *The mark on the crankshaft sprocket and the mark on the VAG tool must align, whilst at the same time the shaft of tool must engage in the drilling in the crankshaft oil seal housing.*

10 The engine is now set to TDC on No.1 cylinder.

4 Camshaft cover – removal and refitting

Removal

1 Remove the fuel injectors (Chapter 4B, Section 4) and fuel rail (Chapter 4B, Section 11).

2 Remove the timing belt upper cover as described in Section 6.

3 Note their fitted positions, then disconnect the vacuum hoses from the camshaft cover, and release them, and the wiring loom from the retaining clips at the rear of the cover **(see illustration)**.

4 Squeeze together the sides of the collar, and disconnect the breather hose from the camshaft cover **(see illustration)**.

5 Release the wiring from the clips at the rear of the cover, then unscrew the camshaft cover retaining bolts and lift the cover away. If the cover sticks, do not attempt to lever it off – instead free it by working around the cover and tapping it lightly with a soft-faced mallet **(see illustration)**.

6 Recover the camshaft cover gasket. Inspect the gasket carefully, and renew it if damage or deterioration is evident – note that the retaining bolts and seals must be pushed fully through the cover **(see illustration)**.

7 Clean the mating surfaces of the cylinder head and camshaft cover thoroughly, removing all traces of oil – take care to avoid damaging the surfaces as you do this.

Refitting

8 Refit the camshaft cover by following the removal procedure in reverse, tightening the cover retaining bolts to the specified torque, starting with the centre bolts and working outwards.

5 Crankshaft pulley – removal and refitting

Removal

1 Switch off the ignition and all electrical consumers and remove the ignition key.

2 Raise the front right-hand side of the vehicle, and support securely on axle stands (see *Jacking and vehicle support*). Remove the roadwheel.

3 Remove the securing fasteners and withdraw the lower section of the front wheel arch liner.

3.9a Fit the tool to the hole in the oil seal housing (arrowed)…

3.9b …so the marks on the tool and sprocket align (arrowed)

3.9c Insert a 6 mm locking tool into the camshaft hub…

3.9d …with the arrow almost at the 12 o'clock position

4 Slacken the bolts securing the crankshaft pulley to the sprocket. If necessary, the pulley can be prevented from turning by counterholding with a spanner or socket on the crankshaft sprocket bolt **(see illustration)**.

4.3 Unclip the wiring from the retaining clips

4.4 Squeeze together the sides of the collar to disconnect the breather hose

4.5 Undo the bolts and lift away the camshaft cover

4.6 Bolts must be pushed fully through the cover before fitting the gasket

5.4 Undo the pulley bolts, counterholding it with a socket on the centre sprocket bolt

6.1 Pull the plastic cover upwards from the mountings

6.2a Release the securing clips (arrowed)…

6.2b …and manoeuvre the cover from place

5 Remove the auxiliary drivebelt, as described in Chapter 1B, Section 25.
6 Unscrew the bolts securing the pulley to the sprocket, and remove the pulley. Discard the bolts – new ones must be fitted.

Refitting

7 Refit the pulley over the locating peg on the crankshaft sprocket, then fit the new pulley securing bolts.

8 Refit and tension the auxiliary drivebelt as described in Chapter 1B, Section 25.
9 Prevent the crankshaft from turning as during removal, then fit the pulley securing bolts, and tighten to the specified torque.
10 Refit the wheel arch liner.
11 Refit the roadwheel and lower the vehicle to the ground.

6 Timing belt covers – removal and refitting

Upper outer cover

1 Pull the engine top cover upwards to release the mountings **(see illustration)**.
2 Release the 3 clips and remove the timing belt upper cover **(see illustrations)**.
3 Refitting is a reversal of removal, noting that the lower edge of the upper cover engages with the lower cover.

Lower outer cover

4 Remove the upper cover as described previously.
5 If not already done, remove the crankshaft pulley as described in Section 5.
6 Unscrew the five bolts securing the lower cover, and remove it **(see illustrations)**.
7 Refitting is a reversal of removal; noting that the upper edge of the lower cover engages with the upper cover **(see illustration)**.

Rear cover

8 Remove the timing belt, tensioner and sprockets as described in Sections 7 and Section 8.
9 Undo the retaining bolt and remove the rear hub cover from the end of the camshaft.
10 Slacken and withdraw the retaining bolts and lift the timing belt inner cover from the studs on the end of the engine, and remove it from the engine compartment **(see illustrations)**. It may be required to remove the coolant pump (Chapter 3, Section 7), before the rear cover can be removed.
11 Refitting is a reversal of removal.

6.6a Undo the lower cover retaining bolts (arrowed)…

6.6b …and manoeuvre the lower cover from place

6.7 Make sure the covers overlap correctly

6.10a Remove the retaining bolts…

6.10b …and remove the rear cover

H48705

7.0 Two types of tensioner Type (A) and type (B)

(A) Roller tensions clockwise
(B) Roller tensions anti-clockwise

7 Timing belt – removal, inspection and refitting

Note: *There are two types of tensioner fitted to this engine and they are not interchangeable*

7.4 Slacken the sprocket-to-hub bolts (arrowed)

7.5 Slacken the high-pressure fuel pump sprocket bolts (arrowed)

(see illustration). *Check to see which type is fitted before removing the timing belt. Type A tensioner requires a locking pin for installation and it tensions the belt by rotating clockwise. Type B tensioner does not require a locking pin for installation and it tensions the belt by rotating anti-clockwise. See text.*

Removal

1 The primary function of the toothed timing belt is to drive the camshaft, but it also drives the coolant pump and high-pressure fuel pump. Should the belt slip or break in service, the valve timing will be disturbed and piston-to-valve contact may occur, resulting in serious engine damage. For this reason, it is important that the timing belt is tensioned correctly, and inspected regularly for signs of wear or deterioration.

2 Switch off the ignition and all electrical consumers and remove the ignition key.

3 Set the engine to TDC on No. 1 cylinder as described in Section 3.

4 Slacken the three bolts securing the sprocket to the camshaft hub by 90° **(see illustration)**.

5 Slacken the three bolts securing the sprocket to the high-pressure fuel pump by 90° **(see illustration)**.

Type A tensioner

6 Insert a suitable Allen key into the tensioner hub, then slacken the retaining nut and rotate the tensioner hub anti-clockwise until it can be locked in place using a 2.0 m pin/drill bit **(see illustration)**.

7 Leaving the pin in place, now rotate the tensioner hub clockwise to the stop, and hand-tighten the retaining nut **(see illustration)**.

Type B tensioner

8 Insert a suitable Allen key into the tensioner hub, then slacken the retaining nut and rotate the tensioner hub clockwise, until the tensioner hub is loosened. When in position hand-tighten the retaining nut.

All engines

9 If the original timing belt is to be refitted, mark the running direction of the belt, to ensure correct refitting.

Caution: If the belt appears to be in good condition and can be re-used, it is essential that it is refitted the same way around, otherwise accelerated wear will result, leading to premature failure.

10 Slide the belt from the sprockets, taking care not to twist or kink the belt excessively if it is to be re-used.

7.6 Insert an Allen key, slacken the nut, and rotate the hub anti-clockwise until a 2 mm rod/drill bit (arrowed) can be inserted to lock the hub to the pulley

7.7 Rotate the tensioner hub clockwise until it hits the stop

7.16 Rotate the high-pressure fuel pump clockwise until a 6 mm drill bit/rod can be inserted into the housing and hub (arrowed)

7.17a Rotate the sprockets fully clockwise until the fuel pump sprocket...

7.17b ...and camshaft sprocket bolts are at the end of the elongated holes

Inspection

11 Examine the belt for evidence of contamination by coolant or lubricant. If this is the case, find the source of the contamination before progressing any further. Check the belt for signs of wear or damage, particularly around the leading edges of the belt teeth. Renew the belt if its condition is in doubt; the cost of belt renewal is negligible compared with potential cost of the engine repairs, should the belt fail in service. The belt must be renewed if it has covered the mileage given in Chapter 1B, however, if it has covered less, it is prudent to renew it regardless of condition, as a precautionary measure.

12 If the timing belt is not going to be refitted for some time, it is a wise precaution to hang a warning label on the steering wheel, to remind yourself (and others) not to attempt to start the engine. Have the battery disconnected to prevent any engine damage.

13 If the tensioner roller is to be renewed, the engine mounting will need to be removed, as described in Section 16. Then the tensioner removed as described in Section 8.

Refitting

14 Ensure that the crankshaft and camshaft are still set to TDC on No 1 cylinder, as described in Section 3. The camshaft sprocket bolts should be renewed, and slackened at this point.

15 Renew the high-pressure fuel pump sprocket bolts one at a time. They should also be slackened.

16 Using a screwdriver on the bolts heads, rotate the high-pressure fuel pump clockwise until a 6.0 mm locking pin/drill bit can be inserted into the housing adjacent to the sprocket, locking the pump in place **(see illustration)**.

17 Rotate the camshaft sprocket and high-pressure fuel pump sprocket fully clockwise so that the securing bolts are at the end of the elongated holes **(see illustrations)**.

18 Loop the timing belt loosely under the crankshaft sprocket. **Note:** *Observe any direction of rotation markings on the belt.*

19 Fit the belt around the tensioner pulley, engage the timing belt teeth with the camshaft sprockets, then manoeuvre it into position around the coolant pump sprocket and the fuel pump sprocket. Make sure that the belt teeth seat correctly on the sprockets. **Note:** *Slight adjustment to the position of the camshaft sprocket may be necessary to achieve this. Avoid bending the belt back on itself or twisting it excessively as you do this.*

20 Finally, fit the belt around the idler roller **(see illustration)**. Ensure that any slack in the belt is in the section of belt that passes over the tensioner roller.

Type A tensioner

21 Loosen the timing belt tensioner securing nut, and pull out the tensioner locking pin. Turn the tensioner clockwise with an Allen key until the pointer is just past the middle of the gap in the tensioner base plate **(see illustrations)**. With the tensioner held in this position, tighten the securing nut to the specified torque and angle.

Type B tensioner

22 Loosen the timing belt tensioner securing nut, and turn the tensioner anti-clockwise with

7.20 Timing belt routing

7.21a Rotate the tensioner clockwise...

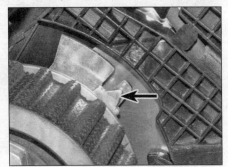

7.21b ...until the pointer (arrowed) is just past the gap in the base plate

7.22 Turn the tensioner anti-clockwise and secure the retaining nut

7.23a Counterhold the camshaft sprocket...

7.23b ...and the pump sprocket, while the bolts are tightened

an Allen key until the pointer is just past the middle of the gap in the tensioner base plate **(see illustration)**. With the tensioner held in this position, tighten the securing nut to the specified torque and angle.

All engines

23 Counterhold the camshaft sprocket and fuel pump sprocket with a home made tool to prevent any rotation, and then tighten the camshaft sprocket and fuel pump sprocket bolts to 20 Nm **(see illustrations)**.

24 Remove the sprockets' locking tools and the crankshaft locking tool **(see illustrations)**.

25 Using a spanner or wrench and socket on the crankshaft pulley centre bolt, rotate the crankshaft clockwise through two complete revolutions. Reset the engine to TDC on No.1 cylinder, with reference to Section 3 and refit the crankshaft locking tool.

26 Check that the tensioner roller indicator arm is centred, or within a maximum of 5 mm to the right of the notch in the base plate **(see illustration)**. If not, hold the tensioner hub stationary with an Allen key, slacken the retaining nut and position the arm in the centre of the notch. Tighten the retaining nut to the specified torque. Remove the Allen key.

27 Check that the camshaft sprocket locking pin can still be inserted. **Note:** *It's very difficult to align the locking point of the fuel pump hub again* **(see illustration)**. *However, a slight*

7.24a Remove the upper locking pins...

7.24b ...and crankshaft locking tool

misalignment of holes will not affect engine performance.

28 If the camshaft sprocket locking pin cannot be inserted, pull the crankshaft locking tool slight away from the engine, and rotate the crankshaft *anti-clockwise* slightly past TDC. Now slowly rotate the crankshaft clockwise until the camshaft sprocket locking tool can be inserted.

29 If the locating pin of the crankshaft locking tool is to the left of the corresponding hole, slacken the camshaft sprocket bolts, slowly rotate the crankshaft clockwise until the locking tool can be fully inserted. Tighten the camshaft sprocket bolts to 20 Nm.

30 If the locating pin of the crankshaft locking

tool is to the right of the corresponding hole, slacken the camshaft sprocket bolts, rotate the crankshaft anti-clockwise slightly until the pin is to the left of the hole, then slowly rotate it clockwise until the lock tool can be fully inserted. Tighten the camshaft sprocket bolts to 20 Nm.

31 Remove the crankshaft and camshaft locking tools, then rotate the crankshaft 2 complete revolutions clockwise and check the locking tools can be reinserted. If necessary, repeat the adjustment procedure described previously.

32 Tighten the camshaft and fuel pump sprocket bolts to the specified torque.

33 The remainder of refitting is a reversal of removal.

7.26 Check the pointer (arrowed) is centred or within 5mm to the right of the gap in the base plate

7.27 Slight misalignment of the pump sprocket timing hole (arrowed) is acceptable

8.5 Engine mounting bracket bolts (arrowed)

8.7 Ensure the lug on the backplate engages with the cut-out in the timing belt cover (arrowed)

8.10 Timing belt idler pulleys

8.16 Using a puller to remove the crankshaft sprocket

8 Timing belt tensioner and sprockets – removal and refitting

Timing belt tensioner

Removal

1 In order to remove the timing belt tensioner, then engine mounting bracket must first be removed. Either support the engine from above using a crossbeam or an engine hoist or support if from underneath with a trolley jack and block of wood.
2 Remove the timing belt as described in Section 7.
3 Undo the bolts and remove the right-hand engine mounting.
4 Working in the wheelarch area, undo the nut securing the lower end of the coolant pipe.

8.26 Fabricate a home made tool to counterhold the hub. Undo the bolt...

5 Undo the 3 retaining bolts and remove the engine mounting bracket (see illustration).
6 Unscrew the timing belt tensioner nut, and remove the tensioner from the engine.

Refitting

7 When refitting the tensioner to the engine, ensure that the lug on the tensioner backplate engages with the corresponding cut-out in the rear timing belt cover, then refit the tensioner nut (see illustration).
8 The remainder of refitting is a reversal of removal.

Idler pulleys

Removal

9 Remove the timing belt as described in Section 7.
10 Unscrew the relevant idler pulley/roller securing bolt/nut, and then withdraw the pulley (see illustration).

Refitting

11 Refit the pulley and tighten the securing bolt or nut to the specified torque. **Note:** *Renew the large roller/pulley retaining bolt (where applicable).*
12 Refit and tension the timing belt as described in Section 7.

Crankshaft sprocket

Note: *A new crankshaft sprocket securing bolt must be used on refitting.*

Removal

13 Remove the timing belt as described in Section 7.

14 The sprocket securing bolt must now be slackened, and the crankshaft must be prevented from turning as the sprocket bolt is unscrewed. To hold the sprocket, make up a suitable tool, and screw it to the sprocket using two bolts screwed into two of the crankshaft pulley bolt holes.
15 Hold the sprocket using the tool, then slacken the sprocket securing bolt. Take care, as the bolt is very tight. Do not allow the crankshaft to turn as the bolt is slackened.
16 Unscrew the bolt, and slide the sprocket from the end of the crankshaft, noting which way round the sprocket's raised boss is fitted. If required, use a puller to withdraw the sprocket from the end of the crankshaft (see illustration).

Refitting

17 Commence refitting by positioning the sprocket on the end of the crankshaft.
18 Fit a new sprocket securing bolt, then counterhold the sprocket using the method employed on removal, and tighten the bolt to the specified torque in the two stages given in the Specifications.
19 Refit the timing belt as described in Section 7.

Camshaft sprocket

Removal

20 Remove the timing belt as described in Section 7, then rotate the crankshaft 90° anti-clockwise to prevent any accidental piston-to-valve contact.
21 Unscrew and remove the three retaining bolts and remove the camshaft sprocket from the camshaft hub.

Refitting

22 Refit the sprocket ensuring that it is fitted the correct way round, as noted before removal, then insert the new sprocket bolts, and tighten by hand only at this stage.
23 If the crankshaft has been turned, turn the crankshaft clockwise 90° back to TDC.
24 Refit and tension the timing belt as described in Section 7.

Camshaft hub

Note: *VAG technicians use special tool T10051 to counterhold the hub, however it is possible to fabricate a suitable alternative.*

Removal

25 Remove the camshaft sprocket as described previously in this Section.
26 Engage special tool T10051 with the three locating holes in the face of the hub to prevent the hub from turning. If this tool is not available, fabricate a suitable alternative. Whilst holding the tool, undo the central hub retaining bolt about two turns (see illustration).
27 Slide the hub from the camshaft. If necessary, attach VW tool T10052 (or a similar three-legged puller) to the hub, and evenly tighten the puller until the hub is free of the camshaft taper (see illustration).

Refitting

28 Ensure that the camshaft taper and the hub centre is clean and dry, locate the hub on the taper, noting that the built-in key in the hub taper must align with the keyway in the camshaft taper **(see illustration)**.

29 Hold the hub in this position with tool T10051 (or similar home-made tool), and tighten the central bolt to the specified torque.

30 Refit the camshaft sprocket as described previously in this Section.

Coolant pump sprocket

31 The coolant pump sprocket is integral with the coolant pump. Refer to Chapter 3 for details of coolant pump removal.

9 Camshaft and hydraulic tappets – removal, inspection and refitting

Note: *A new camshaft oil seal(s) will be required on refitting. VW removal tool T40094 (or similar tool) will be required to refit the camshafts – this is necessary to prevent damage to the retaining frame and cylinder head as the camshafts are refitted.*

Removal

1 With the timing set at TDC, remove the camshaft hub (see Section 8).

2 Remove the camshaft cover (see Section 4).

3 Remove the brake vacuum pump as described in Chapter 9, Section 24.

4 If the camshafts are not going to be renewed, use two flat pieces of metal flat bar and cable ties and secure the two camshafts to the retaining frame **(see illustrations)**. Progressively unscrew the camshaft retaining frame bolts in the reverse of the sequence shown in illustration 9.27, and carefully remove the retaining frame, complete with camshafts. Remove the oil seal from the end of the camshaft and discard it – a new one will be required for refitting.

5 If the camshafts are going to be renewed, progressively unscrew the camshaft retaining frame bolts in the reverse of the sequence shown in illustration 9.27, and carefully remove the retaining frame. Then carefully lift the camshafts from the cylinder head, keeping them identified for location. Remove the oil seal from the end of the camshaft and discard it – a new one will be required for refitting.

6 Lift the rocker arms and hydraulic tappets from place. Store the rockers and tappets in a container with numbered compartments to ensure they are refitted to their correct locations. It is recommended that the tappets are kept immersed in oil for the period they are removed from the cylinder head.

Inspection

7 If the camshafts are still secured to the retaining frame, mark the two sprockets in relation with each other, then cut the cable

8.27 ...and slide the hub from the camshaft

ties to remove them from the frame **(see illustration)**. With the camshafts removed, examine the retaining frame and the bearing locations in the cylinder head for signs of obvious wear or pitting. If evident, a new cylinder head will probably be required. Also check that the oil supply holes in the cylinder head are free from obstructions.

8 Visually inspect the camshafts for evidence of wear on the surfaces of the lobes and journals. Normally their surfaces should be smooth and have a dull shine; look for scoring, erosion or pitting and areas that appear highly polished, indicating excessive wear. Accelerated wear will occur once the hardened exterior of the camshaft has been damaged, so always renew worn items. **Note:** *If these symptoms are visible on the tips of the camshaft lobes, check the corresponding rocker arm, as it will probably be worn as well.*

9.4a Using flat metal bar and cable ties to secure the camshafts...

9.7 Make alignment marks for the position of the sprockets

8.28 Ensure the integral key aligns with the keyway in the camshaft (arrowed)

9 If the machined surfaces of the camshaft appear discoloured or blue, it is likely that it has been overheated at some point, probably due to inadequate lubrication. This may have distorted the shaft, so have the camshaft runout and endfloat checked by an automotive engine reconditioning specialist.

10 Inspect the hydraulic tappets for obvious signs of wear or damage **(see illustration)**, and renew if necessary. Check that the oil holes in the tappets are free from obstructions.

Refitting

11 Oil the rocker arms and hydraulic tappets, and then refit them to their original positions.

⚠️ *Warning: After fitting hydraulic tappets, wait a minimum of 30 minutes (or preferably, leave overnight) before starting the engine; to allow the tappets time to settle, otherwise the valve heads will strike the pistons.*

9.4b ...to the upper ladder frame for removal

9.10 Check the tappets for wear

9.12 VW special tool no. T40094 shown

9.13a Position the inlet camshaft on the tool with the head bolt indent facing outwards…

9.13b …then slide the end of the special tool, in to the slot in the end of the camshaft

9.14a Position the exhaust camshaft on the tool with the head bolt indent facing outwards…

9.14b …then fit special tool clamp into the slot in the end of the exhaust camshaft

then slide the end support into the slot in the end of the camshaft **(see illustrations)**.

14 Position the exhaust camshaft on the supports, again with the cylinder head bolt indents facing outwards, and then fit the locating clamp into the slot in the end of the camshaft **(see illustrations)**.

15 Fit the VW clamping tool No.T40096 to the double gear on the exhaust camshaft, tightening the knurled thumb wheel until the faces of the gear teeth are in alignment **(see illustration)**. Note some camshafts only have a single sprocket, so will not require this procedure.

16 Slide the exhaust camshaft towards the inlet camshaft until the gear teeth engage **(see illustration)**.

17 Ensure the gasket faces of the retaining frame are clean, then apply a smear of clean engine oil to the bearing surfaces and lower the frame into position over the camshafts **(see illustrations)**. Ensure the bearing surfaces locate correctly on the camshafts.

18 Fit the clamping tool No.T40095 over the camshafts and frame, and tighten the thumbwheels to hold the camshafts in position in the frame **(see illustration)**.

19 Slide out locking clamps from each end of the camshafts **(see illustrations)**, and then lift the camshafts, retaining frame and clamping tool from the VW special tool no. 40094.

Without VW special tool

20 Ensure the gasket faces of the retaining frame are clean, then apply a smear of clean engine oil to the bearing surfaces and turn it upside down on a clean surface.

Using VW special tool No.T40094

12 If the camshafts were removed from the retaining frame, use the VW special tool No.T40094, as shown in the following procedures **(see illustration)**.

13 Position the inlet camshaft as shown with the cylinder head bolt indents facing outwards,

9.15 Tighten the thumbwheel to align the gear teeth. Ensure the clamping jaw with the arrow is seated on the wider gear

9.16 Slide the exhaust camshaft to the inlet camshaft until the teeth are in mesh

9.17a Lubricate the bearing mountings…

9.17b …and fit the upper ladder frame to the camshafts

9.18 Secure the camshafts in place in the frame using tool No. T40095

9.19a Slide the locking tool out from the end of the inlet camshaft...

9.19b ...and remove the locking clamp from the end of the exhaust camshaft

9.22a VW special tool for aligning teeth on sprocket

9.22b Using two flat bladed screwdrivers and a pair of pliers to align teeth

9.23a inlet camshaft slot needs to be horizontal

9.23b Slot in end of exhaust camshaft should be at the 12 o'clock position

21 Position the camshafts on the retaining frame with the cylinder head bolt indents facing outwards. Align the marks made on the camshaft sprockets on removal **(see illustration 9.7)**.

22 If a double gear is fitted to the exhaust camshaft, fit the VW clamping tool No.T40096 (or similar) to align the faces of the teeth. If the VW clamping tool is not available use two flat bladed screwdrivers and a pair of pliers, this will need an assistant to keep firm pressure on the camshafts to make sure they locate in the retaining frame correctly **(see illustrations)**. Note some camshafts only have a single sprocket, so will not require this procedure.

23 With the marks on the sprockets aligned and the cylinder head bolt indents facing outwards, the slot in the end of the inlet camshaft (that drives the vacuum pump) should be horizontal and the slot in the end of the exhaust camshaft (that locates the timing belt sprocket) should be at the top when fitted **(see illustrations)**.

24 With the camshafts correctly in position, ensuring the camshafts locate correctly in the bearing surfaces on the retaining frame, use two flat pieces of metal flat bar and cable ties to secure them in position **(see illustration)**.
Caution: Make sure the camshafts are located correctly in the bearing surfaces on the retaining frame, otherwise damage can occur, and this could damage the retaining frame when tightening down onto the cylinder head. The retaining frame is matched to the cylinder head and can only be purchased with a new cylinder head. If there is any doubt, then the VW special

tool should be used, see previous refitting procedure.

All

25 Ensure the sealing surfaces of the cylinder

9.24 Camshafts are secured to the ladder frame with two pieces of flat bar and cable ties

head are clean, and then apply a 2.0 mm wide bead of sealant (D 176 501 A1 or equivalent) as shown. Take care not to apply too much sealant, ensuring the oil holes supply holes are not blocked **(see illustrations)**.

9.25a Apply a 2.0 mm thick bead of sealant...

9.25b ...to the area shown by the thick, black line, taking care not to block the oil holes (arrowed)

9.26a Fit a new seal/end cap to the cylinder head

9.26b Check that the locating dowels are in place

9.27 Camshaft retaining frame bolt tightening sequence

26 Fit a new sealing cap to the timing belt end of the cylinder head and make sure the locating dowels are fitted to the cylinder head **(see illustrations)**.

27 Apply a smear of clean engine oil to the bearing surfaces and place the camshafts, frame and clamping tool in place on the cylinder head. Progressively, carefully,

hand tighten the frame retaining bolts in the sequence shown **(see illustration)**, until the retaining frame makes contact with the cylinder head over the complete surface, then tighten the bolts to the specified torque, again in the correct sequence.

28 Remove the gear aligning tool (T40096) and the clamping tool (T40095), or the metal flat bars and cable ties from the top of the camshaft retaining frame **(see illustration)**.

29 Renew the camshaft oil seal as described in Section 10.

30 The remainder of refitting is a reversal of removal.

10 Camshaft oil seals – renewal

Right-hand oil seal

1 Remove the camshaft sprocket and hub, as described in Section 8.

2 Drill two small holes into the existing oil seal, diagonally opposite each other. Take great care to avoid drilling through into the seal housing or camshaft sealing surface. Thread two self-tapping screws into the holes, and using a pair of pliers, pull on the heads of the screws to extract the oil seal **(see illustration)**.

3 Clean out the seal housing and the sealing surface of the camshaft by wiping it with a lint-free cloth. Remove any swarf or burrs that may cause the seal to leak.

4 Do not lubricate the lip and outer edge of the new oil seal, push it over the camshaft until it is positioned in place above it's housing. To prevent damage to the sealing lips, wrap some adhesive tape around the end of the camshaft **(see illustration)**.

5 Using a hammer and a socket of suitable diameter, drive the seal squarely into its housing. Make sure the seal is fitted the correct way around, some have 'OUTSIDE' stamped on the seal **(see illustration)**. Note: Select a socket that bears only on the hard outer surface of the seal, not the inner lip that can easily be damaged.

6 Refit the camshaft sprocket and its hub, as described in Section 8.

Left-hand oil seal

7 The left-hand camshaft oil seal is formed by the brake vacuum pump seal. Refer to Chapter 9, Section 24, for details of brake vacuum pump removal and refitting.

11 Cylinder head – removal, inspection and refitting

Note: *The cylinder head must be removed with the engine cold. New cylinder head bolts and a new cylinder head gasket will be required on refitting, and suitable studs will be required to guide the cylinder head into position – see text.*

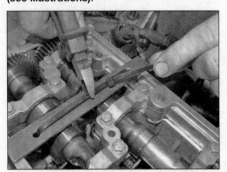

9.28 Remove the cable ties and flat bar from the top of the ladder frame

10.2 Screw-in a self-tapping screw, then pull the screw and seal from place

10.4 Using a plastic sleeve to slide seal over end of camshaft

10.5 Note some seals have 'OUTSIDE' (arrowed) to show fitted position

11.9 Remove the charge air pipe from the turbocharger

11.12 Disconnect the vacuum pipe

11.15a Disconnect the oil pressure switch wiring connector

Removal

1 Remove the battery and battery tray, as described in Chapter 5A, Section 3.
2 Drain the cooling system (Chapter 1B, Section 30) and engine oil (Chapter 1B, Section 3).
3 Pull the plastic cover on the top of the engine upwards to release it from its mountings.
4 Remove the air filter housing as described in Chapter 4B, Section 2.
5 Undo the bolts and remove the air hose/duct from the intercooler to the turbocharger. Release the wiring looms from the clips as necessary to enable the duct to be manoeuvred from place.
6 Remove the camshaft cover as described in Section 4.
7 Remove the camshaft sprocket and hub as described in Section 8.
8 Remove the inlet manifold as described in Chapter 4B, Section 5.
9 Undo the retaining bolts, and remove the charge air pipe from the turbocharger (see illustration).
10 Remove the EGR pipes from the cylinder head as described in Chapter 4D, Section 3.
11 Remove the exhaust manifold/turbocharger as described in Chapter 4D, Section 5. There is no need to completely remove the particulate filter from the vehicle. Slacken the Allen bolt and release the clamp securing the diesel particulate filter/catalytic converter to the turbocharger, then undo the bolts/nuts securing the brackets to the cylinder block/head and lay the filter/converter to one side.
12 Apply a little lubrication spray to the rubber sleeve, pull up the pipe from the vacuum pump, then undo the 4 retaining bolts and remove the vacuum pump from the left-hand end of the cylinder head (see illustration). Renew the pump-to-cylinder head seal/gasket (Chapter 9, Section 24).
13 Disconnect the coolant temperature sensor wiring plug at the left-hand end of the cylinder head, and release the wiring loom from any retaining clips.
14 Note their fitted locations, then release the clamps and disconnect the various coolant hoses from the cylinder head.
15 Disconnect the wiring connector from the oil pressure switch, undo the bolt securing

11.15b Undo the retaining bolt/screw and remove the lifting bracket

the pipe bracket at the left-hand end of the cylinder head (see illustrations), and the bolt securing the lifting bracket on the rear of the head.
16 Undo the bolt securing the timing belt guard adjacent to the timing belt tensioner, and the bolt securing the camshaft position sensor, then remove the tensioner retaining nut (see illustration).
17 Using an M12 multi-splined tool (12 pointed star), undo the cylinder head bolts, working from the outside-in, evenly and gradually. Remove the bolts and recover the washers. Check that nothing remains connected, and starting at the gearbox side, lift the cylinder head from the engine block, sliding the belt tensioner from the mounting stud as the cylinder head is removed. Seek assistance if possible, as it is a heavy assembly, especially as it is being removed complete with the manifolds.

11.20 The holes (arrowed) identify the thickness of the cylinder head gasket

11.16 Undo the bolt (arrowed) securing the timing belt guard

18 Remove the gasket from the top of the block, noting the locating dowels. If the dowels are a loose fit, remove them and store them with the head for safekeeping. Do not discard the gasket yet – it will be needed for identification purposes.

Inspection

19 Dismantling and inspection of the cylinder head is covered in Chapter 2E.

Cylinder head gasket selection

Note: A dial test indicator (DTI) will be required for this operation.
20 Examine the old cylinder head gasket for manufacturer's identification markings (see illustration). These will be in the form of holes, and a part number on the edge of the gasket. Unless new pistons have been fitted, the new cylinder head gasket must be of the same type as the old one.
21 If new piston assemblies have been fitted as part of an engine overhaul, or if a new short engine is to be fitted, the projection of the piston crowns above the cylinder head mating face of the cylinder block at TDC must be measured. This measurement is used to determine the thickness of the new cylinder head gasket required.
22 Anchor a dial test indicator (DTI) to the top face (cylinder head gasket mating face) of the cylinder block, and zero the gauge on the gasket mating face.
23 Rest the gauge probe on No 1 piston crown, and turn the crankshaft slowly by hand until the piston reaches TDC. Measure and

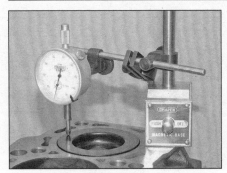

11.23 Measure the piston protrusion using a DTI gauge

11.35 Ensure the dowels are in place, then fit the new gasket with the part number uppermost (arrowed)

11.38 Cylinder head bolt tightening sequence

record the maximum piston projection at TDC **(see illustration)**.

24 Repeat the measurement for the remaining pistons, and record the results.

25 If the measurements differ from piston-to-piston, take the highest figure, and use this to determine the thickness of the head gasket required as follows.

Piston projection	Gasket identification (number of holes)
0.91 to 1.00 mm	1
1.01 to 1.10 mm	2
1.11 to 1.20 mm	3

26 Purchase a new gasket according to the results of the measurements.

Refitting

27 The mating faces of the cylinder head and block must be perfectly clean before refitting the head. Use a scraper to remove all traces of gasket and carbon, also clean the tops of the pistons. Take particular care with the aluminium surfaces, as the soft metal is easily damaged.

28 Make sure that debris is not allowed to enter the oil and water passages – this is particularly important for the oil circuit,

as carbon could block the oil supply to the camshaft and crankshaft bearings. Using adhesive tape and paper, seal the water, oil and bolt holes in the cylinder block.

29 To prevent carbon entering the gap between the pistons and bores, smear a little grease in the gap. After cleaning a piston, rotate the crankshaft to that the piston moves down the bore, and then wipe out the grease and carbon with a cloth rag. Clean the other piston crowns in the same way.

11.40 Use an angle-tightening gauge

30 Check the head and block for nicks, deep scratches and other damage. If slight, they may be removed carefully with a file. More serious damage may be repaired by machining, but this is a specialist job.

31 If warpage of the cylinder head is suspected, use a straight-edge to check it for distortion, as described in Chapter 2E, Section 7.

32 Ensure that the cylinder head bolt holes in the crankcase are clean and free of oil. Syringe or soak up any oil left in the bolt holes. This is most important in order that the correct bolt tightening torque can be applied, and to prevent the possibility of the block being cracked by hydraulic pressure when the bolts are tightened.

33 Turn the crankshaft anti-clockwise all the pistons at an equal height, approximately half-way down their bores from the TDC position (see Section 3). This will eliminate any risk of piston-to-valve contact as the cylinder head is refitted.

34 Where applicable, refit the manifolds with reference to Chapter 4B, Section 5 and/or Chapter 4D, Section 5.

35 Ensure that the cylinder head locating dowels are in place in the cylinder block, and then fit the new cylinder head gasket over the dowels, ensuring that the part number is uppermost **(see illustration)**. Note that VW recommend that the gasket is only removed from its packaging immediately prior to fitting.

36 Lower the cylinder head into position on the gasket, ensuring that it engages correctly over the dowels. Refit the timing belt tensioner as the cylinder head is refitted.

37 Fit the washers in place then fit the new cylinder head bolts to the locations, and screw them in as far as possible by hand. Do not oil the bolt threads.

38 Working progressively, in sequence, tighten all the cylinder head bolts to the specified Stage 1 torque **(see illustration)**.

39 Again working progressively, in sequence, tighten all the cylinder head bolts to the specified Stage 2 torque.

40 Tighten all the cylinder head bolts, in sequence, through the specified Stage 3 angle **(see illustration)**.

41 Finally, tighten all the cylinder head bolts, in sequence, through the specified Stage 4 angle.

42 The remainder of the refitting procedure is a reversal of the removal procedure, noting the following points:

a) Tighten all fasteners to their specified torque where given.

b) Renew all seals and gaskets.

c) Refill the cooling system as described, in Chapter 1B, Section 30.

d) Refill the engine oil, as described in Chapter 1B, Section 3.

e) Ensure all wiring is correctly routed.

f) Run the vehicle and make sure the cooling fans operate when the engine gets up to temperature.

12.3 Undo the dipstick tube lower securing bolt – arrowed

12.4 Undo the air intake pipe securing bolt - arrowed

12.5 Undo the mounting bracket securing bolts – arrowed

12.7 Release the securing clips – one shown

12.8a Undo the three transmission to sump bolts (arrowed)...

12.8b ...and also the four bolts (arrowed), at the transmission end of the sump

12 Sump –
removal and refitting

Removal

1 Apply the handbrake, then jack up the front of the vehicle and support securely on axle stands (see *Jacking and vehicle support*). Remove the securing screws and withdraw the engine undershield.
2 Drain the engine oil as described in Chapter 1B, Section 3.
3 Working at the front lower part of the cylinder block, undo the retaining bolt and remove the dipstick tube from the top of the sump **(see illustration)**.
4 Undo the retaining bolt and move the lower part of the air intake pipes away from the sump **(see illustration)**.
5 Undo the retaining screws and release the coolant hose mounting brackets from the sump **(see illustration)**.
6 Disconnect the wiring connector from the oil level/temperature sender on the lower rear part of the sump.
7 Release the retaining clips and remove the sump insulation cover from the sump **(see illustration)**.
8 Unscrew and remove the bolts securing the sump to the cylinder block, and the bolts securing the sump to the transmission casing, then withdraw the sump **(see illustrations)**. If necessary, release the sump by tapping with a soft-faced hammer.

Refitting

9 Begin refitting by thoroughly cleaning the mating faces of the sump and cylinder block. Ensure that all traces of old sealant are removed.
10 Ensure that the cylinder block mating face of the sump is free from all traces of old sealant, oil and grease, and then apply a 2.0 to 3.0 mm thick bead of silicone sealant (VW D 176 404 A2 or equivalent) to the sump **(see illustrations)**. Note that the sealant should be run around the inside of the bolt holes in the sump. The sump must be fitted within 5 minutes of applying the sealant.
11 Offer the sump up to the cylinder block, then refit the sump-to-cylinder block bolts, and lightly tighten them by hand, working progressively in a diagonal sequence. **Note:**

If the sump is being refitted with the engine and transmission separated, make sure that the sump is flush with the flywheel end of the cylinder block.
12 Refit the sump-to-transmission casing bolts, and tighten them lightly, using a socket.
13 Again working in a diagonal sequence, lightly tighten the sump-to-cylinder block bolts, using a socket.
14 Tighten the sump-to-transmission casing bolts to the specified torque.
15 Working in a diagonal sequence, progressively tighten the sump-to-cylinder block bolts to the specified torque.
16 The remainder of refitting is a reversal of removal, noting to allow at least 30 minutes from the time of refitting the sump for the sealant to dry, then refill the engine with oil, with reference to Chapter 1B, Section 3.

12.10a Apply a bead of sealant...

12.10b ...around the inside of the bolt holes

13.4 Undo the cover bolts - arrowed

13.5 Lock the tensioner with a metal rod

13.6 Undo the sprocket bolt – arrowed

13.7 Undo the tensioner bolts – arrowed

13.8 Balancer shaft assembly bolted to the cylinder block

13 Oil pump and balancer shaft unit – removal, inspection and refitting

Removal

1 Remove the timing belt as described in Section 7.
2 Remove the sump as described in Section 12.
3 Remove the oil seal housing from the timing belt end of the engine, as described in Section 15.
4 Undo the three retaining bolts and remove the plastic cover from below the oil pump/balancer shaft unit **(see illustration)**. As the cover is removed the oil pick-up pipe/filter will need to be disengaged from the O-ring seal in the lower part of the oil pump/balancer shaft unit. Carefully pull the cover downwards to disengage it from the seal. Discard the O-ring seal, as a new one will be required for refitting.
5 Press down on the chain tensioner and lock it in position using a thin metal rod (VW tool no. T40011) **(see illustration)**.
6 Unscrew the bolt from the idler sprocket and remove it out from the chain **(see illustration)**.
7 Undo the retaining bolts and remove the chain tensioner assembly from the end of the end of the cylinder block **(see illustration)**. Discard the bolts, as new ones will be required for refitting. Remove the chain from around the sprockets and keep it in a safe clean place.
8 Unscrew and remove the mounting bolts, then release the oil pump/balancer shaft

unit from the dowels in the crankcase **(see illustration)**.

Oil pump inspection

9 Clean the pump thoroughly, and inspect for signs of damage or wear. If evident, renew the oil pump. *Note: The oil pump and balancer shaft can only be renewed as a complete unit.*

Refitting

10 Prime the pump with oil by pouring oil into the pick-up pipe aperture while turning the shaft.
11 Before offering the unit back into position, make sure the alignment dowels are in position and a new O-ring seal is fitted to the lower part of the crankcase.
12 Refit the oil pump/balancer shaft unit to the cylinder block and tighten the bolts by hand to start. With the unit in position, align the timing belt end of the unit with the edge of

13.14 Align the coloured links with the markings

the cylinder block. With the timing belt end of the unit flush with the end of the cylinder block tighten the retaining bolts to the specified torque.
13 Check that the marking on the crankshaft sprocket is positioned at the top.
14 Making sure the chain is clean and the correct way around, with the coloured links facing the outside when fitted. Feed the chain into place around the sprockets on the oil pump, balancer shaft and crankshaft. The marking on the crankshaft sprocket must be aligned with the single coloured chain link, and the marking on the balancer shaft sprocket should be aligned between the two coloured chain links **(see illustration)**.
15 With the chain aligned with the timing marks, fit the idler sprocket back into the chain and tighten the retaining bolt to the specified torque.
16 Fit the chain tensioner assembly to the centre of the sprockets and fit the new retaining bolts, tighten the bolts in the stages shown and to the torque specified at the beginning of this Chapter.
17 With the tensioner assembly in place, and the markings on the sprockets and chain in the correct position, remove the locking pin (VW tool no. T40011) from the chain tensioner.
18 Refit the plastic cover/pick-up pipe to the oil pump assembly, using a new O-ring seal, and tighten the securing bolts to the specified torque.
19 Refit the oil seal housing to the timing belt end of the engine, as described in Section 15.
20 Refit the sump as described in Section 12.
21 Refit the timing belt as described in Section 7.

14 Flywheel – removal, inspection and refitting

Removal

1 On manual gearbox models, remove the gearbox (see Chapter 7A, Section 3) and clutch (see Chapter 6, Section 6).
2 On semi-automatic (DSG) transmission models, remove the transmission as described in Chapter 7B, Section 2.

14.3 Flywheel bolts are offset and can only be fitted in one position - DSG transmission (0AM) shown

14.5 Use a locking tool to counterhold the flywheel

14.7a Flywheel warpage check – see text

14.7b Flywheel free rotational movement check alignment marks – see text

14.7c Flywheel lateral movement check marks – see text

14.8 Use new bolts when refitting

3 The flywheel can only be fitted in one position due to the offset of the flywheel mounting holes in the end of the crankshaft **(see illustration)**. Note, manual models are fitted with a dual-mass flywheel.

4 Rotate the outside of the dual-mass flywheel so that the bolts align with the holes (if necessary).

5 Unscrew the bolts and remove the flywheel. Using a locking tool, counter-hold the flywheel to prevent it from turning (see illustration). Discard the bolts, as new ones must be fitted. **Note:** *In order not to damage the flywheel, do not allow the bolt heads to make contact with the flywheel during the unscrewing procedure.*

Inspection

6 Check the dual-mass flywheel for wear and damage. Examine the starter ring gear for excessive wear to the teeth. If the driveplate or its ring gear are damaged, the complete driveplate must be renewed. The flywheel ring gear, however, may be renewed separately from the flywheel, but the work should be entrusted to a VW dealer. If the clutch friction face is discoloured or scored excessively, it may be possible to regrind it, but this work should also be entrusted to a VW dealer.

7 The following are guidelines only, but should indicate whether professional inspection is necessary. The dual-mass flywheel should be checked as follows:

Warpage: Place a straight edge across the face of the drive surface, and check by trying to insert a feeler gauge between the straight edge and the drive surface **(see illustration)**.

The flywheel will normally warp like a bowl – ie. Higher on the outer edge. If the warpage is more than 0.40 mm, the flywheel may need replacing.

Free rotational movement: This is the distance the drive surface of the flywheel can be turned independently of the flywheel primary element, using finger effort alone. Move the drive surface in one direction and make a mark where the locating pin aligns with the flywheel edge. Move the drive surface in the other direction (finger pressure only) and make another mark **(see illustration)**. The total of free movement should not exceed 20.0 mm. If it's more, the flywheel may need replacing.

Total rotational movement: This is the total distance the drive surface can be turned independently of the flywheel primary element. Insert two bolts into the clutch pressure plate/damper unit mounting holes, and with the crankshaft/flywheel held stationary, use a lever/pry bar between the bolts and use some effort to move the drive surface fully in one direction – make a mark where the locating pin aligns with the flywheel edge. Now force the drive surface fully in the opposite direction, and make another mark. The total rotational movement should not exceed 44.00 mm. If it does, have the flywheel professionally inspected.

Lateral movement: The lateral movement (up and down) of the drive surface in relation to the primary element of the flywheel, should not exceed 2.0 mm. If it does, the flywheel may need replacing. This can be checked by pressing the drive surface down on one side

into the flywheel (flywheel horizontal) and making an alignment mark between the drive surface and the inner edge of the primary element. Now press down on the opposite side of the drive surface, and make another mark above the original one. The difference between the two marks is the lateral movement **(see illustration)**.

There should be no cracks in the drive surface of the flywheel. If cracks are evident, the flywheel may need replacing.

Refitting

8 Refitting is a reversal of removal. Use new bolts when refitting the flywheel or driveplate **(see illustration)**, and coat the threads of the bolts (if not already coated with locking compound) with locking fluid before inserting them. Tighten them to the specified torque.

15 Crankshaft oil seals – renewal

Note: *The oil seals are a PTFE (Teflon) type and are fitted dry, without using any grease or oil. These have a wider sealing lip and have been introduced instead of the coil spring type oil seal.*

Timing belt end oil seal

1 Remove the timing belt as described in Section 7, and the crankshaft sprocket with reference to Section 8.

2 To remove the seal without removing the housing, drill two small holes diagonally

15.2 Pull the screw and seal from place using pliers

15.5 Using a plastic sleeve to slide the seal over the end of the crankshaft

15.6 Carefully tap the seal into position

opposite each other, insert self-tapping screws, and pull on the heads of the screws with pliers **(see illustration)**.

3 Alternatively, to remove the oil seal complete with its housing, proceed as follows.

 a) *Remove the sump as described in Section 12. This is necessary to ensure a satisfactory seal between the sump and oil seal housing on refitting.*

 b) *Unbolt and remove the oil seal housing.*

 c) *Working on the bench, lever the oil seal from the housing using a suitable screwdriver. Take care not to damage the seal seating in the housing.*

4 Thoroughly clean the oil seal seating in the housing.

5 Wind a length of tape around the end of the crankshaft (or a plastic sleeve) to protect the oil seal lips as the seal (and housing, where applicable) is fitted **(see illustration)**.

6 Fit a new oil seal to the housing, pressing or driving it into position using a socket or tube of suitable diameter. Ensure that the socket or tube bears only on the hard outer ring of the seal, and take care not to damage the seal lips. Press or drive the seal into position until it is seated on the shoulder in the housing **(see illustration)**. Make sure that the closed end of the seal is facing outwards.

7 If the oil seal housing has been removed, proceed as follows, otherwise proceed to paragraph 11.

8 Clean all traces of old sealant from the crankshaft oil seal housing and the cylinder block, then coat the cylinder block mating faces of the oil seal housing with a 2.0 to 3.0 mm thick bead of silicone sealant (VW D 176 404 A2, or equivalent). Note that the seal housing must be refitted within 5 minutes of applying the sealant.

Caution: DO NOT put excessive amounts of sealant onto the housing as it may get into the sump and block the oil pick-up pipe.

9 Refit the oil seal housing, and tighten the bolts progressively to the specified torque.

10 Refit the sump as described in Section 12.

11 Refit the crankshaft sprocket with reference to Section 8, and the timing belt as described in Section 7.

Flywheel end oil seal

Note: *In these engines, the seal, sealing flange and sender wheel are a complete unit. Special tools are required to refit the sealing flange, and press the sender wheel onto the end of the crankshaft. It is not possible to accurately fit these parts without the tools, which may be available from VW (part no. T10134) and are available from aftermarket automotive tool specialists. E.g. Laser tools).*

12 Remove the flywheel as described in Section 14, then prise the intermediate plate from the locating dowels on the cylinder block and unhook it from behind the top of the seal housing **(see illustrations)**.

13 Undo the bolt securing the crankshaft speed sensor and remove it from the seal housing, then undo the bolts securing the sealing flange to the cylinder block **(see illustrations)**.

14 Insert three 6 x 35 mm bolts into the threaded holes in the sealing flange. Tighten the bolts gradually and evenly, and press the sealing flange, and sender wheel from the crankshaft/cylinder block **(see illustrations)**. The seal, sender wheel and sealing flange are supplied as a complete unit.

15.12a Remove the intermediate plate from the dowels…

15.12b …and from behind the top of the crankshaft seal housing

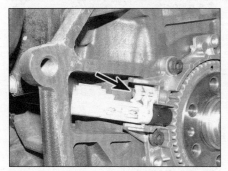

15.13a Undo the crankshaft speed sensor retaining bolt - arrowed

15.13b Sealing flange bolts (arrowed)

15.14a Screw in three 6 x 35 mm bolts…

15.14b ...and draw the sealing flange and sender wheel from place

15.16a Rotate the nut until it's level with the end of the flat clamping surface...

15.16b ...then clamp it in a vice

15.17a Rotate the nut until the inner part of the tool...

15.17b ...is flush with the flat surface of the housing

15.18a Remove the securing clip...

15 Ensure the mating face of the cylinder block is clean and free from debris. The new sealing flange/seal/sender wheel assembly is supplied with a sealing lip support ring, which serves as a fitting sleeve, and must not be removed prior to installation. Equally, the sender wheel must not be separated from the assembly.

16 If using the VW tool, proceed as follows. If using an aftermarket tool specialist's product, follow the instructions supplied with the tool. Rotate the large spindle nut until it's level with the end of the clamping surface of the spindle, then clamp the spindle in a vice (see illustrations).

17 Press the tool housing downwards until it rests on the nut and washer. Rotate the nut until the inner part of the tool is at the same height as the housing (see illustrations).

18 Remove the seal securing clip. The hole on the sender wheel must align with the marking on the sealing flange (see illustrations).

19 Place the flange outer side down on a clean, flat surface, then press the seal guide fitting sleeve (supplied ready fitted), housing, and sender wheel downwards until all the components are flat on the surface. In this position the upper edge of the sender wheel should be level with the edge of the sealing flange (see illustrations).

20 Place the sealing flange on the assembly tool, so the pin locates in the hole in the sender wheel (see illustration).

21 Push the sealing flange and guide fitting sleeve against the tool whilst tightening the 3 knurled screws. Ensure the pin is still located in the sender wheel (see illustration).

22 Ensure the end of the crankshaft is clean, and is locked at TDC on No. 1 cylinder as described in Section 3.

23 Unscrew the large nut to the end

15.18b ...the hole in the sender wheel should align with the marking on the flange (arrowed)

15.19b ...so the upper edge of the sender wheel is level with the edge of the flange

of the spindle threads, then press the spindle inwards as far as possible (see illustrations).

24 Align the flat side of the assembly with

15.19a Press the assembly downwards on a clean, flat surface...

15.20 Fit the flange to the tool, ensuring the pin locates in the hole (arrowed)

15.21 With the pin engaged in the hole, tighten the 3 knurled screws to secure the flange to the tool

15.23a Unscrew the nut to the end of the thread...

15.23b ...and push the spindle in as far as possible

15.24 Hand-tighten the Allen bolts (arrowed), to secure the tool to the crankshaft

15.25 Use two M7 x 35 mm bolts (arrowed) to guide the sealing flange

15.26 Push the black knob into the hole in the crankshaft

the sump flange, then secure the tool to the crankshaft using the integral Allen bolts **(see illustration)**. Only hand tighten the bolts.

25 Insert two M7x 35 mm bolts to guide

the sealing flange to the cylinder block **(see illustration)**.

26 Using hand pressure alone, push the tool assembly onto the crankshaft until the seal

guide fitting sleeve contacts the crankshaft flange, then push the guide pin (black knob) into the hole in the crankshaft. This is to ensure the sender wheel reaches its correct installation position **(see illustration)**.

27 Rotate the large nut until it makes contact with the tool housing, then tighten it to 35 Nm. After tightening this nut, a small air gap must still be present between the sealing flange and cylinder block **(see illustrations)**.

28 Unscrew the large nut; the two M7 x 35 Nm screws, the three knurled screws and the Allen bolts securing the tool to the crankshaft. Remove the tool, and pull the seal guide fitting sleeve from place (if it didn't come out with the tool) **(see illustration)**.

29 Use a vernier caliper or feeler gauge to measure the fitted depth of the sender wheel in relation to the crankshaft flange **(see illustration)**. The correct depth is 0.5 mm.

30 If the gap is correct, fit the sealing flange bolts and tighten them to the specified torque.

31 If the gap is too small, re-attach the tool to the sealing flange and crankshaft, then refit the two M7 x 35 mm guide bolts to the flange. Tighten the large spindle nut to 40 Nm, remove the tool and re-measure the air gap. If the gap is still too small, re-attach the tool and tighten the spindle nut to 45 Nm. Re-measure the gap. When the gap is correct, refit the flange retaining bolts, and tighten them to the specified torque.

32 The remainder of refitting is a reversal of removal.

15.27a After tightening the spindle nut to 35 Nm...

15.27b ...there should be an air gap between the sealing flange and the cylinder block (arrowed)

15.28 Remove the tool and seal fitting guide sleeve

15.29 Measure the fitted depth of the sender wheel in relation to the end of the crankshaft

16.9 Undo the earth cable securing nut – arrowed

16.10a Undo the mounting bracket to engine bolts - arrowed

16.10b Undo the mounting bracket-to-body bolts - arrowed

16 Engine/transmission mountings – inspection and renewal

Inspection

1 If improved access is required, jack up the front of the car, and support it securely on axle stands (see *Jacking and vehicle support*). Remove the securing screws and remove the engine under shield.

2 Check the mounting rubbers to see if they are cracked, hardened or separated from the metal at any point; renew the mounting if any such damage or deterioration is evident.

3 Check that all the mountings are securely tightened; use a torque wrench to check if possible.

4 Using a large screwdriver or a crowbar, check for wear in the mounting by carefully levering against it to check for free play. Where this is not possible, enlist the aid of an assistant to move the engine/transmission back-and-forth, or from side-to-side, whilst you observe the mounting. While some free play is to be expected, even from new components, excessive wear should be obvious. If excessive free play is found, check first that the fasteners are correctly secured, and then renew any worn components as described in the following paragraphs.

5 When working on the right-hand mounting and rear lower mounting (torque arm), remove the mounting as a complete unit. VW state that the mounting bracket-to-flexible mounting nut/bolt should not be slackened, see following procedures for each individual mounting.

Renewal

Right-hand mounting

Note: *New mounting securing bolts will be required on refitting.*

6 Attach a hoist and lifting tackle to the engine lifting brackets on the cylinder head, and raise the hoist to just take the weight of the engine. Alternatively the engine can be supported on a trolley jack under the engine. Use a block of wood between the sump and the head of the jack, to prevent any damage to the sump.

7 To gain access to the engine mounting-to-body bolts, undo the two screws and move the coolant reservoir to one side, leaving the coolant hoses connected.

8 Unclip any wiring harness, pipes or hoses from over the upper mounting bracket and move them to one side.

9 Undo the securing nut and disconnect the earth wiring connector (where fitted), from the top of the engine mounting bracket **(see illustration)**.

10 Unscrew the three bolts securing the mounting bracket-to-engine, and the four bolts securing the engine mounting-to-body, then remove the complete right-hand mounting from the engine compartment **(see illustrations)**.

Caution: Do NOT undo the engine mounting centre nut, securing the bracket to the flexible mounting.

11 Refitting is a reversal of removal, but use new mounting securing bolts, and tighten all fixings to the specified torque.

Left-hand mounting

Note: *New mounting bolts will be required on refitting.*

12 Remove the air filter housing as described in Chapter 4A, Section 2.

13 Remove the battery and battery tray, as described in Chapter 5A, Section 3.

14 Attach a hoist and lifting tackle to the engine lifting brackets on the engine/transmission, and raise the hoist to just take the weight. Alternatively the engine/transmission can be supported on a trolley jack under the transmission. Use a block of

wood between the transmission and the head of the jack, to prevent any damage to the transmission.

15 Release any relevant wiring or hoses from the clips on the battery tray, then unscrew the three securing bolts and remove the battery tray. Disconnect the drain hose from the front of the tray as it is being removed.

16 Unscrew the two bolts securing the mounting to the transmission bracket, and the three remaining bolts securing the mounting to the body **(see illustration)**, then lift the mounting from the engine compartment.

17 To remove the mounting bracket from the transmission, remove the left-hand front wheel and wheel arch liner, then lower the transmission slightly and undo the three retaining bolts **(see illustration)**.

18 Refitting is a reversal of removal, but use new mounting securing bolts, and tighten all fixings to the specified torque.

Rear lower mounting (torque arm)

Note: *New mounting bolts will be required on refitting.*

19 Apply the handbrake, then jack up the front of the car and support securely on axle stands (see *Jacking and vehicle support*). Remove the engine undershield for access to the rear mounting (torque arm).

20 Support the rear of the transmission beneath the final drive housing. To do this, use a trolley jack and block of wood, or alternatively wedge a block of wood between the transmission and the subframe.

21 Working under the car, unscrew and remove the bolt securing the mounting to

16.16 Transmission mounting bolts – arrowed

16.17 Mounting bracket to transmission mounting bolts - arrowed

16.21 Rear lower torque arm mounting bolts – arrowed

the subframe and the two bolts securing the mounting to the transmission **(see illustration)**, then withdraw the complete mounting from under the car.

Caution: Do NOT undo the lower mounting centre bolt, securing the bracket to the flexible mounting.

22 Refitting is a reversal of removal, but use new mounting securing bolts, and tighten all fixings to the specified torque.

17 Engine oil cooler/ filter housing – removal and refitting

Removal

1 The oil cooler is mounted on the lower part of the oil filter housing on the front of the cylinder block.

2 Position a container beneath the oil filter housing to catch escaping oil and coolant.

3 Clamp the oil cooler coolant hoses to minimise coolant spillage, or drain the cooling system as described in Chapter 1B, Section 30.

4 Unscrew the oil cooler retaining screws and remove the oil cooler from the front of the oil filter housing **(see illustrations)**. Recover the O-rings from between the cooler and the oil filter housing, new ones will be required for refitting.

5 If required, disconnect the coolant hose, unclip the dipstick from the side of the housing, then undo the retaining bolts and remove the oil filter housing from the cylinder block **(see illustrations)**.

Refitting

6 Refitting is a reversal of removal, bearing in mind the following points:

a) Use new oil cooler and housing O-rings **(see illustration)**.

b) Tighten the oil cooler and filter housing bolts to the correct torque.

c) On completion, check and if necessary top-up the oil and coolant levels.

18 Oil pressure warning light switch – removal and refitting

Removal

1 The oil pressure warning light switch is fitted to the left-hand rear of the cylinder head **(see**

illustration)**. Remove the engine top cover to gain access to the switch.

2 Slacken the retraining clips and remove the air intake hose from the turbocharger to the air filter housing.

3 Disconnect the wiring connector and wipe clean the area around the switch.

4 Unscrew the switch and remove it, along with its sealing washer (where fitted). If the switch is to be left removed from the engine for any length of time, plug the aperture in the cylinder head.

Refitting

5 Examine the sealing washer for signs of damage or deterioration and if necessary renew.

6 Refit the switch, complete with washer (where fitted), and tighten it to the specified torque.

7 Securely reconnect the wiring connector, refit the air intake hose and then, if necessary, top-up the engine oil as described in *Weekly checks*. On completion, refit the engine top cover.

19 Oil level/temperature sender – removal and refitting

Removal

1 The oil level/temperature sender is fitted to bottom of the sump **(see illustration)**.

2 Drain the engine oil as described in Chapter 1B, Section 3.

17.4a Undo the engine oil cooler retaining screws

17.4b Renew the seals/gaskets

17.5a Disconnect the coolant hoses...

17.5b ...and undo the filter housing retaining bolts (arrowed)

17.6 Renew the seals/gaskets

18.1 Oil pressure warning light switch location - arrowed

3 Disconnect the wiring connector from the sender.

4 Release the retaining clips and remove the insulation cover from the sump.

5 Wipe clean the area around the sender, then undo the three retaining bolts and remove the sender.

Refitting

6 Examine the sealing washer for signs of damage or deterioration and if necessary renew.

7 Refit the switch and tighten the retaining bolts to the specified torque.

8 Refit the insulation cover, then reconnect the wiring connector and refill the engine with oil (refer to Chapter 1B, Section 3).

9 On completion, check and, if necessary, top-up the engine oil as described in *Weekly checks*.

19.1 Oil level/temperature sensor location

Notes

Chapter 2 Part D:
1.6 litre diesel engine in-car repair procedures

Contents

Degrees of difficulty

Easy, suitable for novice with little experience	**Fairly easy,** suitable for beginner with some experience	**Fairly difficult,** suitable for competent DIY mechanic	**Difficult,** suitable for experienced DIY mechanic	**Very difficult,** suitable for expert DIY or professional

Specifications

General

Type	Four-cylinder in-line, belt-driven double overhead camshaft (DOHC), four stroke, 16-valve, liquid-cooled
Cubic capacity	1599 cc
Manufacturer's engine codes*	CAYB, CAYC and CLNA
Maximum power output:	
CAYB	66 kW @ 4200 rpm
CAYC	77 kW @ 4400 rpm
CLNA	77 kW @ 4000 rpm
Maximum torque output:	
CAYB	230 Nm @ 1500 to 2500 rpm
CAYC and CLNA.	250 Nm @ 1500 to 2500 rpm
Bore	79.5 mm
Stroke.	80.5 mm
Compression ratio	16.5 :1
Compression pressures (oil temperature 80°C minimum):	
New	25.0 to 31.0 bars
Minimum	19.0 bars
Maximum difference between cylinders.	5.0 bars
Firing order.	1 – 3 – 4 – 2
No.1 cylinder location.	Timing belt end

* **Note:** *See 'Vehicle identification' at the end of this manual for the location of engine code markings.*

Lubrication system

Oil pump type.	Gear type, belt-driven from crankshaft
Oil pressure switch (green)	0.5 bar
Oil pressure (oil temperature 80°C):	
Minimum @ idling:	
CAYB and CAYC.	0.6 bar
CLNA	0.8 bar
Minimum @ 2000 rpm:	
CAYB and CAYC.	1.0 bar
CLNA	1.5 bar
Maximum @ high rpm.	5.0 bar

Torque wrench settings

	Nm	lbf ft
Ancillary (alternator, etc) bracket mounting bolts*:		
Stage 1 (all six bolts)..	40	30
Stage 2 (for two lower bolts)...............................	Angle-tighten a further 45°	
Stage 2 (for four upper bolts)	Angle-tighten a further 90°	
Auxiliary drivebelt tensioner securing bolt:		
Stage 1..	20	15
Stage 2..	Angle-tighten a further 180°	
Big-end bearing caps bolts*:		
Stage 1..	30	22
Stage 2..	Angle-tighten a further 90°	
Camshaft retaining frame bolts	10	7
Camshaft cover bolts.......................................	10	7
Camshaft sprocket hub centre bolt	100	74
Camshaft sprocket-to-hub bolts*:		
Stage 1..	20	15
Stage 2..	Angle-tighten a further 45°	
Common rail bolts	22	16
Coolant pump bolts	15	11
Crankshaft oil seal housing bolts..........................	15	11
Crankshaft pulley-to-sprocket bolts*:		
Stage 1..	10	7
Stage 2..	Angle-tighten a further 90°	
Crankshaft sprocket bolt*:		
Stage 1..	120	89
Stage 2..	Angle-tighten a further 90°	
Cylinder head bolts*:		
Stage 1..	30	22
Stage 2..	60	44
Stage 3..	Angle-tighten a further 90°	
Stage 4..	Angle-tighten a further 90°	
Engine mountings:		
RH engine mounting*:		
Mounting bracket to engine:		
Stage 1..	40	30
Stage 2..	Angle-tighten a further 180°	
Mounting to body:		
Stage 1..	40	30
Stage 2..	Angle-tighten a further 90°	
Mounting to bracket:		
Stage 1..	60	44
Stage 2..	Angle-tighten a further 90°	
LH engine/transmission mounting*:		
Mounting to body:		
Stage 1..	40	30
Stage 2..	Angle-tighten a further 90°	
Mounting to bracket on transmission:		
Stage 1..	60	44
Stage 2..	Angle-tighten a further 90°	
Rear mounting link*:		
Link-to-transmission:		
Short (front) bolt:		
Stage 1..	40	30
Stage 2..	Angle-tighten a further 90°	
Long (rear) bolt:		
Stage 1..	60	44
Stage 2..	Angle-tighten a further 90°	
Link-to-subframe:		
Stage 1..	100	74
Stage 2..	Angle-tighten a further 90°	
Flywheel*:		
Stage 1..	60	44
Stage 2..	Angle-tighten a further 90°	
Fuel pump hub nut..	95	70
Fuel pump sprocket bolts*.................................	20	15
Main bearing cap bolts*:		
Stage 1..	65	48
Stage 2..	Angle-tighten a further 90°	

Torque wrench settings (continued)

	Nm	lbf ft
Oil cooler screws	11	7
Oil drain plug*	30	22
Oil filter housing-to-cylinder block bolts*:		
Stage 1	14	10
Stage 2	Angle-tighten a further 180°	
Oil filter cover	25	18
Oil level/temperature sensor-to-sump bolts	9	7
Oil pick-up pipe securing bolts	9	7
Oil pressure warning light switch	22	16
Oil pump securing bolts	16	11
Piston oil spray jet bolt	27	19
Sump-to-cylinder block bolts	13	9
Sump-to-transmission bolts	40	30
Thermostat housing	15	11
Timing belt outer cover bolts	10	7
Timing belt tensioner roller securing nut:		
Stage 1	20	15
Stage 2	Angle-tighten a further 45°	
Timing belt idler pulleys:		
Lower idler roller nut	20	15
Upper idler roller (small) bolt	15	11
Upper idler roller (large) bolt*:		
Stage 1	50	37
Stage 2	Angle-tighten a further 90°	

Do not re-use fasteners

1 General information

How to use this Chapter

This Part of Chapter 2 describes those repair procedures that can reasonably be carried out on the engine while it remains in the vehicle. If the engine has been removed from the vehicle and is being dismantled as described in Part E, any preliminary dismantling procedures can be ignored.

Note that while it may be possible physically to overhaul certain items while the engine is in the vehicle, such tasks are not usually carried out as separate operations, and usually require the execution of several additional procedures (not to mention the cleaning of components and of oilways); for this reason, all such tasks are classed as major overhaul procedures, and are described in Part E of this Chapter.

Engine description

Throughout this Chapter, engines are referred to by type, and are identified and referred to by the manufacturer's code letters. A listing of all engines covered, together with their code letters, is given in the Specifications at the start of this Chapter.

The engines are water-cooled, double overhead camshafts (DOHC), in-line four-cylinder units, with cast-iron cylinder blocks and aluminium-silicone alloy cylinder heads. All are mounted transversely at the front of the vehicle, with the transmission bolted to the left-hand end of the engine.

The crankshaft is of five-bearing type, and thrustwashers are fitted to the centre main bearing (No.3) to control crankshaft endfloat.

Drive for the exhaust camshaft is by a toothed timing belt from the crankshaft, with the intake camshaft driven by interlocking gears at the left-hand end of both camshafts. The gears incorporate a toothed backlash compensator element. Each camshaft is mounted at the top of the cylinder head, and is secured by a bearing frame/ladder.

The valves are closed by coil springs, and run in guides pressed into the cylinder head. The valves are operated by roller rocker arms incorporating hydraulic tappets.

The gear-type oil pump is driven by a belt from the right-hand (timing belt) end of the crankshaft. Oil is drawn from the sump through a strainer, and then forced through an externally mounted, renewable filter. From there, it is distributed to the cylinder head, where it lubricates the camshaft journals and hydraulic tappets, and also to the crankcase, where it lubricates the main bearings, connecting rod big-ends, gudgeon pins and cylinder bores. A coolant-fed oil cooler is fitted to the oil filter housing on all engines. Oil jets are fitted to the base of each cylinder – these spray oil onto the underside of the pistons, to improve cooling.

All engines are fitted with a combined brake servo vacuum pump, driven by the camshaft on the transmission end of the cylinder head.

On all engines, engine coolant is circulated by a pump, driven by the timing belt. For details of the cooling system, refer to Chapter 3.

Operations with engine in car

The following operations can be performed without removing the engine:

a) Compression pressure – testing.
b) Camshaft cover – removal and refitting.
c) Crankshaft pulley – removal and refitting.
d) Timing belt covers – removal and refitting.
e) Timing belt – removal, refitting and adjustment.
f) Timing belt tensioner and sprockets – removal and refitting.
g) Camshaft oil seals – renewal.
h) Camshafts and hydraulic tappets – removal, inspection and refitting.
i) Cylinder head – removal and refitting.
j) Cylinder head and pistons – decarbonising.
k) Sump – removal and refitting.
l) Oil pump – removal, overhaul and refitting.
m) Crankshaft oil seals – renewal.
n) Engine/transmission mountings – inspection and renewal.
o) Flywheel/driveplate – removal, inspection and refitting.

Note: *It is possible to remove the pistons and connecting rods (after removing the cylinder head and sump) without removing the engine. However, this is not recommended. Work of this nature is more easily and thoroughly completed with the engine on the bench, as described in Chapter 2E.*

2 Compression and leakdown tests – description and interpretation

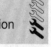

Compression test

Note: *A compression tester suitable for use with diesel engines will be required for this test.*

1 When engine performance is down, or if misfiring occurs which cannot be attributed to the ignition or fuel systems, a compression test can provide diagnostic clues as to the engine's condition. If the test is performed regularly, it can give warning of trouble before any other symptoms become apparent.

3.8 The alignment mark (arrowed) on the crankshaft sprocket should be almost vertical

2 The engine must be fully warmed-up to normal operating temperature, the battery must be fully charged, and you will require the aid of an assistant.

3 Remove the glow plugs as described in Chapter 5C, Section 2, and then fit a compression tester to the No.1 cylinder glow plug hole. The type of tester that screws into the plug thread is preferred. **Note:** *Part of the glow plug removal procedure is to disconnect the fuel injector wiring plugs. As a result of the plugs being disconnected and the engine cranked, faults may be stored in the ECU memory. These must be erased after the compression test.*

4 Have your assistant crank the engine for several seconds on the starter motor. After one or two revolutions, the compression pressure should build-up to a maximum figure and then stabilise. Record the highest reading obtained.

5 Repeat the test on the remaining cylinders, recording the pressure in each.

3.9a Fit the tool to the hole in the oil seal housing (arrowed)...

3.9c Insert a 6 mm locking tool into the camshaft hub...

6 The cause of poor compression is less easy to establish on a diesel engine than on a petrol engine. The effect of introducing oil into the cylinders (wet testing) is not conclusive, because there is a risk that the oil will sit in the recess on the piston crown, instead of passing to the rings. However, the following can be used as a rough guide to diagnosis.

7 All cylinders should produce very similar pressures. Any difference greater than that specified indicates the existence of a fault. Note that the compression should build-up quickly in a healthy engine. Low compression on the first stroke, followed by gradually increasing pressure on successive strokes, indicates worn piston rings. A low compression reading on the first stroke, which does not build-up during successive strokes, indicates leaking valves or a blown head gasket (a cracked head could also be the cause).

8 A low reading from two adjacent cylinders is almost certainly due to the head gasket having blown between them and the presence of coolant in the engine oil will confirm this.

9 On completion, remove the compression tester, and refit the glow plugs, with reference to Chapter 5C, Section 2.

10 Reconnect the wiring to the injector solenoids. Finally, have a VW dealer or suitably equipped specialist erase any fault codes from the ECU memory.

Leakdown test

11 A leakdown test measures the rate at which compressed air fed into the cylinder is lost. It is an alternative to a compression test, and in many ways it is better, since the

3.9b ...so the marks on the tool and sprocket align (arrowed)

3.9d ...with the arrow almost at the 12 o'clock position

escaping air provides easy identification of where pressure loss is occurring (piston rings, valves or head gasket).

12 The equipment required for leakdown testing is unlikely to be available to the home mechanic. If poor compression is suspected, have the test performed by a suitably equipped garage.

3 Engine assembly and valve timing marks – general information and usage

General information

1 TDC is the highest point in the cylinder that each piston reaches as it travels up-and-down when the crankshaft turns. Each piston reaches TDC at the end of the compression stroke and again at the end of the exhaust stroke, but TDC generally refers to piston position on the compression stroke. No 1 piston is at the timing belt end of the engine.

2 Positioning No 1 piston at TDC is an essential part of many procedures, such as timing belt removal and camshaft removal.

3 The design of the engines covered in this Chapter is such that piston-to-valve contact may occur if the camshaft or crankshaft is turned with the timing belt removed. For this reason, it is important to ensure that the camshaft and crankshaft do not move in relation to each other once the timing belt has been removed from the engine.

Setting TDC on No 1 cylinder

Note: *VAG special tool T10050 is required to lock the crankshaft sprocket in the TDC position. Alternatively obtain a tool from automotive tool specialists. Try asttools.co.uk.*

4 Raise the front of the vehicle and support it securely on axle stands (see *Vehicle jacking and support*). Remove the front right-hand road wheel, then release the fasteners and remove the lower section of the wheelarch liner.

5 Remove the auxiliary drivebelt as described in Chapter 1B, Section 25.

6 Remove the crankshaft pulley/vibration damper as described in Section 5.

7 Remove the timing belt outer covers as described in Section 6.

8 Using a spanner or socket on the crankshaft sprocket bolt, turn the crankshaft in the normal direction of rotation (clockwise) until the alignment mark on the face of the sprocket is almost vertical, and the hole in the camshaft sprocket hub aligns with the hole in the cylinder head **(see illustration)**.

9 While in this position it should be possible to insert the VAG tool T10050 to lock the crankshaft, and a 6 mm diameter rod/drill bit to lock the camshafts **(see illustrations)**. **Note:** *The mark on the crankshaft sprocket and the mark on the VAG tool must align, whilst at the same time the shaft of tool must engage in the drilling in the crankshaft oil seal housing.*

10 The engine is now set to TDC on No.1 cylinder.

4.3 Unclip the wiring from the retaining clips

4.4 Squeeze together the sides of the collar to disconnect the breather hose

4.5 Undo the bolts and lift away the camshaft cover

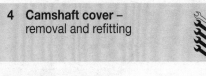

4 Camshaft cover – removal and refitting

Removal

1 Remove the fuel injectors (Chapter 4B, Section 4) and fuel rail (Chapter 4B, Section 11).
2 Remove the timing belt upper cover as described in Section 6.
3 Note their fitted positions, then disconnect the vacuum hoses from the camshaft cover, and release them, and the wiring loom from the retaining clips at the rear of the cover (see illustration).
4 Squeeze together the sides of the collar, and disconnect the breather hose from the camshaft cover (see illustration).
5 Release the wiring from the clips at the rear of the cover, then unscrew the camshaft cover retaining bolts and lift the cover away. If the cover sticks, do not attempt to lever it off – instead free it by working around the cover and tapping it lightly with a soft-faced mallet (see illustration).
6 Recover the camshaft cover gasket. Inspect the gasket carefully, and renew it if damage or deterioration is evident – note that the retaining bolts and seals must be pushed fully through the cover (see illustrations).
7 Clean the mating surfaces of the cylinder head and camshaft cover thoroughly, removing all traces of oil – take care to avoid damaging the surfaces as you do this.

Refitting

8 Refit the camshaft cover by following the removal procedure in reverse, tightening the cover retaining bolts to the specified torque, starting with the centre bolts and working outwards.

5 Crankshaft pulley – removal and refitting

Removal

1 Switch off the ignition and all electrical consumers and remove the ignition key.

4.6a Renew the cover seal if necessary

2 Raise the front right-hand side of the vehicle, and support securely on axle stands (see *Jacking and vehicle support*). Remove the roadwheel.
3 Remove the securing fasteners and withdraw the lower section of the front wheel arch liner.
4 Slacken the bolts securing the crankshaft pulley to the sprocket (see illustration). If necessary, the pulley can be prevented from turning by counterholding with a spanner or socket on the crankshaft sprocket bolt.
5 Remove the auxiliary drivebelt, as described in Chapter 1B, Section 25.
6 Unscrew the bolts securing the pulley to the sprocket, and remove the pulley. Discard the bolts – new ones must be fitted.

Refitting

7 Refit the pulley over the locating peg on the

5.4 Undo the pulley bolts, counterholding it with a socket on the centre sprocket bolt

4.6b Bolts and seals must be pushed fully through the cover before fitting the gasket

crankshaft sprocket, then fit the new pulley securing bolts.
8 Refit and tension the auxiliary drivebelt as described in Chapter 1B, Section 25.
9 Prevent the crankshaft from turning as during removal, then fit the pulley securing bolts, and tighten to the specified torque.
10 Refit the wheel arch liner.
11 Refit the roadwheel and lower the vehicle to the ground.

6 Timing belt covers – removal and refitting

Upper outer cover

1 Pull the engine top cover upwards to release the mountings (see illustration).

6.1 Pull the plastic cover upwards from the mountings

6.2 Unclip the hoses from the retaining clips

6.3a Disconnect the wiring connector...

6.3b ...undo the two retaining bolts...

6.3c ...and withdraw the mounting bracket

6.4 Remove the washer reservoir filler neck

6.5a Undo the filter retaining bolts/nut (arrowed)...

2 Release the hoses from the retaining clips on the right-hand side of the cylinder head and move them to one side **(see illustration)**.

3 Disconnect the wiring plug, undo the retaining bolts, and remove the pressure differential sender (for particulate filter)

including bracket from the top of the engine mounting and move it to one side **(see illustrations)**.

4 Undo the retaining bolt, then twist the washer reservoir filler neck to remove it from engine compartment **(see illustration)**.

5 Undo the retaining bolts and nut, then remove the fuel filter from the engine mounting and move it to one side **(see illustrations)**. The fuel hoses do not need to be disconnected from the filter.

6 To make access easier, undo the retaining

6.5b ...and release the fuel pipe retaining clip

6.6 Move the coolant reservoir to one side

6.7 Disconnect the temperature sensor wiring connector

6.8a Release the rear lower clip (arrowed)...

6.8b ...the two upper front clips (arrowed)...

6.8c ...and manoeuvre the upper cover from place

bolt, disconnect the wiring connector and move the coolant reservoir to one side **(see illustration)**.

7 Disconnect the radiator outlet temperature sensor wiring plug **(see illustration)**.

8 Release the 3 clips and remove the timing belt upper cover **(see illustrations)**.

9 Refitting is a reversal of removal, noting that the lower edge of the upper cover engages with the lower cover.

Lower outer cover

10 Remove the upper cover as described previously.

11 If not already done, remove the crankshaft pulley as described in Section 5.

12 Unscrew the five bolts securing the lower cover, and remove it **(see illustrations)**.

13 Refitting is a reversal of removal; noting that the upper edge of the lower cover engages with the upper cover.

Rear cover

14 Remove the timing belt, tensioner and sprockets as described in Section 7 and Section 8.

15 Undo the retaining bolt and remove the rear hub cover from the end of the camshaft.

16 Slacken and withdraw the retaining bolts and lift the timing belt inner cover from the studs on the end of the engine, and remove it from the engine compartment **(see**

7.0 Two types of tensioner Type (A) and type (B)

(A) Roller tensions clockwise
(B) Roller tensions anti-clockwise

6.12a Undo the lower cover retaining bolts (arrowed)

6.12b ...and manoeuvre the lower cover from place

16.16a Remove the retaining bolts...

16.16b ...and remove the rear cover

illustrations). It may be required to remove the coolant pump (Chapter 3, Section 7), before the rear cover can be removed.

17 Refitting is a reversal of removal.

7 Timing belt – removal, inspection and refitting

Note: *There are two types of tensioner fitted to this engine and they are not interchangeable* **(see illustration)**. *Check to see which type is fitted before removing the timing belt. Type A tensioner requires a locking pin for installation and it tensions the belt by rotating clockwise. Type B tensioner does not require a locking pin for installation and it tensions the belt by rotating anti-clockwise. See text.*

Removal

1 The primary function of the toothed timing

7.4 Slacken the sprocket-to-hub bolts (arrowed)

belt is to drive the camshaft, but it also drives the coolant pump and high-pressure fuel pump. Should the belt slip or break in service, the valve timing will be disturbed and piston-to-valve contact may occur, resulting in serious engine damage. For this reason, it is important that the timing belt is tensioned correctly, and inspected regularly for signs of wear or deterioration.

2 Switch off the ignition and all electrical consumers and remove the ignition key.

3 Set the engine to TDC on No. 1 cylinder as described in Section 3.

4 Slacken the three bolts securing the sprocket to the camshaft hub by 90° **(see illustration)**.

5 Slacken the three bolts securing the sprocket to the high-pressure fuel pump by 90° **(see illustration)**.

Type A tensioner

6 Insert a suitable Allen key into the tensioner

7.5 Slacken the high-pressure fuel pump sprocket bolts (arrowed)

7.6 Insert an Allen key, slacken the nut, and rotate the hub anti-clockwise until a 2 mm rod/drill bit (arrowed) can be inserted to lock the hub to the pulley

7.7 Rotate the tensioner hub clockwise until it hits the stop

hub, then slacken the retaining nut and rotate the tensioner hub anti-clockwise until it can be locked in place using a 2.0 m pin/drill bit **(see illustration)**.

7 Leaving the pin in place, now rotate the tensioner hub clockwise to the stop, and hand-tighten the retaining nut **(see illustration)**.

Type B tensioner

8 Insert a suitable Allen key into the tensioner hub, then slacken the retaining nut and rotate the tensioner hub clockwise, until the tensioner hub is loosened. When in position hand-tighten the retaining nut.

All engines

9 If the original timing belt is to be refitted, mark the running direction of the belt, to ensure correct refitting.

Caution: If the belt appears to be in good condition and can be re-used, it is essential that it is refitted the same way around, otherwise accelerated wear will result, leading to premature failure.

10 Slide the belt from the sprockets, taking care not to twist or kink the belt excessively if it is to be re-used.

Inspection

11 Examine the belt for evidence of contamination by coolant or lubricant. If this is the case, find the source of the contamination before progressing any further. Check the belt for signs of wear or damage, particularly around the leading edges of the belt teeth. Renew the belt if its condition is in doubt; the cost of belt renewal is negligible compared with potential cost of the engine repairs, should the belt fail in service. The belt must be renewed if it has covered the mileage given in Chapter 1B, however, if it has covered less, it is prudent to renew it regardless of condition, as a precautionary measure.

12 If the timing belt is not going to be refitted for some time, it is a wise precaution to hang a warning label on the steering wheel, to remind yourself (and others) not to attempt to start the engine. Have the battery disconnected to prevent any engine damage.

13 If the tensioner roller is to be renewed, the engine mounting will need to be removed, as described in Section 16. Then the tensioner removed as described in Section 8.

Refitting

14 Ensure that the crankshaft and camshaft are still set to TDC on No 1 cylinder, as described in Section 3. The camshaft sprocket bolts should be renewed, and slackened at this point.

15 Renew the high-pressure fuel pump sprocket bolts one at a time. They should also be slackened.

16 Using a screwdriver on the bolts heads, rotate the high-pressure fuel pump clockwise until a 6.0 mm locking pin/drill bit can be inserted into the housing adjacent to the sprocket, locking the pump in place **(see illustration)**.

17 Rotate the camshaft sprocket and high-pressure fuel pump sprocket fully clockwise so that the securing bolts are at the end of the elongated holes **(see illustrations)**.

18 Loop the timing belt loosely under the crankshaft sprocket. Note: *Observe any direction of rotation markings on the belt.*

19 Fit the belt around the tensioner pulley, engage the timing belt teeth with the camshaft sprockets, then manoeuvre it into position around the coolant pump sprocket and the fuel pump sprocket. Make sure that the belt teeth

7.16 Rotate the high-pressure fuel pump clockwise until a 6 mm drill bit/rod can be inserted into the housing and hub (arrowed)

7.17a Rotate the sprockets fully clockwise until the fuel pump sprocket...

7.17b ...and camshaft sprocket bolts are at the end of the elongated holes

7.20 Timing belt routing

7.21a Rotate the tensioner clockwise...

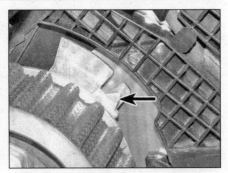

7.21b ...until the pointer (arrowed) is just past the gap in the base plate

7.22 Turn the tensioner anti-clockwise and secure the retaining nut

7.23a Counterhold the camshaft sprocket...

7.23b ...and the pump sprocket, while the bolts are tightened

seat correctly on the sprockets. **Note:** *Slight adjustment to the position of the camshaft sprocket may be necessary to achieve this. Avoid bending the belt back on itself or twisting it excessively as you do this.*
20 Finally, fit the belt around the idler roller (**see illustration**). Ensure that any slack in the belt is in the section of belt that passes over the tensioner roller.

Type A tensioner

21 Loosen the timing belt tensioner securing nut, and pull out the tensioner locking pin. Turn the tensioner clockwise with an Allen key until the pointer is just past the middle of the gap in the tensioner base plate (**see illustrations**). With the tensioner held in this position, tighten the securing nut to the specified torque and angle.

Type B tensioner

22 Loosen the timing belt tensioner securing nut, and turn the tensioner anti-clockwise with an Allen key until the pointer is just past the middle of the gap in the tensioner base plate (**see illustration**). With the tensioner held in this position, tighten the securing nut to the specified torque and angle.

All engines

23 Counterhold the camshaft sprocket and fuel pump sprocket with a home made tool to prevent any rotation, and then tighten the camshaft sprocket and fuel pump sprocket bolts to 20 Nm (**see illustrations**).
24 Remove the sprockets' locking tools and the crankshaft locking tool (**see illustrations**).

25 Using a spanner or wrench and socket on the crankshaft pulley centre bolt, rotate the crankshaft clockwise through two complete revolutions. Reset the engine to TDC on No.1 cylinder, with reference to Section 3 and refit the crankshaft locking tool.
26 Check that the tensioner roller indicator arm is centred, or within a maximum of 5 mm to the right of the notch in the base plate (**see illustration**). If not, hold the tensioner hub stationary with an Allen key, slacken the retaining nut and position the arm in the centre of the notch. Tighten the retaining nut to the specified torque. Remove the Allen key.
27 Check that the camshaft sprocket locking pin can still be inserted. **Note:** *It's very difficult to align the locking point of the fuel pump*

7.24a Remove the upper locking pins...

7.24b ...and crankshaft locking tool

7.26 Check the pointer (arrowed) is centred or within 5mm to the right of the gap in the base plate

7.27 Slight misalignment of the pump sprocket timing hole (arrowed) is acceptable

hub again **(see illustration)**. *However, a slight misalignment of holes will not affect engine performance.*

28 If the camshaft sprocket locking pin cannot be inserted, pull the crankshaft locking tool slight away from the engine, and rotate the crankshaft *anti-clockwise* slightly past TDC. Now slowly rotate the crankshaft clockwise until the camshaft sprocket locking tool can be inserted.

29 If the locating pin of the crankshaft locking tool is to the left of the corresponding hole, slacken the camshaft sprocket bolts, slowly rotate the crankshaft clockwise until the locking tool can be fully inserted. Tighten the camshaft sprocket bolts to 20 Nm.

30 If the locating pin of the crankshaft locking tool is to the right of the corresponding hole, slacken the camshaft sprocket bolts, rotate the crankshaft anti-clockwise slightly until the

pin is to the left of the hole, then slowly rotate it clockwise until the lock tool can be fully inserted. Tighten the camshaft sprocket bolts to 20 Nm.

31 Remove the crankshaft and camshaft locking tools, then rotate the crankshaft 2 complete revolutions clockwise and check the locking tools can be reinserted. If necessary, repeat the adjustment procedure described previously.

32 Tighten the camshaft and fuel pump sprocket bolts to the specified torque.

33 The remainder of refitting is a reversal of removal.

8 Timing belt tensioner and sprockets – removal and refitting

Timing belt tensioner

Removal

1 In order to remove the timing belt tensioner, then engine mounting bracket must first be removed. Either support the engine from above using a crossbeam or an engine hoist or support if from underneath with a trolley jack and block of wood.

2 Remove the timing belt as described in Section 7.

3 Undo the bolts and remove the right-hand engine mounting.

4 Undo the bolt securing the coolant pipe to the mounting bracket **(see illustration)**.

5 Working in the wheelarch area, undo the nut securing the lower end of the coolant pipe.

6 Undo the 3 retaining bolts and remove the engine mounting bracket **(see illustration)**.

7 Unscrew the timing belt tensioner nut, and remove the tensioner from the engine.

Refitting

8 When refitting the tensioner to the engine, ensure that the lug on the tensioner backplate engages with the corresponding cut-out in the rear timing belt cover, then refit the tensioner nut **(see illustration)**.

9 The remainder of refitting is a reversal of removal.

Idler pulleys

Removal

10 Remove the timing belt as described in Section 7.

11 Unscrew the relevant idler pulley/roller securing bolt/nut, and then withdraw the pulley **(see illustration)**.

Refitting

12 Refit the pulley and tighten the securing bolt or nut to the specified torque. **Note:** *Renew the large roller/pulley retaining bolt (where applicable).*

13 Refit and tension the timing belt as described in Section 7.

Crankshaft sprocket

Note: *A new crankshaft sprocket securing bolt must be used on refitting.*

Removal

14 Remove the timing belt as described in Section 7.

15 The sprocket securing bolt must now be slackened, and the crankshaft must be prevented from turning as the sprocket bolt is unscrewed. To hold the sprocket, make up a suitable tool, and screw it to the sprocket using two bolts screwed into two of the crankshaft pulley bolt holes.

16 Hold the sprocket using the tool, then slacken the sprocket securing bolt. Take care, as the bolt is very tight. Do not allow the crankshaft to turn as the bolt is slackened.

17 Unscrew the bolt, and slide the sprocket from the end of the crankshaft, noting which way round the sprocket's raised boss is fitted. If required, use a puller to withdraw the sprocket from the end of the crankshaft **(see illustration)**.

8.4 Coolant pipe upper mounting bolt and lower mounting nut (arrowed)

8.6 Engine mounting bracket bolts (arrowed)

8.8 Ensure the lug on the backplate engages with the cut-out in the timing belt cover (arrowed)

8.11 Timing belt idler pulleys

8.17 Using a puller to remove the crankshaft sprocket

8.27 Fabricate a home made tool to counterhold the hub. Undo the bolt...

8.28 ...and slide the hub from the camshaft

8.29 Ensure the integral key aligns with the keyway in the camshaft (arrowed)

Refitting

18 Commence refitting by positioning the sprocket on the end of the crankshaft.
19 Fit a new sprocket securing bolt, then counterhold the sprocket using the method employed on removal, and tighten the bolt to the specified torque in the two stages given in the Specifications.
20 Refit the timing belt as described in Section 7.

Camshaft sprocket

Removal

21 Remove the timing belt as described in Section 7, then rotate the crankshaft 90° anti-clockwise to prevent any accidental piston-to-valve contact.
22 Unscrew and remove the three retaining bolts and remove the camshaft sprocket from the camshaft hub.

Refitting

23 Refit the sprocket ensuring that it is fitted the correct way round, as noted before removal, then insert the new sprocket bolts, and tighten by hand only at this stage.
24 If the crankshaft has been turned, turn the crankshaft clockwise 90° back to TDC.
25 Refit and tension the timing belt as described in Section 7.

Camshaft hub

Note: *VAG technicians use special tool T10051 to counterhold the hub, however it is possible to fabricate a suitable alternative.*

Removal

26 Remove the camshaft sprocket as described previously in this Section.
27 Engage special tool T10051 with the three locating holes in the face of the hub to prevent the hub from turning. If this tool is not available, fabricate a suitable alternative. Whilst holding the tool, undo the central hub retaining bolt about two turns **(see illustration)**.
28 Slide the hub from the camshaft. If necessary, attach VW tool T10052 (or a similar three-legged puller) to the hub, and evenly tighten the puller until the hub is free of the camshaft taper **(see illustration)**.

Refitting

29 Ensure that the camshaft taper and the hub centre is clean and dry, locate the hub on the taper, noting that the built-in key in the hub taper must align with the keyway in the camshaft taper **(see illustration)**.
30 Hold the hub in this position with tool T10051 (or similar home-made tool), and tighten the central bolt to the specified torque.
31 Refit the camshaft sprocket as described previously in this Section.

Coolant pump sprocket

32 The coolant pump sprocket is integral with the coolant pump. Refer to Chapter 3 for details of coolant pump removal.

9 Camshaft and hydraulic tappets – removal, inspection and refitting

Note: *A new camshaft oil seal(s) will be required on refitting. VW removal tool T40094 (or similar tool) will be required to refit the camshafts – this is necessary to prevent damage to the retaining frame and cylinder head as the camshafts are refitted.*

Removal

1 With the timing set at TDC, remove the camshaft hub (see Section 8).
2 Remove the camshaft cover (see Section 4).
3 Remove the brake vacuum pump as described in Chapter 9, Section 24.

4 If the camshafts are not going to be renewed, use two flat pieces of metal flat bar and cable ties and secure the two camshafts to the retaining frame **(see illustrations)**. Progressively unscrew the camshaft retaining frame bolts in the reverse of the sequence shown in illustration 9.27, and carefully remove the retaining frame, complete with camshafts. Remove the oil seal from the end of the camshaft and discard it – a new one will be required for refitting.
5 If the camshafts are going to be renewed, progressively unscrew the camshaft retaining frame bolts in the reverse of the sequence shown in illustration 9.27, and carefully remove the retaining frame. Then carefully lift the camshafts from the cylinder head, keeping them identified for location. Remove the oil seal from the end of the camshaft and discard it – a new one will be required for refitting.
6 Lift the rocker arms and hydraulic tappets from place. Store the rockers and tappets in a container with numbered compartments to ensure they are refitted to their correct locations. It is recommended that the tappets are kept immersed in oil for the period they are removed from the cylinder head.

Inspection

7 If the camshafts are still secured to the retaining frame, mark the two sprockets in relation with each other, then cut the cable ties to remove them from the frame **(see**

9.4a Using flat metal bar and cable ties to secure the camshafts...

9.4b ...to the upper ladder frame for removal

9.7 Make alignment marks for the position of the sprockets

9.10 Check the tappets for wear

9.12 VW special tool no. T40094 shown

illustration). With the camshafts removed, examine the retaining frame and the bearing locations in the cylinder head for signs of obvious wear or pitting. If evident, a new cylinder head will probably be required. Also check that the oil supply holes in the cylinder head are free from obstructions.

8 Visually inspect the camshafts for evidence of wear on the surfaces of the lobes and journals. Normally their surfaces should be smooth and have a dull shine; look for scoring, erosion or pitting and areas that appear highly polished, indicating excessive wear. Accelerated wear will occur once the hardened exterior of the camshaft has been damaged, so always renew worn items. **Note:** *If these symptoms are visible on the tips of the camshaft lobes, check the corresponding rocker arm, as it will probably be worn as well.*

9 If the machined surfaces of the camshaft appear discoloured or blued, it is likely that it has been overheated at some point, probably due to inadequate lubrication. This may have distorted the shaft, so have the camshaft runout and endfloat checked by an automotive engine reconditioning specialist.

10 Inspect the hydraulic tappets for obvious signs of wear or damage (see illustration), and renew if necessary. Check that the oil holes in the tappets are free from obstructions.

Refitting

11 Oil the rocker arms and hydraulic tappets, and then refit them to their original positions.

 Warning: After fitting hydraulic tappets, wait a minimum of 30 minutes (or preferably, leave overnight) before starting the

engine; to allow the tappets time to settle, otherwise the valve heads will strike the pistons.

Using VW special tool No.T40094

12 If the camshafts were removed from the retaining frame, use the VW special tool No.T40094, as shown in the following procedures (see illustration).

13 Position the inlet camshaft as shown with the cylinder head bolt indents facing outwards, then slide the end support into the slot in the end of the camshaft (see illustrations).

14 Position the exhaust camshaft on the supports, again with the cylinder head bolt indents facing outwards, and then fit the locating clamp into the slot in the end of the camshaft (see illustrations).

15 Fit the VW clamping tool No.T40096 to the double gear on the exhaust camshaft, tightening the knurled thumb wheel until the faces of the gear teeth are in alignment (see illustration). Note some camshafts only have a single sprocket, so will not require this procedure.

16 Slide the exhaust camshaft towards the inlet camshaft until the gear teeth engage (see illustration).

17 Ensure the gasket faces of the retaining frame are clean, then apply a smear of clean engine oil to the bearing surfaces and lower the frame into position over the camshafts (see illustrations). Ensure the bearing surfaces locate correctly on the camshafts.

18 Fit the clamping tool No.T40095 over the camshafts and frame, and tighten the

9.13a Position the inlet camshaft on the tool with the head bolt indent facing outwards...

9.13b ...then slide the end of the special tool, in to the slot in the end of the camshaft

9.14a Position the exhaust camshaft on the tool with the head bolt indent facing outwards...

9.14b ...then fit special tool clamp into the slot in the end of the exhaust camshaft

9.15 Tighten the thumbwheel to align the gear teeth. Ensure the clamping jaw with the arrow is seated on the wider gear

9.16 Slide the exhaust camshaft to the inlet camshaft until the teeth are in mesh

9.17a Lubricate the bearing mountings...

9.17b ...and fit the upper ladder frame to the camshafts

9.18 Secure the camshafts in place in the frame using tool No. T40095

9.19a Slide the locking tool out from the end of the inlet camshaft...

9.19b ...and remove the locking clamp from the end of the exhaust camshaft

thumbwheels to hold the camshafts in position in the frame (see illustration).

19 Slide out locking clamps from each end of the camshafts (see illustrations), and then lift the camshafts, retaining frame and clamping tool from the VW special tool no. 40094.

Without VW special tool

20 Ensure the gasket faces of the retaining frame are clean, then apply a smear of clean engine oil to the bearing surfaces and turn it upside down on a clean surface.

21 Position the camshafts on the retaining frame with the cylinder head bolt indents facing outwards. Align the marks made on the camshaft sprockets on removal (see illustration 9.7).

22 If a double gear is fitted to the exhaust camshaft, fit the VW clamping tool No.T40096 (or similar) to align the faces of the teeth. If the VW clamping tool is not available use two flat bladed screwdrivers and a pair of pliers, this will need an assistant to keep firm pressure on the camshafts to make sure they locate in the retaining frame correctly (see illustrations). Note some camshafts only have a single sprocket, so will not require this procedure.

23 With the marks on the sprockets aligned and the cylinder head bolt indents facing outwards, the slot in the end of the inlet camshaft (that drives the vacuum pump) should be horizontal and the slot in the end of the exhaust camshaft (that locates the timing belt sprocket) should be at the top when fitted (see illustrations).

24 With the camshafts correctly in position, ensuring the camshafts locate correctly in the

bearing surfaces on the retaining frame, use two flat pieces of metal flat bar and cable ties to secure them in position (see illustration). *Caution: Make sure the camshafts are located correctly in the bearing surfaces*

on the retaining frame, otherwise damage can occur, and this could damage the retaining frame when tightening down onto the cylinder head. The retaining frame is matched to the cylinder head and can only

9.22a VW special tool for aligning teeth on sprocket

9.22b Using two flat bladed screwdrivers and a pair of pliers to align teeth

9.23a inlet camshaft slot needs to be horizontal

9.23b Slot in end of exhaust camshaft should be at the 12 o'clock position

9.24 Camshafts are secured to the ladder frame with two pieces of flat bar and cable ties

9.25a Apply a 2.0 mm thick bead of sealant…

9.25b …to the area shown by the thick, black line, taking care not to block the oil holes (arrowed)

9.26a Fit a new seal/end cap to the cylinder head

9.26b Check that the locating dowels are in place

9.27 Camshaft retaining frame bolt tightening sequence

be purchased with a new cylinder head. If there is any doubt, then the VW special tool should be used, see previous refitting procedure.

All

25 Ensure the sealing surfaces of the cylinder head are clean, and then apply a 2.0 mm wide bead of sealant (D 176 501 A1 or equivalent) as shown. Take care not to apply too much sealant, ensuring the oil holes supply holes are not blocked **(see illustrations)**.

26 Fit a new sealing cap to the timing belt end of the cylinder head and make sure the locating dowels are fitted to the cylinder head **(see illustrations)**.

27 Apply a smear of clean engine oil to the bearing surfaces and place the camshafts, frame and clamping tool in place on the cylinder head. Progressively, carefully, hand tighten the frame retaining bolts in the sequence shown **(see illustration)**, until the retaining frame makes contact with the cylinder head over the complete surface, then tighten the bolts to the specified torque, again in the correct sequence.

28 Remove the gear aligning tool (T40096) and the clamping tool (T40095), or the metal flat bars and cable ties from the top of the camshaft retaining frame **(see illustration)**.

29 Renew the camshaft oil seal as described in Section 10.

30 The remainder of refitting is a reversal of removal.

10 Camshaft oil seals – renewal

Right-hand oil seal

1 Remove the camshaft sprocket and hub, as described in Section 8.

2 Drill two small holes into the existing oil seal, diagonally opposite each other. Take great care to avoid drilling through into the seal housing or camshaft sealing surface. Thread two self-tapping screws into the holes, and using a pair of pliers, pull on the heads of the screws to extract the oil seal **(see illustration)**.

9.28 Remove the cable ties and flat bar from the top of the ladder frame

10.2 Screw-in a self-tapping screw, then pull the screw and seal from place

10.4 Using a plastic sleeve to slide seal over end of camshaft

10.5 Note some seals have 'OUTSIDE' (arrowed) to show fitted position

3 Clean out the seal housing and the sealing surface of the camshaft by wiping it with a lint-free cloth. Remove any swarf or burrs that may cause the seal to leak.

4 Do not lubricate the lip and outer edge of the new oil seal, push it over the camshaft until it is positioned in place above it's housing. To prevent damage to the sealing lips, wrap some adhesive tape around the end of the camshaft **(see illustration)**.

5 Using a hammer and a socket of suitable diameter, drive the seal squarely into its housing. Make sure the seal is fitted the correct way around, some have 'OUTSIDE' stamped on the seal **(see illustration)**. Note: Select a socket that bears only on the hard outer surface of the seal, not the inner lip that can easily be damaged.

6 Refit the camshaft sprocket and its hub, as described in Section 8.

Left-hand oil seal

7 The left-hand camshaft oil seal is formed by the brake vacuum pump seal. Refer to Chapter 9, Section 24, for details of brake vacuum pump removal and refitting.

11 Cylinder head – removal, inspection and refitting

Note: *The cylinder head must be removed with the engine cold. New cylinder head bolts and a new cylinder head gasket will be required on*

refitting, and suitable studs will be required to guide the cylinder head into position – see text.

Removal

1 Remove the battery and battery tray, as described in Chapter 5A, Section 3.

2 Drain the cooling system (Chapter 1B, Section 30) and engine oil (Chapter 1B, Section 3).

3 Pull the plastic cover on the top of the engine upwards to release it from its mountings.

4 Remove the air filter housing as described in Chapter 4B, Section 2.

5 Remove the radiator cooling fan(s) and shroud as described in Chapter 3, Section 5.

6 Undo the bolts and remove the air hose/duct from the intercooler to the turbocharger. Release the wiring looms from the clips as necessary to enable the duct to be manoeuvred from place.

7 Remove the camshaft cover as described in Section 4.

8 Remove the camshaft sprocket and hub as described in Section 8.

9 Remove the inlet manifold as described in Chapter 4B, Section 5.

10 Undo the retaining bolts, and remove the charge air pipe from the turbocharger **(see illustration)**.

11 Remove the EGR pipes from the cylinder head as described in Chapter 4D, Section 3.

12 Remove the exhaust manifold/turbocharger, as described in Chapter 4D, Section 5.

13 There is no need to completely remove the front pipe/particulate filter from the vehicle. Slacken the Allen bolt and release the clamp securing the diesel particulate filter/catalytic converter to the turbocharger, then undo the bolts/nuts securing the brackets to the cylinder block/head and lay the filter/converter to one side.

14 Apply a little lubrication spray to the rubber sleeve, pull up the pipe from the vacuum pump, then undo the 4 retaining bolts and remove the vacuum pump from the left-hand end of the cylinder head **(see illustration)**. Renew the pump-to-cylinder head seal/gasket (Chapter 9, Section 24).

15 Disconnect the coolant temperature sensor wiring plug at the left-hand end of the cylinder head, and release the wiring loom from any retaining clips.

16 Disconnect the gearchange cables from the levers on the transmission as described in Chapter 7A, Section 2 (manual transmission) or Chapter 7B, Section 4 (DSG transmission).

17 Undo the bolts/nut, securing the gearchange bracket to the top of the transmission. Move the bracket and cables to one side.

18 Note their fitted locations, then release the clamps and disconnect the various coolant hoses from the cylinder head.

19 Disconnect the wiring connector from the oil pressure switch, undo the bolt securing the pipe bracket at the left-hand end of the cylinder head **(see illustrations)**, and the bolt

11.10 Remove the charge air pipe from the turbocharger

11.14 Disconnect the vacuum pipe

11.19a Disconnect the oil pressure switch wiring connector

11.19b Undo the retaining bolt/screw and remove the lifting bracket

11.20 Undo the bolt (arrowed) securing the timing belt guard

11.21 Undo the cylinder head bolts using a M12 multi-splined (12 pointed star) tool

securing the lifting bracket on the rear of the head.

20 Undo the bolt securing the timing belt guard adjacent to the timing belt tensioner, and the bolt securing the camshaft position sensor, then remove the tensioner retaining nut **(see illustration)**.

21 Using an M12 multi-splined tool (12 pointed star), undo the cylinder head bolts, working from the outside-in, evenly and gradually **(see illustration)**. Remove the bolts and recover the washers. Check that nothing remains connected, and starting at the gearbox side, lift the cylinder head from the engine block, sliding the belt tensioner from the mounting stud as the cylinder head is removed. Seek assistance if possible, as it is a heavy assembly, especially as it is being removed complete with the manifolds.

22 Remove the gasket from the top of the block, noting the locating dowels. If the dowels are a loose fit, remove them and store them with the head for safekeeping. Do not discard the gasket yet – it will be needed for identification purposes.

Inspection

23 Dismantling and inspection of the cylinder head is covered in Part Chapter 2E.

Cylinder head gasket selection

Note: *A dial test indicator (DTI) will be required for this operation.*

24 Examine the old cylinder head gasket for manufacturer's identification markings **(see**

illustration). These will be in the form of holes, and a part number on the edge of the gasket. Unless new pistons have been fitted, the new cylinder head gasket must be of the same type as the old one.

25 If new piston assemblies have been fitted as part of an engine overhaul, or if a new short engine is to be fitted, the projection of the piston crowns above the cylinder head mating face of the cylinder block at TDC must be measured. This measurement is used to determine the thickness of the new cylinder head gasket required.

26 Anchor a dial test indicator (DTI) to the top face (cylinder head gasket mating face) of the cylinder block, and zero the gauge on the gasket mating face.

27 Rest the gauge probe on No 1 piston crown, and turn the crankshaft slowly by hand until the piston reaches TDC. Measure and record the maximum piston projection at TDC **(see illustration)**.

28 Repeat the measurement for the remaining pistons, and record the results.

29 If the measurements differ from piston-to-piston, take the highest figure, and use this to determine the thickness of the head gasket required as follows.

Piston projection	Gasket identification (number of holes)
0.91 to 1.00 mm	1
1.01 to 1.10 mm	2
1.11 to 1.20 mm	3

30 Purchase a new gasket according to the results of the measurements.

Refitting

31 The mating faces of the cylinder head and block must be perfectly clean before refitting the head. Use a scraper to remove all traces of gasket and carbon, also clean the tops of the pistons. Take particular care with the aluminium surfaces, as the soft metal is easily damaged.

32 Make sure that debris is not allowed to enter the oil and water passages – this is particularly important for the oil circuit, as carbon could block the oil supply to the camshaft and crankshaft bearings. Using adhesive tape and paper, seal the water, oil and bolt holes in the cylinder block.

33 To prevent carbon entering the gap between the pistons and bores, smear a little grease in the gap. After cleaning a piston, rotate the crankshaft to that the piston moves down the bore, and then wipe out the grease and carbon with a cloth rag. Clean the other piston crowns in the same way.

34 Check the head and block for nicks, deep scratches and other damage. If slight, they may be removed carefully with a file. More serious damage may be repaired by machining, but this is a specialist job.

35 If warpage of the cylinder head is suspected, use a straight-edge to check it for distortion, as described in Chapter 2E, Section 7.

36 Ensure that the cylinder head bolt holes in the crankcase are clean and free of oil. Syringe or soak up any oil left in the bolt holes. This is most important in order that the correct bolt tightening torque can be applied, and to prevent the possibility of the block being cracked by hydraulic pressure when the bolts are tightened.

37 Turn the crankshaft anti-clockwise all the pistons at an equal height, approximately half-way down their bores from the TDC position (see Section 3). This will eliminate any risk of piston-to-valve contact as the cylinder head is refitted.

38 Where applicable, refit the manifolds with reference to Chapters 4B, Section 5 and/or Chapter 4D, Section 5.

39 Ensure that the cylinder head locating dowels are in place in the cylinder block, and then fit the new cylinder head gasket over

11.24 The holes (arrowed) identify the thickness of the cylinder head gasket

11.27 Measure the piston protrusion using a DTI gauge

11.39 Ensure the dowels are in place, then fit the new gasket with the part number uppermost (arrowed)

11.42 Cylinder head bolt tightening sequence

11.44 Use an angle-tightening gauge

the dowels, ensuring that the part number is uppermost **(see illustration)**. Note that VW recommend that the gasket is only removed from its packaging immediately prior to fitting.
40 Lower the cylinder head into position on the gasket, ensuring that it engages correctly over the dowels. Refit the timing belt tensioner as the cylinder head is refitted.
41 Fit the washers in place then fit the new cylinder head bolts to the locations, and screw them in as far as possible by hand. Do not oil the bolt threads.
42 Working progressively, in sequence, tighten all the cylinder head bolts to the specified Stage 1 torque **(see illustration)**.
43 Again working progressively, in sequence, tighten all the cylinder head bolts to the specified Stage 2 torque.
44 Tighten all the cylinder head bolts, in sequence, through the specified Stage 3 angle **(see illustration)**.
45 Finally, tighten all the cylinder head bolts, in sequence, through the specified Stage 4 angle.
46 The remainder of the refitting procedure is a reversal of the removal procedure, noting the following points:
a) Tighten all fasteners to their specified torque where given.
b) Renew all seals and gaskets.
c) Refill the cooling system as described, in Chapter 1B, Section 30.
d) Refill the engine oil, as described in Chapter 1B, Section 3.
e) Ensure all wiring is correctly routed.

f) Run the vehicle and make sure the cooling fans operate when the engine gets up to temperature.

12 Sump –
removal and refitting

Removal

1 Apply the handbrake, then jack up the front of the vehicle and support securely on axle stands (see *Jacking and vehicle support*).
2 Remove the securing screws and withdraw the engine undershield.
3 Drain the engine oil as described in Chapter 1B, Section 3.

12.4 Slacken the two retaining clips - arrowed

12.5b ...and the bolt on the front of the cylinder block...

12.5c ...then disconnect the pressure switch wiring connector

4 Release the retaining clips and remove the air hose from the intercooler outlet to the charge air pipe **(see illustration)**.
5 Undo the retaining bolts, release the clamp and move the charger air pipe from the front of the cylinder block **(see illustrations)**. Disconnect the charger air pressure sensor wiring plug.
6 Disconnect the wiring connector from the oil level/temperature sender in the sump.
7 Release the retaining clips and remove the sump insulation cover from the sump **(see illustrations)**.
8 Unscrew and remove the bolts securing the sump to the cylinder block, and the bolts securing the sump to the transmission casing, then withdraw the sump **(see illustrations)**. If necessary, release the sump by tapping with a soft-faced hammer.

12.5a Undo the retaining bolt on the end of the sump - arrowed...

12.7a Release the two clips (arrowed) at the rear of the sump

12.7b At the front, prise down the centre pin and pull the clip downwards (arrowed)

12.7c Remove the insulation cover from around the sump

H46180

12.10 Apply a bead of sealant to the around the inside of the bolt holes

12.8a Undo the three transmission to sump bolts (arrowed)…

12.8b …and also the four bolts (arrowed), at the transmission end of the sump

Refitting

9 Begin refitting by thoroughly cleaning the mating faces of the sump and cylinder block. Ensure that all traces of old sealant are removed.

10 Ensure that the cylinder block mating face of the sump is free from all traces of old sealant, oil and grease, and then apply a 2.0 to 3.0 mm thick bead of silicone sealant (VW D 176 404 A2 or equivalent) to the sump **(see illustration)**. Note that the sealant should be run around the inside of the bolt holes in the sump. The sump must be fitted within 5 minutes of applying the sealant.

11 Offer the sump up to the cylinder block, then refit the sump-to-cylinder block bolts, and lightly tighten them by hand, working progressively in a diagonal sequence. **Note:** *If the sump is being refitted with the engine*

and transmission separated, make sure that the sump is flush with the flywheel end of the cylinder block.

12 Refit the sump-to-transmission casing bolts, and tighten them lightly, using a socket.

13 Again working in a diagonal sequence, lightly tighten the sump-to-cylinder block bolts, using a socket.

14 Tighten the sump-to-transmission casing bolts to the specified torque.

15 Working in a diagonal sequence, progressively tighten the sump-to-cylinder block bolts to the specified torque.

16 The remainder of refitting is a reversal of removal, noting to allow at least 30 minutes from the time of refitting the sump for the sealant to dry, then refill the engine with oil, with reference to Chapter 1B, Section 3.

13 Oil pump and drive belt – removal, inspection and refitting

Oil pump removal

1 Remove the sump as described in Section 12.

2 Unscrew the flange bolts and remove the oil pick-up pipe/filter from the oil pump **(see illustration)**. Recover the O-ring seal and discard, as a new one will be required for refitting.

3 Unscrew the securing bolt, and remove the oil baffle from the cylinder block **(see illustration)**.

4 Unscrew and remove the mounting bolts, and release the oil pump from the dowels in the crankcase **(see illustration)**. Unhook the oil pump drive sprocket from the belt and withdraw the oil pump and oil pick-up pipe

13.2 Remove the oil pick-up pipe/filter

13.3 Remove the oil baffle plate bolt (which is also one of the oil pump mounting bolts)

13.4 Oil pump mounting bolts - arrowed

from the engine. Note, the bolt holding the baffle plate is also one of the pump mounting bolts.

Oil pump inspection

5 Clean the pump thoroughly, and inspect for signs of damage or wear. If evident, renew the oil pump.

Oil pump refitting

6 Prime the pump with oil by pouring oil into the pick-up pipe aperture while turning the driveshaft.

7 If the drive belt and crankshaft sprocket have been removed, delay refitting them until after the oil pump has been mounted on the cylinder block.

8 Engage the oil pump sprocket with the drive belt, and then locate the oil pump on the dowels. Refit and tighten the mounting bolts to the specified torque.

9 Where applicable, refit the drive belt and crankshaft sprocket using a reversal of the removal procedure.

10 Refit the oil baffle plate, and tighten the securing bolt.

11 Refit the pick-up pipe to the oil pump, using a new O-ring seal, and tighten the securing bolts **(see illustration)**.

12 Refit the sump as described in Section 12.

Oil pump drive belt and sprockets

Note: *VW sealant (D 176 404 A2 or equivalent) will be required to seal the crankshaft oil seal housing on refitting, and it is advisable to fit a new crankshaft oil seal.*

Removal

13 Proceed as described in paragraphs 1 and 2.

14 To remove the belt, remove the timing belt as described in Section 7, then unbolt the crankshaft oil seal housing from the cylinder block, as described in Section 15. Unhook the belt from the sprocket on the end of the crankshaft.

15 The oil pump drive sprocket is a press-fit on the crankshaft, and cannot easily be removed. Consult a VW dealer for advice if the sprocket is worn or damaged.

Inspection

16 It is wise to renew the belt in any case if the engine is to be overhauled, If there is any doubt as to the condition of the belt, renew it.

Refitting

17 If the oil pump has been removed, refit the oil pump as described previously in this Section before refitting the belt and sprocket.

18 Engage the oil pump sprocket with the belt, then engage the belt with the crankshaft sprocket.

19 Fit a new crankshaft oil seal to the housing, and refit the housing as described in Section 15.

20 Where applicable, refit the oil baffle and pick-up pipe, and tighten the securing bolts.

21 Refit the sump as described in Section 12.

14 Flywheel – removal, inspection and refitting

Removal

1 On manual gearbox models, remove the gearbox (see Chapter 7A, Section 3) and clutch (see Chapter 6, Section 6).

2 On semi-automatic (DSG) transmission models, remove the transmission as described in Chapter 7B, Section 2.

3 The flywheel can only be fitted in one position due to the offset of the flywheel mounting holes in the end of the crankshaft **(see illustration)**. Note, manual models are fitted with a dual-mass flywheel.

4 Rotate the outside of the dual-mass flywheel so that the bolts align with the holes (if necessary).

5 Unscrew the bolts and remove the flywheel. Using a locking tool, counter-hold the flywheel to prevent it from turning **(see illustration)**. Discard the bolts, as new ones must be fitted. **Note:** *In order not to damage the flywheel, do not allow the bolt heads to make contact with the flywheel during the unscrewing procedure.*

Inspection

6 Check the dual-mass flywheel for wear and damage. Examine the starter ring gear for excessive wear to the teeth. If the driveplate or its ring gear are damaged, the complete driveplate must be renewed. The flywheel ring gear, however, may be renewed separately

14.3 Flywheel bolts are offset and can only be fitted in one position - DSG transmission (0AM) shown

14.7a Flywheel warpage check – see text

13.11 Fit a new seal to the end of the oil pick-up pipe

from the flywheel, but the work should be entrusted to a VW dealer. If the clutch friction face is discoloured or scored excessively, it may be possible to regrind it, but this work should also be entrusted to a VW dealer.

7 The following are guidelines only, but should indicate whether professional inspection is necessary. The dual-mass flywheel should be checked as follows:

Warpage: Place a straight edge across the face of the drive surface, and check by trying to insert a feeler gauge between the straight edge and the drive surface **(see illustration)**. The flywheel will normally warp like a bowl – ie. Higher on the outer edge. If the warpage is more than 0.40 mm, the flywheel may need replacing.

Free rotational movement: This is the distance the drive surface of the flywheel can be turned independently of the flywheel primary element, using finger effort alone.

14.5 Use a locking tool to counterhold the flywheel

14.7b Flywheel free rotational movement check alignment marks – see text

14.7c Flywheel lateral movement check marks – see text

Move the drive surface in one direction and make a mark where the locating pin aligns with the flywheel edge. Move the drive surface in the other direction (finger pressure only) and make another mark **(see illustration)**. The total of free movement should not exceed 20.0 mm. If it's more, the flywheel may need replacing.

Total rotational movement: This is the total distance the drive surface can be turned independently of the flywheel primary element. Insert two bolts into the clutch pressure plate/damper unit mounting holes, and with the crankshaft/flywheel held stationary, use a lever/pry bar between the bolts and use some effort to move the drive surface fully in one direction – make a mark where the locating pin aligns with the flywheel edge. Now force the drive surface fully in the opposite direction, and make another mark. The total rotational movement should not exceed 44.00 mm. If it does, have the flywheel professionally inspected.

Lateral movement: The lateral movement (up and down) of the drive surface in relation to the primary element of the flywheel, should not exceed 2.0 mm. If it does, the flywheel may need replacing. This can be checked by pressing the drive surface down on one side into the flywheel (flywheel horizontal) and making an alignment mark between the drive surface and the inner edge of the primary element. Now press down on the opposite side of the drive surface, and make another mark above the original one. The difference between the two marks is the lateral movement **(see illustration)**.

14.8 Use new bolts when refitting

There should be no cracks in the drive surface of the flywheel. If cracks are evident, the flywheel may need replacing.

Refitting

8 Refitting is a reversal of removal. Use new bolts when refitting the flywheel or driveplate **(see illustration)**, and coat the threads of the bolts (if not already coated with locking compound) with locking fluid before inserting them. Tighten them to the specified torque.

15 Crankshaft oil seals – renewal

Note: *The oil seals are a PTFE (Teflon) type and are fitted dry, without using any grease or oil. These have a wider sealing lip and have been introduced instead of the coil spring type oil seal.*

Timing belt end oil seal

1 Remove the timing belt as described in Section 7, and the crankshaft sprocket with reference to Section 8.

2 To remove the seal without removing the housing, drill two small holes diagonally opposite each other, insert self-tapping screws, and pull on the heads of the screws with pliers **(see illustration)**.

3 Alternatively, to remove the oil seal complete with its housing, proceed as follows.

a) *Remove the sump as described in Section 12. This is necessary to ensure a satisfactory seal between the sump and oil seal housing on refitting.*

b) *Unbolt and remove the oil seal housing.*

c) *Working on the bench, lever the oil seal from the housing using a suitable screwdriver. Take care not to damage the seal seating in the housing.*

4 Thoroughly clean the oil seal seating in the housing.

5 Wind a length of tape around the end of the crankshaft (or a plastic sleeve) to protect the oil seal lips as the seal (and housing, where applicable) is fitted **(see illustration)**.

6 Fit a new oil seal to the housing, pressing or driving it into position using a socket or tube of suitable diameter. Ensure that the socket or tube bears only on the hard outer ring of the seal, and take care not to damage the seal lips. Press or drive the seal into position until it is seated on the shoulder in the housing **(see illustration)**. Make sure that the closed end of the seal is facing outwards.

7 If the oil seal housing has been removed, proceed as follows, otherwise proceed to paragraph 11.

8 Clean all traces of old sealant from the crankshaft oil seal housing and the cylinder block, then coat the cylinder block mating faces of the oil seal housing with a 2.0 to 3.0 mm thick bead of silicone sealant (VW D 176 404 A2, or equivalent). Note that the seal housing must be refitted within 5 minutes of applying the sealant.

Caution: DO NOT put excessive amounts of sealant onto the housing as it may get into the sump and block the oil pick-up pipe.

9 Refit the oil seal housing, and tighten the bolts progressively to the specified torque.

10 Refit the sump as described in Section 12.

11 Refit the crankshaft sprocket with reference to Section 8, and the timing belt as described in Section 7.

Flywheel end oil seal

Note: *In these engines, the seal, sealing flange and sender wheel are a complete unit. Special tools are required to refit the sealing flange, and press the sender wheel onto the end of the crankshaft. It is not possible to accurately fit these parts without the tools, which may be available from VW (part no. T10134) and are available from aftermarket automotive tool specialists. E.g. Laser tools).*

15.2 Pull the screw and seal from place using pliers

15.5 Using a plastic sleeve to slide the seal over the end of the crankshaft

15.6 Carefully tap the seal into position

15.12a Remove the intermediate plate from the dowels...

15.12b ...and from behind the top of the crankshaft seal housing

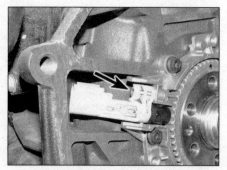

15.13a Undo the crankshaft speed sensor retaining bolt - arrowed

15.13b Sealing flange bolts (arrowed)

15.14a Screw in three 6 x 35 mm bolts...

15.14b ...and draw the sealing flange and sender wheel from place

12 Remove the flywheel as described in Section 14, then prise the intermediate plate from the locating dowels on the cylinder block and unhook it from behind the top of the seal housing **(see illustrations)**.

13 Undo the bolt securing the crankshaft speed sensor and remove it from the seal housing, then undo the bolts securing the sealing flange to the cylinder block **(see illustrations)**.

14 Insert three 6 x 35 mm bolts into the threaded holes in the sealing flange. Tighten the bolts gradually and evenly, and press the sealing flange, and sender wheel from the crankshaft/cylinder block **(see illustrations)**. The seal, sender wheel and sealing flange are supplied as a complete unit.

15 Ensure the mating face of the cylinder block is clean and free from debris. The new sealing flange/seal/sender wheel assembly is supplied with a sealing lip support ring, which serves as a fitting sleeve, and must not be removed prior to installation. Equally, the sender wheel must not be separated from the assembly.

16 If using the VW tool, proceed as follows. If using an aftermarket tool specialist's product, follow the instructions supplied with the tool. Rotate the large spindle nut until it's level with the end of the clamping surface of the spindle, then clamp the spindle in a vice **(see illustrations)**.

17 Press the tool housing downwards until it rests on the nut and washer. Rotate the nut until the inner part of the tool is at the same height as the housing **(see illustrations)**.

18 Remove the seal securing clip. The hole on the sender wheel must align with the marking on the sealing flange **(see illustrations)**.

19 Place the flange outer side down on a

clean, flat surface, then press the seal guide fitting sleeve (supplied ready fitted), housing, and sender wheel downwards until all the components are flat on the surface. In this

15.16a Rotate the nut until its level with the end of the flat clamping surface...

15.16b ...then clamp it in a vice

15.17a Rotate the nut until the inner part of the tool...

15.17b ...is flush with the flat surface of the housing

15.18a Remove the securing clip...

15.18b ...the hole in the sender wheel should align with the marking on the flange (arrowed)

15.19a Press the assembly downwards on a clean, flat surface...

15.19b ...so the upper edge of the sender wheel is level with the edge of the flange

15.20 Fit the flange to the tool, ensuring the pin locates in the hole (arrowed)

15.21 With the pin engaged in the hole, tighten the 3 knurled screws to secure the flange to the tool

position the upper edge of the sender wheel should be level with the edge of the sealing flange **(see illustrations)**.

20 Place the sealing flange on the assembly tool, so the pin locates in the hole in the sender wheel **(see illustration)**.

21 Push the sealing flange and guide fitting sleeve against the tool whilst tightening the 3 knurled screws. Ensure the pin is still located in the sender wheel **(see illustration)**.

22 Ensure the end of the crankshaft is clean, and is locked at TDC on No. 1 cylinder as described in Section 3.

23 Unscrew the large nut to the end of the spindle threads, then press the spindle inwards as far as possible **(see illustrations)**.

24 Align the flat side of the assembly with the sump flange, then secure the tool to the crankshaft using the integral Allen bolts **(see illustration)**. Only hand tighten the bolts.

25 Insert two M7x 35 mm bolts to guide the sealing flange to the cylinder block **(see illustration)**.

26 Using hand pressure alone, push the tool assembly onto the crankshaft until the seal guide fitting sleeve contacts the crankshaft flange, then push the guide pin (black knob) into the hole in the crankshaft. This is to ensure the sender wheel reaches its correct installation position **(see illustration)**.

27 Rotate the large nut until it makes contact with the tool housing, then tighten it to 35 Nm. After tightening this nut, a small air gap must still be present between the sealing flange and cylinder block **(see illustrations)**.

28 Unscrew the large nut; the two M7 x 35 Nm screws, the three knurled screws and the Allen bolts securing the tool to the crankshaft. Remove the tool, and pull the seal guide fitting sleeve from place (if it didn't come out with the tool) **(see illustration)**.

15.23a Unscrew the nut to the end of the thread...

15.23b ...and push the spindle in as far as possible

15.24 Hand-tighten the Allen bolts (arrowed), to secure the tool to the crankshaft

15.25 Use two M7 x 35 mm bolts (arrowed) to guide the sealing flange

15.26 Push the black knob into the hole in the crankshaft

15.27a After tightening the spindle nut to 35 Nm...

15.27b ...there should be an air gap between the sealing flange and the cylinder block (arrowed)

29 Use a vernier caliper or feeler gauge to measure the fitted depth of the sender wheel in relation to the crankshaft flange **(see illustration)**. The correct depth is 0.5 mm.

30 If the gap is correct, fit the sealing flange bolts and tighten them to the specified torque.

31 If the gap is too small, re-attach the tool to the sealing flange and crankshaft, then refit the two M7 x 35 mm guide bolts to the flange. Tighten the large spindle nut to 40 Nm, remove the tool and re-measure the air gap. If the gap is still too small, re-attach the tool and tighten the spindle nut to 45 Nm. Re-measure the gap. When the gap is correct, refit the flange retaining bolts, and tighten them to the specified torque.

32 The remainder of refitting is a reversal of removal.

15.28 Remove the tool and seal fitting guide sleeve

15.29 Measure the fitted depth of the sender wheel in relation to the end of the crankshaft

16 Engine/transmission mountings – inspection and renewal

Inspection

1 If improved access is required, jack up the front of the vehicle, and support it securely on axle stands (see *Jacking and vehicle support*). Remove the engine top cover that also incorporates the air filter, and then remove the engine undershield(s).

2 Check the mounting rubbers to see if they are cracked, hardened or separated from the metal at any point; renew the mounting if any such damage or deterioration is evident.

3 Check that all the mountings are securely tightened; use a torque wrench to check if possible.

4 Using a large screwdriver or a crowbar, check for wear in the mounting by carefully levering against it to check for free play. Where this is not possible, enlist the aid of an assistant to move the engine/transmission back-and-forth, or from side-to-side, whilst you observe the mounting. While some free play is to be expected, even from new components, excessive wear should be obvious. If excessive free play is found, check first that the fasteners are correctly secured, and then renew any worn

components as described in the following paragraphs.

Caution: Do NOT undo the centre bolt, securing the bracket to the flexible mounting.

5 When working on the right-hand mounting and rear lower mounting (torque arm), remove the mounting as a complete unit. VW state that the mounting bracket-to-flexible mounting nut/bolt should not be slackened, see following procedures for each individual mounting.

Renewal

6 The engine mountings on the 1.6 litre engine are similar to those fitted on the 1.2 litre diesel models, see Chapter 2C, Section 16, for the removal and refitting procedures of the engine mountings.

17.4a Undo the engine oil cooler retaining screws

17 Engine oil cooler/ filter housing – removal and refitting

Removal

1 The oil cooler is mounted on the lower part of the oil filter housing on the front of the cylinder block.

2 Position a container beneath the oil filter housing to catch escaping oil and coolant.

3 Clamp the oil cooler coolant hoses to minimise coolant spillage, or drain the cooling system as described in Chapter 1B, Section 30.

4 Unscrew the oil cooler retaining screws and remove the oil cooler from the front of the oil filter housing **(see illustrations)**. Recover the

17.4b Renew the seals/gaskets

17.5a Disconnect the coolant hoses...

17.5b ...release the oil dipstick guide tube retaining clip (arrowed)...

17.5c ...and undo the filter housing retaining bolts (arrowed)

17.6 Renew the seals/gaskets

18.1 Oil pressure warning light switch location - arrowed

19.1 Oil level/temperature sensor location

O-rings from between the cooler and the oil filter housing, new ones will be required for refitting.

5 If required, disconnect the coolant hose, unclip the dipstick from the side of the housing, then undo the retaining bolts and remove the oil filter housing from the cylinder block **(see illustrations)**.

Refitting

6 Refitting is a reversal of removal, bearing in mind the following points:

a) Use new oil cooler and housing O-rings **(see illustration)**.

b) Tighten the oil cooler and filter housing bolts to the correct torque.

c) On completion, check and if necessary top-up the oil and coolant levels.

18 Oil pressure warning light switch – removal and refitting

Removal

1 The oil pressure warning light switch is fitted

to the left-hand rear of the cylinder head **(see illustration)**. Remove the engine top cover to gain access to the switch.

2 Slacken the retraining clips and remove the air intake hose from the turbocharger to the air cleaner housing.

3 Disconnect the wiring connector and wipe clean the area around the switch.

4 Unscrew the switch and remove it, along with its sealing washer (where fitted). If the switch is to be left removed from the engine for any length of time, plug the aperture in the cylinder head.

Refitting

5 Examine the sealing washer for signs of damage or deterioration and if necessary renew.

6 Refit the switch, complete with washer (where fitted), and tighten it to the specified torque.

7 Securely reconnect the wiring connector, refit the air intake hose and then, if necessary, top-up the engine oil as described in *Weekly checks*. On completion, refit the engine top cover.

19 Oil level/temperature sender – removal and refitting

Removal

1 The oil level/temperature sender is fitted to bottom of the sump **(see illustration)**.

2 Drain the engine oil as described in Chapter 1B Section 3.

3 Disconnect the wiring connector from the sender.

4 Release the retaining clips and remove the insulation cover from the sump **(see illustration 12.7)**.

5 Wipe clean the area around the sender, then undo the three retaining bolts and remove the sender.

Refitting

6 Examine the sealing washer for signs of damage or deterioration and if necessary renew.

7 Refit the switch and tighten the retaining bolts to the specified torque.

8 Refit the insulation cover, then reconnect the wiring connector and refill the engine with oil (refer to Chapter 1B, Section 3).

9 On completion, check and, if necessary, top-up the engine oil as described in *Weekly checks*.

Chapter 2 Part E:
Engine removal and overhaul procedures

Contents

Degrees of difficulty

| Easy, suitable for novice with little experience | | Fairly easy, suitable for beginner with some experience | | Fairly difficult, suitable for competent DIY mechanic | | Difficult, suitable for experienced DIY mechanic | | Very difficult, suitable for expert DIY or professional | |

Specifications

Engine codes*

1.2 litre petrol engines:
SOHC	CHFA
DOHC	CGPA and CGPB
1.4 litre petrol engine	CGGB
1.2 litre diesel engine	CFWA
1.6 litre diesel engine	CAYB, CAYC and CLNA

*Note: See 'Vehicle identification' at the end of this manual for the location of engine code markings.

Cylinder head

Minimum permissible dimension between top of valve stem and top surface of cylinder head:
Petrol engines:
  1.2 litre:
Engine code CHFA	N/A
Engine codes CGPA and CGPB	7.6 mm

  1.4 litre:
Inlet valves	7.6 mm
Exhaust valves	7.6 mm
Diesel engines	No reworking permitted

Minimum cylinder head height:
Petrol engines:
  1.2 litre:
Engine code CHFA	N/A
Engine codes CGPA and CGPB	108.25 mm
1.4 litre	108.25 mm
Diesel engines	No reworking permitted

Maximum cylinder head gasket face distortion:
Petrol engines	0.05 mm
Diesel engines	0.10 mm

Valves

Valve stem diameter:	Inlet	Exhaust
Petrol engines:		
1.2 litre:		
Engine code CHFA	5.98 mm	5.96 mm
Engine codes CGPA and CGPB	5.973 mm	5.953 mm
1.4 litre	5.973 mm	5.953 mm
Diesel engines	5.968 to 5.982 mm	5.958 to 5.972 mm
Valve head diameter:		
Petrol engines:		
1.2 litre:		
Engine code CHFA	34.5 mm	28.0 mm
Engine codes CGPA and CGPB	29.5 mm	26.0 mm
1.4 litre	29.5 mm	26.0 mm
Diesel engines	26.50 to 26.70 mm	24.40 to 24.60 mm
Valve length:		
Petrol engines:		
1.2 litre:		
Engine code CHFA	99.25 mm	99.25 mm
Engine codes CGPA and CGPB	100.9 mm	100.5 mm
1.4 litre	100.9 mm	100.5 mm
Diesel engines	99.30 mm	99.10 mm
Valve seat angle (all engines)	45°	45°

Camshaft

Petrol engines:	
Endfloat (axial clearance) - maximum wear limit	0.20 mm
Diesel engines:	
Endfloat (axial clearance):	
New	0.048 to 0.118 mm
Wear limit	0.17 mm
Bearing running (radial) clearances	0.035 to 0.085 mm

Crankshaft

Petrol engines	See Note in Section 2
Diesel engines:	
Main journal diameter	54.00 mm (Nominal)
Big-end journal diameter	47.80 mm (Nominal)
Endfloat (axial clearance):	
New	0.07 to 0.17 mm
Wear limit	0.37 mm
Main bearing running (radial) clearances:	
New	0.03 to 0.08 mm
Wear limit	0.17 mm
Big-end bearing running (radial) clearance	0.03 to 0.08 mm

Pistons/connecting rods

Connecting rod side-play on crankshaft journal:	New	Wear limit
Petrol engines:		
1.2 litre	See Note in Section 2	
1.4 litre	0.10 to 0.35 mm	0.40 mm
Diesel engines	N/A	0.37 mm

Piston and cylinder bore diameters

	Piston	Cylinder bore
Petrol engines:		
1.2 litre	See Note in Section 2	
1.4 litre:		
Standard	76.470 mm	76.510 mm
1st oversize	76.720 mm	76.760 mm
2nd oversize	76.970 mm	77.010 mm
Diesel engines:		
1.2 litre (Standard)	79.450 mm	79.50 mm
1.6 litre (Standard)	79.455 mm	79.50 mm

Piston rings

End gaps:	New	Wear limit
Petrol engines:		
1.2 litre	See Note in Section 2	
1.4 litre:		
Top compression ring	0.20 to 0.50 mm	1.0 mm
Lower compression ring	0.40 to 0.70 mm	1.0 mm
Oil scraper ring	0.40 to 1.40 mm	N/A
Diesel engines:		
Compression rings	0.20 to 0.40 mm	1.0 mm
Oil scraper ring	0.25 to 0.50 mm	1.0 mm
Ring-to-groove clearance:		
Petrol engines:		
1.2 litre	See Note in Section 2	
1.4 litre:		
Compression rings	0.04 to 0.08 mm	0.15 mm
Oil scraper ring	N/A	N/A
Diesel engines:		
1st compression ring	0.06 to 0.09 mm	0.25 mm
2nd compression ring	0.05 to 0.08 mm	0.25 mm
Oil scraper ring	0.03 to 0.06 mm	0.15 mm

Torque wrench settings

Refer to Chapter 2A, 2B, 2C or 2D as applicable.

1 General information

Included in this Part of Chapter 2 are details of removing the engine from the car and general overhaul procedures for the cylinder head, cylinder block and all other engine internal components.

The information given ranges from advice concerning preparation for an overhaul and the purchase of new parts, to detailed step-by-step procedures covering removal, inspection, renovation and refitting of engine internal components.

After Section 6, all instructions are based on the assumption that the engine has been removed from the car. For information concerning in-car engine repair, as well as the removal and refitting of those external components necessary for full overhaul, refer to the relevant in-car repair procedure section (Chapters 2A, 2B, 2C and 2D) and to Section 6 of this Chapter. Ignore any preliminary dismantling operations described in the relevant in-car repair sections that are no longer relevant once the engine has been removed from the car.

Apart from torque wrench settings, which are given at the beginning of the relevant in-car repair procedure in Chapters 2A, 2B, 2C or 2D, all specifications relating to engine overhaul are given at the beginning of this part of Chapter 2.

2 Engine overhaul –
general information

Note 1: *On all petrol engines, the crankshaft must not be removed. Loosening the main bearing cap bolts will cause deformation of the cylinder block. If the crankshaft or main bearing surfaces are worn or damaged, the complete crankshaft/cylinder block assembly must be renewed.*

Note 2: *On 1.2 litre petrol engines, the pistons and connecting rods must not be removed.*

1 It is not always easy to determine when, or if, an engine should be completely overhauled, as a number of factors must be considered.

2 High mileage is not necessarily an indication that an overhaul is needed, while low mileage does not preclude the need for an overhaul. Frequency of servicing is probably the most important consideration. An engine, which has had regular and frequent oil and filter changes, as well as other required maintenance, should give many thousands of miles of reliable service. Conversely, a neglected engine may require an overhaul very early in its life.

3 Excessive oil consumption is an indication that piston rings, valve seals and/or valve guides are in need of attention. Make sure that oil leaks are not responsible before deciding that the rings and/or guides are worn. Perform a compression (or leakdown) test, as described in Part A, B, C or D of this Chapter (as applicable), to determine the likely cause of the problem.

4 Check the oil pressure with a gauge fitted in place of the oil pressure switch, and compare it with that specified (see Specifications in Chapters 2A, 2B, 2C and 2D). If it is extremely low, the main and big-end bearings, and/or the oil pump, are probably worn.

5 Loss of power, rough running, knocking or metallic engine noises, excessive valve gear noise, and high fuel consumption may also point to the need for an overhaul, especially if they are all present at the same time. If a complete service does not remedy the situation, major mechanical work is the only solution.

6 An engine overhaul involves restoring all internal parts to the specification of a new engine. During an overhaul, the pistons and the piston rings are renewed. New main and big-end bearings are generally fitted (where possible); if necessary, the crankshaft may be renewed to restore the journals. The valves are also serviced as well, since they are usually in less-than-perfect condition at this point. While the engine is being overhauled, other components, such as the starter and alternator, can be overhauled as well. The end result should be an as-new engine that will give many trouble-free miles. **Note:** *Critical cooling system components such as the hoses, thermostat and coolant pump should be renewed when an engine is overhauled. The radiator should be checked carefully, to ensure that it is not clogged or leaking. Also, it is a good idea to renew the oil pump whenever the engine is overhauled.*

7 Before beginning the engine overhaul, read through the entire procedure, to familiarise yourself with the scope and requirements of the job. Overhauling an engine is not difficult if you follow carefully all of the instructions, have the necessary tools and equipment, and pay close attention to all specifications. It can, however, be time-consuming. Plan on the car being off the road for a minimum of two weeks, especially if parts must be taken to an engineering works for repair or reconditioning. Check on the availability of parts and make sure that any necessary special tools and equipment are obtained in advance. Most work can be done with typical hand tools, although a number of precision measuring tools are required for inspecting parts to determine if they must be renewed. Often an engineering works will handle the inspection of parts and offer advice concerning reconditioning and renewal. **Note:** *Always wait until the engine has been completely dismantled, and until all*

components (especially the cylinder block and the crankshaft) have been inspected, before deciding what service and repair operations must be performed by an engineering works. The condition of these components will be the major factor to consider when determining whether to overhaul the original engine, or to buy a reconditioned unit. Do not, therefore, purchase parts or have overhaul work done on other components until they have been thoroughly inspected. As a general rule, time is the primary cost of an overhaul, so it does not pay to fit worn or sub-standard parts.

8 As a final note, to ensure maximum life and minimum trouble from a reconditioned engine, everything must be assembled with care, in a spotlessly clean environment.

3 Engine/transmission removal – preparation and precautions

If you have decided that the engine must be removed for overhaul or major repair work, several preliminary steps should be taken.

Locating a suitable place to work is extremely important. Adequate workspace, along with storage space for the vehicle, will be needed. If a workshop or garage is not available, at the very least a solid, level, clean work surface is required.

If possible, clear some shelving close to the work area and use it to store the engine components and ancillaries as they are removed and dismantled. In this manner, the components stand a better chance of staying clean and undamaged during the overhaul. Laying out components in groups, together with their fixings bolts, screws, etc, will save time and avoid confusion when the engine is refitted.

Clean the engine compartment and engine before beginning the removal procedure; this will help visibility and help to keep tools clean.

The help of an assistant is essential; there are certain instances when one person cannot safely perform all of the operations required to remove the engine from the vehicle. Safety is of primary importance, considering the potential hazards involved in this kind of operation. A second person should always be in attendance to offer help in an emergency. If this is the first time you have removed an engine, advice and aid from someone more experienced would also be beneficial.

Plan the operation ahead of time. Before starting work, obtain (or arrange for the hire of) all of the tools and equipment you will need. Access to the following items will allow the task of removing and refitting the engine to be completed safely and with relative ease: a hoist and lifting tackle – rated in excess of the weight of the engine, complete sets of spanners and sockets as described at the rear of this manual, wooden blocks, and plenty of rags and cleaning solvent for mopping-up spilled oil, coolant and fuel. A selection of different-sized plastic storage bins will also prove useful for keeping dismantled components grouped together. If any of the equipment must be hired, make sure that you arrange for it in advance, and perform all of the operations possible without it beforehand; this may save you time and money.

Plan on the vehicle being out of use for quite a while, especially if you intend to carry out an engine overhaul. Read through the whole of this Section and work out a strategy based on your own experience, and the tools, time and workspace available to you. Some of the overhaul processes may have to be carried out by a VW dealer or an engineering works – these establishments often have busy schedules, so it would be prudent to consult them before removing or dismantling the engine, to get an idea of the amount of time required to carry out the work.

When removing the engine from the vehicle, be methodical about the disconnection of external components. Labelling cables and hoses as they are removed will greatly assist the refitting process.

Always be extremely careful when lifting engine from the engine compartment. Serious injury can result from careless actions. If help is required, it is better to wait until it is available rather than risk personal injury and/or damage to components by continuing alone. By planning ahead and taking your time, a job of this nature, although major, can be accomplished successfully and without incident.

4 Engine and transmission – removal and refitting

Removal

1 Access to the front of the engine is gained by moving the lock carrier assembly to its Service position, or alternatively removing it completely after evacuating the air conditioning system (by an air conditioning specialist).

2 Remove the battery and battery tray, as described in Chapter 5A, Section 3.

3 Remove the engine top cover and air filter assembly (Chapter 4A, Section 2 or Chapter 4B, Section 2) and all associated air ducting.

4 Apply the handbrake, then jack up the front of the vehicle and support it on axle stands (see Jacking and vehicle support). Remove both front roadwheels.

5 Drain the cooling system as described in Chapter 1A, Section 30 or Chapter 1B, Section 30.

6 Remove the front bumper, as described in Chapter 11, Section 6.

7 Move the lock carrier, located at the front of the engine compartment, to its Service position as follows.

a) Disconnect the bonnet release cable over the right-hand headlight (see illustration).

b) Undo the retaining screws and remove the metal brackets from above the headlight apertures (see illustration), mark the position of the screws for refitting.

c) Undo the retaining screws and disconnect the ends of the front cross member from the lower part of the front wing panels (see illustration), mark the position of the screws for refitting.

d) On models with a turbocharger, remove the charge air hoses from the intercooler (see illustration), which is positioned across the lower part of the radiator.

e) Where applicable, disconnect the air intake duct from the upper cross panel (see illustration).

f) Unclip the washer reservoir filler neck from the front panel (see illustration).

4.7a Disconnect the bonnet release cable...

4.7b ...undo the upper mounting bracket screws (arrowed)...

4.7c ...and lower mounting bracket screws (arrowed)

4.7d Disconnect the charge air hoses from the intercooler

4.7e Disconnect the air intake ducting

4.7f Unclip the washer reservoir filler neck

g) *Support the front panel/lock carrier, then unscrew the 6 mounting bolts (3 each side) and substitute one of them with a threaded rod at each side of the car* **(see illustration)**.

h) *Carefully pull the lock carrier forwards approximately 10 cm* **(see illustration)**, *to hold the panel in position, we used a couple of pieces of wood (10cm wide) to put between the front panel and the chassis leg. As the panel is moved forward, check to make sure no components will get damaged.*

Alternatively, have the air conditioning system evacuated by a specialist. Then with the air-conditioning pipes disconnected, the lock carrier can be removed completely from the front of the car.

⚠️ *Warning: Have the air conditioning system discharged by a suitably qualified specialist before attempting to remove the compressor.*

8 Noting their locations, disconnect all wiring, coolant hoses, vacuum hoses and fuel lines from the engine/transmission, with reference to the relevant Chapters of this Manual. Alternatively, the engine wiring loom may remain on the engine by disconnecting it from the left-hand side rear of the engine compartment, and removing the engine management ECU (Chapter 4A, Section 3 or Chapter 4B, Section 3) located on the bulkhead. Tape over or plug fuel lines to prevent entry of dust and dirt.

9 Remove the front exhaust pipe with reference to Chapter 4C, Section 5 or Chapter 4D, Section 9.

10 Unbolt the rear engine support/torque arm from the transmission.

11 Disconnect the gearchange mechanism with reference to Chapter 7A, Section 2 (manual transmission) or Chapter 7B, Section 4 (DSG transmission) **(see illustration)**.

12 On manual transmission models, remove the clutch slave cylinder. **Note:** *Do not depress the clutch pedal once the slave cylinder has been removed.*

13 Refer to Chapter 3, Section 10, and unbolt the air conditioning compressor from the front of the engine, without disconnecting the refrigerant lines. Suspend the compressor to one side of the engine compartment.

14 Refer to Chapter 8, Section 2, and

4.7g Substitute one of the bolts with a threaded rod (arrowed) and securing nuts

disconnect the driveshafts from the transmission drive flanges. Suspend them from the underbody **(see illustration)**.

15 Unbolt the washer fluid reservoir for access to the right-engine mounting. Also unbolt the coolant expansion tank and place to one side.

16 Connect a hoist and lifting tackle to the engine lifting brackets on the cylinder head, and raise the hoist to just take the weight of the engine/transmission.

17 Unbolt the right- and left-hand engine mountings with reference to Chapter 2A, 2B, 2C or 2D.

18 Make a final check to ensure that all relevant wiring, hoses and pipes have been disconnected, then carefully swivel the engine/transmission assembly away from the sides of the engine compartment, lift it upwards or lower it (see paragraph 1), and withdraw forwards from the front of the car.

4.11 Disconnect the gearchange cables

4.7h Insert a block (arrowed) to hold carrier 10cm forwards

Separation

Engine and manual transmission

19 Remove the starter motor (Chapter 5A, Section 8).

20 Where applicable, unscrew the bolt securing the small engine-to-transmission plate to the transmission.

21 Ensure that both engine and transmission are adequately supported, and then unscrew the remaining engine-to-transmission bolts, noting the location of each bolt, and the locations of any brackets secured by the bolts.

22 Carefully withdraw the transmission from the engine, ensuring that the weight of the transmission is not allowed to hang on the input shaft while it is engaged with the clutch friction disc. Recover the engine-to-transmission plate.

4.14 Suspend the driveshafts clear of the transmission

Engine and DSG (dual clutch) transmission

23 Remove the starter motor (Chapter 5A, Section 8).

24 Disconnect the coolant hoses from the gearbox oil cooler. Plug the openings to prevent contamination.

25 Disconnect the wiring harness between the engine and gearbox, and move to one side.

26 Ensure that both engine and transmission are adequately supported, and then unscrew the engine-to-transmission bolts, noting the location of each bolt, and the locations of any brackets secured by the bolts.

27 Carefully withdraw the transmission from the engine (take care – the transmission is heavy).

Reconnection and refitting

Engine and manual transmission

28 Reconnection and refitting are a reversal of removal, bearing in mind the following points:

a) Smear the splines of the transmission input shaft with a little high melting-point grease.

b) Ensure that any brackets noted before removal are in place on the engine-to-transmission bolts.

c) Tighten all fixings to the specified torque, where given.

d) Where applicable, have the air conditioning system recharged with refrigerant by a suitably qualified professional.

e) Ensure that all wiring, hoses and pipes are correctly reconnected and routed as noted before removal.

f) Ensure that the fuel lines are correctly reconnected.

g) On completion, refill the cooling system as described in Chapter 1A, Section 30 or Chapter 1B, Section 30.

h) Have the engine management system checked for fault codes by a VW dealer.

Engine and DSG (dual clutch) transmission

29 Reconnection and refitting are a reversal of removal, bearing in mind the following points:

a) When fitting the torque converter (where applicable), make sure that both the drive pins engage with the transmission fluid pump.

b) On completion, check and if necessary top-up the transmission fluid level as described in Chapter 1A, Section 13 or Chapter 1B, Section 13.

5 Engine overhaul – preliminary information

1 It is much easier to dismantle and work on the engine if it is mounted on a portable engine stand. These stands can often be hired from a tool hire shop. Before the engine is mounted on a stand, the flywheel should be removed, so that the stand bolts can be tightened into the end of the cylinder block/crankcase. **Note:** *Do not measure cylinder bore dimensions with the engine mounted on this type of stand.*

2 If a stand is not available, it is possible to dismantle the engine with it blocked up on a sturdy workbench, or on the floor. Be very careful not to tip or drop the engine when working without a stand.

3 If you intend to obtain a reconditioned engine, all ancillaries must be removed first, to be transferred to the new engine (just as they will if you are doing a complete engine overhaul yourself). These components include the following (it may be necessary to transfer additional components, such as the oil level dipstick/tube assembly, oil filter housing, etc, depending on which components are supplied with the reconditioned engine):

Petrol engines

a) Alternator (including mounting brackets) and starter motor (Chapter 5A).

b) The ignition system components including all sensors and spark plugs (Chapter 1A and Chapter 5B).

c) The fuel injection system components (Chapter 4A).

d) All electrical switches, actuators and sensors, and the engine wiring harness (Chapter 3, Chapter 4A and Chapter 5B).

e) Inlet and exhaust manifolds (Chapter 4A and Chapter 4C).

f) Engine mountings (Chapter 2A or Chapter 2B).

g) Clutch components (Chapter 6).

h) Oil separator (where applicable).

Diesel engines

a) Alternator (including mounting brackets) and starter motor (Chapter 5A).

b) The glow plug/preheating system components (Chapter 5C).

c) All fuel system components, including the fuel injection pump (engine code ASY), fuel injectors, all sensors and actuators (Chapter 4B).

d) The brake vacuum/tandem pump (Chapter 9).

e) All electrical switches, actuators and sensors, and the engine wiring harness (Chapter 3, Chapter 4B and Chapter 5C).

f) Inlet and exhaust manifolds, and turbocharger (Chapter 4B and Chapter 4C).

g) Engine mountings (Chapter 2C or Chapter 2D).

h) Clutch components (Chapter 6).

All engines

Note: *When removing the external components from the engine, pay close attention to details that may be helpful or important during refitting. Note the fitted position of gaskets, seals, spacers, pins, washers, bolts, and other small components.*

4 If you are obtaining a short engine (the engine cylinder block/crankcase, crankshaft, pistons and connecting rods, all fully assembled), then the cylinder head, sump, oil pump, timing belt(s) and chain (as applicable – together with tensioner(s) and covers), auxiliary drivebelt (together with its tensioner), coolant pump, thermostat housing, coolant outlet elbows, oil filter housing and where applicable oil cooler will also have to be removed.

5 If you are planning a full overhaul, the engine can be dismantled in the order given below:

a) Inlet and exhaust manifolds (see the relevant parts of Chapter 4).

b) Timing chain/belt(s), sprockets and tensioner(s) (see Chapters 2A, 2B, 2C and 2D).

c) Cylinder head (see Chapters 2A, 2B, 2C and 2D).

d) Flywheel/driveplate (see Chapters 2A, 2B, 2C and 2D).

e) Sump (see Chapters 2A, 2B, 2C and 2D).

f) Oil pump (see Chapters 2A, 2B, 2C and 2D).

g) Piston/connecting rod assemblies (see Section 9).

h) Crankshaft (see Section 10).

6 Cylinder head – dismantling

Note: *A valve spring compressor tool will be required for this operation.*

Petrol engines

1 With the cylinder head removed as described in the relevant part of Chapter 2, proceed as follows.

2 Remove the inlet and exhaust manifolds as described in Chapter 4A or Chapter 4C.

3 Remove the camshaft(s) and hydraulic tappets/roller rocker fingers as described in Chapter 2A or Chapter 2B.

4 If desired, unbolt the coolant housing from the rear of the cylinder head, and recover the seal.

5 Where applicable, remove the camshaft position sensor, with reference to Chapter 4A, Section 4.

6 Where applicable, unscrew the securing nut, and recover the washer, and remove the timing belt tensioner pulley from the stud on the cylinder head.

7 Unbolt any remaining auxiliary brackets and/or engine lifting brackets from the cylinder head as necessary, noting their locations to aid refitting. Where applicable, unscrew the securing bolt and remove the secondary timing belt tensioner from the timing belt end of the cylinder head.

8 Turn the cylinder head over, and rest it on one side.

9 Using a valve spring compressor, compress each valve spring in turn, until the split collets can be removed. Release the compressor, and lift off the spring cap and spring. If, when the valve spring compressor is screwed down, the spring cap refuses to free and expose the split

6.9a Compress a valve spring with a compressor tool

6.9b Remove the spring cap...

6.9c ...and valve spring

6.10a Use a removal tool...

6.10b ...to remove the valve stem oil seals

6.11 Removing a valve

collets, gently tap the top of the tool, directly over the spring cap, with a light hammer. This will free the retainer **(see illustrations)**.

10 Using a pair of pliers, or a removal tool, carefully extract the valve stem oil seal from the top of the valve guide **(see illustrations)**.

11 Withdraw the valve from the gasket side of the cylinder head **(see illustration)**.

12 It is essential that each valve is stored together with its collets, cap, spring and spring seat. The valves should be kept in their correct sequences, unless they are so badly worn that they are to be renewed.

> **HAYNES HiNT**
> *If they are going to be kept and used again, place each valve assembly in a labelled polythene bag or similar small container. Label each bag, noting that No 1 valve is nearest to the timing belt/chain end of the cylinder head.*

Diesel engines

13 With the cylinder head removed as described in Chapter 2C or Chapter 2D, proceed as follows.

14 Remove the inlet and exhaust manifolds (and turbocharger, where applicable) as described in Chapter 4B and Chapter 4C.

15 Remove the camshaft and hydraulic tappets, as described in Chapter 2C or Chapter 2D.

16 Remove the glow plugs, with reference to Chapter 5C.

17 Remove the fuel injectors, with reference to Chapter 4B.

18 Unscrew the nut and remove the timing belt tensioner pulley from the stud on the timing belt end of the cylinder head.

19 Unbolt any remaining auxiliary brackets and/or engine lifting brackets from the cylinder head as necessary, noting their locations to aid refitting.

20 Proceed as described in paragraphs 8 to 12.

---

7 Cylinder head and valves – cleaning and inspection

---

1 Thorough cleaning of the cylinder head and valve components, followed by a detailed inspection, will enable you to decide how much valve service work must be carried out during engine overhaul. **Note:** *If the engine has been severely overheated, it is best to assume that the cylinder head is warped – check carefully for signs of this.*

Cleaning

2 Using a suitable degreasing agent, remove all traces of oil deposits from the cylinder head, paying particular attention to the camshaft bearing surfaces, hydraulic tappet bores, valve guides and oilways. Scrape off any traces of old gasket from the mating surfaces, taking care not to score or gouge them. If using emery paper, do not use a grade of less than 100. Turn the head over and, using a blunt blade, scrape any carbon deposits from the combustion chambers and ports. Finally, wash the entire head casting with a suitable solvent to remove the remaining debris.

3 Clean the valve heads and stems using a fine wire brush (or a power-operated wire brush). If the valve is covered with heavy carbon deposits, scrape off the majority of the deposits with a blunt blade first, then use the wire brush.

4 Thoroughly clean the remainder of the components using solvent and allow them to dry completely. Discard the oil seals, as new ones must be fitted when the cylinder head is reassembled.

Inspection

Cylinder head

Note: *If the valve seats are to be reground, ensure that the maximum permissible reworking dimension is not exceeded (the maximum dimension will only allow minimal reworking to produce a perfect seal between valve and seat). If the maximum dimension is exceeded, the function of the hydraulic tappets cannot be guaranteed, and the cylinder head must be renewed. Refer to paragraph 6 for details of how to calculate the maximum permissible reworking dimension.*

5 Examine the head casting closely to identify any damage or cracks that may have developed. Cracks can often be identified from evidence of coolant or oil leakage. Pay particular attention to the areas around the valve seats and spark plug/fuel injector holes. If cracking is discovered in this area, VW state that, on diesel engines, the cylinder head may be re-used, provided the cracks are no larger than 0.5 mm wide. More serious damage will mean the renewal of the cylinder head casting.

7.6 Measure the distance (A) between the top face of the valve stem and the top surface of the cylinder head

6 Moderately pitted and scorched valve seats can be repaired by lapping the valves in during reassembly, as described later in this Chapter, however the maximum permissible reworking dimension **must** not be exceeded, which will only allow minimal reworking (see note at beginning of paragraph 5). To calculate the maximum permissible reworking dimension, proceed as follows **(see illustration)**:

a) *If a new valve is to be fitted, use the new valve for the following calculation.*
b) *Insert the valve into its guide in the cylinder head, and push the valve firmly on to its seat.*
c) *Measure the distance between the top face of the valve stem, and either the top surface of the cylinder head or spring*

7.7 Measure the distortion of the cylinder head gasket surface

7.13 Measure the free length of each valve spring

seat surface (as applicable). Record the measurement obtained.
d) *Consult the Specifications, and compare the measured distance with that given in the Specifications.*

7 Measure any distortion of the gasket surfaces using a straight-edge and a set of feeler blades. Take one measurement longitudinally on the manifold mating surface(s). Take several measurements across the head gasket surface, to assess the level of distortion in all planes **(see illustration)**. Compare the measurements with the figures in the Specifications.

8 On petrol engines, if the head is distorted beyond the specified limit, it may be possible to have it machined by an engineering works, provided that the minimum permissible cylinder head height is maintained.

9 On diesel engines, if the head is distorted beyond the specified limit, the head must be renewed.

Valves and associated components

Note: *On all engines, the valve heads cannot be recut, although they may be lapped in.*

10 Examine each valve closely for signs of wear. Inspect the valve stems for wear ridges, scoring or variations in diameter; measure their diameters at several points along their lengths with a micrometer, and compare with the figures given in the Specifications **(see illustration)**.

11 The valve heads should not be cracked, badly pitted or charred. Note that light pitting of the valve head can be rectified by lapping-in the valves during reassembly, as described in Section 8.

7.10 Measure the diameter of the valve stems using a micrometer

7.14 Check the squareness of a valve spring

12 Check that the valve stem end face is free from excessive pitting or indentation; this could be caused by defective hydraulic tappets.

13 Using vernier calipers, measure the free length of each of the valve springs. As a manufacturer's figure is not quoted, the only way to check the length of the springs is by comparison with a new component. Note that valve springs are usually renewed during a major engine overhaul **(see illustration)**.

14 Stand each spring on its end on a flat surface, against an engineer's square **(see illustration)**. Check the squareness of the spring visually, and renew it if it appears distorted.

15 Renew the valve stem oil seals regardless of their apparent condition.

8 Cylinder head – reassembly

Note: *A valve spring compressor tool will be required for this operation.*

1 To achieve a gas-tight seal between the valves and their seats, it will be necessary to lap-in (or grind-in) the valves. To complete this process you will need a quantity of fine/coarse grinding paste and a grinding tool – this can either be of the rubber sucker type, or the automatic type which is driven by a rotary power tool.

2 Smear a small quantity of *fine* grinding paste on the sealing face of the valve head. Turn the cylinder head over so that the combustion chambers are facing upwards and insert the valve into the correct guide. Attach the grinding tool to the valve head and using a backward/forward rotary action, grind the valve head into its seat. Periodically lift the valve and rotate it to redistribute the grinding paste **(see illustration)**.

3 Continue this process until the contact between valve and seat produces an unbroken, matt grey ring of uniform width, on both faces. Repeat the operation on the remaining valves.

4 If the valves and seats are so badly pitted that coarse grinding paste must be used, bear in that there is a maximum permissible reworking dimension for the valves and seats.

8.2 Grinding-in a valve

8.8a Lubricate the valve stem with clean engine oil

8.8b Fit a protective sleeve over the valve stem before fitting the stem seal

8.9 Use a long-reach socket to fit a valve stem oil seal

Refer to the Specifications at the beginning of this Chapter for the limits, and note that if exceeded due to excessive lapping-in, the hydraulic tappets may not operate correctly, and the cylinder head must be renewed.

5 Assuming the repair is feasible, work as described previously, but use coarse grinding paste initially, to achieve a dull finish on the valve face and seat. Wash off the coarse paste with solvent and repeat the process using fine grinding paste to obtain the correct finish.

6 When all the valves have been ground in, remove all traces of grinding paste from the cylinder head and valves using solvent, and allow the head and valves to dry completely.

7 Turn the cylinder head on its side.

8 Working on one valve at a time, lubricate the valve stem with clean engine oil, and insert the valve into its guide. Fit one of the protective plastic sleeves supplied with the new valve stem oil seals over the end of the valve stem – this will protect the oil seal as it is being fitted (see illustrations).

9 Dip a new valve stem seal in clean engine oil, and carefully push it over the valve stem and onto the top of the valve guide – take care not to damage the stem seal as it is fitted. Use a suitable long-reach socket or a suitable valve stem seal fitting tool to press the seal firmly into position (see illustration). Remove the protective sleeve from the valve stem.

10 Locate the valve spring over the valve stem, ensuring that the lower end of the spring seats correctly on the cylinder head (see illustration).

11 Fit the upper spring seat over the top of the spring then, using a valve spring compressor, compress the spring until the upper seat is pushed beyond the collet grooves in the valve stem. Refit the split collets. Gradually release the spring compressor, checking that the collets remain correctly seated as the spring extends. When correctly seated, the upper spring seat should force the collets securely into the grooves in the end of the valve stem (see illustrations).

 HAYNES HINT *Use a little dab of grease to hold the collets in position on the valve stem while the spring compressor is released.*

12 Repeat this process for the remaining sets of valve components, ensuring that all components are refitted to their original locations. To settle the components after installation, strike the end of each valve stem with a mallet, using a block of wood to protect the stem from damage. Check before progressing any further that the split collets remain firmly seated in the grooves in the end of the valve stem.

Petrol engines

13 Refit the brackets previously removed, and also where applicable refit the secondary timing belt tensioner.

14 Where applicable, refit the timing belt tensioner pulley on the stud, and loosely refit the securing nut and washer.

15 Where applicable, refit the camshaft position sensor, with reference to Chapter 4A.

16 If removed, refit the coolant housing to the

8.10 Fit a valve spring...

8.11b ... then compress a valve spring using a compressor tool

cylinder head, together with a new seal, and tighten the mounting bolts.

17 Refit the camshaft(s) and hydraulic tappets/roller rocker fingers with reference to Chapter 2A or Chapter 2B.

18 Refit the inlet and exhaust manifolds with reference to Chapter 4A and Chapter 4C.

Diesel engines

19 Refit the brackets previously removed, then refit the timing belt tensioner pulley on the stud, and loosely refit the securing nut and washer.

20 Refit the fuel injectors, with reference to Chapter 4B.

21 Refit the glow plugs, with reference to Chapter 5C.

22 Refit the camshaft and hydraulic tappets, with reference to Chapter 2C or Chapter 2D.

23 Refit the inlet and exhaust manifolds (and turbocharger, where applicable) with reference to Chapter 4B and Chapter 4C.

8.11a ...and upper spring seat ...

8.11c Use grease to hold the split collets in the groove

9.3 Mark the big-end caps and connecting rods with their cylinder numbers (arrowed)

9.6a Unscrew the big-end bearing cap bolts...

9.6b ...and remove the cap

9.7 Wrap the threaded ends of the bolts with tape

9 Piston/connecting rod assemblies – removal

Caution: The pistons and connecting rods must not be removed on 1.2 litre petrol engines.

1 Remove the cylinder head, sump, oil baffle and oil pump pick-up pipe, as applicable, with reference to Chapters 2A, 2B, 2C and 2D. On 3-cylinder diesel engines, also remove the balancer shaft assembly.

2 Inspect the tops of the cylinder bores for ridges at the point where the pistons reach top dead centre. These must be removed otherwise, the pistons may be damaged when they are pushed out of their bores. Use a scraper or ridge reamer to remove the ridges. Such a ridge indicates excessive wear of the cylinder bore.

3 Check the connecting rods and big-end caps for identification markings. Both connecting rods and caps should be marked with the cylinder number on one side of each assembly. Note that No 1 cylinder is at the timing belt end of the engine. If no marks are present, using a hammer and centre-punch, paint or similar, mark each connecting rod and big-end bearing cap with its respective cylinder number – note on which side of the connecting rods and caps the marks are made **(see illustration)**.

4 Similarly, check the piston crowns for direction markings. An arrow on each piston crown should point towards the timing belt end of the engine. On some engines, this mark may be obscured by carbon build-up, in which case the piston crown should be cleaned to check for a mark. In some cases, the direction arrow may have worn off, in which case a suitable mark should be made on the piston

crown using a scriber – do not deeply score the piston crown, but ensure that the mark is easily visible.

5 Turn the crankshaft to bring No 1 piston to bottom dead centre (on 4-cylinder engines, No 4 piston will also be at BDC).

6 Unscrew the bolts or nuts, as applicable, from No 1 piston big-end bearing cap. Lift off the cap, and recover the bottom half bearing shell. If the bearing shells are to be re-used, tape the cap and bearing shell together. Note that if the bearing shells are to be re-used, they must be fitted to the original connecting rod and cap **(see illustrations)**.

7 Where the bearing caps are secured with nuts, wrap the threaded ends of the bolts with insulating tape to prevent them scratching the crankpins and bores when the pistons are removed **(see illustration)**.

8 Using a hammer handle, push the piston up through the bore, and remove it from the top of the cylinder block. Where applicable, take care not to damage the piston cooling oil spray jets in the cylinder block as the piston/ connecting rod assembly is removed. Recover the upper bearing shell, and tape it to the connecting rod for safe-keeping.

9 Loosely refit the big-end cap to the connecting rod, and secure with the bolts or nuts, as applicable – this will help to keep the components in their correct order.

10 On 4-cylinder engines, remove No 4 piston assembly in the same way.

11 Turn the crankshaft as necessary to bring No 2 piston to bottom dead centre, and remove them in the same way (on 4-cylinder engines, No 3 piston will also be at BDC).

12 Where applicable, remove the securing bolts, and withdraw the piston cooling oil spray jets from the bottom of the cylinder block **(see illustrations)**.

10 Crankshaft (diesel engines) – removal

Caution: On petrol engines, the crankshaft must not be removed. Loosening the main bearing cap bolts will cause deformation of the cylinder block. On these engines, if the crankshaft or main bearing surfaces

9.12a Remove the securing bolts...

9.12b ...and withdraw the piston cooling oil spray jets

9.12c Piston cooling spray jet and retainer

are worn or damaged, the complete crankshaft/cylinder block assembly must be renewed. The following procedure only applies to diesel engines.

Note: *If no work is to be done on the pistons and connecting rods, there is no need to remove the cylinder head and push the pistons out of the cylinder bores. The pistons should just be pushed far enough up the bores so that they are positioned clear of the crankshaft journals.*

1 Remove the timing belt and crankshaft sprocket, sump and oil baffle plate, oil pump and pick-up pipe, flywheel, and the crankshaft oil seal housings, as described in Chapter 2C or Chapter 2D.

2 Remove the pistons and connecting rods, or disconnect them from the crankshaft, as described in Section 9.

3 Check the crankshaft endfloat as described in Section 13, then proceed as follows.

4 The main bearing caps should be numbered 1 to 5 (4-cylinder) or 1 to 4 (3-cylinder) from the timing belt end of the engine. If the bearing caps are not marked, mark them accordingly using a centre-punch. Note the orientation of the markings to ensure correct refitting.

5 Slacken and remove the main bearing cap bolts, and lift off each cap. If the caps appear to be stuck, tap them with a soft-faced mallet to free them from the cylinder block **(see illustration)**. Recover the lower bearing shells, and tape them to their caps for safe-keeping.

6 Lift the crankshaft from the cylinder block. Take care, as the crankshaft is heavy. On engines with a crankshaft speed/position sensor fitted, lay the crankshaft on wooden blocks – **do not** rest the crankshaft on the sensor wheel.

7 Recover the upper bearing shells from the cylinder block, and tape them to their respective caps for safe-keeping. Similarly, recover the upper crankshaft endfloat control thrustwasher halves from either side of No 3 main bearing, noting their orientation.

8 On engines with a crankshaft speed/position sensor wheel fitted, unscrew the securing bolts, and remove the sensor wheel, noting which way round it is fitted.

---

11 Cylinder block/crankcase – cleaning and inspection

Cleaning

1 Remove all external components and electrical switches/sensors from the block, including mounting brackets, the coolant pump, the oil filter/cooler housing, etc. For complete cleaning, the core plugs should ideally be removed. Drill a small hole in the plugs, and then insert a self-tapping screw into the hole. Extract the plugs by pulling on the screw with a pair of grips, or by using a slide hammer.

2 Scrape all traces of gasket and sealant from the cylinder block/crankcase, taking care not to damage the sealing surfaces.

3 Remove all oil gallery plugs (where fitted). The plugs are usually very tight – they may have to be drilled out, and the holes re-tapped. Use new plugs when the engine is reassembled.

4 If the casting is extremely dirty, it should be steam-cleaned. After this, clean all oil holes and galleries one more time. Flush all internal passages with warm water until the water runs clear. Dry thoroughly, and apply a light film of oil to all mating surfaces and cylinder bores, to prevent rusting. If you have access to compressed air, use it to speed up the drying process, and to blow out all the oil holes and galleries.

 Warning: Wear eye protection when using compressed air.

5 If the castings are not very dirty, you can do an adequate cleaning job with hot, soapy water and a stiff brush. Take plenty of time, and do a thorough job. Regardless of the cleaning method used, be sure to clean all oil holes and galleries very thoroughly, and to dry all components well. Protect the cylinder bores as described above, to prevent rusting.

6 Where applicable, check the piston cooling oil spray jets for damage, and renew if necessary. Check the oil spray hole and the oil passages for blockage.

7 All threaded holes must be clean, to ensure accurate torque readings during reassembly. To clean the threads, run the correct-size tap into each of the holes to remove rust, corrosion, thread sealant or sludge, and to restore damaged threads **(see illustration)**. If possible, use compressed air to clear the holes free of debris produced by this operation. **Note:** *Take extra care to exclude all cleaning liquid from blind tapped holes, as the casting may be cracked by hydraulic action if a bolt is threaded into a hole containing liquid.*

  A good alternative is to inject aerosol-applied water dispersant lubricant into each hole, using the long spout usually supplied.
Warning: Wear eye protection when cleaning out these holes in this way.

8 After coating the mating surfaces of the new core plugs with suitable sealant, fit them to the cylinder block. Make sure that they are driven in straight and seated correctly, or leakage could result.

 A large socket with an outside diameter which will just fit into the core plug can be used to drive the core plug into position.

10.5 Slacken and remove the main bearing cap bolts

9 Apply suitable sealant to the new oil gallery plugs, and insert them into the holes in the block. Tighten them securely.

10 If the engine is not going to be reassembled immediately, cover it with a large plastic bag to keep it clean; protect all mating surfaces and the cylinder bores, to prevent rusting.

Inspection

11 Visually check the castings for cracks and corrosion. Look for stripped threads in the threaded holes. If there has been any history of internal coolant leakage, it may be worthwhile having an engine overhaul specialist check the cylinder block/crankcase for cracks with special equipment. If defects are found, have them repaired, if possible, or renew the assembly.

12 Check each cylinder bore for scuffing and scoring.

13 If in any doubt as the condition of the cylinder block have the block/bores inspected and measured by an engine reconditioning specialist. They will be able to advise on whether the block is serviceable, whether a rebore is necessary, and supply the appropriate pistons and rings.

14 If the bores are in reasonably good condition and not excessively worn, then it may only be necessary to renew the piston rings.

15 If this is the case, the bores should be honed, to allow the new rings to bed-in correctly and provide the best possible seal. Consult an engine reconditioning specialist.

16 On diesel engines, if the oil filter/cooler housing was removed, it can be refitted at this

11.7 To clean the cylinder block threads, run a correct-size tap into the holes

12.4 Old feeler blades can be used to prevent piston rings from dropping into empty grooves

stage if wished. Use a new gasket, and before fully tightening the bolts, align the housing faces with those of the engine block.

17 The cylinder block/crankcase should now be completely clean and dry, with all components checked for wear or damage, and repaired or overhauled as necessary.

18 Apply a light coating of engine oil to the mating surfaces and cylinder bores to prevent rust forming.

19 Refit as many ancillary components as possible, for safe-keeping. If reassembly is not to start immediately, cover the block with a large plastic bag to keep it clean, and protect the machined surfaces as described above to prevent rusting.

12 Piston/connecting rod assemblies – cleaning and inspection

Cleaning

1 Before the inspection process can begin, the piston/connecting rod assemblies must be cleaned, and the original piston rings removed from the pistons.

2 The rings should have smooth, polished working surfaces, with no dull or carbon-coated sections (showing that the ring is not sealing correctly against the bore wall, so allowing combustion gases to blow-by) and no traces of wear on their top and bottom surfaces. The end gaps should be clear of carbon, but not polished (indicating a too-small end gap), and all the rings (including the elements of the oil

control ring) should be free to rotate in their grooves, but without excessive up-and-down movement. If the rings appear to be in good condition, they are probably fit for further use; check the end gaps (in an unworn part of the bore) as described in Section 16.

3 If any of the rings appears to be worn or damaged, or has an end gap significantly different from the specified value, the usual course of action is to renew all of them as a set. **Note:** *While it is usual to renew piston rings when an engine is overhauled, they may be re-used if in acceptable condition. If re-using the rings, make sure that each ring is marked during removal to ensure that it is refitted correctly.*

4 Carefully expand the old rings over the top of the pistons. The use of two or three old feeler blades will be helpful in preventing the rings dropping into empty grooves **(see illustration)**. Be careful not to scratch the piston with the ends of the ring. The rings are brittle, and will snap if they are spread too far. They are also very sharp – protect your hands and fingers. Note that the third ring incorporates an expander. Keep each set of rings with its piston if the old rings are to be re-used. Note which way up each ring is fitted to ensure correct refitting.

5 Scrape away all traces of carbon from the top of the piston. A hand-held wire brush (or a piece of fine emery cloth) can be used, once the majority of the deposits have been scraped away.

6 Remove the carbon from the ring grooves in the piston, using an old ring. Break the ring in half to do this (be careful not to cut your fingers – piston rings are sharp). Be careful to remove only the carbon deposits – do not remove any metal, and do not nick or scratch the sides of the ring grooves.

7 Once the deposits have been removed, clean the piston/connecting rod assembly with paraffin or a suitable solvent, and dry thoroughly. Make sure that the oil return holes in the ring grooves are clear.

Inspection

8 If the pistons and cylinder bores are not damaged or worn excessively, and if the cylinder block does not need to be rebored, the original pistons can be refitted.

9 Using a micrometer, measure the diameter of all four pistons at a point 10 mm from the bottom of the skirt, at right-angles to the gudgeon pin axis **(see illustration)**. Compare the measurements with those listed in the Specifications. Note that the piston size grades are stamped on the piston crowns.

10 If the piston diameter is incorrect for its particular size, then it must be renewed. **Note:** *If the cylinder block was rebored during a previous overhaul, oversize pistons may already have been fitted.* Record all of the measurements and use them to check the piston clearances against the cylinder bore measurements made in Section 11.

11 Normal piston wear shows up as even vertical wear on the piston thrust surfaces, and slight looseness of the top ring in its groove. New piston rings should always be used when the engine is reassembled.

12 Carefully inspect each piston for cracks around the skirt, around the gudgeon pin holes, and at the piston ring 'lands' (between the ring grooves).

13 Look for scoring and scuffing on the piston skirt, holes in the piston crown, and burned areas at the edge of the crown. If the skirt is scored or scuffed, the engine may have been suffering from overheating, and/or abnormal combustion that caused excessively high operating temperatures. The cooling and lubrication systems should be checked thoroughly.

14 Scorch marks on the sides of the pistons show that blow-by has occurred.

15 A hole in the piston crown, or burned areas at the edge of the piston crown, indicates that abnormal combustion (pre-ignition, knocking, or detonation) has been occurring.

16 If any of the above problems exist, the causes must be investigated and corrected, or the damage will occur again. The causes may include incorrect ignition/injection pump timing, inlet air leaks or incorrect air/fuel mixture (petrol engines), or a faulty fuel injector (diesel engines).

17 Corrosion of the piston, in the form of pitting, indicates that coolant has been leaking into the combustion chamber and/or the crankcase. Again, the cause must be corrected, or the problem may persist in the rebuilt engine.

18 Locate a new piston ring in the appropriate groove and measure the ring-to-groove clearance using a feeler blade **(see illustration)**. Note that the rings are of different widths, so use the correct ring for the groove. Compare the measurements with those listed; if the clearances are outside of the tolerance band, then the piston must be renewed. Confirm this by checking the width of the piston ring with a micrometer.

19 New pistons can be purchased from a VW dealer.

20 Examine each connecting rod carefully for signs of damage, such as cracks around the big-end and small-end bearings. Check that the rod is not bent or distorted. Damage

12.9 Using a micrometer to measure the diameter of a piston

12.18 Measure the piston ring-to-groove clearance using a feeler blade

is highly unlikely, unless the engine has been seized or badly overheated. Detailed checking of the connecting rod assembly can only be carried out by a VW dealer or engine repair specialist with the necessary equipment.

21 The gudgeon pins are of the floating type, secured in position by two circlips. The pistons and connecting rods can be separated as follows.

22 Using a small flat-bladed screwdriver, prise out the circlips, and push out the gudgeon pin **(see illustrations)**. Hand pressure should be sufficient to remove the pin. Identify the piston and rod to ensure correct reassembly. Discard the circlips – new ones *must* be used on refitting. If the gudgeon pin proves difficult to remove, heat the piston to 60°C with hot water – the resulting expansion will then allow the two components to be separated.

23 Examine the gudgeon pin and connecting rod small-end bearing for signs of wear or damage. It should be possible to push the gudgeon pin through the connecting rod bush by hand, without noticeable play. Wear can be cured by renewing both the pin and bush. Bush renewal, however, is a specialist job – press facilities are required, and the new bush must be reamed accurately.

24 Examine all components, and obtain any new parts from your VW dealer. If new pistons are purchased, they will be supplied complete with gudgeon pins and circlips. Circlips can also be purchased individually.

25 The orientation of the piston with respect to the connecting rod must be correct when the two are reassembled. The piston crown is marked with an arrow (which may be obscured by carbon deposits). The arrow must point towards the timing belt end of the engine when the piston is installed. The connecting rod and its bearing cap both have recesses machined into them on one side, close to their mating surfaces – these recesses must both face the same way as the arrow on the piston crown when correctly installed. Reassemble the two components to satisfy this requirement **(see illustrations)**.

26 Apply a smear of clean engine oil to the gudgeon pin. Slide it into the piston and through the connecting rod small-end. Check that the piston pivots freely on the rod, then secure the gudgeon pin in position with two new circlips. Ensure that each circlip is correctly located in its groove in the piston.

27 Repeat the cleaning and inspection process for the remaining pistons and connecting rods.

13 Crankshaft (diesel engines) – checking endfloat and inspection

Checking endfloat

1 If the crankshaft endfloat is to be checked, this must be done when the crankshaft is still

12.22a Use a small flat-bladed screwdriver to prise out the circlip...

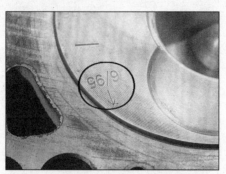

12.25a The piston crown is marked with an arrow which must point towards the timing belt/chain end of the engine

installed in the cylinder block/crankcase, but is free to move (see Section 10).

2 Check the endfloat using a dial gauge in contact with the end of the crankshaft. Push the crankshaft fully one way, and then zero the gauge. Push the crankshaft fully the other way, and check the endfloat. The result can be compared with the specified amount, and will give an indication as to whether new thrustwasher halves are required **(see illustration)**. Note that all thrustwashers must be of the same thickness.

3 If a dial gauge is not available, feeler blades can be used. First push the crankshaft fully towards the flywheel end of the engine, and then use feeler blades to measure the gap between the web of No 3 crankpin and the thrustwasher halves **(see illustration)**.

13.2 Measure crankshaft endfloat using a dial gauge

12.22b ...then push out the gudgeon pin and separate the piston and connecting rod

12.25b The recesses (arrowed) in the connecting rod and bearing cap must face the timing belt/chain end of the engine

Spigot bearing

Note: *On 7-speed DSG semi-automatic transmissions, the spigot needle roller bearing needs to be renewed; every time the transmission is removed from the engine.*

4 On some models, there is a bearing positioned in the end of the crankshaft, which supports the transmission shaft.

5 Remove the transmission as described in Chapter 7A, Section 3 (manual transmission) or Chapter 7B, Section 2 (DSG transmissions)

6 On manual models, remove the clutch assembly as described in Chapter 6, Section 6.

7 Before removing the bearing, check the fitted depth of the bearing inside the end of the crankshaft **(see illustration)**. See specifications at the beginning of this Chapter to find the relevant depth for each engine.

13.3 Measure crankshaft endfloat using feeler blades

13.7 Check the depth of the bearing using a vernier gauge

13.8a Using an internal bearing puller...

13.8b ...to withdraw the bearing

13.9 Using a drift to carefully tap the bearing back into position

8 Using an internal puller, slide the bearing out from the centre of the crankshaft **(see illustrations)**.

9 Using a drift, drive the bearing into the end of the crankshaft **(see illustration)**, taking care not to drive it in to far, as noted on removal. Also see specifications at the beginning of Chapter for depth of bearing.

 Warning: If the new bearing is driven into the end of the crankshaft to far, then it will need

14.1 Typical bearing failures

FATIGUE FAILURE — CRATERS OR POCKETS

IMPROPER SEATING — BRIGHT (POLISHED) SECTIONS

SCRATCHED BY DIRT — DIRT EMBEDDED INTO BEARING MATERIAL

LACK OF OIL — OVERLAY WIPED OUT

EXCESSIVE WEAR — OVERLAY WIPED OUT

TAPERED JOURNAL — RADIUS RIDE

H 28395

to be completely removed and another new one fitted.

Inspection

10 Clean the crankshaft using paraffin or a suitable solvent, and dry it, preferably with compressed air if available. Be sure to clean the oil holes with a pipe cleaner or similar probe, to ensure that they are not obstructed.

 Warning: Wear eye protection when using compressed air.

11 Check the main and big-end bearing journals for uneven wear, scoring, pitting and cracking.

12 Big-end bearing wear is accompanied by distinct metallic knocking when the engine is running (particularly noticeable when the engine is pulling from low speed) and some loss of oil pressure.

13 Main bearing wear is accompanied by severe engine vibration and rumble – getting progressively worse as engine speed increases – and again by loss of oil pressure.

14 Check the bearing journal for roughness by running a finger lightly over the bearing surface. Any roughness (which will be accompanied by obvious bearing wear) indicates that the crankshaft requires regrinding (where possible) or renewal.

15 If the crankshaft has been reground, check for burrs around the crankshaft oil holes (the holes are usually chamfered, so burrs should not be a problem unless regrinding has been carried out carelessly). Remove any burrs with a fine file or scraper, and thoroughly clean the oil holes as described previously.

16 Using a micrometer, measure the diameter of the main and big-end bearing journals, and compare the results with the Specifications, where given. By measuring the diameter at a number of points around each journal's circumference, you will be able to determine whether or not the journal is out-of-round. Take the measurement at each end of the journal, near the webs, to determine if the journal is tapered.

17 Check the oil seal contact surfaces at each end of the crankshaft for wear and damage. If the seal has worn a deep groove in the surface of the crankshaft, consult an engine overhaul specialist; repair may be possible, but otherwise a new crankshaft will be required.

18 If the crankshaft journals have not already been reground, it may be possible to have the crankshaft reconditioned, and to fit oversize shells (see Section 17). If no oversize shells are available and the crankshaft has worn beyond the specified limits, it will have to be renewed. Consult your VW dealer or engine specialist for further information on parts availability.

14 Main and big-end bearings – inspection

Inspection

1 Even though the main and big-end bearings should be renewed during the engine overhaul, the old bearings should be retained for close examination, as they may reveal valuable information about the condition of the engine **(see illustration)**.

2 Bearing failure can occur due to lack of lubrication, the presence of dirt or other foreign particles, overloading the engine, or corrosion. Regardless of the cause of bearing failure, the cause must be corrected before the engine is reassembled, to prevent it from happening again.

3 When examining the bearing shells, remove them from the cylinder block/crankcase, the main bearing caps, the connecting rods and the connecting rod big-end bearing caps. Lay them out on a clean surface in the same general position as their location in the engine. This will enable you to match any bearing problems with the corresponding crankshaft journal. Do not touch any shell's internal bearing surface with your fingers while checking it, or the delicate surface may be scratched.

4 Dirt and other foreign matter get into the engine in a variety of ways. It may be left in the engine during assembly, or it may pass through filters or the crankcase ventilation system. It may get into the oil, and from there into the bearings. Metal chips from machining operations and normal engine wear are often present. Abrasives are sometimes left in engine components after reconditioning, especially when parts are not thoroughly cleaned using the proper cleaning methods. Whatever the source, these foreign objects often end up embedded in the soft bearing material, and are easily recognised. Large particles will not embed in the bearing, but will score or gouge the bearing and journal. The best prevention for this cause of bearing failure is to clean all parts thoroughly, and keep everything spotlessly clean during engine assembly. Frequent and regular engine oil and filter changes are also recommended.

5 Lack of lubrication (or lubrication breakdown) has a number of interrelated causes. Excessive heat (which thins the oil), overloading (which squeezes the oil from the bearing face) and oil leakage (from excessive bearing clearances, worn oil pump or high engine speeds) all contribute to lubrication breakdown. Blocked oil passages, which usually are the result of misaligned oil holes in a bearing shell, will also oil-starve a bearing, and destroy it. When lack of lubrication is the cause of bearing failure, the bearing material is wiped or extruded from the steel backing of the bearing. Temperatures may increase to the point where the steel backing turns blue from overheating.

6 Driving habits can have a definite effect on bearing life. Full-throttle, low-speed operation (labouring the engine) puts very high loads on bearings, tending to squeeze out the oil film. These loads cause the bearings to flex, which produces fine cracks in the bearing face (fatigue failure). Eventually, the bearing material will loosen in pieces, and tear away from the steel backing.

7 Short-distance driving leads to corrosion of bearings, because insufficient engine heat is produced to drive off the condensed water and corrosive gases. These products collect in the engine oil, forming acid and sludge. As the oil is carried to the engine bearings, the acid attacks and corrodes the bearing material.

8 Incorrect bearing installation during engine assembly will lead to bearing failure as well. Tight-fitting bearings leave insufficient bearing running clearance, and will result in oil starvation. Dirt or foreign particles trapped behind a bearing shell result in high spots on the bearing, which lead to failure.

9 Do not touch any shell's internal bearing surface with your fingers during reassembly, as there is a risk of scratching the delicate surface, or of depositing particles of dirt on it.

10 As mentioned at the beginning of this Section, the bearing shells should be renewed as a matter of course during engine overhaul. To do otherwise is false economy.

Bearings selection

11 Main and big-end bearings for the engines described in this Chapter are available in standard sizes and a range of undersizes to suit reground crankshafts.

12 The running clearances will need to be checked when the crankshaft is refitted with its new bearings (see Section 17 and Section 18).

15 Engine overhaul – reassembly sequence

1 Before reassembly begins, ensure that all new parts have been obtained, and that all necessary tools are available. Read through the entire procedure to familiarise yourself with the work involved, and to ensure that all items necessary for reassembly of the engine are at hand. In addition to all normal tools and materials, thread-locking compound will be needed. A suitable tube of liquid sealant will also be required for the joint faces that are fitted without gaskets.

2 In order to save time and avoid problems, engine reassembly can be carried out in the following order, referring to Part A, B, C or D of this Chapter. Where applicable, use new gaskets and seals when refitting the various components.

   a) *Crankshaft (Section 17).*
   b) *Piston/connecting rod assemblies (Section 18).*
   c) *Oil pump.*
   d) *Sump.*
   e) *Flywheel/driveplate.*
   f) *Cylinder head.*
   g) *Timing chain/belt(s), tensioner and sprockets.*
   h) *Inlet and exhaust manifolds.*
   i) *Engine external components.*

3 At this stage, all engine components should be absolutely clean and dry, with all faults repaired. The components should be laid out (or in individual containers) on a completely clean work surface.

16 Piston rings – refitting

1 Before fitting new piston rings, the ring end gaps must be checked as follows.

2 Lay out the piston/connecting rod assemblies and the new piston ring sets, so that the ring sets will be matched with the same piston and cylinder during the end gap measurement and subsequent engine reassembly.

3 Insert the top ring into the first cylinder, and push it down the bore using the top of the piston. This will ensure that the ring remains square with the cylinder walls. Position the ring approximately 15.0 mm the bottom of the cylinder bore, at the lower limit of ring travel. Note that the top and second compression rings are different.

4 Measure the end gap using feeler blades, and compare the measurements with the figures given in the Specifications **(see illustration)**.

5 If the gap is too small (unlikely if genuine VW parts are used), it must be enlarged, or the ring ends may contact each other during engine operation, causing serious damage.

16.4 Check a piston ring end gap using a feeler blade

Ideally, new piston rings providing the correct end gap should be fitted. As a last resort, the end gap can be increased by filing the ring ends very carefully with a fine file. Mount the file in a vice equipped with soft jaws, slip the ring over the file with the ends contacting the file face, and slowly move the ring to remove material from the ends. Take care, as piston rings are sharp, and are easily broken.

6 With new piston rings, it is unlikely that the end gap will be too large. If the gaps are too large, check that you have the correct rings for your engine and for the particular cylinder bore size.

7 Repeat the checking procedure for each ring in the first cylinder, and then for the rings in the remaining cylinders. Remember to keep rings, pistons and cylinders matched up.

8 Once the ring end gaps have been checked and if necessary corrected, the rings can be fitted to the pistons.

9 Fit the piston rings using the same technique as for removal. Fit the bottom (oil control) ring first, and work up. Note that a two- or three-section oil control ring may be fitted; where a two-section ring is fitted, first insert the wire expander, then fit the ring. Ensure that the rings are fitted the correct way up – the top surface of the rings is normally marked TOP **(see illustration)**. Offset the piston ring gaps by 120° from each other. **Note:** *Always*

16.9 Piston ring TOP marking

17.4 Bearing shell correctly refitted

A Recess in cylinder block
B Lug on bearing shell
C Oil hole

follow any instructions supplied with the new piston ring sets – different manufacturers may specify different procedures. Do not mix up the top and second compression rings, as they have different cross-sections.

17 Crankshaft (diesel engines) – refitting and main bearing clearance check

Main bearing clearance check

1 The running clearance check can be carried out using the original bearing shells. However, it is preferable to use a new set, since the results obtained will be more conclusive. If new shells are being fitted, ensure that all traces of the protective grease are cleaned off using paraffin.

2 If still fitted, carefully lift the crankshaft out of the cylinder block, and wipe off the surfaces of the bearing shells in the crankcase and bearing cap(s).

3 Clean the backs of the bearing shells, and the bearing locations in both the cylinder block/crankcase and the main bearing cap(s).

4 With the cylinder block positioned on a clean work surface, with the crankcase uppermost, press the bearing shells into their locations, ensuring that the tab on each shell engages in the notch in the cylinder block or bearing cap, and that the oil holes in the cylinder block and bearing shell are aligned **(see illustration)**. Take care not to touch any shell's bearing surface with your fingers. If the original bearing shells are being used for the check, ensure that they are refitted in their original locations.

5 Fit the crankshaft endfloat control thrustwasher halves either side of the No 3 main bearing location. Use a small quantity of grease to hold them in place. Ensure that the thrustwashers are seated correctly in the machined recesses, with the oil grooves facing outwards.

6 The running clearance can be checked, although this will be difficult to achieve without a range of internal micrometers or internal/external expanding calipers. Refit the main bearing cap(s) to the cylinder block/crankcase, with bearing shells in place. With the original cap retaining bolts tightened to the specified torque, measure the internal diameter of each assembled pair of bearing shells. If the diameter of each corresponding crankshaft journal is measured and then subtracted from

the bearing internal diameter, the result will be the main bearing running clearance.

Final crankshaft refitting

7 Where applicable, refit the speed/position sensor wheel to the crankshaft, and tighten the securing bolts to the specified torque. Make sure that the sensor wheel is correctly orientated as noted before removal.

8 Liberally coat the bearing shells in the crankcase with clean engine oil of the appropriate grade **(see illustration)**. Make sure that the bearing shells are still correctly seated in their locations.

9 Lower the crankshaft into position so that No 1 cylinder crankpin is at BDC, ready for fitting No 1 piston. Ensure that the crankshaft endfloat control thrustwasher halves, either side of the No 3 main bearing location, remain in position. Where applicable, take care not to damage the crankshaft speed/position sensor wheel as the crankshaft is lowered into position.

10 Lubricate the lower bearing shells in the main bearing caps with clean engine oil. Make sure that the crankshaft endfloat control thrustwasher halves are still correctly seated either side of No 3 bearing cap **(see illustrations)**.

11 Fit the main bearing cap(s) in the correct location and orientation – where applicable, No 1 bearing cap must be at the timing end of the engine and the bearing shell tab locating recesses in the crankcase and bearing caps must be adjacent to each other **(see illustration)**. Insert the bearing cap bolts (using new bolts where necessary – see

17.8 Lubricate the upper bearing shells

17.10a Lubricate the lower bearing shells...

17.10b ...and make sure that the thrustwashers are correctly seated

17.11 Fitting No 1 main bearing cap

17.12a Tighten the main bearing cap bolts to the specified torque...

17.12b ...then through the specified angle

Torque wrench settings in the Specifications), and hand-tighten them only.

12 Working from the centre bearing cap outwards, tighten the bearing cap bolts to their specified torque. On diesel engines where two Stages are given for the torque, tighten all bolts to the Stage 1 torque, then go round again, and tighten all bolts through the Stage 2 angle **(see illustrations)**.

13 Check that the crankshaft rotates freely by turning it by hand. If resistance is felt, recheck the bearing running clearances, as described previously.

14 Check the crankshaft endfloat as described at the beginning of Section 13. If the thrust surfaces of the crankshaft have been checked and new thrustwashers have been fitted, then the endfloat should be within specification.

15 Refit the pistons and connecting rods or reconnect them to the crankshaft as described in Section 18.

16 Refit the crankshaft oil seal housings, flywheel, oil pump and pick-up pipe, sump and oil baffle plate, crankshaft sprocket and timing belt as described in Chapter 2C or Chapter 2D.

18 Piston/connecting rod assemblies – refitting and big-end bearing clearance check

Note: *A piston ring compressor tool will be required for this operation.*

Big-end bearing clearance check

1 The running clearance check can be carried out using the original bearing shells. However, it is preferable to use a new set, since the results obtained will be more conclusive.

2 Clean the backs of the bearing shells, and the bearing locations in both the connecting rods and the big-end bearing caps.

3 Press the bearing shells into their locations, ensuring that the tab on each shell engages in the notch in the connecting rod or cap. Take care not to touch any shell's bearing surface with your fingers. If the original bearing shells are being used for the check, ensure that they are refitted in their original locations.

4 The running clearance can be checked, although this will be difficult to achieve without a range of internal micrometers or internal/external expanding calipers. Refit the big-end bearing cap to the connecting rod, using the marks made or noted on removal to ensure that they are fitted the correct way around, with the bearing shells in place. With the original cap retaining bolts or nuts (as applicable) correctly tightened, use an internal micrometer or vernier caliper to measure the internal diameter of each assembled pair of bearing shells. If the diameter of each corresponding crankshaft journal is measured, and then subtracted from the bearing internal diameter, the result will be the big-end bearing running clearance.

18.9a Lubricate the pistons...

Piston/connecting rods refitting

5 Note that the following procedure assumes that the crankshaft main bearing caps are in place.

6 Where applicable, refit the piston cooling oil spray jets to the bottom of the cylinder block, and tighten the securing bolts to the specified torque.

7 On engines where the big-end bearing caps are secured by nuts, renew the bolts/studs in the connecting rods. Tap the old bolts/studs out of the connecting rods using a soft-faced mallet, and tap the new bolts/studs into position. On engines where the caps are secured by bolts, renew the bolts.

8 Ensure that the bearing shells are correctly fitted, as described at the beginning of this Section. If new shells are being fitted, ensure that all traces of the protective grease are cleaned off using paraffin. Wipe dry the shells and connecting rods with a lint-free cloth.

9 Lubricate the cylinder bores, the pistons, piston rings and upper bearing shells with clean engine oil **(see illustrations)**. Lay out each piston/connecting rod assembly in order on a clean work surface. Where the bearing caps are secured with nuts, pad the threaded ends of the bolts with insulating tape to prevent them scratching the crankpins and bores when the pistons are refitted.

10 Start with piston/connecting rod assembly No 1. Make sure that the piston rings are still spaced as described in Section 16, then clamp them in position with a piston ring compressor tool.

11 Insert the piston/connecting rod assembly into the top of No 1 cylinder. Lower the big-end in first, guiding it to protect the cylinder bores.

18.13 Using a hammer handle to tap the piston into its bore

18.9b ...and big-end upper bearing shells with clean engine oil

Where oil jets are located at the bottoms of the bores, take particular care not to damage them when guiding the connecting rods onto the crankpins.

12 Ensure that the orientation of the piston in its cylinder is correct – refer to Section 12 for details.

13 Using a block of wood or hammer handle against the piston crown, tap the assembly into the cylinder until the piston crown is flush with the top of the cylinder **(see illustration)**.

14 Ensure that the bearing shell is still correctly installed in the connecting rod, and then liberally lubricate the crankpin and both bearing shells with clean engine oil.

15 Taking care not to mark the cylinder bores; tap the piston/connecting rod assembly down the bore and onto the crankpin. On engines where the big-end caps are secured by nuts, remove the insulating tape from the threaded ends of the connecting rod bolts. Oil the bolt threads, and on engines where the big-end caps are secured by bolts, oil the undersides of the bolt heads.

16 Fit the big-end bearing cap, tightening its new retaining nuts or bolts (as applicable) finger-tight at first. On diesel engines, the connecting rod and its bearing cap both have recesses machined into them on one side, close to their mating surfaces – these recesses must both face the same way as the arrow on the piston crown (i.e. towards the timing belt end of the engine) when correctly installed. Reassemble the two components to satisfy this requirement.

17 Tighten the retaining bolts or nuts to the specified torque and angle as given in the Specifications **(see illustrations)**.

18.17a Tighten the big-end bearing cap bolts/nuts to the specified torque...

18.17b ...then through the specified angle

18 Refit the remaining piston/connecting rod assemblies in the same way.

19 Rotate the crankshaft by hand. Check that it turns freely; some stiffness is to be expected if new parts have been fitted, but there should be no binding or tight spots.

20 On diesel engines, if new pistons have been fitted, or if a new short engine has been fitted, the projection of the piston crowns above the cylinder head mating face of the cylinder block at TDC must be measured. This measurement is used to determine the thickness of the new cylinder head gasket required. This procedure is described as part of the Cylinder head – removal, inspection and refitting procedure in Chapter 2C or Chapter 2D.

21 Proceed as follows according to engine type:

a) *On the 3-cylinder diesel engine, refit the balancer shaft assembly as described in Chapter 2C.*

b) *On the 1.4 litre petrol engine and all diesel engines, refit the oil pump pick-up pipe and oil baffle, the sump and the cylinder head as described in Chapters 2B, 2C or 2D.*

19 Engine – initial start-up after overhaul and reassembly

1 Refit the remainder of the engine components in the order listed in Section 5 of this Chapter. Refit the engine to the vehicle as described in Section 4 of this Chapter. Double-check the engine oil and coolant levels, and make a final check that everything has been reconnected. Make sure that there are no tools or rags left in the engine compartment.

2 Reconnect the battery negative lead (refer to *Disconnecting the battery* in the *Reference* Chapter at the end of this manual).

Petrol models

3 Remove the spark plugs, referring to Chapter 1A, Section 24, for details.

4 The engine must be immobilised such that it can be turned over using the starter motor, without starting – refer to Section 2 of Chapters 2A, 2B, 2C and 2D. Also, disable the fuel pump by unplugging the fuel pump power relay from the relay board with reference to Chapter 12.

Caution: To prevent damage to the catalytic converter, it is important to disable the fuel system.

5 Turn the engine using the starter motor until the oil pressure warning light goes out. If the light fails to extinguish after several seconds of cranking, check the engine oil level and oil filter security. Assuming these are correct, check the security of the oil pressure switch wiring – do not progress any further until you are satisfied that oil is being pumped around the engine at sufficient pressure.

6 Refit the spark plugs, and reconnect the ignition and fuel pump wiring.

Diesel models

7 Disconnect the injector solenoids by disconnecting the connector at the end of the cylinder head. **Note:** *As a result of the wiring being disconnected, faults will be stored in the ECU memory. These must be erased after starting the engine.*

8 Turn the engine using the starter motor until the oil pressure warning light goes out.

9 If the light fails to extinguish after several seconds of cranking, check the engine oil level and oil filter security. Assuming these are correct, check the security of the oil pressure switch cabling – do not progress any further until you are satisfied that oil is being pumped around the engine at sufficient pressure.

10 Reconnect the wiring as applicable.

All models

11 Start the engine, but be aware that as fuel system components have been disturbed, the cranking time may be a little longer than usual.

12 While the engine is idling, check for fuel, water and oil leaks. Don't be alarmed if there are some odd smells and the occasional plume of smoke as components heat up and burn off oil deposits.

13 Assuming all is well; keep the engine idling until hot water is felt circulating through the top hose.

14 After a few minutes, stop the engine then recheck the oil and coolant levels, and top-up as necessary.

15 There is no need to retighten the cylinder head bolts once the engine has been run following reassembly.

16 If new pistons, rings or crankshaft bearings have been fitted, the engine must be treated as new, and run-in for the first 600 miles (1000 km). Do not operate the engine at full-throttle, or allow it to labour at low engine speeds in any gear. It is recommended that the engine oil and filter be changed at the end of this period.

Chapter 3
Cooling, heating and ventilation systems

Contents

Degrees of difficulty

Easy, suitable for novice with little experience	Fairly easy, suitable for beginner with some experience	Fairly difficult, suitable for competent DIY mechanic	Difficult, suitable for experienced DIY mechanic	Very difficult, suitable for expert DIY or professional

Specifications

Cooling system pressure cap
Opening pressure.................................... 1.4 to 1.6 bar

Thermostat

Petrol engines
Begins to open .... 84°C
Fully open .... 98°C

Diesel engines
Begins to open .... 92°C
Fully open .... 107°C

Cooling fan
Fan speeds:
  1st speed cut-in .... 92 to 97°C
  1st speed cut-out .... 91 to 84°C
  2nd speed cut-in .... 99 to 105°C
  2nd speed cut-out .... 98 to 91°C

Coolant temperature sensor
Resistances:
    At 30°C.. 1500 to 2000 ohms
    At 80°C.. 275 to 375 ohms

Air-conditioning
Refrigerant:
  Capacity .... 500 ± 15g
  Type R134a
Compressor make/type:
  Delphi 6CVC 140
  Denso 6SEU14
  Sanden .... 6PXE14 or 7PXE16
Refrigerant oil type:
  Delphi .... G 052 300 A2 or G 052 154 A2
  Denso .... G 052 300 A2
  Sanden .... G 052 154 A2
Refrigerant oil capacity for replacement compressor:
  Delphi 6CVC 140 .... $110cm^3 \pm 10cm^3$
  Denso 6SEU14 .... $85cm^3 \pm 10cm^3$
  Sanden 6PXE14 & 7PXE16........................... $110cm^3 \pm 10cm^3$

Torque wrench settings

	Nm	lbf ft
Air conditioning condenser	5	4
Coolant pump:		
1.2 litre petrol engines	24	18
1.4 litre petrol engines	20	15
Diesel engines	15	11
Coolant pump pulley (1.2 litre petrol engines)	22	16
Distribution housing (diesel engines)	10	7
Radiator	5	4
Radiator cooling fan shroud bolts	10	7
Radiator cooling fan thermo-switch	35	26
Thermostat cover (diesel engines)	15	11
Thermostat/distribution housing:		
1.2 litre petrol engines	8	6
1.4 litre petrol engines	10	7

1 General information and precautions

The cooling system comprises a centrifugal pump, crossflow radiator, electric cooling fan, thermostat and a heater matrix, as well as the interconnecting hoses. The system functions as follows. Cold coolant from the radiator passes through the bottom hose to the coolant pump where it is pumped around the cylinder block and head passages. After cooling the cylinder bores, combustion surfaces and valve seats, the coolant reaches the top of the engine and passes through the top hose to the radiator. The coolant also passes through the heater matrix where it heats incoming air to the inside of the car.

When the engine is cold the coolant circulation is restricted to the cylinder block, cylinder head, expansion tank, and heater by a thermostat positioned in the radiator circuit. On petrol engines the thermostat is located in the coolant distribution housing on the left-hand end of the cylinder head, however, on diesel engines it is located in the coolant return on the front of the cylinder block. When the coolant reaches a predetermined temperature, the wax-filled thermostat opens and the coolant passes through to the radiator. As the coolant circulates through the radiator it is cooled by the inrush of air when the car is in forward motion. Airflow is supplemented by the action of the electric cooling fan(s) when

necessary. Upon leaving the radiator, the coolant has cooled and the cycle is repeated.

A thermostatic switch controls the electric cooling fan(s) mounted on the rear of the radiator. At a preset coolant temperature, the switch actuates the fan(s).

Precautions

⚠️ *Warning: Do not attempt to remove the expansion tank filler cap or disturb any part of the cooling system while the engine is hot, as there is a high risk of scalding. If the expansion tank filler cap must be removed before the engine and radiator have fully cooled (even though this is not recommended) the pressure in the cooling system must first be relieved. Cover the cap with a thick layer of cloth, to avoid scalding, and slowly unscrew the filler cap until a hissing sound can be heard. When the hissing has stopped, indicating that the pressure has reduced, slowly unscrew the filler cap until it can be removed; if more hissing sounds are heard, wait until they have stopped before unscrewing the cap completely. At all times keep well away from the filler cap opening.*

• *Do not allow antifreeze to come into contact with skin or the car's painted surfaces. Rinse off spills immediately with plenty of water. Never leave antifreeze lying around in an open container or in a puddle in the driveway or on the garage floor. Children and pets are attracted by its sweet smell. Antifreeze can be fatal if ingested.*

• *If the engine is hot, the electric cooling fan may start rotating even if the engine is*

not running, so be careful to keep hands, hair and loose clothing well clear when working in the engine compartment.

• *Refer to Section 8 for additional precautions to be observed when working on models with air conditioning.*

2 Cooling system hoses – disconnection and renewal

Note: *Refer to the warnings given in Section 1 of this Chapter before proceeding.*

1 If the checks described in the relevant part of Chapter 1 reveal a faulty hose, it must be renewed as follows.

2 First drain the cooling system as described in Chapter 1A, Section 30 for petrol engines or Chapter 1B, Section 30 for diesel engines. If the coolant is not due for renewal, it may be re-used if it is collected in a clean container.

3 To disconnect a hose, release its retaining clips (see illustration), and then move them along the hose, clear of the relevant inlet/outlet union. Carefully work the hose free.

4 In order to disconnect the heater matrix inlet and outlet hoses, apply pressure to hold the hose on to the relevant union, pull out the spring clip and pull the hose from the union (see illustration). Note that the radiator inlet and outlet unions are fragile; do not use excessive force when attempting to remove the hoses. If a hose proves to be difficult to remove, try to release it by rotating the hose ends before attempting to free it.

> **HAYNES HINT** *If all else fails, cut the hose with a sharp knife, then slit it so that it can be peeled off in two pieces. Although this may prove expensive if the hose is otherwise undamaged, it is preferable to buying a new radiator.*

5 When fitting a hose, first slide the clips onto the hose, and then work the hose into position. If clamp type clips were originally fitted, it is a good idea to use screw-type clips when refitting the hose. If the hose is stiff, use a little soapy water as a lubricant, or soften the hose by soaking it in hot water.

2.3 Using grips to release the hose clip

2.4 Pull out the retaining clip

6 Work the hose into position, checking that it is correctly routed, and then slide each clip along the hose until it passes over the flared end of the relevant union, before securing it in position with the retaining clip.

7 Prior to refitting a radiator inlet or outlet hose renew the connection O-ring regardless of condition. The connections are a push-fit over the radiator unions.

8 Refill the cooling system as described in Chapter 1A, Section 30 or Chapter 1B, Section 30.

9 Check thoroughly for leaks as soon as possible after disturbing any part of the cooling system.

3 Radiator –
removal, inspection and refitting

Removal

1 Disconnect the battery negative lead. **Note:** *Before disconnecting the battery, refer to 'Disconnecting the battery' in the Reference section at the rear of this manual.*

2 To give better access, apply the handbrake, and then jack up the front of the vehicle and support it on axle stands (see *Jacking and vehicle support*).

3 Drain the cooling system as described in Chapter 1A, Section 30 or 1B, Section 30, then disconnect the upper and lower hoses from the radiator.

4 The front cross member/lock carrier needs to be moved forward and set in the service position, as described in Chapter 2E, Section 4. This will allow more room for the radiator assembly to be removed.

5 Disconnect the wiring from the cooling fan thermo-switch and the cooling fan on the left-hand side of the radiator **(see illustration)**.

6 Release the securing clips (two at each side), and then slide the cooling fan and cowling upwards and out from the rear of the radiator (See Section 5).

7 Working at the front of the panel **(see illustration)**, undo the retaining screws (one at each side on diesel engines and two at each side on petrol engines), and carefully tilt the radiator backwards.

3.5 Disconnect the cooling fan and switch wiring connectors – arrowed

Models with air-conditioning

8 With the radiator tilted back, undo the retaining screw that secures the air-conditioning pipe mounting bracket to the right-hand lower side of the radiator **(see illustration)**.

9 Undo the four screws at the front of the condenser that secure it to the radiator, then using cable ties (or similar) secure the condenser to the front cross panel **(see illustrations)**.

All models

10 The radiator can now be removed from inside the front of the engine compartment. On turbo charged diesel engines, the intercooler is attached across the lower part of the radiator; lift the radiator complete with intercooler out from the front panel.

Inspection

11 If the radiator has been removed due

3.8 Undo the mounting bracket securing screw - arrowed

3.7 Undo the radiator mounting screws (one side shown)

to suspected blockage, reverse flush it as described in the relevant part of Chapter 1.

12 Clean dirt and debris from the radiator fins, using an air-line (in which case, wear eye protection) or a soft brush. Be careful, as the fins are sharp and easily damaged.

13 If necessary, a radiator specialist can perform a 'flow test' on the radiator, to establish whether an internal blockage exists.

14 A leaking radiator must be referred to a specialist for permanent repair. Do not attempt to weld or solder a leaking radiator, as damage may result.

15 If the radiator is to be sent for repair or renewed, remove the cooling fan and thermo-switch.

Refitting

16 Refitting is a reversal of removal, but check the condition of the mounting rubbers and renew if necessary **(see illustration)**. On

3.9a Undo the lower securing screws (one side shown)...

3.9b ...and upper securing screws (one side shown)...

3.9c ...then use cable ties (arrowed) to secure the condenser

3.16 Check the radiator mounting rubbers

4.13 Disconnect the coolant hose

(4.14 Remove and discard the seal)

4.14 Remove and discard the seal

4.15 Remove the thermostat

completion, refill the cooling system using the correct type of antifreeze as described in Chapter 1A, Section 30 or Chapter 1B, Section 30.

4 Thermostat – removal, testing and refitting

1 As the thermostat ages, it will become slower to react to changes in water temperature ('lazy'). Ultimately, the unit may stick in the open or closed position, and this causes problems. A thermostat that is stuck open will result in a very slow warm-up; a thermostat, which is stuck shut, will lead to rapid overheating.
2 Before assuming the thermostat is to blame for a cooling system problem, check the coolant level. If the system is draining due to a leak, or has not been properly filled, there may be an airlock in the system (refer to the coolant renewal procedure in Chapter 1A, Section 30 or Chapter 1B, Section 30).
3 If the engine seems to be taking a long time to warm up (based on heater output), the thermostat could be stuck open. Don't necessarily believe the temperature gauge reading – some gauges never seem to register very high in normal driving.
4 A lengthy warm-up period might suggest that the thermostat is missing - it may have been removed or inadvertently omitted by a previous owner or mechanic. Don't drive the car without a thermostat – the engine management system's ECU will then stay in warm-up mode for longer than necessary,

causing emissions and fuel economy to suffer.
5 If the engine runs hot, use your hand to check the temperature of the radiator top hose. If the hose isn't hot, but the engine clearly is, the thermostat is probably stuck closed, preventing the coolant inside the engine from escaping to the radiator – renew the thermostat. Again, this problem may also be due to an airlock (refer to the coolant renewal procedure in Chapter 1A, Section 30 or Chapter 1B, Section 30).
6 If the radiator top hose is hot, it means that the coolant is flowing (at least as far as the radiator) and the thermostat is open. Consult the *Fault diagnosis* section at the end of this manual to assist in tracing possible cooling system faults, but a lack of heater output would now definitely suggest an airlock or a blockage.
7 To gain a rough idea of whether the thermostat is working properly when the engine is warming up, without dismantling the system, proceed as follows.
8 With the engine completely cold, start the engine and let it idle, while checking the temperature of the radiator top hose. Periodically check the temperature indicated on the coolant temperature gauge – if overheating is indicated, switch the engine off immediately.
9 The top hose should feel cold for some time as the engine warms up, and should then get warm quite quickly as the thermostat opens.
10 The above is not a precise or definitive test of thermostat operation, but if the system does not perform as described, remove and test the thermostat as described below.

Removal

Petrol engines

11 The thermostat is located beneath a cover in a housing on the left-hand end of the cylinder head.
12 Drain the cooling system as described in Chapter 1A, Section 30.
13 Release the retaining clip and disconnect the coolant radiator bottom hose from the thermostat cover **(see illustration)**.
14 Unscrew the retaining bolts and remove the thermostat housing cover and sealing ring from the engine. Discard the sealing ring; a new one must be used on refitting **(see illustrations)**.
15 Remove the thermostat from the housing **(see illustration)**. Note that the thermostat is only available together with its spring housing.

Diesel engines

16 The thermostat is located behind the alternator at the front right-hand side of the engine cylinder block. There are two types of thermostat fitted to diesel models:
  1) Single hose to the thermostat cover, and the thermostat can be renewed separately.
  2) Four hoses to the thermostat housing, the thermostat is part of the housing and can only be renewed as a complete assembly.
17 Drain the cooling system as described in Chapter 1B, Section 30. If the coolant is not due for renewal, it may be re-used if it is collected in a clean container.
18 Slacken the retaining clips and remove the rubber hose from the intercooler and charge air ducting to the throttle housing/inlet manifold.
19 Undo the bolt on the right-hand end of the engine, and disconnect the wiring connector from the charge pressure/temperature sensor on the charge air ducting.
20 Slacken the clip securing the charge air ducting to the throttle housing/inlet manifold, then undo the bolt at the rear of the air-conditioning compressor and withdraw the ducting out from the front of the engine.
21 To make access easier, remove the alternator as described in Chapter 5A, Section 5.
22 Release the securing clip(s) and disconnect the coolant hose(s) from the thermostat cover/housing **(see illustrations)**.

4.22a Release the hose securing clip(s) – arrowed...

4.22b ...there could be up to four hoses depending on model

23 Unscrew the two securing bolts, and remove the thermostat cover/housing complete with the thermostat. Note the locations of any brackets secured by the bolts. Recover the O-ring if it is loose (see illustrations). **Note:** *On thermostat housing with four hose connections, there is a collar that fits into the cylinder block, which is a tight fit, and will need to be rotated from side to side to release it. Damage may occur, so a new one will be required for refitting.*

24 On models with one hose connections to the thermostat cover, remove the thermostat by twisting the thermostat 90° clockwise, and then pull it from the cover.

25 On models with three (or four) hose connections to the thermostat housing, the thermostat cannot be removed, renew the complete unit.

Testing

Note: *If there is any question about the operation of the thermostat, it's best to renew it – they are not expensive items. Testing involves heating in, or over, an open pan of boiling water, which carries with it the risk of scalding. A thermostat that has seen more than five years' service may well be past its best already.*

26 If the thermostat remains in the open position at room temperature, it is faulty, and must be renewed as a matter of course.

27 Check to see if there's an open temperature marking stamped on the thermostat.

28 Using a thermometer and container of water, heat the water until the temperature corresponds with the temperature marking stamped on the thermostat. If no marking is found, start the test with the water hot, and heat slowly until it boils.

29 Suspend the (closed) thermostat on a length of string in the water, and check that maximum opening occurs before the water boils.

30 Remove the thermostat and allow it to cool down, check that it closes fully.

31 If the thermostat does not open and close as described, or if it sticks in either position, it must be renewed.

Refitting

32 Refitting is a reversal of removal, bearing in mind the following points:
a) Refit the thermostat using a new O-ring (see illustrations).
b) Insert the thermostat into the cover and twist 90° anti-clockwise (diesel engines).
c) Ensure that any brackets are in place on the thermostat cover bolts as noted before removal.
d) Refit the alternator (where applicable) with reference to Chapter 5A, Section 5.
e) Refill the cooling system with the correct type and quantity of coolant as described in Chapter 1A, Section 30 or Chapter 1B, Section 30.

4.23a Undo the retaining bolts (arrowed) - four hose fitment...

4.23b ...and remove the thermostat housing – single hose fitment

4.32a Renew the O-ring seal – single hose fitment

4.32b Renew the O-ring seal – four hose fitment

5 Electric cooling fan – testing, removal and refitting

Testing

1 The cooling fan is supplied with current through the ignition switch, cooling fan control unit (where applicable), the relay(s) and fuses/fusible link (see Chapter 12). The circuit is completed by the cooling fan thermostatic switch, which is mounted in the left-hand end of the radiator. The cooling fan has two speed settings; the thermostatic switch actually contains two switches, one for the stage 1 fan speed setting and another for the stage 2 fan speed setting. Testing of the cooling fan circuit is as follows, noting that the following check should be carried out on both the stage 1 speed circuit and speed 2 circuit (see wiring diagrams at the end of Chapter 12).

5.7 Removing the air ducting panel

2 If the fan does not appear to work, first check the fuses/fusible links. If they are good, run the engine until normal operating temperature is reached, then allow it to idle. If the fan does not cut in within a few minutes, switch off the ignition and disconnect the wiring plug from the cooling fan switch. Bridge the relevant two contacts in the wiring plug using a length of spare wire, and switch on the ignition. If the fan now operates, the switch is probably faulty and should be renewed.

3 If the switch appears to work, the motor can be checked by disconnecting the motor wiring connector and connecting a 12-volt supply directly to the motor terminals. If the motor is faulty, it must be renewed, as no spares are available.

4 If the fan still fails to operate, check the cooling fan circuit wiring (Chapter 12). Check each wire for continuity and ensure that all connections are clean and free of corrosion.

5 On models with a cooling fan control unit, if no fault can be found with the fuses/fusible links, wiring, fan switch, or fan motor, then it is likely that the cooling fan control unit is faulty. Testing of the unit should be entrusted to a VW dealer or specialist; if the unit is faulty it must be renewed.

Removal and refitting

6 Disconnect the battery negative lead. **Note:** *Before disconnecting the battery, refer to 'Disconnecting the battery' in the Reference section at the rear of this manual.*

7 Where applicable, undo the retaining screws and disconnect the air intake duct from the upper cross panel (see illustration).

5.8 Unclip the wiring connector from the cowling

8 Disconnect the wiring plug from the cooling fan motor, and slide the connector from the retaining bracket **(see illustration)**.

9 Release the retaining clips (two at each side) and slide the cooling fan and shroud upwards and away from the radiator **(see illustration)**. Take care not to damage the radiator fins as the fan assembly is removed.

10 If required, undo the nuts securing the fan to the radiator shroud, and withdraw the fan.

11 Refitting is a reversal of removal.

---

6 Cooling system electrical switches and sensors – testing, removal and refitting

Cooling fan thermostatic switch

Testing

1 Testing of the switch is described in

6.6 Unscrew the thermo-switch

5.9 Cooling fan and shroud removed from the radiator

Section 5, as part of the electric cooling fan test procedure.

Removal

2 The thermo-switch is located in the left-hand side of the radiator. The engine and radiator must be cold before removing the switch.

3 Disconnect the battery negative lead. **Note:** *Before disconnecting the battery, refer to 'Disconnecting the battery' in the Reference section at the rear of this manual.*

4 Either drain the radiator to below the level of the switch (as described in Chapter 1A, Section 30 or Chapter 1B, Section 30), or have ready a suitable plug which can be used to plug the switch aperture in the radiator whilst the switch is removed. If a plug is used, take great care not to damage the radiator, and do not use anything that will allow foreign matter to enter the radiator.

5 Disconnect the wiring plug from the thermo-switch.

6.9 Coolant temperature sensor – petrol models

6 Carefully unscrew the thermo-switch from the radiator **(see illustration)**.

Refitting

7 Refitting is a reversal of removal, but apply a smear of suitable grease to the threads of the switch and tighten it to the specified torque. On completion, refill the cooling system with the correct type and quantity of coolant as described in Chapter 1A, Section 30 or Chapter 1B, Section 30, or top-up as described in *Weekly checks*.

8 Start the engine and run it until it reaches normal operating temperature, then continue to run the engine and check that the cooling fan cuts in and functions correctly.

Coolant temperature sensors

Testing

9 On petrol engines the coolant temperature sensor is located on the coolant distribution housing on the left-hand end of the cylinder head **(see illustration)**.

10 On diesel engines there are two coolant temperature sensors, one is located on the coolant distribution housing on the left-hand end of the cylinder head, the other one is in the coolant hose which goes around the rear of the engine to the EGR cooler. On 1.2 litre engines it is in the hose at the front right-hand side of the sump and on 1.6 litre engines it is in the hose which goes around the right-hand side of the top of the engine, by the timing belt cover **(see illustrations)**.

11 The sensor contains a thermistor, which consists of an electronic component whose electrical resistance decreases at a predetermined rate as its temperature rises. When the coolant is cold, the sensor resistance is high, current flow through the gauge is reduced, and the gauge needle points towards the 'cold' end of the scale. Typical resistances are given in the Specifications; however, the sensor can also be checked by a VW dealer, or specialist using diagnostic equipment. If the sensor is faulty, it must be renewed.

Removal and refitting

12 Disconnect the wiring plug from the relevant temperature sensor. Partially drain the cooling system to below the level of the sensor (as described in Chapter 1A, Section 30 or Chapter 1B, Section 30).

6.10a Coolant temperature sensor – diesel models

6.10b Coolant temperature sensor – 1.2 litre diesel models

6.10c Coolant temperature sensor – 1.6 litre diesel models

13 Carefully withdraw the retaining clip and pull the sensor from the housing/hose connection **(see illustrations)**. Recover the O-ring
14 Refitting is a reversal of removal, bearing in mind the following points:
a) *Refit the sensor with a new O-ring.*
b) *Refill the cooling system as described in Chapter 1A, Section 30 or Chapter 1B, Section 30, or top-up as described in 'Weekly checks'.*

7 Coolant pump – removal and refitting

Note: *New coolant pumps may be of a modified design, which do not require gaskets. Use a suitable sealer.*

1.2 litre petrol engines

Removal

1 Drain the cooling system as described in Chapter 1A, Section 30.
2 Before removing the auxiliary drivebelt, loosen only the coolant pump pulley mounting bolts.
3 Remove the auxiliary drivebelt as described in Chapter 1A, Section 25.
4 Fully unscrew the bolts and remove the pulley from the coolant pump **(see illustration)**.
5 Unscrew the coolant pump retaining bolts, and withdraw the pump and gasket (if fitted) from the engine block. Identify the front retaining bolt, as it has sealant on its threads. If faulty, the pump must be renewed **(see illustration)**.

6.13a **Pull out the clip and sensor...**

6.13b **...and recover the sealing ring – diesel model shown**

Refitting

6 Refitting is a reversal of removal, bearing in mind the following points:
a) *Refit the pump using a new gasket (refer to note above).*
b) *Apply suitable sealant to the threads of the front retaining bolt.*
c) *Refill the cooling system as described in Chapter 1A, Section 30.*

1.4 litre petrol engines
Removal

7 Remove the main timing belt as described in Chapter 2B, Section 6. If the belt is to be re-used, note the direction of rotation.
8 Remove the timing belt idler roller, and rear timing belt cover.
9 Unscrew the coolant pump retaining bolts, and withdraw the pump from the engine block. Note the gasket is integral with the pump and must not be removed. If faulty, the pump must be renewed **(see illustration)**.

Refitting

10 Refitting is a reversal of removal, bearing in mind the following points:
a) *Clean the surface of the engine block before refitting the pump.*
b) *Refill the cooling system as described in Chapter 1A, Section 30.*

Diesel engines

11 Drain the cooling system as described in Chapter 1B, Section 30.
Belt driven coolant pump

12 Remove the camshaft timing belt as described in Chapter 2C, Section 7 or Chapter 2D, Section 7.
13 Unscrew the coolant pump retaining bolts, and remove the pump from the engine block. Recover the O-ring seal from the groove in the pump. If the pump is faulty, it must be renewed **(see illustrations)**.

7.4 **Removing the coolant pump pulley – 1.2 litre petrol engine**

7.5 **Removing the coolant pump – 1.2 litre petrol engine**

7.9 **Withdraw the coolant pump – 1.4 litre petrol engines**

7.13a **Undo the coolant pump bolts...**

7.13b **...remove it from the cylinder block...**

7.13c **...and recover the sealing ring – diesel engines**

7.16 Electric circulation pump – 1.2 litre engines

7.18 Disconnect the coolant hoses (1.6 litre shown)

14 Refitting is a reversal of removal, bearing in mind the following points.
 a) *Fit the coolant pump with a new O-ring.*
 b) *Lubricate the O-ring with coolant.*
 c) *Refill the cooling system as described in Chapter 1B, Section 30.*

Electric circulation pump

15 Raise the front of the vehicle and support is securely on axle stands (see *Jacking and vehicle support*).
16 Undo the fasteners and remove the engine undertray. On 1.2 litre engines the pump is fitted to the right-hand end of the sump **(see illustration)**, on 1.6 litre engines the pump is fitted to the front of the sump.
17 Disconnect the wiring plug connector to the pump **(see illustration)**.
18 Fit hose clamps to the coolant hoses connected to the pump, and release the clips and disconnect the hoses from the pump **(see**

7.17 Disconnect the wiring connector – arrowed

7.19 Undo the mounting bracket securing bolt - arrowed

illustration). Be prepared for some loss of coolant.
19 Undo the retaining bolt and remove the pump **(see illustration)**.
20 Refitting is a reversal of removal. Refill the cooling system as described in Chapter 1A, Section 30 or Chapter 1B, Section 30, or top-up as described in 'Weekly checks'.

8 Heating and ventilation system – general information

Heating system

1 The heating/ventilation system consists of a four-speed blower motor (housed in the passenger compartment), face-level vents in the centre and at each end of the facia, and air ducts to the front and rear footwells.

2 The control unit is located in the facia, and the controls operate flap valves to deflect and mix the air flowing through the various parts of the heating/ventilation system. The flap valves are contained in the air distribution housing, which acts as a central distribution unit, passing air to the various ducts and vents.
3 Cold air enters the system through the grille at the rear of the engine compartment. A pollen filter is fitted in the heater assembly to filter out dust, soot, pollen and spores from the air entering the car.
4 If warm air is required, the cold air is passed over the heater matrix, which is effectively a small radiator, with engine coolant flowing through it. Diesel models are fitted with an additional electric heating element below the matrix, to ensure quick heater output – this heating element only operates when the coolant temperature is below 80°C.
5 The airflow, which can be boosted by the blower, then flows through the various ducts, according to the settings of the controls. Stale air is expelled through ducts below the rear window.
6 If necessary, the outside air supply can be closed off, allowing the air inside the car to be recirculated. This can be useful to prevent unpleasant odours entering from outside the car, but should only be used briefly, as the recirculated air inside the car will soon deteriorate.

9 Heating and ventilation system components – removal and refitting

Heater control panel

1 Carefully unclip the trim cover from around the radio/CD unit and the heater control panel **(see illustrations)**.
2 Remove the front part of the centre console, as described in Chapter 11, Section 26.
3 Undo the two screws from the base of the heater control panel **(see illustration)**, then carefully withdraw the unit slightly.
4 Reach behind the right-hand side of the panel and disconnect the heater/ventilation control cable, the cable is released by pressing down the back half of the securing clip **(see illustration)**.

9.1a Carefully unclip the radio/CD trim panel...

9.1b ...and unclip the heater trim panel

9.3 Remove the two screws from the base of the control panel

9.4 Release the cable from the control panel

9.8 Use hose clamps to prevent coolant leaking

9.11 Remove the rubber air vent sleeve

9.12a Pull back the insulation…

9.12b …and release the securing clips (arrowed)

9.13 Withdraw the heater matrix and lower housing

5 Withdraw the control panel and disconnect the wiring plug connectors, then remove it from the facia.

6 Refitting is a reversal of removal, ensuring that the control cable is refitted correctly.

Heater matrix

7 At the rear of the engine compartment, remove the bulkhead trim from the plenum chamber, as described in Chapter 12, Section 18 (wiper motor/linkage removal). This will make access to the coolant hoses on the bulkhead easier.

8 Using hose clamps, clamp the heater matrix inlet and return hoses located on the bulkhead at the rear of the engine compartment **(see illustration)**. Place a container beneath the hoses, then release the retaining clips and disconnect them. Note the location of the hoses for correct refitting. Alternatively drain the cooling system as described in Chapter 1A, Section 30 or Chapter 1B, Section 30.

9 With the hoses disconnected, remove the

coolant from the matrix by blowing air into the inlet tube; preferably using an airline, then the coolant can be caught coming out of the outlet tube using a container.

Caution: Always use eye protection when using an airline.

10 Remove the centre console, as described in Chapter 11, Section 26.

11 Unclip the rubber sleeve from the air vent on the heater lower housing **(see illustration)**.

12 Pull back the insulation from around the heater housing and release the securing clips that hold the lower part of the housing to the upper part **(see illustrations)**.

13 Withdraw the lower part of the housing complete with heater matrix from inside the passenger compartment **(see illustration)**. Take care not to damage the pipes, as they are withdrawn from the bulkhead grommet. Place cloth rags or similar on the floor beneath the heater matrix to catch any

coolant that may be lost, as the heater matrix is removed.

14 On diesel engine models with auxiliary air heater element, undo the securing nut and disconnect the earth connections from the body panel and disconnect the auxiliary heater element wiring connector from the right-hand side of the heater housing **(see illustrations)**.

15 Withdraw the heater matrix out from the lower housing **(see illustration)**.

16 Refitting is a reversal of removal, noting the following.

a) *Make sure the foam seal is fitted correctly around the perimeter of the matrix.*

b) *Make sure the matrix is located correctly in the housing.*

c) *Check that the coolant pipes locate correctly in the rubber grommet in the bulkhead.*

d) *Refill the cooling system and top-up the coolant level with reference to 'Weekly checks' at the beginning of this Manual.*

9.14a Undo the earth cable securing nut (arrowed)…

9.14b …and disconnect the heater wiring connector – arrowed

9.15 Lift the heater matrix from the housing

9.20 Undo the bulkhead bolt - arrowed

Heater housing

Warning: Refer to the precautions given in Section 11.

17 It is not possible to remove the housing without opening the refrigerant circuit to the air-conditioning evaporator; therefore this task must be entrusted to a VW dealer or an air conditioning specialist, before removal of the heater housing.
Caution: The air conditioning compressor is driven permanently by the auxiliary drivebelt, and is not fitted with a magnetic clutch. It is not recommended that the engine is started without refrigerant being present in the system, as the compressor may overheat causing internal damage. Note also that if the refrigerant circuit is not opened within 10 minutes of evacuation, slight pressure may develop due to re-evaporation.
18 Remove the facia panel and crossmember, as described in Chapter 11, Section 27.
19 At the rear of the engine compartment, remove the bulkhead trim from the plenum chamber, as described in Chapter 12, Section 18 (wiper motor/linkage removal).
20 Undo the heater housing securing bolt, behind the wiper motor at the rear of the bulkhead **(see illustration)**.
21 Using hose clamps, clamp the heater matrix inlet and return hoses located on the bulkhead at the rear of the engine compartment **(see illustration 9.8)**. Place a container beneath the hoses, then pull out the clips and disconnect them. Note the location of the hoses for correct refitting.

9.23 Unbolt the refrigerant lines from the evaporator expansion valve

22 With the hoses disconnected, remove the coolant from the matrix by blowing air into the inlet tube; preferably using an airline, then the coolant can be caught coming out of the outlet tube using a container.
Caution: Always use eye protection when using an airline.
23 With the refrigerant evacuated, unscrew the bolts securing the refrigerant lines to the evaporator on the bulkhead at the rear of the engine compartment, and detach them. Recover the seals and plug the lines and evaporator openings to prevent entry of foreign matter and water vapour. Discard the seals, as new ones must be used on refitting **(see illustration)**.
24 Inside the car, place cloth rags or similar on the floor beneath the heater unit.
25 Note the location and routing of all wiring then disconnect it from the heater unit, also note the location of plastic cable ties to ensure correct refitting.
26 Carefully pull the heater unit from the bulkhead, taking care not to damage the matrix tubes on the bulkhead. The help of an assistant may be required. Be prepared for coolant spillage as the assembly is removed from inside the car. As the heater unit assembly is removed, check to see if there is any wiring still attached to the housing.
27 If necessary, the heater may be further dismantled on the bench.
28 Refitting is a reversal of removal, but refill the cooling system and top-up the coolant with reference to *Weekly checks* at the beginning of this Manual. Have the air-conditioning system refilled by a VW dealer or an air conditioning specialist, when finished.

Fresh air/recirculating/temperature/ flap positioning servomotors

Note: *Depending on model, there may be up to five air flap servomotors fitted.*
29 On the model being worked on, there are two air flap motors to the left-hand side of the heater housing and one on the right.
30 To access the servo motors, remove the facia panel and crossmember, as described in Chapter 11, Section 27.
31 Disconnect the wiring, undo the motor retaining bolt(s), then remove it from its mountings, and where applicable, separate it from the air flap lever. Note the position of the drive/gear on the rear of the servomotor, as it needs to be re-aligned when refitting. If the drive/gear is not aligned correctly, the flaps will not operate correctly.
32 Refitting is a reversal of removal. Note that if the motor is renewed, its basic settings may need to be reprogrammed by a VW dealer using specialist equipment.

Heater blower motor

33 Remove the glovebox, as described in Chapter 11, Section 25.
34 Switch off the ignition and all electrical consumers.
35 Disconnect the wiring connector from the blower motor, and unclip the wiring and connector from the housing **(see illustration)**.
36 Release the cable tie and wiring from the right-hand side of the blower housing **(see illustration)**.
37 Undo the five retaining screws and remove the blower motor from the housing **(see illustration)**.
38 Refitting is a reversal of removal.

Heater blower motor series resistor

39 Remove the heater blower motor as described previously in paragraphs 33 to 38.
40 Pull the resistor upwards to remove it from the housing **(see illustration)**, if required it can be pushed upwards by reaching inside the air duct.
Caution: The resistor may be very hot if the heater has recently been in use.
41 Disconnect the wiring from the resistor, after it has been withdrawn from the housing.
42 Refitting is the reverse of removal.

9.35 Disconnect the wiring connector – arrowed

9.36 Cut the cable tie from the wiring loom

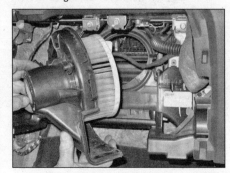

9.37 Removing the heater blower motor

Auxiliary heater

43 Some diesel engine models are equipped with an auxiliary electrically powered heating element within the heating unit, below the heater matrix. In order to remove the element, remove the heater matrix, as described previously in paragraphs 7 to 16.

44 Withdraw the auxiliary heater out from the lower housing, noting its fitted position **(see illustration)**.

45 Refitting is a reversal of removal.

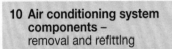

10 Air conditioning system components – removal and refitting

⚠ *Warning: Refer to the precautions given in Section 11, before working on the air-conditioning system.*

1 Before working on any components in the air-conditioning system, have the refrigerant evacuated from the air conditioning system by a VW dealer or refrigeration specialist.

Caution: The air conditioning compressor is driven permanently by the auxiliary drivebelt, and is not fitted with a magnetic clutch. It is not recommended that the engine be started without refrigerant being present in the system, as the compressor may overheat causing internal damage. Note also that if the refrigerant circuit is not opened within 10 minutes of evacuation, slight pressure may develop due to re-evaporation.

Evaporator

2 Remove the heater housing and heater matrix, as described earlier in Section 9.

3 Remove the rubber gaiter and foam cushion from around the refrigerant pipes.

4 Working your way around the housing, undo the retaining screws and release the securing clips and split the housing, then withdraw the evaporator from the housing.

5 Refitting is a reversal of removal, fit new seals and have the system recharged by a VW dealer or refrigeration specialist.

Condenser

6 Have the refrigerant evacuated from the air conditioning system by a VW dealer or refrigeration specialist.

7 Undo the two bolts securing the refrigerant lines to the condenser **(see illustration)**. As the pipes are disconnected, recover the seals and plug the lines and condenser openings to prevent entry of foreign matter and water vapour.

8 Remove the radiator as described in Section 3 of this Chapter, there is no need to carry out the procedures in paragraphs 8 and 9 at this point, as the condenser can be removed whilst still attached to the front of the radiator.

9 With the radiator and condenser removed from the engine compartment, undo the retaining screws and split the condenser from the radiator, taking care not to damage its fins.

9.40 Pull the resistor out from the housing

10 Refitting is a reversal of removal, but fit new seals, and have the system recharged by a VW dealer or refrigeration specialist.

Compressor

11 Have the refrigerant evacuated from the air conditioning system by a VW dealer or refrigeration specialist.

12 Remove the auxiliary drivebelt as described in Chapter 1A, Section 25 or Chapter 1B, Section 25.

13 Unscrew the retaining bolts and disconnect the refrigerant lines from the compressor **(see illustration)**. Remove the O-ring seals and renew them if necessary. Plug the open pipes and ports to prevent the ingress of moisture.

14 Disconnect the wiring plug connector from the rear of the compressor **(see illustration)**.

15 Undo the retaining bolts **(see illustration)**, and withdraw the compressor from the mounting bracket.

10.7 Refrigerant lines to the condenser

10.14 Disconnect the wiring connector

9.44 Remove the auxiliary heater from the lower housing

16 Refitting is a reversal of the removal procedure, ensure that all the fixings are tightened to the specified torque settings, where given. On completion, have new O-rings fitted to the refrigerant lines, and then have the system recharged by a VW dealer or refrigeration specialist.

Receiver/drier

Note: *Check for the availability of parts before removal, there are different makes of receiver/drier and some cannot be renewed separately from the condenser.*

17 The receiver/drier is attached to the left-hand side of the condenser.

18 Remove the condenser, as described in paragraphs 6 to 10.

19 Unscrew the cap (with a T50 torx socket) from the top of the receiver/drier **(see illustration)**.

Caution: DO NOT remove this cap if the

10.13 Refrigerant lines to the compressor

10.15 Unscrew the compressor mounting bolts - arrowed

10.19 Use cable ties to secure the condenser

system has not been evacuated, as it will be under high pressure.

20 Push downwards slightly on sealing cover and extract the retaining circlip from inside the same end of the condenser. Pull the receiver/drier filter element from place.

21 Refitting is a reversal of the removal procedure, ensure that all the fixings are tightened to the specified torque settings, where given. On completion, fit new O-rings and then have the system recharged by a VW dealer or refrigeration specialist.

Evaporator temperature sensor

22 To access the sensor, remove the facia panel and crossmember, as described in Chapter 11, Section 27.

23 The sensor is located to the right-hand side, upper part of the heater housing, behind the evaporator.

24 Disconnect the wiring plug connector, then pull the sensor out from the housing.

25 Refitting is a reversal of the removal procedure.

11 Air conditioning system – general information and precautions

General information

Air conditioning is fitted as standard to most models, and is available as manually operated (Climatic) or automatically-operated (Climatronic). The Climatronic system works in conjunction with the heating and air conditioning systems to maintain a selected vehicle interior temperature fully automatically.

The air conditioning system enables the temperature of incoming air to be lowered, and dehumidifies the air, which makes for rapid demisting and increased comfort. The cooling side of the system works in the same way as a domestic refrigerator. Refrigerant gas is drawn into a belt-driven compressor and passes into a condenser mounted in front of the radiator, where it loses heat and becomes liquid. The liquid passes through an expansion valve to an evaporator, where it changes from liquid under high pressure to gas under low pressure. This change is accompanied by a drop in temperature, which in turn cools the evaporator. The refrigerant returns to the compressor and the cycle begins again.

Air blown through the evaporator passes to the air distribution unit, where it is mixed with hot air blown through the heater matrix to achieve the desired temperature in the passenger compartment.

The operation of the system is controlled electronically by coolant temperature switches, and pressure switches which are screwed into the compressor high-pressure line. Any problems with the system should be referred to a VW dealer or an air conditioning specialist.

The only operation that can be carried out easily without discharging the refrigerant is the renewal of the compressor drivebelt, which is covered in the relevant part of Chapter 1. Removal of the evaporator and condenser requires the evacuation of the refrigerant. If necessary the compressor can be unbolted and moved aside, without disconnecting its flexible hoses, after removing the drivebelt.

Precautions

• *When an air conditioning system is fitted, it is necessary to observe special precautions whenever dealing with any part of the system, its associated components and any items which require disconnection of the system. If for any reason the system must be disconnected, entrust this task to your VW dealer or an air conditioning specialist.*

⚠️ *Warning: The refrigeration circuit contains a refrigerant and it is therefore dangerous to disconnect any part of the system without specialised knowledge and equipment. The refrigerant is potentially dangerous and should only be handled by qualified persons. If it is splashed onto the skin it can cause frostbite. It is not itself poisonous, but in the presence of a naked flame (including a cigarette) it forms a poisonous gas. Uncontrolled discharging of the refrigerant is dangerous and potentially damaging to the environment.*

• *Do not operate the air conditioning system if it is known to be short of refrigerant, as this may damage the compressor.*

Chapter 4 Part A:
Petrol engine fuel systems

Contents

Degrees of difficulty

Easy, suitable for novice with little experience		**Fairly easy,** suitable for beginner with some experience		**Fairly difficult,** suitable for competent DIY mechanic		**Difficult,** suitable for experienced DIY mechanic		**Very difficult,** suitable for expert DIY or professional	

Specifications

Engine codes

1.2 litre:
SOHC	CHFA
DOHC	CGPA and CGPB
1.4 litre	CGGB

System type

1.2 litre engines:
Engine code CHFA	Siemens Simos 3PG
Engine codes CGPA and CGPB	Siemens Simos 9.1 SRE

1.4 litre engines:
Engine codes CGGB	Magneti Marelli 4HV

Recommended fuel

Minimum octane rating:

All models . . . . 95 RON unleaded
(91 RON unleaded may be used, but with reduced performance)

Fuel system data

Fuel pump type	Electric, immersed in fuel tank
Fuel pump delivery rate	540 cc/30 secs (battery voltage of 10.5 V)
Regulated fuel pressure	3.9 to 4.2 bar
Minimum fuel pressure	3.0 bar

Engine idle speed (non-adjustable, electronically controlled):

1.2 litre engines:
Engine code CHFA	600 to 850 rpm
Engine codes CGPA and CGPB	650 to 870 rpm

1.4 litre engine:
Engine code CGGB	630 to 850 rpm
Idle CO content (non-adjustable, electronically controlled)	0.5 % max
Injector electrical resistance (typical)	12 to 17 ohms

Torque wrench settings

	Nm	lbf ft
Camshaft position sensor	8	6
Fuel rail mounting bolts	10	7
Fuel tank strap securing bolts	25	18
Fuel sender unit/pump retaining ring	80	58
Inlet air temperature/pressure sensor	3	2
Inlet manifold	20	15
Knock sensor(s)	20	15
Oxygen sensor(s)	50	37
Throttle valve control unit:		
1.2 litre engines	10	7
1.4 litre engines	8	6

1 General information and precautions

General information

The systems described in this Chapter are all self-contained engine management systems, which control both the fuel injection and ignition. This Chapter deals with the fuel system components only – see Chapter 4C for information on the exhaust and emission control systems, and to Chapter 5B for details of the ignition system.

The fuel injection system comprises a fuel tank, an electric fuel pump/level sender unit, a fuel filter, fuel supply and return lines, a throttle valve control unit, a fuel rail, four electronic fuel injectors, and an Electronic Control Unit (ECU) together with its associated sensors, actuators and wiring. All the fuel systems used operate in the same manner, but there are some detail differences. The electronic power control system (EPC) is completely electronic, and no accelerator cable is fitted. The position of the accelerator pedal is signalled from the pedal control unit by two variable resistors, and the throttle valve is then activated by an electric motor in the throttle valve control unit on the inlet manifold. With the engine stopped, the position of the throttle valve is directly comparable to the position of the accelerator pedal, however, when the engine is running the engine control unit opens and closes the throttle valve independently according to the prevailing conditions. This may mean, for example, that the throttle valve may be fully open even though the accelerator pedal is only half open. The engine electronic control unit (ECU) determines the best position for the throttle valve in the interests of exhaust gas emission and fuel consumption. In the event of a fault in the system, the EPC warning light will illuminate on the instrument panel and the fault will be stored in the fault memory. The system then switches to its emergency settings and the engine speed is increased to allow the driver to take the car to a VW dealer, however, the accelerator pedal position senders are no longer operational.

The fuel pump is immersed in the fuel inside the tank, and delivers a constant supply of fuel through a cartridge filter to the fuel rail. The pressure regulator is integral with the fuel filter located next to the fuel tank, and the return line is taken from the filter to the fuel tank. The fuel pressure regulator maintains a constant fuel pressure to the fuel injectors, and returns excess fuel to the tank through the return line. This constant flow system also helps to reduce fuel temperature, and prevents vaporisation.

The fuel injectors are opened and closed by the Electronic Control Unit (ECU), which calculates the injection timing and duration according to engine speed, crankshaft/camshaft position, throttle position and rate of opening, inlet manifold depression, inlet air temperature, coolant temperature and exhaust gas oxygen content information, received from sensors mounted on and around the engine.

Inlet air is drawn into the engine through the air cleaner, which contains a renewable paper filter element. On 1.4 litre engines, the air cleaner is integral with the engine top cover, however, on 1.2 litre engines, it is located at the left-hand rear corner of the engine compartment. On all engines, the inlet air temperature is regulated by a valve mounted in the air cleaner inlet trunking, which blends air at ambient temperature with hot air, drawn from over the exhaust manifold.

The temperature and pressure of the air entering the engine is measured by a sensor located on the inlet manifold. This information is used by the ECU to fine-tune the fuelling requirements for different operating conditions.

Idle speed is determined by the ECU, and manual adjustment of the engine idle speed is not necessary or possible.

The exhaust gas oxygen content is constantly monitored by the ECU through two oxygen sensors (also known as lambda sensors). One is fitted before the catalytic converter, and the other after – this improves sensor response time and accuracy, and the ECU compares the signals from each sensor to confirm that the converter is working correctly. The ECU uses the information from the sensors to modify the injection timing and duration to maintain the optimum air/fuel ratio – a result of this is that manual adjustment of the idle exhaust CO content is not necessary or possible. Refer to Chapter 4C for more information.

On all engines, the ECU controls the operation of the activated charcoal filter evaporative loss system – refer to Chapter 4C for further details.

It should be noted that fault diagnosis of all the engine management systems described in this Chapter is only possible with dedicated electronic test equipment. Problems with the systems operation should therefore be referred to a VW dealer for assessment. Once the fault has been identified, the removal/refitting sequences detailed in the following Sections will then allow the appropriate component(s) to be renewed as required.

Note: *The engine code may be found on the vehicle data sticker, inside the luggage compartment, by the spare wheel.*

Precautions

 Warning: Petrol is extremely flammable – great care must be taken when working on any part of the fuel system.

• *Do not smoke, or allow any naked flames or uncovered light bulbs near the work area. Note that gas-powered domestic appliances with pilot flames, such as heaters boilers and tumble-dryers, also present a fire hazard – bear this in mind if you are working in an area where such appliances are present. Always keep a suitable fire extinguisher close to the work area, and familiarise yourself with its operation before starting work. Wear eye protection when working on fuel systems, and wash off any fuel spilt on bare skin immediately with soap and water. Note that fuel vapour is just as dangerous as liquid fuel – possibly more so; a vessel that has been emptied of liquid fuel will still contain vapour, and can be potentially explosive.*

• *Many of the operations described in this Chapter involve the disconnection of fuel lines, which may cause an amount of fuel spillage. Before commencing work, refer to the above 'Warning' and the information in 'Safety first!' at the beginning of this manual.*

• *Residual fuel pressure always remains in the fuel system; long after the engine has been switched off. This pressure must be relieved in a controlled manner before work can commence on any component in the fuel system – refer to Section 8 for details.*

• *When working with fuel system components, pay particular attention to* cleanliness – dirt entering the fuel system may cause blockages, which will lead to poor running.

• In the interests of personal safety and equipment protection, many of the procedures in this Chapter suggest that the negative lead be removed from the battery terminal. This firstly eliminates the possibility of accidental short-circuits being caused as the car is being worked upon, and secondly prevents damage to electronic components (e.g. sensors, actuators, ECUs) which are particularly sensitive to the power surges caused by disconnection or reconnection of the wiring harness whilst they are still 'live'. Refer to 'Disconnecting the battery' at the rear of this manual.

2 Air cleaner and inlet system – removal and refitting

Removal

1.2 litre engine

1 The air cleaner is located at the left-hand rear corner of the engine compartment, behind the battery.

2 Disconnect the air inlet hose from the air cleaner cover by releasing the spring clip with a pair of grips.

3 Undo the screw and remove the hot air control flap duct from the air cleaner base.

4 Undo the retaining screw and remove the air cleaner assembly from its mounting rubbers.

5 To remove the intake pipe and hose from the throttle valve control unit, first disconnect the crankcase ventilation hose, then unscrew the mounting bolts and withdraw.

1.4 litre engine

6 Remove the air filter element as described in Chapter 1A, Section 23.

7 Release the catches, and disconnect the hose from the intake duct at the slam panel.

8 Pull the hose from the non-return valve at the left-hand side of the air cleaner, and pull the vacuum hose and valve from the rear corner.

9 Pull the air cleaner assembly upwards from the locating pins. Unclip the fuel hose, as the assembly is withdrawn.

Refitting

10 Refitting is a reversal of removal, but check that the adapter ring is correctly located and ensure that all hoses are securely fitted.

3 Inlet air temperature control system – general information

1 The inlet air temperature control system consists of a temperature-controlled flap valve, mounted on the air cleaner housing,

4.4 Disconnecting the wiring from the throttle valve control unit

and a hose to the warm-air collector plate over the exhaust manifold.

2 The temperature sensor in the flap valve housing senses the temperature of the inlet air, and opens the valve when a preset lower limit is reached. As the flap valve opens, warm air drawn from around the exhaust manifold blends with the inlet air.

3 As the temperature of the inlet air rises, the sensor closes the flap progressively, until the warm-air supply from the exhaust manifold is completely closed off, and only air at ambient temperature is admitted to the air cleaner.

4 With the warm-air hose removed from the temperature control flap valve housing, a hairdryer may be used to test the action of the sensor.

4 Fuel system components – removal and refitting

Note: Observe the precautions in Section 1 before working on any component in the fuel system. Information on the engine management system sensors which are more directly related to the ignition system will be found in Chapter 5B. After fitting any of the components in this Section, have the engine management ECU's fault memory interrogated and any resident faults erased by a VW dealer or suitably-equipped specialist.

Throttle valve control unit

Caution: If the throttle valve control unit is renewed, it will be necessary to program the new unit to the car before it can be used – this will need to be carried out by a VW dealer or specialist.

1 Remove the engine top cover and, where applicable, remove the air intake pipe from the top of the throttle valve control unit as described in Section 2.

2 On 1.2 litre engine code CHFA, disconnect the hose for the evaporative loss charcoal canister, and the hose for the crankcase ventilation hose from the intermediate plate located between the throttle valve control unit and inlet manifold.

3 On 1.2 litre engine codes CGPA and CGPB, unbolt the EGR valve pipe from the intermediate plate.

4.5 Throttle valve control unit mounting screws

4 Disconnect the wiring plug from the throttle valve control unit (see illustration).

5 Progressively unscrew the mounting screws and lift the throttle valve control unit from the top of the inlet manifold (see illustration). Recover the O-ring or gasket (as applicable) and discard it, as a new one will be required on refitting.

6 Where applicable, remove the intermediate plate from the inlet manifold and recover the O-ring. Discard the O-ring as a new one will be required on refitting.

7 Clean the contact faces of the control unit, inlet manifold and intermediate plate as applicable.

8 Refitting is a reversal of removal, but use new O-rings/gaskets and progressively tighten the mounting screws to the specified torque.

Fuel injectors and fuel rail

Note: If a faulty injector is suspected, before removing the injectors, it is worth trying the effect of one of the proprietary injector-cleaning treatments. These can be added to the petrol in the tank, and are intended to clean the injectors as you drive.

9 Remove the engine top cover as described in Section 2.

10 Unplug the injector harness connectors, labelling them to aid correct refitting later (see illustration). Release the wiring harness clips from the top of the fuel rail, and lay the harness to one side.

11 Refer to Section 8 and depressurise the fuel system.

12 On 1.2 litre engine code CHFA only, disconnect the vacuum hose from the fuel pressure regulator on the fuel rail.

4.10 Fuel injector wiring and fuel rail – DOHC engine

4.14a Unscrew the mounting bolts...

4.14b ...and lift the fuel rail with injectors from the inlet manifold...

4.14c ...then recover the injector lower O-ring seals

4.15a Extract the metal clip...

4.15b ...withdraw the injector from the fuel rail...

4.15c ...and recover the injector upper O-ring seal

13 Squeeze the catch on the quick-release fitting(s), and disconnect the fuel supply hose (and return where applicable) from the bulkhead. Alternatively, release the spring clip(s) securing the hose(s) to the fuel rail.
14 Unscrew and remove the fuel rail mounting bolts, then carefully lift the rail away from the inlet manifold, together with the injectors. Recover the injector lower O-ring seals as they emerge from the manifold **(see illustrations)**.
15 The injectors can be removed individually from the fuel rail by extracting the relevant metal clip and easing the injector out of the rail. Recover the injector upper O-ring seals **(see illustrations)**.
16 Check the electrical resistance of the injectors using a multi-meter, and compare it with the Specifications.
17 Refit the injectors and fuel rail by following the removal procedure in reverse, noting the following points:

a) *Renew the injector O-ring seals if they appear worn or damaged. Apply a little engine oil to the seals to assist their refitting* **(see illustration)**.
b) *Ensure that the injector retaining clips are securely seated.*
c) *Check that all electrical connections are remade correctly.*
d) *On 1.2 litre engines, purge air from the fuel rail by loosening the vent valve and temporarily switching on the ignition in order to operate the fuel pump. Tighten the vent valve when the fuel is free of air bubbles.*
e) *On completion, check for fuel leaks before bringing the car back into service.*

Fuel pressure regulator

Note: *Observe the precautions in Section 1 before working on any component in the fuel system.*

18 The fuel pressure regulator is part of the fuel filter and is renewed when changing the fuel filter, as described in Section 5.

Engine speed sensor

19 The engine speed sensor is mounted at the left-hand rear of the cylinder block, next to the transmission bellhousing, and access is very difficult. Where necessary, prise out the rubber bung for access to the sensor.
20 Trace the wiring back from the sensor, and unplug the harness connector.
21 Unscrew the retaining bolt and withdraw the sensor from the cylinder block/transmission **(see illustrations)**.
22 Refitting is a reversal of removal.

Inlet air temperature/ pressure sensor

23 The combined inlet air temperature and pressure sensor is located on the inlet

4.17 Apply a little engine oil to the O-ring seals to assist their refitting

4.21a Unscrew the bolt...

4.21b ...and remove the engine speed sensor – 1.2 litre engine

manifold. On the 1.2 litre engine code CHFA, it is located on the left-hand rear (as seen from the driver's seat), and on engine codes CGPA and CGPB, it is on the right-hand end of the manifold. On 1.4 litre engines it is clipped into the rear, right-hand end of the inlet manifold.

24 Remove the engine top cover and disconnect the wiring from the sensor.

25 On 1.2 litre engines, undo the two mounting screws and remove the sensor from the inlet manifold. Recover the O-ring seal(s). **Note:** *On 1.4 litre engines the sensor is clipped into the manifold, release the retaining clips and withdraw the sensor from the manifold. Recover the O-ring seal(s).*

26 Refitting is a reversal of removal, but renew the O-ring(s) and guide plate if necessary.

Knock sensor

27 The knock sensor is located on the rear of the cylinder block and is difficult to access **(see illustration)**.

28 Remove the engine top cover to gain access from above. Alternatively, firmly apply the handbrake then jack up the front of the car and support it on axle stands (see *Jacking and vehicle support*), and then remove the engine undertray.

29 Disconnect the wiring connector from the sensor or trace the wiring back from the sensor and disconnect its wiring connector.

30 Unscrew the mounting bolt and remove the sensor from the cylinder block.

31 Refitting is the reverse of removal. Ensure the mating surfaces of the sensor and cylinder block are clean and dry, and ensure the mounting bolt is tightened to the specified torque to ensure correct operation.

Camshaft position sensor

Note: *No camshaft position sensor is fitted to 1.4 litre engines.*

32 On 1.2 litre engines, the camshaft position sensor is located on the left-hand end of the cylinder head.

33 Remove the engine top cover, and disconnect the wiring from the sensor.

34 Unscrew the mounting bolt, and remove the sensor **(see illustration)**.

35 Refitting is a reversal of removal.

Coolant temperature sensor

36 Refer to Chapter 3, Section 6.

Oxygen (lambda) sensor(s)

37 On 1.2 litre engines, one oxygen sensor is located on the exhaust manifold and a second sensor is located at the top of the exhaust downpipe **(see illustrations)**. Access to the upstream sensor is from above, and to the downstream sensor from below.

38 On 1.4 litre engines, one oxygen sensor is located upstream of the catalytic converter in the exhaust manifold, and a second sensor is located downstream of the catalytic converter in the exhaust front

4.27 The knock sensor is located on the rear of the cylinder block

4.34 Removing the camshaft position sensor

pipe. The upstream sensor is accessible after removing the engine top cover and the exhaust hot air cowl; however, it is difficult to access as it is hidden between the manifold and the cylinder head. Access to the downstream sensor is possible after raising the front of the car and supporting on axle stands.

⚠️ **Warning: Working on the sensor(s) is only advisable with the engine (and therefore the exhaust system) completely cold. The catalytic converter in particular will be very hot for some time after the engine has been switched off.**

39 Working from the sensor, trace the wiring harness from the oxygen sensor back to the connector, and disconnect it. Typically, the wiring plug is coloured black for the upstream sensor, and brown for the downstream sensor.

40 Release the sensor wiring from any retaining clips, noting how it is routed.

41 Slacken and withdraw the sensor, taking care to avoid damaging the sensor probe as it is removed. **Note:** *As a flying lead remains connected to the sensor after it has been disconnected, if the correct-size spanner is not available, a slotted socket will be required to remove the sensor* **(see illustrations)**.

42 Apply a little high-temperature anti-seize grease to the sensor threads – avoid contaminating the probe tip.

43 Refit the sensor, tightening it to the correct torque. Restore the harness connection.

Throttle pedal/position sensor

44 Release the securing clip and disconnect the wiring connector from the top of the accelerator pedal **(see illustration)**.

45 Undo the retaining nuts and remove the

4.37a Oxygen (lambda) sensor on the exhaust manifold

4.37b Oxygen (lambda) sensor on the exhaust downpipe

4.41a Using a slotted socket to loosen the oxygen (lambda) sensor

4.41b Removing the oxygen (lambda) sensor from the exhaust manifold

**4.44 Disconnect the wiring connector -
arrowed**

throttle pedal from the mounting bracket **(see
illustration)**.

46 Refitting is a reversal of removal.

Clutch pedal switch

47 Fitted to all engines, the clutch switch is
mounted on the clutch pedal bracket, and
sends a signal to the ECU **(see illustration)**.
The purpose of the switch is to avoid engine
over-revving and load change jolts when the
clutch is released. The switch also deactivates
the cruise control system (where fitted) when
the pedal is pressed.

48 To remove the switch, first remove the
facia lower trim panel on the driver's side, as
described in Chapter 11, Section 27.

49 Locate the switch wiring plug in front of
the clutch pedal, and disconnect it.

50 Rotate the switch anti-clockwise and
remove it.

51 When refitting the switch, first extend the

switch plunger to its fullest extent, and then
hold the clutch pedal depressed when offering
it into position. Once the switch has been
clipped into place, release the pedal – this
sets the switch adjustment. Further refitting is
a reversal of removal.

Electronic control unit (ECU)

*Caution: Always wait at least 30 seconds
after switching off the ignition before
disconnecting the wiring from the ECU.
When the wiring is disconnected, all the
learned values are erased, although any
contents of the fault memory are retained.
After reconnecting the wiring, the basic
settings must be reinstated by a VW
dealer using a special test instrument.
Note also that if the ECU is renewed, the
identification of the new ECU must be
transferred to the immobiliser control unit
by a VW dealer.*

52 The ECU is located on the engine
compartment bulkhead, behind the air cleaner
assembly **(see illustration)**. Remove the air
cleaner assembly, as described in Section 2.

53 Disconnect the battery negative lead and
position it away from the terminal. **Note:** *Refer
to 'Disconnecting the battery' at the rear of
this manual first.*

54 Release the retaining clips and remove
the ECU from the mounting bracket on the
bulkhead **(see illustration)**.

55 Disconnect the wiring plugs from the ECU
by sliding the locking levers outwards, then
release them from the ECU **(see illustration)**.
Remove the ECU from the vehicle.

56 If required release the securing clips at
the rear of the bulkhead panel, to remove the
mounting bracket **(see illustration)**.

57 Refitting is a reversal of removal. Bear
in mind the comments made in the Caution
above – the ECU will not work correctly until it
has been electronically coded.

| 5 | Fuel filter – renewal | |

Note: *Observe the precautions in Section 1
before working on any component in the fuel
system.*

1 Depressurise the fuel system as described
in Section 8. Remember, however, that this
procedure merely relieves the fuel pressure,
reducing the risk of fuel spraying when the
connections are disturbed – fuel will still be
spilt during filter renewal, so take precautions
accordingly.

2 The fuel filter is located under the vehicle, to
the front right-hand side of the fuel tank **(see
illustration)**.

3 Jack up the right-hand rear of the car, and
support it on an axle stand (see *Jacking and
vehicle support*). When positioning the axle
stand, ensure that it will not inhibit access to
the filter.

4 To further improve access, if necessary,
unhook the handbrake cable from the adjacent
wire clip.

5 Disconnect the fuel hoses at either end of
the filter, noting their locations for refitting

**4.45 Undo the pedal retaining nuts -
arrowed**

4.47 Clutch pedal switch - arrowed

4.52 The location of the ECU - arrowed

**4.54 Unclip the ECU from the mounting
bracket**

**4.55 Disconnecting the wiring and
removing the ECU**

**4.56 Unclip the mounting bracket from the
bulkhead panel**

5.2 Fuel filter location next to fuel tank

5.5a Release the locking clips...

5.5b ...and disconnect the fuel lines

5.7 Slide the filter from the bracket

5.8a Make sure the arrow is facing forwards when fitted...

5.8b ...and the peg (arrowed) locates in the bracket

(see illustrations). There are two hoses, a feed hose coloured black and a return hose coloured blue at one end, and there is one hose at the engine/fuel rail end of the filter which is coloured black. The connections are of quick-release type, disconnected by squeezing the catch on each. It may be necessary to release the hoses from the clips on the underside of the car, to allow greater movement.

6 Before removing the filter, look for an arrow marking, which points in the direction of fuel flow – in this case, towards the front of the car/engine. The new filter must be fitted the same way round.

7 The filter sits in a support collar – undo the retaining screw and release the collar by carefully pulling the retaining arm off the peg on the filter body, and slide the filter out (see illustration). Try to keep it as level as possible, to reduce fuel spillage. Dispose of the old filter carefully – even if the fuel inside is tipped out, the filter element will still be soaked in fuel, and will be highly flammable.

8 Offer the new filter into position, ensuring that the direction-of-flow arrow is pointing towards the front of the car. Turn the filter so that the peg can be engaged with the retaining arm, and push the arm onto the peg to secure. Ensure that the filter is securely mounted on the car (see illustrations).

9 Connect the fuel hoses to each end of the filter, in the same positions as noted on removal. Push the hoses fully onto the filter stubs and, if necessary, clip them back to the underside of the car. Hook the handbrake cable back in place, if it was disturbed.

10 Switch on the ignition to activate the fuel pump. Check for signs of fuel leakage at both ends of the filter.

11 If all is well, lower the car to the ground, and then start the engine. Check under the car for signs of fuel leaks from the filter.

6 Fuel pump and gauge sender unit – removal and refitting

Note: Observe the precautions in Section 1 before working on any component in the fuel system.

⚠ Warning: Avoid direct skin contact with fuel – wear protective clothing and gloves when handling fuel system components. Ensure that the work area is well ventilated to prevent the build-up of fuel vapour.

6.5 Lift the fuel pump access hatch...

General information

1 The fuel pump and gauge sender unit are combined in one assembly, which is mounted in the top of the fuel tank. Access is through a hatch provided in the load space floor.
Caution: Removal of the sender unit involves exposing the contents of the fuel tank to the atmosphere.

Removal

2 Depressurise the fuel system as described in Section 8.

3 Ensure that the car is parked on a level surface, and then disconnect the battery negative lead (refer to Disconnecting the battery in the Reference Chapter at the end of this manual).

4 Fold the rear seat cushion forwards, and lift the carpet section from the load space floor.

5 Unclip the access panel, and lift the hatch away from the floorpan, noting its fitted position (see illustration).

6 Unplug the wiring harness connector from the pump/sender unit.

7 Pad the area around the supply and return fuel hoses with rags to absorb any spilt fuel, then squeeze the catch to release the hose clips and disconnect them from the ports at the sender unit (see illustration). Observe the supply and return arrow markings on the ports – label the fuel hoses accordingly to ensure correct refitting later. The supply pipe is black, and may have white markings, while the return pipe is blue, or has blue markings.

8 Note the position of the alignment marks, then unscrew the plastic securing ring and

6.7 Note the location of the connections for refitting

6.8a Note the alignment marks...

6.8b ...then unscrew the plastic securing ring

6.9 Lift out the pump/sender unit and recover the flange seal

6.14 Sender unit retaining clips - arrowed

6.15 Checking the resistance of the sender unit

remove it. Use a pair of water pump pliers or a suitable tool to grip and rotate the plastic securing ring, if necessary **(see illustrations)**.
9 Lift out the pump/sender unit, holding it above the level of the fuel in the tank until the excess fuel has drained out. Recover the flange seal **(see illustration)**.
10 Remove the pump/sender unit from the car, and lay it on an absorbent card or rag. Inspect the float at the end of the sender unit swinging arm for punctures and fuel ingress – renew the unit if it appears damaged.
11 The fuel pick-up incorporated in the assembly is spring-loaded to ensure that it always draws fuel from the lowest part of the tank. Check that the pick-up is free to move under spring tension with respect to the sender unit body.
12 Inspect the rubber seal from the fuel tank aperture for signs of fatigue – renew it if necessary.
13 Inspect the sender unit wiper and track; clean off any dirt and debris that may have accumulated, and look for breaks in the track.
14 If required, the sender unit can be separated from the assembly, as follows. Disconnect the two small wires (note their positions), then release the retaining clips and slide the unit out from the housing **(see illustration)**.
15 Connect a hand-held multi-meter to the brown and black wires terminals in the sender/pump unit socket. With the float arm at its lower stop position (tank empty) the resistance should be approx 50 ohms. With the float arm at its upper stop position (tank full) the resistance should be 290 ohms **(see**

illustration)**. There are five terminals inside the connector socket, the outer terminals are for the pump and are larger. Use the two smaller outer terminals of the three in the centre, terminals 2 and 4.

Refitting

16 Refit the pump/sender unit by following the removal procedure in reverse, noting the following points:
a) *Smear the outside of tank aperture rubber seal with clean fuel or lubricating spray, to ease fitting. Unless a new seal is required, the seal should be left on the pump unit before fitting* **(see illustration)**. *When the unit is almost fully in place, slide the seal down and locate it on the rim of the tank aperture, then slide the unit fully home.*
b) *Take care not to bend the float arm as the unit is refitted.*
c) *The arrow markings on the sender unit*

6.16 Fit the new seal to the fuel pump

body and the access aperture must be aligned.
d) *Reconnect the fuel hoses to the correct ports – observe the direction-of-flow arrow markings, and refer to paragraph 7.*
e) *On completion, check that all associated pipes are securely clipped to the tank.*
f) *Before refitting the access hatch and rear seat, run the engine and check for fuel leaks.*

7 Fuel tank –
removal and refitting

Note: *Observe the precautions in Section 1 before working on any component in the fuel system.*

Removal

1 Before the tank can be removed, it must be drained of as much fuel as possible. As no drain plug is provided, it is preferable to carry out this operation with the tank almost empty.
2 Open the fuel filler flap, and unscrew the fuel filler cap – leave the cap loosely in place.
3 Disconnect the battery negative lead (refer to *Disconnecting the battery* in the *Reference* Chapter at the end of this manual). Using a hand pump or syphon, remove any remaining fuel from the bottom of the tank.
4 Gain access to the top of the fuel pump/sender unit as described in Section 6, and disconnect the wiring harness from the top of the pump/sender unit at the multi-plug connector.

5 Loosen the right-hand rear wheel bolts, then jack up the rear of the car and remove the right-hand rear wheel.

6 Remove the right-hand rear wheel arch liner.

7 Remove the activated charcoal (evaporative) filter from its location behind the filler tube under the right-hand rear wheel arch, as described in Chapter 4C, Section 2.

8 Open the fuel filler flap and unscrew the retaining screw (on the side opposite the flap hinge), then ease the flap unit out of position in the wing panel. Recover the rubber seal that fits around the filler neck.

9 Working back under the wheel arch, undo the screw securing the filler tube to the body.

10 On some models, the fuel tank is protected from below by plastic covers, undo the fasteners and remove the covers.

11 Referring to Chapter 4C, Section 5, if necessary, unbolt the exhaust rear silencer mounting, and carefully lower the rear section of the exhaust system. Given that the rear axle assembly has to be removed (or at least lowered) to allow the tank to be removed, it is preferable to remove the rear section of the exhaust system completely.

12 Refer to Chapter 10, Section 13, and remove the rear axle assembly. Alternatively, it is possible to just lower the axle out of position, rather than completely removing it.

13 Depressurise the fuel system as described in Section 8.

14 Remove the fuel filter from the side of the fuel tank, as described in Section 5, or alternatively disconnect the single outlet hose from the engine side of the filter.

15 Unscrew and remove the retaining bolts and detach the tensioning strap from under the centre of the tank **(see illustration)**.

16 Position a trolley jack under the centre of the tank. Insert a flat block of wood between the jack head and the tank to prevent damage to the tank surface. Raise the jack to support the weight of the tank.

17 Unscrew and remove the tank mounting bolts.

18 Lower the tank from the underside of the car. If necessary, detach the various pipes and hoses from the tank, and remove the fuel pump and gauge sender unit with reference to Section 6.

19 If the tank is contaminated with sediment or water, swill the tank out with clean fuel. The tank is injection-moulded from a synthetic material and, if damaged, should be renewed. However, in certain cases it may be possible to have small leaks or minor damage repaired. Seek the advice of a suitable specialist before attempting to repair the fuel tank.

Refitting

20 Refitting is the reverse of the removal procedure, noting the following points:

a) When lifting the tank back into position, take care to ensure none of the hoses get trapped between the tank and vehicle body.

b) Ensure that all pipes and hoses are correctly routed, are not kinked, and are securely held in position with their retaining clips.

c) Tighten the tank strap retaining bolts to the specified torque.

d) On completion, refill the tank with fuel, and check for signs of leakage prior to taking the car out on the road.

8 Fuel injection system – depressurisation

Note: *Observe the precautions in Section 1 before working on any component in the fuel system.*

⚠️ *Warning: The following procedure will merely relieve the pressure in the fuel system – remember that fuel will still be present in the system components and take precautions accordingly before disconnecting any of them.*

1 The fuel system referred to in this Section is defined as the tank-mounted fuel pump, the fuel filter, the fuel injectors, and the metal pipes and flexible hoses of the fuel lines between these components. All these contain fuel, which will be under pressure while the engine is running and/or while the ignition is switched on. The pressure will remain for some time after the ignition has been switched off, and must be relieved before any of these components are disturbed for servicing work. Ideally, the engine should be allowed to cool completely before work commences.

2 Place a suitable container beneath the relevant connection/union to be disconnected, and then wrap clean cloth around it. Where a union connection is fitted, loosen it slightly before wrapping the cloth around.

3 Slowly open the connection to avoid a sudden release of pressure. Once the pressure has been released, disconnect the fuel line. Insert plugs to minimise fuel loss and prevent the entry of dirt into the fuel system.

9 Inlet manifold – removal and refitting

Note: *Observe the precautions in Section 1 before working on any component in the fuel system.*

Removal

1 A one-piece inlet manifold is fitted to the rear of the cylinder head on all models. First, disconnect the battery negative lead (refer to *Disconnecting the battery* in the *Reference* Chapter at the end of this manual).

2 Remove the engine top cover. Where applicable, unclip the hose from the top of the inlet manifold **(see illustration)**.

3 With reference to Section 4, remove the throttle valve control unit from the inlet manifold.

7.15 Fuel tank tensioning strap - arrowed

4 Disconnect the vacuum hose for the brake vacuum servo noting how it is routed.

5 To allow the manifold to be removed completely, and to improve access to the manifold mounting bolts, remove the fuel rail and injectors as described in Section 4. However, if the manifold is being removed as part of another procedure (such as cylinder head or engine removal), the fuel rail can be left in place.

6 Disconnect the wiring plug from the inlet air temperature/pressure sensor, referring if necessary to Section 4 for more details. Alternatively, remove it completely.

7 On the 1.2 litre engine code CHFA, unscrew the two lower mounting bolts and recover the mounting rubbers and sleeves.

8 Progressively loosen the bolts and withdraw the manifold from the cylinder head. Recover the O-ring seals – all should be renewed when refitting the manifold.

Refitting

9 Refitting is a reversal of removal. Use a new gasket or seals, as applicable, and tighten the retaining bolts/nuts to the specified torque.

10 Fuel injection system – testing and adjustment

1 If a fault appears in the fuel injection system, first ensure that all the system wiring connectors are securely connected and free

9.2 Coolant purge hose retaining clips on the top of the inlet manifold

10.2 Diagnostic connector located under the driver's side of the facia

of corrosion. Then ensure that the fault is not due to poor maintenance; i.e. check that the air cleaner filter element is clean, the spark plugs are in good condition and correctly gapped, the cylinder compression pressures are correct, the ignition system wiring is in good condition and securely connected, and the engine breather hoses are clear and undamaged, referring to Chapter 1A, Chapter 2A or 2B and Chapter 5B.

2 If these checks fail to reveal the cause of the problem, the car should be taken to a suitably equipped VW dealer for testing. A diagnostic connector is incorporated in the engine management system wiring harness, into which dedicated electronic test equipment can be plugged (the purple-coloured connector is located at the front of the facia, above the pedals) **(see illustration)**. The test equipment is capable of 'interrogating' the engine management system ECU electronically and accessing its internal fault log (reading fault codes).

3 Fault codes can only be extracted from the ECU using a dedicated fault code reader. A VW dealer will obviously have such a reader, but they are also available from other suppliers. It is unlikely to be cost-effective for the private owner to purchase a fault code reader, but a well-equipped local garage or auto-electrical specialist will have one.

4 Using this equipment, faults can be pinpointed quickly and simply, even if their occurrence is intermittent. Testing all the system components individually in an attempt to locate the fault by elimination is a time-consuming operation that is unlikely to be fruitful (particularly if the fault occurs dynamically), and carries a high risk of damage to the ECU's internal components.

5 Experienced home mechanics equipped with an accurate tachometer and a carefully-calibrated exhaust gas analyser may be able to check the exhaust gas CO content and the engine idle speed; if these are found to be out of specification, then the car must be taken to a suitably-equipped VW dealer for assessment. Neither the air/fuel mixture (exhaust gas CO content) nor the engine idle speed are manually adjustable.

11 Cruise control system – general information

1 Certain models may be equipped with a cruise control system, in which the driver can set a chosen speed, which the system will then try to maintain regardless of gradients, etc.

2 Once the desired speed has been set, the system is entirely under the control of the engine management ECU, which regulates the speed via the throttle valve control unit.

3 The system refers to signals from the engine speed sensor (see Section 4) and roadspeed sensor (on the transmission).

4 The system is deactivated if the clutch or brake pedals are pressed, signalled by the clutch pedal switch (Section 4) or the brake stop-light switch (Chapter 9, Section 21).

5 The cruise control switch is part of the steering column combination switch assembly, which can be removed as described in Chapter 12, Section 4.

6 Any problems with the system which are not caused by wiring faults or failure of the components mentioned in this Section should be referred to a VW dealer. In the event of a problem occurring, it is advisable to first take the car to a suitably equipped dealer for electronic fault diagnosis, using a fault code reader – refer to Section 10.

Chapter 4 Part B:
Diesel engine fuel systems

Contents

Degrees of difficulty

Easy, suitable for novice with little experience	**Fairly easy,** suitable for beginner with some experience	**Fairly difficult,** suitable for competent DIY mechanic	**Difficult,** suitable for experienced DIY mechanic	**Very difficult,** suitable for expert DIY or professional

Specifications

Engine codes*

1.2 litre	CFWA
1.6 litre	CAYB, CAYC and CLNA

***Note:** See 'Vehicle identification' at the end of this manual for the location of engine code markings.*

General

Fuel injection system	Electronic, direct, common rail injection
Firing order.	1-3-4-2
Maximum engine speed.	N/A (ECU controlled)
Engine fast idle speed	N/A (ECU controlled)
Turbocharger type	Garrett or KKK

Torque wrench settings

	Nm	lbf ft
Camshaft position sensor (Hall sender)	10	7
EGR pipe flange-to-inlet manifold bolts.	8	6
Engine speed/TDC sender	5	4
Flap motor housing	10	7
Fuel pressure regulating valve (left-hand end of fuel rail).	80	59
Fuel pressure sender (right-hand end of fuel rail).	100	74
Fuel pump bolts*:		
Two lower bolts (long):		
Stage 1	20	15
Stage 2	Angle-tighten a further 180°	
One upper bolt (short):		
Stage 1	20	15
Stage 2	Angle-tighten a further 45°	
Fuel rail :		
1.2 litre engines:		
Stage 1	20	15
Stage 2	Angle-tighten a further 180°	
1.6 litre engines	22	16
High-pressure fuel pipe unions	28	20
Injector clamp/cover mounting:		
1.2 litre engines		
Clamp bolt*:		
Stage 1	10	7
Stage 2	Angle-tighten a further 180°	
1.6 litre engines		
Clamp bolt*:		
Stage 1	8	6
Stage 2	Angle-tighten a further 180°	
Inlet manifold to cylinder head.	8	6
Oxygen (Lambda probe) sensor.	50	37
Toothed belt pulley on high-pressure pump bolts*	20	15

* Do not re-use

1.6 The diagnostic connector location – arrowed

1 General information and precautions

General information

All engines covered by this Manual are fitted with a direct-injection fuelling system, incorporating a fuel tank, an engine-bay mounted fuel filter with an integral water separator, fuel supply and return lines and four fuel injectors. Also there is a second fuel filter with an integral fuel pressure regulator, located under the vehicle, to the right-hand side front of the fuel tank.

The fuel system is the familiar Common Rail system, where fuel is supplied from a timing belt-driven high-pressure pump to a common fuel rail (or reservoir). The injectors are fitted into the cylinder head and are connected to the fuel rail by rigid metal pipes. The precise timing of the pre-, main, and post-injections are controlled by the engine management ECM and an electrically operated Piezo crystal incorporated into the injector design. All engines are fitted with a turbocharger.

The direct-injection fuelling system is controlled electronically by a diesel engine management system, comprising an Electronic Control Module (ECM) and its associated sensors, actuators and wiring. In addition, the ECM manages the operation of the Exhaust Gas Recirculation (EGR) emission control system (Chapter 4D), the turbocharger boost pressure control system and the glow plug control system (Chapter 5C).

A flap valve/throttle valve module fitted to the intake manifold is closed by the ECM for 3 seconds as the engine is switched off, to minimise the air intake as the engine shuts down. This minimises the vibration felt as the pistons come up against the volume of highly compressed air present in the combustion chambers.

It should be noted that fault diagnosis of the diesel engine management system is only possible with dedicated electronic test equipment. Problems with the system's operation should therefore be referred to a VW dealer or suitably equipped specialist for assessment. Once the fault has been identified, the removal/refitting sequences detailed in the following Sections will then allow the appropriate component(s) to be renewed as required.

The European On-Board Diagnostic (EOBD) connector is located under the driver's side of the facia **(see illustration)**.

2.2 Disconnect the wiring connector (A) and securing clip (B)

2.5 Undo the mounting bolt – arrowed

2.3 Release the vacuum hose securing clips – arrowed

2.6 Release the air ducting

Precautions

Many of the operations described in this Chapter involve the disconnection of fuel lines, which may cause an amount of fuel spillage. Before commencing work, refer to the warnings below and the information in *Safety first!* at the beginning of this manual.

⚠ *Warning: When working on any part of the fuel system, avoid direct contact skin contact with diesel fuel – wear protective clothing and gloves when handling fuel system components. Ensure that the work area is well ventilated to prevent the build-up of diesel fuel vapour.*

• *Fuel injectors operate at extremely high pressures and the jet of fuel produced at the nozzle is capable of piercing skin, with potentially fatal results. When working with pressurised injectors, take care to avoid exposing any part of the body to the fuel spray. It is recommended that a diesel fuel systems specialist should carry out any pressure testing of the fuel system components.*

• *Under no circumstances should diesel fuel be allowed to come into contact with coolant hoses – wipe off accidental spillage immediately. Hoses that have been contaminated with fuel for an extended period should be renewed.*

• *Diesel fuel systems are particularly sensitive to contamination from dirt, air and water. Pay particular attention to cleanliness when working on any part of the fuel system, to prevent the ingress of dirt. Thoroughly clean the area around fuel unions before disconnecting them. Only use lint-free cloths and clean fuel for component cleansing.*

• *Store dismantled components in sealed containers to prevent contamination and the formation of condensation.*

2 Air cleaner assembly – removal and refitting

Removal

1 Disconnect the wiring plug from the air mass meter.

2 Loosen the clip and disconnect the air duct from the air mass meter **(see illustration)**.

3 Unclip the vacuum hoses from across the front of the filter housing **(see illustration)**.

4 Disconnect the pre-heating hose from the side of the air filter housing (only fitted to vehicles in cold climate zones).

5 Undo the retaining bolt at the front left-hand side of the housing and lift the air cleaner assembly upwards to release it from the locating pegs **(see illustration)**.

6 Unclip the plastic air ducting from the front crossmember **(see illustration)**, and as the air cleaner assembly is removed, withdraw the air ducting from under the side of the battery.

3.1a Remove the engine upper trim cover...

3.1b ...and the insulation cover (arrowed), where fitted

3.2 Slacken the two retaining clips (arrowed)

3.3 Disconnect the wiring connector

3.4 Undo the dipstick tube retaining bolt

3.5 Undo the throttle housing retaining bolts

Refitting

7 Refit the air cleaner by following the removal procedure in reverse. Make sure the assembly is located correctly on the lower mounting pegs.

3 Diesel engine management system – component removal and refitting

Throttle valve housing/module

1 Remove the engine upper trim cover **(see illustrations)**.
2 Slacken the retaining clips and remove the air intake rubber hose from the throttle housing **(see illustration)**. If required, undo the bolts securing the air intake plastic hose from the intercooler to the throttle housing, this will allow easier removal of the intake rubber hose.
3 Disconnect the wiring plug connector, from the throttle housing/module **(see illustration)**.
4 On 1.6 litre engines, undo the retaining bolt and disconnect the dipstick guide tube from the throttle housing **(see illustration)**.
5 Unscrew and remove the retaining bolts, then lift the throttle housing/module away from the inlet manifold **(see illustration)**. Recover the O-ring seal; a new one will be required for refitting.
6 Refitting is a reversal of removal, noting the following:
  a) Use a new throttle housing-to-inlet manifold seal **(see illustration)**.
  b) Tighten the throttle housing bolts evenly to the specified torque.

  c) Ensure that all hoses and electrical connectors are refitted securely.

Inlet manifold flap motor

Note: *On some engines there is an electrically operated flap motor located on the inlet manifold, this is not fitted to all models.*
7 Although the manifold flap motor is bolted to the end of the inlet manifold, VW do not recommend that it is removed, check with your local dealer before removing any components.

Air mass meter

8 The air mass meter is located in the outlet from the air cleaner assembly on the left-hand side of the engine compartment.
9 Disconnect the wiring plug connector from the air mass meter.
10 Slacken the retaining clip and disconnect

3.6 Fit new seal (arrowed) to housing on refitting

the air intake ducting from the air mass meter **(see illustration 2.2)**.
11 Undo the retaining screws securing the meter to the air cleaner upper housing. Withdraw the meter and recover the O-ring seal.
Caution: Handle the air mass meter carefully – its internal components are easily damaged.
12 Refitting is a reversal of removal. Renew the O-ring seal if it appears damaged.

Charge air pressure/ temperature sensor

13 The charge air pressure/temperature sensor is fitted in the air ducting from the intercooler to the throttle housing/inlet manifold.
14 On 1.2 litre engines, it is located in the air ducting at the front top corner of the engine **(see illustration)**.

3.14 Sensor location – 1.2 litre engines

**3.15 Sensor location –
1.6 litre engines**

**3.18 Fuel pressure regulator valve
(arrowed)**

3.19 Disconnect the fuel hose (arrowed)

15 On 1.6 litre engines, it is located in the air ducting just below the air-conditioning compressor, at the front of the engine **(see illustration)**. To access the sensor, jack up the front of the vehicle and support it on axle stands (see *Jacking and vehicle support*), and then remove the engine undertray.

16 Disconnect the wiring then undo the two retaining screws and remove the sensor from the intake ducting.

17 Refit the sensor by reversing the removal procedure, using a new O-ring seal.

Fuel pressure regulating valve

18 The fuel pressure regulating valve is fitted to the left-hand end of the fuel rail **(see illustration)**. If the valve is removed from the fuel rail, then it will need to be renewed, as it has a deformable sealing lip as part of the valve.

19 To check the operation of the regulating valve, first disconnect the fuel return hose from the fuel rail and plug the end **(see illustration)**.

**3.21 Pressure regulator valve fitted to the
left-hand end of the fuel rail**

Then fit a piece of hose from the fuel rail and the other end into a container.

On 1.6 litre engines, there are three checks that can be made, the first two with the engine running and the third if the vehicle will not start: *(1) Start the engine and run at idle for 30 seconds, there should be approx. 75ml of fuel in the container. (2) Start engine and increase engine speed to 2000rpm, there should be NO fuel in the container (a few droplets of fuel is allowed). (3) On vehicles that will not run, turn the ignition key and crank the engine, there should be 0ml of fuel in the container (allow for a few droplets of fuel).*

On 1.2 litre engines, there is only one check listed: *(1) Start the engine and run at idle for 30 seconds; there should be NO fuel in the container.*

If any of these readings are not attained, renew the regulating valve.

20 To renew the valve, remove the fuel rail as described in Section 11.

**3.24 Disconnect the wiring connector from
the fuel pressure sensor**

21 Clean around the valve, then slacken the valve from the end of the fuel rail **(see illustration)**; counter hold the fuel rail using the flats on the housing. Plug the end of the rail to prevent dirt from entering.

22 Refit the new valve by reversing the removal procedure, making sure that the threads are all clean before refitting. Check the deformable seal on the new valve, before refitting, to check it is not damaged. Apply a small amount of Molybdenum grease to seal and threads.

Fuel pressure sender

23 The fuel pressure sender is fitted to the right-hand end of the fuel rail. If the engine will not start, disconnect the fuel pressure sender wiring connector and see if the engine will start, if the engine starts, the fuel pressure switch is faulty. With the connector removed a value is taken from the control unit, so that the engine will start, in this mode the maximum engine speed is limited to 3000rpm.

24 To renew the sender, first disconnect the wiring plug connector **(see illustration)**.

25 Clean around the sender, then slacken it from the end of the fuel rail **(see illustration)**; plug the end of the rail to prevent dirt from entering.

26 Refit the pressure sender by reversing the removal procedure, making sure that the threads are all clean before refitting. The sender has a deformable seal, check for damage. Keep the threads free of oil and grease.

Fuel temperature sensor

27 The fuel temperature sensor is located in the fuel supply line at the top of the high-pressure

**3.25 The fuel pressure sensor is fitted to
the right-hand end of the fuel rail**

3.27a Fuel temperature sensor (arrowed)...

3.27b ...or in fuel line (arrowed)

3.31 Camshaft position sensor (arrowed)

3.33a Disconnect the sensor wiring connector (arrowed) – 1.2 litre engine

3.33b Disconnect the sensor wiring connector (arrowed) – 1.6 litre engine

3.34 Unbolt the idler pulley

3.35 Prise up the aperture cover (arrowed)

3.38 Crankshaft position speed sensor (arrowed)

fuel pump **(see illustrations)**, or in the fuel line, depending on model.

28 First, disconnect the wiring connector, then release the securing clips and disconnect the hoses from the sensor assembly.

29 Refit the fuel temperature sensor by reversing the removal procedure.

Coolant temperature sensors

30 Refer to Chapter 3, Section 6.

Camshaft position sensor

31 The camshaft position sensor (Hall sender) is located behind the timing belt cover, below the camshaft sprocket **(see illustration)**.

32 Remove the timing belt, as described in Chapter 2C, Section 7 (1.2 litre engine) or Chapter 2D, Section 7 (1.6 litre engine).

33 Disconnect the sensor wiring plug connector, located at the rear of the oil filter housing against the cylinder block **(see illustrations)**.

34 To make access easier undo the retaining bolt and remove the timing belt idler pulley **(see illustration)**.

35 Using a screwdriver prise out the aperture cover in the rear plastic cover, then withdraw the wiring plug through the cover, unhooking it from the rear cover **(see illustration)**.

36 Undo the retaining bolt and remove the camshaft sensor from the cylinder head.

37 Refitting is a reversal of removal, but tighten the bolt to the specified torque setting and fit rubber plugs to the aperture for the wiring in the rear plastic cover.

Engine speed/TDC sensor

38 The engine speed/TDC sensor is mounted on the front cylinder block, adjacent to the mating surface of the block and transmission bellhousing **(see illustration)**.

39 Access is from beneath the engine compartment. Apply the handbrake, and then

jack up the front of the vehicle and support it on axle stands (see *Jacking and vehicle support*). Remove the engine undertray.

40 Remove the retaining screw and withdraw the sensor from the cylinder block **(see illustrations)**.

41 Refit the sensor by reversing the removal procedure.

Oxygen (lambda probe) sensor

⚠️ *Warning: Working on the sensors is only advisable with the engine (and therefore the exhaust system) completely cold. The catalytic converter in particular will be very hot for some time after the engine has been switched off.*

42 All models have a sensor threaded into the top of the catalytic converter/particulate filter **(see illustrations)**. Note, on some models there may be a second sensor in the front pipe after the catalytic converter/particulate filter.

3.40a Undo the retaining bolt...

3.40b ...and withdraw the sensor

3.42a Oxygen sensor (arrowed) – 1.2 litre engine

3.42b Oxygen sensor (arrowed) –
1.6 litre engine

3.42c Gas sensor (arrowed) fitted to
models with particulate filter

3.43 Upper oxygen sensor connector
(arrowed) – 1.2 litre engine

Note: *Do not confuse exhaust gas sensors fitted to the exhaust system; these are only fitted to models with particulate filter.*

43 Working from the sensor, trace the wiring harness from the oxygen sensor back to the connector, and disconnect it **(see illustration)**. Unclip the sensor wiring from any retaining clips, noting how it is routed.

44 Access to the upstream sensor is possible on some models from above, while the downstream sensor (where fitted) is only accessible from below.

45 Unscrew and remove the sensor, taking care to avoid damaging the sensor probe as it is removed. **Note:** *As a flying lead remains connected to the sensor after it has been disconnected, if the correct-size spanner is not available, a slotted socket will be required to remove the sensor.*

46 Apply a little high-temperature anti-seize grease to the sensor threads – avoid contaminating the probe tip.

47 Refit the sensor, tightening it to the correct torque. Reconnect the wiring; making sure that the wiring loom is secured in its retaining clips.

Throttle pedal/position sensor

48 Release the securing clip and disconnect the wiring connector from the top of the accelerator pedal **(see illustration)**.

49 Undo the retaining nuts and remove the throttle pedal from the mounting bracket **(see illustration)**.

50 Refitting is a reversal of removal.

Clutch pedal switch

51 The clutch switch is mounted on the clutch pedal bracket, and sends a signal to the ECU **(see illustration)**. The purpose of the switch is to avoid engine over-revving and load change

jolts when the clutch is released. The switch also deactivates the cruise control system (where fitted) when the pedal is pressed.

52 To remove the switch, first remove the facia lower trim panel on the driver's side, as described in Chapter 11, Section 27.

53 Locate the switch wiring plug in front of the clutch pedal, and disconnect it.

54 Rotate the switch anti-clockwise and remove it.

55 When refitting the switch, first extend the switch plunger to its fullest extent, and then hold the clutch pedal depressed when offering it into position. Once the switch has been clipped into place, release the pedal – this sets the switch adjustment. Further refitting is a reversal of removal.

Electronic control unit (ECU)

Caution: *Always wait at least 30 seconds after switching off the ignition before disconnecting the wiring from the ECU. When the wiring is disconnected, all the learned values are erased, although any contents of the fault memory are retained. After reconnecting the wiring, the basic settings must be reinstated by a VW dealer using a special test instrument. Note also that if the ECU is renewed, the identification of the new ECU must be transferred to the immobiliser control unit by a VW dealer.*

56 The ECU is located on the engine compartment bulkhead, behind the air cleaner assembly **(see illustration)**. Remove the air cleaner assembly, as described in Section 2.

3.48 Release the wiring connector -
arrowed

3.49 Undo the pedal mounting nuts -
arrowed

3.51 Clutch pedal switch – arrowed

3.56 Location of ECU - arrowed

3.58 Unclip the control unit from the
mounting bracket

57 Disconnect the battery negative lead and position it away from the terminal. **Note:** *Refer to 'Disconnecting the battery' at the rear of this manual first.*
58 Release the retaining clips and remove the ECU from the mounting bracket on the bulkhead **(see illustration)**.
59 Disconnect the wiring plugs from the ECU by sliding the locking levers outwards, then release them from the ECU **(see illustration)**. Remove the ECU from the vehicle.
60 If required release the securing clips at the rear of the bulkhead panel, to remove the mounting bracket **(see illustration)**.
61 Refitting is a reversal of removal. Bear in mind the comments made in the Caution above – the ECU will not work correctly until it has been electronically coded.

4 Injectors –
general information, removal and refitting

Warning: Exercise extreme caution when working on the fuel injectors. Never expose the hands or any part of the body to injector spray, as the high pressure can cause the fuel to penetrate the skin, with possibly fatal results. You are strongly advised to have any work, which involves testing the injectors under pressure carried out, by a dealer or fuel injection specialist. Refer to the precautions given in Section 1 of this Chapter before proceeding.

General information

1 Injectors do deteriorate with prolonged use, and it is reasonable to expect them to need reconditioning or renewal after 60,000 miles (100,000 km) or so. Accurate testing, overhaul and calibration of the injectors must be left to a specialist.

Removal

Note: *Take care not to allow dirt into the injectors or fuel pipes during this procedure. Do not drop the injectors or allow the needles at their tips to become damaged. The injectors are precision-made to fine limits, and must not be handled roughly. Keep the injectors*

3.59 Pull out the locking slides to disconnect the wiring

identified for position to ensure correct refitting.
2 Pull the plastic cover over the engine upwards from its' mountings. Where fitted, remove the foam insulation over the injectors **(see illustrations 3.1a & 3.1b)**.
3 Ensure the area around the injectors and the pipes/return hoses is clean and free from debris. The use of a vacuum cleaner is recommended. Plug all fuel lines when they have been disconnected to prevent any dirt ingress **(see illustration)**.

1.2 litre engine

4 Release the retaining clips and remove the fuel return hoses from the injectrors **(see illustration)**. Discard the o-ring seals, as new ones will be required for refitting.
5 Disconnect the injector wiring plug connectors **(see illustration)**.

4.3 Fit sealing caps to prevent dirt ingress

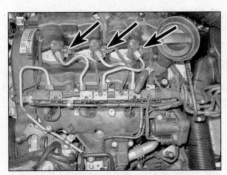
4.5 Disconnect the wiring plugs (arrowed) from the injectors

3.60 Unclip the mounting bracket from the bulkhead

6 Counterhold the injector with an open-ended spanner when releasing the pipe union. Undo the unions and remove the high-pressure pipes from between the fuel rail and the injectors **(see illustration)**. Plug the openings to prevent contamination.
7 Undo the bolt securing the injector clamp and withdraw the injector **(see illustration)**.
8 VW technicians use a slide hammer (tool T10055) and adapter (T10426) to pull the injector from the cylinder head. If this tool is not available, it may be possible to fabricate an equivalent tool to pull the injector out of the cylinder head.
9 Recover the copper seal and O-rings and discard. New ones must be used for refitting **(see illustration)**. **Note:** *The injectors can only be refitted to their original positions. Mark the injectors to avoid confusion if refitting the original injectors.*

4.4 Release the fuel return hoses

4.6 Remove the high pressure fuel pipes

4.7 Remove the injector clamp and injector

4.9 Fit a new sealing washer

4.10 Disconnect the wiring plugs from the injectors

4.11a Remove the retaining clips…

4.11b …and disconnect the fuel return pipes

4.12a Use two spanners to counterhold the fuel pipe to the injector…

4.12b …and remove the high pressure fuel pipes

1.6 litre engine

10 Disconnect the injector wiring plug connectors **(see illustration)**.
11 Using a pair of long-nose pliers, withdraw the retaining clip from the side of the injector

and remove the fuel return hose **(see illustrations)**. Discard the o-ring seals, as new ones will be required for refitting.
12 Counterhold the injector with an open-ended spanner when releasing the

pipe union. Undo the unions and remove the high-pressure pipes from between the fuel rail and the injectors **(see illustrations)**. Plug the openings to prevent contamination.
13 Undo the bolt securing the injector clamp **(see illustration)**, note that one clamp secures two injectors in place.
14 VW technicians use a slide hammer (tool T10055) and adapter (T10402) to pull the injector from the cylinder head. If this tool is not available, it may be possible to fabricate an equivalent tool to pull the injector out of the cylinder head.
15 Two injectors will need to be removed together, as the clamping piece is slotted into both injectors. Recover the copper seal and O-rings and discard. New ones must be used for refitting **(see illustration)**. **Note:** *The injectors can only be refitted to their original positions. Mark the injectors to avoid confusion if refitting the original injectors.*

Refitting

16 If required, renew the injector seals in the top of the camshaft cover. Using a screwdriver, prise the seal out from the cover; the new seal can then be pressed firmly into the cover **(see illustrations)**. There are different size seals depending on engine code, make sure the correct seals are supplied. Also make sure the spring on the inside lip of the seal does not drop into the camshaft cover.
17 Ensure the areas around the injector locations in the cylinder head are clean and free from debris. Use a vacuum cleaner if available. Clean any carbon deposits from the injector and sealing surfaces with a cloth

4.13 Remove the injector clamp retaining bolts

4.15 Remove two injectors at a time with retaining clamp

4.16a Carefully prise out the seal…

4.16b …and fit the new seal…

4.16c ...making sure the spring does not fall into the cover

4.18a Clean off the carbon around the end of the injector...

4.18b ...and fit a new sealing washer

soaked in clean engine oil or rust-releasing spray.

18 To remove the copper sealing washer, spray rust-releasing spray around the injector nozzle, then clamp the seal in a vice, and use a twisting motion to pull the injector from the seal. Push the new copper seal into place **(see illustrations)**. Do not touch the very end of the injector, or you could block up the nozzle.

19 Apply a little clean engine oil to the return pipe connection, and fit the new O-ring **(see illustration)**.

20 To renew the main injector O-ring seal, VW specify the use of tool no. T10377. This tool allows the O-ring to slide over the end of the injector without twisting. With care, the seals can be fitted without the tool **(see illustration)**.

21 Apply a smear of clean engine oil to the main O-ring seal, and insert the injector into place in the cylinder head **(see illustrations)**. Note that if the original injectors are being refitted, they must go into their original positions. Tighten the injector clamping bolt/nut to the specified torque.

22 Refit the high-pressure fuel pipes and tighten the unions to the specified torque. Note that the pipes may be re-used providing the tapered seats are undamaged; the pipes are not deformed, constricted or corroded. Counterhold the injector with an open-ended spanner when tightening the pipe union.

23 On 1.6 litre engines, when fitting the return hoses to the sides of the injector, use new securing clips **(see illustration)**.

24 The remainder of refitting is a reversal of removal, noting the following:

a) On 1.2 litre engines, check the seal inside

4.19 Fit new O-ring seals to the fuel return lines

the wiring connector is not damaged, renew seal if required **(see illustration)**.

b) If one or more injectors have been renewed, the 'injector delivery calibration values' and 'injector voltage calibration values' must be entered into the ECM

4.20 Fit a new main O-ring seal without twisting it

using VW diagnostic equipment. Entrust this task to a VW dealer or suitably equipped specialist.

c) After completion of the work, the fuel system must be bled as described in Section 10.

4.21a Lubricate the seal with some clean oil...

4.21b ...then fit the injectors and clamps – 1.2 litre engine

4.21c ...and on 1.6 litre engines

4.23 Fit new clips to secure the fuel return lines

4.24 Check the seals on the wiring connectors – 1.2 litre engines

5.3a Undo the coolant pipe retaining screw (arrowed) – 1.2 litre engines

5.3b Undo the coolant pipe retaining screws (arrowed) – 1.6 litre engines

5.4a Undo the fuel line retaining screws (arrowed) – 1.2 litre engines

5.4b Undo the fuel line retaining screws (arrowed) – 1.6 litre engines

5.5a Disconnect the wiring connector (arrowed) – 1.2 litre engines

5.5b Disconnect the wiring connector (arrowed) – 1.6 litre engines

5.6 Undo the mounting bracket securing bolt – 1.6 litre engine

5.7 Charge air pressure sensor (A) – EGR coler changeover valve (B) – 1.2 litre engine

5.8 Slacken the EGR pipe retaining clamp (arrowed)

5.9a Undo the retaining bolts (arrowed)...

5 Inlet manifold –
removal and refitting

Removal

1 Remove the throttle housing, as described in Section 3 of this Chapter.

2 Remove the fuel rail from the top of the inlet manifold, as described in Section 11 of this Chapter.

3 Undo the retaining screw(s) and move the coolant return pipe to one side (see illustrations).

4 Undo the two retaining screws and move the fuel return pipe to one side (see illustrations).

5 Where fitted, disconnect the wiring plug connector from the manifold flap motor (see illustrations).

6 Undo the retaining screw and remove the EGR cooler changeover valve from the manifold (see illustration).

7 On 1.2 litre engines, disconnect the wiring plug connector from the charge air pressure sensor (see illustration).

8 Slacken the retaining clamp and disconnect the EGR pipe (see illustration).

9 Undo the manifold retaining bolts, starting from the outside and working inwards in a diagonal sequence (see illustrations). Lift the

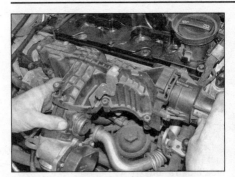

5.9b ...and remove the inlet manifold –
1.6 litre engine

5.9c Cover the inlet manifold recess with
tape

5.10 Refit new seals and gaskets

manifold from the cylinder head and retrieve the gasket seals; discard, as new ones will be required for refitting.

Refitting

10 Refitting is a reversal of removal, using new seals and gaskets **(see illustration)**. Remember to renew any self-locking nuts. Tighten the manifold retaining bolts to the specified torque setting, starting from the inside and working outwards in a diagonal sequence.

6 Fuel filter – renewal

Note: *Observe the precautions in Section 1 before working on any component in the fuel system.*

Engine compartment fuel filter

1 Refer to Chapter 1B, Section 24.

Fuel filter and pressure regulator

2 Depressurise the fuel system as described in Chapter 4A, Section 8. Remember, however, that this procedure merely relieves the fuel pressure, reducing the risk of fuel spraying when the connections are disturbed – fuel will still be spilt during filter renewal, so take precautions accordingly.
3 The fuel filter/pressure regulator is located

under the vehicle, to the front right-hand side of the fuel tank **(see illustration)**.
4 Jack up the right-hand rear of the car, and support it on an axle stand (see *Jacking and vehicle support*). When positioning the axle stand, ensure that it will not inhibit access to the filter.
5 To further improve access, if necessary, unhook the handbrake cable from the adjacent wire clip.
6 Disconnect the fuel hoses at either end of the filter, noting their locations for refitting. There are two hoses, a feed hose coloured black and a return hose coloured blue at one end, and there is one hose at the engine/fuel rail end of the filter which is coloured black. The connections are of quick-release type, disconnected by squeezing the catch on each **(see illustrations)**. It may be

necessary to release the hoses from the clips on the underside of the car, to allow greater movement.
7 Before removing the filter, look for an arrow marking, which points in the direction of fuel flow – in this case, towards the front of the car/engine **(see illustration)**. The new filter must be fitted the same way round.
8 The filter sits in a support collar – release the collar by unscrewing the retaining bolt and carefully pulling the filter body, and sliding it out **(see illustration)**. Try to keep it as level as possible, to reduce fuel spillage. Dispose of the old filter carefully – even if the fuel inside is tipped out, the filter element will still be soaked in fuel, and will be highly flammable.
9 Offer the new filter into position, ensuring that the direction-of-flow arrow is pointing

6.3 Fuel filter location next to fuel tank

6.6a Release the locking clips...

6.6b ...and disconnect the fuel lines

6.7 Make sure the arrow is facing forwards
when fitted

6.8 Slide the filter from the bracket

6.9 Make sure the peg (arrowed) locates in the bracket

towards the front of the car. Turn the filter so that the peg can be engaged with the retaining clip in the support bracket **(see illustration)**, and push the arm onto the peg to secure. Ensure that the filter is securely mounted on the car.

10 Connect the fuel hoses to each end of the filter, in the same positions as noted on removal. Push the hoses fully onto the filter stubs and, if necessary, clip them back to the underside of the car. Hook the handbrake cable back in place, if it was disturbed.

11 Switch on the ignition to activate the fuel pump. Check for signs of fuel leakage at both ends of the filter.

12 If all is well, lower the car to the ground, and then start the engine. Check under the car for signs of fuel leaks from the filter.

7 Fuel gauge sender unit – removal and refitting

Note: Observe the precautions in Section 1 before working on any component in the fuel system.

⚠ *Warning: Avoid direct skin contact with fuel – wear protective clothing and gloves when handling fuel system components. Ensure that the work area is well ventilated to prevent the build-up of fuel vapour.*

1 The fuel gauge sender unit is mounted in the top of the fuel tank. Access is beneath a cover in the load space floor. The unit protrudes into the fuel tank, and its removal involves exposing the contents of the tank to the atmosphere.

2 Refer to the procedures in Chapter 4A, Section 6, for removal and refitting procedures.

8 Fuel tank – removal and refitting

Note: Observe the precautions in Section 1 before working on any component in the fuel system.

Refer to the procedures in Chapter 4A, Section 7, for the removal of the fuel tank, as the procedure will be the same as petrol models.

9 Fuel pump – removal and refitting

Removal

1 Remove the timing belt and pump sprocket as described in Chapter 2C, Section 7 or Chapter 2D, Section 7.

2 Disconnect the wiring connector from the fuel metering valve on top of the fuel pump **(see illustration)**.

3 Undo the two retaining screws and move the coolant return pipe to one side **(see illustration 5.3a & 5.3b)**.

4 Undo the two retaining screws and move the fuel return pipe to one side **(see illustration 5.4a & 5.4b)**.

5 Undo the pipe retaining bracket screw and the two retaining bolts, then remove the lifting eye from the front of the engine **(see illustration)**.

6 Slacken the fuel pipe unions and remove the high-pressure pipe from the pump to the fuel rail **(see illustration)**.

7 Release the retaining clips and disconnect the two fuel hoses from the top of the fuel pump **(see illustration)**.

8 Counterhold the pump hub using VW tool No. T10051, and undo the pump hub nut. In the absence of this special tool, counterhold the hub using something to lock the sprocket, whilst the centre nut is slackened **(see illustration)**.

9 Using a suitable two-legged puller (VW tool

9.2 Disconnect the pump wiring connector

9.5 Remove the lifting bracket from above the fuel pump

9.6 Remove the high pressure fuel line from the pump

9.7 Disconnect the fuel hoses (arrowed) from the pump

9.8 Remove the fuel pump center hub nut

9.10 Fuel pump mounting bolts (arrowed)

No. T40064) and two bolts, remove the hub complete with sprocket from the pump shaft.
10 Undo the 3 retaining bolts and remove the pump **(see illustration)**.

Refitting

11 Refitting is a reversal of removal, noting the following points:
 a) *Ensure all fuel pipes/hose connections are clean and free from debris.*
 b) *The high-pressure fuel pipe from the pump to the common rail maybe re-used providing it's not been damaged.*
 c) *Tighten all fasteners to their specified torque where given.*
 d) *Fill the pump with clean fuel through the fuel supply pipe aperture prior to starting.*
 e) *Bleed the fuel system as described in Section 10.*

10 Fuel system bleeding

1 Prime the high pressure fuel pump by filling it with clean diesel through the fuel supply aperture, then operate the starter for shorts bursts (no more than 10 seconds at a time) until the engine starts. Operate the engine at a fast idle (approx 2000 rpm) for several minutes before allowing it to return to its normal idle speed.
2 If the engine fails to start, it must be filled/bled using VW diagnostic equipment (VAS5051 etc.). Using this equipment operates the electric fuel pumps for 3 minutes.
3 Once the engine has been started, test-drive the vehicle over a distance of at least 15 miles with at least one period of full acceleration. If there is any air left in the fuel system, the engine management ECU may switch to 'limp home' mode, and store a fault code. Have the fault code cleared and road test the vehicle again.

11 Fuel rail –
removal and refitting

Note: *Observe the precautions in Section 1*

11.3a Remove the high pressure pipes from the rail and injectors...

11.3b ...and fit sealing caps to prevent dirt ingress

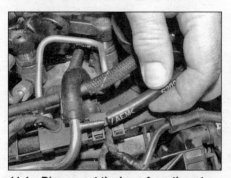
11.4a Disconnect the hose from the return pipe...

11.4b ...and the return pipe from the fuel rail

before working on any component in the fuel system.

Removal

1 Pull the plastic cover on the top of the engine upwards from its' mountings and remove the foam insulation (where fitted) **(see illustrations 3.1a and 3.1b)**. Ensure the area around the fuel rail and pipes is clean and free from debris. If available, use a vacuum cleaner.
2 Disconnect the wiring connectors from the fuel injectors.
3 Counterhold the injector with an open-ended spanner when releasing the pipe union. Undo the unions and remove the high-pressure pipes from between the fuel rail and the injectors **(see illustrations)**. Plug the openings to prevent contamination.
4 Release the retaining clips and disconnect

the fuel return hose from the fuel rail **(see illustrations)**.
5 Undo the retaining bolts, disconnect the coolant return hose from the expansion tank, and move the coolant pipe/hose to one side **(see illustration 5.3)**.
6 Slacken the fuel pipe unions and remove the high-pressure pipe from the pump to the fuel rail **(see illustration 9.6)**.
7 Disconnect the wiring plugs from the glow plugs, fuel pressure regulating valve, and the fuel pressure sensor at each end of the fuel rail. Unclip the wiring loom retaining bracket from the top of the fuel rail and move it to one side **(see illustration)**.
8 Undo the multi-spline retaining bolts and remove the fuel rail **(see illustrations)**.
9 If required, note their fitted positions, then unscrew the fuel pressure sensor and pressure regulating valve from the fuel rail, as

11.7 Lift the wiring loom over and place to one side

11.8a Undo the fuel rail mounting bolts (arrowed) – 1.2 litre engines

11.8b Undo the fuel rail mounting bolts (arrowed) – 1.6 litre engines

described in Section 3. **Note:** *VW insist that once removed, the pressure regulating valve cannot be re-used.*

Refitting

10 Where applicable, refit the fuel pressure sensor and the new regulating valve to the fuel rail, and tighten them to the specified torque. Note that the threads of the sensors must be clean and free from oil and grease.

11 The remainder of refitting is a reversal of removal, noting the following points:

a) *Refit the high-pressure fuel pipes and tighten the unions to the specified torque.*

Note that the high-pressure fuel pipes may be re-used providing the tapered seats are undamaged; the pipes are not deformed, constricted or corroded.

b) *After completion of the work, the fuel system must be bled as described in Section 10.*

Chapter 4 Part C:
Emission control and exhaust systems – petrol engines

Contents

Degrees of difficulty

| **Easy,** suitable for novice with little experience | | **Fairly easy,** suitable for beginner with some experience | | **Fairly difficult,** suitable for competent DIY mechanic | | **Difficult,** suitable for experienced DIY mechanic | | **Very difficult,** suitable for expert DIY or professional | |

Specifications

Engine codes*
1.2 litre:
  SOHC . . . . CHFA
  DOHC . . . . CGPA and CGPB
1.4 litre . . . . CGGB
* Note: *See 'Vehicle identification' at the end of this manual for the location of engine code markings.*

Emission control applications
1.2 litre engine codes CHFA, CGPA and CGPB . . . . Catalytic converter complete with exhaust manifold, pre-cat oxygen sensor in top of exhaust manifold, after-cat sensor behind cat in exhaust front pipe, No EGR system.

1.4 litre engine code CGGB . . . . Pre-Catalytic converter complete with exhaust manifold, main catalytic converter in exhaust front pipe. Pre-cat oxygen sensor in top of exhaust manifold, after-cat sensor in the rear of the intermediate/ flexible pipe. No EGR system.

Torque wrench settings
	Nm	lbf ft
Catalytic converter support bracket to engine bolt (CAXA engine)* . . .	20	15
Exhaust manifold nuts*	25	18
Exhaust front flexible pipe-to-catalytic converter:		
1.2 litre (CHFA engine) exhaust nuts*	40	30
1.2 litre (CGPA and CGPB engines) exhaust nuts*	25	18
1.4 litre (CGGB engine):		
Bolts	20	15
Nuts*	40	30
Exhaust pipe clamp bolts	25	18
Exhaust mounting bracket bolts	25	18
Oxygen (Lambda probe) sensors:		
1.2 litre (CHFA, CGPA and CGPB engines)	50	37
1.4 litre (CGGB) engine:		
Oxygen sensor before catalytic converter	50	37
Oxygen sensor after catalytic converter	55	41

* Do not re-use

1 General information

Emission control systems

All petrol models are designed to use unleaded petrol, and are controlled by engine management systems that are programmed to give the best compromise between driveability, fuel consumption and exhaust emission production. In addition, a number of systems are fitted that help to minimise other harmful emissions. A crankcase emission control system is fitted, which reduces the release of pollutants from the engine's lubrication system, and a catalytic converter is fitted which reduces exhaust gas pollutant. An evaporative loss emission control system is fitted which reduces the release of gaseous hydrocarbons from the fuel tank.

Crankcase emission control

To reduce the emission of unburned hydrocarbons from the crankcase into the atmosphere, the engine is sealed and the blow-by gases and oil vapour are drawn from inside the crankcase, through a wire-mesh oil separator, into the inlet tract to be burned by the engine during normal combustion.

Under conditions of high manifold depression, the gases will be sucked positively out of the crankcase. Under conditions of low manifold depression, the gases are forced out of the crankcase by the (relatively) higher crankcase pressure. If the engine is worn, the raised crankcase pressure (due to increased blow-by) will cause some of the flow to return under all manifold conditions.

Exhaust emission control

To minimise the amount of pollutants that escape into the atmosphere, all petrol models are fitted with one (1.2 litre engines) or two (1.4 litre engine) catalytic converters in the exhaust system. The fuelling system is of the closed-loop type, in which an oxygen (lambda) sensor in the exhaust system provides the engine management system ECU with constant feedback, enabling the ECU to adjust the air/fuel mixture to optimise combustion.

The oxygen sensor has a built-in heating element, controlled by the ECU through

4.3 Cable guide bracket on the shroud lower mounting bolts

the oxygen sensor relay, to quickly bring the sensor's tip to its optimum operating temperature. The sensor's tip is sensitive to oxygen, and sends a voltage signal to the ECU that varies according to the amount of oxygen in the exhaust gas. If the inlet air/fuel mixture is too rich, the exhaust gases are low in oxygen so the sensor sends a low-voltage signal, the voltage rising as the mixture weakens and the amount of oxygen rises in the exhaust gases. Peak conversion efficiency of all major pollutants occurs if the inlet air/fuel mixture is maintained at the chemically correct ratio for the complete combustion of petrol of 14.7 parts (by weight) of air to 1 part of fuel (the stoichiometric ratio). The sensor output voltage alters in a large step at this point, the ECU using the signal change as a reference point and correcting the inlet air/fuel mixture accordingly by altering the fuel injector pulse width.

All models covered in this manual have two oxygen (lambda probe) sensors, one before and one after the catalytic converter(s). This enables more efficient monitoring of the exhaust gas, allowing a faster response time. The overall efficiency of the converter itself can also be checked. Details of the oxygen (lambda probe) sensor removal and refitting are given in Chapter 4A, Section 4.

Evaporative emission control

To minimise the escape of unburned hydrocarbons into the atmosphere, an evaporative loss emission control system is fitted to all petrol models. The fuel tank filler cap is sealed and a charcoal canister is mounted under the right-hand rear wing panel next to the fuel filler neck, this collects the petrol vapours released from the fuel contained in the fuel tank. It stores them until they can be drawn from the canister (under the control of the fuel injection/ignition system ECU) via the purge valve(s) into the inlet tract, where the engine then burns them during normal combustion.

To ensure that the engine runs correctly when it is cold and/or idling and to protect the catalytic converter from the effects of an over-rich mixture, the purge control valve(s) are not opened by the ECU until the engine has warmed-up, and the engine is under load; the valve solenoid is then modulated on and off to allow the stored vapour to pass into the inlet tract.

Exhaust systems

On most models, the exhaust system is the exhaust manifold, front pipe(s), intermediate pipe and silencer, and tailpipe and silencer. The systems fitted differ in detail depending on the engine fitted – for example, in how the catalytic converter is incorporated into the system. On 1.2 litre engines, there is one catalytic converter that is incorporated in the exhaust manifold. On 1.4 litre engines, there are two catalytic converters, one is part of the exhaust manifold and the second one is part of the middle section of exhaust, fitted behind the front flexible pipe.

The system is supported by various metal brackets screwed to the vehicle floor, with rubber vibration dampers fitted to suppress noise, refer to Section 5, of this Chapter.

2 Evaporative loss emission control system – information and component renewal

1 The evaporative loss emission control system consists of the purge valve, the activated charcoal filter canister and connecting vacuum hoses.
2 The purge (or solenoid) valve is located in the right-hand rear corner of the engine compartment, and the charcoal canister is located near the fuel tank behind the right-hand rear wheel arch liner.
3 To remove the purge valve, check that the ignition is switched off, then disconnect the wiring plug and the two hoses.
4 To remove the canister, chock the front wheels, and then jack up the rear of the car and support it on axle stands (see *Jacking and vehicle support*). Remove the right-hand rear roadwheel and the wheel arch liner. Disconnect the hose leading to the solenoid valve from the top of the adapter, and then disconnect the hose from the fuel tank from the side of the adapter. Unscrew the mounting bolt and lower the canister from the body.
5 Refitting is a reversal of removal.

3 Crankcase emission system – general information

1 The crankcase emission control system consists of hoses connecting the crankcase to the air cleaner or inlet manifold. Oil separator units are fitted to some petrol engines, usually at the back of the engine.
2 The system requires no attention other than to check at regular intervals that the hoses, valve and oil separator are free of blockages and in good condition.

4 Exhaust manifold – removal and refitting

Removal

1 Apply the handbrake, then jack up the front of the vehicle and support it on axle stands (see *Jacking and vehicle support*).
2 The exhaust manifold/catalytic converter is located on the front of the engine. To make access easier, first move the lock carrier/front cross member assembly to its service position as described in Chapter 2E, Section 4.
3 Undo the retaining bolts and remove the hot-air shroud from over the exhaust manifold. On some models, it may be necessary to remove the cable guide bracket on the lower bolts **(see illustration)**.

4.4 Front pipe flange with mounting bracket – 1.4 litre engine

4.6a Unbolt and remove the exhaust manifold...

4.6b ...and recover the gasket

4 Working under the vehicle, unbolt the exhaust front pipe/catalytic converter to front flexible flange bolts/nuts **(see illustration)**. Lower the front pipe and recover the gasket; a new one will be required on refitting.
Caution: Handle the flexible, braided section of the front pipe carefully, and do not bend it excessively, if it is bent more than 10° it could get damaged.
5 Trace the wiring back from the oxygen sensor, located above the catalytic converter on the manifold, and then disconnect the wiring plug connector. Release the wiring from its retaining clips, noting its routing and fitted position.
6 Unscrew the nuts and withdraw the exhaust manifold from the cylinder head. Discard the nuts, as new ones must be used on refitting. Also, recover the gasket and discard **(see illustrations)**.

Refitting

7 Refitting is a reversal of the removal procedure, but fit new gaskets and tighten all nuts and bolts to the specified torque where given.

5 Exhaust system –
 component renewal

⚠️ *Warning: Allow ample time for the exhaust system to cool before starting work. In particular, note that the catalytic converter runs at very high temperatures. If there is any*

chance that the system may still be hot, wear suitable gloves. When removing the exhaust sections, take care not to damage the oxygen sensors if they are not removed from their locations.

Removal

1 The original VW exhaust system fitted in the factory is in two sections:
 a) *1.2 litre engines: Front flexible pipe and silencer section, and the rear section with one silencer*
 b) *1.4 litre engines: Front flexible pipe and catalytic converter section, and the rear section with two silencers*
There is also a catalytic converter, which is part of the exhaust manifold (see Section 4) on all engines. The rear section of the exhaust on all models, can be cut at the middle of the pipe and a joining clamp be fitted. On 1.4 litre engines, the rear section has two silencers, however each silencer may be renewed separately by cutting the middle of the pipe and fitting a joining clamp. See paragraph 13, in this Section.
2 To remove part of the system, first jack up the front or rear of the car and support it on axle stands (see *Jacking and vehicle support*). Alternatively, position the car over an inspection pit or on car ramps.

Front flexible pipe/silencer

Note: *Handle the flexible, braided section of the front pipe carefully, and do not bend it more than 10°, as it may get damaged.*
3 Trace the wiring back from the oxygen sensor, which is fitted at the front of the flexible

section **(see illustration)**. Trace the wiring back from the sensor and disconnect the wiring connector. Unclip the oxygen sensor wiring from any clips or brackets, noting how it is routed for refitting. If a new front flexible section is being fitted, unscrew the oxygen sensors from the pipe, as applicable.
4 Unscrew the clamp bolts and release the rear of the pipe/silencer from the centre section **(see illustration)**.
5 Unscrew and remove the nuts securing the front flange to the lower part of the catalytic converter **(see illustration 4.4)**. Discard the nuts, as new ones will be required for refitting.
6 Release the rubber mountings from the brackets under the vehicle **(see illustration)** and separate the front joint, carefully moving it down sufficiently to clear the mounting studs.
Caution: Handle the flexible, braided section of the front pipe carefully, and do not bend it excessively, if it is bent more than 10° it could get damaged.
7 Supporting the front of the pipe, detach the rear of the pipe from the centre section and withdraw it forwards and remove it from under the car. Recover the gasket from the end of the pipe, as a new one will be required on refitting.

Rear pipe and silencer(s)

8 If the factory-fitted VW rear section is being worked on, examine the pipe just in front of the rear axle (between the two silencers on 1.4 litre engines), for three pairs of punch marks, or three line markings. The centre marking indicates the point at which to cut the pipe, while the outer marks indicate the position

5.3 Disconnect the sensor connectors - arrowed

5.4 Slacken the securing clamp retaining bolts

5.6 Unclip the exhaust rubber mounting - arrowed

5.10 Exhaust rubber mountings

for the ends of the new clamp required when refitting. Cut through the pipe using the centre mark as a guide, making the cut as square to the pipe as possible if either section is to be re-used.

9 If the factory-fitted rear section has already been renewed, loosen the nuts securing the clamp between the silencers so that the clamp can be moved.

Rear silencers

10 The rear silencers are supported by rubber mountings that locate on mounting brackets, which are bolted to the underside of the car **(see illustration)**.

11 Undo the clamp bolts at the front of the rear silencers and slide it along the pipe to release it from the centre section. Lower the silencers out of position and release the mounting(s) from the underside of the car.

Refitting

12 Each section is refitted by a reversal of the removal sequence, noting the following points:
  a) *Ensure that all traces of corrosion have*

been removed from the flanges or pipe ends, and renew all necessary gaskets.
b) *If necessary, renew the clamps, and use the markings on the pipes as a guide to the clamp's correct fitted position.*
c) *Inspect the mountings for signs of damage or deterioration, and renew as necessary.*
d) *If using exhaust assembly paste, make sure this is only applied to joints downstream of the catalyst.*
e) *Prior to tightening the exhaust system mountings and clamps, ensure that all rubber mountings are correctly located and that there is adequate clearance between the exhaust system and vehicle underbody. Try to ensure that no unnecessary twisting stresses are applied to the pipes – move the pipes relative to each other at the clamps to relieve this.*

6 Catalytic converter – general information and precautions

The catalytic converter is a reliable and simple device which needs no maintenance in itself, but there are some facts of which an owner should be aware if the converter is to function properly for its full service life:
a) *DO NOT use leaded or lead-replacement petrol in a car equipped with a catalytic converter – the lead (or other additives) will coat the precious metals, reducing their converting efficiency and will eventually destroy the converter.*
b) *Always keep the ignition and fuel systems well maintained in accordance with the manufacturer's schedule (see Chapter 1A).*

c) *If the engine develops a misfire, do not drive the car at all (or at least as little as possible) until the fault is cured.*
d) *DO NOT push- or tow-start the car – this will soak the catalytic converter in unburned fuel, causing it to overheat when the engine does start.*
e) *DO NOT switch off the ignition at high engine speeds – i.e. do not 'blip' the throttle immediately before switching off the engine.*
f) *DO NOT use fuel or engine oil additives – these may contain substances harmful to the catalytic converter.*
g) *DO NOT continue to use the car if the engine burns oil to the extent of leaving a visible trail of blue smoke.*
h) *Remember that the catalytic converter operates at very high temperatures. DO NOT, therefore, park the car in dry undergrowth, over long grass or piles of dead leaves after a long run.*
i) *Remember that the catalytic converter is FRAGILE – do not strike it with tools during servicing work, and take care handling it when removing it from the car for any reason.*
j) *In some cases, a sulphurous smell (like that of rotten eggs) may be noticed from the exhaust. This is common to many catalytic converter-equipped cars, and has more to do with the sulphur content of the brand of fuel being used than the converter itself.*
k) *The catalytic converter, used on a well-maintained and well-driven car, should last for between 50,000 and 100,000 miles – if the converter is no longer effective, it must be renewed.*

Chapter 4 Part D:
Emission control and exhaust systems – diesel engines

Contents

Degrees of difficulty

Easy, suitable for novice with little experience	Fairly easy, suitable for beginner with some experience	Fairly difficult, suitable for competent DIY mechanic	Difficult, suitable for experienced DIY mechanic	Very difficult, suitable for expert DIY or professional

Specifications

Engine codes*
1.2 litre - common rail injection . . . . CHFA
1.6 litre - common rail injection . . . . CAYB, CAYC and CLNA
* Note: *See 'Vehicle identification' at the end of this manual for the location of engine code markings.*

Emission control applications
All engines . . . . Particulate filter in the front downpipe with catalytic converter and oxygen (lambda probe) sensor. EGR system fitted, with exhaust gas temperature sensors and exhaust gas pressure sensor.

Torque wrench settings

	Nm	lbf ft
Catalytic converter/particulate filter mounting bracket nuts/bolts.	25	18
EGR cooler mounting bolts	9	6
EGR recirculation metal pipes:		
to-cooler bolts	9	6
to-cylinder head bolts.	9	6
to-exhaust manifold nuts	24	18
to-inlet manifold clamp bolt	5	4
Exhaust clamp nuts	25	18
Exhaust gas temperature senders	45	33
Exhaust/turbo manifold to cylinder head	24	18
Turbocharger pulsation damper bolts	10	7
Turbocharger oil return pipe flange bolts*	17	13
Turbocharger oil return banjo bolt*	40	30
Turbocharger oil supply banjo bolt	30	22
Turbocharger-to-downpipe/catalytic converter clamp.	7	5

* Do not re-use

2.1 Disconnecting the breather hose

1 General information

Emission control systems

All diesel-engined models have a crankcase emission control system, and in addition, are fitted with a catalytic converter. All diesel engines are fitted with an Exhaust Gas Recirculation (EGR) system to reduce exhaust emissions.

Crankcase emission control

To reduce the emission of unburned hydrocarbons from the crankcase into the atmosphere, the engine is sealed and the blow-by gases and oil vapour are drawn from inside the crankcase, through a wire mesh oil separator, into the inlet tract to be burned by the engine during normal combustion.

Under conditions of high manifold depression, the gases will be sucked positively out of the crankcase. Under conditions of low manifold depression, the gases are forced out of the crankcase by the (relatively) higher crankcase pressure. If the engine is worn, the raised crankcase pressure (due to increased blow-by) will cause some of the flow to return under all manifold conditions.

Exhaust emission control

An oxidation catalyst is fitted in the exhaust system of all diesel-engined models. This has the effect of removing a large proportion of the gaseous hydrocarbons, carbon monoxide and particulates present in the exhaust gas. Some models have a particulate filter, which is fitted behind the catalytic converter in order to filter out soot particles.

An Exhaust Gas Recirculation (EGR) system is fitted to all diesel-engined models. This reduces the level of nitrogen oxides produced during combustion by introducing a proportion of the exhaust gas back into the inlet manifold under certain engine operating conditions. The system is controlled electronically by the diesel engine management ECU.

Exhaust systems

The exhaust system consists of the exhaust manifold, front flexible pipe with catalytic converter/particulate filter and rear pipe section including silencer. The turbocharger is integral with the exhaust manifold, and is driven by the exhaust gases.

The system is supported by various metal brackets screwed to the vehicle floor, with rubber vibration dampers fitted to suppress noise.

2 Crankcase emission system – general information

1 The crankcase emission control system consists of hoses connecting the crankcase to the air cleaner, cylinder head cover and/or inlet manifold **(see illustration)**.
2 The system requires no attention other than to check at regular intervals that the hoses and pressure-regulating valve are free of blockages and in good condition.

3 Exhaust Gas Recirculation (EGR) system – component removal

1 The EGR system consists of the EGR valve, which directs exhaust gas from the exhaust manifold to the inlet manifold, and a control (change-over) valve that actuates the system according to engine load and speed **(see**

3.1 Vacuum hose layout - diesel engines

1) EGR cooler change over vacuum unit
2) Cylinder head cover
3) EGR cooler change over valve
4) Non-return valve
5) Vacuum pump connection
6) To brake servo
7) Air filter
8) Silencer
9) Charge pressure control solenoid valve
10) Vacuum unit on turbocharger (with position sensor)

3.3a EGR cooler solenoid valve (arrowed)
– 1.2 litre engine

3.3b EGR cooler solenoid valve (arrowed)
– 1.6 litre engine

3.4 Disconnect the wiring connector...

3.5 ...then unclip the valve from the
bracket

3.10a EGR cooler hoses – 1.2 litre engine

3.10b Disconnect the hoses...

illustration). There is a vacuum-operated changeover unit, which is fitted on the EGR cooler for recirculating the exhaust gas. All this is connected by a series of vacuum hoses, and metal corrugated cooler pipes. There is also a recirculation potentiometer fitted to the EGR valve, this is controlled directly from the engine management ECU, which then activates the control motor.

2 The EGR valve is integral with the exhaust gas cooler, which is bolted to the rear of the cylinder block. It is joined to the exhaust manifold and cylinder head, by flanged corrugated metal pipes. The system is activated by a solenoid valve mounted at the front of the inlet manifold, which is controlled by the ECU.

EGR cooler 'change-over' solenoid valve

3 The EGR vacuum-solenoid valve is

mounted on the front of the inlet manifold **(see illustrations)**. Do not confuse the EGR solenoid with the turbo charge pressure control solenoid, which is mounted on the bulkhead.

4 Disconnect the wiring plug from the solenoid valve **(see illustration)**.

5 Unclip the valve from the mounting bracket **(see illustration)**, then identify the vacuum hoses for refitting and disconnect them from the valve.

6 Refitting is a reversal of removal. Ensure that the hoses and wiring plug are reconnected securely and correctly.

EGR valve

7 The EGR valve is incorporated into the EGR cooler, remove the cooler as described in paragraphs 8 to 16. At the time of writing, it was not possible to separate the EGR valve from the cooler.

EGR cooler

8 Remove the exhaust front pipe/catalytic converter/ particulate filter as described in Section 8.

9 Drain the cooling system as described in Chapter 1B, Section 30. If required the coolant hoses can be clamped before removal, to save draining the complete system.

10 Release the retaining clips and disconnect the coolant hoses from each end of the EGR cooler **(see illustrations)**. Be prepared for coolant spillage.

11 Undo the two retaining screws from the cooler, the two retaining nuts from the exhaust manifold and remove the EGR metal connecting pipe **(see illustration)**.

12 Undo the two retaining screws from the cooler, the two retaining screws from the cylinder head and remove the EGR metal connecting pipe **(see illustrations)**.

13 Undo the upper bolts and lower banjo

3.10c ...from the EGR cooler – 1.6 litre
engine

3.11 Remove the EGR pipe from the cooler
to the manifold

3.12a Undo the EGR pipe bolts (arrowed)
to the cooler

3.12b Undo the EGR pipe bolts (arrowed) to the cylinder head

3.13a Undo the upper bolts (arrowed)…

3.13b …and lower banjo bolts…

3.13c …then remove the pipes and support bracket

3.14 Disconnect the wiring connector from the EGR valve

bolt and remove the turbocharger oil return pipe/support from the rear of the engine (see illustrations).

14 Disconnect the wiring plug connector from the EGR valve (see illustration).

15 Disconnect the vacuum hose from vacuum unit on the lower part of the cooler, then undo the four retaining bolts (see illustration), and remove the cooler from the rear of the engine.

16 Refitting is a reversal of removal, using new gaskets (see illustration), and tightening the retaining bolts to the specified torque.

4 Turbocharger – general information and precautions

General information

A turbocharger is fitted to all engines, and is integral with the exhaust manifold.

3.15 EGR cooler securing bolts (arrowed)

The turbocharger increases engine efficiency by raising the pressure in the inlet manifold above atmospheric pressure. Instead of the air simply being sucked into the cylinders, it is forced in.

Energy for the operation of the turbocharger comes from the exhaust gas. The gas flows through a specially shaped housing (the turbine housing) and in so doing, spins the turbine wheel. The turbine wheel is attached to a shaft, at the end of which is another vaned wheel, known as the compressor wheel. The compressor wheel spins in its own housing, and compresses the inducted air on the way to the inlet manifold.

Between the turbocharger and the inlet manifold, the compressed air passes through an intercooler (see Section 7 for details). The purpose of the intercooler is to remove from the inducted air some of the heat gained in being compressed. Because cooler air is

3.16 Fit new gaskets to the EGR pipes

denser, removal of this heat further increases engine efficiency.

Boost pressure (the pressure in the inlet manifold) is limited by a wastegate, which diverts the exhaust gas away from the turbine wheel in response to a pressure-sensitive actuator.

The turbo shaft is pressure-lubricated by an oil feed pipe from the engine oil filter mounting. The shaft 'floats' on a cushion of oil. Oil is returned to the sump through a return pipe that connects to the rear of the cylinder block.

Precautions

The turbocharger operates at extremely high speeds and temperatures. Certain precautions must be observed to avoid premature failure of the turbo, or injury to the operator.

• *Do not operate the turbo with any parts exposed – foreign objects falling onto the rotating vanes could cause excessive damage and (if ejected) personal injury.*

• *Cover the turbocharger air inlet ducts to prevent debris entering, and clean using lint-free cloths only.*

• *Do not race the engine immediately after start-up, especially if it is cold. Give the oil a few seconds to circulate.*

• *Observe the recommended intervals for oil and filter changing, and use a reputable oil of the specified quality. Neglect of oil changing, or use of inferior oil, can cause carbon formation on the turbo shaft and subsequent failure. Thoroughly clean the area around all oil pipe unions before disconnecting them, to prevent the ingress of dirt. Store dismantled components in a sealed container to prevent contamination.*

5 Turbocharger and exhaust manifold – removal and refitting

Note: *This Section describes removal of the turbocharger together with the exhaust manifold. On all diesel engines covered in this Manual, the turbocharger cannot be removed from the exhaust manifold.*

Removal

1 Apply the handbrake, then jack up the front

5.5a Disconnecting the breather hose...

5.5b ...undo the retaining screw...

5.5c ...and disconnect the air intake hose

5.6a Disconnect the wiring connector...

5.6b ...and vacuum hose from the charge pressure valve

5.7 Trace the wiring back from the gas temperature sensor (arrowed)

of the vehicle and support it on axle stands (see *Jacking and vehicle support*). Remove the engine compartment undertray and the engine top cover.

2 Remove the bulkhead panel from the rear of the engine compartment, as described in Chapter 12, Section 18 (wiper motor/linkage removal).

3 Remove the air cleaner assembly and ducting as described in Chapter 4B, Section 2.

4 Undo the clamp securing the exhaust front pipe/catalytic converter/ particulate filter to the turbocharger and move front pipe to one side, refer to the information given in Section 8.

5 Undo the retaining bolt, unclip the breather pipe and disconnect the air intake hose from the turbocharger **(see illustrations)**.

6 Disconnect the wiring connector and vacuum pipe from the charge pressure valve on top of the turbocharger **(see illustrations)**.

7 Located at the engine compartment bulkhead, disconnect the exhaust gas temperature sensor wiring plugs **(see illustration)**, and detach the connector from the bulkhead bracket. Note that there is one wiring connector behind the mounting plate on the bulkhead, trace the wiring back from the relevant sensor, noting its routing and releasing it from any retaining clips.

8 Slacken the retaining clips, undo the two retaining bolts and withdraw the pulsation damper from the charge air ducting to the turbo **(see illustration)**.

9 Undo the retaining screws and remove the EGR metal connecting pipes, with reference to Section 3.

10 Undo the two upper securing bolts and the lower banjo bolts for the oil supply and return for the turbocharger. Then remove the oil return pipe/support from the rear of

the engine **(see illustrations 3.13a, 3.13b & 3.13c)**.

11 Undo the two retaining screws and remove the heat shield from the manifold **(see illustration)**.

12 Check around the turbocharger/exhaust manifold and unclip any wiring or hoses still connected, noting their fitted position and the routing of all cables.

13 Undo the retaining nuts and manoeuvre the exhaust manifold/turbocharger assembly out from the engine compartment **(see illustration)**.

Refitting

14 Refit the turbocharger by following the removal procedure in reverse, noting the following points:

a) *Renew exhaust manifold gaskets, sealing washers and O-rings* **(see illustration)**.

5.8 Disconnect the charge air pipe/ pulsation damper from the turbo

5.11 Undo the two retaining screws from the heat shield

5.13 Remove the turbocharger/manifold from the engine compartment

5.14a Fit new exhaust manifold gasket...

5.14b ...oil return/supply pipe gasket...

5.14c ...oil return banjo bolt...

5.14d ...and oil supply sealing washers

b) *Fit new gasket to the oil return pipe upper flange* **(see illustration)**.

c) *Fit new banjo bolt to oil return pipe* **(see illustration)**.

d) *Fit new sealing washers to the oil supply pipe* **(see illustration)**.

e) *Before reconnecting the oil supply pipe, fill the turbocharger with fresh oil using an oil can.*

f) *Tighten all nuts and bolts to the specified torque, where given.*

g) *Ensure that the air hose clips are securely tightened, to prevent air leaks.*

h) *When the engine is started after refitting, allow it to idle for approximately one minute to give the oil time to circulate around the turbine shaft bearings. Check for signs of oil or coolant leakage from the relevant unions.*

6 Turbocharger charge control system components – description, removal and refitting

Description

1 The turbocharger wastegate valve is operated by vacuum supplied by the brake vacuum pump mounted on the left-hand end of the cylinder head. The vacuum supply is controlled by an electrically operated solenoid valve activated by the engine management ECU. The solenoid valve is mounted on the left-hand inner wing panel at the side of the air cleaner houisng. The valve has three hoses connecting it to the air cleaner, turbocharger vacuum unit and vacuum pump. It is important that the hoses are connected correctly to the solenoid valve **(see illustration 3.1)**.

Charge pressure control solenoid valve

2 The charge pressure solenoid valve is mounted on the left-hand inner wing panel **(see illustration)**, at the rear of the battery.

3 Disconnect the wiring from the solenoid valve.

4 Undo the two retaining nuts and withdraw the solenoid valve away from the wing panel, unclipping the vacuum hoses from their retaining clips.

5 Remove the vacuum hoses from the ports on the control solenoid valve, noting their order of connection carefully as they need to be fitted in the correct position on refitting **(see illustration)**.

6 Refitting is a reversal of removal.

Charge pressure valve (wastegate)

7 The Charge pressure 'boost' valve is fitted to the top of the turbocharger and cannot be renewed separately as it is an integral part of the turbocharger **(see illustration)**.

7 Intercooler – general information, removal and refitting

General information

1 The intercooler is effectively an 'air radiator', used to cool the pressurised inlet air before it enters the engine.

2 When the turbocharger compresses the inlet air, one side effect is that the air is heated, causing the air to expand. If the inlet air can be cooled, a greater effective volume of air will be inducted, and the engine will produce more power.

3 The compressed air from the turbocharger, which would normally be fed straight into the inlet manifold, is instead ducted around the engine to the base of the intercooler. The intercooler is mounted at the front of the car, in the airflow. The heated air entering one side of the intercooler is cooled by the airflow over the intercooler fins, much as with the radiator.

4 There is a charge air pressure/temperature sensor fitted to the air inlet ducting from the intercooler to the inlet manifold. See Chapter 4B, Section 3, for removal and refitting procedure.

6.2 Boost pressure solenoid valve (arrowed)

6.5 Disconnect the wiring connector and disconnect the vacuum hoses

6.7 Charge pressure valve (arrowed)

7.6a Release the retaining clip...

7.6b ...and disconnect the intercooler

7.7 Check the rubber grommets in the crossmember

Removal

5 The intercooler is attached to the lower part of the radiator on the lock carrier (the crossmember incorporating the radiator grille and air-conditioning condenser). Remove the radiator as described in Chapter 3, Section 3, for access to the intercooler. This procedure may include moving the lock carrier to its Service position, See Chapter 2E, Section 4.

6 Release the retaining clips and disconnect the intercooler from the lower part of the radiator **(see illustrations)**.

Refitting

7 Refitting is a reversal of removal, noting the following points:

a) Check the rubber grommets are still located in the lower crossmember **(see illustration)**.

b) Refer to Chapter 3, Section 3, when refitting the radiator.

c) Ensure that the air hose clips are securely refitted, to prevent air leaks.

8 Catalytic converter/ particulate filter – removal and refitting

⚠️ **Warning: Allow ample time for the exhaust system to cool before starting work. In particular, note that the catalytic converter runs at very high temperatures. If there is any chance that the system may still be hot, wear suitable gloves.**

Note: *This Section describes removal of the exhaust front flexible pipe/catalytic converter/particulate filter, which is one complete assembly. The subframe will need to be removed, to allow enough room for the assembly to be lowered out from under the rear of the engine.*

1 Disconnect the battery negative lead and position it away from the terminal. **Note:** *Refer to 'Disconnecting the battery' at the rear of this manual first.*

2 Working at the engine compartment bulkhead, disconnect the wiring plugs for the oxygen sensor and exhaust gas temperature sensors.

3 Trace the wiring back from the sensors, noting their routing and release the wiring harness from the retaining clips **(see illustration)**. Note the sensors can stay fitted to the exhaust at this point, if a new catalytic converter/particulate is fitted, then the sensors can be swapped over with the system of the vehicle.

4 Slacken the retaining bolt to release the clamp between the turbocharger and the catalytic converter/particulate filter **(see illustration)**.

5 On 1.6 litre engines, release the hoses from the timing cover **(see illustration)**, release the retaining clip and disconnect the pressure hose from the exhaust to the differential pressure sender.

6 On models with particulate filter, slacken and remove the upper mounting bolt at the right-hand rear corner of the cylinder head, **(see illustration)**.

7 Apply the handbrake, then jack up the front of the vehicle and support it on axle stands (see *Jacking and vehicle support*). Remove the engine compartment undertray.

8 Where fitted, undo the two retaining bolts and remove the heat shield from above the right-hand drive shaft **(see illustration)**.

9 To prevent any damage to the front flexible

8.3 Unclip the wiring loom

8.4 Undo the exhaust/turbo securing clamp (arrowed)

8.5 Unclip the hoses from the retaining clips on the timing cover

8.6 Undo the retaining bolt (arrowed)

8.8 Remove the heat shield from the cylinder block

8.9 Support the flexible pipe with flat metal bar and securing clips

8.10a Slide the exhaust clamp along the exhaust…

8.10b …and release the rubber mountings

8.11a Undo the upper securing nuts…

8.11b …and lower securing nuts…

8.11c …then remove the lower mounting bracket

pipe use a couple of pieces of metal bar and some retaining clips to prevent the flexible pipe from bending to far and getting damaged **(see illustration)**.

Caution: Handle the flexible, braided section of the front pipe carefully, and do not bend it excessively, if it is bent more than 10° it could get damaged.

10 Slacken the retaining bolts and slide the exhaust clamp to the rear of the vehicle, and disengage the exhaust front pipe rubber mountings from the rear of the subframe **(see illustrations)**.

11 Undo the nuts securing the catalytic converter/particulate filter lower support bracket to the cylinder block **(see illustrations)**.

12 Lower the front subframe, as described in Chapter 10, Section 18, when removing the steering gear assembly.

13 Carefully manoeuvre the catalytic

8.14 Renew the gasket between the particulate filter and the turbo

converter/particulate filter downwards from place. Take care not to damage any wiring, making sure that all wiring has been disconnected and release from their retaining clips. Also take care not to bend the flexible section of the exhaust pipe at an angle of more than 10°.

Refitting

14 Refit the exhaust catalytic converter/particulate filter assembly by following the removal procedure in reverse, but renew all gaskets **(see illustration)** and tighten all nuts and bolts to the specified torque, where given.

9 Exhaust system – component renewal

⚠️ *Warning: Allow ample time for the exhaust system to cool before starting work. In particular, note that the catalytic converter runs at very high temperatures. If there is any chance that the system may still be hot, wear suitable gloves.*

Removal

1 The original VW system fitted in the factory is in two sections. The front section includes the catalytic converter (or 'catalyst'), and particulate filter. The rear section, which connects to the front section under the centre of the vehicle, has a silencer fitted at the rear **(see illustration)**.

2 To remove part of the system, first jack up the front or rear of the car and support it on axle stands (see *Jacking and vehicle support*). Alternatively, position the car over an inspection pit or on car ramps.

Front pipe (catalytic converter/ particulate filter)

Caution: Handle the flexible, braided section of the front pipe carefully, and do not bend it excessively, if it is bent more than 10° it could get damaged.

3 The front flexible pipe section is part of the catalytic converter/particulate filter, remove the front pipe assembly as described in Section 8.

Rear pipe and silencer

4 Unscrew the clamp bolt securing the rear section of exhaust to the front section **(see illustration)**.

9.1 Rear exhaust system - 1.2 litre engines

5 Release the silencer from the rubber mountings, then twist it from the centre section and withdraw it from under the car **(see illustrations)**.

6 If required, undo the retaining bolts and remove the mounting brackets from across the exhaust tunnel, to make removal easier **(see illustration)**.

7 If the factory-fitted VW rear section is being worked on, examine the pipe in front of the rear axle for three pairs of punch marks, or three line markings. The centre marking indicates the point at which to cut the pipe, while the outer marks indicate the position for the ends of the new clamp required when refitting. Cut through the pipe using the centre mark as a guide, making the cut as square to the pipe as possible if either resulting section is to be re-used.

8 If the factory-fitted rear section has already been renewed, unscrew the clamp bolts between the two sections, to remove individual sections.

Refitting

9 Each section is refitted by a reversal of the removal sequence, noting the following points:

a) *Ensure that all traces of corrosion have been removed from the flanges or pipe ends, and renew all necessary gaskets.*

b) *The design of the clamps used between the exhaust sections means that they play a greater role in ensuring a gas-tight seal – fit new clamps if they are in less than perfect condition.*

c) *When fitting the clamps, use the markings on the pipes as a guide to the clamps correct fitted position.*

d) *Inspect the mountings for signs of damage or deterioration, and renew as necessary.*

e) *If using exhaust assembly paste, make sure this is only applied to joints downstream of the catalyst.*

f) *Prior to tightening the exhaust system mountings and clamps, ensure that all rubber mountings are correctly located and that there is adequate clearance*

9.4 Slacken the bolts on the exhaust pipe clamp

9.5b Rubber mounting on centre section of exhaust

between the exhaust system and vehicle underbody.

10 Catalytic converter – general information and precautions

The catalytic converter fitted to diesel models is simpler than that fitted to petrol models, but it still needs to be treated with respect to avoid problems. The converter is a reliable and simple device which needs no maintenance in itself, but there are some facts of which an owner should be aware if the converter is to function properly for its full service life:

9.5a Rear silencer exhaust rubber mounting

9.6 Mounting bracket across exhaust tunnel

a) *DO NOT use fuel or engine oil additives – these may contain substances harmful to the catalytic converter.*

b) *DO NOT continue to use the car if the engine burns (engine) oil to the extent of leaving a visible trail of blue smoke.*

c) *Remember that the catalytic converter is FRAGILE – do not strike it with tools during servicing work, and take care handling it when removing it from the car for any reason.*

d) *The catalytic converter, used on a well-maintained and well-driven car, should last for between 50,000 and 100,000 miles – if the converter is no longer effective, it must be renewed.*

Chapter 5 Part A:
Starting and charging systems

Contents

Degrees of difficulty

Easy, suitable for novice with little experience	**Fairly easy,** suitable for beginner with some experience	**Fairly difficult,** suitable for competent DIY mechanic	**Difficult,** suitable for experienced DIY mechanic	**Very difficult,** suitable for expert DIY or professional

Specifications

Engine codes

Petrol engines

1.2 litre:	
SOHC	CHFA
DOHC (12V)	CGPA and CGPB
1.4 litre	CGGB

Diesel engines

1.2 litre	CFWA
1.6 litre	CAYB, CAYC and CLNA

General

System type	12-volt, negative-earth

Starter motor

Rating:	
Petrol engines	12V, 1.1 kW
Diesel engines	12V, 2.0 kW

Battery

Ratings	36 to 72 Ah (depending on model and market)

Alternator

Rating	55, 60, 70 or 90 amp
Minimum brush length	5.0 mm

Torque wrench settings

	Nm	lbf ft
Alternator mounting bolts:		
M8 bolts	23	17
M10 bolts	50	37
Battery clamping plate bolt	20	15
Battery terminal clamp bolts	6	4
Battery tray	10	8
Starter motor mounting bolts:		
M10 bolts	40	30
M12 bolts	80	59

1 General information and precautions

General information

The engine electrical system consists mainly of the charging and starting systems. Because of their engine-related functions, these are covered separately from the body electrical devices such as the lights, instruments, etc (which are covered in Chapter 12). On petrol engine models refer to Part B of this Chapter for information on the ignition system, and on diesel models refer to Part C for information on the preheating system.

The electrical system is of the 12-volt negative-earth type.

The battery is of the low-maintenance or maintenance-free (sealed for life) type and is charged by the alternator, which is belt-driven from the crankshaft pulley.

The starter motor is of the pre-engaged type, with an integral solenoid. On starting, the solenoid moves the drive pinion into engagement with the flywheel ring gear before the starter motor is energised. Once the engine has started, a one-way clutch prevents the motor armature being driven by the engine until the pinion disengages from the flywheel.

Further details of the various systems are given in the relevant Sections of this Chapter. While some repair procedures are given, the usual course of action is to renew the component concerned. The owner whose interest extends beyond mere component renewal should obtain a copy of the *Automotive Electrical & Electronic Systems Manual*, available from the publishers of this manual.

Precautions

⚠️ *Warning: It is necessary to take extra care when working on the electrical system to avoid damage to semi-conductor devices (diodes and transistors), and to avoid the risk of personal injury. In addition to the precautions given in 'Safety first!' observe the following when working on the system:*

• *Always remove rings, watches, etc, before working on the electrical system. Even with the battery disconnected, capacitive discharge could occur if a component's live terminal is earthed through a metal object. This could cause a shock or nasty burn.*

• *Do not reverse the battery connections. Components such as the alternator, electronic control units, or any other components having semi-conductor circuitry could be irreparably damaged.*

• *Never disconnect the battery terminals, the alternator, any electrical wiring or any test instruments when the engine is running.*

• *Do not allow the engine to turn the alternator when the alternator is not connected.*

• *Never test for alternator output by flashing the output lead to earth.*

• *Always ensure that the battery negative lead is disconnected when working on the electrical system.*

• *If the engine is being started using jump leads and a slave battery, connect the batteries positive-to-positive and negative-to-negative (see Jump starting at the beginning of the manual). This also applies when connecting a battery charger.*

• *Before using electric-arc welding equipment on the car, disconnect the battery, alternator and components such as the electronic control units (where applicable) to protect them from the risk of damage.*

Caution: Certain radios fitted as standard equipment by VW have a built-in security code to deter thieves. If the power source to the unit is cut, the anti-theft system will activate. Even if the power source is immediately reconnected, the radio will not function until the correct security code has been entered. Therefore, if you do not know the correct security code for the radio do not disconnect the battery negative terminal or remove the radio/cassette unit from the car. Refer to your VW dealer for further information on whether the unit fitted to your car has a security code. Refer to 'Disconnecting the battery' in the Reference section at the rear of this manual.

2 Battery – testing and charging

Testing

Standard and low-maintenance battery

1 If the car covers a small annual mileage, it is worthwhile checking the specific gravity of the electrolyte every three months to determine the state of charge of the battery. Remove the battery (see Section 3) then remove the cell caps/cover (as applicable) and use a hydrometer to make the check, comparing the results with the following table. Note that the specific gravity readings assume an electrolyte temperature of 15°C; for every 10°C below 15°C subtract 0.007. For every 10°C above 15°C add 0.007. If the electrolyte level of any cell is low, top it up to the MAX level mark with distilled water.

	Above 25°C	Below 25°C
Fully-charged	1.210 to 1.230	1.270 to 1.290
70% charged	1.170 to 1.190	1.230 to 1.250
Discharged	1.050 to 1.070	1.110 to 1.130

2 If the battery condition is suspect, first check the specific gravity of electrolyte in each cell. A variation of 0.040 or more between any cells indicates loss of electrolyte or deterioration of the internal plates.

3 If the specific gravity variation is 0.040 or more, the battery should be renewed. If the cell variation is satisfactory but the battery is discharged, it should be charged as described later in this Section.

Maintenance-free battery

4 In cases where a sealed for life maintenance-free battery is fitted, topping-up and testing of the electrolyte in each cell is not possible. The condition of the battery can therefore only be tested using a battery condition indicator or a voltmeter.

5 Certain models may be fitted with a maintenance-free battery with a built-in charge condition indicator. The indicator is located in the top of the battery casing, and indicates the condition of the battery from its colour. If the indicator shows green, then the battery is in good condition and charged up. If the indicator turns darker, eventually to black, then the battery requires charging, as described later in this Section. If the indicator shows clear/yellow, then the electrolyte is low and in a critical condition, and should be topped-up with distilled water. If charging the battery does not return the eye to green, the battery should be scrapped.

All battery types

6 If testing the battery using a voltmeter, connect the voltmeter across the battery and note the voltage. The test is only accurate if the battery has not been subjected to any kind of charge for the previous six hours. If this is not the case, switch on the headlights for 30 seconds, then wait four to five minutes before testing the battery after switching off the headlights. All other electrical circuits must be switched off, so check that the doors and tailgate are fully shut when making the test.

7 If the voltage reading is less than 12.2 volts, then the battery is discharged, whilst a reading of 12.2 to 12.4 volts indicates a partially discharged condition.

Charging

Note: *The following is intended as a guide only. Always refer to the manufacturer's recommendations (often printed on a label attached to the battery) before charging a battery.*

8 If the battery is to be recharged, we recommend that you use a low current battery charger. If the battery is disconnected (e.g. if it is to be removed and recharged on the bench), note that certain 'learned' values will be lost from the engine management ECU memory, requiring the car to be driven over a short distance after refitting the battery. Also, when the battery is reconnected, the warning lights for the ESP and electro-mechanical steering will light up and stay on. They will extinguish if you drive briefly in a straight line at a speed of 9 to 13 mph.

Standard and low-maintenance battery

9 Charge the battery at a rate equivalent to 10% of the battery capacity (e.g. for a 45 Ah

battery, charge at 4.5 A) and continue to charge the battery at this rate until no further rise in specific gravity is noted over a four-hour period.

10 Alternatively, a trickle charger charging at the rate of 1.5 amps can safely be used overnight.

11 Specially rapid boost charges that are claimed to restore the power of the battery in 1 to 2 hours are not recommended, as they can cause serious damage to the battery plates through overheating.

12 While charging the battery, note that the temperature of the electrolyte should never exceed 38°C.

Maintenance-free battery

13 This battery type takes considerably longer to fully recharge than the standard type, the time taken being dependent on the extent of discharge, but it can take anything up to three days.

14 A constant voltage type charger is required, to be set, when connected, to 13.9 to 14.9 volts with a charger current below 25 amps. Using this method, the battery should be useable within three hours, giving a voltage reading of 12.5 volts, but this is for a partially discharged battery and, as mentioned, full charging can take far longer.

15 If the battery is to be charged from a fully discharged state (condition reading less than 12.2 volts), have it recharged by your local automotive electrician, as the charge rate is higher and constant supervision during charging is necessary.

3 Battery – removal and refitting

Note: *If the car has a security-coded radio, make sure that you have the code number before disconnecting the battery. If necessary, a 'code-saver' or 'memory-saver' can be used to preserve the radio code and any other relevant memory values whilst the battery is disconnected.*

Removal

1 The battery is located in the front, left-hand corner of the engine compartment.

2 Loosen the clamp nut and disconnect the battery negative (–) lead from the terminal **(see illustration)**.

3 Open the plastic cover and loosen the clamp nut and disconnect the positive (+) lead from the battery terminal **(see illustration)**.

4 Lift the fused panel and plastic bracket from over the battery and move it to one side **(see illustration)**.

5 Unscrew the bolt and remove the battery mounting clamp **(see illustration)**. The battery can then be lifted out of position.

6 To remove the battery tray, undo the two retaining nuts and the one bolt, then as the tray is lifted out from the engine compartment, disconnect the water drain hose from the front of the tray **(see illustrations)**.

Refitting

7 Refit the battery by following the removal procedure in reverse. Tighten the mounting clamp bolt to the correct torque. Tighten the terminal clamp nuts securely, but do not over-tighten them to the point where the clamps are distorted.

8 Where applicable, enter the code on the security-coded radio. Adjust the clock to the correct time, and (where applicable) reset the electric windows as described in *Disconnecting the battery*.

4 Alternator/charging system – testing in car

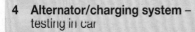

Note: *Refer to Section 1 of this Chapter before starting work.*

1 If the charge warning light fails to illuminate when the ignition is switched on, first check the alternator wiring connections for security. If the light still fails to illuminate, check the continuity of the warning light feed wire from the alternator to the bulbholder. If all is satisfactory, the alternator is at fault and should be renewed or taken to an auto-electrician for testing and repair.

2 Similarly, if the charge warning light comes on with the ignition, but is then slow to go out when the engine is started, this may indicate an impending alternator problem. Check all the items listed in the preceding paragraph, and refer to an auto-electrical specialist if no obvious faults are found.

3.2 Disconnecting the negative terminal – arrowed

3.3 Lift the plastic cover to access the positive terminal

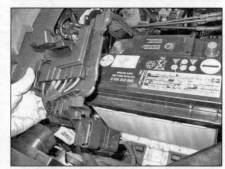

3.4 Unclip the panel from the top of the battery

3.5 Unscrew the clamp bolt – arrowed

3.6a Unscrew the mounting bolts (arrowed)…

3.6b …and disconnect the drain hose

5.5 Unplug the wiring connector

5.6 Disconnect the positive lead securing nut – arrowed

5.7 Undo the cable guide retaining nut – arrowed

5.8a Alternator mounting bolts – petrol engines

3 If the charge warning light illuminates when the engine is running, stop the engine and check that the auxiliary drivebelt is intact and correctly tensioned, and that the alternator connections are secure. If all is so far satisfactory, check the alternator brushes and slip-rings as described in Section 6. If the fault persists, the alternator should be renewed, or taken to an auto-electrician for testing and repair.

4 If the alternator output is suspect even though the warning light functions correctly, the regulated voltage may be checked as follows.

5 Connect a voltmeter across the battery terminals, and start the engine.

6 Increase the engine speed until the voltmeter reading remains steady; the reading should be approximately 12 to 13 volts, and no more than 14 volts.

7 Switch on as many electrical accessories

(e.g. the headlights, heated rear window and heater blower) as possible, and check that the alternator maintains the regulated voltage at around 13 to 14 volts.

8 If the regulated voltage is not as stated, this may be due to worn brushes, weak brush springs, a faulty voltage regulator, a faulty diode, a severed phase winding or worn or damaged slip-rings. The brushes and slip-rings may be checked as described in Section 6, but if the fault persists, the alternator should be renewed or taken to an auto-electrician.

5 Alternator – removal and refitting

Removal

1 Disconnect the battery negative lead (refer

5.8b Alternator mounting bolts – diesel engines

5.10 Tap the spacer (arrowed) down slightly to aid refitting

to *Disconnecting the battery* in the *Reference* Chapter at the end of this manual).

2 To give better access, apply the handbrake, and then jack up the front of the vehicle and support it on axle stands (see *Jacking and vehicle support*).

3 Remove the auxiliary drivebelt from the alternator pulley (see Chapter 1A, Section 25 or Chapter 1B, Section 25). Mark the drivebelt for direction of rotation to ensure it is refitted correctly.

4 It is necessary to unbolt the air conditioning compressor from below the alternator, and then suspend it to one side, making sure that the hoses are not damaged. Refer to Chapter 3, Section 10 for further information on removing the compressor.

5 Release the securing clip and disconnect the wiring connector from the alternator **(see illustration)**.

6 Remove the protective cap (where fitted), unscrew and remove the nut and washers, then disconnect the battery positive cable from the alternator terminal **(see illustration)**.

7 Where applicable, unscrew the retaining nut and remove the cable guide **(see illustration)**.

8 Unscrew and remove the lower, then upper bolts, then lift the alternator away from its bracket **(see illustrations)**. On some models, it may be necessary to remove the auxiliary belt tensioner, to access the alternator mounting bolt.

Refitting

9 The alternator mounting bushes are self-centralising and should be carefully tapped back approximately 1.0 mm before refitting.

10 Refitting is a reversal of removal. Refer to Chapter 1A, Section 25 or Chapter 1B, Section 25, for details of refitting the auxiliary drivebelt. Before fitting the alternator, it may be necessary to tap the sliding sleeve in the alternator housing back a couple of millimeters **(see illustration)**. So that it can be fitted back to the mounting bracket easier. Tighten the alternator mounting bolts to the specified torque.

6 Alternator – brush holder/ regulator module renewal

1 Remove the alternator, as described in Section 5.

2 Place the alternator on a clean work surface, with the pulley facing down.

3 Undo the screw and the two retaining nuts, and lift away the outer plastic cover **(see illustration)**.

4 Undo the three screws, and remove the voltage regulator **(see illustrations)**.

5 Measure the free length of the brush contacts **(see illustration)**. Check the measurement with the Specifications; renew the module if the brushes are worn below the minimum limit.

6.3 On the Bosch type, remove the outer cover nuts/screw...

6.4a ...undo the screws...

6 Clean and inspect the surfaces of the slip-rings, at the end of the alternator shaft **(see illustration)**. If they are excessively worn, or damaged, the alternator must be renewed.

7 Before refitting the module, depress the brushes in their released position, and hold them there by pulling out the cap – with the module in position, press the cap to release the brushes. The remaining reassembly is a reversal of the dismantling procedure. On completion, refer to Section 5 and refit the alternator.

7 Starting system – testing

Note: *Refer to Section 1 of this Chapter before starting work.*

1 If the starter motor fails to operate when the ignition key is turned to the appropriate position, the following faults may be the cause:

a) *The battery is faulty.*
b) *The electrical connections between the switch, solenoid, battery and starter motor are somewhere failing to pass the necessary current from the battery through the starter to earth.*

c) *The solenoid is faulty.*
d) *The starter motor is mechanically or electrically defective.*

2 To check the battery, switch on the headlights. If they dim after a few seconds, this indicates that the battery is discharged – recharge (see Section 2) or renew the battery. If the headlights glow brightly, operate the ignition switch and observe the lights. If they dim, then this indicates that current is reaching the starter motor; therefore the fault must lie in the starter motor. If the lights continue to glow brightly (and no clicking sound can be heard from the starter motor solenoid), this indicates that there is a fault in the circuit or solenoid – see following paragraphs. If the starter motor turns slowly when operated, but the battery is in good condition, then this indicates that either the starter motor is faulty, or there is considerable resistance somewhere in the circuit.

3 If a fault in the circuit is suspected, disconnect the battery leads (including the earth connection to the body), the starter/solenoid wiring and the engine/transmission earth strap. **Note:** *Before disconnecting the battery, refer to 'Disconnecting the battery' in the Reference section at the rear of this manual.* Thoroughly clean the connections, and reconnect the leads and wiring, then use a

voltmeter or test light to check that full battery voltage is available at the battery positive lead connection to the solenoid, and that the earth is sound.

4 If the battery and all connections are in good condition, check the circuit by disconnecting the wire from the solenoid blade terminal. Connect a voltmeter or test light between the wire end and a good earth (such as the battery negative terminal), and check that the wire is live when the ignition switch is turned to the start position. If it is, then the circuit is sound, if not, the circuit wiring can be checked as described in Chapter 12.

5 The solenoid contacts can be checked by connecting a voltmeter or test light between the battery positive feed connection on the starter side of the solenoid, and earth. When the ignition switch is turned to the start position, there should be a reading or lighted bulb, as applicable. If there is no reading or lighted bulb, the solenoid is faulty and should be renewed.

6 If the circuit and solenoid are proved sound, the fault must lie in the starter motor. It may be possible to have the starter motor overhauled by a specialist, but check on the availability and cost of spares before proceeding, as it may prove more economical to obtain a new or exchange motor.

6.4b ...and remove the brush holder/ regulator

6.5 Measure the brush length

6.6 Clean and inspect the surfaces of the slip-rings

8.3 Starter wiring plug connector (A) – Battery positive cable (B)

8.5 Removing the wiring loom support bracket

8.6 Remove the earth cable (where fitted)

8.7 The starter bolt also secures the transmission

6 On some models, it may be necessary to undo the retaining nut and disconnect the earth cable from the upper starter motor mounting bolt **(see illustration)**.

7 Unscrew the two mounting bolts and withdraw the starter motor from the engine compartment **(see illustration)**.

Refitting

8 Refit the starter motor by following the removal procedure in reverse. Tighten the mounting bolts to the specified torque.

8 Starter motor – removal and refitting

Removal

1 Disconnect the battery negative lead (refer to *Disconnecting the battery* in the *Reference* Chapter at the end of this manual). Remove the engine top cover.

2 Remove the battery and battery tray with reference to Section 3.

3 Release the securing clip and disconnect the wiring plug from the starter **(see illustration)**.

4 Remove the protective cap, unscrew and remove the nut and washers **(see illustration 8.3)**, then disconnect the battery positive cable from the solenoid terminal.

5 Undo the retaining nut and disconnect the wiring bracket from the lower starter motor mounting bolt **(see illustration)**.

9 Starter motor – testing and overhaul

If the starter motor is thought to be defective, it should be removed from the car and taken to an auto-electrician for assessment. In the majority of cases, new starter motor brushes can be fitted at a reasonable cost. However, check the cost of repairs first as it may prove more economical to purchase a new or exchange motor.

Chapter 5 Part B:
Ignition system – petrol engines

Contents

Degrees of difficulty

Easy, suitable for novice with little experience	Fairly easy, suitable for beginner with some experience	Fairly difficult, suitable for competent DIY mechanic	Difficult, suitable for experienced DIY mechanic	Very difficult, suitable for expert DIY or professional

Specifications

Engine codes*
1.2 litre:
   SOHC . . . . CHFA
   DOHC . . . . CGPA and CGPB
1.4 litre . . . . CGGB
* **Note:** *See 'Vehicle identification' at the end of this manual for the location of code marking on the engine.*

System type
1.2 litre engines:
   Engine code CHFA . . . . Siemens Simos 3PG
   Engine codes CGPA and CGPB . . . . Siemens Simos 9.1 SRE
1.4 litre engines . . . . Magneti Marelli 4HV SRE

Ignition coil
Type . . . . Individual coil per cylinder (no HT leads), camshaft position sensor (in cylinder head), knock sensor

Spark plugs
See Chapter 1A Specifications

Torque wrench settings

	Nm	lbf ft
Camshaft position sensor mounting bolt	10	7
Knock sensor mounting bolt	20	15
Spark plugs:		
1.2 litre engine	30	22
1.4 litre engine	25	18

1 General information

The Siemens and Magneti-Marelli ignition systems described in this Chapter, are part of the self-contained engine management systems which control both the fuel injection and ignition. This Chapter deals with the ignition system components only – refer to Chapter 4A for details of the fuel system components.

The ignition system comprises the spark plugs, ignition coils, and the Electronic Control Unit (ECU) together with its associated sensors, actuators and wiring. The component layout varies from system to system but the basic operation is the same for all models.

The ECU supplies a voltage to the input stage of the ignition coil, which causes the primary windings in the coil to be energised. The supply voltage is periodically interrupted by the ECU and this results in the collapse of the primary magnetic field, which then induces a much larger voltage (called the HT voltage) in the secondary coil. This voltage is directed to the spark plug in the cylinder where the piston is currently at the end of its compression stroke. The spark plug electrodes form a gap small enough for the HT voltage to arc across, and the resulting spark ignites the fuel/air mixture in the cylinder. The timing of this sequence of events is critical and is regulated solely by the ECU.

Each spark plug has its own dedicated 'plug-top' HT coil that fits directly onto the spark plug; on these models a spark is generated at each plug once every engine cycle.

The ECU calculates and controls the ignition timing primarily according to engine speed, crankshaft/camshaft position; throttle position and inlet air temperature, received from sensors mounted on and around the engine. Other parameters that affect ignition timing are coolant temperature and engine knock, these being monitored by sensors mounted on the engine.

2.2 Location of diagnostic connector

3.1a Ignition coils on 1.2 litre engine

3.1b Ignition coils on 1.4 litre engine

5.1 Knock sensor (arrowed) on the rear of the cylinder block

The knock sensor is mounted on the cylinder block in order to detect engine pre-ignition (or 'pinking'). If pre-ignition occurs, the ECU retards the ignition timing in steps until the pre-ignition ceases. The ECU then advances the ignition timing in steps until it is restored to normal, or until pre-ignition occurs again.

Idle speed control is achieved partly by the electronic throttle valve positioning module, and partly by the ignition system, which gives fine control of the idle speed by altering the ignition timing. Manual adjustment of the engine idle speed or ignition timing is not necessary or possible.

It should be noted that comprehensive fault diagnosis of all the engine management systems described in this Chapter is only possible with dedicated electronic test equipment. Problems with the system's operation that cannot be pinpointed by following the basic guidelines in Section 2 should therefore be referred to a VW dealer for assessment. Once the fault has been identified, the removal/refitting sequences detailed in the following Sections will then allow the appropriate components to be renewed as required.

2 Ignition system – testing

⚠ *Warning: Extreme care must be taken when working on the system with the ignition switched on; it is*
possible to get a substantial electric shock from a vehicle's ignition system. Persons with cardiac pacemaker devices should keep well clear of the ignition circuits, components and test equipment. Always switch off the ignition before disconnecting or connecting any component and when using a multi-meter to check resistances.

1 If a fault appears in the engine management (fuel injection/ignition) system which is thought to be ignition related, first ensure that the fault is not due to a poor electrical connection or poor maintenance; i.e. check that the air cleaner filter element is clean, the spark plugs are in good condition and correctly gapped, that the engine breather hoses are clear and undamaged, referring to Chapter 1A for further information. If the engine is running very roughly, check the compression pressures as described in Chapter 2A, Section 2 or Chapter 2B, Section 2.

2 If these checks fail to reveal the cause of the problem the vehicle should be taken to a VW dealer for testing. A diagnostic connector is incorporated in the engine management circuit into which a special electronic diagnostic tester can be plugged **(see illustration)**. The tester will locate the fault quickly and simply, alleviating the need to test all the system components individually, which is a time consuming operation that carries a high risk of damaging the ECU.

3 The only ignition system checks which can be carried out by the home mechanic are those described in Chapter 1A, Section 24,

relating to the spark plugs. If necessary, the system wiring and wiring connectors can be checked as described in Chapter 12 ensuring that the ECU wiring connector has first been disconnected.

3 HT coil – removal and refitting

1 Removal of the ignition coils is covered in the spark plug renewal procedure in Chapter 1A, Section 24, since the coils must be removed for access to the plugs **(see illustrations)**.
2 Refitting is a reversal of the relevant removal procedure.

4 Ignition timing – checking and adjusting

The ignition timing is under the control of the engine management system ECU and is not manually adjustable without access to dedicated electronic test equipment. A basic setting cannot be quoted because the ignition timing is constantly being altered to control engine idle speed (see Section 1 for details).

The vehicle must be taken to a VW dealer if the timing requires checking or adjustment.

5 Knock sensor – removal and refitting

Removal

1 The knock sensor is located on the rear of the cylinder block, beneath the inlet manifold **(see illustration)**.
2 Remove the engine top cover to gain access to the sensor from above. Alternatively for access from below, apply the handbrake, then jack up the front of the vehicle and support it on axle stands (see *Jacking and vehicle support*). Access to the knock sensor is very awkward, and can only be improved by either removing the inlet manifold (see Chapter 4A, Section 9) or removing the right-hand driveshaft (see Chapter 8, Section 2).
3 Disconnect the wiring from the sensor or trace the wiring back from the sensor and disconnect its wiring connector.
4 Unscrew the mounting bolt and remove the sensor from the cylinder block, noting its fitted position.

Refitting

5 Refitting is the reverse of removal. Ensure the mating surfaces of the sensor and cylinder block are clean and dry and ensure the mounting bolt is tightened to the specified torque to ensure correct operation.

Chapter 5 Part C:
Pre-heating system – diesel engines

Contents

Degrees of difficulty

Easy, suitable for novice with little experience		Fairly easy, suitable for beginner with some experience		Fairly difficult, suitable for competent DIY mechanic		Difficult, suitable for experienced DIY mechanic		Very difficult, suitable for expert DIY or professional	

Specifications

Glow plugs

Electrical resistance (max. with cold engine)	1.0 ohm
Current consumption (typical – no value quoted by VW)	8 amps (per plug)

Torque wrench setting	Nm	lbf ft
Glow plug to cylinder head	18	13

1 General information

To assist cold starting, diesel engine models are fitted with a preheating system, which consists of glow plugs, a glow plug control unit, a facia-mounted warning light and the associated electrical wiring. The glow plug control unit on some models, is incorporated in the ECU, other models have a control unit/relay located on the mounting bracket on the front of the battery.

The glow plugs are miniature electric heating elements, encapsulated in a metal case with a probe at one end and electrical connection at the other. Each inlet tract has a glow plug threaded into it, which is positioned directly in line with the incoming spray of fuel. When the glow plug is energised, the fuel passing over it is heated, allowing its optimum combustion temperature to be achieved more readily in the combustion chamber.

The duration of the preheating period is governed by the ECU, which monitors the temperature of the engine through the coolant temperature sensor and alters the preheating time to suit the conditions. Pre-heating only takes place at coolant temperature below 9°C.

A facia-mounted warning light informs the driver that preheating is taking place. The light extinguishes when sufficient preheating has taken place to allow the engine to be started, but power will still be supplied to the glow plugs for a further period until the engine

is started. If no attempt is made to start the engine, the power supply to the glow plugs is switched off to prevent battery drain and glow plug burn-out. If the warning light flashes, or comes on during normal driving, this indicates a fault with the diesel engine management system, which should be investigated by a VW dealer as soon as possible.

After the engine has been started, the glow plugs continue to operate for a further period of time. This helps to improve fuel combustion whilst the engine is warming-up, resulting in quieter, smoother running and reduced exhaust emissions.

2 Glow plugs – testing, removal and refitting

⚠️ **Warning: A correctly functioning glow plug will become red-hot in a very short time. This should be in mind when removing the glow plugs, if they have recently been in use. If a glow plug is dropped, it may be damaged internally, which could result in ceramic fragments entering the engine causing extensive damage. Do not fit a glow plug that has been dropped.**

Testing

1 If the system malfunctions, testing is ultimately by substitution of known good units, but some preliminary checks may be made as described in the following paragraphs.

2 Before testing the system, use a multi-meter to check that the battery voltage is at least 11.5. Switch off the ignition.

3 Pull the engine upper trim cover upwards to remove it from the top of the engine.

4 Disconnect the wiring plug from the coolant temperature sender at the left-hand end of the engine (left as seen from the driver's seat) – **(see illustration)**. Disconnecting the sender in this way simulates a cold engine, which is a requirement for the glow plug system to activate.

5 Disconnect the wiring connector from the most convenient glow plug, and connect a suitable multimeter between the wiring connector and a good earth.

6 Have an assistant switch on the ignition for approximately 20 seconds.

7 Battery voltage should be displayed – note that the voltage will drop to zero when the preheating period ends.

8 If no supply voltage can be detected at the glow plug, then either the glow plug relay (where applicable) or the supply wiring must

2.4 Temperature sensor location (arrowed)

2.10 Testing the glow plugs using a multimeter

2.15a Glow plug wiring

2.15b Disconnect the wiring plugs from the injectors

be faulty. Also check that the glow plug fuse or fusible link has not blown – if it has, this may indicate a serious wiring fault; consult a VW dealer for advice.

9 To locate a faulty glow plug, first disconnect the battery negative cable and position it away from the terminal.

10 Disconnect the wiring plug from the glow plug terminal. Measure the electrical resistance between the glow plug terminal and the engine earth **(see illustration)**. At the time of writing, this information is not available – as a guide, a resistance of more than a few ohms indicates that the plug is defective.

11 If a suitable ammeter is available, connect it between the glow plug and its wiring connector, and measure the steady-state current consumption (ignore the initial current surge, which will be about 50% higher). As a guide, high current consumption (or no current draw at all) indicates a faulty glow plug.

12 As a final check, remove the glow plugs and inspect them visually, as described in the next sub-Section. A badly burned or charred stem may be an indication of a faulty fuel injector.

Removal

Note: *Refer to the Warning at the start of this Section before proceeding.*

13 Pull the plastic cover on the top of the engine upwards from its' mountings.

14 Where fitted, remove the noise insulation from above the injectors.

15 Due to the wiring loom to the glow plugs being short **(see illustrations)**, it may be necessary to disconnect the wiring plugs from the injectors, exhaust gas pressure sensor, and fuel rail pressure sensor, then when the loom is released and unclipped from the top of the cylinder head.

16 To remove the wiring loom upwards it will be necessary to undo the retaining bolts

and detach the coolant pipe from the intake manifold, then move it to the front of the manifold.

17 Also release the retaining clips and disconnect the fuel return hose from the fuel rail and the fuel return pipe connectors from the top of the fuel rail **(see illustration)**. Plug the openings to prevent contamination. Move the entire fuel return pipe assembly to the one side, be prepared for fuel spillage.

18 Pull the connectors from the top of the glow plugs and move the wiring loom to one side. Be sure to only pull on the underside of the ridge at the top of the connectors **(see illustrations)**.

19 Clean the area around the glow plugs; use a vacuum cleaner if possible. Spray brake cleaner (or similar) around the glow plug opening, letting it penetrate briefly, and then blow out with compressed air.

Caution: Always wear protective goggles to protect your eyes, when using compressed air.

20 Using a universal joint, extension and a deep 10 mm socket, unscrew and remove the glow plug(s) from the cylinder head. Note that the plug must be kept 'straight' when being removed, as it can be easily damaged.

Refitting

21 Refitting is a reversal of removal, but tighten the glow plugs to the specified torque.

3 Glow plug control unit – removal and refitting

Note: *The glow plug control unit may be incorporated inside the engine management ECU. Follow the procedure below for models with separate glow plug control unit.*

Removal

1 The glow plug control unit (where applicable) is located on the fuse box in front of the battery **(see illustration)**.

2 Release the retaining clip and slide the control unit from the mounting bracket.

3 Disconnect the wiring connector and remove the control unit

Refitting

4 Refitting is a reversal of removal.

2.17 Disconnect the return hose from the fuel rail

2.18a Using long nose pliers...

2.18b ...pull the connectors from the top of the glow plugs

3.1 Glow plug control unit location (arrowed)

Chapter 6
Clutch

Contents

Degrees of difficulty

Easy, suitable for novice with little experience	Fairly easy, suitable for beginner with some experience	Fairly difficult, suitable for competent DIY mechanic	Difficult, suitable for experienced DIY mechanic	Very difficult, suitable for expert DIY or professional

Specifications

Engine codes

Petrol engines

1.2 litre:	
SOHC	CHFA
DOHC	CGPA and CGPB
1.4 litre	CGGB

Diesel engines

1.2 litre	CFWA
1.6 litre	CAYB, CAYC and CLNA

General

Type	Single dry plate, diaphragm spring
Operation	Hydraulic with master and slave cylinders
Application:	
Petrol models	5-speed transmission 02T
Diesel models	5-speed transmission 02R
Friction disc diameter:	
5-speed transmission 02T	200 mm
5-speed transmission 02R	228 mm

Torque wrench settings

	Nm	lbf ft
Clutch master cylinder mounting nuts*	28	21
Clutch pedal mounting bracket nuts*	28	21
Clutch pedal pivot nut*	25	18
Clutch pressure plate-to-flywheel bolts:		
M6 bolts	13	9
M7 bolts	20	15
Clutch slave cylinder mounting bolts	20	15
Guide tube-to-transmission bolts:		
02R transmission	20	15
02T transmission*:		
Stage 1	5	3
Stage 2	Angle-tighten a further 90°	

* Use new bolts/nuts.

1 General information

The clutch is of single dry plate type, incorporating a diaphragm spring pressure plate, and is hydraulically operated.

The pressure plate is bolted to the rear face of the flywheel, and the friction disc is located between the pressure plate and the flywheel friction surface. The friction disc hub is splined to the transmission input shaft and is free to slide along the splines. Friction lining material is riveted to each side of the disc, and the disc hub incorporates cushioning springs to absorb transmission shocks and ensure a smooth take-up of drive.

When the clutch pedal is depressed, the slave cylinder pushrod moves the top of the release lever towards the engine, and the lower end of the lever pivots on a ball-stud located in the transmission bellhousing. The release bearing is forced onto the pressure plate diaphragm spring fingers. As the centre of the diaphragm spring is pushed in, the outer part of the spring moves out and releases the pressure plate from the friction disc. Drive then ceases to be transmitted to the transmission.

When the clutch pedal is released, the diaphragm spring forces the pressure plate into contact with the linings on the friction disc, and at the same time pushes the disc slightly forward along the input shaft splines into engagement with the flywheel. The friction disc is now firmly sandwiched between the pressure plate and flywheel. This causes drive to be taken up.

As the linings wear on the friction disc, the pressure plate rest position moves closer to the flywheel resulting in the 'rest' position of the diaphragm spring fingers being raised. The hydraulic system requires no adjustment since the quantity of hydraulic fluid in the circuit automatically compensates for wear every time the clutch pedal is operated.

2 Hydraulic system – bleeding

Warning: Hydraulic fluid is poisonous; thoroughly wash off spills from bare skin without delay. Seek immediate medical advice if any fluid is swallowed or gets into the eyes. Certain types of hydraulic fluid are inflammable and may ignite when brought into contact with hot components. Hydraulic fluid is also an effective paint stripper. If spillage occurs onto painted bodywork or fittings, it should be washed off immediately, using copious quantities of cold water. It is also hygroscopic (it absorbs moisture from the air) therefore old fluid should never be re-used.

1 The correct operation of any hydraulic system is only possible after removing all air from the components and circuit; this is achieved by bleeding the system.

2 During the bleeding procedure, add only clean, unused hydraulic fluid of the recommended type; never re-use fluid that has already been bled from the system. Ensure that sufficient fluid is available before starting work.

3 If there is any possibility of incorrect fluid being already in the system, the hydraulic circuit must be flushed completely with uncontaminated, correct fluid.

4 If hydraulic fluid has been lost from the system, or air has entered because of a leak, ensure that the fault is cured before continuing further.

5 The bleed screw is located on the slave cylinder located on the left-hand upper side of the transmission **(see illustration)**. As access to the bleed screw is limited it will be necessary to jack up the front of the vehicle and support it on axle stands so that the screw can be reached from below.

6 Check that all pipes and hoses are secure, unions tight and the bleed screw is closed. Clean any dirt from around the bleed screw.

7 Unscrew the master cylinder fluid reservoir cap (the clutch shares the same fluid reservoir as the braking system), and top the master cylinder reservoir up to the upper (MAX) level line. Refit the cap loosely, and remember to maintain the fluid level at least above the lower (MIN) level line throughout the procedure, or there is a risk of further air entering the system.

8 There are a number of one-man, do-it-yourself bleeding kits currently available from motor accessory shops. It is recommended that one of these kits is used whenever possible, as they greatly simplify the bleeding operation, and reduce the risk of expelled air and fluid being drawn back into the system. If such a kit is not available, the basic (two-man) method must be used, which is described in detail below.

9 If a kit is to be used, prepare the vehicle as described previously, and follow the kit manufacturer's instructions, as the procedure may vary slightly according to the type being used; generally, they are as outlined below in the relevant sub-section.

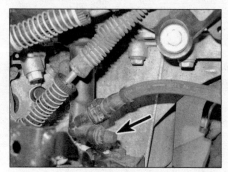

2.5 Slave cylinder bleed screw - arrowed

Bleeding

Basic (two-man) method

10 Collect a clean glass jar, a suitable length of plastic or rubber tubing which is a tight fit over the bleed screw, and a ring spanner to fit the screw. The help of an assistant will also be required.

11 Remove the dust cap from the bleed screw. Fit the spanner and tube to the screw, place the other end of the tube in the jar, and pour in sufficient fluid to cover the end of the tube.

12 Ensure that the fluid level is maintained at least above the lower level line in the reservoir throughout the procedure.

13 Have the assistant fully depress the clutch pedal several times to build up pressure, and then maintain it on the final down stroke.

14 While pedal pressure is maintained, unscrew the bleed screw (approximately one turn) and allow the compressed fluid and air to flow into the jar. The assistant should maintain pedal pressure and should not release it until instructed to do so. When the flow stops, tighten the bleed screw again, have the assistant release the pedal slowly, and recheck the reservoir fluid level.

15 Repeat the steps given in paragraphs 13 and 14 until the fluid emerging from the bleed screw is free from air bubbles. If the master cylinder has been drained and refilled allow approximately five seconds between cycles for the master cylinder passages to refill.

16 When no more air bubbles appear, tighten the bleed screw securely, remove the tube and spanner, and refit the dust cap. Do not overtighten the bleed screw.

Using a one-way valve kit

17 As their name implies, these kits consist of a length of tubing with a one-way valve fitted, to prevent expelled air and fluid being drawn back into the system; some kits include a translucent container, which can be positioned so that the air bubbles can be more easily seen flowing from the end of the tube.

18 The kit is connected to the bleed screw, which is then opened. The user returns to the driver's seat, depresses the clutch pedal with a smooth, steady stroke, and slowly releases it; this is repeated until the expelled fluid is clear of air bubbles.

19 Note that these kits simplify work so much that it is easy to forget the fluid reservoir level; ensure that this is maintained at least above the lower level line at all times.

Using a pressure-bleeding kit

20 These kits are usually operated by the reservoir of pressurised air contained in the spare tyre. However, note that it will probably be necessary to reduce the pressure to a lower level than normal; refer to the instructions supplied with the kit.

21 By connecting a pressurised, fluid-filled container to the fluid reservoir, bleeding can

H48710

3.5 Clutch pedal assembly

1) Clutch pedal
2) Pivot pin
3) Bearing bushes
4) Over centre spring
5) Mounting bracket
6) Seal
7) Master cylinder
8) Seal
9) Pivot bolt
10) Pedal securing clip

H48707

3.6 Master cylinder pushrod to pedal securing clip

1) Master cylinder pushrod
2) Securing clip
3) Clutch pedal

6 Working at each side of the clutch pedal, release the retaining clip to disengage the master cylinder push-rod from the pedal **(see illustration)**. The pedal can now be removed from the mounting bracket.

7 If required, undo the three mounting nuts and remove the mounting bracket from the bulkhead. Discard the self-locking nuts, as new ones will be required for refitting

Refitting

8 Refitting is a reversal of removal, bearing in mind the following points:
a) *Press the pushrod retaining clip firmly into the pedal until it is heard to engage.*
b) *Tighten all fixings to the specified torque, where given.*
c) *On completion, check the brake/clutch fluid level, and top-up if necessary*

be carried out simply by opening the bleed screw and allowing the fluid to flow out until no more air bubbles can be seen in the expelled fluid.

22 This method has the advantage that the large reservoir of fluid provides an additional safeguard against air being drawn into the system during bleeding.

All methods

23 When bleeding is complete, and correct pedal feel is restored, tighten the bleed screw securely and wash off any spilt fluid. Refit the dust cap to the bleed screw.

24 Check the hydraulic fluid level in the master cylinder reservoir, and top-up if necessary (see *Weekly checks*).

25 Discard any hydraulic fluid that has been bled from the system; it will not be fit for re-use.

26 Check the operation of the clutch pedal. If the clutch is still not operating correctly, air must still be present in the system, and further bleeding is required. Failure to bleed satisfactorily after a reasonable repetition of the bleeding procedure may be due to worn master cylinder/release cylinder seals.

3 Clutch pedal – removal and refitting

Removal

1 Move the driver's seat fully to the rear, and adjust the steering column to its highest position.

2 Disconnect the battery negative lead and position it away from the terminal. **Note:** *Before disconnecting the battery, refer to 'Disconnecting the battery' in the reference section at the rear of this manual.*

3 Remove the driver's side lower facia trim panel, with reference to Chapter 11, Section 27.

4 Where fitted, release the securing clips and remove the insulation padding from around the clutch pedal mounting bracket.

5 Undo the retaining nut and remove the pedal pivot bolt, move the pedal downwards and withdraw the over-centre spring from inside the top of the mounting bracket **(see illustration). Note:** *The clutch pedal will still be attached to the master cylinder operating-rod.*

4 Master cylinder – removal, overhaul and refitting

Note: *Refer to the warning at the beginning of Section 2.*

Removal

1 The clutch master cylinder is located inside the car on the clutch and brake pedal mounting bracket **(see illustration)**. Hydraulic

4.1 Clutch master cylinder

4.4 Hydraulic hose to master cylinder - arrowed

fluid for the unit is supplied from the brake master cylinder reservoir.

2 On LHD models, remove the air cleaner assembly as described in Chapter 4A, Section 2 or Chapter 4B, Section 2, then unclip the auxiliary relay carrier on the left-hand side of the engine compartment, and position it to one side.

3 Before proceeding, place cloth rags on the carpet inside the car to prevent damage from spilt hydraulic fluid.

4 Working in the engine compartment, clamp the hydraulic fluid hose leading from the brake fluid reservoir to the clutch master cylinder **(see illustration)**, using a brake hose clamp.

5 Similarly, clamp the rubber section of the hydraulic hose leading from the master cylinder to the slave cylinder using a brake hose clamp, to prevent loss of hydraulic fluid.

6 Position a suitable container, or some cloth rags, beneath the master cylinder to catch escaping hydraulic fluid.

7 Pull the hydraulic supply hose from the clutch master cylinder on the bulkhead.

8 Pull the fluid outlet hose retaining clip from the union on the master cylinder, then pull the pipe from the union. Again, be prepared for fluid spillage.

9 Remove the driver's side lower facia trim panel, with reference to Chapter 11, Section 27.

10 Where fitted, remove the clutch pedal switch from the pedal bracket by turning it 90° anti-clockwise.

11 The pedal must now be disconnected from the master cylinder pushrod by squeezing together the tabs of the securing clip (see

5.6 Fluid pipe retaining clip - arrowed

4.13 Undo the pedal bracket nuts (arrowed)

Section 3), and moving the pushrod away from the pedal.

12 Twist the clutch pedal stop anti-clockwise, and remove it from the bulkhead.

13 Unscrew the three nuts securing the clutch pedal mounting bracket to the bulkhead, and then remove the mounting bracket complete with pedal from the bulkhead **(see illustration)**.

14 With the mounting bracket on the bench, the over-centre spring must be disconnected and removed from the pedal – see Section 3.

15 With the over-centre spring removed, remove the spring seat from the pedal bracket. The seat must be renewed whenever removed.

16 Remove the master cylinder from the bracket.

Overhaul

17 No spare parts are available from VW for the master cylinder. If the master cylinder is faulty or worn, the complete assembly must be renewed.

Refitting

18 Refitting is a reversal of removal, bearing in mind the following points:
  a) *Ensure that the pedal-to-master cylinder pushrod retaining clip is fitted to the master cylinder pushrod before attempting to reconnect the pushrod to the pedal.*
  b) *Push the pedal onto the pushrod to engage the retaining clip. Make sure that the clip is securely engaged.*
  c) *On completion, bleed the clutch hydraulic system as described in Section 2.*

5.7a Slave cylinder mounting bolts - arrowed

5 Slave cylinder – removal, overhaul and refitting

Note: *Refer to the warning at the beginning of Section 2 regarding the hazards of working with hydraulic fluid.*

Removal

1 The slave cylinder is located on the top of the transmission casing. First remove the engine top cover.

2 Remove the battery and battery tray, as described in Chapter 5A, Section 3.

3 Where necessary, remove the air cleaner and air ducting with reference to Chapter 4A, Section 2 or Chapter 4B, Section 2.

4 If required, to make access to the slave cylinder easier, remove the gear change cables and mounting bracket from the top of the transmission housing, as described in Chapter 7A Section 2.

5 Clamp the rubber section of the hydraulic hose leading from the master cylinder to the slave cylinder using a brake hose clamp, to prevent loss of hydraulic fluid. Place a wad of clean rag beneath the fluid line connection on the slave cylinder to catch escaping fluid.

6 Pull the fluid pipe retaining clip from the union on the slave cylinder **(see illustration)**, then disconnect the pipe from the union. Release the fluid line from the bracket, and position it clear of the slave cylinder. Be prepared for fluid spillage.

7 Unscrew the two bolts securing the slave cylinder to the transmission casing, and withdraw the slave cylinder **(see illustration)**.

Overhaul

8 No spare parts are available from VW for the slave cylinder. If the slave cylinder is faulty or worn, the complete assembly must be renewed.

Refitting

9 Refitting is a reversal of removal, bearing in mind the following points:
  a) *Apply a little molybdenum sulphide-based grease to the end of the slave cylinder plunger.*

5.7b Removing the clutch slave cylinder

b) *Tighten the slave cylinder securing bolts to the specified torque.*
c) *On completion, bleed the clutch hydraulic system as described in Section 2.*

6 Clutch friction disc and pressure plate – removal, inspection and refitting

⚠️ **Warning:** *Dust created by clutch wear and deposited on the clutch components may contain asbestos, which is a health hazard. DO NOT blow it out with compressed air or inhale any of it. DO NOT use petrol or petroleum-based solvents to clean off the dust. Brake system cleaner or methylated spirit should be used to flush the dust into a suitable receptacle. After the clutch components are wiped clean with clean rags, dispose of the contaminated rags and cleaner in a sealed container.*

Removal

1 Access to the clutch is obtained by removing the transmission as described in Chapter 7A, Section 3.
2 Mark the clutch pressure plate and flywheel in relation to each other **(see illustration)**.
3 Hold the flywheel stationary, and then unscrew the clutch pressure plate bolts progressively in diagonal sequence. With the bolts unscrewed two or three turns, check that the pressure plate is not binding on the dowel pins. If necessary, use a screwdriver to release the pressure plate.
4 Remove all the bolts, then lift the clutch pressure plate and friction disc from the flywheel **(see illustration)**.

Inspection

5 Clean the pressure plate, disc and flywheel. Do not inhale the dust, as it may contain asbestos, which is dangerous to health.
6 Examine the fingers of the diaphragm spring for wear or scoring. If the depth of wear exceeds half the thickness of the fingers, a new pressure plate assembly must be fitted.
7 Examine the pressure plate for scoring, cracking and discoloration. Light scoring is acceptable, but if excessive, a new pressure plate assembly must be fitted.

6.2 Mark the clutch pressure plate and flywheel in relation to each other

8 Examine the friction disc linings for wear and cracking, and for contamination with oil or grease. The linings are worn excessively if they are worn down to, or near, the rivets. Check the disc hub and splines for wear, by temporarily fitting it on the transmission input shaft. Renew the friction disc as necessary.
9 Examine the flywheel friction surface for scoring, cracking and discoloration (caused by overheating). If excessive, it may be possible to have the flywheel machined by an engineering works, otherwise it should be renewed.
10 Ensure that all parts are clean, and free of oil or grease, before reassembling. Apply just a small amount of high-melting-point grease to the splines of the friction disc hub. Note that new pressure plates may be coated with protective grease. It is only permissible to clean the grease away from the friction disc lining contact area. Removal of the grease from other areas will shorten the service life of the clutch.

Refitting

11 Commence reassembly by locating the friction disc on the flywheel, with the raised, torsion spring side of the hub facing outwards. If necessary, the centralising tool (see paragraph 14) may be used to hold the disc on the flywheel at this stage **(see illustration)**.
12 Locate the clutch pressure plate on the disc, and fit it onto the location dowels **(see illustration)**. If refitting the original pressure plate, make sure that the previously-made marks are aligned.

6.4 Lift the pressure plate and friction disc away from the flywheel

13 Insert the bolts finger-tight to hold the pressure plate in position **(see illustration)**.
14 The friction disc must now be centralised, to ensure correct alignment of the transmission input shaft with the spigot bearing in the crankshaft. To do this, a proprietary tool may be used, or alternatively, use a wooden mandrel made to fit inside the friction disc and flywheel spigot bearing. Insert the tool through the friction disc into the spigot bearing, and make sure that it is central.
15 Tighten the pressure plate bolts progressively and in diagonal sequence, until the specified torque setting is achieved, and then the centralising tool can be removed.
16 Check the release bearing in the transmission bellhousing for smooth operation, and if necessary renew it with reference to Section 7.
17 Refit the transmission with reference to Chapter 7A, Section 3.

7 Release bearing and lever – removal, inspection and refitting

Removal

1 First, remove the transmission as described in Chapter 7A, Section 3. If a long bolt was fitted through the top of the transmission to prevent the release lever from moving while the transmission was removed, it can now be removed **(see illustration)**.

6.11 Locating the friction disc on the flywheel

6.12 Locating the clutch pressure plate over the friction disc

6.13 Insert the bolts finger-tight initially

7.1 Bolt (arrowed) securing the release lever in position

7.2 Unscrew the retaining bolts

7.3 Push the spring clip to release the arm from the ball-stud

7.5 Removing the guide tube from the release bearing. Note the tab and slot (arrowed)

2 On 02T transmissions, unscrew and remove the guide tube retaining bolts **(see illustration)**, on these transmissions the release bearing and lever are removed together with the guide tube, and then separated on the bench.

3 Prise the release lever from the ball-stud on the transmission housing, to do this, press the retaining spring through the release lever **(see illustration)**.

4 Slide the release lever and bearing (together

7.6a Depress the clips...

7.6b ...and remove the bearing from the release lever

with the guide tube on 02T transmissions), over the transmission input shaft.

5 On 02T transmissions, turn the guide tube 90° to align the tabs with the slots in the release bearing, and withdraw the tube **(see illustration)**.

6 Using a screwdriver, depress the clips and remove the bearing from the release lever **(see illustrations)**.

Inspection

7 Spin the release bearing by hand, and check it for smooth running. Any tendency to seize or run rough will necessitate renewal of the bearing. If the bearing is to be re-used, wipe it clean with a dry cloth; the bearing should not be washed in a liquid solvent, as this will remove the internal grease.

8 Clean the release lever, ball-stud and guide sleeve.

Refitting

9 Lubricate the ball-stud in the transmission bellhousing with molybdenum disulphide-based grease. Also smear a little grease on the release bearing surface which contacts the diaphragm spring fingers in the clutch cover.

10 If removed, refit the ball-stud spring to the release lever **(see illustrations)**.

11 Locate the bearing on the lever, and press until the clips engage.

12 On 02T transmissions, locate the guide tube on the bearing, align the tabs with the slots, then insert and turn through 90°.

13 Locate the release lever on the ball-stud, and press until the retaining spring holds it in position **(see illustration)**.

14 Slide the bearing and lever (and guide tube on 02T transmissions), over the input shaft and locate it in position.

15 On 02T transmissions, insert the guide tube retaining bolts and tighten to the specified torque.

16 Refit the transmission as described in Chapter 7A, Section 3. If required, refit a long bolt through the top of the transmission to prevent the release lever from moving while the transmission is fitted **(see illustration 7.1)**. Remember to remove the bolt from the top of the transmission, before fitting the clutch slave cylinder.

7.10a Hook the spring over the end of the lever...

7.10b ...and press the other end into the hole

7.13 Locating the release lever and spring onto the ball-stud

Chapter 7 Part A:
Manual transmission

Contents

Degrees of difficulty

Easy, suitable for novice with little experience	Fairly easy, suitable for beginner with some experience	Fairly difficult, suitable for competent DIY mechanic	Difficult, suitable for experienced DIY mechanic	Very difficult, suitable for expert DIY or professional

Specifications

Engine codes

Petrol engines

1.2 litre:
SOHC	CHFA
DOHC	CGPA and CGPB
1.4 litre	CGGB

Diesel engines

1.2 litre	CFWA
1.6 litre	CAYB, CAYC and CLNA

General

Type	Transversely mounted, front-wheel-drive layout with integral transaxle differential/final drive. Five forward speeds, one reverse.

Application:
Petrol models	5-speed transmission 02T
Diesel models	5-speed transmission 02R

Torque wrench settings

	Nm	lbf ft
Driveshaft flange bolt	25	18
Guide tube-to-transmission bolts:		
02R transmission (2 bolts)	20	15
02T transmission (3 bolts)*:		
Stage 1	5	3
Stage 2	Angle-tighten a further 90°	
Reversing light switch	20	15
Filler/level and drain plug		
02R transmission (diesel engines)	35	26
02T transmission (petrol engines):		
Multi-splined (12-point) plug	25	18
Hexagon (Allen key) plug	30	22
Mounting bracket to transmission:		
Stage 1	40	30
Stage 2	Angle-tighten a further 90°	
Small cover plate bolt	10	7
Transmission to engine:		
M12 bolts	80	59
M10 bolts	40	30

1.3 Gearchange cable components

1 Shift cable	5 Shift housing	8 Relay lever	12 Shift lever with	15 Grommet
2 Selector cable	6 Pivot	9 Bushes	weight	16 Spacer
3 Press-stud	7 Selector cable	10 Circlip	13 Shift cable lock	17 Circlip
4 Circlip	lock	11 Sliding shoe	14 Nut	18 Bolt

H45885

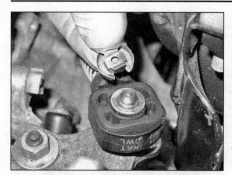

2.3a Release the locking clips…

2.3b …and prise off the inner cables …

2.3c …and outer cable securing clips - arrowed

1 General information

The manual transmission is bolted directly to the left-hand end of the engine. This layout has the advantage of providing the shortest possible drive path to the front wheels, as well as locating the transmission in the airflow through the engine bay, optimising cooling. The unit is cased in aluminium alloy.

Drive from the crankshaft is transmitted by the clutch to the gearbox input shaft, which is splined to accept the clutch friction disc.

All forward gears are fitted with synchromesh. The floor-mounted gear lever is connected to the gearbox by selector and shift cables **(see illustration)**. This actuates selector forks inside the gearbox, which are slotted onto the synchromesh sleeves. The sleeves, which are locked to the gearbox shafts but can slide axially by means of splined hubs, press baulk rings into contact with the respective gear/pinion. The coned surfaces between the baulk rings and the pinion/gear act as a friction clutch, that progressively matches the speed of the synchromesh sleeve (and hence the gearbox shaft) with that of the gear/pinion. This allows gearchanges to be carried out smoothly.

Drive is transmitted to the differential crownwheel, which rotates the differential case and planetary gears, thus driving the sun gears and driveshafts. The rotation of the differential planetary gears on their shaft allows the inner roadwheel to rotate at a slower speed than the outer roadwheel during cornering.

2 Gear change housing and cables – removal, refitting and adjustment

Removal

1 Remove the battery and battery tray as described in Chapter 5A, Section 3.
2 Remove the air cleaner housing as described in Chapter 4A, Section 2 (petrol) or Chapter 4B, Section 2 (diesel).
3 Prise out the clips securing the inner cable to the lever on the transmission, and the outer cable to the support bracket **(see illustrations)**. Withdraw the cable from the support bracket and discard the clips – new ones must be fitted.
4 Working inside the vehicle, remove the centre console, as described in Chapter 11, Section 26.
5 Remove the insulation around the base of the gear change housing to access the mounting nuts **(see illustration)**.
6 Raise the front of the vehicle and support it securely on axle stands (see *Jacking and vehicle support*).
7 Remove the centre tunnel front heat shield from the underside of the vehicle to gain access to the base of the selector lever housing and cables **(see illustration)**. Note: *It may be necessary to separate the exhaust downpipe from the intermediate pipe to remove the housing.*
8 Working back inside the vehicle, undo the retaining nuts, then remove the bracket and lower the gear change housing downwards.

Withdraw it complete with selector cables out from under the vehicle. It may be useful having the aid of an assistant at this point, to be under the vehicle when lowering the gear change housing.
9 To remove the cables from the gear change housing, prise out the clips securing the inner cable to the lower part of the gear lever, and then withdraw the securing clips from the outer cable to the gear change housing **(see illustration 1.3)**. Withdraw the cables and discard the clips – new ones must be fitted.

Refitting

10 Refitting is the reversal of the removal procedure, noting the following points:
 a) *Ensure that the cables are correctly routed and secured, as noted on removal.*
 b) *Take care not to bend or kink the cables.*
 c) *Carry out the cable adjustment procedure described below before reconnecting the cable at the transmission end.*
 d) *When refitting the cables, use new clips.*

Adjustment

11 If not already done remove the battery and battery tray, as described in Chapter 5A, Section 3. If required remove the air cleaner housing, and air ducting for better access to the top of the transmission.
12 With the gearchange set in the neutral position, push the two locking collars (one on each cable) forwards to compress the springs, turn them clockwise (looking from the driver's seat) to lock into position **(see illustration)**.
13 Press down on the selector shaft on the top of the transmission, and push the locking

2.5 Gearchange housing mounting nuts - arrowed

2.7 Lower section of gearchange housing, viewed from under the vehicle

2.12 Push the collar down and lock in position

2.13a Press down on (A), then turn the angle lever (B) - 02R transmssion

2.13b Press down on (A), then turn the angle lever (B) - 02T transmssion

pin into the transmission while turning it clockwise 90°, until it engages and the selector shaft cannot move **(see illustrations)**.

14 Working inside the vehicle, unclip the gear lever gaiter from the centre console and lift out the insulator. Still in the neutral position, move the gear lever as far to the left as possible and insert the locking pin (or drill bit) through the hole in the base of the gear lever and into the hole in the housing **(see illustration)**.

15 Working back in the engine bay, turn the two locking collars on the cables anti-clockwise (looking from the driver's seat) so that the springs will release them back into position and lock the cables **(see illustration)**.

2.14 Locking the gear lever in position with a drill bit

3.6 Mounting bracket bolts - arrowed

16 With the cable adjustment set, the locking pin in the transmission housing, can now be turned anti-clockwise 90°, to its original position. Pointing upwards on 02T transmissions and pointing to the rear on 02R transmissions.

17 Inside the vehicle, remove the locking pin (or drill bit) from the gear lever, and then check the operation of the selector mechanism. When the gear lever is at rest in neutral, it should be central, ready to select 3rd or 4th. The gear lever gaiter and insulator can now be refitted to the centre console.

18 Refit the air ducting, engine top cover/ air filter and battery/tray as described in Chapter 5A, Section 3.

2.15 Release the two locking collars (arrowed)

3.8 Insert bolt (arrowed) to secure the release lever

3 Manual transmission – removal and refitting

Removal

1 Select a solid, level surface to park the vehicle upon. Give yourself enough space to move around it easily. Apply the handbrake and chock the rear wheels.

2 Raise the front of the vehicle and support it securely on axle stands (see *Jacking and vehicle support*). Where fitted, remove the engine/transmission undertray sections. Position a suitable container beneath the transmission, then unscrew the drain plug and drain the transmission oil.

3 The front cross member/lock carrier will need to be moved into its Service Position to allow for the transmission to be removed. Refer to Chapter 2E, Section 4, to move the lock carrier into the Service Position.

4 Remove the air cleaner housing as described in Chapter 4A, Section 2 or Chapter 4B, Section 2.

5 Remove the battery and battery tray with reference to Chapter 5A, Section 3.

6 Release the retaining clips and disconnect the gear selector cables from the gear selector levers, as described in Section 2. Also, unbolt and remove the cable mounting bracket from the top of the transmission **(see illustration)**.

7 The clutch slave cylinder is on the top of the transmission, undo the retaining bolts and place the cylinder to one side, with reference to Chapter 6, Section 5.

Caution: Do not depress the clutch pedal with the slave cylinder removed or disconnected.

8 Insert a long bolt (approx. 60mm) through the bolt hole above the clutch slave cylinder aperture, this will prevent the clutch fork falling of into the bell housing, as the transmission is removed or refitted **(see illustration)**.

3.14 Undo the heat shield mounting bolts - arrowed

3.17 Undo the mounting bolts - arrowed

3.18 Cover plate retaining bolt - arrowed

9 Unbolt the earth cable from the engine/transmission or subframe.

10 Unscrew and remove the upper bolts securing the transmission to the engine.

11 With reference to Chapter 5A, Section 8, remove the starter motor.

12 Remove the lower left-hand wheel arch liner.

13 Disconnect the wiring from the reversing light switch, and where fitted, the neutral position switch on vehicles with a start/stop system.

14 Where fitted, unbolt the shield from the rear of the cylinder block **(see illustration)**, which goes around the top of the right-hand driveshaft.

15 Slacken the clamp securing the exhaust intermediate pipe to the rear section and undo the front mounting bracket bolts. This will allow the engine to be moved forwards and backwards during the transmission removal and alignment procedures. Consequently, there is no need to completely separate the exhaust pipe sections. Take care not to damage the front flexible pipe as the engine is being moved.

16 With reference to the Chapter 8, Section 2, unscrew and remove the bolts securing the driveshafts to the transmission output flanges. Tie the right-hand driveshaft to one side, and then tie the left-hand driveshaft to the suspension strut, so that the shaft is as high as possible. Alternatively, completely remove the driveshaft as described in Chapter 8, Section 2.

17 Unbolt the engine rear mounting torque

3.20a Transmission mounting...

3.20b ...mounting bracket to transmission bolts - arrowed

arm from the bottom of the transmission **(see illustration)**. **Note: Do Not** *undo the centre bolt that goes through the rubber mounting, as this is set in position.*

18 Where applicable, unbolt the small flywheel cover plate from the rear of the transmission bellhousing **(see illustration)**. This is removed to allow the driveshaft flange to be able to clear the flywheel.

19 Using a suitable hoist, support the weight of the engine.

20 Unscrew the bolts securing the transmission mounting to the body. Also, unbolt the mounting bracket from the transmission **(see illustrations)**.

21 Lower the engine/transmission assembly slightly and, using a trolley jack, support the transmission. Position the jack so that it can be withdrawn from the left-hand side of the car. As the engine/transmission is moved,

make sure any wiring or hoses are not damaged.

22 Unscrew and remove the remaining lower transmission-to-engine mounting bolts, including the bolt located on the left-hand rear of the engine **(see illustrations)**.

23 Carefully pull the transmission directly away from the engine, taking care not to allow its weight to rest on the clutch friction disc hub. A second person is helpful to pull the engine as far forwards as possible.

24 On models with driveshafts that have a bolted flange, it will be necessary to manoeuvre the right-hand driveshaft flange, from around the flywheel on removal. If required, hold the drive flange in position and undo the centre securing bolt, then the drive flange can be removed **(see illustration)**, as described in Section 6, to make removal of the transmission easier.

3.22a Upper transmission bolts...

3.22b ...lower transmission bolts...

3.22c ...and rear transmission bolt - arrowed

3.24 Removing the left-hand drive flange

3.26 Remove the bolt (arrowed) securing the clutch fork

During dismantling of the transmission, make careful notes of how each component is fitted to make reassembly easier and accurate.

Before dismantling the transmission, it will help if you have some idea of where the problem lies. Certain problems can be closely related to specific areas in the transmission, which can make component examination and renewal easier. Refer to the *Fault finding* Section in this manual for more information.

> ⚠️ **Warning: Support the transmission to ensure that it remains steady on the jack head. Keep the transmission level until the input shaft is fully withdrawn from the clutch friction disc.**

25 When the transmission is clear of the locating dowels and clutch components, lower the transmission to the ground and withdraw from under the car.

h) Refill the transmission with the correct grade and quantity of oil. Refer to 'Lubricants and fluids' in Chapter 1A or Chapter 1B, as appropriate.

4 Manual transmission overhaul – general information

Refitting

26 Refitting the transmission is essentially a reversal of the removal procedure, but note the following points:

a) Apply a smear of high melting-point grease to the clutch friction disc hub splines; take care to avoid contaminating the friction surfaces.

b) In order to align the transmission with the flywheel; gently pull the engine forward as the transmission is manoeuvred into place.

c) Tighten the transmission-to-engine bolts to the specified torque.

d) Remember to remove the bolt that was holding the clutch fork in position for refitting, once the transmission is bolted in place (see illustration).

e) Refer to the relevant part of Chapter 2 and tighten the engine mounting bolts to the correct torque.

f) Refer to Chapter 8, Section 2, and then tighten the driveshaft bolts to the specified torque.

g) On completion, refer to Section 2 and check the gearchange linkage/cable adjustment.

The overhaul of the manual transmission is a complex and often expensive task for the DIY home mechanic to undertake, which requires access to specialist equipment. It involves dismantling and reassembly of many small components, measuring clearances precisely and, if necessary, adjusting them by selecting shims and spacers. Internal transmission components are also often difficult to obtain and in many instances, extremely expensive. Because of this, if the transmission develops a fault or becomes noisy, the best course of action is to have the unit overhauled by a specialist repairer or to obtain an exchange reconditioned unit.

Nevertheless, it is not impossible for the more experienced mechanic to overhaul the transmission if the special tools are available and the job is carried out in a deliberate step-by-step manner, to ensure nothing is overlooked.

The tools necessary for an overhaul include internal and external circlip pliers, bearing pullers, a slide hammer, a set of pin punches, a dial test indicator and possibly a hydraulic press. In addition, a large, sturdy workbench and a vice will be required.

5 Reversing light switch – testing, removal and refitting

Testing

1 Ensure that the ignition switch is turned to the 'off' position.
2 Disconnect the wiring from the reversing light switch **(see illustrations)**. The switch is screwed into the front of the casing on 02T transmissions, and into the shift cover on the top of the 02R transmission.
3 Connect the probes of a continuity tester, or multi-meter set to the resistance measurement function, across the terminals of the reversing light switch.
4 The switch contacts are open when any gear other than reverse is selected; the tester/meter should indicate an open circuit or infinite resistance. When reverse gear is selected, the switch contacts should close, causing the tester/meter to indicate continuity or zero resistance.
5 If the switch does not operate correctly, it should be renewed.

Removal

6 Ensure that the ignition switch is turned to the 'off' position.
7 Disconnect the wiring from the reversing light switch.
8 Unscrew and remove the switch from the casing. On the 02T transmissions, recover the sealing ring.

Refitting

9 Refitting is a reversal of removal, but tighten the switch to the specified torque. On the 02T transmissions, renew the sealing ring. On the 02R transmission, apply some molybdenum disulphide grease to the peg.

6 Oil seals – renewal

Driveshaft oil seals

1 Remove the appropriate driveshaft as described in Chapter 8, Section 2.
2 Undo the retaining bolt and remove the appropriate driveshaft flange from the transmission **(see illustrations)**.
3 Carefully prise the oil seal out of the

5.2a Reversing light switch - 02R transmission

5.2b Reversing light switch - 02T transmission

6.2a Hold the drive flange in position...

6.2b ...remove the centre bolt...

6.2c ...then slide the drive flange from the transmission

transmission, using a large flat-bladed screwdriver, noting its fitted position.

4 Remove all traces of dirt from the area around the oil seal aperture, then apply a smear of grease to the outer lip of the new oil seal. Fit the new seal into its aperture, and drive it squarely into position using a suitable tubular drift (such as a socket), which bears only on the hard outer edge of the seal until it abuts its locating shoulder. If the seal was supplied with a plastic protector sleeve, leave this in position until the driveshaft has been refitted.

5 Apply a thin film of grease to the oil seal lip.

6 When refitting the driveshaft flange, pressure will need to be applied to the flange to compress the spring, when fitting the flange centre bolt. Tighten the bolt to the specified torque setting.

7 Refit the driveshaft as described in Chapter 8, Section 2.

Input shaft oil seal

Note: *On some transmissions, the oil seal appears to be integral with the guide sleeve. Check with your VW parts specialist before removal.*

8 Remove the transmission as described in Section 3, and the clutch release mechanism as described in Chapter 6, Section 7.

9 Undo the bolts (two or three bolts, depending on model) securing the clutch release bearing guide sleeve in position, and slide the guide off the input shaft, along with its sealing ring or gasket (as applicable). Recover any shims or thrustwashers, which have stuck to the rear of the guide sleeve, and refit them to the input shaft.

10 Where applicable, carefully lever the oil seal out of the guide using a suitable flat-bladed screwdriver or remove the seal using a drift.

11 Before fitting a new seal, check the input shaft's seal rubbing surface for signs of burrs, scratches or other damage, which may have caused the seal to fail in the first place. It may be possible to polish away minor faults of this sort using fine abrasive paper; however, more serious defects will require the renewal of the input shaft. Ensure that the input shaft is clean and greased, to protect the seal lips on refitting.

12 Lubricate the lips of the seal before refitting to the transmission or guide tube.

13 Fit a new sealing ring or gasket (as applicable) to the rear of the guide sleeve, then carefully slide the sleeve into position over the input shaft. Refit the retaining bolts and tighten them to the specified torque setting.

14 Take the opportunity to inspect the clutch components if not already done (Chapter 6, Section 6). Finally, refit the transmission as described in Section 3.

Chapter 7 Part B:
DSG semi-automatic transmission

Contents

Degrees of difficulty

Easy, suitable for novice with little experience 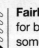	**Fairly easy,** suitable for beginner with some experience	**Fairly difficult,** suitable for competent DIY mechanic	**Difficult,** suitable for experienced DIY mechanic	**Very difficult,** suitable for expert DIY or professional

Specifications

General

Description	DSG (Direct Shift Gearbox) semi-automatic 7-forward speeds and 1 reverse. Integral transaxle differential/final drive transmission with dual-clutch.
Transmission type number:	0AM
Transmission capacity (after draining)	1.7 litres
Mechatronic unit capacity (cannot be renewed)	1.0 litres
Clutch type	Two (Dual-clutch) dry friction discs, with spring loaded centre hub.
Clutch operation.	Mechatronic unit (mechanical and electronic).

Torque wrench settings

	Nm	lbf ft
Driveshaft flange bolt	30	22
Transmission-to-engine bolts:		
M10 bolts	40	30
M12 bolts	80	59
Transmission mounting bracket-to-casing bolts*:		
Stage 1	40	30
Stage 2	Angle-tighten a further 90°	
Transmission mounting-to-bracket bolts*:		
Stage 1	60	44
Stage 2	Angle-tighten a further 90°	
Drain plug	30	22

*Do not re-use

1.2 Mechatronic unit fitted to front of transmission

1.3 Dual clutch assembly

1 General information

The VW semi-automatic Direct Shift Gearbox (DSG) covered in this manual has seven-forward speeds (and one reverse). In contrast to traditional automatic transmissions where a fluid flywheel (torque converter) transmits the power from the engine to the gearbox, the DSG has a dual-clutch operate by a mechatronic unit. The main advantages of the DSG transmission, is near-instant gear changes, with seamless, highly efficient drive, resulting in less exhaust emissions and improved fuel consumption.

On the front of the transmission housing is a mechatronic unit, this is made up of mechanical and electronic components. The electronic part of the unit uses information from sensors (e.g. engine speed, road speed, driving mode etc...) to determine the optimum gear and shift commands, the mechanical part then selects the correct gear required. It is a sealed unit, and is bolted to the front of the transmission **(see illustration)**.

The clutch is of a dual-clutch dry plate type, which has two friction discs and a spring loaded centre hub **(see illustration)**. The clutch friction disc nearest the engine is operated by the larger outer release lever (K1) and operates 1st, 3rd, 5th & 7th gears. The clutch friction disc nearest the transmission is operated by the smaller inner release lever (K2) and operates 2nd, 4th, 6th & Reverse gears. With this system whilst 'K1' has a gear

engaged, then 'K2' will pre-select the next gear ready to change gear. The clutch assembly can only be purchased as a complete unit, and if renewed, new release levers will also need to be renewed.

A fault diagnosis system is integrated into the control unit, but analysis can only be undertaken with specialised equipment. It is important that any transmission fault be identified and rectified at the earliest possible opportunity. A VW dealer or suitable equipped specialist can 'interrogate' the ECM fault memory for stored fault codes, enabling him to pinpoint the fault quickly. Once the fault has been corrected and any fault codes have been cleared, normal transmission operation is restored.

Because of the need for special test equipment, the complexity of some of the parts, and the need for scrupulous cleanliness when these transmissions, the work which the owner can do is limited. Most major repairs and overhaul operations should be left to a VW dealer or specialist, who will be equipped with the necessary equipment for fault diagnosis and repair. The information in this Chapter is therefore limited to a description of the removal and refitting of the transmission as a complete unit. The removal, refitting and adjustment of the selector cable is also described.

In the event of a transmission problem occurring, consult a VW dealer or transmission specialist before removing the transmission from the vehicle, since the majority of fault diagnosis is best carried out with the transmission still in the vehicle.

2.0 Breather cap on mechatronic unit

2.9a Disconnect the wiring plug connections...

2 Transmission – removal and refitting

Note: *The mechatronic unit on the front of the transmission is a sealed unit. If any oil is lost from this mechatronic unit, it will need to be renewed, as it cannot be refilled. Remove the breather cap from the top of the unit and cover with blanking plug, to prevent any loss of oil as the transmission is removed (see illustration).*

Removal

1 The transmission is removed downwards from the engine compartment. First, select a solid, level surface to park the vehicle upon. Give yourself enough space to move around it easily. Select P, apply the handbrake, and chock the rear wheels.

2 Loosen the front wheel bolts, and the driveshaft hub bolts. Do not undo the hub bolt more than 90° at this point; otherwise the wheel bearing could be damaged, whilst the weight is still on the wheels.

3 Raise the front of the vehicle and rest it securely on axle stands (see *Jacking and vehicle support*). Remove the front wheels. Allow a suitable working clearance underneath for the eventual withdrawal of the transmission. Undo the fasteners and remove the engine/transmission undershield.

4 Drain the transmission oil, as described in Section 6.

⚠️ *Warning: The mechatronic unit on the front of the transmission is a sealed unit. If any oil is lost from this unit, it will need to be renewed, as it cannot be refilled. Remove the breather cap from the top of the unit and cover with blanking plug, to prevent any loss of oil.*

5 Remove the air cleaner housing as described in Chapter 4A, Section 2 (petrol) or Chapter 4B, Section 2 (diesel).

6 The front cross member/lock carrier will need to be moved into its Service Position to allow for the transmission to be removed. Refer to Chapter 2E, Section 4, to move the lock carrier into the Service Position.

7 Remove the starter motor as described in Chapter 5A, section 8.

8 Disconnect the selector cable from the selector shaft lever on the top of the transmission, as described in Section 4. Position the cable to one side, noting that the retaining clip/circlip must be renewed.

9 Disconnect the wiring plug connectors from the front of the transmission **(see illustrations)**. If required, undo the nuts and detach the wiring loom retainer from the gearbox cover – slide the locking lever upwards to disconnect.

10 Disconnect the earth cable from either the transmission or the vehicle body **(see illustration)**.

11 Remove the upper engine-to-transmission mounting bolts.

2.9b ...on the front of the transmission

2.10 Undo the earth cable securing nut

2.13 Disconnect the oil level/temperature sensor wiring connector

12 Slacken the clamp securing the exhaust intermediate pipe to the rear section and undo the front mounting bracket bolts. This will allow the engine to be moved forwards and backwards during the transmission removal and alignment procedures. Consequently, there is no need to completely separate the exhaust pipe sections. Take care not to damage the front flexible pipe as the engine is being moved.

13 Disconnect the wiring plug from the engine oil level/temperature sensor on the sump **(see illustration)**; this is to prevent it getting damaged when the engine moves forward.

14 With reference to the Chapter 8, Section 2, unscrew and remove the bolts securing the driveshafts to the transmission output flanges. Tie the right-hand driveshaft to one side, and then tie the left-hand driveshaft to the suspension strut, so that the shaft is as high as possible. Alternatively, completely remove the driveshaft as described in Chapter 8, Section 2.

15 Support the engine with a hoist or support bar located on the front wing inner channels. Depending on the engine, temporarily remove components as necessary to attach the hoist.

16 Position a trolley jack underneath the transmission, and raise it to just take the weight of the unit.

17 Undo and remove the bolts securing the left-hand gearbox mounting. By controlling both the engine hoist/support bar and the trolley jack, lower the transmission slightly. To make removal easier undo the retaining bolts

and remove the mounting bracket from the top of the transmission casing.

18 Lower the engine/transmission until there is sufficient clearance between the upper edge of the transmission and the left-hand chassis member.

19 Unscrew and remove the lower bolts securing the transmission to the engine, noting the bolt locations, as they are of different sizes and lengths.

20 On models with driveshafts that have a bolted flange, hold the right-hand side flange in position and undo the flange securing bolt, then the flange can be removed **(see illustrations)**.

21 Check that all the fixings and attachments are clear of the transmission. Enlist the aid of an assistant to help in guiding and supporting the transmission during its removal.

22 The transmission is located on engine alignment dowels, and if stuck on them, it may be necessary to carefully tap and prise the transmission free of the dowels to allow separation. Once the transmission is disconnected from the location dowels, swivel the unit out and lower it out of the vehicle.

 Warning: Support the transmission to ensure that it remains steady on the jack head.

23 When the transmission is clear of the locating dowels and clutch components, lower the transmission to the ground and withdraw from under the car. Make sure that the transmission does not fall and lose any transmission oil. Also make sure that the clutch

assembly comes away with the transmission, and stays inside the bell-housing.

Refitting

24 Refitting the transmission is essentially a reversal of the removal procedure, but note the following points:
   a) Renew the needle (spigot) bearing in the end of the crankshaft (see Chapter 2E, Section 13).
   b) When reconnecting the transmission to the engine, ensure that the location dowels are in position, and that the transmission is correctly aligned with them before pushing it fully into engagement with the engine.
   c) Tighten all retaining bolts to their specified torque wrench settings.
   d) Be sure to guide the selector cable into the support bracket as the transmission is refitted – renew the retaining clips.
   e) Adjust the selector cable, as described in Section 4.
   f) Refer to Chapter 8, Section 2, and tighten the driveshaft bolts to the specified torque.
   g) On completion, check the coolant level.
   h) If a new transmission unit has been fitted, it may be necessary to have the transmission ECM 'matched' to the engine management ECM electronically, to ensure correct operation – seek the advice of your VW dealer or suitably equipped specialist.
   j) Refill the transmission with the correct grade and quantity of oil, as described in Section 6.

2.20a Hold the drive flange in position...

2.20b ...whilst removing the centre bolt...

2.20c ...then slide the drive flange from the transmission

4.4 Disconnect the wiring connector

4.5 Prise the inner cable from the ball joint

4.6 Release the outer cable securing clip

4.9 Gearchange housing mounting nuts (arrowed)

3 Transmission overhaul – general information

In the event of a fault occurring, it will be necessary to establish whether the fault is electrical, mechanical or hydraulic in nature, before repair work can be contemplated. Diagnosis requires detailed knowledge of the transmission's operation and construction, as well as access to specialised test equipment, and so is deemed to be beyond the scope of this manual. It is therefore essential that problems with the automatic transmission be referred to a VW dealer or specialist for assessment.

Although it is possible to remove the clutch assembly from out of the bell housing, it is not possible to fit a new assembly without

the use of special tools. When a new clutch is purchased, there are a number of shims and retaining clips of different thickness in the kit, therefore without the correct tools, it is not possible to correctly install the assembly back in place.

Note that a faulty transmission should not be removed before the vehicle has been assessed by a dealer or specialist, as fault diagnosis is best carried out with the transmission still in the vehicle.

4 Selector lever housing and cable – removal, refitting and adjustment

Removal

1 Move the selector lever to the P position,

4.14a Secure the outer cable in the bracket...

4.14b ...and slacken the cable adjustment screw (arrowed)

and remove the battery and battery tray as described in Chapter 5A, Section 3.

2 Remove the air cleaner housing as described in Chapter 4A, Section 2 (petrol) or Chapter 4B, Section 2 (diesel).

3 Working inside the vehicle, remove the centre console and gear selector knob, as described in Chapter 11, Section 26.

4 Disconnect the wiring connector from the front of the gear selector housing **(see illustration)**.

5 Working inside the engine compartment, use a pair of long-nose pliers to release the cable end fitting from the ball head on the selector lever **(see illustration)**.

6 Prise out the clip securing the outer cable and withdraw the cable from the support bracket on the transmission **(see illustration)**. Discard the retaining clip – as a new one must be fitted.

7 Raise the front of the vehicle and support it securely on axle stands (see *Vehicle jacking and support*).

8 Remove the centre tunnel front heat shield from the underside of the vehicle to gain access to the base of the selector lever housing and cable. It may be necessary to separate the exhaust downpipe from the intermediate pipe.

9 Working inside the vehicle, undo the retaining nuts **(see illustration)**, then remove the bracket and lower the gear selector housing downwards. Withdraw it complete with selector cable out from under the vehicle. It may be useful having the aid of an assistant at this point, to be under the vehicle when lowering the selector housing.

Refitting

10 Refitting is the reversal of the removal procedure, noting the following points:
a) *Do not grease the cable end fittings. This is stated by VW.*
b) *Ensure that the cable is correctly routed and secured, as noted on removal.*
c) *Take care not to bend or kink the cable.*
d) *Carry out the cable adjustment procedure described below before reconnecting the cable at the transmission end.*
e) *When refitting the outer cable to the support bracket, use new clips.*

Adjustment

11 Inside the car, move the selector lever to the P position.

12 If not already done, disconnect the cable from the selector lever on the transmission.

13 Move the selector lever inside the vehicle from 'P' to 'S' and back, repeatedly, to check that everything moves easily. VW recommend that you **Do Not** grease the cable.

14 Reconnect the cable to the lever at the transmission, and then slacken the cable adjusting bolt **(see illustrations)**.

15 Check that both the selector lever inside the car and the lever on the transmission are in their P positions. Gently rock the levers backwards and forwards to make sure the

4.16 Push the lever in the direction of the arrow

5.2 Prise up the selector lever gaiter surround trim

5.3 Press down the yellow plastic peg

cable is settled. Do not move either lever out of the P position.

16 The transmission lever is in the P position, when it's pushed back towards the selector cable mounting bracket **(see illustration)**.

17 When in position, tighten the cable adjusting bolt.

18 Verify the operation of the selector lever by shifting through all gear positions and checking that every gear can be selected smoothly and without delay.

5 Emergency release of selector lever

1 If the vehicles battery is disconnected or discharged, it is possible to release the selector lever from its locked position. First, ensure the handbrake is fully applied.

2 Carefully prise up the selector lever gaiter surround trim from the console and move it to one side **(see illustration)**.

3 Press the yellow plastic wedge downwards **(see illustration)**. It should now be possible to move the selector lever to the desired position.

6 Transmission oil renewal

Note: *This transmission is fitted to 1.4-litre petrol and 1.6-litre diesel engines. The transmission is filled for life, and does not have an oil level checking procedure. If there has been an oil leak from the transmission, after the leak has been rectified, renew the transmission oil as described in the following paragraphs.*

1 Take the vehicle on a short journey to warm the transmission oil, and then park the car on a level surface. For improved access to the drain plug, apply the handbrake, then jack up the front of the vehicle and support it on axle

6.2 Transmission oil drain plug - arrowed

stands (see *Jacking and vehicle support*), but note that the rear of the vehicle should also be raised to ensure all oil is drained.

2 Undo the retaining screws and remove the engine undertray. Wipe clean the area around the transmission drain plug, which is situated on the lower rear of the transmission **(see illustration)**.

3 Place a container under the transmission casing, then unscrew the drain plug from the base of the differential housing, and allow the oil to drain.

4 Remove the battery and battery tray as described in Chapter 5A, Section 3.

5 Remove the air cleaner housing as described in Chapter 4A, Section 2 (petrol) or Chapter 4B, Section 2, (diesel).

6 When the oil has finished draining, clean the surrounding area, refit the drain plug and tighten it to the specified torque.

7 Unclip the breather cap from the selector cover plate on the top of the transmission casing **(see illustration)**.

8 Using a length of hose, and funnel, add 1.7 litres of new oil to the transmission. Only use VW recommended oil, for 7-speed dual clutch 0AM transmission.

9 Refit the breather cap, making sure that it is secure. Renew if damaged.

10 The remainder of refitting is a reversal of removal.

6.7 Breather cap on selector cover - arrowed

7 Driveshaft oil seals – renewal

Driveshaft oil seals

1 Remove the appropriate driveshaft as described in Chapter 8, Section 2.

2 Undo the retaining bolt and remove the appropriate driveshaft flange from the transmission **(see illustrations 2.20a, 2.20b & 2.20c)**.

3 Carefully prise the oil seal out of the transmission, using a large flat-bladed screwdriver, noting its fitted position.

4 Remove all traces of dirt from the area around the oil seal aperture, then apply a smear of grease to the outer lip of the new oil seal. Fit the new seal into its aperture, and drive it squarely into position using a suitable tubular drift (such as a socket), which bears only on the hard outer edge of the seal until it abuts its locating shoulder. If the seal was supplied with a plastic protector sleeve, leave this in position until the driveshaft has been refitted.

5 Apply a thin film of grease to the oil seal lip.

6 Refit the driveshaft as described in Chapter 8, Section 2.

Chapter 8
Driveshafts

Contents

Degrees of difficulty

Easy, suitable for novice with little experience	**Fairly easy,** suitable for beginner with some experience	**Fairly difficult,** suitable for competent DIY mechanic	**Difficult,** suitable for experienced DIY mechanic	**Very difficult,** suitable for expert DIY or professional

Specifications

General

Driveshaft type	Steel shafts with outer constant velocity joints and inner tripod or constant velocity joints (according to type).
Type code differences:	
VL 90, VL 100 or VL107	CV joints each end, inner joint diameter 90mm, 100mm or 107mm, bolted to transmission drive flanges on each side
AAR 2000/108	CV outer joint, tripod inner joint body diameter 108mm, bolted to transmission drive flanges on each side

Lubrication

Overhaul and repair	Use only special grease supplied in sachets with gaiter/overhaul kits
Joint grease type	Refer to VW dealer

Torque wrench settings

	Nm	lbf ft
Driveshaft-to-transmission flange bolts:		
Stage 1	10	7
Stage 2:		
M8 x 48 bolts* - (VL90 & VL100 type joint)	40	30
M10 x 52 bolts* - (VL107 type joint)	70	52
M10 x 23 bolts - (AAR 2000/108 type joint)	70	52
Driveshaft/Hub nut (12 point – 36mm): *		
Stage 1	50	37
Stage 2	Angle-tighten a further 45°	
Lower arm-to-balljoint nuts*	100	74
Lower rear mounting-to-transmission bolts: *		
Stage 1	50	37
Stage 2	Angle-tighten a further 90°	
Wheel bolts	120	89

* Use new bolt/nuts

---

1   General information

Drive is transmitted from the differential to the front wheels by means of two steel driveshafts of either solid or hollow construction (depending on model, and which side of the vehicle). Both driveshafts are splined at their outer ends, to accept the wheel hubs, and are secured to the hub by a large bolt. The inner end of each driveshaft is either bolted to a transmission drive flange or splined directly onto the differential splined shaft.

The outer ends of each driveshaft are fitted with ball-bearing type constant velocity (CV) joints, to ensure the smooth and efficient transmission of drive at all the angles possible, as the roadwheels move up-and-down with the suspension, and as they turn from side to side under steering.

The inner ends of each driveshaft (except for the AAR 2000/108 type joint) are fitted with ball and cage type constant velocity (CV) joint. The AAR 2000/108 driveshaft has a triple roller type (tripod) joint fitted to the inner end of the driveshaft.

Hytrel (thermoplastic elastomer) gaiters are fitted over the CV joints with steel clips. These gaiters combine the flexibility of rubber with the strength and durability of thermoplastics.

The gaiters contain the grease that lubricates the joints, and also protect the joints from the entry of dirt and debris.

2   Driveshafts – removal and refitting

Removal

1 Remove the wheel trim/centre cap (as applicable) then apply the handbrake, and partially unscrew the relevant hub bolt with the vehicle resting on its wheels, by a maximum of 90° – note that the bolt is very tight, and a suitable extension bar will probably be

2.3 Remove the heat shield

2.4a Remove the driveshaft/hub nut

2.4b A new nut will be required for refitting

required to aid unscrewing. Also slacken the road wheel securing bolts by half a turn. **Note:** *Do not loosen the bolt more than 90° with the vehicle standing on the ground, as the wheel bearings may be damaged.*

2 Apply the handbrake, then jack up the front of the vehicle and support it on axle stands (see *Jacking and vehicle support*). Remove the appropriate front roadwheel.

3 Remove the retaining screws and/or clips, and remove the undershields from beneath the engine/transmission unit to gain access to the driveshafts. Where necessary, also unbolt the heat shield from the rear of the cylinder block to improve access to the right-hand driveshaft inner joint **(see illustration)**.

4 Unscrew and remove the driveshaft/hub nut **(see illustrations)**. **Note:** *Discard the nut and obtain a new one.*

5 Unscrew the three nuts securing the front suspension lower arm balljoint to the lower

arm **(see illustration)**. Discard the nuts, as new ones must be used on refitting.

6 Lever the lower arm downwards to release it from the balljoint studs, then pull the hub carrier outwards, and at the same time withdraw the driveshaft outer constant velocity joint from the hub **(see illustration)**. If the joint splines are a tight fit in the hub, tap the joint out of the hub using a soft-faced mallet and drift. If this fails to free the driveshaft from the hub, the joint will have to be pressed out using a suitable tool bolted to the hub.

7 On some models, in order to gain the necessary clearance required to withdraw the left-hand driveshaft, it may be necessary to unbolt the rear engine transmission mounting **(see illustration)**, and move the engine slightly. Taking care not to damage the exhaust flexible front pipe. **Note: Do Not** *undo the centre bolt that goes through the rubber mounting, as this is set in position.*

8 Proceed as follows according to driveshaft type.
Caution: Support the driveshaft by suspending it with wire or string – do not allow it to hang under its own weight, or the joint may be damaged.

Inner joint with drive flange – VL90, VL100 and VL107

9 Mark the inner joint in relation to the drive flange for refitting. Using a multi-splined tool, unscrew and remove the six bolts securing the inner driveshaft joint to the transmission flange and, recover the retaining plates from underneath the bolts **(see illustrations)**.

Inner joint triple roller (tripod) located in joint body – AAR 2000/108

10 Mark the inner joint body and driveshaft in relation to each other, as the tripod joint will need to be refitted in the joint body in the same position. Loosen the larger retaining clip, ease off the rubber gaiter, and pull the triple roller out of the joint body.

All types

11 Manoeuvre the driveshaft out from underneath the vehicle and (where fitted) recover the gasket from the end of the inner constant velocity joint. **Note:** *Discard the gasket and obtain a new one.*
Caution: Do not allow the vehicle to rest on its wheels with one or both driveshaft(s) removed, as damage to the wheel bearings may result.

12 If moving the vehicle is unavoidable, temporarily insert the outer end of the driveshaft(s) in the hub(s), and tighten the

2.5 Undo the lower ball joint retaining nuts

2.6 Slide the driveshaft out from the hub assembly

2.7 Unbolt the lower rear mounting bracket

2.9a Make alignment marks (arrowed)…

2.9b …and remove the drive flange bolts and plates

driveshaft retaining bolt(s); in this case, the inner end(s) of the driveshaft(s) must be supported, for example by suspending with string from the vehicle underbody.

Refitting

13 Where applicable, check the condition of the circlip on the inner end of the driveshaft, and if necessary, renew it.

14 As applicable, clean the splines on each end of the driveshaft and in the hub and apply a little oil, and where applicable wipe clean the oil seal in the transmission casing. Check the oil seal and if necessary renew it as described in Chapter 7A, Section 6 or Chapter 7B, Section 7. Smear a little oil on the lips of the oil seal before fitting the driveshaft.

Inner joint with bolted drive flange – VL90, VL100 and VL107

15 Ensure that the transmission flange and inner joint mating surfaces are clean and dry. Where necessary, fit a new gasket to the joint by peeling off its backing foil and sticking it in position **(see illustration)**.

16 Manoeuvre the driveshaft into position, aligning the previously made marks, and then align the inner joint holes with those on the transmission flange. Refit the new retaining bolts and locking plates, and then tighten the retaining bolts to the specified torque.

2.15 Locate a new gasket on the inner joint

Inner joint triple roller (tripod) located in joint body – AAR 2000/108

17 Fill the inner joint with the specified quantity of grease, and then locate the driveshaft tripod into the joint body, aligning the previously made marks. Ease the gaiter onto the joint body, and secure the gaiter with a new retaining clip.

All types

18 With the lower arm levered downwards, engage the outer joint with the hub. Fit the new hub bolt and use it to draw the joint fully into position.

19 Align the balljoint studs with the holes in the lower arm, then release the arm and fit

the three new nuts. Tighten the nuts to the specified torque.

20 Where applicable, refit the lower rear mounting-to-transmission bolts, and then tighten the new bolts to the specified torque.

21 Tighten the driveshaft/hub bolt to the Stage 1 torque setting. **Note:** *The bolt must be tightened with the wheel clear of the ground.*

22 Refit the roadwheel and lower the vehicle to the ground, then angle-tighten the driveshaft bolt through the Stage 2 angle (see Specifications).

23 Once the driveshaft bolt is correctly tightened, tighten the wheel bolts to the specified torque and refit the wheel trim/centre cap.

3 Driveshaft rubber gaiters – renewal

1 Remove the driveshaft from the car, as described in Section 2. Continue as described under the relevant sub-heading. Driveshafts with a tripod type inner joint can be identified by the shape of the inner CV joint; the driveshaft retaining bolt holes are in extensions from the joint, giving it a six-pointed star-shaped exterior, in contrast to the smooth, circular shape of the ball-and-cage joint **(see illustrations)**.

3.1a Driveshaft components – models with VL90 or VL100 CV joint

1 Hub bolt	5 Inner joint	8 Thrust washer	11 Gasket
2 Outer joint gaiter	6 Flange bolts	9 Circlip	12 Inner joint gaiter
3 Gaiter securing clip	7 Bolt retaining plate	10 Washer	13 Outer joint
4 Driveshaft			

H48695

3.1b Driveshaft joint components – models with VL107 CV joint

1 Outer joint
2 Hub bolt
3 Circlip
4 Thrust washer
5 Washer
6 Gaiter securing clip
7 Outer joint gaiter
8 Driveshaft
9 Inner joint gaiter
10 Flange bolts
11 Bolt retaining plate
12 Metal cover
13 Inner 'bolt-on' joint
14 Gasket
15 Circlip
16 Metal end cover

H48696

3.1c Driveshaft joint components – models with AAR2000/108 triple roller joints

1 Outer joint
2 Hub bolt
3 Circlip
4 Thrust washer
5 Washer
6 Gaiter securing clip
7 Outer joint gaiter
8 Driveshaft
9 Inner joint gaiter
10 Triple roller joint
11 Flange bolts
12 Inner joint housing

H48698

3.2 Release the outer joint gaiter clips...

3.3 ...and slide the gaiter away from the joint

3.4 Use a mallet to drive the outer joint from the driveshaft

Outer CV joint gaiter – all types of driveshafts

2 Secure the driveshaft in a vice equipped with soft jaws, and release the two outer joint gaiter retaining clips **(see illustration)**. If necessary, the retaining clips can be cut to release them.

3 Slide the rubber gaiter down the shaft to expose the constant velocity joint, and scoop out excess grease **(see illustration)**.

4 Using a soft-faced mallet, tap the joint off the end of the driveshaft **(see illustration)**.

5 Remove the circlip from the driveshaft groove, and slide off the thrustwasher and dished washer, noting which way around it is fitted **(see illustration)**.

6 Slide the rubber gaiter off the driveshaft and discard it **(see illustration)**.

7 Thoroughly clean the constant velocity joint(s) using paraffin, or a suitable solvent, and dry thoroughly. Carry out a visual inspection as follows.

8 Move the inner splined driving member from side-to-side to expose each ball in turn at the top of its track. Examine the balls for cracks, flat spots or signs of surface pitting.

9 Inspect the ball tracks on the inner and outer members. If the tracks have widened, the balls will no longer be a tight fit. At the same time, check the ball cage windows for wear or cracking between the windows.

10 If on inspection any of the constant velocity joint components are found to be worn or damaged, it will be necessary to renew the complete joint assembly. If the joint is in satisfactory condition, obtain a new gaiter and retaining clips, a constant velocity joint circlip and the correct type of grease. Grease is often supplied with the joint repair kit – if not, use good-quality molybdenum disulphide grease.

11 Tape over the splines on the end of the driveshaft, to protect the new gaiter as it is slid into place **(see illustration)**.

12 Slide the new gaiter onto the end of the driveshaft, then remove the protective tape from the driveshaft splines.

13 Slide on the dished washer, making sure its convex side is innermost, followed by the thrustwasher.

14 Pack the joint with half the quantity of the specified type of grease. Work the grease well into the bearing tracks whilst twisting the joint, and fill the rubber gaiter with the remaining half **(see illustrations)**.

15 Fit a new circlip to the driveshaft, then tap the joint onto the driveshaft until the circlip engages in its groove **(see illustrations)**. Make sure that the joint is securely retained by the circlip.

16 Ease the gaiter over the joint, and ensure

3.5 Removing the circlip, thrustwasher and dished washer

3.6 Removing the outer gaiter

3.11 Temporarily tape over the splines to protect the new gaiter

3.14a Pack half of the grease in the joint...

3.14b ...and the remaining half in the gaiter

3.15a Fit a new circlip...

3.15b ...then refit the outer joint

3.16 Seat the gaiter on the outer joint and driveshaft, then lift its inner lip to equalise the air pressure

3.17a Fit the large metal retaining clip...

3.17b ...and use a suitable tool to tighten it

that the gaiter lips are correctly located on both the driveshaft and constant velocity joint. Lift the outer sealing lip of the gaiter to equalise air pressure within the gaiter **(see illustration)**.

17 Fit the large metal retaining clip to the gaiter. Pull the clip as tight as possible, and locate the hooks on the clip in their slots. Remove any slack in the gaiter retaining clip by carefully compressing the raised section

of the clip. In the absence of the special tool, a pair of side-cutters may be used, taking care not to cut the clip **(see illustrations)**. Secure the small retaining clip using the same procedure.

18 Check the constant velocity joint moves freely in all directions, then refit the driveshaft to the vehicle, as described in Section 2.

Inner gaiter with bolted drive flange – VL90, VL100 and VL107

19 Secure the driveshaft in a vice equipped with soft jaws, then release the gaiter small securing clip, securing the gaiter to the driveshaft **(see illustration)**.

20 Using a hammer and a small drift, carefully drive the gaiter metal ring from the joint outer member **(see illustration)**.

21 Slide the gaiter down the driveshaft to expose the constant velocity joint, and scoop out excess grease.

22 Remove the circlip from the end of the driveshaft using circlip pliers **(see illustration)**.

23 Press or drive the driveshaft from the joint, taking great care not to damage the joint. Recover the dished washer fitted between the constant velocity joint and the gaiter **(see illustrations)**.

24 Slide the gaiter from the end of the driveshaft **(see illustration)**.

25 Proceed as described previously in paragraphs 7 to 12 **(see illustrations)**.

26 Slide the dished washer onto the driveshaft, making sure its convex side is innermost.

3.19 Release the gaiter small securing clip...

3.20 ...drive the metal ring from the joint outer member

3.22 Remove the circlip...

3.23a ...followed by the joint...

3.23b ...dished washer...

3.24 ...and gaiter

3.25a Tilt the splined hub and cage to remove the ball-bearings...

3.25b ...then separate the hub from the cage

3.25c Inner CV joint gaiter repair kit

27 Fit the joint to the end of the driveshaft, noting that the chamfered edge of the internal splines on the joint should face towards the driveshaft. Drive or press the joint into position until it contacts the shoulder on the driveshaft.

28 Fit a new circlip to retain the joint on the end of the driveshaft.

29 Pack the joint with the half the recommended quantity of grease (see Specifications), and then pack the gaiter with the remaining half **(see illustrations)**.

30 Slide the gaiter up the driveshaft, and press or drive the gaiter metal ring onto the joint outer member. To ensure the bolt holes are correctly positioned, temporarily fit a couple of flange bolts **(see illustrations)**.

31 If the left-hand driveshaft is being worked on, slide the outboard end of the gaiter into position using the mark made previously (see paragraph 29), then secure the outer gaiter securing clip in position as described in paragraph 17.

32 If the right-hand driveshaft is being worked on, slide the outboard end of the gaiter into position on the driveshaft, then secure the outer gaiter securing clip in position as described in paragraph 17 **(see illustration)**.

33 Check the driveshaft joint moves freely in all directions, then refit the driveshaft to the vehicle, as described in Section 2.

3.29a Pack the inner joint with half of the grease...

3.29b ...then pack the gaiter with the remaining half

3.30a Temporarily fit the flange bolts to ensure the bolt holes are correctly aligned...

3.30b ...then drive the metal ring onto the joint outer member

3.32 Installation position of inner joint gaiter on right-hand driveshaft

A Vent chamber in gaiter
B Vent hole

Inner gaiter with triple roller (tripod) joint – AAR 2000/108

34 Secure the driveshaft in a vice equipped with soft jaws, and clean out the old grease from around the triple roller joint and inside the gaiter.

35 Remove the circlip from the end of the driveshaft.

36 Press or drive the driveshaft from the tripod, taking great care not to damage the surfaces of the roller locating arms.

37 Slide the outer member and the rubber gaiter from the end of the driveshaft.

38 Thoroughly clean the joint components using paraffin, or a suitable solvent, and dry thoroughly. Carry out a visual inspection as follows.

39 Inspect the tripod rollers and the joint outer member for signs of wear, pitting or scuffing on their mating surfaces **(see illustration)**.

Check that the joint rollers rotate smoothly, with no traces of roughness.

40 If the rollers or outer member shown signs of wear or damage, it will be necessary

3.39 Check the tripod rollers and outer member for signs of wear

3.45 Work the grease into the joint outer housing

3.47 Lift the gaiter outer end to equalize the air pressure

to renew the complete driveshaft, since the joint is not available separately. If the joint is in satisfactory condition, obtain a repair kit, consisting of a new gaiter, retaining clips, circlip, and the correct type and quantity of grease.

41 Tape over the splines on the end of the driveshaft, to protect the new gaiter as it is slid into place, and then slide the new gaiter over the end of the driveshaft.

42 Press or drive the tripod onto the end of the driveshaft until it contacts the stop, ensuring that the marks made on the end of the driveshaft and the tripod before dismantling are aligned. Note that the chamfered edge of the internal splines on the tripod should face towards the driveshaft.

43 Fit the new circlip to retain the tripod on the end of the driveshaft.

44 Work half of the grease supplied with the repair kit into the inner end of the joint housing, then slide the housing over the tripod, ensuring that the marks made during dismantling are aligned, and clamp the housing in the vice.

45 Work the rest of the grease supplied with the repair kit into the outer end of the joint housing **(see illustration)**.

46 Slide the rubber gaiter along the driveshaft onto the joint housing, ensuring that the end of the gaiter seats in the groove in the joint housing, and secure with the large clip as described in paragraph 17.

47 Lift the gaiter outer end to equalise the air pressure in the gaiter (taking care not to damage the gaiter), then secure the outer gaiter securing clip in position using the same method used previously **(see illustration)**.

48 Check the driveshaft joint moves freely in all directions, then refit the driveshaft to the vehicle, as described in Section 2.

4 Driveshaft overhaul – general information

If any of the checks described in Chapter 1A or Chapter 1B reveal wear in any driveshaft joint, first remove the roadwheel trim or centre cap (as applicable) and check that the hub bolt is tight. If the bolt is loose, obtain a new one, and tighten it to the specified torque (see Section 2). If the bolt is tight, refit the centre cap/trim, and repeat the check on the other hub bolt.

Road test the vehicle, and listen for a metallic clicking from the front of the vehicle as the vehicle is driven slowly in a circle on full-lock. If a clicking noise is heard, this indicates wear in the outer constant velocity joint; this means that the joint must be renewed.

If vibration consistent with roadspeed is felt through the car when accelerating, there is a possibility of wear in the inner constant velocity joints.

To check the joints for wear, remove the driveshafts, then dismantle them as described in Section 3. If any wear or free play is found, the affected joint must be renewed. Refer to a VW dealer for information on the availability of driveshaft components.

Chapter 9
Braking system

Contents

Degrees of difficulty

Easy, suitable for novice with little experience | **Fairly easy,** suitable for beginner with some experience | **Fairly difficult,** suitable for competent DIY mechanic | **Difficult,** suitable for experienced DIY mechanic | **Very difficult,** suitable for expert DIY or professional

Specifications

Front brakes

Caliper type . . . .   FSIII or FN3 (according to model)
Disc diameter:
  FSIII (14" wheels) . . . .   280 mm
  FN3:
    15" wheels . . . .   288 mm
    16" wheels . . . .   310 or 312 mm
Disc thickness.
  New:
    FSIII. . . . .   22.0 mm
    FN3 . . . .   25.0 mm
  Minimum permissible thickness:
    FSIII. . . . .   19.0 mm
    FN3 . . . .   22.0 mm
Maximum disc run-out. . . . .   0.1 mm
Brake pad lining thickness (all models):
  New . . . .   14.0 mm
  Minimum. . . . .   2.0 mm

Rear disc brakes

Caliper type:	
C 38	15" wheels
CI 38	16" wheels
Disc diameter:	
Type C 38	232 mm
Type CI 38..	254 mm
Disc thickness:	
New:	
Type C 38	9.0 mm
Type CI 38	22.0 mm
Minimum thickness:	
Type C 38	7.0 mm
Type CI 38	20.0 mm
Maximum disc run-out..	0.1 mm
Brake pad lining thickness (all models):	
New	12.0 mm
Minimum...	2.0 mm

Rear drum brakes

Drum diameter:	
New	200 mm
Maximum diameter...	201.5 mm
Brake lining width	40 mm
Brake lining thickness:	
New	5 mm
Minimum	2.5 mm

Torque wrench settings

	Nm	lbf ft
ABS control unit retaining bolts	8	6
ABS control unit mounting bracket nuts	20	15
ABS wheel sensor retaining bolts..................................	8	6
Brake pedal pivot shaft nut*......................................	25	18
Brake light switch...	5	4
Brake disc shield bolts..	12	9
Front brake caliper:		
Guide pins	30	22
Mounting bracket bolts (FN3 calipers)	190	141
Hydraulic brake line to caliper banjo bolt......................	35	26
Hydraulic brake line union nuts	14	10
Master cylinder mounting nuts*	20	15
Rear brake caliper:		
Guide pin bolts*	35	26
Mounting bracket bolts (multi-point socket head): *		
Stage 1	90	66
Stage 2	Angle-tighten a further 90°	
Roadwheel bolts...	120	89
Servo unit mechanical vacuum pump (diesel models).............	10	8
Servo unit mounting bolts	25	18
* Use new bolts		

1 General information and precautions

General information

The braking system is of servo-assisted, diagonal dual-circuit hydraulic type. The arrangement of the hydraulic system is such that each circuit operates one front and one rear brake from a tandem master cylinder. Under normal circumstances, both circuits operate in unison, but, if there is hydraulic failure in one circuit, full braking force will still be available at two wheels. On petrol engines with a manual transmission, vacuum for the servo unit is supplied from the inlet manifold, however, on models with the DSG semi-automatic transmission, there is an electric vacuum pump located at the front right-hand side of the engine compartment. On diesel engines a combined fuel lift pump and vacuum pump is driven off the left-hand end of the camshaft.

All models covered by this manual are equipped with disc brakes at the front. Either rear drum brakes or rear disc brakes may be fitted depending on model. ABS is fitted as standard to all models (refer to Section 22 for further information on ABS operation).

The front disc brakes are actuated by single-piston sliding type calipers, which ensure that equal pressure is applied to each disc pad.

On models with rear drum brakes, the rear brakes incorporate leading and trailing shoes, which are actuated by twin-piston wheel cylinders. A self-adjust mechanism is incorporated, to compensate for brake shoe wear. The handbrake lever operates the rear shoes by two cables.

On models with rear disc brakes, the brakes are actuated by single-piston sliding calipers, which incorporate mechanical handbrake mechanisms.

Precautions

• When servicing any part of the system, work carefully and methodically; also observe scrupulous cleanliness when overhauling any part of the hydraulic system. Always renew components in axle sets (where applicable) if in doubt about their condition, and use only genuine VW parts, or at least those of known good quality. Note the warnings given in *Safety first!* and at relevant points in this Chapter concerning the dangers of asbestos dust and hydraulic fluid.

⚠️ *Warning: Brake fluid is poisonous. Take care to keep it off bare skin, and in particular not to get splashes in your eyes. The fluid also attacks paintwork and plastics – wash off spillages immediately with cold water. Finally, brake fluid is highly inflammable, and should be handled with the same care as petrol.*

Make sure the ignition is off (take out the key) before disconnecting any braking system hydraulic union, and do not switch it on until after the hydraulic system has been bled. Failure to do this could lead to air entering the ABS hydraulic unit. If air enters the hydraulic unit pump, it will prove very difficult (in some cases impossible) to bleed the unit.

When servicing any part of the system, work carefully and methodically – do not take short cuts; also observe scrupulous cleanliness when overhauling any part of the hydraulic system.

Always renew components in axle sets, where applicable – this means replacing brake pads on BOTH sides, even if only one set of pads is worn, or one wheel cylinder is leaking (for example). In the instance of uneven brake wear, the cause should be investigated and fixed (on front brakes, sticking caliper pistons is a likely problem).

Although genuine VW brake pads are asbestos-free, the dust created by wear of non-genuine parts may contain asbestos, which is a health hazard. Never blow it out with compressed air, and don't inhale any of it.

DO NOT use petroleum-based solvents to clean brake parts; use brake cleaner or methylated spirit only.

DO NOT allow any brake fluid, oil or grease to contact the brake pads or disc.

2 Hydraulic system – bleeding

⚠️ *Warning: Hydraulic fluid is poisonous; wash off immediately and thoroughly in the case of skin contact, and seek immediate medical advice if any fluid is swallowed or gets into the eyes. Certain types of hydraulic fluid are flammable, and may ignite when allowed into contact with hot components; when servicing any hydraulic system, it is safest to assume that the fluid is flammable, and to take precautions against the risk of fire as though it is petrol that is being handled. Hydraulic fluid is also an effective paint stripper, and will attack*

plastics; if any is spilt, it should be washed off immediately, using copious quantities of fresh water. Finally, it is hygroscopic (it absorbs moisture from the air) – old fluid may be contaminated and unfit for further use. When topping-up or renewing the fluid, always use the recommended type, and ensure that it comes from a freshly opened sealed container.
Note: *VW specify that at least 0.25 litre of brake fluid should be expelled from each caliper.*

General

1 The correct operation of any hydraulic system is only possible after removing all air from the components and circuit; this is achieved by bleeding the system. Since the clutch hydraulic system also uses fluid from the brake system reservoir, it should also be bled at the same time by referring to Chapter 6, Section 2.
2 During the bleeding procedure, add only clean, unused hydraulic fluid of the recommended type; never re-use fluid that has already been bled from the system. Ensure that sufficient fluid is available before starting work.
3 If there is any possibility of incorrect fluid being already in the system, the brake components and circuit must be flushed completely with uncontaminated, correct fluid, and new seals should be fitted to the various components.
4 If hydraulic fluid has been lost from the system, or air has entered because of a leak, ensure that the fault is cured before continuing further.
5 Park the vehicle on level ground, then chock the wheels and release the handbrake.
6 Check that all pipes and hoses are secure, unions tight and bleed screws closed. Clean any dirt from around the bleed screws.
7 Unscrew the master cylinder reservoir cap, and top the reservoir up to the MAX level line; refit the cap loosely, and remember to maintain the fluid level at least above the MIN level line throughout the procedure, or there is a risk of further air entering the system.
8 There is a number of one-man, do-it-yourself brake bleeding kits currently available from motor accessory shops. It is recommended that one of these kits is used whenever possible, as they greatly simplify the bleeding operation, and reduce the risk of expelled air and fluid being drawn back into the system. If such a kit is not available, the basic (two-man) method must be used, which is described in detail below.
9 If a kit is to be used, prepare the vehicle as described previously, and follow the kit manufacturer's instructions, as the procedure may vary slightly according to the type being used; generally, they are as outlined below in the relevant sub-section.
10 Whichever method is used, the same sequence must be followed (paragraph 12) to ensure the removal of all air from the system.

Bleeding sequence

11 If the system has been only partially disconnected, and suitable precautions were taken to minimise fluid loss, it should be necessary only to bleed that part of the system.
12 If the complete system is to be bled, then it should be done working in the following sequence:

RHD models

a) *Right-hand front brake.*
b) *Left-hand front brake.*
c) *Right-hand rear brake.*
d) *Left-hand rear brake.*

LHD models

a) *Left-hand front brake.*
b) *Right-hand front brake.*
c) *Left-hand rear brake.*
d) *Right-hand rear brake.*

If the hydraulic fluid has run dry in either chamber of the reservoir, the system must be pre-bled as follows, before carrying out the bleeding sequence described above:
a) *Bleed the front left and right brakes simultaneously.*
b) *Bleed the rear left and right brakes simultaneously.*

Bleeding

Basic (two-man) method

13 Collect together a clean glass jar of reasonable size, a suitable length of plastic or rubber tubing which is a tight fit over the bleed screw, and a ring spanner to fit the screw. The help of an assistant will also be required.
14 Remove the dust cap from the first screw in the sequence **(see illustration)**. Fit the spanner and tube to the screw, place the other end of the tube in the jar, and pour in sufficient fluid to cover the end of the tube.
15 Ensure that the master cylinder reservoir fluid level is maintained at least above the MIN level line throughout the procedure.
16 Have the assistant fully depress the brake pedal several times to build-up pressure, and then maintain it on the final downstroke.
17 While pedal pressure is maintained, unscrew the bleed screw (approximately one turn) and allow the compressed fluid and air to flow into the jar. The assistant should

2.14 Remove the dust cap (arrowed) from the first bleed screw in the sequence

2.22 Bleeding a brake using a one-way valve kit

maintain pedal pressure, following it down to the floor if necessary, and should not release it until instructed to do so. When the flow stops, tighten the bleed screw again, have the assistant release the pedal slowly, and recheck the reservoir fluid level.

18 Repeat the steps given in paragraphs 16 and 17 until the fluid emerging from the bleed screw is free from air bubbles. If the master cylinder has been drained and refilled, and air is being bled from the first screw in the sequence, allow approximately five seconds between cycles for the master cylinder passages to refill.

19 When no more air bubbles appear, tighten the bleed screw securely, remove the tube and spanner, and refit the dust cap. Do not overtighten the bleed screw.

20 Repeat the procedure on the remaining screws in the sequence, until all air is removed from the system and the brake pedal feels firm again.

Using a one-way valve kit

21 As their name implies, these kits consist of a length of tubing with a one-way valve fitted, to prevent expelled air and fluid being drawn back into the system; some kits include a translucent container, which can be positioned so that the air bubbles can be more easily seen flowing from the end of the tube.

22 The kit is connected to the bleed screw, which is then opened. The user returns to the driver's seat, depresses the brake pedal with a smooth, steady stroke, and slowly releases it; this is repeated until the expelled fluid is clear of air bubbles **(see illustration)**.

23 Note that these kits simplify work so much that it is easy to forget the master cylinder reservoir fluid level; ensure that this is maintained at least above the MIN level line at all times.

Using a pressure-bleeding kit

24 These kits are usually operated by the reservoir of pressurised air contained in the spare tyre. However, note that it will be probably necessary to reduce the pressure to less than 1.0 bar (14.5 psi); refer to the instructions supplied with the kit.

25 By connecting a pressurised, fluid-filled container to the master cylinder reservoir, bleeding can be carried out simply by opening each screw in turn (in the specified sequence), and allowing the fluid to flow out until no more air bubbles can be seen in the expelled fluid.

26 This method has the advantage that the large reservoir of fluid provides an additional safeguard against air being drawn into the system during bleeding.

27 Pressure-bleeding is particularly effective when bleeding 'difficult' systems, or when bleeding the complete system at the time of routine fluid renewal.

All methods

28 When bleeding is complete, and firm pedal feel is restored, wash off any spilt fluid, tighten the bleed screws securely, and refit their dust caps.

29 Check the hydraulic fluid level in the master cylinder reservoir, and top-up if necessary (see Weekly checks).

30 Discard any hydraulic fluid that has been bled from the system; it will not be fit for re-use.

31 Check the feel of the brake pedal. If it feels at all spongy, air must still be present in the system, and further bleeding is required. Failure to bleed satisfactorily after a reasonable repetition of the bleeding procedure may be due to worn master cylinder seals.

3 Hydraulic pipes and hoses – renewal

Note: Refer to the note in Section 2 concerning the dangers of hydraulic fluid.

1 If any pipe or hose is to be renewed, minimise fluid loss by first removing the master cylinder reservoir cap, then tightening it down onto a piece of polythene to obtain an airtight seal. Alternatively, flexible hoses can be sealed, if required, using a proprietary brake hose clamp; metal brake pipe unions can be plugged (if care is taken not to allow dirt into the system) or capped immediately they are disconnected. Place a wad of rag under any union that is to be disconnected, to catch any spilt fluid.

2 If a flexible hose is to be disconnected, where applicable unscrew the brake pipe union nut before removing the spring clip which secures the hose to its mounting bracket.

3 To unscrew the union nuts, it is preferable to obtain a brake pipe spanner of the correct size; these are available from most large motor accessory shops. Failing this, a close-fitting open-ended spanner will be required, though if the nuts are tight or corroded, their flats may be rounded-off if the spanner slips. In such a case, a self-locking wrench is often the only way to unscrew a stubborn union, but it follows that the pipe and the damaged nuts must be renewed on reassembly. Always clean a union and surrounding area before disconnecting it. If disconnecting a component with more than one union, make a careful note of the connections before disturbing any of them.

4 If a brake pipe is to be renewed, it can be obtained, cut to length and with the union nuts and end flares in place, from VW dealers. All that is then necessary is to bend it to shape, following the line of the original, before fitting it to the car. Alternatively, most motor accessory shops can make up brake pipes from kits, but this requires very careful measurement of the original, to ensure that the new pipe is of the correct length. The safest answer is usually to take the original to the shop as a pattern.

5 On refitting, do not overtighten the union nuts. It is not necessary to exercise brute force to obtain a sound joint.

6 Ensure that the pipes and hoses are correctly routed, with no kinks, and that they are secured in the clips or brackets provided **(see illustrations)**. After fitting, remove the polythene from the reservoir, and bleed the hydraulic system as described in Section 2. Wash off any spilt fluid, and then check carefully for fluid leaks.

3.6a Brake hose retaining clip in strut...

3.6b ...and on inner wing panel (arrowed)

3.6c Locating peg (arrowed) for brake hose end fitting

4.4a Remove the plastic caps...

4.4b ...unscrew the caliper guide pins (arrowed)...

4.4c ...and remove them from the caliper

4.5a Removing the outer pad...

4.5b ...and inner pad from the caliper

4.5c Front brake pads

4 Front brake pads – removal, inspection and refitting

Warning: Renew both sets of brake pads at the same time – never renew the pads on only one wheel, as uneven braking may result. Note that the dust created by wear of the pads may contain asbestos, which is a health hazard. Never blow it out with compressed air, and do not inhale any of it. An approved filtering mask should be worn when working on the brakes. DO NOT use petrol or petroleum-based solvents to clean brake parts; use brake cleaner or methylated spirit only.

FSIII calipers

Removal

1 Apply the handbrake, then jack up the front of the vehicle and support it on axle stands (see *Jacking and vehicle support*). Remove the front roadwheels.
2 Trace the brake pad wear sensor wiring (where fitted) back from the pads, and disconnect it from the wiring connector. Note the routing of the wiring, and free it from any relevant retaining clips.
3 Where applicable, to improve access, undo the retaining bolts and remove the air deflector shield from the caliper.
4 Remove the two protective rubber caps and, using a suitable hexagon key, slacken

and remove the two caliper guide pins from the caliper **(see illustrations)**. Then lift the caliper, together with pads, away from the hub carrier, and tie it to the suspension strut using a suitable piece of wire. Do not allow the caliper to hang unsupported on the flexible brake hose.
5 Remove the two brake pads from the caliper, noting that the inner pad is retained in the piston by a spring clip **(see illustrations)**. If the outer pad remains on the carrier, remove it. If the original pads are to be refitted, mark them so that they can be refitted in their original positions.

Inspection

6 First measure the thickness of each brake pad. If either pad is worn at any point to the specified minimum thickness or less, all four pads must be renewed. Also, the pads should be renewed if any are fouled with oil or grease; there is no satisfactory way of degreasing friction material, once contaminated. If any of the brake pads are worn unevenly, or are fouled with oil or grease, trace and rectify the cause before reassembly. New brake pad kits are available from VW dealers.
7 If the brake pads are still serviceable, carefully clean them using a clean, fine wire brush or similar, paying particular attention to the sides and back of the metal backing. Clean out the grooves in the friction material (where applicable), and pick out any large embedded particles of dirt or debris. Carefully clean the pad locations in the caliper body/mounting bracket.

8 Prior to fitting the pads, check that the guide pins are free to slide easily in the caliper body bushes, and are a reasonably tight fit. Brush the dust and dirt from the caliper and piston, but *do not* inhale it, as it is injurious to health. Inspect the dust seal around the piston for damage, and the piston for evidence of fluid leaks, corrosion or damage. If attention to any of these components is necessary, refer to Section 5.

Refitting

9 If new brake pads are to be fitted, the caliper piston must be pushed back into the cylinder to make room for them. Either use a G-clamp or similar tool, or use suitable pieces of wood as levers. To avoid any dirt entering the ABS solenoid valves, connect a pipe to the bleed nipple and, as the piston is pushed back, open the nipple and allow the displaced

4.9 Open the bleed nipple as the piston is pushed back into the caliper

4.10 The inboard pad is labelled 'Piston side'

4.11 Ensure the pads and caliper are correctly located on the carrier

4.12 Apply copper grease to the guide pins before inserting them

fluid to flow through the pipe into a suitable container **(see illustration)**.
10 Fit the new pads into the caliper. The inboard pad (piston side) is marked 'Piston side' **(see illustration)**.
11 Position the caliper and pads over the brake disc ensuring that the lug on the caliper engages correctly with the hub carrier **(see illustration)**. Pass the pad warning sensor wiring (where fitted) through the caliper aperture.
12 Position the caliper until it is possible to install the caliper guide pins. Apply a little copper grease to the pins before refitting them, and tighten them to the specified torque **(see illustration)**. Note: *Do not exert excess pressure on the caliper, as this will deform the pad springs, resulting in noisy operation of the brakes.*

13 Where applicable, reconnect the brake pad wear sensor wiring connectors, ensuring that the wiring is correctly routed. Where applicable, refit the air deflector shield to the caliper.
14 Depress the brake pedal repeatedly, until the pads are pressed into firm contact with the brake disc, and normal (non-assisted) pedal pressure is restored.
15 Repeat the above procedure on the remaining front brake caliper.
16 Refit the roadwheels, then lower the vehicle to the ground and tighten the roadwheel bolts to the specified torque.
17 New pads will not give full braking efficiency until they have bedded-in. Be prepared for this, and avoid hard braking as far as possible for the first hundred miles or so after pad renewal.

FN3 calipers

Removal

18 Proceed as described in paragraphs 1 and 2.
19 Using a screwdriver, lever the brake pad retaining spring from the caliper housing **(see illustration)**.
20 Remove the two protective rubber caps and using a suitable hexagon key, slacken and remove the two caliper guide pins from the caliper **(see illustration)**. Then lift the caliper away from the brake pads and hub, and tie it to the suspension strut using a suitable piece of wire. Do not allow the caliper to hang unsupported on the flexible brake hose.
21 Withdraw the two brake pads from the caliper mounting bracket. If the original pads are to be refitted, identify them so that they can be refitted in their original locations. Where applicable, disconnect the pad wear sensor wiring connector.

Inspection

22 Examine the pads and caliper as described previously in paragraphs 6 to 8. If new pads are to be refitted, refer to paragraph 9 before attempting to push the piston back into the caliper.

Refitting

23 Where applicable, remove the protective foil from the outer pad backplate. Install the outer pad in the caliper mounting bracket, ensuring that the friction material of the pad is against the brake disc. Install the inner (piston side) pad into the caliper. If the original pads are being refitted, ensure that they are refitted to their original locations as noted before removal. The inner pad is fitted with a retaining clip, which engages with the recess in the piston **(see illustrations)**. Where applicable, note that the pad with the wear sensor wiring should be installed as the inner pad. New pads are marked with an arrow on the backing plate, which identifies the direction of rotation. Consequently, the pads should be fitted with the arrows pointing to the ground.
24 Press the caliper into position. Install and tighten the guide pins to the specified torque **(see illustration)**.
25 Refit the brake pad retaining spring to the caliper housing **(see illustration)**.

4.19 Lever the spring from the caliper housing

4.20 Undo the caliper guide pins

4.23a Fit the outer pad to the caliper mounting bracket...

4.23b ...and the inner pad to the caliper piston

26 Where applicable, reconnect the brake pad wear sensor wiring connectors, ensuring that the wiring is correctly routed.

27 Depress the brake pedal repeatedly, until the pads are pressed into firm contact with the brake disc, and normal (non-assisted) pedal pressure is restored.

28 Repeat the above procedure on the remaining front brake caliper.

29 Refit the roadwheels, then lower the vehicle to the ground and tighten the roadwheel bolts to the specified torque.

30 Check the hydraulic fluid level as described in *Weekly checks*.

31 New pads will not give full braking efficiency until they have bedded-in. Be prepared for this and avoid hard braking (where possible) in the first hundred miles or so after pad renewal.

4.24 Install the caliper guide pins

4.25 Refit the retaining spring securely

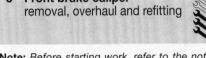

5 Front brake caliper – removal, overhaul and refitting

Note: *Before starting work, refer to the note at the beginning of Section 2 concerning the dangers of hydraulic fluid, and to the warning at the beginning of Section 4 concerning the dangers of asbestos dust.*

Removal

1 Apply the handbrake, then jack up the front of the vehicle and support it on axle stands (see *Jacking and vehicle support*). Remove the appropriate roadwheel.

2 Minimise fluid loss by first removing the master cylinder reservoir cap, and then tightening it down onto a piece of polythene, to obtain an airtight seal. Alternatively, use a brake hose clamp, a G-clamp or a similar tool to clamp the flexible hose.

3 Clean the area around the union, and then loosen the brake hose union nut.

4 Remove the brake pads as described in Section 4.

5 Unscrew the caliper from the end of the brake hose and remove it from the vehicle.

Overhaul

6 With the caliper on the bench, wipe away all traces of dust and dirt, but *avoid inhaling the dust, as it is injurious to health.*

7 Withdraw the partially ejected piston from the caliper body, and remove the dust seal.

8 Using a small screwdriver, extract the piston hydraulic seal, taking great care not to damage the caliper bore **(see illustration)**.

9 Thoroughly clean all components, using only methylated spirit, isopropyl alcohol or clean hydraulic fluid as a cleaning medium. Never use mineral-based solvents such as petrol or paraffin, as they will attack the hydraulic system rubber components. Dry the components immediately, using compressed air or a clean, lint-free cloth. Use compressed air to blow clear the fluid passages.

10 Check all components, and renew any

that are worn or damaged. Check particularly the cylinder bore and piston; these should be renewed if they are scratched, worn or corroded in any way (note that this means the renewal of the complete caliper body assembly). Similarly check the condition of the spacers/guide pins and their bushes/bores (as applicable); both spacers/pins should be undamaged and (when cleaned) a reasonably tight sliding fit in their bores. If there is any doubt about the condition of any component, renew it.

11 If the assembly is fit for further use, obtain the appropriate repair kit; the components are available from VW dealers in various combinations.

12 Renew all rubber seals, dust covers and caps disturbed on dismantling as a matter of course; these should never be re-used.

13 On reassembly, ensure that all components are clean and dry.

14 Thinly coat the piston and piston seal with brake fitting paste (VW part no G 052 150 A2). This should be included in the VW caliper overhaul/repair kit.

15 Fit the new piston (fluid) seal, using only your fingers (no tools) to manipulate it into the cylinder bore groove. Fit the new dust seal to the piston, and refit the piston to the cylinder bore using a twisting motion; ensure that the piston enters squarely into the bore. Press the piston fully into the bore, then press the dust seal into the caliper body.

Refitting

16 Screw the caliper fully onto the flexible hose union.

5.8 Use a small screwdriver to extract the caliper piston hydraulic seal

17 Refit the brake pads as described in Section 4.

18 Securely tighten the brake pipe union nut.

19 Remove the brake hose clamp or polythene, as applicable, and bleed the hydraulic system as described in Section 2. Note that, providing the precautions described were taken to minimise brake fluid loss, it should only be necessary to bleed the relevant front brake.

20 Refit the roadwheel, then lower the vehicle to the ground and tighten the roadwheel bolts to the specified torque.

6 Brake disc – inspection, removal and refitting

Note: *Before starting work, refer to the note at the beginning of Section 4 concerning the dangers of asbestos dust.*

Note: *If either disc requires renewal, BOTH should be renewed at the same time, to ensure even and consistent braking. New brake pads should also be fitted.*

Front brake disc

Inspection

1 Apply the handbrake, then jack up the front of the car and support it on axle stands (see *Jacking and vehicle support*). Remove the appropriate front roadwheel.

2 Slowly rotate the brake disc so that the full area of both sides can be checked; remove the brake pads if better access is required to the inboard surface. Light scoring is normal in the area swept by the brake pads, but if heavy scoring or cracks are found, the disc must be renewed.

3 It is normal to find a lip of rust and brake dust around the perimeter of the disc; this can be scraped off if required. If, however, a lip has formed due to excessive wear of the brake pad swept area, then the disc thickness must be measured using a micrometer. Take measurements at several places around the disc, at the inside and outside of the pad swept area; if the disc has worn at any point to the specified minimum thickness or less, the disc must be renewed.

4 If the disc is thought to be warped, it can be

6.4 Using a DTI gauge to measure disc run-out

6.8 Undo the disc retaining screw

6.13 Remove the rear brake disc

checked for run-out. Either use a dial gauge mounted on any convenient fixed point, while the disc is slowly rotated, or use feeler blades to measure (at several points all around the disc) the clearance between the disc and a fixed point, such as the caliper mounting bracket. If the measurements obtained are at the specified maximum or beyond, the disc is excessively warped, and must be renewed; however, it is worth checking first that the hub bearings are in good condition. If the run-out is excessive, the disc must be renewed **(see illustration)**.

5 Check the disc for cracks, especially around the wheel bolt holes, and any other wear or damage, and renew if necessary.

Removal

6 Remove the brake pads as described in Section 4.

7 On models with FN3 front brake calipers, unscrew the two bolts securing the brake caliper mounting bracket to the hub carrier, then slide the caliper assembly off the disc. Using a piece of wire or string, tie the caliper to the front suspension coil spring, to avoid placing any strain on the brake hose.

8 Use chalk or paint to mark the relationship of the disc to the hub, then remove the screw securing the brake disc to the hub, and remove the disc **(see illustration)**. If it is tight, apply penetrating fluid, and tap its rear face gently with a hide or plastic mallet. The use of excessive force could cause the disc to be damaged.

Refitting

9 Refitting is the reverse of the removal procedure, noting the following points:
  a) *Ensure that the mating surfaces of the disc and hub are clean and flat.*
  b) *Align (if applicable) the marks made on removal, and securely tighten the disc retaining screw.*
  c) *If a new disc has been fitted, use a suitable solvent to wipe any preservative coating from the disc, before refitting the caliper.*
  d) *On models with FN3 brake calipers, slide the caliper into position over the disc, making sure the pads pass either side of the disc. Tighten the caliper bracket mounting bolts to the specified torque.*

  e) *Fit the pads as described in Section 4.*
  f) *Refit the roadwheel, then lower the vehicle to the ground and tighten the roadwheel bolts to the specified torque. On completion, repeatedly depress the brake pedal until normal (non-assisted) pedal pressure returns.*

Rear brake disc

Inspection

10 Firmly chock the front wheels, then jack up the rear of the car and support it on axle stands. Remove the appropriate rear roadwheel.

11 Inspect the disc as described in paragraphs 1 to 5.

Removal

12 Unscrew the two bolts securing the brake caliper mounting bracket in position, then slide the caliper assembly off the disc. Using a piece of wire or string, tie the caliper to the rear suspension coil spring, to avoid placing any strain on the hydraulic brake hose.

13 Use chalk or paint to mark the relationship of the disc to the hub, then remove the screw securing the brake disc to the hub, and remove the disc **(see illustration)**. If it is tight, apply penetrating fluid, and tap its rear face gently with a hide or plastic mallet. The use of excessive force could cause the disc to be damaged.

Refitting

14 Refitting is a reversal of the removal procedure, noting the following points:
  a) *Ensure that the mating surfaces of the disc and hub are clean and flat.*
  b) *Align (if applicable) the marks made on removal, and securely tighten the disc retaining screw.*
  c) *If a new disc has been fitted, use a suitable solvent to wipe any preservative coating from the disc, before refitting the caliper.*
  d) *Slide the caliper into position over the disc, making sure the pads pass either side of the disc. Tighten the caliper bracket mounting bolts to the specified torque. If new discs have been fitted and there is insufficient clearance between the pads to accommodate the new,*

thicker disc, it may be necessary to push the piston back into the caliper body as described in Section 8.
  e) *Refit the roadwheel, then lower the vehicle to the ground and tighten the roadwheel bolts to the specified torque. On completion, repeatedly depress the brake pedal until normal (non-assisted) pedal pressure returns.*

| 7 | **Front brake disc shield** – removal and refitting |

Removal

1 Remove the brake disc as described in Section 6.

2 Unscrew the securing bolts, and remove the brake disc shield.

Refitting

3 Refitting is a reversal of removal. Tighten the shield retaining bolts to the specified torque. Refit the brake disc with reference to Section 6.

| 8 | **Rear brake pads** – removal, inspection and refitting |

Note: *Before starting work, refer to the note at the beginning of Section 4 concerning the dangers of asbestos dust. New caliper mounting bolts will be required on refitting.*

Removal

1 Chock the front wheels, then jack up the rear of the vehicle and support it on axle stands (see *Jacking and vehicle support*). Remove the rear wheels.

2 Slacken the handbrake cable and detach it from the caliper as described in Section 19.

3 Slacken and remove the guide pin bolts, using a slim open-ended spanner to prevent the guide pins from rotating **(see illustration)**. Discard the bolts – new ones must be used on refitting.

4 Lift the caliper away from the brake pads, and tie it to the suspension strut using a

suitable piece of wire **(see illustration)**. Do not allow the caliper to hang unsupported on the flexible brake hose.

5 Withdraw the two brake pads from the caliper mounting bracket **(see illustrations)**, and on the CI 38 type, recover the pad anti-rattle shims from the mounting bracket, noting their correct fitted locations. **Note:** *On the C38 type, the anti-rattle springs are attached to the pads themselves.*

Inspection

6 First measure the thickness of each brake pad. If either pad is worn at any point to the specified minimum thickness or less, **all four** pads must be renewed. Also, the pads should be renewed if any are fouled with oil or grease; there is no satisfactory way of degreasing friction material, once contaminated. If any of the brake pads are worn unevenly, or fouled with oil or grease, trace and rectify the cause before reassembly. New brake pads are available from VW dealers.

7 If the brake pads are still serviceable, carefully clean them using a clean, fine wire brush or similar, paying particular attention to the sides and back of the metal backing. Clean out the grooves in the friction material (where applicable), and pick out any large embedded particles of dirt or debris. Carefully clean the pad locations in the caliper body/ mounting bracket.

8 Prior to fitting the pads, check that the guide pins are free to slide easily in the caliper bracket, and check that the rubber guide pin gaiters are undamaged. Brush the dust and dirt from the caliper and piston, but **do not** inhale it, as it is injurious to health. Inspect the dust seal around the piston for damage, and the piston for evidence of fluid leaks, corrosion or damage. If attention to any of these components is necessary, refer to Section 9.

Refitting

9 If new brake pads are to be fitted, it will be necessary to retract the piston fully; by rotating it in a clockwise direction as it is pushed into the caliper bore **(see Haynes Hint)**. To avoid any dirt entering the ABS solenoid valves, connect a pipe to the bleed nipple, and as the piston is pushed back open the nipple and allow the displaced fluid to flow through the pipe into a suitable container.

10 On the CI 38 type, fit the pad anti-rattle shims to the caliper mounting bracket, ensuring that they are correctly located (see note in paragraph 5). Install the pads in the mounting bracket, ensuring that each pad's friction material is against the brake disc. Remove the protective foil from the outer pad backing plate **(see illustrations)**.

11 Slide the caliper back into position over the pads.

12 Press the caliper into position, then install the new guide pin bolts, tightening them to the specified torque setting while retaining the guide pin with an open-ended spanner **(see illustration)**.

8.3 Counterhold the guide pins

8.4 Remove the caliper

8.5a Remove the outer rear brake pad...

8.5b ...and inner rear brake pad

13 Depress the brake pedal repeatedly, until the pads are pressed into firm contact with the brake disc, and normal (non-assisted) pedal pressure is restored.

14 Repeat the above procedure on the remaining rear brake caliper.

In the absence of the special tool, the piston can be screwed back into the caliper using a pair of circlip pliers.

8.10b ...and install the brake pads

15 Reconnect the handbrake cables to the calipers, and adjust the handbrake as described in Section 17.

16 Refit the roadwheels, then lower the vehicle to the ground and tighten the roadwheel bolts to the specified torque setting.

8.10a Refit the anti-rattle shims...

8.12 Hold the guide pin whilst tightening the guide pin bolt

17 Check the hydraulic fluid level as described in *Weekly checks*.

18 New pads will not give full braking efficiency until they have bedded-in. Be prepared for this, and avoid hard braking as far as possible for the first hundred miles or so after pad renewal.

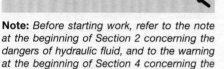

9 Rear brake caliper – removal, overhaul and refitting

Note: *Before starting work, refer to the note at the beginning of Section 2 concerning the dangers of hydraulic fluid, and to the warning at the beginning of Section 4 concerning the dangers of asbestos dust.*

Removal

1 Chock the front wheels, then jack up the rear of the vehicle and support on axle stands (see *Jacking and vehicle support*). Remove the relevant rear wheel.

2 Minimise fluid loss by first removing the master cylinder reservoir cap, and then tightening it down onto a piece of polythene, to obtain an airtight seal. Alternatively, use a brake hose clamp, a G-clamp or a similar tool to clamp the flexible hose.

3 Clean the area around the union on the caliper, and then loosen the brake hose union nut.

4 Lift the caliper from the brake pads as described in Section 8.

5 Unscrew the caliper from the end of the flexible hose and remove it from the vehicle.

Overhaul

Note: *It is not possible to overhaul the brake caliper handbrake mechanism. If the mechanism is faulty, or fluid is leaking from the handbrake lever seal the caliper assembly must be renewed.*

6 With the caliper on the bench, wipe away all traces of dust and dirt, but avoid inhaling the dust, as it is injurious to health.

7 Using a small screwdriver, carefully prise out the dust seal from the caliper, taking care not to damage the piston.

8 Remove the piston from the caliper bore by rotating it in an anti-clockwise direction.

This can be achieved using a suitable pair of circlip pliers engaged in the caliper piston slots. Once the piston turns freely but does not come out any further, the piston can be withdrawn by hand.

9 Using a small screwdriver, extract the piston hydraulic seal(s), taking care not to damage the caliper bore.

10 Withdraw the guide pins from the caliper, and remove the guide sleeve gaiters.

11 Thoroughly clean all components, using only methylated spirit, isopropyl alcohol or clean hydraulic fluid as a cleaning medium. Never use mineral-based solvents such as petrol or paraffin, as they will attack the hydraulic system rubber components. Dry the components immediately, using compressed air or a clean, lint-free cloth. Use compressed air to blow clear the fluid passages.

12 Check all components, and renew any that are worn or damaged. Check particularly the cylinder bore and piston; these should be renewed (note that this means the renewal of the complete caliper body assembly) if they are scratched, worn or corroded in any way. Similarly check the condition of the spacers/guide pins and their bushes/bores (as applicable); both spacers/pins should be undamaged and (when cleaned) a reasonably tight sliding fit in their bores. If there is any doubt about the condition of any component, renew it.

13 If the assembly is fit for further uses obtain the appropriate repair kit; the components are available from VW dealers in various combinations.

14 Renew all rubber seals, dust covers and caps disturbed on dismantling as a matter of course; these should never be re-used.

15 On reassembly, ensure that all components are clean and dry.

16 Smear a thin coat of brake fitting paste (VW part no G 052 150 A2) on the piston, seal and caliper bore. This should be included in the overhaul/repair kit. Fit the new piston (fluid) seal, using only the fingers (no tools) to manipulate into the cylinder bore groove.

17 Fit the new dust seal to the piston groove, then refit the piston assembly. Turn the piston in a clockwise direction, using the method

employed on dismantling, until it is fully retracted into the caliper bore.

18 Press the dust seal into position in the caliper housing.

19 Apply the grease supplied in the repair kit, or a copper-based brake grease or anti-seize compound, to the guide pins. Fit the new gaiters to the guide pins and fit the pins to the caliper ensuring that the gaiters are correctly located in the grooves on both the pins and caliper.

20 Prior to refitting, fill the caliper with fresh hydraulic fluid by slackening the bleed screw and pumping the fluid through the caliper until bubble-free fluid is expelled from the union hole.

Refitting

21 Screw the caliper fully onto the flexible hose union.

22 Refit the caliper over the brake pads as described in Section 8.

23 Securely tighten the brake pipe union nut.

24 Remove the brake hose clamp or remove the polythene from the fluid reservoir, as applicable, and bleed the hydraulic system as described in Section 2. Note that, providing the precautions described were taken to minimise brake fluid loss, it should only be necessary to bleed the relevant rear brake.

25 Connect the handbrake cable to the caliper, and adjust the handbrake as described in Section 17.

26 Refit the roadwheel, then lower the vehicle to the ground and tighten the roadwheel bolts to the specified torque. On completion, check the hydraulic fluid level as described in *Weekly checks*.

10 Rear brake drum – removal, inspection and refitting

Note: *Before starting work, refer to the warning at the beginning of Section 4 concerning the dangers of asbestos dust.*

Removal

1 Remove the wheel trim (where applicable), then loosen the rear roadwheel bolts and chock the front wheels. Jack up the rear of the car, and support on axle stands positioned under the body side members (see *Jacking and vehicle support*). Remove the roadwheel.

2 Fully release the handbrake.

3 Extract the drum securing screw and remove the drum. The drum may be tight due to the brake shoes binding on the inner circumference of the drum. If this is the case, insert a screwdriver through one of the wheel bolt holes in the brake drum and hub, and lever up the wedge key in order to allow the brake shoes to retract fully. The wedge key is located beneath the front of the wheel cylinder **(see illustrations)**. The brake drum can now be withdrawn.

10.3a Rear brake drum securing screw

10.3b If the drum is tight, insert a screwdriver in through one of the wheel bolt holes...

Inspection

Note: *If either drum requires renewal, BOTH should be renewed at the same time, to ensure even and consistent braking. New brake shoes should also be fitted.*

4 Brush the dust and dirt from the drum, taking care not to inhale it.

5 Examine the internal friction surface of the drum. If deeply scored, or so worn that the drum has become ridged to the width of the shoes, then both drums must be renewed.

6 Regrinding of the friction surface may be possible provided the maximum diameter given in the Specifications and on the drum Itself Is not exceeded.

Refitting

7 If a new brake drum is to be fitted, use a suitable solvent to remove any preservative coating that may have been applied to its interior. Prior to refitting the drum, fully retract the brake shoes by lifting up the wedge key.

8 Refit the brake drum and tighten the securing screw.

9 Adjust the brakes by operating the footbrake a number of times. A clicking noise will be heard at the drum as the automatic adjuster operates. When the clicking stops, adjustment is complete.

10 Refit the roadwheel and lower the car to the ground.

11 Repeat the above procedure on the remaining rear brake assembly, then check and, if necessary, adjust the handbrake cable (see Section 17).

12 On completion, refit the roadwheels, then lower the car to the ground and tighten the wheel bolts to the specified torque.

11 Rear brake shoes – removal, inspection and refitting

Note: *Refer to the warning at the start of Section 4 before starting work.*

1 Remove the brake drum (see Section 10), then carefully remove all traces of brake dust from the brake drum, backplate and shoes.

2 Measure the thickness of the friction material of each brake shoe at several points;

10.3c ...and lever up on the wedge key to retract the brake shoes (drum removed for clarity)

if either shoe is worn at any point to the specified minimum thickness or less, **all four** shoes must be renewed as a set. The shoes should also be renewed if any are fouled with oil or grease; there is no way of degreasing friction material, once contaminated.

3 If any of the brake shoes are worn unevenly, or fouled with oil or grease, trace and rectify the cause before reassembly.

4 To renew the brake shoes, continue as follows. If all is well, refit the brake drum as described in Section 10.

5 Note the position of the brake shoes and springs, and mark the webs of the shoes, if necessary, to aid refitting **(see illustration)**.

6 To facilitate easy removal and refitting of the brake shoes, we found it necessary to remove the hub/bearing assembly first (see Chapter 10, Section 9), although this may not be necessary on some models.

11.5 Note the position of the brake shoes before dismantling them

10.3d Removing the rear brake drum

7 Using a pair of pliers, remove the shoe retainer spring cups by depressing and turning them through 90°. With the cups removed, lift off the springs and withdraw the retainer pins **(see illustration)**.

8 Ease the shoes out one at a time from the lower pivot point, to release the tension of the return spring, then disconnect the lower return spring from both shoes **(see illustrations)**.

9 Ease the upper end of both shoes out from their wheel cylinder locations, taking care not to damage the wheel cylinder seals, and disconnect the handbrake cable from the trailing shoe. The brake shoe assembly can then be manoeuvred out of position and away from the backplate. Do not depress the brake pedal until the brakes are reassembled; wrap a strong elastic band or fit a cable tie around the wheel cylinder pistons to retain them **(see illustrations)**.

11.7 Removing the shoe retainer spring cup, spring and retainer pin

11.8a Ease the shoes out from the lower pivot point...

11.8b ...and detach the lower return spring

11.9a Ease the upper ends of the shoes from their wheel cylinder locations...

11.9b ...then disconnect the handbrake cable and remove the shoe assembly

11.9c Use a cable-tie or elastic band to retain the wheel cylinder pistons

11.10 Unhook the adjuster wedge key spring and remove it

11.11a Using a length of bent welding rod to unhook the upper return spring

11.11b Remove the trailing shoe from the leading shoe and strut

in a vice, and use the length of bent welding rod to remove the spring **(see illustrations)**.

13 Examine all components for signs of wear or damage, and renew as necessary.

14 Peel back the rubber protective caps, and check the wheel cylinder for fluid leaks or other damage; check that both cylinder pistons are free to move easily. Refer to Section 12, if necessary, for information on wheel cylinder overhaul.

15 Apply a little brake grease to the contact areas of the pushrod and handbrake lever.

16 Hook the tensioning spring into the leading shoe. Engage the strut with the opposite end of the spring, and pivot the strut into position into the leading shoe slot.

17 Insert the wedge key between the leading shoe and pushrod, making sure it is fitted the correct way around **(see illustration)**.

18 Fit the upper return spring to the leading shoe and engage the spring in its hole in the trailing shoe **(see illustration)**. Ensure the spring is correctly fitted then pivot the trailing shoe into position making sure both the shoe and handbrake lever are correctly engaged with the strut.

19 Fit the spring to the wedge key, and hook it onto the trailing shoe.

20 Prior to installation, clean the backplate, and apply a thin smear of high-temperature brake grease or anti-seize compound to the shoe contact areas **(see illustration)**, and to the wheel cylinder pistons and lower pivot point. Do not allow the lubricant to foul the friction material.

21 Remove the elastic band or cable tie fitted

10 Make a note of the correct fitted positions of all components, then unhook the spring, and disengage the wedge key spring **(see illustration)**.

11 Unhook the upper return spring and remove the trailing shoe from the leading shoe

and strut. A length of bent welding rod may be used to unhook the spring **(see illustrations)**.

12 Withdraw the wedge key, noting which way around it is fitted, then ease the strut out from the leading shoe and detach the tensioning spring. If necessary, mount the strut

11.12a Mount the strut in a vice, and use welding rod to unhook the tensioning spring

11.12b Remove the wedge key and unhook the spring...

11.12c ...then separate the strut from the leading shoe

11.17 Insert the wedge key, ensuring its peg is facing away from the shoe

11.18 Refitting the upper return spring

to the wheel cylinder, and offer up the shoe assembly.

22 Connect the handbrake cable to the handbrake lever, and locate the top of the shoes in the wheel cylinder piston slots.

23 Fit the lower return spring to the shoes, then lever the bottom of the shoes onto the bottom anchor.

24 Tap the shoes to centralise them with the backplate, then refit the shoe retainer pins and springs, and secure them in position with the spring cups.

25 Refit the hub as described in Chapter 10, Section 9, and then refit the brake drum as described in Section 10.

26 Repeat the above procedure on the remaining rear brake.

27 Once both sets of rear shoes have been renewed, adjust the lining-to-drum clearance by repeatedly depressing the brake pedal until normally (non-assisted) pedal pressure returns.

28 Check and, if necessary, adjust the handbrake as described in Section 17.

29 On completion, check the hydraulic fluid level as described in *Weekly checks*.

12 Rear wheel cylinder – removal, overhaul and refitting

Note: *Before starting work, refer to the note at the beginning of Section 2 concerning the dangers of hydraulic fluid, and to the warning at the beginning of Section 4 concerning the dangers of asbestos dust.*

Removal

1 Remove the brake drum (see Section 10).

2 Using pliers, carefully unhook the upper brake shoe return spring, and remove it from both brake shoes. Pull the upper ends of the shoes away from the wheel cylinder to disengage them from the pistons.

3 Minimise fluid loss by first removing the master cylinder reservoir cap, and then tightening it down onto a piece of polythene, to obtain an airtight seal. Alternatively, use a brake hose clamp, a G-clamp or a similar tool to clamp the flexible hose at the nearest convenient point to the wheel cylinder.

4 Wipe away all traces of dirt around the brake pipe union at the rear of the wheel cylinder, and unscrew the union nut. Carefully ease the pipe out of the wheel cylinder, and plug or tape over its end to prevent dirt entry. Wipe off any spilt immediately.

5 Unscrew the two wheel cylinder retaining bolts from the rear of the backplate, and remove the cylinder, taking great care not to allow surplus hydraulic fluid to contaminate the brake shoe linings.

Overhaul

6 Brush the dirt and dust from the wheel cylinder, but take care not to inhale it.

7 Pull the rubber dust seals from the ends of the cylinder body **(see illustration)**.

11.20 Apply high-temperature brake grease to the shoe contact areas on the backplate

8 The pistons will normally be ejected by the pressure of the coil spring, but if they are not, tap the end of the cylinder body on a piece of wood, or apply low air pressure – e.g. from a foot pump – to the hydraulic fluid union hole to eject the pistons from their bores.

9 Inspect the surfaces of the pistons and their bores in the cylinder body for scoring, or evidence of metal-to-metal contact. If evident, renew the complete wheel cylinder assembly.

10 If the pistons and bores are in good condition, discard the seals and obtain a repair kit, which will contain all the necessary renewable items.

11 Remove the seals from the pistons noting their correct fitted orientation. Lubricate the new piston seals with clean brake fluid, and fit them onto the pistons with their larger diameters innermost.

12 Dip the pistons in clean brake fluid, then fit the spring to the cylinder.

13 Insert the pistons into the cylinder bores using a twisting motion.

14 Fit the dust seals, and check that the pistons can move freely in their bores.

Refitting

15 Ensure that the backplate and wheel cylinder mating surfaces are clean, then spread the brake shoes and manoeuvre the wheel cylinder into position. Engage the brake pipe, and screw in the union nut two or three turns to ensure that the thread has started.

16 Insert the two wheel cylinder retaining bolts, and tighten them to the specified torque. Now fully tighten the brake pipe union nut.

17 Remove the clamp from the flexible brake hose, or the polythene from the master cylinder reservoir (as applicable).

18 Ensure that the brake shoes are correctly located in the cylinder pistons, and then refit the brake shoe upper return spring, using a screwdriver to stretch the spring into position.

19 Refit the brake drum (see Section 10).

20 Bleed the brake hydraulic system as described in Section 2. Providing suitable precautions were taken to minimise loss of fluid, it should only be necessary to bleed the relevant rear brake.

13 Brake pedal – removal and refitting

Removal

1 Disconnect the battery negative lead. **Note:** *Before disconnecting the battery, refer to 'Disconnecting the battery' in the reference section at the rear of this manual.*

2 If required, remove the trim panel from below the facia panel on the driver's side, across the top of the pedal assembly.

3 Where fitted, undo the mounting bolt/nut and remove the crash bar from above the brake pedal.

12.7 Exploded view of a rear wheel cylinder

1 Dust seal *2 Piston* *3 Coil spring* *4 Fluid seal*

13.4a Improvised special tool constructed from a modified exhaust clamp, used to release the brake pedal from the servo pushrod

13.4b Using the tool to release the brake pedal from the servo pushrod

13.4c Plastic lugs (arrowed) securing pedal to servo pushrod

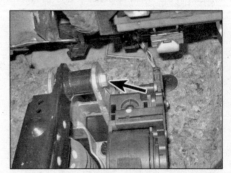

13.5 Undo the securing nut - arrowed

13.6 Remove the upper pivot bolt - arrowed

4 It is now necessary to release the brake pedal from the ball on the vacuum servo pushrod. To do this, a VW special tool is available, but a suitable alternative can be improvised. Note that the plastic lugs in the pedal are very stiff, and it will not be possible to release them by hand. Depress and hold down the pedal, then, using the tool, release the securing lugs, and pull the pedal from the servo pushrod (see illustrations).

5 Slacken and remove the pivot shaft nut (see illustration).

6 Slide the pivot shaft bolt out, until the pedal is free, and then remove the pedal (see illustration).

7 Carefully clean all components, and renew any that are worn or damaged.

Refitting

8 Prior to refitting, apply a smear of multi-purpose grease to the pivot shaft and pedal bearing surfaces.

9 Pull the servo unit pushrod down, and at the same time manoeuvre the pedal into position, ensuring that the pivot bush is correctly located.

10 Hold the servo unit pushrod, and push the pedal back onto the pushrod ball. Make sure the pedal is securely fastened to the pushrod.

11 Insert the pedal pivot bolt and tighten the retaining nut to the specified torque.

12 The remainder of the refitting procedure is the opposite of the removal.

14 Servo unit – testing, removal and refitting

Testing

1 To test the operation of the servo unit, depress the footbrake several times to exhaust the vacuum, then start the engine whilst keeping the pedal firmly depressed. As the engine starts, there should be a noticeable 'give' in the brake pedal as the vacuum builds-up. Allow the engine to run for at least two minutes, and then switch it off. If the brake pedal is now depressed, it should feel normal, but further applications should result in the pedal feeling firmer, with the pedal stroke decreasing with each application.

2 If the servo does not operate as described, first inspect the servo unit non-return valve as described in Section 15. On diesel models, also check the operation of the vacuum pump as described in Section 24 or 25.

3 If the servo unit still fails to operate satisfactorily, the fault lies within the unit itself. Repairs to the unit are not possible – if faulty, the servo unit must be renewed.

Removal

4 Remove the master cylinder as described in Section 16.

5 Where applicable remove the heat shield from the servo, then carefully ease the vacuum valve out from the sealing grommet in the front of the servo (see illustration). Where applicable, also disconnect the wiring from the servo vacuum sensor, then extract the retaining circlip with a screwdriver, and withdraw the sensor from the servo.

6 On LHD models with manual transmission, refer to Chapter 7A, Section 2 and disconnect the gearchange cables from the levers on the transmission, then unbolt the gearchange support bracket and tie it to one side.

7 With reference to Chapter 11 remove the driver's side lower facia trim panels, and the trim panel below the dash, where applicable.

8 It is now necessary to release the brake pedal from the ball on the vacuum servo pushrod.

9 To do this, a VW special tool is available, but a suitable alternative can be improvised. Note that the plastic lugs in the pedal are very stiff, and it will not be possible to release them by hand. Using the tool, release the securing lugs, and pull the pedal from the servo pushrod (see illustrations 13.4a, 13.4b & 13.4c).

10 Again working in the footwell, undo the nuts securing the servo unit to the bulkhead (see illustration).

14.5 Disconnect the vacuum valve - arrowed

14.10 Servo unit mounting nuts – arrowed

11 Return to the engine compartment and manoeuvre the servo unit out of position, and recover the gasket where fitted. Note that, it may be necessary to remove the bulkhead panel **(see illustration)**, to give sufficient clearance to withdraw the servo.

Refitting

12 Check the servo unit vacuum hose sealing grommet for signs of damage or deterioration, and renew if necessary.
13 Where applicable, fit a new gasket to the rear of the servo unit, and then reposition the unit in the engine compartment.
14 From inside the vehicle, ensure that the servo unit pushrod is correctly engaged with the brake pedal, and push the pedal onto the pushrod ball. Check the pushrod ball is securely engaged, then refit the servo unit mounting nuts and tighten them to the specified torque.
15 Refit the facia trim panels, as applicable.
16 On LHD models with manual transmission, refit the gearchange cables and support bracket.
17 Carefully ease the vacuum hose back into position in the servo, taking great care not to displace the sealing grommet. Refit the heat shield to the servo and, where applicable, refit the vacuum sensor and wiring.
18 Refit the master cylinder as described in Section 16 of this Chapter.
19 Where applicable, refit the bulkhead panel.
20 On completion, start the engine and check for air leaks at the vacuum hose-to-servo unit connection; check the operation of the braking system.

15 Servo non-return valve –
testing, removal and refitting

1 The non-return valve is located in the vacuum hose leading from the inlet manifold or vacuum pump to the brake servo **(see illustration)**.

Removal

2 Ease the vacuum hose out of the servo unit, taking care not to displace the grommet.
3 Note the routing of the hose, then slacken the retaining clip(s) and disconnect the opposite end of the hose assembly from the manifold/vacuum pump **(see illustration)**, and remove it from the car.

Testing

4 Examine the check valve and vacuum hose for signs of damage, and renew if necessary.
5 The valve may be tested by blowing through it in both directions; air should flow through the valve in one direction only; when blown through from the servo unit end of the valve. Renew the valve if this is not the case.
6 Examine the servo unit rubber sealing grommet for signs of damage or deterioration, and renew as necessary.

14.11 Remove the bulkhead panel

Refitting

7 Ensure that the sealing grommet is correctly fitted to the servo unit.
8 Ease the hose union into position in the servo, taking great care not to displace or damage the grommet.
9 Ensure that the hose is correctly routed, and connect it to the inlet manifold/vacuum pump, ensuring the hose is secured in the retaining clips.
10 On completion, start the engine and check the valve-to-servo unit connection for signs of air leaks.

16 Master cylinder –
removal, overhaul and refitting

Note: *Before starting work, refer to the warning at the beginning of Section 2 concerning*

15.1 Non-return valve (arrowed) in vacuum pipe

16.3 Brake fluid level warning switch - arrowed

the dangers of hydraulic fluid. A new master cylinder O-ring will be required on refitting.

Removal

1 Disconnect the battery negative lead. **Note:** *Before disconnecting the battery, refer to 'Disconnecting the battery' in the Reference section at the rear of this manual.* Remove the engine top cover and air inlet trunking.
2 On LHD models, remove the battery and tray with reference to Chapter 5A, Section 3.
3 Remove the master cylinder reservoir cap, disconnecting the wiring plug from the brake fluid level warning switch **(see illustration)**, and then syphon the hydraulic fluid from the reservoir. **Note:** *Do not syphon the fluid by mouth, as it is poisonous; use a syringe or an old antifreeze tester.*
4 Disconnect the wiring connector from the brake light switch **(see illustration 21.1)**, at the lower part of the master cylinder.
5 To remove the hydraulic fluid reservoir from the top of the master cylinder, undo the retaining bolt and pull the reservoir upwards from the rubber grommets **(see illustration)**. On manual transmission models, disconnect and plug the clutch master cylinder supply hose from the side of the brake fluid reservoir.
6 Wipe clean the area around the brake pipe unions on the side of the master cylinder, and place absorbent rags beneath the pipe unions to catch any leaking fluid. Make a note of the correct fitted positions of the unions, then unscrew the union nuts and carefully withdraw the pipes. Plug or tape over the pipe ends and master cylinder orifices, to minimise the

15.3 Disconnect hose from vacuum pump

16.5 Reservoir retaining bolt (A) – clutch supply hose (B)

16.7 Master cylinder securing nuts – arrowed

loss of brake fluid, and to prevent the entry of dirt into the system. Wash off any spilt fluid immediately with cold water.

7 Unscrew and remove the two nuts and washers securing the master cylinder to the vacuum servo unit, remove the heat shield (where fitted), then withdraw the unit from the engine compartment **(see illustration)**. Remove the O-ring from the rear of the master cylinder, and check it for damage, renew if required.

Overhaul

8 If the master cylinder is faulty, it must be renewed. Repair kits are not available from VW dealer, so the cylinder must be treated as a sealed unit.

9 The only items that can be renewed are the mounting seals for the fluid reservoir; if these show signs of deterioration, prise them out with a screwdriver. Lubricate the new seals with clean brake fluid, and press them into the master cylinder ports.

Refitting

10 Remove all traces of dirt from the master cylinder and servo unit mating surfaces, and fit a new O-ring to the groove on the master cylinder body.

11 Fit the master cylinder to the servo unit, ensuring that the servo unit pushrod enters the master cylinder bore centrally. Refit the heat shield (where applicable), and the master cylinder mounting nuts, and then tighten them to the specified torque.

12 Wipe clean the brake pipe unions, then refit them to the master cylinder ports and tighten them securely.

17.8 Turn the nuts until a gap (A) of between 1.0 and 1.5 mm can be seen

17.3 Handbrake cable adjuster nut - arrowed

13 Refit the hydraulic fluid reservoir; making sure it is entered correctly in the rubber grommets.

14 On manual transmission models, reconnect the clutch master cylinder supply hose to the reservoir.

15 Refill the master cylinder reservoir with new fluid, and bleed the complete hydraulic system as described in Section 2.

16 Reconnect the wiring to the brake level sender unit and brake light switch as applicable.

17 On LHD models, refit the battery and tray, with reference to Chapter 5A, Section 3.

18 Refit the engine cover and air trunking where necessary, and then reconnect the battery negative lead.

17 Handbrake – adjustment
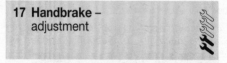

1 To check the handbrake adjustment, first apply the footbrake firmly several times to establish correct shoe-to-drum/pad-to-disc clearance, then apply and release the handbrake three times.

2 Applying normal moderate pressure, pull the handbrake lever to the fully applied position, counting the number of clicks emitted from the handbrake ratchet mechanism. If adjustment is correct, there should be approximately 4 clicks before the handbrake is fully applied. If there are more clicks, adjust as follows.

3 Depending on specification, it will be necessary to either remove the rear trim from

18.3 Handbrake warning light switch

the rear of the centre console or remove the complete centre armrest. See Chapter 11, Section 26, as applicable, to gain access to the handbrake lever adjustment **(see illustration)**.

4 Chock the front wheels, then jack up the rear of the car and support it on axle stands. Continue as described under the relevant sub-heading.

Rear drum brake models

5 With the handbrake set on the 1st notch of the ratchet mechanism, turn the adjustment nut until it is just difficult to turn both rear wheels. Now release the handbrake lever, and check that the wheels rotate freely; if not, back off the adjustment nut. Apply the handbrake fully, and check that the handbrake is fully applied on the 4th notch.

6 Once adjustment is correct, refit the centre console upper rear section as described in Chapter 11, Section 26.

Rear disc brake models

7 With the handbrake fully released, slacken the adjustment nut until both the rear caliper handbrake levers are back against their stops.

8 Tighten the adjustment nut until both handbrake levers just move off the caliper stops. **Note:** *The nut is contoured to prevent it coming loose, and it is important that the adjustment is checked with the nut fully seated in the equaliser bar. The gap between each caliper handbrake lever and its stop must be between 1.0 and 1.5 mm* **(see illustration)**.

9 Fully apply the handbrake lever three times, then release it and check that both wheels still rotate freely. Check the adjustment by applying the handbrake fully, counting the clicks emitted from the handbrake ratchet. The handbrake must be fully applied on the 4th notch.

10 Once adjustment is correct, refit the centre console upper rear section as described in Chapter 11, Section 26.

18 Handbrake lever – removal and refitting

Removal

1 Remove the centre console as described in Chapter 11, Section 26.

2 If desired, remove the handbrake lever cover sleeve by depressing the locating tag with a screwdriver, then sliding the sleeve from the lever.

3 Disconnect the wiring connector from the handbrake 'on' warning light switch **(see illustration)**.

4 Loosen the handbrake cable adjuster nut sufficiently to allow the ends of the cables to be disengaged from the equaliser plate.

5 Unscrew the retaining nuts, and withdraw the lever **(see illustration)**.

Refitting

6 Refitting is a reversal of removal, bearing in mind the following points.
- a) *Before refitting the handbrake lever cover, adjust the handbrake as described in Section 17.*
- b) *Check the operation of the handbrake 'on' warning switch before refitting the centre console.*

19 Handbrake cables – removal and refitting

Removal

1 Remove the centre console as described in Chapter 11, Section 26, to gain access to the handbrake lever. The handbrake cable consists of two sections, a right- and a left-hand section, which are linked to the lever by an equaliser plate **(see illustration 18.5)**. Each section can be removed individually.
2 Loosen the handbrake cable adjuster nut sufficiently to allow the ends of the cables to be disengaged from the equaliser plate, see Section 18.
3 Chock the front wheels, then jack up the rear of the car and support it on axle stands (see *Jacking and vehicle support*).
4 Work back along the length of the cable, noting its correct routing, and free it from all the relevant guides and retaining clips.
5 On rear drum brake models, remove the brake shoes as described in Section 11, and then release the cable from the backplate.
6 On rear disc brake models, disengage the inner cable from the caliper handbrake lever, then remove the outer cable retaining clip and detach the cable from the caliper **(see illustration)**.
7 Withdraw the cable from beneath the car.

Refitting

8 Refitting is a reversal of removal, but adjust the handbrake as described in Section 17 before refitting the centre console.

20 Handbrake 'on' warning light switch – removal and refitting

Removal

1 Disconnect the battery negative lead. **Note:** *Before disconnecting the battery, refer to 'Disconnecting the battery' in the reference section at the rear of this manual.*
2 Remove the centre console, with reference to Chapter 11, Section 26.
3 Disconnect the wiring plug from the switch.
4 Release the securing lugs, and remove the switch from the handbrake lever assembly **(see illustration)**.

Refitting

5 Refitting is a reversal of removal.

18.5 Handbrake lever mounting nuts (A) and cable equaliser plate (B)

21 Brake light switch – removal and refitting

Removal

1 The brake light switch is located on the lower part of the master cylinder **(see illustration)**. Remove the engine top cover, and where applicable, remove the air inlet trunking to improve access.
2 Disconnect the wiring from the switch.
3 Unscrew the mounting bolt, then pull the switch from the bottom of the master cylinder, and remove it from the locking lug at the top.

Refitting

4 Refitting is a reversal of removal, but tighten the mounting bolt to the specified torque.

22 Anti-lock braking system (ABS) – general information and precautions

The anti-lock braking system (ABS) fitted as standard to all models, prevents wheel lock-up under heavy braking, and not only optimises stopping distances, but also improves steering control. By electronically monitoring the speed of each roadwheel in relation to the other wheels, the system can detect when a wheel is about to lock-up, before control is actually lost. The brake fluid pressure applied to that wheel's brake caliper is then decreased

20.4 Unclip the handbrake warning light switch

19.6 Release the cable inner from its lever and withdraw the cable from the caliper

and restored ('modulated') several times a second until control is regained. The system components are: four wheel-speed sensors, a hydraulic unit with integral Electronic Control Unit (ECU), brake lines and a dashboard-mounted warning light. The four wheel-speed sensors are mounted on the wheel hub carriers. Each wheel has a rotating toothed hub mounted on the driveshaft (front) or on the hub (rear). The wheel speed sensors are mounted in close proximity to these hubs. The teeth produce a voltage waveform whose frequency varies with the speed of the hubs. These waveforms are transmitted to the ECU, and used to calculate the rotational speed of each wheel. The ECU has a self-diagnostic facility, to inhibit the operation of the ABS if a fault is detected, lighting the dashboard-mounted warning light. The braking system will then revert to conventional, non-ABS operation. If the nature of the fault is not immediately obvious upon inspection, the vehicle *must* be taken to a VW dealer, who will have the diagnostic equipment required to interrogate the ABS ECU electronically and pin-point the problem.

There are two ABS systems fitted to the models covered in this Manual.

One version includes a traction control system (TCS), which uses the basic ABS system, with an additional pump and valves fitted to the hydraulic actuator. If wheelspin is detected at a speed below 30 mph, one of the valves opens, to allow the pump to pressurise the relevant brake, until the spinning wheel

21.1 Brake light switch (arrowed)

23.1 ABS hydraulic unit

23.4 Disconnect the wiring connector...

23.5 ...and unbolt the front wheel sensor

slows to a rotational speed corresponding to the speed of the vehicle. This has the effect of transferring torque to the wheel with most traction. At the same time, the throttle plate is closed slightly, to reduce the torque from the engine.

The second version includes electronic differential locking (EDL) and an electronic stability programme (ESP). The EDL system applies the brake of the spinning wheel in order to transfer torque to the wheel with the better grip. On models with ESP, the system recognises critical driving conditions and stabilises the vehicle by individual wheel braking and by intervention in the engine control, which occurs independently of the position of the brake and accelerator pedals.

The operation of the ABS system is entirely dependent on electrical signals. To prevent the system responding to any inaccurate signals, a built-in safety circuit monitors all signals received by the ECU. If an inaccurate signal or low battery voltage is detected, the ABS system is automatically shut down, and the warning light on the instrument panel is illuminated, to inform the driver that the ABS system is not operational. Normal braking will still be available, however.

If a fault does develop in the ABS system, the car must be taken to a VW dealer for fault diagnosis and repair.

23 Anti-lock braking system (ABS) components – removal and refitting

Hydraulic unit

1 Removal and refitting of the hydraulic unit is best entrusted to a VW dealer. It is positioned in the left-hand rear corner of the engine compartment, behind the battery **(see illustration)**. If the fluid is lost from the hydraulic unit, there is no guarantee that the unit can be sufficiently filled or the fluid bled through the unit. Also a fault diagnosis check must be performed on completion using specialist equipment.

Electronic control module (ECM)

2 The ECM is mounted at the rear of the

hydraulic unit, secured by three Torx screws. Although it can be separated from the hydraulic unit, due to the delicacy of the components and the need for absolute cleanliness, it is recommended that the work be entrusted to a VW dealer. See hydraulic unit information in paragraph 1.

Front wheel sensor

Removal

3 Chock the rear wheels, then firmly apply the handbrake, jack up the front of the car and support on axle stands (see *Jacking and vehicle support*). Remove the appropriate front roadwheel.
4 Disconnect the electrical connector from the sensor by carefully lifting up the retaining tag, and pulling the connector from the sensor **(see illustration)**.
5 Slacken and remove the hexagon socket-head bolt securing the sensor to the hub carrier, and remove the sensor from the car **(see illustration)**.

Refitting

6 Ensure that the sensor and hub carrier sealing faces are clean.
7 Apply a thin coat of multi-purpose grease to the mounting hole inner surface, then fit the sensor to the hub carrier. Refit the retaining bolt and tighten it to the specified torque.
8 Ensure that the sensor wiring is correctly routed and retained by all the necessary clips, and reconnect the wiring connector.
9 Refit the roadwheel, then lower the car to the ground and tighten the roadwheel bolts to the specified torque.

24.5 Disconnect the small vacuum pipe

Rear wheel sensor

Removal

10 Chock the front wheels, then jack up the rear of the car and support it on axle stands (see *Jacking and vehicle support*). Remove the appropriate roadwheel.
11 Remove the sensor as described in paragraphs 4 and 5, for front wheel speed sensor.

Refitting

12 Refit the sensor as described above in paragraphs 6 to 9.

Reluctor rings

13 The reluctor rings are integral with the wheel bearings (front and rear), and can only be inspected after removal of the hub assembly. If faulty, the bearings must be renewed as described in Chapter 10, Section 3 (front and Chapter 10, Section 9 (rear).

24 Servo unit vacuum pump (diesel models) – testing, removal and refitting

Testing

1 The operation of the braking system vacuum pump can be checked using a vacuum gauge. First, remove the engine top cover to access the vacuum hose.
2 Disconnect the vacuum hose from the pump, and connect the gauge to the pump union using a suitable length of hose.
3 Start the engine and allow it to idle, and then measure the vacuum created by the pump. As a guide, after one minute, a minimum of approximately 500 mm Hg should be recorded. If the vacuum registered is significantly less than this, it is likely that the pump is faulty. However, seek the advice of a VW dealer before condemning the pump.
4 Reconnect the vacuum hose. Overhaul of the vacuum pump is not possible, since no major components are available separately for it. If faulty, the complete pump assembly must be renewed.

Removal

Note: *A new pump O-ring will be required on refitting.*

5 Disconnect the small vacuum pipe from the vacuum hose connector on the top of the vacuum pump **(see illustration)**.
6 Release the securing clips and remove the air intake hose from across the end of the cylinder head, to access the vacuum pump.
7 Pull the vacuum hose from the top of the pump, noting the rubber seal may stay on the vacuum pump outlet pipe **(see illustration)**.
8 Unscrew the four mounting bolts and withdraw the vacuum pump from the cylinder head **(see illustration)**. Recover the O-ring seal and discard, as a new one will be required for refitting.

Refitting

9 Fit the new O-ring seal to the vacuum pump, and apply a smear of oil to aid installation.
10 Manoeuvre the vacuum pump into position, making sure that the slot in the pump drive gear aligns with the slot on the pump driveshaft.
11 Refit the pump retaining bolts, and tighten to the specified torque.
12 Reconnect the vacuum hoses and secure with the retaining clip (where fitted). If the vacuum hose seal is still fitted to the outlet pipe on the vacuum pump, remove it and fit it inside the end of the vacuum hose before refitting.
13 Refit the air intake pipe and engine top cover.

24.7 Remove the vacuum hose and rubber seal

25 Servo unit electric vacuum pump – testing, removal and refitting

Note: *The electric vacuum pump is only fitted to petrol models with dual clutch (automatic) transmission.*

Testing

1 With the engine stopped, depress the brake pedal several times to exhaust the vacuum in the servo unit. The pedal will become firm.
2 Start the engine, and then slowly depress the brake pedal. An audible 'click' must be heard as the electric vacuum pump is activated, and the pedal will be easier to depress. Confirmation that the pump is running can be made by an assistant touching the pump as the pedal is depressed.

24.8 Vacuum pump securing bolts (arrowed)

3 Overhaul of the electric vacuum pump is not possible, therefore, if faulty, the pump must be renewed.

Removal

4 The electric brake vacuum pump is located on a bracket on the front right-hand side of the engine compartment, behind the headlamp unit.
5 Disconnect the vacuum hose from the pump.
6 Disconnect the wiring from the vacuum pump and release it from the clip.
7 Unscrew the bolts securing the bracket to the inner wing panel and withdraw the assembly from the engine compartment.
8 Unbolt the bracket from the vacuum pump.

Refitting

9 Refitting is a reversal of removal.

Chapter 10
Suspension and steering

Contents

Degrees of difficulty

Easy, suitable for novice with little experience	**Fairly easy,** suitable for beginner with some experience	**Fairly difficult,** suitable for competent DIY mechanic	**Difficult,** suitable for experienced DIY mechanic	**Very difficult,** suitable for expert DIY or professional

Specifications

Front suspension

Type . . . . Independent, with MacPherson struts incorporating coil springs and telescopic shock absorbers. Anti-roll bar fitted to all models

Rear suspension

Type . . . . Transverse torsion beam axle with trailing arms. Separate gas-filled telescopic shock absorbers and coil springs. Anti-roll bar fitted to all models

Steering

Type . . . . Rack-and-pinion. Power assistance standard

Roadwheels

Type . . . . Aluminium alloy

Tyres

Standard sizes . . . . 175/70R14, 185/60R15, 195/55R15 and 215/45R16
Pressures . . . . See Weekly checks on page 0•16

Wheel alignment and steering angles*

Front wheel:

Camber angle:

Standard suspension	-28' ± 30'
Sports suspension	-39' ± 30'
Heavy duty suspension	-15' ± 30'
Maximum difference between sides (all models)	30'

Castor angle:

Standard suspension	4° 54' ± 30'
Sports suspension	5° 09' ± 30'
Heavy duty suspension	4° 40' ± 30'
Maximum difference between sides (all models)	30'
Toe setting	+10' ± 10'

Toe-out on turns (20° left or right):

Standard suspension	1° 19' ± 20'
Sports suspension	1° 20' ± 20'
Heavy duty suspension	1° 18' ± 20'

Rear wheel:

Camber angle	-1°30' ± 10'
Maximum difference between sides	30'

Toe setting (total track):

Standard suspension	+21' ± 10'
Sports suspension	+26' ± 10'
Heavy duty suspension	+16' ± 10'
Maximum difference between sides	20'

*Refer to a VW dealer for the latest recommendations.

Torque wrench settings

	Nm	lbf ft
Front suspension		
Anti-roll bar:		
Drop link nuts	40	30
Mounting clamp bolts*:		
Stage 1	20	15
Stage 2	Angle-tighten a further 90°	
Driveshaft/Hub nut (12 point – 36mm)*:		
Stage 1	50	37
Stage 2	Angle-tighten a further 45°	
Engine rear mounting link:		
To transmission bolts*:		
Stage 1	30	22
Stage 2	Angle-tighten a further 90°	
To subframe bolt*:		
Stage 1	40	30
Stage 2	Angle-tighten a further 90°	
Lower arm:		
Front pivot bolt*:		
Stage 1	70	52
Stage 2	Angle-tighten a further 90°	
Lower arm mounting bracket rear plate:		
Small bolts*:		
Stage 1	20	15
Stage 2	Angle-tighten a further 90°	
Large bolt*:		
Stage 1	70	52
Stage 2	Angle-tighten a further 90°	
Balljoint-to-lower arm nuts*	100	74
Balljoint nut*:		
Stage 1	20	15
Stage 2	Angle-tighten a further 90°	
Subframe-to-underbody bolts*:		
Stage 1	70	52
Stage 2	Angle-tighten a further 90°	
Suspension strut:		
Bottom clamp bolt nut*:		
Stage 1	60	44
Stage 2	Angle-tighten a further 90°	
Piston rod nut*	60	44
Upper mounting-to-body nut*	60	44

Torque wrench settings continued)

	Nm	lbf ft
Rear suspension		
Axle mounting bolts and nuts*:		
Stage 1	45	33
Stage 2	Angle-tighten a further 90°	
Hub nut (12-point)*:		
Stage 1	70	52
Stage 2	Angle-tighten a further 30°	
Shock absorber:		
Lower mounting bolt and nut*:		
Stage 1	40	30
Stage 2	Angle-tighten a further 90°	
Upper mounting bracket-to-body bolts*:		
Stage 1	30	22
Stage 2	Angle-tighten a further 90°	
Upper mounting nut to bracket*	25	18
Stub axle/bearing hub bolts*:		
Stage 1	30	22
Stage 2	Angle-tighten a further 90°	
Vehicle level sender:		
Sender to underbody (pop-rivet screw)	8	6
Sender link to lower arm.	6	4
Steering		
Power steering hose union to electric pump	30	22
Power steering hose union to steering gear:		
Supply (banjo bolt)	40	30
Return (union)	30	22
Steering column mounting bolts	23	17
Steering column lower universal joint clamp bolt*:		
Stage 1	20	15
Stage 2	Angle-tighten a further 180°	
Steering gear mounting bolts*:		
Stage 1	50	37
Stage 2	Angle-tighten a further 90°	
Steering wheel bolt*:		
Stage 1	30	22
Stage 2	Angle-tighten a further 90°	
Track rod balljoint nut*:		
Stage 1	20	15
Stage 2	Angle-tighten a further 90°	
Track rod balljoint locknut	50	37
Track rod inner balljoint to steering rack	80	59
Roadwheels		
Roadwheel bolts.	120	89

* Renew the nut/bolt every time it is removed

1 General information

The independent front suspension is of the MacPherson strut type, incorporating coil springs and integral telescopic shock absorbers. The struts are located by transverse lower suspension arms, which use rubber inner mounting bushes, and incorporate a balljoint at the outer ends. The front wheel bearing housings, which carry the wheel bearings, brake calipers and the hub/disc assemblies, are attached to the MacPherson struts by clamp bolts, and connected to the lower arms through the balljoints. A front anti-roll bar is fitted to all models. The anti-roll bar is rubber-mounted, and is connected to both lower suspension arms by short links.

The rear suspension consists of a torsion beam axle with telescopic shock absorbers and coil springs. An anti-roll bar is incorporated into the rear axle beam. One of three different rear axles may be fitted, according to which engine is fitted – each axle has different geometry and rigidity characteristics.

The safety steering column incorporates an intermediate shaft at its lower end. The intermediate shaft is connected to both the steering column and steering gear by universal joints, although the shaft is supplied as part of the column assembly and cannot be separated. Both the inner steering column and intermediate shaft have splined sections, which collapse during a major frontal impact. The outer column is also telescopic with two sections, to facilitate reach adjustment.

The steering gear is mounted onto the front subframe, and is connected by two track rods, with balljoints at their inner and outer ends, to the steering arms projecting rearwards from the wheel bearing housings. The track rod ends are threaded to the track rods in order to allow adjustment of the front wheel toe setting.

Electrically Powered Hydraulic Steering (EPHS) is fitted as standard on all UK models. The system electric pump and hydraulic fluid reservoir are located behind the front bumper, on the left-hand side.

All UK models are fitted with an Anti-lock Brake System (ABS), and most models can also be fitted with a Traction Control System (TCS), an Electronic Differential Lock (EDL) system and an Electronic Stability Program (ESP). The ABS may also be referred to as including EBD (Electronic Brake Distribution), which means it adjusts the front and rear braking forces according to the weight being carried, and the TCS may also be referred to as ASR (Anti Slip Regulation).

The TCS system prevents the front wheels from losing traction during acceleration by reducing the engine output. The system is switched on automatically when the engine is started, and it utilises the ABS system sensors to monitor the rotational speeds of the front wheels.

The ESP system extends the ABS, TCS and EDL functions to reduce wheel spin in difficult driving conditions. It does this by using highly sensitive sensors that monitor the speed of the car, lateral movement of the car, the brake pressure, and the steering angle of the front wheels. If, for example, the car is tending to oversteer, the brake will be applied to the front outer wheel to correct the situation. If the car is tending to understeer, the brake will be applied to the rear inside wheel. The steering angle of the front wheels is monitored by an angle sensor on the top of the steering column.

The TCS/ESP systems are switched on automatically each time the engine is started, and should be left on except when driving with snow chains, driving in snow or driving on loose surfaces, when some wheel spin may be advantageous. The ESP switch is located in the centre of the facia.

Some models are also fitted with an Electronic Differential Lock (EDL) that reduces unequal traction from the front wheels. If one front wheel spins 100 rpm or more faster than the other, the faster wheel is slowed down by applying the brake to that wheel. The system is not the same as the traditional differential lock, where the actual differential gears are locked. Because the system applies a front brake, in the event of a brake disc overheating the system will shut down until the disc has cooled. No warning light is displayed if the system shuts down. As is the case with the TCS system, the EDL system uses the ABS sensors to monitor front wheel speeds.

2 Front wheel bearing housing – removal and refitting

Note: *All self-locking nuts and bolts disturbed on removal must be renewed as a matter of course.*

2.3 Removing the 12-point driveshaft retaining nut

2.9a Unscrew the ball joint-to-lower arm nuts…

2.9b …and detach the lower arm from the ball joint studs

2.11 Undo the strut lower securing bolt - arrowed

Removal

1 Remove the wheel trim/hub cap (as applicable) and loosen the driveshaft retaining nut with the car resting on its wheels. Also loosen the wheel bolts.

2 Apply the handbrake, then jack up the front of the car and support it on axle stands (see *Jacking and vehicle support*). Remove the front roadwheel and also remove the engine compartment undershield.

3 Unscrew and remove the driveshaft retaining nut **(see illustration)**. Discard, as a new one will be required for refitting.

4 Unscrew the nut securing the link to the anti-roll bar, and separate the link.

5 Remove the ABS wheel sensor as described in Chapter 9 Section 23.

6 Remove the brake disc as described in Chapter 9, Section 6. This procedure includes removing the brake caliper; however **do not** disconnect the hydraulic brake hose from the caliper. Using a piece of wire or string, tie the caliper to the front suspension coil spring, to avoid placing any strain on the hydraulic brake hose.

7 Unbolt the splash plate from the wheel bearing housing.

8 Loosen the nut securing the steering track rod balljoint to the wheel bearing housing. To do this, fit a ring spanner to the nut, then, where applicable, hold the balljoint pin stationary using an Allen key. With the nut removed, it may be possible to release the balljoint from the wheel bearing housing by turning the balljoint pin with an Allen key. If not, leave the nut on by a few turns to protect the threads, then use a universal balljoint separator to release the balljoint. Remove the nut completely once the taper has been released.

9 Unscrew the front suspension lower balljoint-to-lower arm retaining nuts **(see illustrations)**, then lever down the lower arm to release the arm from the balljoint studs.

10 Now use a soft-faced mallet to tap the driveshaft from the hub splines while pulling out the bottom end of the wheel bearing housing. If the driveshaft is tight on the splines, it may be necessary to use a puller bolted to the hub to remove it.

11 Note which way round it is fitted, then unscrew the nut and remove the clamp bolt securing the wheel bearing housing to the bottom of the strut **(see illustration)**.

12 The wheel bearing housing must now be released from the strut. To do this, VW technicians insert a special tool into the split wheel bearing housing, and turn it through 90° to open up the clamp. A similar tool can be made out of an old screwdriver, or alternatively a suitable cold chisel can be driven into the split as a wedge. Slightly press inwards the top of the wheel bearing housing, and then push it downwards from the bottom of the strut **(see illustrations)**.

13 If required, unscrew the nut and remove the balljoint from the bottom of the wheel bearing housing. If it is tight, use a balljoint separator.

Refitting

14 Note that all self-locking nuts and bolts disturbed on removal must be renewed as a matter of course.

15 If removed, refit the balljoint to the wheel bearing housing and tighten the nut to the specified torque.

16 Lift the wheel bearing housing into position and engage the top of the wheel bearing housing with the bottom of the suspension strut; making sure that the hole in the side plate aligns with the holes in the split housing. Once in position, remove the tool used to open the split.

17 Ensure that the driveshaft outer joint and hub splines are clean and dry, and then engage the hub with the driveshaft. Fit the new hub nut, tightening it by hand only at this stage.

18 Insert the strut-to-wheel bearing housing clamp bolt from the rear, and fit the new retaining nut. Tighten the nut to the specified torque.

19 Refit the lower arm balljoint and tighten the new nuts to the specified torque.

20 Refit the track rod balljoint to the wheel bearing housing, then fit a new retaining nut and tighten it to the specified torque. If necessary, hold the balljoint pin with an Allen key while tightening the nut.

21 Refit the splash plate and tighten the bolts.

22 Refit the brake disc and caliper with reference to Chapter 9, Section 6.

23 Refit the ABS wheel sensor as described in Chapter 9, Section 23.

24 Refit the link to the anti-roll bar and tighten the nut to the specified torque.

25 Ensure the outer joint is drawn fully into the hub, tighten the new driveshaft retaining nut in the stages given in the Specifications, then refit the roadwheel and engine compartment undershield.

26 Lower the vehicle to the ground, and tighten the roadwheel bolts to the specified torque.

3 Front hub and bearings – renewal

Note: *The front hub is supplied complete with bearings, and it is not possible to renew the bearings separately. Note that the hub and bearing assembly must be assembled to the hub carrier in one single operation, by applying force to the bearing and* **not** *the hub. VW technicians use special tools that locate only on the bearing, however, it is possible to fabricate spacers to insert between the hub flange and the bearing, making it possible to apply pressure to the hub itself. If these tools cannot be obtained of fabricated, it is recommended that a VW dealer carry out the work.*

1 Remove the wheel bearing housing as described in Section 2.

2.12a Tool used by VW technicians to open up the split wheel bearing housing

2.12c Withdrawing the suspension strut from the wheel bearing housing

2.12b Using a cold chisel to open up the wheel bearing housing

2.12d Wheel bearing housing

2 A press will be required to remove the hub and bearing, however, if such a tool is not available, a large bench vice and spacers (such as large sockets) will serve as an adequate substitute. As a last resort, it is possible to use a lump hammer to drive out the hub and bearing **(see illustration)**.

3 Support the wheel bearing housing securely on blocks or in a vice. Using a metal tube, which bears on the inner end of the hub, press the hub and bearing out of the housing **(see illustration)**. Note that the internal circlip, retaining the bearing in the housing, will be destroyed during the removal operation.

4 Thoroughly clean the wheel bearing housing, removing all traces of dirt and grease, and polish away any burrs or raised edges, which might hinder reassembly. Check for cracks or any other signs of wear or damage, and

renew if necessary. Note that the new hub and bearing is supplied with a new circlip, which locates automatically if the special VW tool is used.

5 On reassembly, apply a light coating of molybdenum disulphide grease to the bearing outer race and bearing surface of the wheel bearing housing.

6 If using the special VW tool fit it to the bearing, then draw the assembly into the hub carrier until the circlip is heard to click into position. **Note:** *The tools include grippers and spacers that cannot be fabricated locally.* Check that the hub rotates freely, and wipe off any excess oil or grease.

7 If not using the special tools, make up suitable spacers to fit firmly between the hub flange and the bearing, then press the hub with bearing fully into the wheel bearing housing.

3.2 Driving out the hub and bearing with a lump hammer

3.3 Using a press to remove the hub and bearing from the wheel bearing housing

3.7a Pressing the hub and bearing into the wheel bearing housing

Using this method, it may be necessary to tap the circlip into its groove **(see illustrations)**.

8 Refit the wheel bearing housing as described in Section 2.

4 Front suspension strut – removal, overhaul and refitting

Note: *This section describes removal of the suspension strut leaving the wheel bearing housing in situ, however, if necessary it can be removed together with the wheel bearing housing, then separated on the bench. All self-locking nuts and bolts disturbed on removal must be renewed as a matter of course.*

Removal

1 Remove the wheel trim/hub cap (as

4.3 Undo the link rod upper securing nut - arrowed

4.10 Unclip the cover and undo the retaining nut

3.7b Make sure the circlip is fully entered in its groove

applicable) and loosen the driveshaft retaining bolt (hub bolt) with the vehicle resting on its wheels. **Note:** *Do not loosen the hub bolt more than 90° at this stage, or the wheel bearing may be damaged.* Also loosen the wheel bolts.

2 Apply the handbrake, then jack up the front of the vehicle and support it on axle stands (see *Jacking and vehicle support*). Remove the appropriate roadwheel.

3 Unscrew the nut and disconnect the anti-roll bar link from the strut **(see illustration)**.

4 Release the ABS sensor wiring from the base of the strut.

5 Unscrew and remove the driveshaft retaining nut **(see illustration)**.

6 Note which way round it is fitted, then unscrew the nut and remove the clamp bolt securing the wheel bearing housing to the bottom of the strut **(see illustration 2.11)**.

7 The wheel bearing housing must now

4.5 Removing the 12-point driveshaft retaining nut

4.12 Compress the coil spring with the tool

be released from the strut. To do this, VW technicians insert a special tool into the split wheel bearing housing, and turn it through 90° to open up the clamp. A similar tool such as an Allen key can be used, or alternatively a suitable cold chisel can be driven into the split as a wedge. Slightly press inwards the top of the wheel bearing housing, and then push it downwards to release it from the bottom of the strut **(see illustrations 2.12a, 2.12b & 2.12c)**.

8 As the wheel bearing housing is pressed downwards, use a soft-faced mallet to tap the driveshaft from the hub splines. If the driveshaft is tight on the splines, it may be necessary to use a puller bolted to the hub to remove it. Remove the bottom of the suspension strut from the top of the wheel bearing housing. Support the wheel bearing housing to one side without straining the hydraulic brake hose.

9 Remove the wiper arms and the plenum chamber cover (Chapter 12, Section 17 & Chapter 12, Section 18).

10 Support the strut, then unclip the cover and unscrew the upper mounting nut and lower the strut from under the wheel arch **(see illustration)**.

Overhaul

⚠ *Warning: Before attempting to dismantle the suspension strut, a suitable tool to hold the coil spring in compression must be obtained. Adjustable coil spring compressors are readily available, and are recommended for this operation. Any attempt to dismantle the strut without such a tool is likely to result in damage or personal injury.*

11 With the strut removed from the car, clean away all external dirt. If necessary, mount it upright in a vice during the dismantling procedure.

12 Fit the spring compressor, and compress the coil spring until all tension is relieved from the upper spring seat **(see illustration)**.

13 Unscrew and remove the upper centre retaining nut, whilst retaining the strut piston with a suitable Allen key, then remove the rubber mounting, thrust bearing, and spring upper plate **(see illustrations)**.

4.13a Unscrew the upper centre nut...

4.13b ...remove the rubber mounting...

4.13c ...thrust bearing...

4.13d ...and spring upper plate

4.14 Withdraw the coil spring with compressor

4.15a Remove the protective sleeve/ gaiter...

4.15b ...and slide the bump stop from the strut piston rod

14 Carefully withdraw the coil spring, still with the spring compressor attached and move it to one side **(see illustration)**. Put it in a safe place to prevent it from getting knocked, whilst still in the compressed position.

15 Remove the protective gaiter/sleeve, and then remove the bump stop from the strut piston rod **(see illustrations)**.

16 With the strut assembly now completely dismantled, examine all the components for wear, damage or deformation, and check the bearing for smoothness of operation. Renew any of the components as necessary.

17 Examine the strut for signs of fluid leakage. Check the strut piston for signs of pitting along its entire length, and check the strut body for signs of damage. While holding it in an upright position, test the operation of the strut by moving the piston through a full stroke, and then through short strokes of 50 to 100 mm. In both cases, the resistance

felt should be smooth and continuous. If the resistance is jerky, or uneven, or if there is any visible sign of wear or damage to the strut, renewal is necessary.

18 If any doubt exists about the condition of the coil spring, carefully remove the spring compressors, and check the spring for distortion and signs of cracking. Renew the spring if it is damaged or distorted, or if there is any doubt as to its condition.

19 Inspect all other components for signs of damage or deterioration, and renew as necessary.

20 Assemble the bump stop and protective gaiter/sleeve to the strut piston, and then refit the coil spring (together with the compressor tool) onto the strut, making sure its lower (larger diameter) end is correctly located against the spring seat stop **(see illustration)**.

21 Fit the spring upper plate, upper bearing race and rubber mounting, making sure the

rubber mounting is fitted the correct way up **(see illustration)**.

22 Refit the new upper retaining nut and tighten to the specified torque while holding the piston rod with an Allen key. The spring compressor can now be removed from the spring assembly.

Refitting

23 Manoeuvre the strut into position under the wheel arch, and locate in the suspension strut turret. Fit the stop plate on top of the strut and fit a new retaining nut. Tighten the nut to the specified torque.

24 With the outer end of the driveshaft engaged with the splines in the centre of the hub, engage the top of the wheel bearing housing with the bottom of the suspension strut.

25 Make sure the hole in the strut side plate aligns with the holes in the split housing for retaining bolt **(see illustration)**. Raise the

4.20 The end of the coil springs must locate correctly in the seatings

4.25 Make sure the hole in the side plate (arrowed) is aligned for the bolt

4.21 Make sure the rubber mounting is fitted the correct way up

5.3a Lower arm front mounting bolt - arrowed

housing, while pressing it inwards to assist entry. Use a trolley jack if necessary. When fully entered, remove the tool used to open the split.

26 Insert the new strut-to-wheel bearing housing bolt from the rear, and fit the new retaining nut. Tighten the nut to the specified torque. Also fit the new driveshaft/hub nut, tightening it by hand only at this stage.

27 Refit the ABS sensor wiring to the bracket at the base of the strut.

28 Connect the anti-roll bar link to the strut and fit a new retaining nut and tighten to the specified torque.

29 Refit the plenum chamber cover and wiper arms.

30 Ensure that the outer joint is drawn fully into the hub, and then refit the roadwheel. Have an assistant depress the brake pedal, and then tighten the driveshaft retaining nut in the stages given in the Specifications. It is recommended that an angle gauge be used to ensure the correct tightening angle. **Note:** *The car must not be standing on its wheels when tightening the nut, or the wheel bearing may be damaged.*

31 Lower the vehicle to the ground and tighten the roadwheel bolts to the specified torque.

---

5 Front suspension lower arm –
removal, overhaul and refitting

Note: *All self-locking nuts and bolts disturbed on removal must be renewed as a matter of course.*

6.2a The front suspension lower balljoint on the wheel bearing housing

5.3b Lower arm rear mounting bolt - arrowed

Removal

1 Apply the handbrake, then jack up the front of the car and support it on axle stands (see *Jacking and vehicle support*). Remove the appropriate front roadwheel and the engine compartment undershield.

2 Unscrew the front suspension lower balljoint-to-lower arm retaining nuts, then lever down the lower arm to release the arm from the balljoint studs **(see illustration 2.9a & 2.9b)**.

3 Unscrew and remove the lower arm front and rear pivot bolts from the subframe **(see illustrations)**.

4 Swivel out the front of the lower arm, and withdraw it forwards to release it from the subframe.

Overhaul

5 Thoroughly clean the lower arm and bracket, then check carefully for cracks or any other signs of wear or damage, paying particular attention to the pivot and rear mounting rubber bushes. If either bush requires renewal, the lower arm and bracket should be taken to a VW dealer or suitably equipped garage. A hydraulic press and suitable spacers are required to press out the bushes and install the new ones. When fitting a new mounting bush, make sure that it is correctly aligned with any markings on the arm. If no alignment marks are visible, then alignment marks should be made, so that correct fitting of the bushes is carried out.

Refitting

6 Locate the lower arm into the subframe.

6.2b Using a universal balljoint separator tool to remove the lower balljoint

7 Insert the front and rear pivot bolts and tighten to the specified torque.

8 Refit the balljoint to the lower arm using new nuts, then tighten the nuts to the specified torque.

9 Refit the roadwheel and undershield, and then lower the car to the ground.

---

6 Front suspension lower arm balljoint – removal, inspection and refitting

Note: *All self-locking nuts and bolts disturbed on removal must be renewed as a matter of course.*

Removal

Method 1

1 Remove the wheel bearing housing as described in Section 2.

2 Unscrew and remove the balljoint retaining nut **(see illustrations)**, then release the balljoint from the wheel bearing housing using a universal balljoint separator. Withdraw the balljoint.

Method 2

3 Remove the wheel trim/hub cap (as applicable) and loosen the driveshaft retaining nut (hub nut) with the vehicle resting on its wheels. **Note:** *Do not loosen the hub nut more than 90° at this stage, or the wheel bearing may be damaged.* Also loosen the wheel bolts.

4 Apply the handbrake, then jack up the front of the vehicle and support it on axle stands (see *Jacking and vehicle support*). Remove the appropriate roadwheel.

5 Unscrew and remove the driveshaft retaining nut. Discard, as a new one will be required for refitting.

6 Unscrew the front suspension lower balljoint-to-lower arm retaining nuts, then lever the lower arm down to release the balljoint studs **(see illustrations 2.9a & 2.9b)**. Now use a soft-faced mallet to tap the driveshaft from the hub splines while pulling out the bottom end of the wheel bearing housing. If the driveshaft is tight on the splines, it may be necessary to use a puller bolted to the hub to remove it. It is not necessary to remove the driveshaft completely from the hub. Retain the wheel bearing housing away from the lower arm by inserting a block of wood between the strut and the inner body panel.

7 Unscrew and remove the balljoint retaining nut, then release the balljoint from the wheel bearing housing using a universal balljoint separator **(see illustration 6.2a & 6.2b)**. Withdraw the balljoint.

Inspection

8 With the balljoint removed, check that it moves freely, without any sign of roughness. Check also that the balljoint rubber gaiter shows no sign of deterioration, and is free from cracks and splits. Renew as necessary.

Refitting

Method 1

9 Fit the balljoint to the wheel bearing housing and fit the new retaining nut. Tighten the nut to the specified torque setting, noting that the balljoint shank can be retained with an Allen key if necessary to prevent it from rotating.

10 Refit the wheel bearing housing with reference to Section 2.

Method 2

11 Fit the balljoint to the wheel bearing housing and fit the new retaining nut. Tighten the nut to the specified torque setting, noting that the balljoint shank can be retained with an Allen key if necessary to prevent it from rotating.

12 Remove the wooden block and move the strut inwards, then refit the balljoint to the lower arm using new nuts, and tighten them to the specified torque.

13 Refit the driveshaft retaining nut and tighten it sufficiently to draw the driveshaft fully into the hub, and then refit the roadwheel.

14 Have an assistant depress the brake pedal, and then tighten the driveshaft retaining nut in the stages given in the Specifications. It is recommended that an angle gauge be used to ensure the correct tightening angle. **Note:** *The car must not be standing on its wheels when tightening the nut, or the wheel bearing may be damaged.*

15 Lower the vehicle to the ground and tighten the roadwheel bolts.

7 Front anti-roll bar – removal and refitting

Note: *All self-locking nuts and bolts disturbed on removal must be renewed as a matter of course.*

Removal

1 Apply the handbrake, then jack up the front of the car and support it on axle stands (see *Jacking and vehicle support*). Remove both front roadwheels and the engine compartment undershield.

2 Unscrew the bolts securing the engine rear mounting link to the bottom of the transmission.

3 Unscrew the bolts securing the anti-roll bar clamps to the rear of the lower arm brackets **(see illustration)**. Note that the lower right-hand bolt cannot be completely removed at this stage.

4 Unscrew the nuts and disconnect the lower part of the connecting/drop links from the ends of the anti-roll bar **(see illustration)**.

5 Unscrew the steering gear mounting bolts from the bottom of the subframe. Tie the steering gear to the underbody.

6 Mark the position of the subframe on the underbody to retain the wheel alignment. Also, mark the anti-roll bar to indicate which way round it is fitted, and the position of the rubber mounting bushes. This will aid refitting.

7.3 Anti-roll bar clamp securing bolts - arrowed

7 Support the subframe on a trolley jack, then unscrew the mounting bolts and lower the subframe approximately 4 cm.

8 Remove the clamp, then turn the anti-roll bar upwards and withdraw towards the rear of the car. Remove the rubber mounting bushes from the bar.

9 Carefully examine the anti-roll bar components for signs of wear, damage or deterioration, paying particular attention to the rubber mounting bushes. Renew worn components as necessary.

Refitting

10 Fit the rubber mounting bushes to the anti-roll bar, aligning them with the marks made prior to removal.

11 Manoeuvre the anti-roll bar into position, then refit the mounting clamps and insert the retaining bolts. Ensure that the bush markings are still aligned with the marks on the bars, and then tighten the mounting clamp retaining bolts to the specified torque.

12 Raise the subframe and align with the previously made marks. Insert the mounting bolts and tighten to the specified torque and angle.

13 Untie the steering gear, then secure it to the subframe with the bolts tightened to the specified torque.

14 Refit the anti-roll bar side connecting links and tighten the nuts to the specified torque.

15 Refit the engine rear mounting link bolts, then push the transmission forwards as far as possible and tighten the bolts to the specified torque.

16 Refit the roadwheels and engine compartment undershield, then lower the car to the ground and tighten the wheel bolts to the specified torque.

8 Front anti-roll bar connecting link – removal and refitting

Note: *All self-locking nuts and bolts disturbed on removal must be renewed as a matter of course.*

Removal

1 Apply the handbrake, then jack up the front of the car and support it on axle stands (see

7.4 Connecting link/drop link lower ball joint - arrowed

Jacking and vehicle support). Remove the relevant front roadwheel.

2 Unscrew the nuts securing the anti-roll bar drop link to the front suspension strut and anti-roll bar and remove it **(see illustration)**.

3 Inspect the link rubbers for signs of damage or deterioration. If evident, renew the drop link complete.

Refitting

4 Refitting is a reversal of removal, but delay fully tightening the link bolts until the weight of the car is on the front suspension.

9 Rear hub assembly – removal and refitting

Note: *The rear wheel bearings cannot be renewed independently of the rear hub, because the outer races are formed in the hub itself. If excessive wear is evident, the rear hub must be renewed complete. The rear hub nut must always be renewed after removal.*

Removal

1 Chock the front roadwheels, then jack up the rear of the car and support on axle stands (see *Jacking and vehicle support*). Release the handbrake and remove the relevant rear roadwheel.

2 Remove the rear brake disc or drum (as applicable) with reference to Chapter 9, Section 6 for brake disc or Chapter 9, Section 10 for brake drum.

8.2 Connecting link/drop link upper and lower securing nuts - arrowed

9.3 Use a cold chisel or screwdriver to remove the rear hub dust cap

9.4 Unscrew the self-locking 12-point hub nut...

9.5 ...and remove the hub and bearings from the stub axle

9.8 Using a socket to drive the hub onto the stub axle

3 Remove the dust cap from the centre of the hub using a screwdriver or cold chisel (see illustration).

4 Unscrew and remove the self-locking 12-point hub nut. Note that it is tightened to a high torque and a socket extension bar may be required to loosen it (see illustration). It is recommended that the nut is renewed whenever removed.

5 Using a suitable puller if necessary, pull the hub and bearings from the stub axle (see illustration). Take care not to damage the ABS sensor ring on the inside of the hub.

6 Examine the hub and bearings for wear, pitting and damage. If all the bearing surfaces and balls appear to be in good order upon inspection, the hub may be re-used.

Refitting

7 Wipe clean the stub axle, then check that

10.3 ABS rear wheel speed sensor

the bearing races are adequately lubricated with suitable grease.

8 Locate the hub as far as possible onto the stub axle. VW technicians use a special drift to drive the inner race onto the stub; however, a suitable metal tube or deep socket will do the same (see illustration). Make sure that the tube is only located on the inner race.

9 Screw on the new self-locking nut and tighten it to the specified torque and angle.

10 Check the dust cap for damage and renew it if necessary. Use a hammer to carefully tap the cap into the hub. **Note:** *A badly fitting dust cap will allow moisture to enter the bearing, reducing its service life.*

11 Refit the brake disc or drum (as applicable) with reference to Chapter 9, Section 6 for brake disc or Chapter 9, Section 10 for brake drum.

12 Refit the roadwheel and lower the car to the ground.

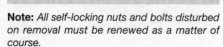

10 Rear stub axle – removal and refitting

Note: *All self-locking nuts and bolts disturbed on removal must be renewed as a matter of course.*

Removal

1 Chock the front roadwheels, then jack up the rear of the car and support on axle stands (see *Jacking and vehicle support*). Release the handbrake and remove the relevant roadwheel.

2 Remove the rear hub as described in Section 9.

3 Disconnect the wiring, then unscrew the bolt and remove the ABS speed sensor from the rear axle trailing arm (see illustration).

4 Unscrew the mounting bolts securing the stub axle and backplate to the rear axle trailing arm. Carefully withdraw the backplate and stub axle, taking care not to bend the brake line excessively. If necessary, remove the rear wheel cylinder or rear caliper as applicable with reference to Chapter 9.

5 Inspect the stub axle for signs of damage and renew if necessary. **Do not** attempt to straighten the stub axle.

Refitting

6 Ensure the mating surfaces of the axle; stub axle and backplate are clean and dry. Check the backplate for signs of damage.

7 Refit the stub axle together with the backplate, then insert the new bolts and progressively tighten to the specified torque.

8 If removed, refit the rear wheel cylinder or rear caliper as applicable with reference to Chapter 9.

9 Refit the speed sensor, tighten the bolt, and reconnect the wiring.

10 Refit the rear hub with reference to Section 9.

11 Refit the roadwheel and lower the car to the ground.

11 Rear suspension shock absorber and coil spring – removal, inspection and refitting

Note: *All self-locking nuts and bolts disturbed on removal must be renewed as a matter of course.*

Shock absorber

Removal

1 Before removing the shock absorber, an idea of how effective it is can be gained by depressing the rear corner of the car. If the shock absorber is in good condition, the body should rise then settle in its normal position. If the body oscillates more than this, the shock absorber is defective. **Note:** *The rear shock absorbers can be renewed individually if necessary.*

2 Chock the front roadwheels, then jack up the rear of the car and support on axle stands (see *Jacking and vehicle support*). Remove the relevant rear roadwheel.

3 Position a trolley jack and block of wood beneath the coil spring position on the trailing arm, and raise the arm so that the shock absorber is slightly compressed (see illustration). Note that on some models, it may be necessary to remove the stone protection guard first.

4 On models with gas-discharge (Xenon) headlights, disconnect the tension rod for the rear sender.

11.3 Position the trolley jack and block of wood beneath the trailing arm

11.5 Remove the shock absorber lower mounting bolt

11.6 Unscrew the shock absorber upper mounting bolts - arrowed

5 Unscrew and remove the shock absorber lower mounting nut and bolt, and lever the bottom of the shock absorber from the trailing arm **(see illustration)**.

6 Support the shock absorber, then unscrew the upper mounting bolts located in the rear wheel arch. Lower the shock absorber and withdraw from under the wheel arch **(see illustration)**.

7 With the shock absorber on the bench, prise off the cover, then unscrew the nut from the top of the piston rod and remove the upper mounting bracket. The piston rod can be held stationary with a pair of grips on the raised peg on the top of the rod. Remove the rubber stop and protectors from the top of the rod.

Inspection

8 If necessary, the action of the shock absorber can be checked by mounting it upright in a vice. Fully depress the rod, and then pull it up fully. The piston rod must move smoothly over its complete length.

Refitting

9 Locate the rubber stop and protectors on the piston rod followed by the upper mounting bracket. Fit the new nut and tighten to the specified torque while holding the piston rod as for removal, then refit the cover.

10 Locate the shock absorber in the rear wheel arch, then insert the upper mounting bolts and tighten to the specified torque.

11 Locate the bottom of the shock absorber in the trailing arm, insert the bolt from the outside, then screw on the nut. Raise the trailing arm with the jack to take the weight of the rear suspension, then tighten the lower mounting bolt to the specified torque.

12 Lower the jack, and where necessary refit the stone protection guard.

13 On models with gas-discharge (Xenon) headlights, reconnect the tension rod and adjust it so that the lever points towards the rear and not upwards when the rear suspension is flexed.

14 Refit the roadwheel and lower the car to the ground.

Coil spring

Note: *It is possible to remove the rear coil spring without the use of a coil spring compressor; both methods are described in the following paragraphs.*

 Warning: Adjustable coil spring compressors are readily available, and are recommended for this operation.

15 Chock the front roadwheels, then jack up the rear of the car and support on axle stands (see *Jacking and vehicle support*). Remove the relevant rear roadwheel.

16 If removing the left-hand rear coil spring, it may be necessary to release the exhaust rubber mountings and move the exhaust tail pipe/silencer to one side.

With a spring compressor

17 Support the trailing arm with a trolley jack, then fit the tool to the coil spring and compress it until it can be removed from the trailing arm and underbody. With the coil spring on the bench, carefully release the tension of the tool and remove it.

11.20 Release the ABS sensor wiring from the bracket on the trailing arm

11.21b ...then release the coil spring from its lower seat...

Without a spring compressor

18 Position a trolley jack and block of wood beneath the coil spring position on the trailing arm, and raise the arm so that the shock absorber is slightly compressed. Note on some models, it may be necessary to remove the stone protection guard first.

19 Unscrew and remove the shock absorber lower mounting nut and bolt, and lever the bottom of the shock absorber from the trailing arm.

20 Release the ABS sensor wiring from the bracket on the trailing arm **(see illustration)**.

21 Lower the trolley jack and remove it from under the trailing arm, then carefully lever the arm down until the coil spring can be removed. Lever against a block of wood to prevent damage to the underbody. Make sure that the car is adequately supported on the axle stands **(see illustrations)**.

11.21a Lever down the trailing arm...

11.21c ...and underbody seat

11.22 Recover the upper and lower spring seats

Inspection

22 With the coil spring removed, recover the upper and lower spring seats and check them for damage **(see illustration)**. Obtain new ones if necessary. Also clean the spring locations on the underbody and trailing arm.

Refitting

23 Refitting is a reversal of removal, but make sure that the upper spring seat is located correctly on the top of the coil spring, with the spring end abutting the shoulder on the seat. The lower seat is circular and locates only in the centre of the spring. Before tightening the shock absorber lower mounting bolt to the specified torque, raise the trailing arm to its normal running position. If removed, make sure the exhaust rear tail pipe/silencer is secured in the rubber mountings.

12 Rear anti-roll bar –
removal and refitting

The rear anti-roll bar runs along the length of the rear axle beam. It is an integral part of the axle assembly, and cannot be removed. If the anti-roll bar is damaged, which is unlikely, the complete axle assembly must be renewed.

13 Rear axle assembly –
removal and refitting

Note: *All self-locking nuts and bolts disturbed*

13.7 Flexible brake hose on the rear axle and underbody

on removal must be renewed as a matter of course.

Removal

1 Chock the front roadwheels, then jack up the rear of the car and support on axle stands positioned beneath the underbody (see *Jacking and vehicle support*). Remove both rear roadwheels. Fully release the handbrake.
2 Working on each side at a time, slightly raise the trailing arm so that the shock absorber is not fully extended, then unscrew and remove the shock absorber upper mounting bolts from inside the rear wheel arch. Carefully lower the trailing arm to relieve the tension in the coil spring.
3 On models fitted with gas-discharge (Xenon) headlights, disconnect the tension rod at the rear of the vehicle level sensor. If necessary, disconnect the wiring and unbolt the sensor.
4 With both shock absorber upper mountings detached, lower the trailing arms until the coil springs and seats can be removed.
5 Remove the stone protection plates from the trailing arms where fitted, then unscrew the lower mounting bolts and remove the shock absorbers from the rear axle.
6 Release the handbrake cable from the supports/clips on the rear axle and underbody.
7 Pull out the clips and disconnect the flexible brake hoses from the supports on the rear axle and underbody bracket on both sides **(see illustration)**. **Do not** disconnect the rigid brake lines from the hoses.
8 Refer to Section 10 and remove the rear stub axles from the rear trailing arms. Release the rigid pipes from their clips and place the rear wheel cylinders or calipers (as applicable) to one side, together with the handbrake cables. Where fitted, also unbolt the rear brake load regulator.
9 Support the rear axle with a trolley jack, and then unscrew and remove the rear axle front mounting bolts from the underbody brackets **(see illustration)**.
10 Manoeuvre the rear axle down from the underbody brackets and withdraw from under the car. The help of an assistant is recommended.
11 Inspect the rear axle mountings for signs of damage or deterioration, and refer to Section 14 if renewal is necessary.

13.9 Rear axle front mounting bolt - arrowed

Refitting

12 Apply a little brake grease or soapy water to the kidney-shaped cavity in the front mounting rubbers, then manoeuvre the rear axle into the underbody brackets and insert the mounting bolts from the outside. Screw on the nuts finger-tight at this stage. **Note:** *Make sure that the bolts are inserted through the centres of the rubber mountings and are not located in one of the three off-centre cut-outs. If the bolts are not correctly centred, the rear wheel alignment will be incorrect causing excessive tyre wear.*
13 Refit the rear stub axles as described in Section 10. Secure the brake lines to their clips, and where applicable refit the rear brake load regulator.
14 Refit the flexible brake hoses to the supports and secure with the clips.
15 Refit the handbrake cables and locate them in the supports/clips.
16 Locate the shock absorbers on the trailing arms and insert the lower mounting bolts loosely.
17 On models with gas-discharge (Xenon) headlights, refit the vehicle level sensor if removed, then reconnect the wiring and tension rod.
18 Carefully locate the coil springs and seats on the rear axle with reference to Section 11.
19 Working on each side at a time, raise the trailing arm until the shock absorber upper mounting bolts can be inserted. Tighten the bolts to the specified torque.
20 Working on each side at a time, raise the trailing arm with a trolley jack until the weight of the car is taken on the coil spring. Fully tighten the front mounting bolts to the specified torque, and then tighten the shock absorber mounting bolts to the specified torque.
21 Refit the stone protection plates under the trailing arms.
22 Check and if necessary adjust the handbrake as described in Chapter 9, Section 17.
23 Refit the roadwheels and lower the car to the ground.

14 Rear axle rubber mountings – renewal

Note: *It is recommended that the rubber mountings are renewed on both sides at the same time to ensure the correct rear wheel alignment.*

1 Chock the front roadwheels, and then jack up the rear of the car and support it on axle stands positioned beneath the underbody (see *Jacking and vehicle support*). Remove both rear roadwheels.
2 Release the handbrake cables from the supports/clips on the rear axle and underbody.
3 Pull out the clips and disconnect the flexible brake hoses from the supports on the rear axle and underbody brackets.
4 Unscrew and remove both rear axle front mounting bolts from the underbody brackets.

5 Working on one side at a time, pull the front end of the trailing arm down from the underbody bracket and retain it in this position by placing a block of wood between the arm and underbody.

6 When fitting a new mounting bush, make sure that it is correctly aligned with any markings on the arm. If no alignment marks are visible, then alignment marks should be made, so that correct fitting of the bushes is carried out.

7 VW technicians use a special tool to remove the rubber mounting from the rear axle. If a similar tool is not available, use a long bolt with suitable-sized metal tubing and washers to force out the mounting.

8 The new mounting must be located correctly in the rear axle. Using a suitable tool, pull the mounting into the rear axle until it is positioned as noted on removal.

9 Renew the mounting on the other side using the same procedure described in paragraphs 5 to 8.

10 Apply a little brake grease or soapy water to the mounting rubbers, and then locate the rear axle in the underbody brackets. Insert the mounting bolts from the outside, hand-tight at this stage.

11 Refit the flexible brake hoses and handbrake cables, and secure with the clips.

12 Working on one side at a time, raise the trailing arm with a trolley jack until the weight of the car is taken on the coil spring, then fully tighten the front mounting bolt to the specified torque.

13 Refit the roadwheels and lower the car to the ground.

15 Steering wheel – removal and refitting

Removal

1 Set the front wheels in the straight-ahead position, and release the steering lock by inserting the ignition key.

2 Disconnect the battery negative lead (refer to *Disconnecting the battery* in the *Reference* Chapter at the end of this manual), and position it away from the terminal.

3 Remove the driver's airbag as described in Chapter 12, Section 26.

4 Using a multi-spline socket, unscrew and remove the retaining bolt, while holding the steering wheel stationary – do not use the steering lock to hold the wheel, as it may be damaged **(see illustration)**.

5 The wheel should have an alignment mark already, to indicate its correct fitted position. If necessary, use a centre-punch or dab of paint to mark the steering wheel in relation to the column in order to aid refitting **(see illustration)**.

6 Refit the steering wheel retaining bolt a couple of threads, and then ease the steering wheel from the column splines by firmly rocking it side-to-side. With the steering wheel loose on the column, remove the retaining bolt

15.4 Steering wheel multi-spline retaining bolt

16.8a Undo the earth wire securing screw…

again and discard, as a new one must be used on refitting.

Refitting

7 Locate the steering wheel on the column splines making sure that the previously made marks are correctly aligned and the electrical connector is aligned with the opening in the steering wheel.

8 Fit a new bolt to the top of the steering column and tighten to the specified torque while holding the steering wheel stationary.

9 Refit the driver's airbag as described in Chapter 12, Section 26.

10 Reconnect the battery negative (earth) lead.

16 Steering column – removal, inspection and refitting

Removal

1 Disconnect the battery negative lead (see *Reference* at end of Manual), and position it away from the terminal.

2 Remove the steering wheel as described in Section 15.

3 Return the steering to the straight-ahead position. Adjust the steering column to its lowest position and extend it into the passenger compartment as far as possible, and then lock it in this position.

4 Unclip and remove the upper shroud from the steering column, then undo the two upper screws and single lower screw and remove

15.5 Alignment marks for steering wheel in relation to column

16.8b …and unclip the wiring loom from under the column

the lower shroud from the steering column, as described in Chapter 11, Section 25.

5 Remove the lower facia panels located around the steering column as described in Chapter 11, Section 27.

6 Remove the switch assembly from the top of the steering column as described in Chapter 12, Section 4.

7 Disconnect the wiring connector from the transponder around the ignition switch, and then release the wiring retaining clips and earth cables from the steering column.

8 Follow the wiring loom down the length of the steering column, undo the earth cable retaining screw, release the retaining clips and remove the wiring loom from under the steering column, noting its fitted position **(see illustrations)**.

9 Working in the footwell, release the retaining clips and remove the plastic trim panel from over the steering column lower universal joint **(see illustration)**.

16.9 Removing the plastic cover from the steering column lower universal joint

16.10 Steering column lower universal joint

16.12a Undo the lower mounting bolt (arrowed)...

16.12b ...and upper mounting bolts - arrowed

10 Unscrew the clamp bolt and pull the universal joint from the steering gear pinion. Note that the pinion shaft has a cut-out to enable fitting of the clamp bolt, and the splined pinion shaft incorporates a flat making it impossible to assemble the joint to the shaft in the wrong position (see illustration). Discard the clamp bolt; a new one should be used on refitting.

11 Note that the inner and outer columns, and the intermediate shaft, are telescopic, to facilitate the reach adjustment. It is important to keep the splined sections of the inner steering column engaged with each other while the steering column is removed. If they become detached due to the outer column sections being separated, especially on a vehicle, which has completed a high mileage, it is possible that rattling noises may occur.

12 Support the steering column, then unscrew and remove the mounting bolts. Withdraw the steering column from inside the car (see illustrations). Note that the mounting bracket on the bulkhead has locating lug, which aligns with a slot on the top of the steering column.

Caution: Do not carry the steering column by suspending it from the universal joint or intermediate shaft, as this will damage the universal joint and steering column bushes. Also, do not bend the joints by more than 90°.

13 If necessary, remove the ignition switch/ steering column lock with reference to Section 17.

Inspection

14 The steering column is designed to

17.6 Disconnecting the ignition switch wiring plug

collapse in the event of a front-end crash, to prevent the steering wheel injuring the driver. Before refitting the steering column, examine the column and mountings for signs of damage and deformation.

15 Check the inner column sections for signs of free play in the column bushes. If any damage or wear is found on the steering column bushes, the column must be renewed as an assembly.

16 The intermediate shaft is permanently attached to the inner column and cannot be renewed separately. Inspect the universal joints for excessive wear. If evident, the complete steering column must be renewed.

Refitting

17 Where removed, refit the ignition switch/ steering column lock/switch carrier with reference to Section 22.

18 Refit the steering column to the bulkhead bracket, making sure it located on the locating lug. Insert the mounting bolts, and tighten to the specified torque, starting with the upper bolts first and then the lower bolts.

19 Attach the universal joint on the steering gear pinion splines, making sure the road wheels and steering wheel are in the correct position. Insert the new clamp bolt, and tighten to the specified torque.

20 Reconnect the earth cable and tighten the retaining nut, then refit the wiring harness under the steering column.

21 Reconnect the wiring to the ignition switch transponder and secure the wiring in its retaining clips.

17.7 Switch retaining screws - arrowed

22 Refit the plastic trim panel over the steering column lower universal joint.

23 Refit the light switch assembly with reference to Chapter 12, Section 4.

24 Refit the lower facia panels, as described in Chapter 11, Section 27.

25 Refit the lower and upper shrouds, as described in Chapter 11, Section 25.

26 Refit the steering wheel with reference to Section 15.

27 Reconnect the battery negative lead.

28 On models with ESP (electronic stability programme), the steering angle sensor basic settings must be set by a VW dealer using specialist diagnostic equipment.

17 Ignition switch and steering column lock – removal and refitting

Ignition switch

Removal

1 Disconnect the battery negative lead (refer to *Disconnecting the battery* in the *Reference* Chapter at the end of this manual).

2 Remove the steering wheel as described in Section 15.

3 With the steering in the straight-ahead position, adjust the steering column to its lowest position, then extend it into the passenger compartment as far as possible, and then lock it in this position.

4 Unclip and remove the upper shroud from the steering column, then undo the two upper screws and single lower screw and remove the lower shroud from the steering column, as described in Chapter 11, Section 25.

5 Remove the switch assembly from the top of the steering column as described in Chapter 12, Section 4.

6 Release the securing clip and carefully pull the wiring plug from the ignition switch (see illustration).

7 Remove the locking paint from the switch retaining screw heads (see illustration), then loosen them slightly and pull out the switch from the rear of the steering lock housing.

Refitting

8 Insert the ignition key and turn it to the 'on'

position. Also turn the switch in the same position.

9 Carefully insert the switch into the housing, then insert the screws and tighten securely. Lock the screws by applying some paint over their heads and onto the housing.

10 Reconnect the wiring plug to the ignition switch.

11 Refit the light switch assembly with reference to Chapter 12, Section 4.

12 Refit the lower and upper shrouds, as described in Chapter 11, Section 25.

13 Refit the steering wheel as described in Section 15.

14 Reconnect the battery negative lead (refer to *Disconnecting the battery* in the *Reference* Chapter at the end of this manual).

Steering column lock

Removal

15 Carry out the procedures as described in paragraphs 1 to 5.

16 Release the securing clips and disconnect the wiring plug connectors from the ignition switch and ignition key immobiliser coil. Also undo the retaining screw and disconnect the earth wiring terminal from the top of the housing.

17 The lock is secured to the outer column by shear-head bolts (see illustration), and the heads are broken off in the tightening procedure. To remove the old bolts, either drill them out, or use a sharp cold chisel to cut off their heads or turn them anti-clockwise. Withdraw the lock from the steering column.

18 If necessary, the lock cylinder can be removed from the steering lock housing as described later in this section.

Refitting

19 If removed, refit the lock cylinder as described later in this section.

20 Locate the lock on the outer column and insert the new shear-head bolts. Tighten the bolts until their heads break off.

21 Reconnect the wiring plug to the ignition switch and ignition key immobiliser coil.

22 Attach the earth terminal to the housing and tighten the retaining screw.

23 Refit the light switch assembly with reference to Chapter 12, Section 4.

17.17 Steering column lock shear-head bolts - arrowed

24 Refit the lower and upper shrouds, as described in Chapter 11, Section 25.

25 Refit the steering wheel as described in Section 15.

26 Reconnect the battery negative lead (refer to *Disconnecting the battery* in the *Reference* Chapter at the end of this manual).

Lock cylinder

Removal

27 Carry out the procedures as described in paragraphs 1 to 4.

28 Disconnect the wiring connector from the immobiliser transponder around the ignition switch (see illustration).

29 Insert the ignition key and turn the lock cylinder to the drive position (which is 90° from off position).

30 Insert a piece of wire 1.2 mm in diameter in the drilling next to the ignition key, slide it in to release the locking lever, then withdraw the lock cylinder from the housing (see illustrations). To make the piece of wire locate in the locking lever easier, file an angle on the end of the wire.

Refitting

31 Refit the lock cylinder with the ignition key in the Drive position, then remove the wire.

32 Reconnect the wiring connector to the immobiliser/transponder.

33 Refit the upper and lower shrouds, and tighten the screws.

34 Refit the steering wheel with reference to Section 15.

35 Reconnect the battery negative lead.

18 Steering gear assembly (EPHS) – removal, overhaul and refitting

Note: *New subframe mounting bolts, track rod balljoint nuts, steering gear retaining bolts, and an intermediate shaft universal joint clamp bolt will be required on refitting.*

Removal

1 Apply the handbrake, then jack up the front of the car and support it on axle stands positioned on the underbody, leaving the subframe free (see *Jacking and vehicle support*). Position the steering straight-ahead, and then remove both front roadwheels. Also remove the engine compartment undershield. As a precaution against the steering wheel turning and damaging the airbag contact spring, use adhesive tape to secure it to the facia or steering column.

2 Beneath the pedal bracket, undo the plastic nuts and remove the cover for access to the steering column lower universal joint.

3 Unscrew and remove the clamp bolt and free the steering column universal joint from the steering gear pinion (the shaft is telescopic to enable it to be easily disconnected). Discard the clamp bolt, as a new one should be used on refitting. Note that the pinion shaft has a cut-out to enable fitting of the clamp bolt, and the splined pinion shaft incorporates a flat making it impossible to assemble the joint to the shaft in the wrong position. Some models may have a clamp ring securing the universal joint to the inner column.

4 Remove the battery and battery tray as described in Chapter 5A, Section 3.

5 Remove the air filter and air ducting from the engine compartment with reference to Chapter 4A, Section 2 or Chapter 4B, Section 2.

6 Release the power-assisted steering sensor wiring from the holder on the inner panel above the left-hand driveshaft.

7 On models where the front exhaust pipe runs beneath the front subframe, remove it with reference to Chapter 4C (petrol engines) or Chapter 4D (diesel engines).

8 Unscrew the two bolts securing the rear

17.28 Disconnect the wiring connector

17.30a insert a thin rod through the hole in the Ignition switch...

17.30b ...to release the locking lever - arrowed

engine/transmission mounting link to the underside of the transmission unit. Discard both bolts, new ones must be used on refitting, and leave the mounting attached to the subframe.

9 Unscrew the nuts and disconnect the links from the anti-roll bar on each side.

10 Working on each side at a time, unscrew the nuts from the track rod ends, then use a balljoint separator tool to release the ends from the steering arms on the front wheel bearing housings.

11 Unscrew the filler cap from the top of the hydraulic fluid reservoir on top of the electric power steering pump, then syphon all the fluid into a suitable container. Note that there will still be fluid in the system lines. Discard the removed fluid. **Note:** *VW specifically state that a hose clamp* **must not** *be fitted to the hydraulic fluid line.*

12 Support the weight of the subframe with a trolley jack, then mark the position of the bolts securing the subframe to the underbody, and unscrew them.

13 Position a suitable container beneath the steering gear to catch spilt fluid.

14 Lower the subframe approximately 4 cm, at the same time guiding the pinion shaft from the rubber grommet in the floor, and making sure that the hydraulic lines are not damaged.

15 Unscrew the union nut and disconnect the supply line and return lines from the steering gear, then recover the copper sealing washers. Tape over or plug the ends of the lines and the apertures in the steering gear to prevent entry of dust and dirt into the hydraulic system. The line ends can be wrapped in a plastic bag if preferred.

16 Unscrew the bolts and remove the power-assisted steering sensor from the steering gear pinion housing. Be prepared for some loss of fluid.

17 Unscrew the mounting bolts and withdraw the steering gear from the subframe to the rear. Note that the mounting on the passenger side of the gear incorporates a clamp and rubber mounting. Examine the mounting for wear and damage, and renew it if necessary. Discard the steering gear mounting bolts; new ones should be used on refitting.

19.2 Steering rack gaiter securing clips - arrowed

Overhaul

18 Examine the steering gear assembly for signs of wear or damage, and check that the rack moves freely throughout the full length of its travel, with no signs of roughness or excessive free play between the steering gear pinion and rack. It is not possible to overhaul the steering gear assembly housing components, and if it is faulty the assembly must be renewed. The only components, which can be renewed individually, are the steering gear gaiters, the track rod end balljoints and the track rods, as described later in this Chapter.

Refitting

19 Locate the steering gear on the subframe, and insert the new mounting bolts. Make sure that the location dowel is correctly fitted. Tighten the bolts to the specified torque and Stage 2 angle.

20 Refit the power-assisted steering sensor together with a new seal to the steering gear pinion housing, and tighten the bolts.

21 Refit the hydraulic supply and return lines to the steering gear together with new copper sealing washers, and tighten to the specified torque.

22 Raise the subframe and at the same time guide the steering gear pinion shaft through the rubber grommet in the floor. Align the subframe with the previously made marks, then insert the new mounting bolts and tighten them to the specified torque and angle.

23 Align the engine/transmission rear mounting with the transmission unit and fit the new mounting bolts. Tighten the bolts to the specified torque and angle.

24 Refit the track rod ends to the steering arms, screw on the new nuts, and tighten them to the specified torque.

25 Refit the links to the anti-roll bar and tighten the nuts to the specified torque.

26 Where applicable, refit the exhaust front pipe with reference to Chapter 4C or 4D.

27 Secure the power-assisted steering sensor to the holder on the inner panel.

28 Refit the air filter and ducting with reference to Chapter 4A, Section 2 or Chapter 4B, Section 2.

29 Refit the battery and battery tray with reference to Chapter 5A, Section 3. **Note:** *On some models access to the hydraulic fluid reservoir is restricted by the battery, therefore delay refitting the battery until the hydraulic system has been bled.*

30 Working inside the car, locate the steering column universal joint on the pinion shaft, making sure that the cut-out is aligned with the bolt holes. Insert the new bolt and tighten to the specified torque.

31 Check that the rubber grommet is located correctly in the floor, then refit the plastic cover and secure with the screws.

32 Refit the engine compartment undershield and roadwheels, and then lower the car to the ground. On completion check and, if necessary, adjust the front wheel alignment as described in Section 23.

33 Refill and bleed the hydraulic system as described in Section 20.

34 Have the system checked for fault codes by a VW dealer at the earliest opportunity.

19 Steering gear rubber gaiters and track rods – renewal

Steering gear rubber gaiters

1 Remove the track rod end balljoint as described in Section 22.

2 Note the fitted position of the gaiter on the track rod, then release the retaining clips and slide the gaiter off the steering gear housing and track rod **(see illustration)**.

3 Wipe clean the track rod and the steering gear housing, and then apply a film of suitable grease to the surface of the rack. To do this, turn the steering wheel as necessary to fully extend the rack from the housing, then reposition it in its central position.

4 Carefully slide the new gaiter onto the track rod, and locate it on the steering gear housing. Position the gaiter as previously noted on removal, making sure that it is not twisted, then lift the outer sealing lip of the gaiter to equalise air pressure within the gaiter.

5 Secure the gaiter in position with new retaining clips. Where crimped-type clips are used, pull the clip as tight as possible, and locate the hooks in their slots. Remove any slack in the clip by carefully compressing the raised section. In the absence of the special crimping tool, a pair of side-cutters may be used, taking care not to cut the clip.

6 Refit the track rod end balljoint as described in Section 22.

Track rods

7 Remove the relevant steering gear rubber gaiter as described earlier. If there is insufficient working room with the steering gear mounted in the car, remove it as described in Section 18 and hold it in a vice while renewing the track rod.

8 Hold the steering rack stationary with one spanner on the flats provided, then loosen the balljoint nut with another spanner. Fully unscrew the nut and remove the track rod from the rack.

9 Locate the new track rod on the end of the steering rack and screw on the nut. Hold the rack stationary with one spanner and tighten the balljoint nut to the specified torque. A crow's foot adapter may be required since the track rod prevents access with a socket, and care must be taken to apply the exact torque in this situation.

10 Refit the steering gear or rubber gaiter with reference to the earlier paragraphs or Section 18. On completion check and, if necessary, adjust the front wheel alignment as described in Section 23.

21.1 Electric power steering pump viewed with the front bumper removed

21.6 Radiator fan control unit

21.9 Wiring plugs on the electric power steering pump

20 Power steering system – bleeding

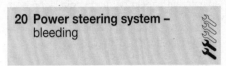

1 Apply the handbrake, then jack up the front of the car and support it on axle stands (see *Jacking and vehicle support*). Turn the front roadwheels to their straight-ahead position.

2 Unscrew the filler cap from the electric power steering hydraulic fluid reservoir and top-up the level to the MAX mark.

3 With the engine switched off, turn the steering from lock-to-lock ten times, then check and top-up the level again.

4 Screw on the filler cap loosely, then start the engine and allow it to idle for approximately 10 seconds.

5 Switch off the engine and top-up the fluid level.

6 Screw on the filler cap loosely, start the engine, and turn the steering from lock-to-lock ten times.

7 Switch off the engine and top-up the fluid level.

8 Repeat the procedure in paragraphs 6 and 7 until the fluid level no longer requires topping-up.

9 Refit and tighten the filler cap.

21 Electric power steering pump – removal and refitting

Removal

1 The electric power steering hydraulic pump is located behind the front bumper in front of the left-hand front wheel **(see illustration)**.

2 On models where access to the fluid reservoir is restricted by the battery, remove the battery and battery tray as described in Chapter 5A, Section 3.

3 Apply the handbrake, then jack up the front of the car and support it on axle stands (see *Jacking and vehicle support*).

4 Remove the front bumper as described in Chapter 11, Section 6.

5 Unscrew the filler cap from the top of the hydraulic fluid reservoir on top of the electric power steering pump, then syphon all the fluid

into a suitable container. Note that there will still be fluid in the system lines. Discard the removed fluid. **Note:** *VW specifically state that a hose clamp* **must not** *be fitted to the hydraulic fluid line.*

6 On models with a radiator fan control unit **(see illustration)**, disconnect the wiring and unscrew the mounting nuts, then remove the radiator fan control unit from the left-hand front chassis leg.

7 Release the support clip and remove the supply and return hydraulic lines from the inner body.

8 Locate a suitable container beneath the electric power steering pump to catch spilled hydraulic fluid.

9 Note their location, and then disconnect the three wiring plugs from the electric power steering pump **(see illustration)**.

10 Unscrew the union nut and disconnect the pressure line from the pump. Recover the O-ring seal, then loosen the clip and disconnect the return line from the pump reservoir. Tape over or plug the ends of the lines and the apertures in the steering gear to prevent entry of dust and dirt into the hydraulic system. The line ends can be wrapped in a plastic bag if preferred.

11 Unscrew the mounting bolts and lower the electric power steering pump and bracket from the underbody.

12 Unscrew the nuts/bolts and remove the mounting bracket from the pump. Where applicable, unscrew the rubber mountings from the pump.

Caution: The power steering control

unit and the electric motor must not be separated.*

Refitting

13 Refitting is a reversal of removal, but finally bleed the system as described in Section 20. At the earliest opportunity, have a VW dealer perform a system self-diagnosis and erase any fault codes.

22 Track rod end – removal and refitting

Note: *A new balljoint retaining nut will be required on refitting.*

Removal

1 Apply the handbrake, then jack up the front of the car and support it on axle stands (see *Jacking and vehicle support*). Remove the relevant roadwheel.

2 If the track rod end is to be re-used, mark its position in relation to the track rod to facilitate refitting.

3 Unscrew the track rod end locknut by a quarter of a turn. Do not move the locknut from this position, as it will serve as a handy reference mark on refitting.

4 Loosen and remove the nut securing the track rod end balljoint to the wheel bearing housing, and release the balljoint tapered shank using a universal balljoint separator. Note that the balljoint shank has a hexagon hole – hold the shank with an Allen key while loosening the nut **(see illustrations)**.

22.4a Using an Allen key to hold the balljoint shank while loosening the nut

22.4b Using a balljoint separator to release the track rod balljoint

22.5 Unscrewing the track rod end from the track rod

5 Counting the exact number of turns necessary to do so, unscrew the track rod end from the track rod **(see illustration)**.

6 Carefully clean the balljoint and the threads. Renew the balljoint if its movement is sloppy or too stiff, if excessively worn, or if damaged in any way; carefully check the stud taper and threads. If the balljoint gaiter is damaged, the complete balljoint assembly must be renewed; it is not possible to obtain the gaiter separately.

Refitting

7 Screw the track rod end onto the track rod by the number of turns noted on removal. This should bring the track rod end to within a quarter of a turn of the locknut, with the alignment marks that were made on removal (if applicable) lined up. Tighten the locknut.

8 Refit the balljoint shank to the steering arm on the wheel bearing housing, then fit a new retaining nut and tighten it to the specified torque. Hold the shank with an Allen key if necessary.

9 Refit the roadwheel, then lower the car to the ground and tighten the roadwheel bolts to the specified torque.

10 Check and, if necessary, adjust the front wheel toe setting as described in Section 23.

23 Wheel alignment and steering angles – general information

Definitions

1 A car's steering and suspension geometry is defined in three basic settings – all angles are expressed in degrees; the steering axis is defined as an imaginary line drawn through the axis of the suspension strut, extended where necessary to contact the ground.

2 **Camber** is the angle between each roadwheel and a vertical line drawn through its centre and tyre contact patch, when viewed from the front or rear of the car. Positive camber is when the roadwheels are tilted outwards from the vertical at the top; negative camber is when they are tilted inwards.

3 Camber angle is only adjustable by loosening the front suspension subframe mounting bolts and moving it slightly to one side. This also alters the Castor angle. The camber angle can be checked using a camber checking gauge.

4 **Castor** is the angle between the steering axis and a vertical line drawn through each roadwheel's centre and tyre contact patch, when viewed from the side of the car. Positive castor is when the steering axis is tilted so that it contacts the ground ahead of the vertical; negative castor is when it contacts the ground behind the vertical. Slight castor angle adjustment is possible by loosening the front suspension subframe bolts and moving it slightly to one side. This also alters the Camber angle.

5 Castor is not easily adjustable, and is given for reference only; while it can be checked using a castor checking gauge, if the figure obtained is significantly different from that specified, the car must be taken for careful checking by a professional, as the fault can only be caused by wear or damage to the body or suspension components.

6 **Toe** is the difference, viewed from above, between lines drawn through the roadwheel centres and the car's centre-line. Toe-in is when the roadwheels point inwards, towards each other at the front, while toe-out is when they splay outwards from each other at the front.

7 The front wheel toe setting is adjusted by screwing the track rod(s) in/out of the outer balljoint(s) to alter the effective length of the track rod assembly.

8 Rear wheel toe setting is not adjustable, and is given for reference only. While it can be checked, if the figure obtained is significantly different from that specified, the car must be taken for careful checking by a professional, as the fault can only be caused by wear or damage to the body or suspension components.

Checking and adjustment

Front wheel toe setting

9 Due to the special measuring equipment necessary to check the wheel alignment, and the skill required to use it properly, the checking and adjustment of these settings is best left to a VW dealer or similar expert. Note that most tyre-fitting centres now possess sophisticated checking equipment.

10 To check the toe setting, a tracking gauge must first be obtained. Two types of gauge are available, and can be obtained from motor accessory shops. The first type measures the distance between the front and rear inside edges of the roadwheels, as previously described, with the car stationary – however, VW do not quote settings in millimetres, so this type of gauge would not be suitable for the Polo. The second type, known as a 'scuff plate', measures the actual position of the contact surface of the tyre, in relation to the road surface, with the car in motion. This is achieved by pushing or driving the front tyre over a plate, which then moves slightly according to the scuff of the tyre, and shows this movement on a scale.

11 Make sure that the steering is in the straight-ahead position when making measurements.

12 If adjustment is necessary, apply the handbrake, then jack up the front of the car and support it securely on axle stands (see Jacking and vehicle support). Turn the steering wheel onto full-left lock, and record the amount of exposed thread on the right-hand track rod. Now turn the steering onto full-right lock, and record the number of threads on the left-hand track rod. If there is the same amount of thread visible on both sides, then subsequent adjustment should be made equally on both sides. If there are more thread is visible on one side than the other, it will be necessary to compensate for this during adjustment.

13 First clean the track rod threads; if they are corroded, apply penetrating fluid before starting adjustment. Release the rubber gaiter outer clips, peel back the gaiters and apply a smear of grease. This will ensure that both gaiters are free and will not be twisted or strained as there respective track rods are rotated.

14 Retain the track rod with a suitable spanner, and loosen the balljoint locknut fully. Alter the length of the track rod, by screwing it into or out of the balljoint. Rotate the track rod using an open-ended spanner fitted to the track rod flats provided; shortening the track rod (screwing it onto its balljoint) will reduce toe-in/increase toe-out.

15 When the setting is correct, hold the track rod and tighten the balljoint locknut to the specified torque setting. If after adjustment, the steering wheel spokes are no longer horizontal when the wheels are in the straight-ahead position, remove the steering wheel and reposition it (see Section 15).

16 Check that the toe setting has been correctly adjusted by lowering the car to the ground and rechecking the toe setting; re-adjust if necessary. Ensure that the rubber gaiters are seated correctly and are not twisted or strained, and secure them in position with the retaining clips; where necessary, fit a new retaining clip (refer to Section 19).

Rear wheel toe setting

17 The procedure for checking the rear toe setting is the same as described for the front setting in paragraph 10. The setting is not adjustable – see paragraph 8.

Front wheel camber and castor angles

18 Checking and adjusting the front wheel camber angle should be entrusted to a VW dealer or other suitably equipped specialist. Note that most tyre-fitting centres now possess sophisticated checking equipment. For reference, adjustments are made by loosening the front suspension subframe mounting bolts, and repositioning the subframe.

Chapter 11
Bodywork and fittings

Contents

Degrees of difficulty

Easy, suitable for novice with little experience	**Fairly easy,** suitable for beginner with some experience	**Fairly difficult,** suitable for competent DIY mechanic	**Difficult,** suitable for experienced DIY mechanic	**Very difficult,** suitable for expert DIY or professional

Specifications

Torque wrench settings	Nm	lbf ft
Bonnet hinge nuts	20	15
Bonnet lock bolts	12	9
Door hinges:		
To body*	32	23
To door*	32	23
Locking bolt	23	18
Door Check strap (arrester):		
To body	30	22
To door	10	7
Door lock	18	14
Door lock striker	20	15
Front seat belt adjuster upper bolt	20	15
Front seat belt lower mounting bolt (microencapsulated)*	40	30
Front seat belt stalk to seat frame bolt (microencapsulated)*	40	30
Front seat mounting retaining bolts	40	30
Front window glass clamp bolts (left-hand thread)	8	6
Front window regulator nuts	18	14
Inertia reel mounting bolts	40	30
Rear window regulator nuts	8	6
Seat belt and stalk anchorage bolts	40	30
Tailgate hinge upper retaining bolts	10	7
Tailgate hinge lower retaining nut	24	18
Tailgate lock bolts	23	18

* *Renew the bolts*

1 General information

The body shell is made of pressed-steel sections, and is available in both three- and five-door Hatchback versions. Most components are welded together, and some use is made of structural adhesives; the front wings are bolted on.

The bonnet, door, and some other vulnerable panels are made of zinc-coated metal, and are further protected by being coated with an anti-chip primer before being sprayed.

Extensive use is made of plastic materials, mainly in the interior, but also in exterior components. The front and rear bumpers, and front grille, are injection-moulded from a synthetic material that is very strong and yet light. Plastic components such as wheel arch liners are fitted to the underside of the vehicle, to improve the body's resistance to corrosion.

2 Maintenance – bodywork and underframe

The general condition of a vehicle's bodywork is the one thing that significantly affects its value. Maintenance is easy, but needs to be regular. Neglect, particularly after minor damage, can lead quickly to further deterioration and costly repair bills. It is important also to keep watch on those parts of the vehicle not immediately visible, for instance the underside, inside all the wheel arches, and the lower part of the engine compartment.

The basic maintenance routine for the bodywork is washing – preferably with a lot of water, from a hose. This will remove all the loose solids, which may have stuck to the vehicle. It is important to flush these off in such a way as to prevent grit from scratching the finish. The wheel arches and underframe need washing in the same way, to remove any accumulated mud, which will retain moisture and tend to encourage rust. Paradoxically enough, the best time to clean the underframe and wheel arches is in wet weather, when the mud is thoroughly wet and soft. In very wet weather, the underframe is usually cleaned of large accumulations automatically, and this is a good time for inspection.

Periodically, except on vehicles with a wax-based underbody protective coating, it is a good idea to have the whole of the underframe of the vehicle steam-cleaned, engine compartment included, so that a thorough inspection can be carried out to see what minor repairs and renovations are necessary. Steam cleaning is available at many garages, and is necessary for the removal of the accumulation of oily grime, which sometimes is allowed to become thick in certain areas. If steam-cleaning facilities are

not available, there are some excellent grease solvents available which can be brush-applied; the dirt can then be simply hosed off. Note that these methods should not be used on vehicles with wax-based underbody protective coating, or the coating will be removed. Such vehicles should be inspected annually, preferably just prior to Winter, when the underbody should be washed down, and any damage to the wax coating repaired. Ideally, a completely fresh coat should be applied. It would also be worth considering the use of such wax-based protection for injection into door panels, sills, box sections, etc, as an additional safeguard against rust damage, where such protection is not provided by the vehicle manufacturer.

After washing paintwork, wipe off with a chamois leather to give an unspotted clear finish. A coat of clear protective wax polish will give added protection against chemical pollutants in the air. If the paintwork sheen has dulled or oxidised, use a cleaner/polisher combination to restore the brilliance of the shine. This requires a little effort, but such dulling is usually caused because regular washing has been neglected. Care needs to be taken with metallic paintwork, as special non-abrasive cleaner/polisher is required to avoid damage to the finish. Always check that the door and ventilator opening drain holes and pipes are completely clear, so that water can be drained out. Brightwork should be treated in the same way as paintwork. Windscreens and windows can be kept clear of the smeary film that often appears, by the use of proprietary glass cleaner. Never use any form of wax or other body or chromium polish on glass.

3 Maintenance – upholstery and carpets

Mats and carpets should be brushed or vacuum-cleaned regularly, to keep them free of grit. If they are badly stained, remove them from the vehicle for scrubbing or sponging, and make quite sure they are dry before refitting. Seats and interior trim panels can be kept clean by wiping with a damp cloth. If they do become stained (which can be more apparent on light-coloured upholstery), use a little liquid detergent and a soft nail brush to scour the grime out of the grain of the material. Do not forget to keep the headlining clean in the same way as the upholstery. When using liquid cleaners inside the vehicle, do not over-wet the surfaces being cleaned. Excessive damp could get into the seams and padded interior, causing stains, offensive odours or even rot.

If the inside of the vehicle gets wet accidentally, it is worthwhile taking some trouble to dry it out properly, particularly where carpets are involved. Do not leave oil or electric heaters inside the vehicle for this purpose.

4 Minor body damage – repair

Scratches

If the scratch is very superficial, and does not penetrate to the metal of the bodywork, repair is very simple. Lightly rub the area of the scratch with a paintwork renovator, or a very fine cutting paste, to remove loose paint from the scratch, and to clear the surrounding bodywork of wax polish. Rinse the area with clean water.

Apply touch-up paint to the scratch using a fine paintbrush; continue to apply fine layers of paint until the surface of the paint in the scratch is level with the surrounding paintwork. Allow the new paint at least two weeks to harden, and then blend it into the surrounding paintwork by rubbing the scratch area with a paintwork renovator or a very fine cutting paste. Finally, apply wax polish.

Where the scratch has penetrated right through to the metal of the bodywork, causing the metal to rust, a different repair technique is required. Remove any loose rust from the bottom of the scratch with a penknife, and then apply rust-inhibiting paint to prevent the formation of rust in the future. Using a rubber or nylon applicator, fill the scratch with bodystopper paste. If required, this paste can be mixed with cellulose thinners to provide a very thin paste that is ideal for filling narrow scratches. Before the stopper-paste in the scratch hardens, wrap a piece of smooth cotton rag around the top of a finger. Dip the finger in cellulose thinners, and quickly sweep it across the surface of the stopper-paste in the scratch; this will ensure that the surface of the stopper-paste is slightly hollowed. The scratch can now be painted over as described earlier in this Section.

Dents

When deep denting of the vehicle's bodywork has taken place, the first task is to pull the dent out, until the affected bodywork almost attains its original shape. There is little point in trying to restore the original shape completely, as the metal in the damaged area will have stretched on impact, and cannot be reshaped fully to its original contour. It is better to bring the level of the dent up to a point, which is about 3 mm below the level of the surrounding bodywork. In cases where the dent is very shallow anyway, it is not worth trying to pull it out at all. If the underside of the dent is accessible, it can be hammered out gently from behind, using a mallet with a wooden or plastic head. Whilst doing this, hold a suitable block of wood firmly against the outside of the panel, to absorb the impact from the hammer blows and thus prevent a large area of the bodywork from being 'belled-out'.

Should the dent be in a section of the

bodywork that has a double skin, or some other factor making it inaccessible from behind, a different technique is called for. Drill several small holes through the metal inside the area – particularly in the deeper section. Then screw long self-tapping screws into the holes, just sufficiently for them to gain a good purchase in the metal. Now the dent can be pulled out by pulling on the protruding heads of the screws with a pair of pliers.

The next stage of the repair is the removal of the paint from the damaged area, and from an inch or so of the surrounding 'sound' bodywork. This is accomplished most easily by using a wire brush or abrasive pad on a power drill, although it can be done just as effectively by hand, using sheets of abrasive paper. To complete the preparation for filling, score the surface of the bare metal with a screwdriver or the tang of a file, or alternatively, drill small holes in the affected area. This will provide a really good 'key' for the filler paste.

To complete the repair, see the Section on filling and respraying.

Rust holes or gashes

Remove all paint from the affected area, and from an inch or so of the surrounding 'sound' bodywork, using an abrasive pad or a wire brush on a power drill. If these are not available, a few sheets of abrasive paper will do the job most effectively. With the paint removed, you will be able to judge the severity of the corrosion, and therefore decide whether to renew the whole panel (if this is possible) or to repair the affected area. New body panels are not as expensive as most people think, and it is often quicker and more satisfactory to fit a new panel than to attempt to repair large areas of corrosion.

Remove all fittings from the affected area, except those, which will act as a guide to the original shape of the damaged bodywork (e.g. headlight shells etc). Then, using tin snips or a hacksaw blade, remove all loose metal and any other metal badly affected by corrosion. Hammer the edges of the hole inwards, in order to create a slight depression for the filler paste.

Wire-brush the affected area to remove the powdery rust from the surface of the remaining metal. Paint the affected area with rust-inhibiting paint, if the back of the rusted area is accessible, treat this also.

Before filling can take place, it will be necessary to block the hole in some way. This can be achieved by the use of aluminium or plastic mesh, or aluminium tape.

Aluminium or plastic mesh, or glassfibre matting, is probably the best material to use for a large hole. Cut a piece to the approximate size and shape of the hole to be filled, then position it in the hole so that its edges are below the level of the surrounding bodywork. It can be retained in position by several blobs of filler paste around its periphery.

Aluminium tape should be used for small or very narrow holes. Pull a piece off the roll, trim it to the approximate size and shape required, then pull off the backing paper (if used) and stick the tape over the hole; it can be overlapped if the thickness of one piece is insufficient. Burnish down the edges of the tape with the handle of a screwdriver or similar, to ensure that the tape is securely attached to the metal underneath.

Filling and respraying

Before using this Section, see the Sections on dent, deep scratch, rust holes and gash repairs.

Many types of bodyfiller are available, but generally speaking, those proprietary kits, which contain a tin of filler paste and a tube of resin hardener, are best for this type of repair. A wide, flexible plastic or nylon applicator will be found invaluable for imparting a smooth and well-contoured finish to the surface of the filler.

Mix up a little filler on a clean piece of card or board – measure the hardener carefully (follow the maker's instructions on the pack), otherwise the filler will set too rapidly or too slowly. Using the applicator, apply the filler paste to the prepared area; draw the applicator across the surface of the filler to achieve the correct contour and to level the surface. As soon as a contour that approximates to the correct one is achieved, stop working the paste – if you carry on too long, the paste will become sticky and begin to 'pick-up' on the applicator. Continue to add thin layers of filler paste at 20-minute intervals, until the level of the filler is just proud of the surrounding bodywork.

Once the filler has hardened, the excess can be removed using a metal plane or file. From then on, progressively finer grades of abrasive paper should be used, starting with a 40-grade production paper, and finishing with a 400-grade wet-and-dry paper. Always wrap the abrasive paper around a flat rubber, cork, or wooden block – otherwise the surface of the filler will not be completely flat. During the smoothing of the filler surface, the wet-and-dry paper should be periodically rinsed in water. This will ensure that a very smooth finish is imparted to the filler at the final stage.

At this stage, the dent should be surrounded by a ring of bare metal, which in turn should be encircled by the finely 'feathered' edge of the good paintwork. Rinse the repair area with clean water, until all of the dust produced by the rubbing-down operation has gone.

Spray the whole area with a light coat of primer – this will show up any imperfections in the surface of the filler. Repair these imperfections with fresh filler paste or bodystopper, and once more smooth the surface with abrasive paper. Repeat this spray-and-repair procedure until you are satisfied that the surface of the filler, and the feathered edge of the paintwork, are perfect. Clean the repair area with clean water, and allow to dry fully.

The repair area is now ready for final spraying. Paint spraying must be carried out in a warm, dry, windless and dust-free atmosphere. This condition can be created artificially if you have access to a large indoor working area, but if you are forced to work in the open, you will have to pick your day very carefully. If you are working indoors, dousing the floor in the work area with water will help to settle the dust, which would otherwise be in the atmosphere. If the repair area is confined to one body panel, mask off the surrounding panels; this will help to minimise the effects of a slight mis-match in paint colours. Bodywork fittings (e.g. chrome strips, door handles etc) will also need to be masked off. Use genuine masking tape, and several thicknesses of newspaper, for the masking operations.

Before commencing to spray, agitate the aerosol can thoroughly, and then spray a test area (an old tin, or similar) until the technique is mastered. Cover the repair area with a thick coat of primer; the thickness should be built up using several thin layers of paint, rather than one thick one. Using 400-grade wet-and-dry paper, rub down the surface of the primer until it is really smooth. While doing this, the work area should be thoroughly doused with water, and the wet-and-dry paper periodically rinsed in water. Allow to dry before spraying on more paint.

Spray on the top coat, again building up the thickness by using several thin layers of paint. Start spraying at one edge of the repair area, and then, using a side-to-side motion, work until the whole repair area and about 2 inches of the surrounding original paintwork is covered. Remove all masking material 10 to 15 minutes after spraying on the final coat of paint.

Allow the new paint at least two weeks to harden, then, using a paintwork renovator, or a very fine cutting paste, blend the edges of the paint into the existing paintwork. Finally, apply wax polish.

Plastic components

With the use of more and more plastic body components by the vehicle manufacturers (e.g. bumpers. spoilers, and in some cases major body panels), rectification of more serious damage to such items has become a matter of either entrusting repair work to a specialist in this field, or renewing complete components. Repair of such damage by the DIY owner is not really feasible, owing to the cost of the equipment and materials required for effecting such repairs. The basic technique involves making a groove along the line of the crack in the plastic, using a rotary burr in a power drill. The damaged part is then welded back together, using a hot-air gun to heat up and fuse a plastic filler rod into the groove. Any excess plastic is then removed, and the area rubbed down to a smooth finish. It is important that a filler rod of the correct plastic is used, as body components can be made of a variety of different types (e.g. polycarbonate, ABS, polypropylene).

6.3 Undo the screws (arrowed)

6.4 Undo the retaining screws (arrowed)

Damage of a less serious nature (abrasions, minor cracks etc) can be repaired by the DIY owner using a two-part epoxy filler repair material. Once mixed in equal proportions, this is used in similar fashion to the bodywork filler used on metal panels. The filler is usually cured in twenty to thirty minutes, ready for sanding and painting.

If the owner is renewing a complete component himself, or if he has repaired it with epoxy filler, he will be left with the problem of finding a suitable paint for finishing which is compatible with the type of plastic used. At one time, the use of a universal paint was not possible, owing to the complex range of plastics encountered in body component applications. Standard paints, generally speaking, will not bond to plastic or rubber satisfactorily. However, it is now possible to obtain a plastic body parts finishing kit, which consists of a pre-primer treatment, a primer

and coloured top coat. Full instructions are normally supplied with a kit, but basically, the method of use is to first apply the pre-primer to the component concerned, and allow it to dry for up to 30 minutes. Then the primer is applied, and left to dry for about an hour before finally applying the special-coloured top coat. The result is a correctly coloured component, where the paint will flex with the plastic or rubber, a property that standard paint does not normally possess.

5 Major body damage – repair

Where serious damage has occurred, or large areas need renewal due to neglect, it means that complete new panels will need welding-in, and this is best left to professionals. If the damage

is due to impact, it will also be necessary to check completely the alignment of the body shell, and this can only be carried out accurately by a VW dealer using special jigs. If the body is left misaligned, it is primarily dangerous, as the car will not handle properly, and secondly, uneven stresses will be imposed on the steering, suspension and possibly transmission, causing abnormal wear, or complete failure, particularly to such items as the tyres.

6 Front bumper – removal and refitting

Note: *Depending on the model, it is possible that slight changes to the removal and refitting procedures may be necessary.*

Removal

1 Apply the handbrake, then jack up the front of the vehicle and support it on axle stands (see *Jacking and vehicle support*).
2 Remove the both headlamps as described in Chapter 12, Section 7.
3 Open the bonnet, and undo the screws securing the top of the grille trim panel to the engine compartment crossbar **(see illustration)**.
4 Working at each side in turn, undo the screws securing the wheel arch liners to the ends of the bumper and inner wheel arch liner **(see illustration)**. Note the upper screw points upwards into the wing panel.
5 Undo the lower screws from under the front edge of the bumper (two at each end and three in the centre).
6 With the help of an assistant, unclip each end of the bumper from the edge of the front wing panels and release from the securing clips inside the headlamp apertures **(see illustrations)**. Then withdraw the front bumper from the vehicle until it is possible to disconnect the wiring from the foglights and parking sensors (where fitted). Also, where applicable, release the headlamp washer hoses.
7 If required, remove the grille from the top of the bumper trim panel by using a lever, and starting from the outer edges, carefully unclip the retaining clips along the lower part of the grille. Withdraw the grille forwards away from the top of the front bumper trim **(see illustrations)**.

6.6a Unclip the sides of the bumper...

6.6b ...release the securing clips (arrowed)...

6.6c ...and withdraw the bumper

6.7a Insert plastic tool...

6.7b ...to release the securing clips (arrowed)

7.3 Undo the wheel arch retaining screws (arrowed)...

7.4 ...and the lower end retaining screw

7.5 Undo the fasteners under the rear of the bumper

Refitting

8 Refitting is a reverse of the removal procedure, ensuring that the bumper ends engage correctly with the locating clips on the edge of the front wing panels. Make sure all wiring plugs are reconnected.

7 Rear bumper – removal and refitting

Note: *Depending on the model, it is possible that slight changes to the removal and refitting procedures may be necessary.*

Removal

1 To improve access, chock the front wheels, and then jack up the rear of the vehicle and support it on axle stands (see *Jacking and vehicle support*).
2 Remove the rear light clusters as described in Chapter 12, Section 7.
3 Working at each side in turn, undo the screws securing the wheel arch liners to the ends of the bumper and inner wheel arch liner **(see illustration)**. Note the upper screw points upwards into the wing panel.
4 Undo the two screws (one at each side) from under the lower edge of the bumper **(see illustration)**.
5 Release the lower fasteners from under the rear edge of the bumper **(see illustration)**. Two outer screws and one clip in the centre. Note depending on model the amount of fasteners may vary.
6 With the help of an assistant, release the bumper from the rear wing panels at the left- and right-hand ends, and from the rear light apertures **(see illustrations)**. Then withdraw the bumper from the rear of the vehicle until it is possible to disconnect the wiring from the number plate lights and parking sensors (where fitted).

Refitting

7 Refitting is a reverse of the removal procedure, ensuring that the bumper ends engage correctly with the rear wing panels, as the bumper is refitted. Where applicable, retrieve the centre pins for the plastic rivets from the plastic slides before refitting the bumper - renew if necessary.

7.6a Unclip the sides of the bumper...

8 Bonnet – removal, refitting and adjustment

Removal

1 Open the bonnet and using a pencil or felt tip pen, mark the outline of each bonnet hinge relative to the bonnet, to use as a guide on refitting.
2 Unclip the washer jets from under the rear edge of the bonnet and disconnect the washer hose **(see illustrations)**, release the rubber grommet from the bonnet and withdraw the washer hose from inside the bonnet. Where necessary, disconnect the wiring from the jet heating elements.
3 Before disconnecting the gas support strut, get help from an assistant to support

8.2b ...then release the rubber grommet and hose from the bonnet

7.6b ...and release the rear securing clips

the bonnet. Using a small screwdriver release the retaining clip, and then disconnect the gas support strut from the bonnet **(see illustration)**.

8.2a Unclip the washer jet and disconnect the hose...

8.3 Unclip the bonnet strut securing clip

8.4 Bonnet to hinge securing nuts

4 Undo the bonnet retaining nuts **(see illustration)**, and then carefully lift the bonnet clear. Store the bonnet out of the way in a safe place.

5 Inspect the bonnet hinges for signs of wear and free play at the pivots, and if necessary renew. Each hinge is secured to the body by two bolts, mark the position of the hinge on the body then undo the retaining bolts and remove it from the vehicle. On refitting, align the new hinge with the marks and tighten the retaining bolts.

Refitting and adjustment

6 With the aid of an assistant, offer up the bonnet and loosely fit the retaining bolts. Align the hinges with the marks made on removal, and then tighten the retaining bolts/nuts securely.

7 Refit the washer hose, wiring and gas strut in the reverse order of removal.

8 Close the bonnet, and check for alignment with the adjacent panels. If necessary, unscrew the hinge bolts and re-align the bonnet. Once the bonnet is correctly aligned, tighten the hinge bolts. Check that the bonnet fastens and releases satisfactorily.

9 Bonnet release cable – removal and refitting

Removal

1 The bonnet release cable is in two sections, with a coupling located over the right-hand headlight. To remove the shorter front section cable, remove the bonnet lock as described in Section 10.

2 To remove the rear section, first release the coupling from over the right-hand headlight, as described in Section 10, paragraph 3

3 Working inside the vehicle, locate the release lever and pull it out slightly, then insert a small screwdriver into the gap between the release lever and its securing clip. Let the lever return to its original position, then release the clip with a screwdriver (note that the clip may fall behind the trim) **(see illustration)**.

4 Unscrew the plastic screws, and then unclip the trim at the centre and at the lower edge from the sill trim to remove **(see illustration)**.

5 Undo the two retaining screws and withdraw the bonnet release lever from the bottom of the A-pillar **(see illustration)**.

6 Release the outer cable from the mounting bracket, and then detach the inner cable from the lever **(see illustration)**.

7 Working along the length of the cable and noting it's correct routing, free it from any retaining clips/ties and release the cable sealing grommet from the bulkhead.

8 Tie a length of string to the end of the cable inside the vehicle, and then withdraw the cable through into the engine compartment.

9 Once the cable is free, untie the string and leave it in position in the vehicle; the string can then be used to draw the new cable back into position.

Refitting

10 Tie the inner end of the string to the end of the cable, and then use the string to draw the bonnet release cable back from the engine compartment. Once the cable is through, untie the string.

11 Refitting is a reversal of the removal. **Note:** *Before refitting the bonnet release lever, fit the securing clip back into the lever first* **(see illustration)**, *and then push the lever back into place.*

12 Ensure the rubber grommet in the bulkhead is fitted correctly, and the cable is correctly routed and secured to all the relevant retaining clips.

13 Before closing the bonnet, check the operation of the release lever and cable.

10 Bonnet lock – removal and refitting

Removal

1 Open the bonnet then remove the front bumper/grille, as described in Section 6.

2 Disconnect the wiring for the contact micro switch at the connector located by the washer reservoir filler neck.

3 Disconnect the bonnet cable at the join adapter located above the right-hand headlight, unclip the outer cable and release the two parts of the release cable **(see illustrations)**. This will allow the cable to be disconnected from the bonnet lock.

4 Note the location of the mounting bolts in

9.3 Insert a screwdriver to release the securing clip

9.4 Remove the retaining screw/clip from the panel

9.5 Release handle mounting bracket screws (arrowed)

9.6 Unclip the release cable from the lever

9.11 Slide the securing clip into the handle before refitting

10.3a Unclip the cable joiner from under the panel...

10.3b ...and disconnect the two parts of the cable

10.4 Unscrew the two lock mounting bolts

their slots to ensure correct adjustment on refitting, then unscrew and remove them **(see illustration)**.
5 Prise the lock from the crossmember, and withdraw the cable and wiring from the front panel, release them from any retaining clips. If required lift the cover and unhook the release cable end fitting from the lock lever.

Refitting
6 Refitting is a reversal of removal. Check that the bonnet fastens and releases satisfactorily before refitting the radiator grille. If adjustment is necessary, loosen the bonnet lock retaining bolts, and adjust the position of the lock to suit. Finally, tighten the bolts.

11 Door –
removal, refitting and adjustment

Note: The hinge bolts must always be renewed if loosened.

Removal
1 Open the door then disconnect the wiring at the A- or B-pillar as applicable. To do this, first release the rubber bellows by pressing the small tab at the top. Pull down the locking lever and disconnect the wiring plug **(see illustrations)**.
2 Undo the retaining bolt and disconnect the check strap from the door pillar **(see illustration)**. With this disconnected the door can swing fully open, take care it does not go to far and damage the body panels.

3 Remove the plastic cap and unscrew and remove the bolt from the upper and lower hinge **(see illustration)**, then the door can be lifted upwards and removed from the vehicle.
4 Examine the hinges for signs of wear or damage. If renewal is necessary, the hinges can be unbolted from the A- or B-pillar; however, one of the hinge retaining bolts is fitted from inside the vehicle making it necessary to remove the A- or B-pillar trim for access to them. Before removing them, accurately mark their position to ensure correct refitting.

Refitting
5 Where renewed, fit the hinges and tighten the bolts to the specified torque. Refit the trim.
6 With the aid of an assistant, offer up the door to the vehicle and locate it on the guide

11.1a Release the rubber bellows for wiring protection...

bolts. Fit the new hinge bolts and tighten to the specified torque.
7 Reconnect the wiring plug and secure with the locking lever, then refit the rubber bellows.

Adjustment
8 Close the door and check the door alignment with the surrounding body panels. There must be an even gap all around, and the door must be level with the surrounding body panels.
9 Check that the striker enters the door lock centrally as the door is closed, and if necessary adjust the position of the striker by loosening its mounting bolts **(see illustration)**.

12 Door inner trim panel –
removal and refitting

Note: As the trim panel is removed, the retaining studs/clips may be damaged; it may

11.1b ...and pull down the locking lever

11.2 Check strap securing bolt

11.3 Remove the plastic cap (arrowed)

11.9 Door lock striker mounted on pillar

12.2a Carefully prise out the trim panel (rear door shown)...

12.2b ...and release it from the grab handle (front drivers door shown)...

12.3 ...then undo the retaining screws (arrowed)

12.4 Undo the door trim lower screw

12.5 Unclip cover and undo retaining screw

12.6 Release the switch wiring connectors

be necessary to get new retaining studs/clips before proceeding.

Removal

1 Switch off the ignition, before disconnecting any wiring connectors.

12.7a Press the spacer/clip...

12.7b ...and slide the handle from the splines

12.8 Carefully prise the door panel from the securing studs

12.10 Unclip the operating cable from the inner handle

2 Using a lever, carefully unclip the trim cover from the door grab handle and remove it (see illustrations).
3 Undo the two screws located in the door trim panel, behind the trim cover (see illustration).

4 Undo the retaining screw from the lower edge of the trim panel (see illustration).
5 On front door trim panels, unclip the plastic cover and undo the retaining screws on the rear edge of the door trim panel (see illustration).
6 On the driver's door panel, disconnect the wiring connectors from the door locking switch, mirror switch and the red LED warning light (where fitted) on the top of the trim panel (see illustration).
7 On models with manually operated rear windows, note the closed position of the handle, then press the spacer/clip located under the handle towards the front of the car, and slide the handle from the splines (see illustrations).
8 Release the door trim panel studs, carefully levering between the panel and door with a flat-bladed lever (see illustration). Work around the outside of the panel, and when all the studs are released, lift the door trim panel upwards and off the window slot. Support the panel away from the door.
9 Disconnect the wiring connectors from the door switch in the trim panel.
10 Release the retaining clip and unhook the cable from the inner door handle (see illustration), and then remove the trim panel from the vehicle.
11 On front doors, if required, undo the retaining screw and unclip the trim panel from the door frame (see illustration).

Refitting

12 Before refitting, check whether any of the trim panel retaining studs where broken

12.11 Undo the retaining screw (arrowed) to remove trim

12.12 Clip on the left shows how it should be, before refitting the trim panel

13.2 Unclip the cover from the lock securing screws

on removal, and renew them as necessary. If the retaining clip part of the stud has been pressed down onto the stud, then it will need to be withdraw back into position to the end of the centre stud **(see illustration)**. The Refitting of the trim panel is then a reversal of removal. Check the operation of the door electrical equipment.

---

13 Door handle and lock components – removal and refitting

Removal

Front door lock cylinder/ door handle end cap

1 If working on the right-hand door handle, using a small screwdriver in the slot provided,

carefully release the trim cover from the door lock cylinder.
2 Open the door, then remove the plastic cap in the rear edge of the door to locate the two retaining screws **(see illustration)**.
3 Unscrew both of the retaining screws until they stop, and then push the outer screw inwards to release the locking clamp **(see illustration)**.
4 Pull out the door handle, and hold it in this position whilst withdrawing the lock cylinder/end cap out of the door handle, then release the handle to its original position **(see illustration)**.

Rear door handle end cap

5 Open the door, then remove the rubber cap at the rear edge of the door **(see illustration)**.
6 VW technicians use a special tool (T10389) to release the locking clamp. A tool can be made out of a length of metal rod, put a small

hook on the end, and then wrap a piece of insulation tape 40mm up from the end.
7 Insert the special tool approx 40mm (up to the insulation tape) through the hole in the door. With the hook facing to the inside of the vehicle, hook the locking clamp and pull, to release the clamp **(see illustration)**.
8 Pull out the door handle, and hold it in this position whilst withdrawing the end cap out of the door handle, then release the handle to its original position **(see illustration)**.

Exterior door handle

9 Depending on door being worked on, either remove the door lock cylinder or door handle end cap, as described previously in this Section.
10 Slide the handle to the rear edge of the door, to release it from the door handle mounting plate, and then pull it outwards and disengage it from the door **(see illustration)**.

13.3 Push on the outer screw to release the locking clamp

13.4 Pull out the door handle, and withdraw the door lock cylinder

13.5 Remove the rubber grommet/seal

13.7 Insert hooked rod and pull to release the locking clamp

13.8 Pull out the door handle, and remove the end cap

13.10 Slide the door handle to the rear of the door, then pull it out to remove

13.11 Unclip the seal from the door panel

13.14 Undo the retaining screw (arrowed)

13.16a Unclip the outer cable...

13.16b ...hinge the outer cable upwards...

13.16c ...and unhook the inner cable from the lever

11 If required recover the gasket from the handle aperture **(see illustration)**.

Exterior door handle mounting plate

12 Remove the exterior door handle as described in paragraphs 9 and 10.

13.18 Undo the door lock retaining bolts and screw (arrowed)

13.20a Release the outer cable locking pegs...

13 Remove the window regulator as described in Section 14.

14 On the outside of the door, undo the retaining screw from the front of the door handle aperture **(see illustration)**.

13.19 Remove the lock assembly from inside the door panel

13.20b ...then disconnect the inner cable from the lever

15 Reaching up inside the door, slide the mounting plate to the rear edge of the door, and then disengage it from the outer panel.

16 Unhook the operating cable from the mounting bracket, unclip the end of the outer cable and release the inner cable from the mechanism **(see illustrations)**.

Door lock

17 Remove the window regulator as described in Section 14.

18 Undo the two lock retaining screws, on the rear edge of the door and the one screw from the inside of the door **(see illustration)**.

19 Reaching up inside the door, remove the door lock assembly, releasing the grommet for the wiring connector, as it is removed **(see illustration)**.

20 To remove the operating cables, release the locking pegs, twist the outer cable and then unhook the inner cable from the operating lever **(see illustrations)**.

Refitting

Front door lock cylinder/ door handle end cap

21 Pull out the door handle and insert the lock cylinder housing/end cap into the door handle mounting-bracket.

22 Whilst keeping pressure on the lock cylinder/end cap, tighten both retaining screws in the rear edge of the door to 4Nm.

23 Where applicable, refit the plastic trim cover to the door lock cylinder.

24 Refit the plastic cap to cover the screws at the rear edge of the door.

25 Check the operation of the lock before closing the door, by sliding a screwdriver into the lock to operate the mechanism.

Rear door handle end cap

26 Pull out the door handle and insert the end cap into the door handle mounting-bracket.

27 Whilst keeping pressure on the handle end cap, use a screwdriver through the hole in the rear edge of the door to press the locking clamp back into position.

28 Refit the rubber grommet to cover the hole at the rear edge of the door.

29 Check the operation of the lock before closing the door, by sliding a screwdriver into the lock to operate the mechanism.

14.2 Prise out the access cap (arrowed)

14.3 Remove the access panel

14.4 Window glass clamp securing screws (arrowed)

Exterior door handle

30 If removed, locate the gasket on the door handle aperture.

31 Insert the handle into the door at the front end first, and then pivot the handle back into position. Slide the handle towards the front of the door, to lock it back in position in the mounting bracket.

32 Refit the lock cylinder or handle end cap, as described previously in this Section and check that it functions correctly.

Exterior door handle mounting plate

33 Refitting is a reversal of removal, making sure the operating cable is attached to the mounting bracket securely. Tighten the securing screw securely. Refit the window regulator as described in Section 14.

Door lock

34 Refitting is a reversal of removal, making sure the operating cables are attached to the lock securely. Tighten the mounting bolts to the specified torque. Refit the window regulator as described in Section 14.

14 Door window glass and regulator – removal and refitting

Removal

Front door window glass

1 Remove the door inner trim panel as described in Section 12.

14.6 Lifting the window glass from the front door

2 Prise out the access cap from the inner door panel **(see illustration)**.

3 Release the wiring loom, and then unclip the plastic trim panel from the inside of the door **(see illustration)**.

4 Temporarily connect the wiring to the switches, then switch on the ignition, and lower the window glass until the bolts attaching it to the regulator are visible through the access holes **(see illustration)**. If there is a fault with the electric motor, remove the motor in order to lower the glass.

5 Loosen the bolts on the regulator to release the window glass clamps (do not remove bolts completely).

6 Lift the rear of the window glass so that it is tilted, then remove it upwards from the door **(see illustration)**.

Rear door window glass

7 Remove the door inner trim panel as described in Section 12.

14.8 Remove the rubber grommet to access the roll pins (arrowed)

8 Prise out the access cap from the inner door panel and lower the window glass until the plastic roll-pins are visible through the access hole **(see illustration)**. On models with electric windows, temporarily reconnect the switch to operate the glass. If there is a fault with the electric motor, remove the motor in order to lower the glass.

9 Screw a 5.0 mm diameter bolt into the plastic centre roll-pin and pull it out, then screw an 8.0 mm diameter bolt into the outer part of the roll-pin and remove **(see illustrations)**. Do not apply too much pressure, as the roll-pin may drop inside the door, causing further dismantling of the window regulator to retrieve it. It is recommended that the roll-pin is renewed whenever removed.

10 Carefully unclip the outer window seal trim from the upper edge of the door panel **(see illustration)**.

11 Pull out the window channel rubber from

14.9a Use a 5.0 mm bolt to pull out the plastic centre roll-pin...

14.9b ...then use an 8.0 mm bolt to pull out the plastic outer roll-pin

14.10 Unclip the outer window seal

14.11a Pull out the window channel rubber moulding…

14.11b …and undo the retaining screw (arrowed)…

14.11c …then remove the door frame trim panel

14.12 Lifting the window glass from the rear door

14.15 Door window regulator motor

14.16 Release the motor from the locating pegs

the rear of the door frame, undo the retaining screw and slide the small trim panel upwards and disengage it from the outside of the door frame **(see illustrations)**.

12 Lift the window glass and withdraw it from the outside of the door **(see illustration)**.

Window regulator motor

13 Remove the door inner trim panel as described in Section 12.

14 With the window fully closed, use strong tape to hold the glass in position.

15 Release the locking clips and disconnect the wiring plugs from the motor/control unit **(see illustration)**.

16 Undo the three mounting screws and remove the motor from the mounting plate **(see illustration)**.

Window regulator assembly

17 Remove the door inner trim panel as described in Section 12.

18 Remove the door window glass as described earlier or disconnect the glass from the regulator and slide it to the top of the frame, securing it in place with strong tape.

19 Remove the window regulator motor as described in paragraphs 13 to 16.

20 Undo the retaining nuts, release the regulator drive plate from the door panel and remove the window regulator assembly out from the door **(see illustrations)**.

Refitting

Front door window glass

21 Carefully lower the tilted window glass into the door and engage it with the regulator clamps. Apply light downwards pressure to the glass to make sure it is correctly located in the channels, then tighten the regulator clamp bolts. Note that the bolts are fitted from the outside, so will have to be turned anti-clockwise to tighten them

22 If necessary, the window may be checked for correct operation at this stage by connecting the wiring to the switches.

23 Refit the access caps and plastic trim panel, making sure the wiring loom is routed correctly.

24 Refit the door inner trim panel with reference to Section 12.

Rear door window glass

25 Before fitting the window glass to the door, fit the new outer roll-pin so that it extends by equal amounts on each side of the glass, then secure with the new inner roll-pin.

26 Lower the window glass into the door and locate the roll-pin on the regulator clip. Press directly downwards until the roll-pin engages with the clip.

27 If necessary, the window may be checked for correct operation at this stage by connecting the wiring to the switches.

28 Refit the access cap.

14.20a Window regulator securing nuts (arrowed) – front door

14.20b Window regulator securing nuts (arrowed) – rear door

14.20c Withdraw the window regulator – rear door shown

29 Refit the door inner trim panel with reference to Section 12.

Window regulator motor

30 Locate the motor on the mounting plate and insert the mounting bolts hand-tight.
31 Reconnect the wiring plug, then remove the adhesive tape and operate the window down and up a short distance to allow the splines between the motor and cable drum to engage.
32 Fully tighten the motor mounting bolts.
33 Operate the window twice to its upper and lower stops to normalise the window operation.
34 Refit the door inner trim panel with reference to Section 12.

Window regulator assembly

35 Refit the window regulator assembly inside the door panel, locating the regulator drive plate lugs in position, then tighten the regulator assembly retaining nuts.
36 Refit the window regulator motor as described in paragraphs 30 to 34.
37 Refit the door window glass as described earlier in this section.
38 Refit the door inner trim panel with reference to Section 12.

15 Tailgate and support struts – removal and refitting

Removal

Tailgate

1 With the tailgate open, undo the trim panel retaining screws inside the grab handles **(see illustration)**.
2 Release the trim panel clips, carefully levering between the panel and tailgate with a flat-bladed lever. Work around the outside of the panel, and when all the clips are released, remove the panel.
3 Disconnect all of the wiring connectors situated behind the trim panel.
4 Working at the top of the tailgate, disconnect the wiring connectors from the heated rear screen terminals.
5 Remove the high level brake light from the top of the tailgate as described in Chapter 12, Section 7.

15.1 Undo the screws (arrowed) in the grab handle recesses

6 Free the wiring grommet from the tailgate **(see illustration)**, and then tie a piece of string to each end of the wiring and washer hose, then noting the correct routing, release the harness rubber grommets from the tailgate and withdraw the wiring and washer hose. When the end of the wiring and washer hose appears, untie the string and leave it in position in the tailgate; it can then be used on refitting to draw the wiring and washer hose back into position.
7 Using a suitable marker pen draw around the outline of each hinge marking its correct position on the tailgate.
8 With the help of an assistant to support the tailgate, remove the support struts as described below.
9 Unscrew and remove the bolts securing the hinges to the tailgate. Where necessary, recover the gaskets that are fitted between the hinge and vehicle body.
10 Inspect the hinges for signs of wear or damage and renew if necessary. The hinges are secured to the vehicle roof panel by nuts, which can be accessed once the headlining rear cover strip has been removed.

Support struts

⚠️ *Warning: The support struts are filled with a gas and must be disposed of safely.*

11 With the help of an assistant, support the tailgate in the open position.
12 Using a small flat-bladed screwdriver lift the locking clip, and pull the gas support strut off its balljoint mounting on the tailgate (see

15.6 Release the wiring grommet (arrowed) from the tailgate

illustration). Repeat the procedure on the lower strut mounting and remove the strut from the vehicle body. **Note:** *If the gas strut is to be re-used, the locking clip must not be taken all the way out, or the clip will be damaged.*

Refitting

Tailgate

13 Refitting is the reverse of removal, aligning the hinges with the marks made before removal. Tighten retaining bolts to the specified torque.
14 On completion, close the tailgate and check its alignment with the surrounding panels. If necessary slight adjustment can be made by unscrewing the retaining bolts and repositioning the tailgate on its hinges. If the tailgate buffers are in need of adjustment, continue as follows.
15 Locate the adjustment buffers on the tailgate. Through the hole in the rubber cap, insert an Allen key and undo the screw until the centre notched slide will move freely in or out, in the housing. When the adjustment buffer has been set to the correct position tighten the centre screw. When renewing buffers the notched slide is preset at 12.5 mm from the housing. To remove the adjustment buffer, turn anti-clockwise 90° with a spanner **(see illustrations)**.

Support struts

16 Refitting is a reverse of the removal procedure, ensuring that the strut is securely retained by its retaining clips.

15.12 Lift locking clip (arrowed) to release strut from the balljoint

15.15a Slacken the centre screw to adjust the tailgate buffer...

15.15b ...check the setting on each buffer to line up tailgate

16.0 Slide the key in the slot in the trim panel, to operate the lever to open the tailgate

16.3 Undo the lock retaining screws (arrowed)

16.5 Disconnect the wiring connector...

16.6 ...and remove the tailgate handle/ release unit

16 Tailgate lock components – removal and refitting

Removal

Note: *If the lock is inoperative, the tailgate can be opened manually by inserting the key into the slot provided, in the lower part of the inner tailgate trim, and then sliding it to the left-hand side of the vehicle (see illustration).*

Tailgate lock

1 Open up the tailgate and remove the trim panel as described in Section 15.
2 Disconnect the wiring connector from the rear of the lock.
3 Undo the retaining bolts and remove the lock from the lower edge of the tailgate (see illustration).

17.5a Release the securing clips (arrowed)...

Tailgate handle/release unit

4 Open up the tailgate and remove the trim panel as described in Section 15.
5 Disconnect the wiring from the handle/ release unit (see illustration).
6 Undo the retaining screws, and then turn the handle/release unit clockwise slightly, to release it from the tailgate (see illustration).

Refitting

7 Refitting is reversals of removal, however, before refitting the trim panel, check the operation of the lock components.

17 Central locking components – description, removal and refitting

Description

1 The central locking system consists of the

17.3 Onboard supply control unit (arrowed)

17.5b ...then withdraw the control unit downwards

17.4 Disconnect the two wiring block connectors (arrowed)

following main components. Note that the central locking and anti-theft alarm systems share some components (see Chapter 12):
a) Convenience system onboard supply control unit located behind the driver's side facia panel.
b) Door control units integrated in the window regulator motors.
c) Electric door lock actuators integrated in the door locks.
d) Fuel tank filler cap flap actuator located behind the luggage compartment trim.
e) Tailgate lock actuator located in the tailgate, together with the release button.
f) Bonnet contact switch located on the bonnet lock.
g) Remote control transmitter on the ignition key fob.

Removal

2 Before working on any electrical circuit, disconnect the battery negative lead (refer to *Disconnecting the battery* in the *Reference* Chapter at the end of this manual).

Convenience system onboard supply control unit

3 The control unit is located behind the fuse/ relay box at the right-hand side of the facia, this can be accessed from under the driver's side facia above the throttle pedal (see illustration).
4 Release the locking clips and disconnect the wiring connectors from the rear of the control unit (see illustration).
5 Release the two securing clips, push the control unit forwards slightly, and then withdraw it downwards and out from under the facia (see illustrations).

Electric door lock actuator

6 Remove the door lock as described in Section 13.

Tailgate/boot lid lock activator

7 Remove the tailgate handle/release unit as described in Section 16.

Bonnet contact switch

8 Remove the bonnet lock as described in Section 10. If necessary, the operating cable may remain attached to the lock.
9 On the lock, release the tab and push the switch from the slotted holes.

Fuel tank filler cap flap actuator

10 Open the tank filler flap and removed the filler cap, then undo the screw from inside the aperture and peel the rubber grommet from around the filler neck.
11 Carefully pull the tank flap, complete with water drain hose from the wing panel. Move the flap to the rear of the vehicle and swing it outwards to remove it from the wing panel.
12 Side the actuator upwards and release it from the inner body panel.
13 Trace the wiring from the actuator and disconnect the connector.

Remote control transmitter battery

14 Using a screwdriver inserted in the slot, separate the transmitter unit cover from the key (see illustration).
15 Carefully prise out the battery, noting which way round it is fitted (see illustration).

Refitting

16 Refitting is a reversal of removal; on completion check the operation of the central locking system.

---

18 Mirrors and associated components – removal and refitting

Removal

Exterior mirror

1 Remove the door inner trim panel as described in Section 12.
2 If not already removed, undo the retaining

17.14 Unclip the battery cover...

17.15 ...and remove the battery

screw and unclip the small inner trim panel from the door frame (see illustration).
3 Trace the wiring from the exterior mirror and disconnect the wiring plug, also release the wiring support clips from the door panel (see illustration).
4 Unscrew the mounting bolt while supporting the exterior mirror, then withdraw the exterior mirror from the door while guiding the wiring through the hole (see illustration).

Mirror glass

Note: *The mirror glass is clipped into place. Removal of the glass without the VW special forked tool (number 80-200) may result in breakage of the glass. Wear protective gloves and glasses to prevent personal injury.*
5 Press in the bottom of the mirror glass so that the top edge is furthest from the housing. If required, protect the edge of the housing with masking tape, then insert the special tool

and lever the mirror glass from its mounting clips. Take great care when removing the glass; do not use excessive force, as the glass is easily broken. If the VW special tool is not available, use a flat-bladed lever (see illustration).
6 Disconnect the wiring connectors from the mirror heating element (see illustration).

Mirror housing

7 Remove the mirror glass as described in paragraphs 5 and 6.
8 Release the two upper retaining clips and pull the housing from the mirror base (see illustrations).
9 If required, release the securing clip, disconnect the wiring connector for the indicator side repeater and then remove (see illustration). Check for the availability of parts for the side repeater, it may only be available as part of the mirror assembly.

18.2 Remove the inner trim panel

18.3 Disconnect the wiring connector and release the retaining clip (arrowed)

18.4 Undo the mirror retaining bolt (arrowed)

18.5 Remove the exterior mirror glass...

18.6 ...and disconnect the wiring (arrowed)

Mirror switch

10 Refer to Chapter 12, Section 4.

Refitting

11 Refitting is the reverse of the relevant removal procedure. When refitting the mirror glass, press firmly at the centre taking care not to use excessive force, as the glass is easily broken (*Wear protective gloves and glasses to prevent personal injury*).

Interior mirror (with sensors)

12 Switch off the ignition and all electrical consumers and remove the ignition key.
13 Separate the left and right mirror base covers, and disconnect the wiring plug **(see illustrations)**.
14 Slide the mirror downwards to release it from the mirror base **(see illustration)**. The mirror base is bonded to the windscreen. Whilst it is possible to remove the base, great care must be exercised to avoid damaging the windscreen. Due to the hazardous chemicals involved, it is recommended that the bonding of the mirror base to the windscreen be entrusted to a VW dealer or suitably equipped specialist.
15 With the base in place, refit the mirror to the base, reconnect the sensor wiring plugs and refit the two halves of the mirror base covers.

Interior mirror (without sensors)

16 Twist the mirror through 90°, anti-clockwise; this will then release it from the adhesive plate on the windscreen. Take care when removing the mirror as excessive force may damage the windscreen. Refitting is the reversal of the removal procedure.

19 Windscreen and rear window glass – general information

These areas of glass are bonded in position with a special adhesive. Renewal of such fixed glass is a difficult, messy and time-consuming task, which is beyond the scope of the home mechanic. It is difficult, unless one has plenty of practice, to obtain a secure, waterproof fit. Furthermore, the task carries a high risk of breakage; this applies especially to the laminated glass windscreen. In view of this, owners are strongly advised to have this sort of work carried out by one of the many specialist windscreen fitters.

20 Sunroof – general information

Due to the complexity of the sunroof mechanism, considerable expertise is needed to repair, renew or adjust the sunroof components successfully. Removal of the roof first requires the headlining to be removed, which is a complex and tedious operation, and not a task to be undertaken lightly. Therefore, any problems with the sunroof should be referred to a VW dealer. On models with an electric sunroof, if the sunroof motor fails to operate, first check the relevant fuse.

If the fault cannot be traced and rectified, the sunroof can be opened and closed manually using an Allen key to turn the motor spindle (a suitable key is supplied with the vehicle, and should be clipped onto the inside of the sunroof motor trim). To gain access to the motor, unclip the rear of the trim cover to open. Unclip the Allen key, and then insert it fully into the motor opening (against spring pressure). Rotate the key to move the sunroof to the required position.

21 Body exterior fittings – removal and refitting

Wheel arch liners and body under-panels

1 The various plastic covers fitted to the underside of the vehicle are secured in position by a mixture of screws, nuts and retaining clips and removal will be fairly obvious on inspection. Work methodically around the panel removing it's retaining screws and releasing its retaining clips until the panel is free and can be removed from the underside of the vehicle. Most clips used on the vehicle are simply prised out of position. Remove the wheels to ease the removal of the wheel arch liners.
2 On refitting, renew any retaining clips that may have been broken on removal, and ensure that the panel is securely retained by all the relevant clips and screws.

18.8a Release the two securing clips (arrowed)…

18.8b …and unclip the upper outer shell

18.9 Unclip indicator side repeater from mirror housing

18.13a Unclip the sides of mirror housing…

18.13b …disconnect the wiring connector…

18.14 …and slide the mirror from its mounting bracket

22.2 Seat rear mounting bolts (arrowed)

22.3 Seat front mounting bolts (one side shown)

22.8 Push the hooks in the direction of the arrows to release

Body trim strips and badges

3 The various body trim strips and badges are held in position with a special adhesive tape and locating lugs. Removal requires the trim/badge to be heated, to soften the adhesive, and then carefully lifted away from the surface. Due to the high risk of damage to the vehicle's paintwork during this operation, it is recommended that this task should be entrusted to a VW dealer.

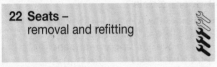

22 Seats – removal and refitting

Note: *Refer to the warnings in Chapter 12, Section 25, on airbags.*

Removal

Front seats

Note: *The amount of wiring connectors under the seat may, vary depending on the vehicle specification.*

1 Disconnect the battery negative lead (refer to *Disconnecting the battery* in the *Reference* Chapter at the end of this manual).

2 Slide the seat forwards as far as possible and unscrew the rear mounting bolts **(see illustration)**.

3 Slide the seat rearwards as far as possible and unscrew the front mounting bolts **(see illustration)**.

⚠️ *Warning: As a precaution against unintentional electrostatic discharge into the airbag, briefly touch part of the vehicle body before disconnecting the wiring.*

4 Tilt the seat back slightly and disconnect the wiring connectors from under the seat. VW technicians fit an adapter to the airbag wiring connector as a safety precaution; however, wrap the wiring connectors with insulation tape or similar, to prevent any contact of the wiring.

5 Check that the wiring harness is released from any retaining clips, and then remove the headrests from the seat back; this will give more room when removing the seat from the vehicle.

6 When removing the seat from the vehicle, do not lift the seat by the seat belt stalk or by the seat adjustment levers. If necessary, have

an assistant help to remove the seat, as it is heavy, and surrounding trim panels may be otherwise damaged. Make sure that the seat runners; do not damage the paintwork as the seat is withdrawn.

Rear seat cushion

7 Pull the front edge of the cushion upwards from the location sockets, and then lift the rear of the seat cushion and fold it forwards.

8 Push the hooks sideways from the pivot brackets and remove the seat cushion from inside the car **(see illustration)**.

Rear seat backrest

9 Remove the seat cushion as described in paragraphs 7 & 8.

10 Fold the backrest forwards, and then remove the plastic trim from the centre mounting **(see illustration)**.

11 Unbolt the clamp, then remove the left backrest by lifting it from the centre mounting

22.10 Unclip the trim cover

22.11b ...and depress the catch to release the outer mounting

and sliding it off the outer mounting pin **(see illustrations)**.

12 Before removing the right-hand seat back it will be necessary to unscrew the bolt and remove the centre stalk from the floor **(see illustration)**.

13 Remove the right backrest by lifting it from the centre mounting and releasing it from the outer mounting bracket, as shown for the left seat back.

Refitting

14 Refitting is a reversal of removal, but tighten the mounting bolts to the specified torque where given.

23 Front seat belt tensioning mechanism – general information

All models covered in this manual are fitted with a front seat belt tensioner system

22.11a Unbolt the centre securing bracket...

22.12 Remove the seat belt stalk securing bolt

incorporated in each of the inertia reels. Rear seat belt inertia reels with the tensioner system are only fitted to some models, other models having standard inertia reels.

The system is designed to instantaneously take up any slack in the seat belt in the case of a sudden frontal impact, therefore reducing the possibility of injury to the front seat occupants. The seat belt tensioner is triggered by a frontal impact above a predetermined force. Lesser impacts, including impacts from behind, will not trigger the system.

When the system is triggered, the explosive gas in the tensioner mechanism retracts and locks the seat belt. This prevents the seat belt moving and keeps the occupant firmly in position in the seat. Once the tensioner has been triggered, the seat belt will be permanently locked and the assembly must be renewed.

There is a risk of personal injury if the system is triggered inadvertently when working on the vehicle, and it is therefore strongly recommended that any work involving the seat belt inertia reels be entrusted to a VW dealer. Note the following warnings before contemplating any work on the front seat belts.

⚠️ *Warning: Do not expose the tensioner mechanism to temperatures in excess of 100°C.*
• *Before removing any components, disconnect the battery negative lead (refer to Disconnecting the battery in the Reference Chapter at the end of this manual).*

• *If the tensioner mechanism is dropped, it must be renewed, even it has suffered no apparent damage.*
• *Do not allow any solvents to come into contact with the tensioner mechanism.*
• *Do not attempt to open the tensioner mechanism as it contains explosive gas.*
• *Tensioners must be discharged before they are disposed of, but this task should be entrusted to a VW dealer.*
• *Some of the bolts securing the seat belts are microencapsulated and need to be heated with a hot air blower before they are slackened. Microencapsulated means that the threads of the bolts are coated with a locking compound from new. New bolts will be required for refitting.*

24 Seat belt components – removal and refitting

⚠️ *Warning: Refer to Section 23 before proceeding.*

Front seat belt removal

5-door models

1 Disconnect the battery negative lead (refer to *Disconnecting the battery* in the *Reference* Chapter at the end of this manual).
2 Remove the upper and lower trim panels from the B-pillar with reference to Section 25.
3 Pull back the carpet, then unscrew and remove the seat belt lower anchor mounting bolt and remove the belt from the floor **(see**

illustration)**. Discard the bolt and obtain a new one. Also, note that the threads of the corresponding nut must be cleaned with a tap before fitting the new bolt.

⚠️ *Warning: As a precaution against unintentional electrostatic discharge, briefly touch part of the vehicle body before disconnecting the wiring.*
4 Release the locking clip and disconnect the wiring connector from the inertia reel **(see illustration)**.
5 Unscrew the mounting bolt and remove the inertia reel from the bottom of the B-pillar **(see illustration)**.
6 Unclip the belt guide from the B-pillar **(see illustration)**.
7 Unscrew and remove the bolt securing the seat belt upper anchor to the height adjuster on the B-pillar **(see illustration)**. The seat belt assembly can then be removed from the vehicle.
8 To remove the belt height adjustment, remove the securing bolt from the top of the adjuster and lift upwards to release from the pillar.

3-door models

9 Remove the relevant rear seat and backrest as described in Section 22.
10 Remove the upper trim panel from the B-pillar with reference to Section 25.
11 Remove the sill and side trim panels with reference to Section 25.
12 Unscrew the bolts securing the anchor rail to the sill, and slide the rail from the end of the seat belt **(see illustrations)**.

24.3 Seat belt lower anchorage bolt (arrowed)

24.4 Release the locking peg (arrowed), to disconnect wiring connector

24.5 Front seat belt inertia reel mounting bolt

24.6 Unclip the front seat belt guide

24.7 Seat belt upper anchorage securing bolt (arrowed)

24.12a Remove the bolt at the front of the belt anchor rail...

13 On models without rear seat belt tensioners, unscrew the mounting bolt and withdraw the inertia reels.

14 On models with rear seat belt tensioners, disconnect the battery negative lead (refer to 'Disconnecting the battery' in the Reference Chapter at the end of this manual), then unscrew the inertia reel mounting bolt, withdraw the reel and disconnect the wiring.

⚠ *Warning: As a precaution against unintentional electrostatic discharge, briefly touch part of the vehicle body before disconnecting the wiring.*

15 Unclip the belt guide from the B-pillar **(see illustration 24.6)**.

16 Unscrew and remove the bolt securing the seat belt upper anchor to the height adjuster on the B-pillar **(see illustration 24.7)**.

17 Remove the seat belt assembly from the vehicle.

18 To remove the belt height adjustment, remove the securing bolt from the top of the adjuster and lift upwards to release from the pillar.

Front seat belt stalk removal

19 Remove the front seat assembly as described in Section 22.

20 Unscrew and remove the bolt securing the stalk to the seat, and remove the stalk **(see illustration)**. Trace the wiring back from the seat belt stalk and disconnect it from under the seat cushion. Discard the bolt and obtain a new one. Also, note that the threads of the corresponding nut must be cleaned with a tap before fitting the new bolt.

Rear seat side belt removal

21 Remove the rear seat as described in Section 22.

22 Remove the side panel trim, luggage compartment side trim and C-pillar trim panel with reference to Section 25. **Note:** *Refer to Chapter 12 on models with rear side airbags.*

23 Unbolt the belt from the floor anchorage **(see illustration)**.

24 Unscrew the mounting bolts and withdraw the inertia reel and upper anchorage bracket, from the rear panel **(see illustration)**

25 On models with rear seat belt tensioners, disconnect the battery negative lead (refer to *Disconnecting the battery* in the *Reference* Chapter at the end of this manual), then disconnect the wiring, as shown in **illustration 24.4**.

⚠ *Warning: As a precaution against unintentional electrostatic discharge, briefly touch part of the vehicle body before disconnecting the wiring.*

Rear seat centre belt and buckle removal

26 Remove the rear seat cushion and backrest as described in Section 22.

27 To remove the inertia reel, first prise the

24.12b ...and the bolt at the rear of the rail – 3-door models

24.23 Undo the seat belt lower anchorage bolt

belt guide from the top of the backrest **(see illustrations)**.

28 Carefully prise the trim moulding from around the edge of the backrest **(see illustration)**.

24.27a Prise out the trim clip...

24.28 Release the seat trim from the seat frame

24.20 Undo the seat belt stalk securing bolt (arrowed)

24.24 Rear seat belt inertia reel and upper anchorage mounting bolts

29 Pull back the padding from the seat back to access the inertia reel securing nut **(see illustration)**.

30 Unbolt and remove the inertia reel, guiding the seat belt out from the seat back.

24.27b ...and remove the belt guide

24.29 Rear centre seat belt inertia reel mounting nut

Refitting

31 Refitting is a reversal of the removal procedure, ensuring that all the seat belt units are located correctly and mounting bolts are securely tightened to their specified torque. Check all the trim panels are securely retained by all the relevant retaining clips. When refitting the B-pillar upper trim panels, ensure that the height adjustment peg engages correctly with the trim panel.

25 Interior trim – removal and refitting

Interior trim panels

1 The interior trim panels are secured using either screws or various types of trim fasteners, usually studs or clips.

2 Check that there are no other panels overlapping the one to be removed; usually there is a sequence that has to be followed, and this will only become obvious on close inspection.

3 Remove all obvious fasteners, such as screws. If the panel will not come free, it will be held by hidden clips or fasteners. These are usually situated around the edge of the panel and can be prised up to release them; note, however, that they can break quite easily so new ones should be available. The best way of releasing such clips, without the correct type of tool, is to use a large flat-bladed screwdriver. Note in many cases that the adjacent sealing strip must be prised back to release a panel.

4 When removing a panel, **never** use excessive force or the panel may be damaged; always check carefully that all fasteners or other relevant components have been removed or released before attempting to withdraw a panel.

5 On models with side airbags, disconnect the battery negative lead (refer to *'Disconnecting the battery'* in the *'Reference'* Chapter at the end of this manual.

6 Refitting is the reverse of the removal procedure; secure the fasteners by pressing them firmly into place and ensure that all disturbed components are correctly secured to prevent rattles.

B-pillar (3-door models)

7 The side trim panels are removed from the lower sill trim panels up to the upper pillar trim panels, as they are overlapped.

8 Remove the rear seat cushion and backrest as described in Section 22.

9 Carefully lever the sill trim panel upwards to release the retaining clips and remove the trim panel.

10 Prise out the clip at the lower part of the seat side trim panel, then starting from the rear of the trim panel unclip it from the side body panel.

11 Pull the upper B-pillar trim panel out at the bottom to release it from the pillar, and then slide it downwards to release it from the headlining. Undo the lower seat belt mounting bracket and pass the seat belt through the panel to remove it completely.

12 Refitting is the reverse of removal.

B-pillar (5-door models)

13 Remove the rear seat cushion and backrest as described in Section 22.

14 Release the securing clip from the rear of the trim panel, and then carefully lever the sill trim panel upwards to release the retaining clips and remove the trim panel **(see illustrations)**.

15 Pull the B-pillar trim panel out at the bottom to release it from the pillar, and then slide it downwards to release it from the headlining **(see illustrations)**. Undo the lower seat belt mounting bracket and pass the seat belt through the panel to remove it completely.

16 Refitting is the reverse of removal.

Luggage compartment trim

17 Open the tailgate and remove the parcel shelf and floor panel from the luggage compartment

18 Remove the rear seat cushion and backrest as described in Section 22.

19 Carefully unclip the trim panel from the rear of the luggage compartment by prising it upwards **(see illustrations)**

20 On 3-door models, remove the seat side trim panel as described in paragraphs 9 and 10.

21 On 5-door models, open the rear door and unclip the side trim panel, from the front of the rear wheel arch **(see illustration)**.

22 Undo the retaining screws from the lower rear edge of the trim panel **(see illustration)**.

23 Undo the retaining screws and remove the

25.14a Release the securing clip...

25.14b ...and remove the sill trim panel

25.15a Unclip the B-pillar trim panel...

25.15b ...and slide it downwards from the headlining

25.19a Carefully lever the rear trim panel...

25.19b ...and unclip it from the rear panel

25.21 Unclip the side trim panel – 5-door models

25.22 Undo the retaining screw (arrowed)

25.23 Undo the shelf support retaining screws (arrowed)

shelf support from the lower front edge of the trim panel (see illustration).

24 Undo the retaining screws from the upper front edge of the trim panel (see illustration).

25 The side trim panel can then be unclipped from the body panel (see illustration). Check around the trim panel to make sure there are no more retaining screws, as some models may have anchor brackets fitted for securing luggage.

26 Pull the upper C-pillar trim panel out at the bottom to release it from the pillar, and then slide it downwards to release it from the headlining. Undo the lower seat belt mounting bracket and pass the seat belt through the panel to remove it completely.

27 Refitting is the reverse of removal.

A-pillar trim

28 Pull the trim panel out from the top of the pillar to release the retaining clips, then work downwards along the length of the trim and pull upwards to release from behind the facia panel.

29 On models with speaker fitted to trim panel, disconnect the wiring connector as the trim panel is removed.

30 Refitting is the reverse of removal.

Steering column shrouds

31 Release the locking lever and move the steering column down and pull it upwards, then lock in position.

32 To make access easier remove the steering wheel, as described in Chapter 10, Section 15.

33 Unclip the upper shroud from the bottom of the instrument panel and the top of the

25.24 Undo the upper front edge retaining screws (arrowed)

steering column, then remove it from the vehicle (see illustrations).

34 Undo the retaining screws from under the steering column lower shroud and the top of the steering column, then remove it from the vehicle (see illustrations).

25.25 Remove the side trim from the luggage compartment

35 Refitting is the reverse of removal.

Glovebox

36 Using a lever, unclip the end panel on the passenger side of the facia (see illustration).

37 Undo the two retaining screws from

25.33a Unclip the upper shroud from the instrument panel...

25.33b ...and at the front from the lower shroud

25.34a Undo the lower retaining screw...

25.34b ...and the two upper screws (arrowed)...

25.36 Unclip the side trim from the facia

25.37 Undo the lower retaining screws (arrowed)

25.38 Undo the upper retaining screws (arrowed)

25.39a Release the upper corner of the glovebox...

25.39b ...and disconnect the cooling hose

25.44a Release the securing clip...

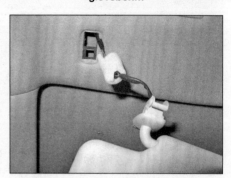

25.44b ...and disconnect the wiring connector

under the lower edge of the glovebox (see illustration).

38 Open up the glovebox lid then unscrew and remove the five retaining screws (see illustration).

39 Release the upper left-hand corner, then slide the glovebox out of position, disconnecting any wiring connectors from the tyre pressure monitor switch and the passenger airbag isolation switch (depending on model), and disconnect the air conditioning cooling hose as they become accessible (see illustrations).

40 Refitting is the reverse of removal.

Carpets

41 The passenger compartment floor carpet is in one piece and is secured at its edges by screws or clips; usually the same fasteners used to secure the various adjoining trim panels.

42 Carpet removal and refitting is reasonably straightforward but very time-consuming because all adjoining trim panels must be removed first, as must components such as the seats, the centre console and seat belt lower anchorages.

Headlining

43 The headlining is clipped to the roof and can be withdrawn only once all fittings such as the grab handles, sun visors, interior lights, sunroof (if fitted), and related upper trim panels have been removed. Also the door, tailgate and sunroof aperture sealing strips need to be prised clear of the headlining.

44 To remove the sun visors, withdraw the plastic retaining clips, then release the securing clips and pull the visor from the headlining, disconnect the wiring connector as the visor is removed (see illustrations)

45 To remove the grab handles, unclip the

plastic cover, then release the securing clips and pull the grab handle from the headlining (see illustrations)

46 Note that headlining removal requires considerable skill and experience if it is to be carried out without damage and is therefore best entrusted to an expert.

26 Centre console – removal and refitting

Removal

1 Switch off the ignition.

2 Carefully unclip the trim panel from around the Radio/CD player and heater control panel (see illustrations).

3 Unclip the trim panel and release the gear lever gaiter from the centre console (see illustration).

25.45a Unclip the covers to access...

25.45b ...the retaining clips

26.2a Unclip the radio/CD trim...

26.2b ...and the heater control panel trim

26.3 Release the gaiter trim from the centre console

26.4a Undo the four screws (arrowed)...

26.4b ...push down on the retaining clips (arrowed)...

26.4c ...and remove the upper trim

26.5 Unclip the trim cover

4 Undo the four retaining screws and then push down on the two retaining clips at the rear of the upper trim to release the upper trim from the centre console **(see illustrations)**.
5 Unclip the plastic trim from in front of the handbrake lever **(see illustration)**.
6 On models without armrest, carefully lever the cup holder from the rear of the centre console **(see illustration)**.
7 On models with armrest fitted, first open the rear cup holder and undo the retaining screw from inside, then unclip the cup holder from the rear of the centre console. Working inside the rear of the centre console, undo the retaining nut and lift the armrest from the centre console.
8 Undo the retaining screw from the rear of the console **(see illustration)**.
9 Undo the four retaining screws from the front of the console **(see illustration)**.

10 Remove the securing clip and remove the foot rest from the driver's side footwell **(see illustration)**.
11 Working at the front edges of the centre console, pull each side outwards to release

the Velcro straps securing each side to the heater unit **(see illustration)**.
12 With the front edges released, slide the centre console to the rear, and then lift it up over the handbrake lever to remove. To make

26.6 Unclip the cup holder

26.8 Undo the rear screw (arrowed)

26.9 Undo the four screws (arrowed)

26.10 Remove the footrest from the drivers side

26.11 Pull the front out to release the Velcro

26.12 Remove the handbrake lever

27.10 Unclip the fusebox cover

27.4 Unclip the cover from the side of the facia

27.18 Retaining screw (arrowed) in the instrument panel aperture

removal easier, undo the mounting bolts and remove the handbrake lever from the floor panel **(see illustration)**.

Refitting

13 Refitting is a reversal of removal, but tighten the screws securing the centre console to the facia first, before tightening the rest.

27 Facia panel assembly – removal and refitting

Note: *Refer to the warnings in Chapter 12 for airbags. Before disconnecting the battery, refer to 'Disconnecting the battery' at the rear of this manual.*

Removal

1 Disconnect the battery negative lead (refer to *Disconnecting the battery* in the *Reference* Chapter at the end of this manual).
2 Remove the steering column shrouds as described in Section 25.
3 Remove the steering column switch assembly, as described in Chapter 12, Section 4.
4 Prise out the trim panels from each end of the facia **(see illustration)**.
5 Remove the A-pillar upper trim panels, as described in Section 25.
6 Remove the glovebox as described in Section 25.
7 Remove the centre console as described in Section 26.
8 Remove the instrument panel as described in Chapter 12, Section 10.
9 Remove the light switch from the driver's side panel, as described in Chapter 12, Section 4.
10 Unclip the fusebox trim cover from the lower part of the facia **(see illustration)**.

11 Working inside the glovebox aperture, undo the three bolts from the passenger side airbag mounting bracket and disconnect the wiring connector from the end of the airbag unit. Refer to Chapter 12, Section 26.
12 Remove the Radio/CD or navigation unit, as described in Chapter 12, Section 21.
13 On models with standard radio/CD fitted, undo the retaining screws and remove the storage compartment from the centre of the facia.
14 Remove the Climatronic/ heater controls, as described in Chapter 3, Section 9.
15 Where fitted, disconnect the wiring connectors from the temperature senders in the air vents at each end of the facia panel.
16 Unbolt the fusebox from the driver's side of the facia, and place to one side.
17 Disconnect the wiring connectors from the switches below the centre air vents in the facia panel.
18 Undo the retaining screw from the instrument panel aperture **(see illustration)**.
19 Working your way around the facia, unscrew the retaining screws from the facia assembly, noting their fitted position. Then, with the help of an assistant, pull out from the bulkhead clips and remove from the vehicle. As the facia is being removed, disconnect any wiring retaining clips, noting it's routing to aid refitting.

Refitting

20 Refitting is a reversal of the removal procedure, noting the following points:
a) *Ensure the facia guides engage correctly with the clips on the bulkhead. As the facia is being fitted, check that all wiring is routed as noted during removal.*
b) *Insert all of the retaining screws hand-tight, then close both front doors and check that the facia is positioned centrally between the door trims. If it needs to be moved one way or another, place a wad of cloth between the facia and door trim, then close the door. This should move the facia as required. When central, fully tighten the securing screws.*
c) *On completion, reconnect the battery and check that all the electrical components and switches function correctly.*

Chapter 12
Body electrical system

Contents

Degrees of difficulty

Easy, suitable for novice with little experience	**Fairly easy,** suitable for beginner with some experience	**Fairly difficult,** suitable for competent DIY mechanic	**Difficult,** suitable for experienced DIY mechanic	**Very difficult,** suitable for expert DIY or professional

Specifications

System type. . . . . 12 volt negative earth

Fuses. . . . . See *Wiring diagrams* commencing on page 12•19

Bulbs

	Wattage/Type
Brake light	21W - bayonet
Brake light – High level.	LEDs
Day time running light (where fitted inside front foglight).	21W - P21W
Front direction indicators:	
All except models with gas discharged headlights	21W – PY bayonet
Models with gas discharged headlights.	24W – PSY
Front foglight	35W - H8
Front sidelight:	
All except models with gas discharged headlight	5W – wedge W5W
Madels with gas discharged headlights.	LEDs
Headlight:	
Halogen (single bulb):	
Twin filament	60/55W – H4
Halogen (two bulbs):	
Dipped beam	55W – H7
Main beam	55W – H7
Gas discharge fitment (two bulbs):	
Static cornering bulb (inner)	55W – H7
Gas discharge bulb (outer)	35W – D3S (high voltage)
Front interior light unit:	
Outer bulbs (reading lights)	5W - wedge
Centre bulb (interior light).	5W – wedge or festoon
Interior light (vanity mirror)	5W - festoon
Luggage compartmant light	3W – wedge W3W
Number plate light (secured by clip)	5W – wedge W5W
Number plate light (secured by screws)	5W – festoon C5W
Rear direction indicators	21W – PY bayonet
Rear fog light	21W – H21W
Rear interior light unit	5W – wedge
Rear sidelight	5W – wedge W5W
Reversing light	21W - bayonet

Torque wrench settings

	Nm	lbf ft
Crash sensor mounting bolt	6	5
Passenger airbag and bracket retaining screws	9	7
Wiper arm securing nut:		
Front	20	15
Rear	12	9
Front wiper motor securing bolts	8	6
Rear wiper motor securing bolts	8	6

1 General information and precautions

⚠ **Warning: Before carrying out any work on the electrical system, read through the precautions given in 'Safety first!' at the beginning of this manual, and in Chapter 5A.**

The electrical system is of 12-volt negative earth type. Power for the lights and all electrical accessories is supplied by a lead-acid type battery, which is charged by the alternator.

This Chapter covers repair and service procedures for the various electrical components not associated with the engine. Information on the battery, alternator and starter motor can be found in Chapter 5A.

It should be noted that prior to working on any component in the electrical system, the ignition and all electrical consumers must be switched off. Additionally, where stated, the battery negative lead must be disconnected, however, note the information given in *Disconnecting the battery* in the *Reference* chapter at the end of this manual, as special procedures have to be carried out when reconnecting the battery.

Some models are fitted with gas discharge headlight systems, which include automatic range control to reduce the possibility of dazzling oncoming drivers. Note the special precautions which apply to these systems as given in Section 5.

2 Electrical fault finding – general information

Note: *Refer to the precautions given in 'Safety first!' and in Chapter 5A before starting work. The following tests relate to testing of the main electrical circuits, and should not be used to test delicate electronic circuits (such as anti-lock braking systems), particularly where an electronic control module is used.*

General

1 A typical electrical circuit consists of an electrical component; any switches, relays, motors, fuses, fusible links or circuit breakers related to that component, and the wiring and connectors which link the component to both the battery and the chassis. To help to pin-point a problem in an electrical circuit, wiring diagrams are included at the end of this Chapter. **Note:** *Many of the circuits are controlled by computerised systems (for instance, the windscreen wipers will only operate with the bonnet closed), so before assuming there are faults, it is worthwhile checking if specific conditions apply.*

2 Before attempting to diagnose an electrical fault, first study the appropriate wiring diagram to obtain a complete understanding of the components included in the particular circuit concerned. The possible sources of a fault can be narrowed down by noting if other components related to the circuit are operating properly. If several components or circuits fail at one time, the problem is likely to be related to a shared fuse or earth connection.

3 Electrical problems usually stem from simple causes, such as loose or corroded connections, a faulty earth connection, a blown fuse, a melted fusible link, or a faulty relay (refer to Section 3 for details of testing relays). Visually inspect the condition of all fuses, wires and connections in a problem circuit before testing the components. Use the wiring diagrams to determine which terminal connections will need to be checked in order to pin-point the trouble spot.

4 The basic tools required for electrical fault finding include a circuit tester or voltmeter (a 12-volt bulb with a set of test leads can also be used for certain tests); a self-powered test light (sometimes known as a continuity tester); an ohmmeter (to measure resistance); a battery and set of test leads; and a jumper wire, preferably with a circuit breaker or fuse incorporated, which can be used to bypass suspect wires or electrical components. Before attempting to locate a problem with test instruments, use the wiring diagram to determine where to make the connections.

5 To find the source of an intermittent wiring fault (usually due to a poor or dirty connection, or damaged wiring insulation), a wiggle test can be performed on the wiring. This involves wiggling the wiring by hand to see if the fault occurs as the wiring is moved. It should be possible to narrow down the source of the fault to a particular section of wiring. This method of testing can be used in conjunction with any of the tests described in the following sub-Sections.

6 Apart from problems due to poor connections, two basic types of fault can occur in an electrical circuit – open-circuit, or short-circuit.

7 Open-circuit faults are caused by a break somewhere in the circuit, which prevents current from flowing. An open-circuit fault will prevent a component from working, but will not cause the relevant circuit fuse to blow.

8 Short-circuit faults are caused by a short somewhere in the circuit, which allows the current flowing in the circuit to escape along an alternative route, usually to earth. Short-circuit faults are normally caused by a breakdown in wiring insulation, which allows a feed wire to touch either another wire, or an earthed component such as the bodyshell. A short-circuit fault will normally cause the relevant circuit fuse to blow.

Finding an open-circuit

9 To check for an open-circuit, connect one lead of a circuit tester or voltmeter to either the negative battery terminal or a known good earth.

10 Connect the other lead to a connector in the circuit being tested, preferably nearest to the battery or fuse.

11 Switch on the circuit, bearing in mind that some circuits are live only when the ignition switch is moved to a particular position.

12 If voltage is present (indicated either by the tester bulb lighting or a voltmeter reading, as applicable), this means that the section of the circuit between the relevant connector and the battery is problem-free.

13 Continue to check the remainder of the circuit in the same fashion.

14 When a point is reached at which no voltage is present, the problem must lie between that point and the previous test point with voltage. Most problems can be traced to a broken, corroded or loose connection.

Finding a short-circuit

15 To check for a short-circuit; first disconnect the load(s) from the circuit (loads are the components which draw current from a circuit, such as bulbs, motors, heating elements, etc).

16 Remove the relevant fuse from the circuit, and connect a circuit tester or voltmeter to the fuse connections.

17 Switch on the circuit, bearing in mind that some circuits are live only when the ignition switch is moved to a particular position.

18 If voltage is present (indicated either by the tester bulb lighting or a voltmeter reading, as applicable), this means that there is a short circuit.

19 If no voltage is present, but the fuse still blows with the load(s) connected, this indicates an internal fault in the load(s).

Finding an earth fault

20 The battery negative terminal is connected to earth – the metal of the engine/transmission and the car body – and most systems are

wired so that they only receive a positive feed, the current returning through the metal of the car body. This means that the component mounting and the body form part of that circuit. Loose or corroded mountings can therefore cause a range of electrical faults, ranging from total failure of a circuit, to a puzzling partial fault. In particular, lights may shine dimly (especially when another circuit sharing the same earth point is in operation), motors (e.g. wiper motors or the radiator cooling fan motor) may run slowly, and the operation of one circuit may have an apparently unrelated effect on another. Note that on many vehicles, earth straps are used between certain components, such as the engine/transmission and the body, usually where there is no metal-to-metal contact between components due to flexible rubber mountings, etc.

21 To check whether a component is properly earthed, disconnect the battery (refer to the warnings given in the Reference section at the rear of the manual) and connect one lead of an ohmmeter to a known good earth point. Connect the other lead to the wire or earth connection being tested. The resistance reading should be zero; if not, check the connection as follows.

22 If an earth connection is thought to be faulty, dismantle the connection and clean back to bare metal both the bodyshell and the wire terminal or the component earth connection mating surface. Be careful to remove all traces of dirt and corrosion, and then use a knife to trim away any paint, so that a clean metal-to-metal joint is made. On reassembly, tighten the joint fasteners securely; if a wire terminal is being refitted, use serrated washers between the terminal and the bodyshell to ensure a clean and secure connection. When the connection is remade, prevent the onset of corrosion in the future by applying a coat of petroleum jelly or silicone-based grease or by spraying on (at regular intervals) a proprietary ignition sealer or a water dispersant lubricant.

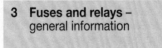

3 Fuses and relays – general information

Fuses and fusible links

1 Fuses are designed to break a circuit when a predetermined current is reached, in order to protect the components and wiring, which could be damaged by excessive current flow. Any excessive current flow will be due to a fault in the circuit, usually a short-circuit (see Section 2).

2 The main fuses are located in the fusebox on the driver's side of the facia; open the driver's door and unclip the fusebox cover from the lower edge of the facia to gain access to the fuses **(see illustration)**. The fuse locations are marked onto the rear of the fusebox cover.

3 To remove a fuse, first switch off the circuit

3.2 Fusebox on lower driver's side of facia

concerned (or the ignition), and then pull the fuse out of its terminals.

4 The wire within the fuse should be visible; if the fuse has blown it will be broken or melted.

5 Always renew a fuse with one of the correct rating; never use a fuse with a different rating from that specified.

6 Refer to the wiring diagrams for details of the fuse ratings and the circuits protected. The fuse rating is stamped on the top of the fuse; the fuses are also colour-coded as follows.

Colour	Rating
Light brown	5A
Brown	7.5A
Red	10A
Blue	15A
Yellow	20A
White or clear	25A
Green	30A
Orange	40A

7 Never renew a fuse more than once without tracing the source of the trouble. If the new fuse blows immediately, find the cause before renewing it again; a short to earth as a result of faulty insulation is most likely. Where a fuse protects more than one circuit, try to isolate the fault by switching on each circuit in turn (where possible) until the fuse blows again. Always carry a supply of spare fuses of each relevant rating on the vehicle.

8 Additional fused links and relays are located in a bracket on top of the battery in the engine compartment. Release the securing clips and withdraw the cover to gain access to the fused link **(see illustration)**.

9 To renew a fusible link, first disconnect the battery negative terminal. Unscrew the

3.11 Glow plug relay (arrowed) – diesel models

3.8 Fusible links and fusebox on top of battery

retaining nuts then remove the blown link. Fit the new link to its terminals and reconnect the leads. Ensure the link and leads are correctly seated then refit the retaining nuts and tighten securely. Clip the cover back into position then reconnect the battery.

Relays

10 A relay is an electrically operated switch, which is used for the following reasons:

a) *A relay can switch a heavy current remotely from the circuit in which the current is flowing, allowing the use of lighter-gauge wiring and switch contacts.*

b) *A relay can receive more than one control input, unlike a mechanical switch.*

c) *A relay can have a timer function – for example, the intermittent wiper relay.*

11 Most of the relays are located on the relay plate behind the driver's side facia, however, the glowplug relay on diesel models is located in the bracket on top of the battery **(see illustration)**.

12 Access to the relays can be obtained from under the driver's side lower facia panel **(see illustration)**. Identification details of the relays are given at the start of the wiring diagrams.

13 If a circuit or system controlled by a relay develops a fault, and the relay is suspect, operate the system. If the relay is functioning, it should be possible to hear it click as it is energised. If this is the case, the fault lies with the components or wiring of the system. If the relay is not being energised, then either the relay is not receiving a main supply or a switching voltage, or the relay itself is faulty. Testing is by the substitution of a known good

3.12 Relays located behind driver's side of facia

4.5 Undo the retaining screw (arrowed)

4.6a Pull the locking clip upwards...

4.6b ...and disconnect the wiring connector

4.7 Removing the airbag clock spring/slip ring

unit, but be careful – while some relays are identical in appearance and in operation, others look similar but perform different functions.

14 To remove a relay, first ensure that the relevant circuit is switched off. The relay can then simply be pulled out from the socket, and pushed back into position.

15 The direction indicator/hazard flasher relay is integral with the hazard warning switch. Refer to Section 4 for the switch removal procedure.

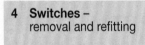 **4 Switches –** removal and refitting

Note: *Before working on any electrical systems switch off the ignition and all electrical consumers and remove the ignition key.*

Ignition switch

1 Refer to Chapter 10, Section 17.

4.9 Press the switch centre inwards and turn it slightly to the right to remove

Wiper and indicator/switches

Note: *The lighting and wiper switch is one unit and cannot be renewed separately.*
2 Check that the front wheels are pointing straight-ahead and the steering wheel is in its centre position, then remove the steering wheel as described in Chapter 10, Section 15.
3 Remove the steering column shrouds, as described in Chapter 11, Section 25.
4 To prevent the airbag clock spring/slip ring from moving from its position use a piece of tape to secure it in position.
5 Slacken the securing screw from the mounting clamp bracket at the rear of the switch assembly **(see illustration)**.
6 Slide the switch assembly off the steering column, then pull the locking clip upwards and disconnect the wiring connector from the rear of the switch assembly **(see illustrations)**.
7 If required, release the securing clips and

4.10 Disconnect the wiring block connector

release the airbag clock spring/slip ring from the switch assembly **(see illustration)**.
8 Refitting is a reversal of removal. Note, it may be necessary to have the airbag clock spring/slip ring reset to its basic settings using a diagnostic tester.

Lighting switch

9 With the light switch in position O, press the switch centre inwards and turn it slightly to the right. Hold this position and pull the switch from the dash **(see illustration)**.
10 As the switch is withdrawn from the dash, disconnect the wiring plug **(see illustration)**.
11 To refit the switch, first reconnect the wiring plug, then hold the switch and press the rotary part inwards and slightly to the right. Insert the switch into the dash, turn the rotary part to position O and release. Check the switch for correct operation.

Headlamp range control and instrument illumination switch

12 Remove the lighting switch as described in paragraphs 9 to 11.
13 Remove the end panel from the driver's side of the facia.
14 Reach in behind the facia and release the clips then remove the switch **(see illustration)**. Disconnect the wiring from the switch.
15 Refitting is a reversal of removal.

Air conditioning/ recirculation switches

16 The switches are integral with the heater control panel, and cannot be removed separately. Refer to Chapter 3, Section 9, for details of heater control panel removal and refitting.

Heater blower motor switch

17 The switch is integral with the heater control panel, and cannot be removed separately. Refer to Chapter 3, Section 9, for details of heater control panel removal and refitting.

Seat heating/Hazard warning/ TCS/HRW/Airbag light/ Start-Stop switches

18 Using a lever carefully unclip the trim panel from around the radio/CD player, then lever the switch from the facia, disconnect the wiring connector on removal **(see illustration)**. Refitting is a reversal of removal.

4.14 Reach inside and unclip the switch from the rear of the facia

4.18 Carefully unclip the trim panel from the facia

4.20 Switches on inside of glovebox

4.22 Unclip the trim panel...

Passenger air bag on/off switch & tyre monitoring switch

19 Remove the glovebox, as described in Chapter 11, Section 25.
20 Release the retaining clips and withdraw the switch from inside the glovebox **(see illustration)**.
21 Refitting is a reversal of removal.

Driver's door locking switch

22 Unclip the trim panel from the door grab handle **(see illustration)**.
23 Disconnect the wiring connector, then release the securing clips and withdraw the switch from the trim panel **(see illustration)**.
24 Refitting is a reversal of removal.

Electric window/ mirror switch assembly

25 Unclip the trim panel from the door grab handle **(see illustration 4.22)**.
26 Release the securing clips and withdraw the switch from the grab handle trim panel **(see illustration)**.
27 Refitting is a reversal of removal.

Handbrake 'on' warning switch

28 Refer to Chapter 9, Section 20.

Brake light switch

29 Refer to Chapter 9, Section 21.

Reversing light switch

30 Refer to Chapter 7A, Section 5.

Courtesy light switches

31 The courtesy light switch is integrated

into the door lock mechanism, and cannot be renewed independently. If the courtesy light switch is faulty, renew the door lock mechanism as described in Chapter 11, Section 13.

Luggage area light switch

32 The luggage compartment light switch is integrated into the tailgate/boot lid lock mechanism, and cannot be renewed independently. If the luggage compartment light switch is faulty, renew the tailgate/boot lid lock mechanism as described in Chapter 11, Section 16.

Rain and light sensor

33 The windscreen wipers/lights (depending on model) are automatically activated, when the sensor located in the interior mirror base, detects droplets of water/darkness.
34 Remove the interior mirror, as described in Chapter 11, Section 18.

4.23 ...and remove the switch

35 Remove the plastic trim/stay, and if disconnect the wiring connector from the sensor **(see illustration)**.
36 The mirror base/sensor is bonded to the windscreen **(see illustration)**. Whilst it is possible to remove the base by means of a scraper, great care must be exercised to avoid damaging the windscreen.
37 Due to the hazardous chemicals involved, it is recommended that the bonding of the mirror base to the windscreen be entrusted to a VW dealer or suitably equipped specialist.
38 With the base/sensor in place, refit the mirror with reference to Chapter 11, Section 18.

Aux in/out & 12 volt supply

39 Remove the centre console, as described in Chapter 11, Section 26.
40 Release the retaining clips under the console and withdraw the switch from the console **(see illustration)**.
41 Refitting is a reversal of removal.

4.26 Unclip the switch from the trim panel

4.35 Disconnect the wiring connector from the sensor

4.36 Sensor and mirror base fitted to windscreen

4.40 Switches in the front of the centre console

5.2 Remove the rubber cover...

5.3a Turn the bulb holder anti-clockwise to remove…

5.3b …and pull the bulb from the holder

5 Bulbs (exterior lights) – renewal

General

1 Whenever a bulb is renewed, note the following points:
a) Switch off the ignition and all electrical consumers before commencing work.
b) Remember that if the light has just been in use the bulb may be extremely hot.
c) Always check the bulb contacts and holder, ensuring that there is clean metal-to-metal contact. Clean off any corrosion or dirt before fitting a new bulb.
d) Wherever bayonet-type bulbs are fitted ensure that the spring-tensioned arms bear firmly against the bulb contacts.
e) Always ensure that the new bulb is of the correct rating and that it is thoroughly clean before fitting it.

Headlight main beam/ daytime running light

Note: Do not touch the glass envelope of the bulb if it is to be re-used.
2 Remove the headlight as described in Section 7, then remove the rubber cover from the rear of the headlight (see illustration).
3 Turn the bulbholder anti-clockwise a quarter of a turn and remove it from the rear of the headlight unit, then pull the bulb from the holder (see illustrations).
4 When handling the new bulb, use a tissue or clean cloth to avoid touching the glass with the fingers; moisture and grease from the skin can cause blackening and rapid failure of this type of bulb. If the glass is accidentally touched, wipe it clean using methylated spirit.
5 Fit the new bulb to the bulbholder, ensuring that the location lugs are aligned, then fit the bulbholder to the headlight and turn clockwise to secure.
6 Refit the rubber cover, making sure that it is secure and then refit the headlight.

Headlight dip beam

Halogen headlights

Note: Do not touch the glass envelope of the bulb if it is to be re-used.
7 Remove the headlight as described in Section 7, then remove the outermost rubber cover from the rear of the headlight unit (see illustration).
8 Turn the bulbholder anti-clockwise a quarter of a turn and remove it from the rear of the headlight unit, then pull the bulb from the holder (see illustration).
9 When handling the new bulb, use a tissue or clean cloth to avoid touching the glass with the fingers; moisture and grease from the skin can cause blackening and rapid failure of this type of bulb. If the glass is accidentally touched, wipe it clean using methylated spirit.
10 Fit the new bulb to the bulbholder, ensuring that the location lugs are aligned, then fit the bulbholder to the headlight and turn clockwise to secure.
11 Refit the rubber cover, making sure that it is secure and then refit the headlight.

Gas discharge headlights

⚠ Warning: The headlight bulb contains gas at very high pressure, and it is recommended that gloves and eye protection be worn to prevent potential personal injury.

Note: Do not touch the glass envelope of the bulb if it is to be re-used.

12 Remove the headlight as described in Section 7.
13 Remove the outermost cover from the rear of the headlight.
14 Disconnect the wiring connector, by releasing the securing clip and pulling the wiring connector from the lower part of the bulb.
15 Turn the gas discharge bulb and holder anti-clockwise and carefully withdraw it from the headlight. Note: The gas discharge bulb is integral with the bulbholder.
16 When handling the new bulb, use a tissue or clean cloth to avoid touching the glass with the fingers; moisture and grease from the skin can cause blackening and rapid failure of this type of bulb. If the glass is accidentally touched, wipe it clean using methylated spirit.
17 Fit the new gas discharge bulb and holder to the headlight and turn clockwise to secure. Reconnect the wiring connector to the lower part of the bulb.
18 Refit the headlight cover, making sure that it is secure and then refit the headlight.
Caution: After refitting a gas discharge headlamp, the basic setting of the Automatic Range Control system should be checked.

Front sidelight

19 Remove the headlight as described in Section 7, and then remove the inner rubber cover from the rear of the headlight (see illustration 5.2).
20 Carefully pull the sidelight bulbholder from the headlight unit. The bulb is a push-fit in the holder and can be removed by grasping the end of the bulb and pulling it out (see illustrations).
21 Refitting is a reversal of removal, making sure that the headlight cover is securely refitted.

5.7 Remove the rubber cover

5.8 Turn the bulb holder anti-clockwise to remove

5.20a Sidelight bulb (arrowed)

5.20b Using long nose pliers to remove the sidelight bulb holder…

5.20c …then pull the bulb from the holder

Front direction indicator

22 Remove the headlight as described in Section 7.
23 Turn the bulbholder anti-clockwise and remove it from the headlight complete with bulb **(see illustration)**.
24 The bulb is a bayonet fit, turn the bulb anti-clockwise and remove it from the holder **(see illustration)**.
25 Refit the bulb to the holder, then fit the bulbholder to the headlight and turn clockwise to secure.
26 Refit the headlight as described in Section 7.

Front foglight

27 Unclip the trim cover from around the fog light unit **(see illustration)**.
28 Undo the two retaining screws from the lower part of the foglight **(see illustration)**.

5.23 Turn the bulbholder anti-clockwise to remove

29 Release the two retaining clips at the top and withdraw the foglight unit from the front bumper **(see illustration)**.
30 Disconnect the wiring connector from the rear of the foglight, then turn the bulbholder anti-clockwise and remove it complete with

5.24 Twist the bayonet type bulb anti-clockwise to remove

bulb **(see illustrations)**. **Note:** *The bulb is integral with the bulbholder.*
31 Fit the new bulb using a reversal of the removal procedure. Adjustment of the foglight can be made through the hole in the trim panel **(see illustration)**.

5.27 Unclip the trim from around the light unit

5.28 Undo the retaining screws (arrowed)

5.29 Release the upper securing clips

5.30a Disconnect the wiring connector…

5.30b …and turn the bulbholder anti-clockwise to remove

5.31 Adjusting the foglight

5.34a Release the securing clips (arrowed)...

5.34b ...and unclip the bulbholder

5.38 Unclip the light unit...

Direction indicator in exterior mirror

32 There are no conventional bulbs in the exterior mirror, but LED's instead, therefore if the direction indicator is not working; the complete unit must be renewed as described in Chapter 11, Section 18.

Rear light cluster

33 Remove the rear light cluster as described in Section 7.
34 Release the securing clips and remove the bulb holder from the rear of the light unit (see illustrations). Recover the rubber seal if required, make sure it is fitted correctly in the rear of the bulbholder before refitting.
35 Depending on bulb being replaced, it is either a bayonet type bulb or a wedge type bulb. If the bulb is a bayonet-fit in the bulbholder – depress and twist the relevant

bulb to remove it. If the bulb is a glass wedge type – pull the relevant bulb to remove.
36 Fit the new bulb using a reversal of the removal procedure.

High-level brake light

Note: *The light is of LED design; therefore if faulty the complete unit must be renewed. Note that the LED's are arranged in groups of four, and if just one group fails, the light still meets legal requirement. Failure of more than one group renders the light illegal.*
37 Remove the high-level light unit as described in Section 7.

Number plate light

Secured with clip

38 Release the securing clip, and withdraw the light unit from the tailgate (see illustration).

39 Twist the bulb holder to remove from light unit, and then pull the bulb to remove it from the holder (see illustrations).
40 Fit the new bulb using a reversal of the removal procedure.

Secured with screws

41 Undo the two securing screws and withdraw the light unit from the tailgate (see illustrations).
42 Unclip the bulb from the light unit; the bulb is a festoon type.
43 Fit the new bulb using a reversal of the removal procedure.

6 Bulbs (interior lights) – renewal

General

1 Whenever a bulb is renewed, note the following points:
   a) Switch off the ignition and all electrical consumers before commencing work.
   b) Remember that if the light has just been in use the bulb may be extremely hot.
   c) Always check the bulb contacts and holder, ensuring that there is clean metal-to-metal contact between them. Clean off any corrosion or dirt before fitting a new bulb.
   d) Wherever bayonet-type bulbs are fitted ensure that the live contact(s) bear firmly against the bulb contact.
   e) Always ensure that the new bulb is of the correct rating and that it is completely clean before fitting it.

5.39a ...twist and remove bulb holder...

5.39b ...then pull the bulb from the holder

Front courtesy/reading light

2 Using a thin screwdriver, carefully release the locking lugs and remove the lens from the light unit (see illustration).
3 Depending on bulb being replaced, it is either a festoon type bulb or a wedge type bulb. The centre interior bulb can now be removed from the light unit.
4 To remove the outer reading light bulbs, it may be necessary to remove the light unit from the headlining. First unclip the cover from the rear of the light console (see illustration).

5.41a Undo the screws...

5.41b ...and remove the rear number plate light

6.2 Unclip the interior light lens

6.4 Remove the rear trim cover

6.5 Release the securing clips to remove

6.6 Twist the bulbholder to remove

6.8 Prise out the footwell light

6.9a Unclip the metal shield...

5 Reach inside the headlining and release the retaining clips from the light console, and then remove it from the headlining **(see illustration)**.

6 To remove the bulb, twist the bulbholder anti-clockwise and remove it from the rear of the light unit, then pull out the wedge-type bulb from the holder **(see illustration)**. Note some wedge type bulbs cannot be removed from the holder and have to be replaced complete with holder.

7 Fit the new bulb and light unit using a reversal of the removal procedure.

Front footwell illumination lights

8 Use a screwdriver to prise out the light, and then disconnect the wiring **(see illustration)**.

9 Unclip the lens from the metal heat shield, and pull out the wedge-type bulb **(see illustrations)**.

10 Refitting is a reverse of the removal procedure.

Rear courtesy/reading lights

11 Using a screwdriver, carefully release the locking lugs and remove the lens from the centre light unit **(see illustration)**.

12 Pull the festoon-type bulb from the light **(see illustration)**.

6.9b ...and pull the bulb from the holder

13 If required the outer courtesy light units can be removed by releasing the retaining clip and removing it from the headlining. Disconnect the wiring connector as it is removed and pull the festoon-type bulb from the light **(see illustrations)**.

6.11 Unclip the interior light lens...

6.12 ...and remove the festoon-type bulb

6.13a Prise out the light unit...

6.13b ...and remove the festoon-type bulb

6.15 Prise out the luggage compartment light and pull out bulb

14 Fit the new bulb and light unit using a reversal of the removal procedure.

Luggage compartment light

15 Carefully prise the light unit from its location in the luggage compartment. The wedge-type bulb is a push-fit in the spring contacts **(see illustration)**.
16 Fit the new bulb using a reversal of the removal procedure.

Instrument panel illumination/ warning lights

17 The instrument panel illumination/warning lights are non-renewable LED's.

Heater/ventilation control panel illumination

18 The control panel is illuminated by LED's built into the panel. Consequently, if a fault develops, renewal of the panel is necessary.

Switch illumination

19 The switch illumination bulbs are integral with the switches. If a bulb fails, the complete switch must be renewed.

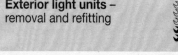

7 Exterior light units – removal and refitting

1 Before removing any light units, switch off the ignition and all electrical consumers, and then remove the ignition key.

Headlight

2 Mark the position of the headlight mountings on the upper mounting bracket, to ensure correct alignment on refitting
3 Undo the two mounting bolts along the top of the headlight unit, and then pull the headlight unit forward, releasing it from the lower securing clips **(see illustrations)**.
4 Unplug the wiring multiplug connector as the headlight is withdrawn **(see illustration)**.
5 Refitting is a reversal of removal, but on completion, check that the headlight is aligned flush with the surrounding bodywork. If not, slacken the mounting bolts and re-align the light unit. Finally, have the headlight alignment checked at the earliest opportunity.
Caution: After refitting a gas discharge headlamp, the basic setting of the Automatic Range Control system should be checked. Because of the requirement for specialised equipment, a VW dealer or suitably equipped specialist can only carry

this out. The headlight bulb contains gas at very high pressure, and it is recommended that gloves and eye protection be worn to prevent potential personal injury.

Gas discharge bulb control unit/ starter

Note: *There are two control units on the base of the headlight unit, one is the output module (three screws) and one is the starter (two screws).*
6 Remove the headlight as described above.
7 Undo the retaining screws, and remove the control unit from the base of the headlight. Note that the electrical connections are automatically separated when the unit is removed.
8 Refitting is a reversal of removal.

Direction indicator in mirror

9 Remove the exterior mirror housing as described in Chapter 11, Section 18.

Front foglight

10 The procedure is described as part of the front foglight bulb renewal procedure in Section 5.

Rear light cluster

11 Open the tailgate and pull back the access panel at the rear of the light unit.
12 Disconnect the wiring connector and unscrew the securing bolt from the rear of the light unit **(see illustrations)**.
13 Using a wide bladed lever, carefully prise the light unit, taking care not to damage the paintwork. This will release the locating pegs from the wing panel, and then the light unit can be removed from the vehicle **(see illustrations)**.

7.3a Undo the retaining screws (arrowed)...

7.3b ...and release the headlamp from the lower securing clips (arrowed)

7.4 Disconnect the wiring connector (arrowed)

7.12a Disconnecting the wiring connector (arrowed)...

7.12b ...and unscrew the securing bolt/ spring - Hatchback

7.13a Prise the light unit from the wing panel...

14 Refitting is a reversal of removal, making sure that the alignment lugs locate in the wing panel, on refitting.

High level brake light

Note: *The light is of LED design; therefore if faulty the complete unit must be renewed.*

15 Using a wide bladed lever, carefully prise the light unit out from the top of the tailgate, taking care not to damage the paintwork **(see illustration)**.

16 Disconnect the wiring connector and the rear washer hose from the rear of the light unit, as the light unit is being removed **(see illustrations)**.

17 Fit the new light unit using a reversal of the removal procedure.

Rear number plate light

18 The procedure is described as part of the rear number plate light bulb renewal procedure in Section 5.

8 Headlight beam adjustment components – removal and refitting

Headlight adjustment switch

1 The switch is integral with the instrument illumination switch.

2 Removal and refitting of the switch assembly is covered in Section 4.

Headlight range adjustment motor

3 Remove the headlight as described in Section 7.

H7 bulb fitment

4 Remove the outer cover from the rear of the headlight **(see illustration)**.

5 Turn the range control motor anti-clockwise and pull it upwards and to the left slightly to disengage the ball-head from the guide on the reflector, then disconnect the wiring connector to remove,

6 Refitting is a reversal of removal, making sure the ball joint mounting is correctly located in the headlight reflector.

H4 and Gas discharge bulb fitment

7 Release the wire clip and remove the cover from the rear of the headlight.

7.13b ...to release the locating pegs (arrowed)

7.16a Disconnect the wiring connector...

8 Turn the range control motor clockwise and pull it out to disengage the ball-head from the guide on the reflector, then disconnect the wiring connector to remove,

9 Refitting is a reversal of removal, making sure the ball joint mounting is correctly located in the headlight reflector.

9 Headlight beam alignment – general information

1 Accurate adjustment of the headlight beam is only possible using optical beam setting equipment and this work should therefore be carried out by a VW dealer or suitably-equipped workshop.

2 For reference, the headlights can be manually adjusted using the adjuster assemblies fitted to the top of each light unit

8.4 Range control motor (arrowed)

9.2 Headlight adjustment screws (arrowed)

7.15 Prise the light unit from the top of the tailgate

7.16b ...and the rear washer hose

(see illustration). The inner adjuster alters the lateral position of the beam whilst the outer adjuster alters the height of the beam.

10 Instrument panel – removal and refitting

Removal

1 Switch off the ignition and all electrical consumers and remove the ignition key. Release the steering wheel adjustment handle, pull the wheel out as far as possible, and set it in the lowest position.

2 Carefully prise out the steering column upper gap cover, and then undo the two screws at the lower part of the instrument panel **(see illustrations)**.

3 Release the upper retaining clip and

10.2a Unclip the upper shroud from the instrument panel...

10.2b ...and undo the retaining screws (arrowed)

10.3a Release the upper retaining clip and withdraw it from the facia...

10.3b ...then release locking clip (arrowed) to disconnect the wiring connector

carefully pull the instrument panel from the facia, release the locking lever and disconnect the wiring plug from the rear of the instrument panel **(see illustrations)**.

Refitting

4 Refitting is a reversal of removal.

11 Instrument panel components – removal and refitting

It is not possible to dismantle the instrument panel. If any of the gauges are faulty, the complete instrument panel must be renewed.

12 Service interval indicator – general information and resetting

1 All models are equipped with a service interval indicator. After all necessary maintenance work has been completed; the service interval display code must be reset. If more than one service schedule is carried out, note that the relevant display intervals must be reset individually.
2 The display is reset using the buttons on the instrument panel (below the speedometer and rev.counter/tachometer). Resetting is described in Chapter 1A, Section 5 or Chapter 1B, Section 5.

15.3 Disconnect the wiring connectors and undo the bolt (arrowed)

13 Clock – removal and refitting

The clock is integral with the instrument panel, and cannot be removed separately. The instrument panel is a sealed unit, and if the clock, or any other components, are faulty, the complete instrument panel must be renewed. Refer to Section 10, for the removal of the instrument panel.

14 Cigarette lighter/12V supply – removal and refitting

Removal

1 Disconnect the battery negative lead (refer to *Disconnecting the battery* in the *Reference* Chapter at the end of this manual).
2 Remove the centre console as described in Chapter 11, Section 26.
3 Remove the bulbholder as described in Section 6.
4 Release the retaining clips and push the centre element out of the outer plastic mounting.

Refitting

5 Refitting is a reversal of removal.

15 Horn – removal and refitting

Removal

1 Switch off the ignition and all electrical consumers and remove the ignition key.
2 Remove the front bumper as described in Chapter 11, Section 6. If required, it may be possible to release the front of the left-hand side inner wheel arch liner and reach up behind the front bumper to access the horn.
3 Disconnect the wiring, then unscrew the mounting bolt and withdraw the horn together with the mounting bracket **(see illustration)**.
4 If required, unscrew the nut on the top of the horn to remove the bracket.

Refitting

5 Refitting is a reversal of removal.

16 Speedometer sensor – general information

All models are fitted with an electronic speedometer sensor. This device measures the rotational speed of the transmission final drive and converts the information into an electronic signal, which is then sent to the speedometer module in the instrument panel. On certain models, the signal is also used as an input by the engine management system ECU, and the trip computer.

Unlike earlier models, no electronic speedometer sensor is fitted to the models covered in this Manual. Vehicle speed is determined from the ABS wheel sensor signals, and processed by the engine management ECU.

17 Wiper arm – removal and refitting

Removal

1 Operate the wiper motor, then switch off so that the wiper arms return to the at-rest position. Alternatively, set the wiper blades to the Winter/Service (vertical) position by operating the wipers within 10 seconds of switching off the ignition. **Note:** *The wiper motor will only operate with the bonnet closed.*
2 Stick a piece of masking tape to the glass along the edge of the wiper blade to use as an alignment aid on refitting.
3 On front wiper arms, prise off the wiper arm spindle nut cover, then slacken but do not completely remove the spindle nut. Lift the blade off the glass and carefully rock the wiper arm from side to side, until it releases from the spindle. Remove the spindle nut and the wiper arm **(see illustrations)**. **Note:** *If both windscreen wiper arms are to be removed at the same time mark them for identification; the arms are not interchangeable.*

4 On rear wiper arms, unclip the spindle nut cover, then slacken but do not completely remove the spindle nut. Lift the blade off the glass and carefully rock the wiper arm from side to side, until it releases from the spindle. Remove the spindle nut and wiper arm **(see illustration)**.

5 If the arm is a tight fit on the spindle, the arm can be removed from the spindle using a small puller **(see illustration)**.

Refitting

6 Ensure that the wiper arm and spindle splines are clean and dry, and then refit the arm to the spindle, aligning the wiper blade with the tape fitted on removal. Refit the spindle nut, tightening it securely, and clip the nut cover back in position.

Note: *Where the wipers were set to the Winter/Service position in paragraph 1, they will only resume their normal position after actuating the wipers twice, or after starting a journey when the speed of the car is greater than 1 mph.*

18 Windscreen wiper motor and linkage – removal and refitting

Removal

1 Remove the wiper arms as described in Section 17.

2 Disconnect the battery negative lead (refer to *Disconnecting the battery* in the *Reference* Chapter at the end of this manual).

3 Pull off the rubber sealing strip from along the top of the bulkhead **(see illustration)**.

4 Working along the lower part of the windscreen, carefully pull the plastic cowling from the windscreen seal and remove the panel from the bulkhead **(see illustration)**.

Caution: Do not use a screwdriver lever between the cowling and windscreen, as this is likely to result in the windscreen cracking.

5 Remove the ECU from the left-hand rear of the bulkhead panel as described in, Chapter 4A, Section 4 (petrol models) or Chapter 4B, Section 3 (diesel models).

6 Working along the rear of the engine compartment, release the fasteners and

remove the insulation padding from the bulkhead panel **(see illustration)**.

7 Undo the retaining bolts and remove the bulkhead panel from the rear of the engine compartment **(see illustration)**.

8 Unscrew the mounting bolts and manoeuvre the windscreen wiper motor and linkage out from the scuttle **(see illustration)**.

9 Disconnect the wiring plug from the wiper motor **(see illustration)**.

17.3a Prise up the cover and remove the nut...

17.3b ...then remove the wiper arm

17.4 Unscrew the rear wiper securing nut

17.5 Use a small puller to remove wiper arm, if required

18.3 Peel back the rubber seal...

18.4 ...then unclip the cowling from along the windscreen seal...

18.6 Remove the insulation padding from the bulkhead

18.7 Unbolt and remove the bulkhead panel

18.8 Undo the wiper motor/linkage mounting bolts (arrowed)

18.9 Disconnect the wiring plug (arrowed)

10 Recover the washers and spacers from the motor mounting rubbers, noting their locations, then inspect the rubbers for signs of damage or deterioration, and renew if necessary.

Refitting

11 Refitting is a reversal of removal, bearing in mind the following points.
  a) *If the motor has been separated from the linkage, ensure that the marks made on the motor spindle and linkage before removal are aligned, and ensure that the linkage is orientated as noted before removal.*
  b) *Ensure that the washers and spacers are fitted to the motor mounting rubbers as noted before removal.*
  c) *Make sure the locating peg aligns with the grommet in the bulkhead, when refitting (see illustration).*

19.5 Removing the tailgate wiper motor

20.5 Disconnect the washer fluid hoses

18.11 Make sure peg (A) is aligned with grommet (B)

  d) *Lubricate the windscreen cowling mounting slots with a silicone-based spray lubricant to ease installation. Do not strike the cowling to seat it in position as this could result in the windscreen cracking.*
  e) *Refit the wiper arms as described in Section 17.*

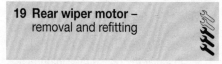

19 Rear wiper motor – removal and refitting

Removal

1 Remove the wiper arm as described in Section 17.
2 Recover the wiper motor shaft sealing ring.
3 Open the tailgate, then remove the trim panel as described in Chapter 11, Section 15.

20.2 Unclip the reservoir filler neck

20.9 Washer fluid reservoir mounting nuts (arrowed)

4 Release the locking clip and unplug the wiring connector from the motor.
5 Unscrew the three nuts securing the motor, and then withdraw the assembly. Note the position of the rubber sealing ring, renew if necessary **(see illustration)**.

Refitting

6 Refitting is a reversal of removal, but ensure that the motor shaft rubber sealing ring/ grommet is correctly refitted to prevent water leaks, and refit the wiper arm with reference to Section 17.

20 Washer system components – removal and refitting

Washer fluid reservoir and pumps

1 Switch off the ignition and all electrical consumers and remove the ignition key.
2 In the engine compartment, unclip the top of the reservoir filler neck from the front panel **(see illustration)**.
3 Remove the front bumper as described in Chapter 11, Section 6. If required, it may be possible to release the front of the right-hand side inner wheel arch liner and reach up behind the front bumper to access the washer reservoir.
4 Disconnect the wiring connector from the top of the washer pump.
5 Note the position of the hoses, and then disconnect them from the washer pump **(see illustration)**. Position a suitable container beneath the reservoir to catch spilt fluid. **Note:** *Depending on model, there may be more than one washer pump.*
6 To remove the washer pump, pull it upwards from the reservoir and out from its rubber grommet.
7 Where fitted, disconnect the wiring plug from the fluid level sender unit.
8 Release the retaining clip and disconnect the wiring loom from the top of the washer reservoir.
9 Unscrew the mounting nuts, then remove the reservoir from the vehicle **(see illustration)**.
10 Refitting is a reversal of removal.

Windscreen washer jets

11 Open the bonnet, and pull down on the washer jet to release it from the bonnet. Release the securing clip and disconnect the washer tube (and wiring where applicable), then remove the washer jet, See Chapter 11, Section 8.
12 Refitting is a reversal of removal. Note that the aim of the jet can be adjusted by moving the jet up or down **(see illustration)**.

Tailgate washer jet

13 Switch off the ignition and all electrical consumers and remove the ignition key.
14 The washer jet is fitted to the high level brake light, remove the light as described

in Section 7. Release the retaining clips and remove the washer jet from the brake light **(see illustration)**.

15 On refitting, ensure that the jet is securely pushed into position. Check the operation of the jet. If necessary, adjust the nozzle, aiming the spray at a point slightly above the area of glass swept by the wiper blade.

21 Radio/CD player/ Multimedia control unit – removal and refitting

Note: *This Section only applies to standard fit audio equipment.*

Radio/CD player

Removal

1 The radio/CD player is equipped with an electronic anti-theft system linked to the instrument panel. If the voltage supply to the radio is temporarily disconnected, the radio will function again when the supply is reconnected, without entering the safety code number, provided the radio is located in the original vehicle. Should the radio operation be blocked, normal operation can be restored by entering the correct anti-theft code.

2 Remove any CDs, which may be in the unit. Switch off the ignition and all electrical consumers, and remove the ignition key.

3 Carefully unclip the trim panel from around the Radio/CD player **(see illustration)**.

4 Undo the radio/CD player mounting screws, and pull out the unit until the wiring plugs can be disconnected **(see illustration)**. Release the locking clips and disconnect the wiring connectors from the rear of the unit.

5 Withdraw the radio/CD player unit from the facia.

Refitting

6 Refitting is a reversal of removal.

Multimedia control unit

Removal

7 The multimedia control unit is located in the top of the glovebox **(see illustration)**.

8 Switch off the ignition and all electrical consumers, and remove the ignition key.

9 Remove the glovebox as described in Chapter 11, Section 25.

10 Release the plastic rivets and slide the control unit out from the top of the glovebox housing.

Refitting

11 Refitting is a reversal of removal.

22 Loudspeakers – removal and refitting

Front treble speaker

1 Switch off the ignition and all electrical consumers, and remove the ignition key.

20.12 Washer jet can be adjusted up and down

2 Remove the A-pillar trim panel as described in Chapter 11, Section 25.

3 Disconnect the speaker wiring plug, and remove the trim from the vehicle.

4 The loudspeaker is integral with the A-pillar trim panel and can only be renewed as a complete unit.

5 Refitting is a reversal of removal.

Front and rear bass speakers

6 Switch off the ignition and all electrical consumers, and remove the ignition key.

7 Remove the relevant door inner trim, as described in Chapter 11, Section 12.

8 On 3-door models, remove the rear inner trim, as described in Chapter 11, Section 25.

9 Disconnect the wiring plug from the top of the loudspeaker.

10 Drill out the retaining rivets, and withdraw the speaker from the door **(see illustration)**. Recover the rubber sealing ring between the

21.3 Carefully remove the trim by releasing the retaining clips

21.7 Multimedia control unit location (arrowed)

20.14 Pull the washer jet from the light unit

speaker and door trim. **Note:** *Where mid-range loudspeakers are fitted, they are secured with screws instead of rivets.*

11 Refitting is a reversal of removal. The special-sized rivets should be available from VW dealers and in-car entertainment specialists.

23 Radio aerials, filters and modules – removal and refitting

Aerials

1 On some models, there is a FM2 radio aerial is integrated into the rear window that is bonded in position with a special adhesive. If the aerial is faulty, a new rear window must be fitted.

2 The standard AM/FM aerial is fitted to the rear of the roof panel.

21.4 Undo the mounting screws (arrowed)

22.10 Door speaker secured by rivets (arrowed)

26.4a Insert screwdriver...

26.4b ...to release the airbag clips...

26.4c ...in both sides of the steering wheel (arrowed)

3 To access the AM/FM aerial, carefully unclip the trim panel from across the rear of the headlining. If required remove the C-pillar trim panels as described in Chapter 11, Section 25. This will allow the rear of the headlining to be lowered further to gain better access.

4 Carefully lower the rear of the headlining, taking care not to damage it. Disconnect the wiring; note the fitted position of the wiring, as there may be more than one connector, depending on model.

5 Unscrew the securing nut and withdraw the aerial base from the roof. Hold the aerial base as the nut is being unscrewed to prevent the base from rotating and scratching the roof panel. Recover the rubber spacer.

6 Refitting is a reversal of removal, but make sure that the two guide lugs on the rubber spacer are correctly located in the aerial base.

Filters

7 The FM2 aerial that is integrated into the rear window has two frequency filters, which are fitted behind the C-pillar trim panels.

8 Remove the C-pillar trim panels as described in Chapter 11, Section 25.

9 Disconnect the wiring connector and unclip the filter from the body panel. **Note:** *The filter behind the C-pillar on the right-hand side is positioned in the negative wire, and the filter behind the C-pillar on the left-hand side is positioned in the positive wire.*

10 Refitting is a reversal of removal.

Modules

11 There is an aerial module that is located behind the tailgate trim on the upper edge, below the rear window. This is for FM reception, diversity aerial for FM2 and an impedance converter.

12 Remove the tailgate inner trim panel as described in Chapter 11, Section 15.

13 Disconnect the wiring connector, undo the retaining screw and slide it to one side to remove the module from the tailgate.

14 Refitting is a reversal of removal.

24 Anti-theft alarm system and engine immobiliser – general information

Note: *This information is applicable only to*

the anti-theft alarm system fitted by VW as standard equipment.

Models in the range are fitted with an anti-theft alarm system as standard equipment. The alarm has switches on all the doors (including the tailgate/boot lid), the bonnet and the ignition switch. If the tailgate/boot lid, bonnet or any of the doors are opened whilst the alarm is set, the alarm horn will sound and the hazard warning lights will flash. Some models are equipped with an internal monitoring system, which will activate the alarm system if any movement in the cabin is detected.

The alarm is set using the key in the driver's or passenger's front door lock, and tailgate/boot lid lock, or with the central locking remote control transmitter. The alarm system will then start to monitor its various switches approximately 30 seconds later.

With the alarm set, if the tailgate/boot lid is unlocked, the lock switch sensing will automatically be switched off but the door and bonnet switches will still be active. Once the tailgate/boot lid is shut and locked again, the switch sensing will be switched back on.

All models are fitted with an immobiliser system, which is activated by the ignition switch. A transponder reading coil on the ignition switch reads a code contained within the ignition key. The system sends a signal to the engine management electronic control unit (ECU), which allows the engine to start if the code is correct. If an incorrect ignition key is used, the engine will not start.

If a fault is suspected with the alarm or immobiliser systems, the vehicle should be taken to a VW dealer for examination. They will have access to a special diagnostic tester that will quickly trace any fault present in the system.

25 Airbag system – general information and precautions

⚠️ *Warning: Before carrying out any operations on the airbag system, disconnect the battery negative terminal (refer to 'Disconnecting the battery' in the Reference section at the rear of this manual). When operations are*

complete, make sure no one is inside the vehicle when the battery is reconnected.

• *Note that the airbags must not be subjected to temperatures in excess of 90°C. When the airbag is removed, ensure that it is stored with the pad upwards to prevent possible inflation.*

• *Do not allow any solvents or cleaning agents to contact the airbag assemblies. They must be cleaned using only a damp cloth.*

• *The airbags and control unit are both sensitive to impact. If either is dropped or damaged they should be renewed.*

A driver's airbag, passenger's airbag and side airbags were fitted as standard to the Polo range. Certain models also have curtain airbags located behind the headlining on each side of the car. The airbag system consists of the airbag unit (complete with gas generator), which is fitted to the steering wheel (driver's side), facia (passenger's side), roof (where applicable) and front seats, an impact sensor, the control unit and a warning light in the instrument panel.

The airbag system is triggered in the event of a heavy frontal or side impact above a predetermined force; depending on the point of impact. The airbag is inflated within milliseconds and forms a safety cushion between the driver and the steering wheel, the passenger and the facia, and in the case of side impact, between front seat occupants and the sides of the cabin. This prevents contact between the upper body and cabin interior, and therefore greatly reduces the risk of injury. The airbag then deflates almost immediately.

Every time the ignition is switched on, the airbag control unit performs a self-test. The self-test takes approximately 3 seconds and during this time the airbag warning light on the facia is illuminated. After the self-test has been completed the warning light should go out. If the warning light fails to come on, remains illuminated after the initial 3-second period or comes on at any time when the vehicle is being driven, there is a fault in the airbag system. The vehicle should then be taken to a VW dealer for examination at the earliest possible opportunity.

26 Airbag system components – removal and refitting

Note: *Refer to the warnings in Section 25 before carrying out the following operations.*
1 Disconnect the battery negative lead (refer to *Disconnecting the battery* in the *Reference* Chapter at the end of this manual), then continue as described under the relevant heading.
Caution: To prevent any discharge of static electricity into the airbag circuit, temporarily touch the vehicle bodywork before disconnecting the wiring from any airbag unit.

Driver's airbag

2 Set the front wheels to the straight-ahead position, and release the steering lock by inserting the ignition key.
3 Adjust the steering column to its highest position by releasing the adjustment handle, then extend the steering wheel as far as possible. Lock the column in this position.
4 With the spokes in the vertical position, insert a screwdriver into the hole in the upper rear of the steering wheel hub, then move it up to release the clip and free the airbag locking lug **(see illustrations)**. Now turn the steering wheel through 180° and release the remaining airbag locking lug.
5 Carefully withdraw the airbag module from the steering wheel, release the locking clip and disconnect the wiring connector.
6 Turn the steering wheel to its central, straight-ahead position.

> **Warning: Position the airbag in a safe and secure place, away from the work area.**

7 When refitting make sure the steering wheel is in the straight-ahead position, then locate the airbag module in position and reconnect the wiring. Carefully press in the module until both locking lugs are heard to engage. Reconnect the battery negative lead, ensuring that nobody is inside the vehicle as the lead is connected.

Passenger's airbag

8 Remove the passenger side glovebox with reference to Chapter 11, Section 25.
9 Release the locking clip and disconnect the wiring from the passenger's airbag **(see illustration)**.
10 Undo the mounting bolts, then remove the airbag from under the facia.

> **Warning: Position the airbag in a safe and secure place, away from the work area.**

11 Refitting is a reversal of removal, but tighten the mounting screws to the specified torque. Reconnect the battery negative lead, ensuring that nobody is inside the vehicle as the lead is connected.

26.9 Airbag wiring connector and mounting bolts (arrowed)

Front seat side impact airbags

12 The side impact air bags are integral with the seats. As seat upholstery removal requires considerable skill and experience, if it is to be carried out without damage, it is best entrusted to an expert.

Roof curtain and rear side airbags

13 This work involves removing the headlining and major dismantling of interior trim panels, and is best entrusted to a VW dealer.

Airbag control unit

14 The airbag control unit is located beneath the centre of the facia, under the heater housing.
15 Remove the centre console as described in Chapter 11, Section 26.
16 Pull back the carpet/insulation, then release the locking lever and disconnect the wiring from the control unit **(see illustration)**.
17 Unscrew the nuts and remove the control unit from the vehicle.
18 Refitting is the reverse of removal making sure the wiring connector is securely reconnected. Reconnect the battery negative lead, ensuring that nobody is inside the vehicle as the lead is connected.

Airbag wiring contact unit

19 The airbag contact unit/clock spring is part of the steering column switch assembly, remove the contact unit as described in Section 4.
20 The airbag clock spring/slip-ring must be

26.24 Airbag crash sensor on front inner door panel

held in its central position while it is removed, to ensure correct refitting. Unclip the airbag clock spring/slip-ring from the combination switch carrier by lifting the retaining hooks.
21 When refitting the switch assembly. Reconnect the battery negative lead, ensuring that nobody is inside the vehicle as the lead is connected.

Passenger airbag on/off switch

22 The switch is located inside the glovebox, remove the switch with reference to Section 4.

Front door crash sensor

23 Remove the inner door trim as described in Chapter 11, Section 12.
24 Disconnect the wiring from the crash sensor, then undo the retaining screws and withdraw the sensor from the door panel **(see illustration)**. Note some models may have rivets, securing the sensor to the panel.
25 Refitting is a reversal of removal. Make sure that nobody is inside the vehicle when first switching on the ignition.

Rear wheel housing crash sensor

26 Remove the rear inner trim panels from the rear wheel arch as described in Chapter 11, Section 25.
27 Release the securing clip and disconnect the wiring from the crash sensor, undo the retaining screw and remove the sensor from the floor panel **(see illustration)**.
28 Refitting is a reversal of removal. Make sure that nobody is inside the vehicle when first switching on the ignition.

26.16 Airbag control unit

26.27 Airbag crash sensor in front of rear wheel arch

27.9 Disconnect the wiring connector...

27.10 ...and unclip the sensor from the bumper

27 Parking aid components – general information, removal and refitting

General information

1 The parking aid system is available as a standard fitment on highline models, and optional on other models. Four ultrasound sensors located in the front and rear bumper. These measure the distance to the closest object behind or in front of the car, and inform the driver using acoustic signals from a warning buzzer. The nearer the object, the more frequent the acoustic signals.

2 The system includes a control unit and self-diagnosis program, and therefore, in the event of a fault, the vehicle should be taken to a VW dealer.

3 Switch off the ignition and all electrical consumers and remove the ignition key, before removing any electrical components.

Control unit

4 The parking aid control unit is located behind the right-hand rear trim panel in the luggage compartment. Refer to Chapter 11, Section 25 to aid removing the trim panels.

5 Withdraw the control unit complete with mounting bracket from the body panel. A new mounting bracket will be required, as the retaining clips break on removal.

6 Disconnect the wiring connectors as the control unit is removed.

7 Refitting is a reversal of removal.

Range/distance sensor

8 Remove the rear bumper as described in Chapter 11, Section 7.

9 Disconnect the wiring from the sensor (see illustration).

10 Release the two retaining clips at each side and pull the sensor from the bumper (see illustration).

11 Refitting is a reversal of removal. Press the sensor firmly into position until the retaining clips engage.

Warning buzzer

12 The warning buzzer is located behind the right-hand luggage compartment trim.

13 To remove the warning buzzer, remove the right-hand inner trim, with reference to Chapter 11, Section 25. Disconnect the wiring, then release the two plastic rivets and remove the warning buzzer.

14 Refitting is a reversal of removal.

* For vehicles with 1.4 ltr engine, engine code CGGB

** For vehicles with automatic transmission from November 2009

*** For vehicles with automatic transmission to November 2009

Starting and charging from May '09
– 1.2 litre CGPA & CGPB and 1.4 litre CGGB petrol engines

IGNITION / STARTER SWITCH

BU ALTERNATOR

ENGINE CONTROL UNIT

ONBOARD SUPPLY CONTROL UNIT

TERMINAL 75 VOLTAGE SUPPLY VOLTAGE

STARTER INHIBITOR RELAY

TERMINAL 50 VOLTAGE SUPPLY VOLTAGE

STARTER MOTOR

*STARTER INHIBITOR RELAY

Battery

**Starting and charging from May '09
– 1.6 litre CAYA, CAYB, CAYC diesel engines**

*** For vehicles with automatic transmission

* For vehicles with automatic transmission
* For vehicles with automatic transmission from November 2009
** For vehicles with automatic transmission to November 2009

RD

IGNITION /
STARTER
SWITCH

ENGINE CONTROL
UNIT

ONBOARD SUPPLY
CONTROL UNIT

ALTERNATOR

STARTER
MOTOR

Battery

**Starting and charging from November '09
– 1.2 litre CGPA & CGPB petrol engines**

✱ For vehicles with 1.2 petrol engine to November 2011

Starting and charging from November '09 – 1.4 litre CGGB petrol engines

* For vehicles with automatic transmission

** According to equipment

Starting and charging from November '09 – 1.6 litre CAYA, CAYB & CAYC diesel engines

T4e For vehicles with automatic transmission
*   For vehicles with automatic transmission

Starting and charging with Stop/Start from November '09 – 1.6 litre CAYB diesel engines

T4   For Vehicles with automatic transmission

Starting and charging from January '10 – 1.2 litre CFWA diesel engines

Starting and charging with Stop/Start from February '10 – 1.2 litre CFWA diesel engines

* For vehicles up to May 2011
** For vehicles from May 2011
** According to equipment

Starting and charging with Stop/Start from May '10 – 1.6 litre CAYB diesel engines

T4   For Vehicles with automatic transmission

Starting and charging with Stop/Start from November '10 – 1.2 litre CGPA petrol engines

* For vehicles up to May 2011

Exterior lighting from May '09

Exterior lighting with Stop/Start from September '09

* For vehicles from November 2009

Exterior lighting from November '09

'1 For vehicles with daytime headlights
'2 For vehicles with halogen headlights
'3 For vehicles with gas discharge headlights
'4 For vehicles up to May 2010
'5 For vehicles from May 2010
'6 According to equipment
'7 For vehicles from November 2011

Exterior lighting with Stop/Start from November '09

Interior lights from May '09

'1 Driver side reading light
'2 Interior light with swich-off delay
'3 Front passenger reading light
'4 Rear centre reading light

Wipers and Washers from May '09

Central Locking from May '09

* For vehicles from May 2011

Electric Windows from May '09

* For vehicles with central locking and manual rear windows

Electric Windows from November '09

* For vehicles with central locking and manual rear windows

ENGINE CONTROL UNIT

ONBOARD SUPPLY CONTROL UNIT

CLUTCH POSITION SWITCH

BRAKE LIGHT SWITCH

DIODE

Battery

CAN

Cruise Control from May '09

T94   For vehicles with diesel engine

T80   For vehicles with gasoline engine

*   Except vehicles with gasoline engines

Cruise Control from November '09

T94 For vehicles with diesel engine

T80 For vehicles with gasoline engine except CGPA and CGPB

T121 For vehicles with CGPA and CGPB

ENGINE CONTROL UNIT

ONBOARD SUPPLY CONTROL UNIT

CLUTCH PEDAL SWITCH

BRAKE LIGHT SWITCH

DIODE

CAN

Battery

Cruise Control with Stop/Start from November '09

* Depending on equipment

** For vehicles with engines CFWA, CGPA

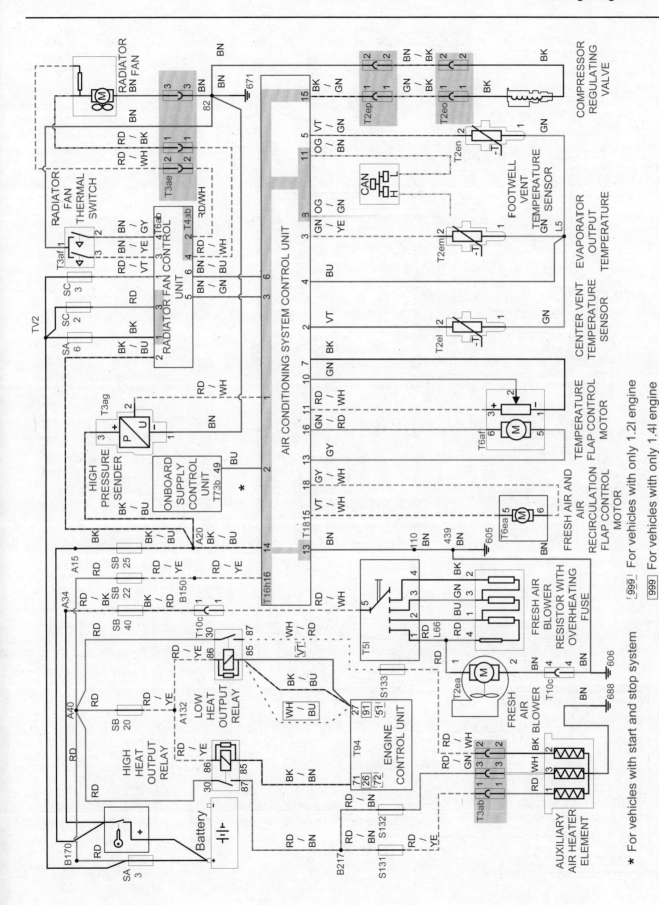

Climatic from May '09

999�月 For vehicles with only 1.2l engine

999 For vehicles with only 1.4l engine

For vehicles with start and stop system

* For vehicles with only 1.2l engine

Climatronic from May '09

Climatic from May '11

[999] For vehicles with only 1.2l engine

999 For vehicles with only 1.4l engine

For vehicles with start and stop system

*

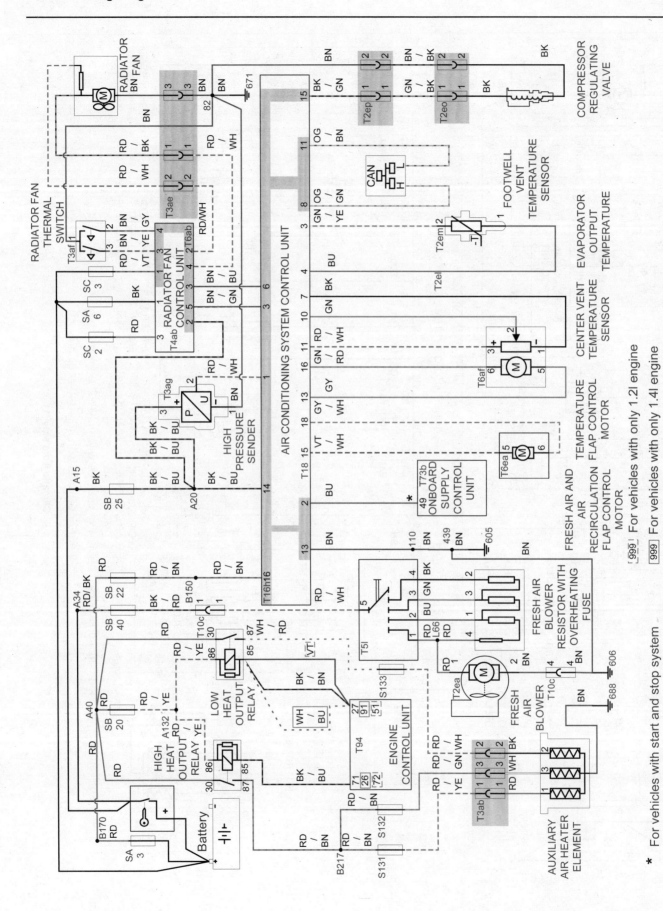

Air Conditioning with manual regulation from November '10 to May '11

999 For vehicles with only 1.2l engine

999 For vehicles with only 1.4l engine

* For vehicles with start and stop system

RADIATOR FAN

RADIATOR BN FAN

COMPRESSOR REGULATING VALVE

RADIATOR FAN THERMAL SWITCH

AIR CONDITIONING SYSTEM CONTROL UNIT

FOOTWELL VENT TEMPERATURE SENSOR

EVAPORATOR OUTPUT TEMPERAT JRE

RADIATOR FAN CONTROL UNIT

CENTER VENT TEMPERATURE SENSOR

TEMPERATURE FLAP CONTROL MOTOR

HIGH PRESSURE SENDER

FRESH AIR AND AIR RECIRCULATION FLAP CONTROL MOTOR

ONBOARD SUPPLY CONTROL UNIT

999 For vehicles with only 1.2l engine

999 For vehicles with only 1.4l engine

Air Conditioning with manual regulation from May '11

FRESH AIR BLOWER RESISTOR WITH OVERHEATING FUSE

HIGH HEAT OUTPUT RELAY

LOW HEAT OUTPUT RELAY

ENGINE CONTROL UNIT

FRESH AIR BLOWER

Battery

AUXILIARY AIR HEATER ELEMENT

* For vehicles with start and stop system

RCD 310, RCD 510, RCD 210 Radio and Navigation

* For vehicles with rear left window aerial

** For vehicles with 4 doors only

*** For vehicles from May 2011

Dimensions and weights

Note: *All figures and dimensions are approximate and may vary according to model. Refer to manufacturer's data for exact figures.*

Overall length
All models. . . . . 3970 to 4077 mm

Overall width
All models. . . . . 1682 to 1698 mm

Overall height (unladen)
All models. . . . . 1438 to 1505 mm

Wheelbase
All models. . . . . 2455 to 2459 mm

Turning circle
All models. . . . . 10.6 m

Front track
All models - depending on wheel and tyre sizes . . . . 1438 to 1463 mm

Rear track
All models - depending on wheel and tyre sizes . . . . 1434 to 1456 mm

Ground clearance
All models. . . . . 133 mm

Weights

Kerb weight*	Manual transmission	DSG transmission
1.2 litre petrol models.	1051 to 1224 kg	N/A
1.4 litre petrol models.	1070 to 1227 kg	1104 to 1263 kg
1.2 litre diesel models.	1132 to 1289 kg	N/A
1.6 litre diesel models.	1157 to 1317 kg	1179 to 1337 kg

Maximum gross vehicle weight*
1.2 litre petrol models . . . . 1540 to 1570 kg
1.4 litre petrol models. . . . . 1550 to 1600 kg
1.2 litre diesel models. . . . . 1590 to 1640 kg
1.6 litre diesel models. . . . . 1650 to 1700 kg

Maximum towing weights**	Unbraked trailer	Braked trailer
1.2 litre petrol models.	530 to 560 kg	800 kg
1.4 litre petrol models:		
Manual transmission.	530 to 560 kg	1000 to 1200 kg
DSG transmission.	550 to 580 kg	1000 to 1200 kg
1.2 litre diesel models.	560 to 600 kg	800 to 1200 kg
1.6 litre diesel models:		
Manual transmission.	570 to 610 kg	1200 kg
DSG transmission.	570 to 620 kg	1200 kg

* *Refer to the Vehicle Identification Plate for the exact figures for your specific vehicle – see 'Vehicle identification numbers'*
** *Ensure the combined weight of the trailer and vehicle never exceeds the gross train weight when towing.*

Fuel economy

Although depreciation is still the biggest part of the cost of motoring for most car owners, the cost of fuel is more immediately noticeable. These pages give some tips on how to get the best fuel economy.

Working it out

Manufacturer's figures

Car manufacturers are required by law to provide fuel consumption information on all new vehicles sold. These 'official' figures are obtained by simulating various driving conditions on a rolling road or a test track. Real life conditions are different, so the fuel consumption actually achieved may not bear much resemblance to the quoted figures.

How to calculate it

Many cars now have trip computers which will

display fuel consumption, both instantaneous and average. Refer to the owner's handbook for details of how to use these.

To calculate consumption yourself (and maybe to check that the trip computer is accurate), proceed as follows.

1. Fill up with fuel and note the mileage, or zero the trip recorder.
2. Drive as usual until you need to fill up again.
3. Note the amount of fuel required to refill the tank, and the mileage covered since the previous fill-up.
4. Divide the mileage by the amount of fuel used to obtain the consumption figure.

For example:

    Mileage at first fill-up (a) = 27,903
    Mileage at second fill-up (b) = 28,346
    Mileage covered (b - a) = 443
    Fuel required at second fill-up = 48.6 litres

The half-completed changeover to metric units in the UK means that we buy our fuel

in litres, measure distances in miles and talk about fuel consumption in miles per gallon. There are two ways round this: the first is to convert the litres to gallons before doing the calculation (by dividing by 4.546, or see Table 1). So in the example:

    48.6 litres ÷ 4.546 = 10.69 gallons
    443 miles ÷ 10.69 gallons = 41.4 mpg

The second way is to calculate the consumption in miles per litre, then multiply that figure by 4.546 (or see Table 2).

So in the example, fuel consumption is:

    443 miles ÷ 48.6 litres = 9.1 mpl
    9.1 mpl x 4.546 = 41.4 mpg

The rest of Europe expresses fuel consumption in litres of fuel required to travel 100 km (l/100 km). For interest, the conversions are given in Table 3. In practice it doesn't matter what units you use, provided you know what your normal consumption is and can spot if it's getting better or worse.

Table 1: conversion of litres to Imperial gallons

litres	1	2	3	4	5	10	20	30	40	50	60	70
gallons	0.22	0.44	0.66	0.88	1.10	2.24	4.49	6.73	8.98	11.22	13.47	15.71

Table 2: conversion of miles per litre to miles per gallon

miles per litre	5	6	7	8	9	10	11	12	13	14
miles per gallon	23	27	32	36	41	46	50	55	59	64

Table 3: conversion of litres per 100 km to miles per gallon

litres per 100 km	4	4.5	5	5.5	6	6.5	7	8	9	10
miles per gallon	71	63	56	51	47	43	40	35	31	28

Maintenance

A well-maintained car uses less fuel and creates less pollution. In particular:

Filters

Change air and fuel filters at the specified intervals.

Oil

Use a good quality oil of the lowest viscosity specified by the vehicle manufacturer (see *Lubricants and fluids*). Check the level often and be careful not to overfill.

Spark plugs

When applicable, renew at the specified intervals.

Tyres

Check tyre pressures regularly. Under-inflated tyres have an increased rolling resistance. It is generally safe to use the higher pressures specified for full load conditions even when not fully laden, but keep an eye on the centre band of tread for signs of wear due to over-inflation.

When buying new tyres, consider the 'fuel saving' models which most manufacturers include in their ranges.

Driving style

Acceleration

Acceleration uses more fuel than driving at a steady speed. The best technique with modern cars is to accelerate reasonably briskly to the desired speed, changing up through the gears as soon as possible without making the engine labour.

Air conditioning

Air conditioning absorbs quite a bit of energy from the engine – typically 3 kW (4 hp) or so. The effect on fuel consumption is at its worst in slow traffic. Switch it off when not required.

Anticipation

Drive smoothly and try to read the traffic flow so as to avoid unnecessary acceleration and braking.

Automatic transmission

When accelerating in an automatic, avoid depressing the throttle so far as to make the transmission hold onto lower gears at higher speeds. Don't use the 'Sport' setting, if applicable.

When stationary with the engine running, select 'N' or 'P'. When moving, keep your left foot away from the brake.

Braking

Braking converts the car's energy of motion into heat – essentially, it is wasted. Obviously some braking is always going to be necessary, but with good anticipation it is surprising how much can be avoided, especially on routes that you know well.

Carshare

Consider sharing lifts to work or to the shops. Even once a week will make a difference.

Electrical loads

Electricity is 'fuel' too; the alternator which charges the battery does so by converting some of the engine's energy of motion into electrical energy. The more electrical accessories are in use, the greater the load on the alternator. Switch off big consumers like the heated rear window when not required.

Freewheeling

Freewheeling (coasting) in neutral with the engine switched off is dangerous. The effort required to operate power-assisted brakes and steering increases when the engine is not running, with a potential lack of control in emergency situations.

In any case, modern fuel injection systems automatically cut off the engine's fuel supply on the overrun (moving and in gear, but with the accelerator pedal released).

Gadgets

Bolt-on devices claiming to save fuel have been around for nearly as long as the motor car itself. Those which worked were rapidly adopted as standard equipment by the vehicle manufacturers. Others worked only in certain situations, or saved fuel only at the expense of unacceptable effects on performance, driveability or the life of engine components.

The most effective fuel saving gadget is the driver's right foot.

Journey planning

Combine (eg) a trip to the supermarket with a visit to the recycling centre and the DIY store, rather than making separate journeys.

When possible choose a travelling time outside rush hours.

Load

The more heavily a car is laden, the greater the energy required to accelerate it to a given speed. Remove heavy items which you don't need to carry.

One load which is often overlooked is the contents of the fuel tank. A tankful of fuel (55 litres / 12 gallons) weighs 45 kg (100 lb) or so. Just half filling it may be worthwhile.

Lost?

At the risk of stating the obvious, if you're going somewhere new, have details of the route to hand. There's not much point in

achieving record mpg if you also go miles out of your way.

Parking

If possible, carry out any reversing or turning manoeuvres when you arrive at a parking space so that you can drive straight out when you leave. Manoeuvering when the engine is cold uses a lot more fuel.

Driving around looking for free on-street parking may cost more in fuel than buying a car park ticket.

Premium fuel

Most major oil companies (and some supermarkets) have premium grades of fuel which are several pence a litre dearer than the standard grades. Reports vary, but the consensus seems to be that if these fuels improve economy at all, they do not do so by enough to justify their extra cost.

Roof rack

When loading a roof rack, try to produce a wedge shape with the narrow end at the front. Any cover should be securely fastened – if it flaps it's creating turbulence and absorbing energy.

Remove roof racks and boxes when not in use – they increase air resistance and can create a surprising amount of noise.

Short journeys

The engine is at its least efficient, and wear is highest, during the first few miles after a cold start. Consider walking, cycling or using public transport.

Speed

The engine is at its most efficient when running at a steady speed and load at the rpm where it develops maximum torque. (You can find this figure in the car's handbook.) For most cars this corresponds to between 55 and 65 mph in top gear.

Above the optimum cruising speed, fuel consumption starts to rise quite sharply. A car travelling at 80 mph will typically be using 30% more fuel than at 60 mph.

Supermarket fuel

It may be cheap but is it any good? In the UK all supermarket fuel must meet the relevant British Standard. The major oil companies will say that their branded fuels have better additive packages which may stop carbon and other deposits building up. A reasonable compromise might be to use one tank of branded fuel to three or four from the supermarket.

Switch off when stationary

Switch off the engine if you look like being stationary for more than 30 seconds or so. This is good for the environment as well as for your pocket. Be aware though that frequent restarts are hard on the battery and the starter motor.

Windows

Driving with the windows open increases air turbulence around the vehicle. Closing the windows promotes smooth airflow and

reduced resistance. The faster you go, the more significant this is.

And finally . . .

Driving techniques associated with good fuel economy tend to involve moderate acceleration and low top speeds. Be considerate to the needs of other road users who may need to make brisker progress; even if you do not agree with them this is not an excuse to be obstructive.

Safety must always take precedence over economy, whether it is a question of accelerating hard to complete an overtaking manoeuvre, killing your speed when confronted with a potential hazard or switching the lights on when it starts to get dark.

Conversion factors

Length (distance)

Inches (in)	x 25.4	= Millimetres (mm)	x 0.0394	= Inches (in)
Feet (ft)	x 0.305	= Metres (m)	x 3.281	= Feet (ft)
Miles	x 1.609	= Kilometres (km)	x 0.621	= Miles

Volume (capacity)

Cubic inches (cu in; in³)	x 16.387	= Cubic centimetres (cc; cm³)	x 0.061	= Cubic inches (cu in; in³)
Imperial pints (Imp pt)	x 0.568	= Litres (l)	x 1.76	= Imperial pints (Imp pt)
Imperial quarts (Imp qt)	x 1.137	= Litres (l)	x 0.88	= Imperial quarts (Imp qt)
Imperial quarts (Imp qt)	x 1.201	= US quarts (US qt)	x 0.833	= Imperial quarts (Imp qt)
US quarts (US qt)	x 0.946	= Litres (l)	x 1.057	= US quarts (US qt)
Imperial gallons (Imp gal)	x 4.546	= Litres (l)	x 0.22	= Imperial gallons (Imp gal)
Imperial gallons (Imp gal)	x 1.201	= US gallons (US gal)	x 0.833	= Imperial gallons (Imp gal)
US gallons (US gal)	x 3.785	= Litres (l)	x 0.264	= US gallons (US gal)

Mass (weight)

Ounces (oz)	x 28.35	= Grams (g)	x 0.035	= Ounces (oz)
Pounds (lb)	x 0.454	= Kilograms (kg)	x 2.205	= Pounds (lb)

Force

Ounces-force (ozf; oz)	x 0.278	= Newtons (N)	x 3.6	= Ounces-force (ozf; oz)
Pounds-force (lbf; lb)	x 4.448	= Newtons (N)	x 0.225	= Pounds-force (lbf; lb)
Newtons (N)	x 0.1	= Kilograms-force (kgf; kg)	x 9.81	= Newtons (N)

Pressure

Pounds-force per square inch (psi; lbf/in²; lb/in²)	x 0.070	= Kilograms-force per square centimetre (kgf/cm²; kg/cm²)	x 14.223	= Pounds-force per square inch (psi; lbf/in²; lb/in²)
Pounds-force per square inch (psi; lbf/in²; lb/in²)	x 0.068	= Atmospheres (atm)	x 14.696	= Pounds-force per square inch (psi; lbf/in²; lb/in²)
Pounds-force per square inch (psi; lbf/in²; lb/in²)	x 0.069	= Bars	x 14.5	= Pounds-force per square inch (psi; lbf/in²; lb/in²)
Pounds-force per square inch (psi; lbf/in²; lb/in²)	x 6.895	= Kilopascals (kPa)	x 0.145	= Pounds-force per square inch (psi; lbf/in²; lb/in²)
Kilopascals (kPa)	x 0.01	= Kilograms-force per square centimetre (kgf/cm²; kg/cm²)	x 98.1	= Kilopascals (kPa)
Millibar (mbar)	x 100	= Pascals (Pa)	x 0.01	= Millibar (mbar)
Millibar (mbar)	x 0.0145	= Pounds-force per square inch (psi; lbf/in²; lb/in²)	x 68.947	= Millibar (mbar)
Millibar (mbar)	x 0.75	= Millimetres of mercury (mmHg)	x 1.333	= Millibar (mbar)
Millibar (mbar)	x 0.401	= Inches of water (inH₂O)	x 2.491	= Millibar (mbar)
Millimetres of mercury (mmHg)	x 0.535	= Inches of water (inH₂O)	x 1.868	= Millimetres of mercury (mmHg)
Inches of water (inH₂O)	x 0.036	= Pounds-force per square inch (psi; lbf/in²; lb/in²)	x 27.68	= Inches of water (inH₂O)

Torque (moment of force)

Pounds-force inches (lbf in; lb in)	x 1.152	= Kilograms-force centimetre (kgf cm; kg cm)	x 0.868	= Pounds-force inches (lbf in; lb in)
Pounds-force inches (lbf in; lb in)	x 0.113	= Newton metres (Nm)	x 8.85	= Pounds-force inches (lbf in; lb in)
Pounds-force inches (lbf in; lb in)	x 0.083	= Pounds-force feet (lbf ft; lb ft)	x 12	= Pounds-force inches (lbf in; lb in)
Pounds-force feet (lbf ft; lb ft)	x 0.138	= Kilograms-force metres (kgf m; kg m)	x 7.233	= Pounds-force feet (lbf ft; lb ft)
Pounds-force feet (lbf ft; lb ft)	x 1.356	= Newton metres (Nm)	x 0.738	= Pounds-force feet (lbf ft; lb ft)
Newton metres (Nm)	x 0.102	= Kilograms-force metres (kgf m; kg m)	x 9.804	= Newton metres (Nm)

Power

Horsepower (hp)	x 745.7	= Watts (W)	x 0.0013	= Horsepower (hp)

Velocity (speed)

Miles per hour (miles/hr; mph)	x 1.609	= Kilometres per hour (km/hr; kph)	x 0.621	= Miles per hour (miles/hr; mph)

Fuel consumption*

Miles per gallon, Imperial (mpg)	x 0.354	= Kilometres per litre (km/l)	x 2.825	= Miles per gallon, Imperial (mpg)
Miles per gallon, US (mpg)	x 0.425	= Kilometres per litre (km/l)	x 2.352	= Miles per gallon, US (mpg)

Temperature

Degrees Fahrenheit = (°C x 1.8) + 32   Degrees Celsius (Degrees Centigrade; °C) = (°F - 32) x 0.56

It is common practice to convert from miles per gallon (mpg) to litres/100 kilometres (l/100km), where mpg x l/100 km = 282

Spare parts are available from many sources, including maker's appointed garages, accessory shops, and motor factors. To be sure of obtaining the correct parts, it will sometimes be necessary to quote the vehicle identification number. If possible, it can also be useful to take the old parts along for positive identification. Items such as starter motors and alternators may be available under a service exchange scheme – any parts returned should be clean.

Our advice regarding spare parts is as follows.

Officially appointed garages

This is the best source of parts which are peculiar to your car, and which are not otherwise generally available (e.g. badges, interior trim, certain body panels, etc). It is also the only place at which you should buy parts if the car is still under warranty.

Accessory shops

These are very good places to buy materials and components needed for the maintenance of your car (oil, air and fuel filters, light bulbs, drivebelts, greases, brake pads, touch-up paint, etc). Components of this nature sold by a reputable shop are usually of the same standard as those used by the car manufacturer.

Besides components, these shops also sell tools and general accessories, usually have convenient opening hours, charge lower prices, and can often be found close to home. Some accessory shops have parts counters where components needed for almost any repair job can be purchased or ordered.

Motor factors

Good factors will stock all the more important components that wear out comparatively quickly, and can sometimes supply individual components needed for the overhaul of a larger assembly (e.g. brake seals and hydraulic parts, bearing shells, pistons, valves). They may also handle work such as cylinder block reboring, crankshaft regrinding, etc.

Engine reconditioners

These specialise in engine overhaul and can also supply components. It is recommended that the establishment is a member of the Federation of Engine Re-Manufacturers, or a similar society.

Tyre and exhaust specialists

These outlets may be independent, or members of a local or national chain. They frequently offer competitive prices when compared with a main dealer or local garage, but it will pay to obtain several quotes before making a decision. When researching prices, also ask what extras may be added – for instance fitting a new valve, balancing the wheel and tyre disposal all both commonly charged on top of the price of a new tyre.

Other sources

Beware of parts or materials obtained from market stalls, car boot sales, on-line auctions or similar outlets. Such items are not invariably sub-standard, but there is little chance of compensation if they do prove unsatisfactory. In the case of safety-critical components such as brake pads, there is the risk not only of financial loss, but also of an accident causing injury or death.

Second-hand components or assemblies obtained from a car breaker can be a good buy in some circumstances, but this sort of purchase is best made by the experienced DIY mechanic.

Jacking and vehicle support

The jack supplied with the vehicle should only be used for changing the roadwheels – see Wheel changing at the front of this manual. When carrying out any other kind of work, raise the vehicle using a hydraulic (or 'trolley') jack, and always supplement the jack with axle stands at the vehicle jacking points.

When using a hydraulic jack or axle stands, always position the jack head or axle stand head under one of the relevant jacking points; the jacking point is the area below the mark on the sill (see illustration). Use a block of wood between the jack or axle stand and the sill – the block of wood should have a groove cut into it, into which the welded flange of the sill will locate.

Do not attempt to jack the vehicle under the front crossmember, rear axle, engine, transmission or any of the suspension components.

The jack supplied with the vehicle locates at the jacking points on the underside of the sills – see Wheel changing. Ensure that the jack head is correctly engaged before attempting to raise the vehicle.

Never work under, around, or near a raised vehicle, unless it is adequately supported in at least two places.

Front and rear jacking points (arrowed)

The jacking points are indicated by an arrow on the sill

Use an axle stand with a suitable block of wood

Whenever servicing, repair or overhaul work is carried out on the car or its components, observe the following procedures and instructions. This will assist in carrying out the operation efficiently and to a professional standard of workmanship.

Joint mating faces and gaskets

When separating components at their mating faces, never insert screwdrivers or similar implements into the joint between the faces in order to prise them apart. This can cause severe damage which results in oil leaks, coolant leaks, etc upon reassembly. Separation is usually achieved by tapping along the joint with a soft-faced hammer in order to break the seal. However, note that this method may not be suitable where dowels are used for component location.

Where a gasket is used between the mating faces of two components, a new one must be fitted on reassembly; fit it dry unless otherwise stated in the repair procedure. Make sure that the mating faces are clean and dry, with all traces of old gasket removed. When cleaning a joint face, use a tool which is unlikely to score or damage the face, and remove any burrs or nicks with an oilstone or fine file.

Make sure that tapped holes are cleaned with a pipe cleaner, and keep them free of jointing compound, if this is being used, unless specifically instructed otherwise.

Ensure that all orifices, channels or pipes are clear, and blow through them, preferably using compressed air.

Oil seals

Oil seals can be removed by levering them out with a wide flat-bladed screwdriver or similar implement. Alternatively, a number of self-tapping screws may be screwed into the seal, and these used as a purchase for pliers or some similar device in order to pull the seal free.

Whenever an oil seal is removed from its working location, either individually or as part of an assembly, it should be renewed.

The very fine sealing lip of the seal is easily damaged, and will not seal if the surface it contacts is not completely clean and free from scratches, nicks or grooves. If the original sealing surface of the component cannot be restored, and the manufacturer has not made provision for slight relocation of the seal relative to the sealing surface, the component should be renewed.

Protect the lips of the seal from any surface which may damage them in the course of fitting. Use tape or a conical sleeve where possible. Where indicated, lubricate the seal lips with oil before fitting and, on dual-lipped seals, fill the space between the lips with grease.

Unless otherwise stated, oil seals must be fitted with their sealing lips toward the lubricant to be sealed.

Use a tubular drift or block of wood of the appropriate size to install the seal and, if the seal housing is shouldered, drive the seal down to the shoulder. If the seal housing is unshouldered, the seal should be fitted with its face flush with the housing top face (unless otherwise instructed).

Screw threads and fastenings

Seized nuts, bolts and screws are quite a common occurrence where corrosion has set in, and the use of penetrating oil or releasing fluid will often overcome this problem if the offending item is soaked for a while before attempting to release it. The use of an impact driver may also provide a means of releasing such stubborn fastening devices, when used in conjunction with the appropriate screwdriver bit or socket. If none of these methods works, it may be necessary to resort to the careful application of heat, or the use of a hacksaw or nut splitter device. Before resorting to extreme methods, check that you are not dealing with a left-hand thread!

Studs are usually removed by locking two nuts together on the threaded part, and then using a spanner on the lower nut to unscrew the stud. Studs or bolts which have broken off below the surface of the component in which they are mounted can sometimes be removed using a stud extractor.

Always ensure that a blind tapped hole is completely free from oil, grease, water or other fluid before installing the bolt or stud. Failure to do this could cause the housing to crack due to the hydraulic action of the bolt or stud as it is screwed in.

For some screw fastenings, notably cylinder head bolts or nuts, torque wrench settings are no longer specified for the latter stages of tightening, "angle-tightening" being called up instead. Typically, a fairly low torque wrench setting will be applied to the bolts/nuts in the correct sequence, followed by one or more stages of tightening through specified angles.

When checking or retightening a nut or bolt to a specified torque setting, slacken the nut or bolt by a quarter of a turn, and then retighten to the specified setting. However, this should not be attempted where angular tightening has been used.

Locknuts, locktabs and washers

Any fastening which will rotate against a component or housing during tightening should always have a washer between it and the relevant component or housing.

Spring or split washers should always be renewed when they are used to lock a critical component such as a big-end bearing retaining bolt or nut. Locktabs which are folded over to retain a nut or bolt should always be renewed.

Self-locking nuts can be re-used in non-critical areas, providing resistance can be felt when the locking portion passes over the bolt or stud thread. However, it should be noted that self-locking stiffnuts tend to lose their effectiveness after long periods of use, and should then be renewed as a matter of course.

Split pins must always be replaced with new ones of the correct size for the hole.

When thread-locking compound is found on the threads of a fastener which is to be re-used, it should be cleaned off with a wire brush and solvent, and fresh compound applied on reassembly.

Special tools

Some repair procedures in this manual entail the use of special tools such as a press, two or three-legged pullers, spring compressors, etc. Wherever possible, suitable readily-available alternatives to the manufacturer's special tools are described, and are shown in use. In some instances, where no alternative is possible, it has been necessary to resort to the use of a manufacturer's tool, and this has been done for reasons of safety as well as the efficient completion of the repair operation. Unless you are highly-skilled and have a thorough understanding of the procedures described, never attempt to bypass the use of any special tool when the procedure described specifies its use. Not only is there a very great risk of personal injury, but expensive damage could be caused to the components involved.

Environmental considerations

When disposing of used engine oil, brake fluid, antifreeze, etc, give due consideration to any detrimental environmental effects. Do not, for instance, pour any of the above liquids down drains into the general sewage system, or onto the ground to soak away, as this is likely to pollute your local environment. Many local council refuse tips provide a facility for waste oil disposal, as do some garages. You can find your nearest disposal point by calling the Environment Agency on 03708 506 506 or by visiting www.oilbankline.org.uk.

Note: It is illegal and anti-social to dump oil down the drain. To find the location of your local oil recycling bank, call 03708 506 506 or visit www.oilbankline.org.uk.

Vehicle identification numbers

Modifications are a continuing and unpublicised process in vehicle manufacture, quite apart from major model changes. Spare parts manuals and lists are compiled upon a numerical basis, the individual vehicle identification numbers being essential for correct identification of the part concerned.

When ordering spare parts, always give as much information as possible. Quote the car model, year of manufacture and registration, chassis and engine numbers, as appropriate.

The *Vehicle Identification Number (VIN) plate* is visible from the outside of the vehicle, through the left-hand lower corner of the windscreen, and is also stamped on the right-hand upper strut inner wing panel, in the engine compartment **(see illustrations)**.

The *Vehicle Data Sticker* is located on the luggage compartment floor panel next to the spare wheel well **(see illustration)**. It contains the VIN, vehicle type, engine power, transmission type, engine and transmission codes, paint number, interior equipment, optional extras and PR number (for maintenance schedule).

The *Type plate and factory plate* is located at the bottom of the front, left-hand door B-pillar **(see illustration)**, and is visible with the door open. It contains the gross vehicle weight, front axle weight and rear axle weight.

The *Engine Number* is stamped into the left-hand end of the cylinder block and on the right-hand end of the cylinder head on petrol engines. On diesel engines it is stamped into the front of the cylinder block, next to the engine to transmission joint. A barcode identification sticker is located on the top of the timing cover or on the right-hand end of the cylinder head **(see illustrations)**. If the engine number is difficult to find, check the *Vehicle Data Sticker* on the luggage compartment floor panel (see above).

Vehicle Identification Number (VIN) located on the left-hand front edge of the windscreen

Vehicle Identification Number (VIN) located on the top of the right-hand inner wing

Vehicle Data Sticker located in the spare wheel well

VIN (A) and engine number (B) located on the left-hand B-pillar label

Engine code sticker on the right-hand end of the cylinder head on petrol engines

Engine code sticker on the top of the timing cover on diesel engines

Introduction

A selection of good tools is a fundamental requirement for anyone contemplating the maintenance and repair of a motor vehicle. For the owner who does not possess any, their purchase will prove a considerable expense, offsetting some of the savings made by doing-it-yourself. However, provided that the tools purchased meet the relevant national safety standards and are of good quality, they will last for many years and prove an extremely worthwhile investment.

To help the average owner to decide which tools are needed to carry out the various tasks detailed in this manual, we have compiled three lists of tools under the following headings: *Maintenance and minor repair*, *Repair and overhaul*, and *Special*. Newcomers to practical mechanics should start off with the *Maintenance and minor repair* tool kit, and confine themselves to the simpler jobs around the vehicle. Then, as confidence and experience grow, more difficult tasks can be undertaken, with extra tools being purchased as, and when, they are needed. In this way, a *Maintenance and minor repair* tool kit can be built up into a *Repair and overhaul* tool kit over a considerable period of time, without any major cash outlays. The experienced do-it-yourselfer will have a tool kit good enough for most repair and overhaul procedures, and will add tools from the *Special* category when it is felt that the expense is justified by the amount of use to which these tools will be put.

Maintenance and minor repair tool kit

The tools given in this list should be considered as a minimum requirement if routine maintenance, servicing and minor repair operations are to be undertaken. We recommend the purchase of combination spanners (ring one end, open-ended the other); although more expensive than open-ended ones, they do give the advantages of both types of spanner.

☐ *Combination spanners:*
  Metric - 8 to 19 mm inclusive
☐ *Adjustable spanner - 35 mm jaw (approx.)*
☐ *Spark plug spanner (with rubber insert) - petrol models*
☐ *Spark plug gap adjustment tool - petrol models*
☐ *Set of feeler gauges*
☐ *Brake bleed nipple spanner*
☐ *Screwdrivers:*
  Flat blade - 100 mm long x 6 mm dia
  Cross blade - 100 mm long x 6 mm dia
  Torx - various sizes (not all vehicles)
☐ *Combination pliers*
☐ *Hacksaw (junior)*
☐ *Tyre pump*
☐ *Tyre pressure gauge*
☐ *Oil can*
☐ *Oil filter removal tool (if applicable)*
☐ *Fine emery cloth*
☐ *Wire brush (small)*
☐ *Funnel (medium size)*
☐ *Sump drain plug key (not all vehicles)*

Repair and overhaul tool kit

These tools are virtually essential for anyone undertaking any major repairs to a motor vehicle, and are additional to those given in the *Maintenance and minor repair* list. Included in this list is a comprehensive set of sockets. Although these are expensive, they will be found invaluable as they are so versatile - particularly if various drives are included in the set. We recommend the half-inch square-drive type, as this can be used with most proprietary torque wrenches.

The tools in this list will sometimes need to be supplemented by tools from the *Special* list:

☐ *Sockets to cover range in previous list (including Torx sockets)*
☐ *Reversible ratchet drive (for use with sockets)*
☐ *Extension piece, 250 mm (for use with sockets)*
☐ *Universal joint (for use with sockets)*
☐ *Flexible handle or sliding T "breaker bar" (for use with sockets)*
☐ *Torque wrench (for use with sockets)*
☐ *Self-locking grips*
☐ *Ball pein hammer*
☐ *Soft-faced mallet (plastic or rubber)*
☐ *Screwdrivers:*
  Flat blade - long & sturdy, short (chubby), and narrow (electrician's) types
  Cross blade – long & sturdy, and short (chubby) types
☐ *Pliers:*
  Long-nosed
  Side cutters (electrician's)
  Circlip (internal and external)
☐ *Cold chisel - 25 mm*
☐ *Scriber*
☐ *Scraper*
☐ *Centre-punch*
☐ *Pin punch*
☐ *Hacksaw*
☐ *Brake hose clamp*
☐ *Brake/clutch bleeding kit*
☐ *Selection of twist drills*
☐ *Steel rule/straight-edge*
☐ *Allen keys (inc. splined/Torx type)*
☐ *Selection of files*
☐ *Wire brush*
☐ *Axle stands*
☐ *Jack (strong trolley or hydraulic type)*
☐ *Light with extension lead*
☐ *Universal electrical multi-meter*

Sockets and reversible ratchet drive

Brake bleeding kit

Torx key, socket and bit

Hose clamp

Angular-tightening gauge

Special tools

The tools in this list are those which are not used regularly, are expensive to buy, or which need to be used in accordance with their manufacturers' instructions. Unless relatively difficult mechanical jobs are undertaken frequently, it will not be economic to buy many of these tools. Where this is the case, you could consider clubbing together with friends (or joining a motorists' club) to make a joint purchase, or borrowing the tools against a deposit from a local garage or tool hire specialist.

The following list contains only those tools and instruments freely available to the public, and not those special tools produced by the vehicle manufacturer specifically for its dealer network. You will find occasional references to these manufacturers' special tools in the text of this manual. Generally, an alternative method of doing the job without the vehicle manufacturers' special tool is given. However, sometimes there is no alternative to using them. Where this is the case and the relevant tool cannot be bought or borrowed, you will have to entrust the work to a dealer.

☐ Angular-tightening gauge
☐ Valve spring compressor
☐ Valve grinding tool
☐ Piston ring compressor
☐ Piston ring removal/installation tool
☐ Cylinder bore hone
☐ Balljoint separator
☐ Coil spring compressors (where applicable)
☐ Two/three-legged hub and bearing puller
☐ Impact screwdriver
☐ Micrometer and/or vernier calipers
☐ Dial gauge
☐ Tachometer
☐ Fault code reader
☐ Cylinder compression gauge
☐ Hand-operated vacuum pump and gauge
☐ Clutch plate alignment set
☐ Brake shoe steady spring cup removal tool
☐ Bush and bearing removal/installation set
☐ Stud extractors
☐ Tap and die set
☐ Lifting tackle

Buying tools

Reputable motor accessory shops and superstores often offer excellent quality tools at discount prices, so it pays to shop around.

Remember, you don't have to buy the most expensive items on the shelf, but it is always advisable to steer clear of the very cheap tools. Beware of 'bargains' offered on market stalls, on-line or at car boot sales. There are plenty of good tools around at reasonable prices, but always aim to purchase items which meet the relevant national safety standards. If in doubt, ask the proprietor or manager of the shop for advice before making a purchase.

Care and maintenance of tools

Having purchased a reasonable tool kit, it is necessary to keep the tools in a clean and serviceable condition. After use, always wipe off any dirt, grease and metal particles using a clean, dry cloth, before putting the tools away. Never leave them lying around after they have been used. A simple tool rack on the garage or workshop wall for items such as screwdrivers and pliers is a good idea. Store all normal spanners and sockets in a metal box. Any measuring instruments, gauges, meters, etc, must be carefully stored where they cannot be damaged or become rusty.

Take a little care when tools are used. Hammer heads inevitably become marked, and screwdrivers lose the keen edge on their blades from time to time. A little timely attention with emery cloth or a file will soon restore items like this to a good finish.

Working facilities

Not to be forgotten when discussing tools is the workshop itself. If anything more than routine maintenance is to be carried out, a suitable working area becomes essential.

It is appreciated that many an owner-mechanic is forced by circumstances to remove an engine or similar item without the benefit of a garage or workshop. Having done this, any repairs should always be done under the cover of a roof.

Wherever possible, any dismantling should be done on a clean, flat workbench or table at a suitable working height.

Any workbench needs a vice; one with a jaw opening of 100 mm is suitable for most jobs. As mentioned previously, some clean dry storage space is also required for tools, as well as for any lubricants, cleaning fluids, touch-up paints etc, which become necessary.

Another item which may be required, and which has a much more general usage, is an electric drill with a chuck capacity of at least 8 mm. This, together with a good range of twist drills, is virtually essential for fitting accessories.

Last, but not least, always keep a supply of old newspapers and clean, lint-free rags available, and try to keep any working area as clean as possible.

Micrometers

Dial test indicator ("dial gauge")

Oil filter removal tool (strap wrench type)

Compression tester

Bearing puller

This is a guide to getting your vehicle through the MOT test. Obviously it will not be possible to examine the vehicle to the same standard as the professional MOT tester. However, working through the following checks will enable you to identify any problem areas before submitting the vehicle for the test.

It has only been possible to summarise the test requirements here, based on the regulations in force at the time of printing. Test standards are becoming increasingly stringent, although there are some exemptions for older vehicles.

An assistant will be needed to help carry out some of these checks.

The checks have been sub-divided into four categories, as follows:

1 Checks carried out **FROM THE DRIVER'S SEAT**

2 Checks carried out **WITH THE VEHICLE ON THE GROUND**

3 Checks carried out **WITH THE VEHICLE RAISED AND THE WHEELS FREE TO TURN**

4 Checks carried out on **YOUR VEHICLE'S EXHAUST EMISSION SYSTEM**

---

1 Checks carried out **FROM THE DRIVER'S SEAT**

Handbrake (parking brake)

☐ Test the operation of the handbrake. Excessive travel (too many clicks) indicates incorrect brake or cable adjustment.
☐ Check that the handbrake cannot be released by tapping the lever sideways. Check the security of the lever mountings.

☐ If the parking brake is foot-operated, check that the pedal is secure and without excessive travel, and that the release mechanism operates correctly.
☐ Where applicable, test the operation of the electronic handbrake. The brake should engage and disengage without excessive delay. If the warning light does not extinguish when the brake is disengaged, this could indicate a fault which will need further investigation.

Footbrake

☐ Depress the brake pedal and check that it does not creep down to the floor, indicating a master cylinder fault. Release the pedal,

wait a few seconds, then depress it again. If the pedal travels nearly to the floor before firm resistance is felt, brake adjustment or repair is necessary. If the pedal feels spongy, there is air in the hydraulic system which must be removed by bleeding.

☐ Check that the brake pedal is secure and in good condition. Check also for signs of fluid leaks on the pedal, floor or carpets, which would indicate failed seals in the brake master cylinder.
☐ Check the servo unit (when applicable) by operating the brake pedal several times, then keeping the pedal depressed and starting the engine. As the engine starts, the pedal will move down slightly. If not, the vacuum hose or the servo itself may be faulty.

Steering wheel and column

☐ Examine the steering wheel for fractures or looseness of the hub, spokes or rim.
☐ Move the steering wheel from side to side and then up and down. Check that the steering wheel is not loose on the column, indicating wear or a loose retaining nut. Continue moving the steering wheel as before, but also turn it slightly from left to right.

☐ Check that the steering wheel is not loose on the column, and that there is no abnormal movement of the steering wheel, indicating wear in the column support bearings or couplings.
☐ Check that the ignition lock (where fitted) engages and disengages correctly.
☐ Steering column adjustment mechanisms (where fitted) must be able to lock the column securely in place with no play evident.

Windscreen, mirrors and sunvisor

☐ The windscreen must be free of cracks or other significant damage within the driver's field of view. (Small stone chips are acceptable.) Rear view mirrors must be secure, intact, and capable of being adjusted.

☐ The driver's sunvisor must be capable of being stored in the "up" position.

Seat belts and seats

Note: *The following checks are applicable to all seat belts, front and rear.*

☐ Examine the webbing of all the belts (including rear belts if fitted) for cuts, serious fraying or deterioration. Fasten and unfasten each belt to check the buckles. If applicable, check the retracting mechanism. Check the security of all seat belt mountings accessible from inside the vehicle, ensuring any height adjustable mountings lock securely in place.

☐ Seat belts with pre-tensioners, once activated, have a "flag" or similar showing on the seat belt stalk. This, in itself, is not a reason for test failure.

☐ The front seats themselves must be securely attached and the backrests must lock in the upright position.

Doors

☐ Both front doors must be able to be opened and closed from outside and inside, and must latch securely when closed.

Bonnet and boot/tailgate

☐ The bonnet and boot/tailgate must latch securely when closed.

2 Checks carried out WITH THE VEHICLE ON THE GROUND

Vehicle identification

☐ Number plates must be in good condition, secure and legible, with letters and numbers correctly spaced – spacing at (A) should be 33 mm and at (B) 11 mm. At the front, digits must be black on a white background and at the rear black on a yellow background. Other background designs (such as honeycomb) are not permitted.

☐ The VIN plate and/or homologation plate must be permanently displayed and legible.

Electrical equipment

☐ Switch on the ignition and check the operation of the horn.

☐ Check the windscreen washers and wipers, examining the wiper blades; renew damaged or perished blades. Also check the operation of the stop-lights.

☐ Check the operation of the sidelights and number plate lights. The lenses and reflectors must be secure, clean and undamaged.

☐ Check the operation and alignment of the headlights. The headlight reflectors must not be tarnished and the lenses must be undamaged.

☐ Switch on the ignition and check the operation of the direction indicators (including the instrument panel tell-tale) and the hazard warning lights. Operation of the sidelights and stop-lights must not affect the indicators - if it does, the cause is usually a bad earth at the rear light cluster. Indicators should flash at a rate of between 60 and 120 times per minute – faster or slower than this could indicate a fault with the flasher unit or a bad earth at one of the light units.

☐ Check the operation of the rear foglight(s), including the warning light on the instrument panel or in the switch.

☐ The warning lights must illuminate in accordance with the manufacturer's design. For most vehicles, the ABS and other warning lights should illuminate when the ignition is switched on, and (if the system is operating properly) extinguish after a few seconds. Refer to the owner's handbook.

Footbrake

☐ Examine the master cylinder, brake pipes and servo unit for leaks, loose mountings, corrosion or other damage. If ABS is fitted, this unit should also be examined for signs of leaks or corrosion.

☐ The fluid reservoir must be secure and the fluid level must be between the upper (**A**) and lower (**B**) markings.

☐ Inspect both front brake flexible hoses for cracks or deterioration of the rubber. Turn the steering from lock to lock, and ensure that the hoses do not contact the wheel, tyre, or any part of the steering or suspension mechanism. With the brake pedal firmly depressed, check the hoses for bulges or leaks under pressure.

Steering and suspension

☐ Have your assistant turn the steering wheel from side to side slightly, up to the point where the steering gear just begins to transmit this movement to the roadwheels. Check for excessive free play between the steering wheel and the steering gear, indicating wear or insecurity of the steering column joints, the column-to-steering gear coupling, or the steering gear itself.

☐ Have your assistant turn the steering wheel more vigorously in each direction, so that the roadwheels just begin to turn. As this is done, examine all the steering joints, linkages, fittings and attachments. Renew any component that shows signs of wear or damage. On vehicles with power steering, check the security and condition of the steering pump, drivebelt and hoses.

☐ Check that the vehicle is standing level, and at approximately the correct ride height.

Shock absorbers

☐ Depress each corner of the vehicle in turn, then release it. The vehicle should rise and then settle in its normal position. If the vehicle continues to rise and fall, the shock absorber is defective. A shock absorber which has seized will also cause the vehicle to fail.

Exhaust system

☐ Start the engine. With your assistant holding a rag over the tailpipe, check the entire system for leaks. Repair or renew leaking sections.

3 Checks carried out **WITH THE VEHICLE RAISED AND THE WHEELS FREE TO TURN**

Jack up the front and rear of the vehicle, and securely support it on axle stands. Position the stands clear of the suspension assemblies. Ensure that the wheels are clear of the ground and that the steering can be turned from lock to lock.

Steering mechanism

☐ Have your assistant turn the steering from lock to lock. Check that the steering turns smoothly, and that no part of the steering mechanism, including a wheel or tyre, fouls any brake hose or pipe or any part of the body structure.
☐ Examine the steering rack rubber gaiters for damage or insecurity of the retaining clips. If power steering is fitted, check for signs of damage or leakage of the fluid hoses, pipes or connections. Also check for excessive stiffness or binding of the steering, a missing split pin or locking device, or severe corrosion of the body structure within 30 cm of any steering component attachment point.

Front and rear suspension and wheel bearings

☐ Starting at the front right-hand side, grasp the roadwheel at the 3 o'clock and 9 o'clock positions and rock gently but firmly. Check for free play or insecurity at the wheel bearings, suspension balljoints, or suspension mount-ings, pivots and attachments.
☐ Now grasp the wheel at the 12 o'clock and 6 o'clock positions and repeat the previous inspection. Spin the wheel, and check for roughness or tightness of the front wheel bearing.

☐ If excess free play is suspected at a component pivot point, this can be confirmed by using a large screwdriver or similar tool and levering between the mounting and the component attachment. This will confirm whether the wear is in the pivot bush, its retaining bolt, or in the mounting itself (the bolt holes can often become elongated).

☐ Carry out all the above checks at the other front wheel, and then at both rear wheels.

Springs and shock absorbers

☐ Examine the suspension struts (when applicable) for serious fluid leakage, corrosion, or damage to the casing. Also check the security of the mounting points.
☐ If coil springs are fitted, check that the spring ends locate in their seats, and that the spring is not corroded, cracked or broken.
☐ If leaf springs are fitted, check that all leaves are intact, that the axle is securely attached to each spring, and that there is no deterioration of the spring eye mountings, bushes, and shackles.

☐ The same general checks apply to vehicles fitted with other suspension types, such as torsion bars, hydraulic displacer units, etc. Ensure that all mountings and attachments are secure, that there are no signs of excessive wear, corrosion or damage, and (on hydraulic types) that there are no fluid leaks or damaged pipes.
☐ Inspect the shock absorbers for signs of serious fluid leakage. Check for wear of the mounting bushes or attachments, or damage to the body of the unit.

Driveshafts (fwd vehicles only)

☐ Rotate each front wheel in turn and inspect the constant velocity joint gaiters for splits or damage. Also check that each driveshaft is straight and undamaged.

Braking system

☐ If possible without dismantling, check brake pad wear and disc condition. Ensure that the friction lining material has not worn excessively, (A) and that the discs are not fractured, pitted, scored or badly worn (B).

☐ Examine all the rigid brake pipes underneath the vehicle, and the flexible hose(s) at the rear. Look for corrosion, chafing or insecurity of the pipes, and for signs of bulging under pressure, chafing, splits or deterioration of the flexible hoses.
☐ Look for signs of fluid leaks at the brake calipers or on the brake backplates. Repair or renew leaking components.
☐ Slowly spin each wheel, while your assistant depresses and releases the footbrake. Ensure that each brake is operating and does not bind when the pedal is released.

□Examine the handbrake mechanism, checking for frayed or broken cables, excessive corrosion, or wear or insecurity of the linkage. Check that the mechanism works on each relevant wheel, and releases fully, without binding.

□It is not possible to test brake efficiency without special equipment, but a road test can be carried out later to check that the vehicle pulls up in a straight line.

Fuel and exhaust systems

□ Inspect the fuel tank (including the filler cap), fuel pipes, hoses and unions. All components must be secure and free from leaks. Locking fuel caps must lock securely and the key must be provided for the MOT test.

□ Examine the exhaust system over its entire length, checking for any damaged, broken or missing mountings, security of the retaining clamps and rust or corrosion.

Wheels and tyres

□ Examine the sidewalls and tread area of each tyre in turn. Check for cuts, tears, lumps, bulges, separation of the tread, and exposure of the ply or cord due to wear or damage. Check that the tyre bead is correctly seated on the wheel rim, that the valve is sound and properly seated, and that the wheel is not distorted or damaged.

□ Check that the tyres are of the correct size for the vehicle, that they are of the same size and type on each axle, and that the pressures are correct.

□Check the tyre tread depth. The legal minimum at the time of writing is 1.6 mm over the central three-quarters of the tread width. Abnormal tread wear may indicate incorrect front wheel alignment or wear in steering or suspension components.

□If the spare wheel is fitted externally or in a separate carrier beneath the vehicle, check that mountings are secure and free of excessive corrosion.

Body corrosion

□Check the condition of the entire vehicle structure for signs of corrosion in load-bearing areas. (These include chassis box sections, side sills, cross-members, pillars, and all suspension, steering, braking system and seat belt mountings and anchorages.) Any corrosion which has seriously reduced the thickness of a load-bearing area (or is within 30 cm of safety-related components such as steering or suspension) is likely to cause the vehicle to fail. In this case professional repairs are likely to be needed.

□Damage or corrosion which causes sharp or otherwise dangerous edges to be exposed will also cause the vehicle to fail.

Towbars

□Check the condition of mounting points (both beneath the vehicle and within boot/hatchback areas) for signs of corrosion, ensuring that all fixings are secure and not worn or damaged. There must be no excessive play in detachable tow ball arms or quick-release mechanisms.

4 Checks carried out on **YOUR VEHICLE'S EXHAUST EMISSION SYSTEM**

Petrol models

□The engine should be warmed up, and running well (ignition system in good order, air filter element clean, etc).

□Before testing, run the engine at around 2500 rpm for 20 seconds. Let the engine drop to idle, and watch for smoke from the exhaust. If the idle speed is too high, or if dense blue or black smoke emerges for more than 5 seconds, the vehicle will fail. Typically, blue smoke signifies oil burning (engine wear);

black smoke means unburnt fuel (dirty air cleaner element, or other fuel system fault).

□An exhaust gas analyser for measuring carbon monoxide (CO) and hydrocarbons (HC) is now needed. If one cannot be hired or borrowed, have a local garage perform the check.

CO emissions (mixture)

□The MOT tester has access to the CO limits for all vehicles. The CO level is measured at idle speed, and at 'fast idle' (2500 to 3000 rpm). The following limits are given as a general guide:

At idle speed – Less than 0.5% CO
At 'fast idle' – Less than 0.3% CO
Lambda reading – 0.97 to 1.03

□If the CO level is too high, this may point to poor maintenance, a fuel injection system problem, faulty lambda (oxygen) sensor or catalytic converter. Try an injector cleaning treatment, and check the vehicle's ECU for fault codes.

HC emissions

□The MOT tester has access to HC limits for all vehicles. The HC level is measured at 'fast idle' (2500 to 3000 rpm). The following limits are given as a general guide:

At 'fast idle' – Less than 200 ppm

□Excessive HC emissions are typically caused by oil being burnt (worn engine), or by a blocked crankcase ventilation system ('breather'). If the engine oil is old and thin, an oil change may help. If the engine is running badly, check the vehicle's ECU for fault codes.

Diesel models

□The only emission test for diesel engines is measuring exhaust smoke density, using a calibrated smoke meter. The test involves accelerating the engine at least 3 times to its maximum unloaded speed.

Note: *On engines with a timing belt, it is VITAL that the belt is in good condition before the test is carried out.*

□With the engine warmed up, it is first purged by running at around 2500 rpm for 20 seconds. A governor check is then carried out, by slowly accelerating the engine to its maximum speed. After this, the smoke meter is connected, and the engine is accelerated quickly to maximum speed three times. If the smoke density is less than the limits given below, the vehicle will pass:

Non-turbo vehicles: 2.5m-1
Turbocharged vehicles: 3.0m-1

□If excess smoke is produced, try fitting a new air cleaner element, or using an injector cleaning treatment. If the engine is running badly, where applicable, check the vehicle's ECU for fault codes. Also check the vehicle's EGR system, where applicable. At high mileages, the injectors may require professional attention.

Engine

- [ ] Engine fails to rotate when attempting to start
- [ ] Engine rotates, but will not start
- [ ] Engine difficult to start when cold
- [ ] Engine difficult to start when hot
- [ ] Starter motor noisy or excessively-rough in engagement
- [ ] Engine starts, but stops immediately
- [ ] Engine idles erratically
- [ ] Engine misfires at idle speed
- [ ] Engine misfires throughout the driving speed range
- [ ] Engine hesitates on acceleration
- [ ] Engine stalls
- [ ] Engine lacks power
- [ ] Engine backfires
- [ ] Oil pressure warning light on with engine running
- [ ] Engine runs-on after switching off
- [ ] Engine noises

Cooling system

- [ ] Overheating
- [ ] Overcooling
- [ ] External coolant leakage
- [ ] Internal coolant leakage
- [ ] Corrosion

Fuel and exhaust systems

- [ ] Excessive fuel consumption
- [ ] Fuel leakage and/or fuel odour
- [ ] Excessive noise or fumes from exhaust system

Clutch

- [ ] Pedal travels to floor – no pressure or very little resistance
- [ ] Clutch fails to disengage (unable to select gears)
- [ ] Clutch slips (engine speed rises, with no increase in vehicle speed)
- [ ] Judder as clutch is engaged
- [ ] Noise when depressing or releasing clutch pedal

Manual transmission

- [ ] Noisy in neutral with engine running
- [ ] Noisy in one particular gear
- [ ] Difficulty engaging gears
- [ ] Jumps out of gear
- [ ] Vibration
- [ ] Lubricant leaks

Automatic/DSG transmission

- [ ] Fluid leakage
- [ ] Transmission fluid brown, or has burned smell
- [ ] General gear selection problems
- [ ] Engine won't start in any gear, or starts in gears other than P or N
- [ ] Transmission slips, shifts roughly, is noisy, or has no drive in forward or reverse gears

Driveshafts

- [ ] Clicking or knocking noise on turns (at slow speed on full-lock)
- [ ] Vibration when accelerating or decelerating

Braking system

- [ ] Vehicle pulls to one side under braking
- [ ] Noise (grinding or high-pitched squeal) when brakes applied
- [ ] Excessive brake pedal travel
- [ ] Brake pedal feels spongy when depressed
- [ ] Excessive brake pedal effort required to stop vehicle
- [ ] Judder felt through brake pedal or steering wheel when braking
- [ ] Brakes binding
- [ ] Rear wheels locking under normal braking

Suspension and steering systems

- [ ] Vehicle pulls to one side
- [ ] Wheel wobble and vibration
- [ ] Excessive pitching and/or rolling around corners, or during braking
- [ ] Wandering or general instability
- [ ] Excessively-stiff steering
- [ ] Excessive play in steering
- [ ] Lack of power assistance
- [ ] Tyre wear excessive

Electrical system

- [ ] Battery will not hold a charge for more than a few days
- [ ] Ignition/no-charge warning light stays on with engine running
- [ ] Ignition/no-charge warning light fails to come on
- [ ] Lights inoperative
- [ ] Instrument readings inaccurate or erratic
- [ ] Horn inoperative, or unsatisfactory in operation
- [ ] Windscreen/tailgate wipers failed, or unsatisfactory in operation
- [ ] Windscreen/tailgate washers failed, or unsatisfactory in operation
- [ ] Electric windows inoperative, or unsatisfactory in operation
- [ ] Central locking system inoperative, or unsatisfactory in operation

Introduction

The vehicle owner who does his or her own maintenance according to the recommended service schedules should not have to use this section of the manual very often. Modern component reliability is such that, provided those items subject to wear or deterioration are inspected or renewed at the specified intervals, sudden failure is comparatively rare. Faults do not usually just happen as a result of sudden failure, but develop over a period of time. Major mechanical failures in particular are usually preceded by characteristic symptoms over hundreds or even thousands of miles. Those components that do occasionally fail without warning are often small and easily carried in the vehicle.

With any fault-finding, the first step is to decide where to begin investigations. Sometimes this is obvious, but on other occasions, a little detective work will be necessary. The owner who makes half a dozen haphazard adjustments or replacements may be successful in curing a fault (or its symptoms), but will be none the wiser if the fault recurs, and ultimately may have spent more time and money than was necessary. A calm and logical approach will be found to be more satisfactory in the long run. Always take into account any warning signs or abnormalities that may have been noticed in the period preceding the fault – power loss, high or low gauge readings, unusual smells,

etc – and remember that failure of components such as fuses or spark plugs may only be pointers to some underlying fault.

The pages that follow provide an easy-reference guide to the more common problems, which may occur during the operation of the vehicle. These problems and their possible causes are grouped under headings denoting various components or systems, such as Engine, Cooling system, etc. The general Chapter that deals with the problem is also shown in brackets; refer to the relevant part of that Chapter for system-specific information. Whatever the fault, certain basic principles apply. These are as follows:

Verify the fault. This is simply a matter of being sure that you know what the symptoms are before starting work. This is particularly important if you are investigating a fault for someone else, who may not have described it very accurately.

Don't overlook the obvious. For example, if the vehicle won't start, is there fuel in the tank? (Don't take anyone else's word on this particular point, and don't trust the fuel gauge either!) If an electrical fault is indicated, look for loose or broken wires before digging out the test gear.

Cure the disease, not the symptom. Substituting a flat battery with a fully charged one will get you off the hard shoulder, but if the underlying cause is not attended to, the new battery will go the same way. Similarly, changing oil-fouled spark plugs (petrol models) for a new set will get you moving again, but remember that the reason for the fouling (if it wasn't simply an incorrect grade of plug) will have to be found and corrected.

Don't take anything for granted. Particularly, don't forget that a 'new' component may itself be defective (especially if it's been rattling around in the boot for months), and don't leave components out of a fault diagnosis sequence just because they are new or recently fitted. When you do finally diagnose a difficult fault, you'll probably realise that all the evidence was there from the start.

Engine

Engine fails to rotate when attempting to start

- [ ] Battery terminal connections loose or corroded (*Weekly checks*).
- [ ] Battery discharged or faulty (Chapter 5A).
- [ ] Broken, loose or disconnected wiring in the starting circuit (Chapter 5A).
- [ ] Defective starter motor (Chapter 5A).
- [ ] Starter pinion or flywheel/driveplate ring gear teeth loose or broken (Chapter 2A, 2B, 2C or 2D and 5A).
- [ ] Engine earth strap broken or disconnected (Chapter 5A).

Engine rotates, but will not start

- [ ] Fuel tank empty.
- [ ] Battery discharged (engine rotates slowly) (Chapter 5A).
- [ ] Battery terminal connections loose or corroded (*Weekly checks*).
- [ ] Worn, faulty or incorrectly-gapped spark plugs – petrol models (Chapter 1A).
- [ ] Preheating system faulty – diesel models (Chapter 5C).
- [ ] Engine management system fault – petrol models (Chapter 4A).
- [ ] Air in fuel system – diesel models (Chapter 4B).
- [ ] Fuel injector/injection pump fault – diesel models (Chapter 4B).
- [ ] Low cylinder compressions (Chapter 2A, 2B, 2C or 2D).
- [ ] Major mechanical failure (e.g. camshaft drive) (Chapter 2A, 2B, 2C or 2D).

Engine difficult to start when cold

- [ ] Battery discharged (Chapter 5A).
- [ ] Battery terminal connections loose or corroded (*Weekly checks*).
- [ ] Worn, faulty or incorrectly-gapped spark plugs – petrol models (Chapter 1A).
- [ ] Preheating system faulty – diesel models (Chapter 5C).
- [ ] Engine management system fault – petrol models (Chapter 4A).
- [ ] Fuel injector/injection pump fault – diesel models (Chapter 4B).

Engine difficult to start when hot

- [ ] Engine management system fault – petrol models (Chapter 4A).
- [ ] Fuel injector/injection pump fault – diesel models (Chapter 4B).
- [ ] Low cylinder compressions (Chapter 2A, 2B, 2C or 2D).

Starter motor noisy or excessively rough in engagement

- [ ] Starter pinion or flywheel/driveplate ring gear teeth loose or broken (Chapters 2A, 2B, 2C or 2D and 5A).
- [ ] Starter motor mounting bolts loose or missing (Chapter 5A).
- [ ] Defective starter motor (Chapter 5A).

Engine starts, but stops immediately

- [ ] Vacuum leak at the throttle housing/inlet manifold – petrol models (Chapter 4A).
- [ ] Engine management system fault – petrol models (Chapter 4A).
- [ ] Air in fuel system – diesel models (Chapter 4B).
- [ ] Fuel injector/injection pump fault – diesel models (Chapter 4B).

Engine idles erratically

- [ ] Vacuum leak at the throttle housing/inlet manifold – petrol models (Chapter 4A).
- [ ] Worn, faulty or incorrectly-gapped spark plugs – petrol models (Chapter 1A).
- [ ] Engine management system fault – petrol models (Chapter 4A).
- [ ] Air in fuel system – diesel models (Chapter 4B).
- [ ] Fuel injector/injection pump fault – diesel models (Chapter 4B).
- [ ] Uneven or low cylinder compressions (Chapter 2A, 2B, 2C or 2D).
- [ ] Camshaft lobes worn (Chapter 2A, 2B, 2C or 2D).
- [ ] Timing belt/chain incorrectly fitted (Chapter 2A, 2B, 2C or 2D).

Engine misfires at idle speed

- [ ] Worn, faulty or incorrectly-gapped spark plugs – petrol models (Chapter 1A).
- [ ] Vacuum leak at the throttle housing/inlet manifold – petrol models (Chapter 4A).
- [ ] Engine management system fault – petrol models (Chapter 4A).
- [ ] Faulty injector(s) – diesel models (Chapter 4B).
- [ ] Uneven or low cylinder compressions (Chapter 2A, 2B, 2C or 2D).
- [ ] Disconnected, leaking, or perished crankcase ventilation hoses (Chapter 4C).

Engine misfires throughout the driving speed range

- [ ] Fuel filter blocked (Chapter 1A or 1B).
- [ ] Fuel pump faulty (Chapter 4A or 4B).
- [ ] Fuel tank vent blocked, or fuel pipes restricted (Chapter 4A or 4B).
- [ ] Worn, faulty or incorrectly-gapped spark plugs – petrol models (Chapter 1A).
- [ ] Vacuum leak at the throttle housing/inlet manifold – petrol models (Chapter 4A).
- [ ] Engine management system fault – petrol models (Chapter 4A).
- [ ] Fuel injector/injection pump fault – diesel models (Chapter 4B).
- [ ] Faulty ignition HT coil – petrol models (Chapter 5B).
- [ ] Uneven or low cylinder compressions (Chapter 2A, 2B, 2C or 2D).

Engine (continued)

Engine hesitates on acceleration

- ☐ Worn, faulty or incorrectly-gapped spark plugs – petrol models (Chapter 1A).
- ☐ Vacuum leak at the throttle housing/inlet manifold – petrol models (Chapter 4A).
- ☐ Engine management system fault – petrol models (Chapter 4A).
- ☐ Fuel injector/injection pump fault – diesel models (Chapter 4B).

Engine stalls

- ☐ Fuel filter blocked (Chapter 1A or 1B).
- ☐ Fuel pump faulty (Chapter 4A or 4B).
- ☐ Fuel tank vent blocked, or fuel pipes restricted (Chapter 4A or 4B).
- ☐ Worn, faulty or incorrectly-gapped spark plugs – petrol models (Chapter 1A).
- ☐ Vacuum leak at the throttle housing/inlet manifold – petrol models (Chapter 4A).
- ☐ Engine management system fault – petrol models (Chapter 4A).
- ☐ Fuel injector/injection pump fault – diesel models (Chapter 4B).

Engine lacks power

- ☐ Timing belt/chain incorrectly fitted (Chapter 2A, 2B, 2C or 2D).
- ☐ Fuel filter blocked (Chapter 1A or 1B).
- ☐ Fuel pump faulty (Chapter 4A or 4B).
- ☐ Uneven or low cylinder compressions (Chapter 2A, 2B, 2C or 2D).
- ☐ Worn, faulty or incorrectly-gapped spark plugs – petrol models (Chapter 1A).
- ☐ Vacuum leak at the throttle housing/inlet manifold – petrol models (Chapter 4A).
- ☐ Engine management system fault – petrol models (Chapter 4A).
- ☐ Fuel injector/injection pump fault – diesel models (Chapter 4B).
- ☐ Brakes binding (Chapters 1A or 1B and 9).
- ☐ Clutch slipping (Chapter 6).

Engine backfires

- ☐ Timing belt/chain incorrectly fitted (Chapter 2A, 2B, 2C or 2D).
- ☐ Vacuum leak at the throttle housing/inlet manifold – petrol models (Chapter 4A).
- ☐ Engine management system fault – petrol models (Chapter 4A).

Oil pressure warning light on with engine running

- ☐ Low oil level, or incorrect oil grade (*Weekly checks*).

- ☐ Faulty oil pressure warning light switch (Chapter 5A).
- ☐ Worn engine bearings and/or oil pump (Chapter 2E).
- ☐ High engine operating temperature (Chapter 3).
- ☐ Oil pressure relief valve defective (Chapter 2A, 2B, 2C or 2D).
- ☐ Oil pick-up strainer clogged (Chapter 2A, 2B, 2C or 2D).

Engine runs-on after switching off

- ☐ Excessive carbon build-up in engine (Chapter 2E).
- ☐ High engine operating temperature (Chapter 3).
- ☐ Engine management system fault – petrol models (Chapter 4A).
- ☐ Fuel injection pump fault – diesel models (Chapter 4B).

Engine noises

Pre-ignition (pinking) or knocking during acceleration or under load

- ☐ Engine management system fault – petrol models (Chapter 4A).
- ☐ Incorrect grade of spark plug – petrol models (Chapter 1A).
- ☐ Incorrect grade of fuel – petrol models (Chapter 4A).
- ☐ Vacuum leak at the throttle housing/inlet manifold – petrol models (Chapter 4A).
- ☐ Excessive carbon build-up in engine (Chapter 2E).

Whistling or wheezing noises

- ☐ Leaking inlet manifold or throttle housing gasket – petrol models (Chapter 4A).
- ☐ Leaking vacuum hose (Chapters 4A or 4B and 9).
- ☐ Blowing cylinder head gasket (Chapter 2A, 2B, 2C or 2D).

Tapping or rattling noises

- ☐ Worn valve gear or camshaft (Chapter 2A, 2B, 2C or 2D).
- ☐ Ancillary component fault (coolant pump, alternator, etc) – (Chapters 3, 5A, etc).

Knocking or thumping noises

- ☐ Worn big-end bearings (regular heavy knocking, perhaps less under load) (Chapter 2E).
- ☐ Worn main bearings (rumbling and knocking, perhaps worsening under load) (Chapter 2E).
- ☐ Piston slap (most noticeable when cold) (Chapter 2E).
- ☐ Ancillary component fault (coolant pump, alternator, etc) – (Chapters 3, 5A, etc).

Cooling system

Overheating

- ☐ Insufficient coolant in system (*Weekly checks*).
- ☐ Thermostat faulty (stuck closed) (Chapter 3).
- ☐ Radiator core blocked, or grille restricted (Chapter 3).
- ☐ Electric cooling fan or sensor faulty (Chapter 3).
- ☐ Pressure cap faulty (Chapter 3).
- ☐ Inaccurate temperature gauge/sensor (Chapter 3).
- ☐ Airlock in cooling system (Chapter 1A or 1B).
- ☐ Engine management system fault (Chapter 4).

Overcooling

- ☐ Thermostat faulty (stuck open) (Chapter 3).
- ☐ Inaccurate temperature gauge/sensor (Chapter 3).

External coolant leakage

- ☐ Deteriorated or damaged hoses or hose clips (Chapter 1A or 1B).

- ☐ Radiator core or heater matrix leaking (Chapter 3).
- ☐ Pressure cap faulty (Chapter 3).
- ☐ Coolant pump leaking (Chapter 3).
- ☐ Boiling due to overheating (Chapter 3).
- ☐ Core plug leaking (Chapter 2E).

Internal coolant leakage

- ☐ Leaking cylinder head gasket (Chapter 2A, 2B, 2C or 2D).
- ☐ Cracked cylinder head or cylinder bore (Chapter 2A, 2B, 2C, 2D or 2E).

Corrosion

- ☐ Infrequent draining and flushing (Chapter 1A or 1B).
- ☐ Incorrect coolant mixture or inappropriate coolant type (Chapter 1A or 1B).

Fuel and exhaust systems

Excessive fuel consumption
☐ Air filter element dirty or clogged (Chapter 1A or 1B).
☐ Engine management system fault (Chapter 4).
☐ Faulty injector(s) (Chapter 4).
☐ Tyres under-inflated (*Weekly checks*).
☐ Brakes binding (Chapters 1A or 1B and 9).

Fuel leakage and/or fuel odour
☐ Damaged or corroded fuel tank, pipes or connections (Chapter 4A or 4B).

Excessive noise or fumes from exhaust system
☐ Leaking exhaust system or manifold joints (Chapters 1A or 1B and 4A or 4B).
☐ Leaking, corroded or damaged silencers or pipe (Chapters 1A or 1B and 4A or 4B).
☐ Broken mountings causing body or suspension contact (Chapters 1A or 1B and 4A or 4B).

Clutch

Pedal travels to floor – no pressure or very little resistance
☐ Air in hydraulic system/faulty master or slave cylinder (Chapter 6).
☐ Broken clutch release bearing or fork (Chapter 6).
☐ Broken diaphragm spring in clutch pressure plate (Chapter 6).

Clutch fails to disengage (unable to select gears)
☐ Air in hydraulic system/faulty master or slave cylinder (Chapter 6).
☐ Clutch disc sticking on gearbox input shaft splines (Chapter 6).
☐ Clutch disc sticking to flywheel or pressure plate (Chapter 6).
☐ Faulty pressure plate assembly (Chapter 6).
☐ Clutch release mechanism worn or incorrectly assembled (Chapter 6).

Clutch slips (engine speed rises, with no increase in vehicle speed)
☐ Faulty hydraulic release system (Chapter 6).

☐ Clutch disc linings excessively worn (Chapter 6).
☐ Clutch disc linings contaminated with oil or grease (Chapter 6).
☐ Faulty pressure plate or weak diaphragm spring (Chapter 6).

Judder as clutch is engaged
☐ Clutch disc linings contaminated with oil or grease (Chapter 6).
☐ Clutch disc linings excessively worn (Chapter 6).
☐ Faulty or distorted pressure plate or diaphragm spring (Chapter 6).
☐ Worn or loose engine or gearbox mountings (Chapter 2A, 2B, 2C or 2D).
☐ Clutch disc hub or gearbox input shaft splines worn (Chapter 6).

Noise when depressing or releasing clutch pedal
☐ Worn clutch release bearing (Chapter 6).
☐ Worn or dry clutch pedal bushes (Chapter 6).
☐ Faulty pressure plate assembly (Chapter 6).
☐ Pressure plate diaphragm spring broken (Chapter 6).
☐ Broken clutch disc cushioning springs (Chapter 6).

Manual transmission

Noisy in neutral with engine running
☐ Input shaft bearings worn (noise apparent with clutch pedal released, but not when depressed) (Chapter 7A).*
☐ Clutch release bearing worn (noise apparent with clutch pedal depressed, possibly less when released) (Chapter 6).

Noisy in one particular gear
☐ Worn, damaged or chipped gear teeth (Chapter 7A).*

Difficulty engaging gears
☐ Clutch fault (Chapter 6).
☐ Worn or damaged gear selection cables (Chapter 7A).
☐ Worn synchroniser units (Chapter 7A).*

Jumps out of gear
☐ Worn or damaged gear selection cables (Chapter 7A).

☐ Worn synchroniser units (Chapter 7A).*
☐ Worn selector forks (Chapter 7A).*

Vibration
☐ Lack of oil (Chapters 1 and 7A).
☐ Worn bearings (Chapter 7A).*

Lubricant leaks
☐ Leaking differential output oil seal (Chapter 7A).
☐ Leaking housing joint (Chapter 7A).*
☐ Leaking input shaft oil seal (Chapter 7A).

Although the corrective action necessary to remedy the symptoms described is beyond the scope of the home mechanic, the above information should be helpful in isolating the cause of the condition, so that the owner can communicate clearly with a professional mechanic.

Automatic/DSG transmission

Note: *Due to the complexity of the automatic transmission, it is difficult for the home mechanic to properly diagnose and service this unit. For problems other than the following, the vehicle should be taken to a VW dealer service department or suitably equipped specialist.*

Fluid leakage

☐ Automatic transmission fluid is usually dark in colour. Fluid leaks should not be confused with engine oil, which can easily be blown onto the transmission by airflow.

☐ To determine the source of a leak, first remove all built-up dirt and grime from the transmission housing and surrounding areas using a degreasing agent, or by steam-cleaning. Drive the vehicle at low speed, so airflow will not blow the leak far from its source. Raise and support the vehicle, and determine where the leak is coming from.

Transmission fluid brown, or has burned smell

☐ Transmission fluid level low, or fluid in need of renewal (Chapter 1A and 7B).

General gear selection problems

☐ Chapter 7B deals with checking and adjusting the selector cable

on automatic transmissions. The following are common problems, which may be caused by a poorly adjusted cable:
a) *Engine starting in gears other than Park or Neutral.*
b) *Indicator panel showing a gear other than that being used.*
c) *Vehicle moves when in Park or Neutral.*
d) *Poor gear shift quality or erratic gear changes.*
☐ Refer to Chapter 7B for the selector cable adjustment procedure.

Engine won't start in any gear, or starts in gears other than Park or Neutral

☐ Incorrect multi-function switch adjustment (Chapter 7B).
☐ Incorrect selector cable adjustment (Chapter 7B).

Transmission slips, shifts roughly, is noisy, or has no drive in forward or reverse gears

☐ There are many probable causes for the above problems, but the home mechanic should be concerned with only one possibility – fluid level. Before taking the vehicle to a dealer or transmission specialist, check the fluid level as described in Chapter 1A. Correct the fluid level as necessary, or change the fluid. If the problem persists, professional help will be necessary.

Driveshafts

Clicking or knocking noise on turns (at slow speed on full-lock)

☐ Lack of constant velocity joint lubricant, possibly due to damaged gaiter (Chapter 8).
☐ Worn outer constant velocity joint (Chapter 8).

Vibration when accelerating or decelerating

☐ Worn inner constant velocity joint (Chapter 8).
☐ Bent or distorted driveshaft (Chapter 8).
☐ Worn intermediate bearing (Chapter 8).

Braking system

Note: *Before assuming that a brake problem exists, make sure that the tyres are in good condition and correctly inflated, that the front wheel alignment is correct, and that the vehicle is not loaded with weight in an unequal manner. Apart from checking the condition of all pipe and hose connections, any faults occurring on the anti-lock braking system should be referred to a VW dealer for diagnosis.*

Vehicle pulls to one side under braking

☐ Worn, defective, damaged or contaminated brake pads on one side (Chapter 9).
☐ Seized or partially-seized front brake caliper (Chapter 9).
☐ A mixture of brake pad materials fitted between sides (Chapter 9).
☐ Brake caliper mounting bolts loose (Chapter 9).
☐ Worn or damaged steering or suspension components (Chapters 1A or 1B and 10).

Noise (grinding or high-pitched squeal) when brakes applied

☐ Brake pad material worn down to metal backing (Chapters 1A or 1B and 9).
☐ Excessive corrosion of brake disc. May be apparent after the vehicle has been standing for some time (Chapter 9).
☐ Foreign object (stone chipping, etc) trapped between brake disc and shield (Chapter 9).

Excessive brake pedal travel

☐ Faulty master cylinder (Chapter 9).
☐ Air in hydraulic system (Chapter 9).
☐ Faulty vacuum servo unit (Chapter 9).

Brake pedal feels spongy when depressed

☐ Air in hydraulic system (Chapter 9).

☐ Deteriorated flexible rubber brake hoses (Chapters 1A or 1B and 9).
☐ Master cylinder mounting nuts loose (Chapter 9).
☐ Faulty master cylinder (Chapter 9).

Excessive brake pedal effort required to stop vehicle

☐ Faulty vacuum servo unit (Chapter 9).
☐ Disconnected, damaged or insecure brake servo vacuum hose (Chapter 9).
☐ Primary or secondary hydraulic circuit failure (Chapter 9).
☐ Seized brake caliper (Chapter 9).
☐ Brake pads incorrectly fitted (Chapter 9).
☐ Incorrect grade of brake pads fitted (Chapter 9).
☐ Brake pads contaminated (Chapter 9).

Judder felt through brake pedal or steering wheel when braking

☐ Excessive run-out or distortion of discs (Chapters 9).
☐ Brake pads worn (Chapters 1A or 1B and 9).
☐ Brake caliper mounting bolts loose (Chapter 9).
☐ Wear in suspension or steering components or mountings (Chapters 1A or 1B and 10).

Brakes binding

☐ Seized brake caliper (Chapter 9).
☐ Incorrectly-adjusted handbrake mechanism (Chapter 9).
☐ Faulty master cylinder (Chapter 9).

Rear wheels locking under normal braking

☐ Rear brake pads contaminated (Chapters 1A or 1B and 9).
☐ ABS system fault (Chapter 9).

Suspension and steering

Note: Before diagnosing suspension or steering faults, be sure that the trouble is not due to incorrect tyre pressures, mixtures of tyre types, or binding brakes.

Vehicle pulls to one side

☐ Defective tyre (*Weekly checks*).
☐ Excessive wear in suspension or steering components (Chapters 1A or 1B and 10).
☐ Incorrect front wheel alignment (Chapter 10).
☐ Damage to steering or suspension components (Chapter 1A or 1B).

Wheel wobble and vibration

☐ Front roadwheels out of balance (vibration felt mainly through the steering wheel) (Chapters 1A or 1B and 10).
☐ Rear roadwheels out of balance (vibration felt throughout the vehicle) (Chapters 1A or 1B and 10).
☐ Roadwheels damaged or distorted (Chapters 1A or 1B and 10).
☐ Faulty or damaged tyre (*Weekly checks*).
☐ Worn steering or suspension joints, bushes or components (Chapters 1A or 1B and 10).
☐ Wheel bolts loose (Chapters 1A or 1B and 10).

Excessive pitching and/or rolling around corners, or during braking

☐ Defective shock absorbers (Chapters 1A or 1B and 10).
☐ Broken or weak spring and/or suspension part (Chapters 1A or 1B and 10).
☐ Worn or damaged anti-roll bar or mountings (Chapter 10).

Wandering or general instability

☐ Incorrect front wheel alignment (Chapter 10).
☐ Worn steering or suspension joints, bushes or components (Chapters 1A or 1B and 10).
☐ Roadwheels out of balance (Chapters 1A or 1B and 10).
☐ Faulty or damaged tyre (Weekly checks).
☐ Wheel bolts loose (Chapters 1A or 1B and 10).
☐ Defective shock absorbers (Chapters 1A or 1B and 10).

Excessively-stiff steering

☐ Lack of power steering fluid (Chapter 10).
☐ Seized track rod end balljoint or suspension balljoint (Chapters 1A or 1B and 10).

☐ Incorrect front wheel alignment (Chapter 10).
☐ Steering rack or column bent or damaged (Chapter 10).
☐ Power steering pump fault (Chapter 10).

Excessive play in steering

☐ Worn steering column universal joint (Chapter 10).
☐ Worn steering track rod end balljoints (Chapters 1A or 1B and 10).
☐ Worn steering rack (Chapter 10).
☐ Worn steering or suspension joints, bushes or components (Chapters 1A or 1B and 10).

Lack of power assistance

☐ Incorrect power steering fluid level (*Weekly checks*).
☐ Restriction in power steering fluid hoses (Chapter 1A or 1B).
☐ Faulty power steering pump (Chapter 10).
☐ Faulty steering rack (Chapter 10).

Tyre wear excessive

Tyre treads exhibit feathered edges
☐ Incorrect toe setting (Chapter 10).

Tyres worn in centre of tread
☐ Tyres over-inflated (*Weekly checks*).

Tyres worn on inside and outside edges
☐ Tyres under-inflated (*Weekly checks*).

Tyres worn on inside or outside edges
☐ Incorrect camber/castor angles (wear on one edge only) (Chapter 10).
☐ Worn steering or suspension joints, bushes or components (Chapters 1A or 1B and 10).
☐ Excessively-hard cornering.
☐ Accident damage.

Tyres worn unevenly
☐ Tyres/wheels out of balance (*Weekly checks*).
☐ Excessive wheel or tyre run-out (Chapter 1A or 1B).
☐ Worn shock absorbers (Chapters 1A or 1B and 10).
☐ Faulty tyre (*Weekly checks*).

Electrical system

Note: For problems associated with the starting system, refer to the faults listed under 'Engine' earlier in this Section.

Battery won't hold a charge for more than a few days

☐ Battery defective internally (Chapter 5A).
☐ Battery terminal connections loose or corroded (*Weekly checks*).
☐ Auxiliary drivebelt broken, worn or incorrectly adjusted (Chapter 1A or 1B).
☐ Alternator not charging at correct output (Chapter 5A).
☐ Alternator or voltage regulator faulty (Chapter 5A).
☐ Short-circuit causing continual battery drain (Chapters 5A and 12).

Ignition/no-charge warning light stays on with engine running

☐ Auxiliary drivebelt broken, worn, or incorrectly adjusted (Chapter 1A or 1B).
☐ Internal fault in alternator or voltage regulator (Chapter 5A).
☐ Broken, disconnected, or loose wiring in charging circuit (Chapter 5A).

Ignition/no-charge warning light fails to come on

☐ Warning light bulb blown (Chapter 12).
☐ Broken, disconnected, or loose wiring in warning light circuit (Chapter 12).
☐ Alternator faulty (Chapter 5A).

Lights inoperative

☐ Bulb blown (Chapter 12).
☐ Corrosion of bulb or bulbholder contacts (Chapter 12).
☐ Blown fuse (Chapter 12).
☐ Faulty relay (Chapter 12).
☐ Broken, loose, or disconnected wiring (Chapter 12).
☐ Faulty switch (Chapter 12).

Instrument readings inaccurate or erratic

Fuel or temperature gauges give no reading
☐ Faulty gauge sensor unit (Chapter 3 or 4).
☐ Wiring open-circuit (Chapter 12).
☐ Faulty gauge (Chapter 12).

Electrical system (continued)

Fuel or temperature gauges give continuous maximum reading

- ☐ Faulty gauge sensor unit (Chapter 3 or 4).
- ☐ Wiring short-circuit (Chapter 12).
- ☐ Faulty gauge (Chapter 12).

Horn inoperative, or unsatisfactory in operation

Horn operates all the time

- ☐ Horn push either earthed or stuck down (Chapter 12).
- ☐ Horn cable-to-horn push earthed (Chapter 12).

Horn fails to operate

- ☐ Blown fuse (Chapter 12).
- ☐ Cable or cable connections loose, broken or disconnected (Chapter 12).
- ☐ Faulty horn (Chapter 12).

Horn emits intermittent or unsatisfactory sound

- ☐ Cable connections loose (Chapter 12).
- ☐ Horn mountings loose (Chapter 12).
- ☐ Faulty horn (Chapter 12).

Windscreen/tailgate wipers failed, or unsatisfactory in operation

Wipers fail to operate, or operate very slowly

- ☐ Wiper blades stuck to screen, or linkage seized or binding (Chapters 1A or 1B and 12).
- ☐ Blown fuse (Chapter 12).
- ☐ Cable or cable connections loose, broken or disconnected (Chapter 12).
- ☐ Faulty built-in system interface (BSI) unit (Chapter 12).
- ☐ Faulty wiper motor (Chapter 12).

Wiper blades sweep over too large or too small an area of the glass

- ☐ Wiper arms incorrectly positioned on spindles (Chapter 12).
- ☐ Excessive wear of wiper linkage (Chapter 12).
- ☐ Wiper motor or linkage mountings loose or insecure (Chapter 12).

Wiper blades fail to clean the glass effectively

- ☐ Wiper blade rubbers worn or perished (*Weekly checks*).
- ☐ Wiper arm tension springs broken, or arm pivots seized (Chapter 12).
- ☐ Insufficient windscreen washer additive to adequately remove road film (*Weekly checks*).

Windscreen/tailgate washers failed, or unsatisfactory in operation

One or more washer jets inoperative

- ☐ Blocked washer jet (*Weekly checks*).
- ☐ Disconnected, kinked or restricted fluid hose (Chapter 12).
- ☐ Insufficient fluid in washer reservoir (*Weekly checks*).

Washer pump fails to operate

- ☐ Broken or disconnected wiring or connections (Chapter 12).
- ☐ Blown fuse (Chapter 12).
- ☐ Faulty washer switch (Chapter 12).
- ☐ Faulty washer pump (Chapter 12).

Electric windows inoperative, or unsatisfactory in operation

Window glass will only move in one direction

- ☐ Faulty switch (Chapter 12).

Window glass slow to move

- ☐ Regulator seized or damaged, or in need of lubricant (Chapter 11).
- ☐ Door internal components or trim fouling regulator (Chapter 11).
- ☐ Faulty motor (Chapter 11).

Window glass fails to move

- ☐ Blown fuse (Chapter 12).
- ☐ Broken or disconnected wiring or connections (Chapter 12).
- ☐ Faulty motor (Chapter 11).
- ☐ Faulty built-in systems interface (BSI) unit (Chapter 12).

Central locking system inoperative, or unsatisfactory in operation

Complete system failure

- ☐ Blown fuse (Chapter 12).
- ☐ Broken or disconnected wiring or connections (Chapter 12).
- ☐ Faulty built-in system interface (BSI) unit (Chapter 12).

Door/tailgate locks but will not unlock, or unlocks but will not lock

- ☐ Broken or disconnected link rod(s) (Chapter 11).
- ☐ Faulty lock motor (Chapter 11).

One lock fails to operate

- ☐ Broken or disconnected wiring or connections (Chapter 12).
- ☐ Faulty lock motor (Chapter 11).
- ☐ Broken, binding or disconnected link rod(s) (Chapter 11).

Disconnecting the battery

Caution: After reconnecting the battery, the safety function of the electric windows will not be re-instated until the windows have been reprogrammed.

Several of the systems require battery power to be available at all times (permanent live). This is either to ensure their continued operation (such as the clock), or to maintain electronic memory settings which would otherwise be erased. Whenever the battery is to be disconnected, first note the following points, to ensure there are no unforeseen consequences:

a) Firstly, on any vehicle with central door locking, it is a wise precaution to remove the key from the ignition, and to keep it with you. This avoids the possibility of the key being locked inside the car, should the central locking engage when the battery is reconnected.

b) If a security-coded audio unit is fitted, and the unit and/or the battery is disconnected, the unit will not function until the correct security code has been entered. Therefore, if you do not know the correct security code for the radio/cassette unit, **do not** disconnect either of the battery terminals, or remove the radio/cassette unit from the car. The code appears on a code card supplied with the car when new. Details for entering the code appear in the handbook. Should the code have been misplaced or forgotten, on production of proof of ownership, a VW dealer or in-car entertainment specialist may be able to help.

c) The engine management system ECU is of the 'self-learning' type, meaning that, as it operates, it adapts to changes in operating conditions, and stores the optimum settings found (this is especially true for idle speed settings). When the battery is disconnected, these 'learned' settings are lost, and the ECU reverts to the base factory settings. When the engine is restarted, it may idle and run roughly until the ECU has 'relearned' the best settings. To further this 'learning' process, take the car for a road test of at least 15 minutes' duration, covering as many engine speeds and loads as possible, and concentrating on the 2000 to 4000 rpm range. On completion, let the engine idle for at least 10 minutes, turning the steering wheel occasionally and switching on high-current-draw equipment such as the heater fan or heated rear window. If the engine does not regain its normal performance, have the system checked for faults by a VW dealer.

d) Where electric windows with 'one-touch' operation are fitted, this function may not work correctly until each window has been reset. This is done by fully opening the window with the button pressed, then keeping the button pressed for a few seconds after opening, so the system can 'learn' the fully-open position. Close the window, and again keep the button pressed for a few seconds after closing.

Devices known as 'memory-savers' or 'code-savers' can be used to avoid some of the above problems. Precise details of use vary according to the device used. Typically, it is plugged into the cigarette lighter socket, and is connected by its own wiring to a spare battery; the battery is then disconnected from the electrical system, leaving the memory-saver to pass sufficient current to maintain audio unit security codes, and other memory values, and also to run permanently-live circuits such as the clock.

⚠️ **Warning: Some of these devices allow a considerable amount of current to pass, which can mean that many of the car's systems are still operational when the main battery is disconnected. If a memory-saver is used, ensure that the circuit concerned is actually 'dead' before carrying out any work on it.**

A

ABS (Anti-lock brake system) A system, usually electronically controlled, that senses incipient wheel lockup during braking and relieves hydraulic pressure at wheels that are about to skid.

Air bag An inflatable bag hidden in the steering wheel (driver's side) or the dash or glovebox (passenger side). In a head-on collision, the bags inflate, preventing the driver and front passenger from being thrown forward into the steering wheel or windscreen.

Air cleaner A metal or plastic housing, containing a filter element, which removes dust and dirt from the air being drawn into the engine.

Air filter element The actual filter in an air cleaner system, usually manufactured from pleated paper and requiring renewal at regular intervals.

Air filter

Allen key A hexagonal wrench which fits into a recessed hexagonal hole.

Alligator clip A long-nosed spring-loaded metal clip with meshing teeth. Used to make temporary electrical connections.

Alternator A component in the electrical system which converts mechanical energy from a drivebelt into electrical energy to charge the battery and to operate the starting system, ignition system and electrical accessories.

Ampere (amp) A unit of measurement for the flow of electric current. One amp is the amount of current produced by one volt acting through a resistance of one ohm.

Anaerobic sealer A substance used to prevent bolts and screws from loosening. Anaerobic means that it does not require oxygen for activation. The Loctite brand is widely used.

Antifreeze A substance (usually ethylene glycol) mixed with water, and added to a vehicle's cooling system, to prevent freezing of the coolant in winter. Antifreeze also contains chemicals to inhibit corrosion and the formation of rust and other deposits that would tend to clog the radiator and coolant passages and reduce cooling efficiency.

Anti-seize compound A coating that reduces the risk of seizing on fasteners that are subjected to high temperatures, such as exhaust manifold bolts and nuts.

Asbestos A natural fibrous mineral with great heat resistance, commonly used in the composition of brake friction materials.

Asbestos is a health hazard and the dust created by brake systems should never be inhaled or ingested.

Axle A shaft on which a wheel revolves, or which revolves with a wheel. Also, a solid beam that connects the two wheels at one end of the vehicle. An axle which also transmits power to the wheels is known as a live axle.

Axleshaft A single rotating shaft, on either side of the differential, which delivers power from the final drive assembly to the drive wheels. Also called a driveshaft or a halfshaft.

B

Ball bearing An anti-friction bearing consisting of a hardened inner and outer race with hardened steel balls between two races.

Bearing The curved surface on a shaft or in a bore, or the part assembled into either, that permits relative motion between them with minimum wear and friction.

Bearing

Big-end bearing The bearing in the end of the connecting rod that's attached to the crankshaft.

Bleed nipple A valve on a brake wheel cylinder, caliper or other hydraulic component that is opened to purge the hydraulic system of air. Also called a bleed screw.

Brake bleeding Procedure for removing air from lines of a hydraulic brake system.

Brake bleeding

Brake disc The component of a disc brake that rotates with the wheels.

Brake drum The component of a drum brake that rotates with the wheels.

Brake linings The friction material which contacts the brake disc or drum to retard the vehicle's speed. The linings are bonded or riveted to the brake pads or shoes.

Brake pads The replaceable friction pads that pinch the brake disc when the brakes are applied. Brake pads consist of a friction material bonded or riveted to a rigid backing plate.

Brake shoe The crescent-shaped carrier to which the brake linings are mounted and which forces the lining against the rotating drum during braking.

Braking systems For more information on braking systems, consult the *Haynes Automotive Brake Manual*.

Breaker bar A long socket wrench handle providing greater leverage.

Bulkhead The insulated partition between the engine and the passenger compartment.

C

Caliper The non-rotating part of a disc-brake assembly that straddles the disc and carries the brake pads. The caliper also contains the hydraulic components that cause the pads to pinch the disc when the brakes are applied. A caliper is also a measuring tool that can be set to measure inside or outside dimensions of an object.

Camshaft A rotating shaft on which a series of cam lobes operate the valve mechanisms. The camshaft may be driven by gears, by sprockets and chain or by sprockets and a belt.

Canister A container in an evaporative emission control system; contains activated charcoal granules to trap vapours from the fuel system.

Canister

Carburettor A device which mixes fuel with air in the proper proportions to provide a desired power output from a spark ignition internal combustion engine.

Castellated Resembling the parapets along the top of a castle wall. For example, a castellated balljoint stud nut.

Castor In wheel alignment, the backward or forward tilt of the steering axis. Castor is positive when the steering axis is inclined rearward at the top.

Catalytic converter A silencer-like device in the exhaust system which converts certain pollutants in the exhaust gases into less harmful substances.

Catalytic converter

Circlip A ring-shaped clip used to prevent endwise movement of cylindrical parts and shafts. An internal circlip is installed in a groove in a housing; an external circlip fits into a groove on the outside of a cylindrical piece such as a shaft.

Clearance The amount of space between two parts. For example, between a piston and a cylinder, between a bearing and a journal, etc.

Coil spring A spiral of elastic steel found in various sizes throughout a vehicle, for example as a springing medium in the suspension and in the valve train.

Compression Reduction in volume, and increase in pressure and temperature, of a gas, caused by squeezing it into a smaller space.

Compression ratio The relationship between cylinder volume when the piston is at top dead centre and cylinder volume when the piston is at bottom dead centre.

Constant velocity (CV) joint A type of universal joint that cancels out vibrations caused by driving power being transmitted through an angle.

Core plug A disc or cup-shaped metal device inserted in a hole in a casting through which core was removed when the casting was formed. Also known as a freeze plug or expansion plug.

Crankcase The lower part of the engine block in which the crankshaft rotates.

Crankshaft The main rotating member, or shaft, running the length of the crankcase, with offset "throws" to which the connecting rods are attached.

Crankshaft assembly

Crocodile clip See Alligator clip

D

Diagnostic code Code numbers obtained by accessing the diagnostic mode of an engine management computer. This code can be used to determine the area in the system where a malfunction may be located.

Disc brake A brake design incorporating a rotating disc onto which brake pads are squeezed. The resulting friction converts the energy of a moving vehicle into heat.

Double-overhead cam (DOHC) An engine that uses two overhead camshafts, usually one for the intake valves and one for the exhaust valves.

Drivebelt(s) The belt(s) used to drive accessories such as the alternator, water pump, power steering pump, air conditioning compressor, etc. off the crankshaft pulley.

Accessory drivebelts

Driveshaft Any shaft used to transmit motion. Commonly used when referring to the axleshafts on a front wheel drive vehicle.

Drum brake A type of brake using a drum-shaped metal cylinder attached to the inner surface of the wheel. When the brake pedal is pressed, curved brake shoes with friction linings press against the inside of the drum to slow or stop the vehicle.

E

EGR valve A valve used to introduce exhaust gases into the intake air stream.

Electronic control unit (ECU) A computer which controls (for instance) ignition and fuel injection systems, or an anti-lock braking system. For more information refer to the *Haynes Automotive Electrical and Electronic Systems Manual*.

Electronic Fuel Injection (EFI) A computer controlled fuel system that distributes fuel through an injector located in each intake port of the engine.

Emergency brake A braking system, independent of the main hydraulic system, that can be used to slow or stop the vehicle if the primary brakes fail, or to hold the vehicle stationary even though the brake pedal isn't depressed. It usually consists of a hand lever that actuates either front or rear brakes mechanically through a series of cables and linkages. Also known as a handbrake or parking brake.

Endfloat The amount of lengthwise movement between two parts. As applied to a crankshaft, the distance that the crankshaft can move forward and back in the cylinder block.

Engine management system (EMS) A computer controlled system which manages the fuel injection and the ignition systems in an integrated fashion.

Exhaust manifold A part with several passages through which exhaust gases leave the engine combustion chambers and enter the exhaust pipe.

F

Fan clutch A viscous (fluid) drive coupling device which permits variable engine fan speeds in relation to engine speeds.

Feeler blade A thin strip or blade of hardened steel, ground to an exact thickness, used to check or measure clearances between parts.

Feeler blade

Firing order The order in which the engine cylinders fire, or deliver their power strokes, beginning with the number one cylinder.

Flywheel A heavy spinning wheel in which energy is absorbed and stored by means of momentum. On cars, the flywheel is attached to the crankshaft to smooth out firing impulses.

Free play The amount of travel before any action takes place. The "looseness" in a linkage, or an assembly of parts, between the initial application of force and actual movement. For example, the distance the brake pedal moves before the pistons in the master cylinder are actuated.

Fuse An electrical device which protects a circuit against accidental overload. The typical fuse contains a soft piece of metal which is calibrated to melt at a predetermined current flow (expressed as amps) and break the circuit.

Fusible link A circuit protection device consisting of a conductor surrounded by heat-resistant insulation. The conductor is smaller than the wire it protects, so it acts as the weakest link in the circuit. Unlike a blown fuse, a failed fusible link must frequently be cut from the wire for replacement.

G

Gap The distance the spark must travel in jumping from the centre electrode to the side electrode in a spark plug. Also refers to the spacing between the points in a contact breaker assembly in a conventional points-type ignition, or to the distance between the reluctor or rotor and the pickup coil in an electronic ignition.

Adjusting spark plug gap

Gasket Any thin, soft material - usually cork, cardboard, asbestos or soft metal - installed between two metal surfaces to ensure a good seal. For instance, the cylinder head gasket seals the joint between the block and the cylinder head.

Gasket

Gauge An instrument panel display used to monitor engine conditions. A gauge with a movable pointer on a dial or a fixed scale is an analogue gauge. A gauge with a numerical readout is called a digital gauge.

H

Halfshaft A rotating shaft that transmits power from the final drive unit to a drive wheel, usually when referring to a live rear axle.
Harmonic balancer A device designed to reduce torsion or twisting vibration in the crankshaft. May be incorporated in the crankshaft pulley. Also known as a vibration damper.
Hone An abrasive tool for correcting small irregularities or differences in diameter in an engine cylinder, brake cylinder, etc.
Hydraulic tappet A tappet that utilises hydraulic pressure from the engine's lubrication system to maintain zero clearance (constant contact with both camshaft and valve stem). Automatically adjusts to variation in valve stem length. Hydraulic tappets also reduce valve noise.

I

Ignition timing The moment at which the spark plug fires, usually expressed in the number of crankshaft degrees before the piston reaches the top of its stroke.
Inlet manifold A tube or housing with passages through which flows the air-fuel mixture (carburettor vehicles and vehicles with throttle body injection) or air only (port fuel-injected vehicles) to the port openings in the cylinder head.

J

Jump start Starting the engine of a vehicle with a discharged or weak battery by attaching jump leads from the weak battery to a charged or helper battery.

L

Load Sensing Proportioning Valve (LSPV) A brake hydraulic system control valve that works like a proportioning valve, but also takes into consideration the amount of weight carried by the rear axle.
Locknut A nut used to lock an adjustment nut, or other threaded component, in place. For example, a locknut is employed to keep the adjusting nut on the rocker arm in position.
Lockwasher A form of washer designed to prevent an attaching nut from working loose.

M

MacPherson strut A type of front suspension system devised by Earle MacPherson at Ford of England. In its original form, a simple lateral link with the anti-roll bar creates the lower control arm. A long strut - an integral coil spring and shock absorber - is mounted between the body and the steering knuckle. Many modern so-called MacPherson strut systems use a conventional lower A-arm and don't rely on the anti-roll bar for location.
Multimeter An electrical test instrument with the capability to measure voltage, current and resistance.

N

NOx Oxides of Nitrogen. A common toxic pollutant emitted by petrol and diesel engines at higher temperatures.

O

Ohm The unit of electrical resistance. One volt applied to a resistance of one ohm will produce a current of one amp.
Ohmmeter An instrument for measuring electrical resistance.
O-ring A type of sealing ring made of a special rubber-like material; in use, the O-ring is compressed into a groove to provide the sealing action.
Overhead cam (ohc) engine An engine with the camshaft(s) located on top of the cylinder head(s).

Overhead valve (ohv) engine An engine with the valves located in the cylinder head, but with the camshaft located in the engine block.
Oxygen sensor A device installed in the engine exhaust manifold, which senses the oxygen content in the exhaust and converts this information into an electric current. Also called a Lambda sensor.

P

Phillips screw A type of screw head having a cross instead of a slot for a corresponding type of screwdriver.
Plastigage A thin strip of plastic thread, available in different sizes, used for measuring clearances. For example, a strip of Plastigage is laid across a bearing journal. The parts are assembled and dismantled; the width of the crushed strip indicates the clearance between journal and bearing.

Plastigage

Propeller shaft The long hollow tube with universal joints at both ends that carries power from the transmission to the differential on front-engined rear wheel drive vehicles.
Proportioning valve A hydraulic control valve which limits the amount of pressure to the rear brakes during panic stops to prevent wheel lock-up.

R

Rack-and-pinion steering A steering system with a pinion gear on the end of the steering shaft that mates with a rack (think of a geared wheel opened up and laid flat). When the steering wheel is turned, the pinion turns, moving the rack to the left or right. This movement is transmitted through the track rods to the steering arms at the wheels.
Radiator A liquid-to-air heat transfer device designed to reduce the temperature of the coolant in an internal combustion engine cooling system.
Refrigerant Any substance used as a heat transfer agent in an air-conditioning system. R-12 has been the principle refrigerant for many years; recently, however, manufacturers have begun using R-134a, a non-CFC substance that is considered less harmful to the ozone in the upper atmosphere.
Rocker arm A lever arm that rocks on a shaft or pivots on a stud. In an overhead valve engine, the rocker arm converts the upward movement of the pushrod into a downward movement to open a valve.

Rotor In a distributor, the rotating device inside the cap that connects the centre electrode and the outer terminals as it turns, distributing the high voltage from the coil secondary winding to the proper spark plug. Also, that part of an alternator which rotates inside the stator. Also, the rotating assembly of a turbocharger, including the compressor wheel, shaft and turbine wheel.

Runout The amount of wobble (in-and-out movement) of a gear or wheel as it's rotated. The amount a shaft rotates "out-of-true." The out-of-round condition of a rotating part.

S

Sealant A liquid or paste used to prevent leakage at a joint. Sometimes used in conjunction with a gasket.

Sealed beam lamp An older headlight design which integrates the reflector, lens and filaments into a hermetically-sealed one-piece unit. When a filament burns out or the lens cracks, the entire unit is simply replaced.

Serpentine drivebelt A single, long, wide accessory drivebelt that's used on some newer vehicles to drive all the accessories, instead of a series of smaller, shorter belts. Serpentine drivebelts are usually tensioned by an automatic tensioner.

Serpentine drivebelt

Shim Thin spacer, commonly used to adjust the clearance or relative positions between two parts. For example, shims inserted into or under bucket tappets control valve clearances. Clearance is adjusted by changing the thickness of the shim.

Slide hammer A special puller that screws into or hooks onto a component such as a shaft or bearing; a heavy sliding handle on the shaft bottoms against the end of the shaft to knock the component free.

Sprocket A tooth or projection on the periphery of a wheel, shaped to engage with a chain or drivebelt. Commonly used to refer to the sprocket wheel itself.

Starter inhibitor switch On vehicles with an automatic transmission, a switch that prevents starting if the vehicle is not in Neutral or Park.

Strut See MacPherson strut.

T

Tappet A cylindrical component which transmits motion from the cam to the valve stem, either directly or via a pushrod and rocker arm. Also called a cam follower.

Thermostat A heat-controlled valve that regulates the flow of coolant between the cylinder block and the radiator, so maintaining optimum engine operating temperature. A thermostat is also used in some air cleaners in which the temperature is regulated.

Thrust bearing The bearing in the clutch assembly that is moved in to the release levers by clutch pedal action to disengage the clutch. Also referred to as a release bearing.

Timing belt A toothed belt which drives the camshaft. Serious engine damage may result if it breaks in service.

Timing chain A chain which drives the camshaft.

Toe-in The amount the front wheels are closer together at the front than at the rear. On rear wheel drive vehicles, a slight amount of toe-in is usually specified to keep the front wheels running parallel on the road by offsetting other forces that tend to spread the wheels apart.

Toe-out The amount the front wheels are closer together at the rear than at the front. On front wheel drive vehicles, a slight amount of toe-out is usually specified.

Tools For full information on choosing and using tools, refer to the *Haynes Automotive Tools Manual*.

Tracer A stripe of a second colour applied to a wire insulator to distinguish that wire from another one with the same colour insulator.

Tune-up A process of accurate and careful adjustments and parts replacement to obtain the best possible engine performance.

Turbocharger A centrifugal device, driven by exhaust gases, that pressurises the intake air. Normally used to increase the power output from a given engine displacement, but can also be used primarily to reduce exhaust emissions (as on VW's "Umwelt" Diesel engine).

U

Universal joint or U-joint A double-pivoted connection for transmitting power from a driving to a driven shaft through an angle. A U-joint consists of two Y-shaped yokes and a cross-shaped member called the spider.

V

Valve A device through which the flow of liquid, gas, vacuum, or loose material in bulk may be started, stopped, or regulated by a movable part that opens, shuts, or partially obstructs one or more ports or passageways. A valve is also the movable part of such a device.

Valve clearance The clearance between the valve tip (the end of the valve stem) and the rocker arm or tappet. The valve clearance is measured when the valve is closed.

Vernier caliper A precision measuring instrument that measures inside and outside dimensions. Not quite as accurate as a micrometer, but more convenient.

Viscosity The thickness of a liquid or its resistance to flow.

Volt A unit for expressing electrical "pressure" in a circuit. One volt that will produce a current of one ampere through a resistance of one ohm.

W

Welding Various processes used to join metal items by heating the areas to be joined to a molten state and fusing them together. For more information refer to the *Haynes Automotive Welding Manual*.

Wiring diagram A drawing portraying the components and wires in a vehicle's electrical system, using standardised symbols. For more information refer to the *Haynes Automotive Electrical and Electronic Systems Manual*.

Note: *References throughout this index are in the form* **"Chapter number"** • **"Page number"**. *So, for example, 2C•15 refers to page 15 of Chapter 2C.*

Note: *References throughout this index are in the form* "**Chapter number**" • "*Page number*"*. So, for example, 2C•15 refers to page 15 of Chapter 2C.*

Note: *References throughout this index are in the form* "**Chapter number**" • "**Page number**". *So, for example, 2C•15 refers to page 15 of Chapter 2C.*